ANTI-KNOWLEDGE

ESSAYS FROM THE ERA OF NEGOTIABLE TRUTH

Christian Schneider

Pelham Press

christianschneiderblog.com

Schneider, Christian.

 Anti-Knowledge: Essays From the Era of Negotiable Truth / Christian Schneider.

ISBN 979-8-9852056-3-3

Pelham Press, LLC

P.O. Box 5372

Madison, Wisconsin, 53705

For Sonja

PRAISE FOR "ANTI-KNOWLEDGE"

"Christian Schneider's range of subject matter and interests, his blend of humor and analysis, his ability to both opine and report, means there's something—a lot of things, actually—here for everyone. Chapter 5 is my favorite, but Schneider's work on the state of college campuses is vital. And to the guys who were behind me at the 9:30 Club last night: please read page 75."

– Christopher J. Scalia, co-editor of Scalia Speaks: Reflections on Law, Faith, and Life Well Lived

"Christian's writing is thoughtful, funny and, most of all in our black and white times, not predictable. His columns, even those from a decade ago, remain relevant and fresh. Christian's incisive essays are a must-read."

-Karol Markowicz, The New York Post

"Do yourself a favor and read these hidden gems. Brilliant, mordant, witty, and insightful, Christian Schneider chronicles our sojourn through Crazytown. Don't let the fact that he's so frequently hilarious distract you from the deep seriousness of his critique of our era of Unknowledge. Highly recommended"

-Charlie Sykes, Founder, editor-at-large, The Bulwark

"If you've never read Christian Schneider, you'll enjoy his wit, style, and keen eye for the ridiculous. If you're reading him for a second time, you'll remember why you loved it the first time. (And if you're reading him for a third time, a little obsessed is ok but please don't show up at his house.)"

-Anneke E. Green, founder of Reach, BBC contributor, former producer of words in George W. Bush speechwriting office

TABLE OF CONTENTS

Introduction

CHAPTER TWO: INTRIGUES 135

CHAPTER THREE: 'SAVE THE PRESIDENCY FROM THE PRESIDENT'

INTRODUCTION

As he barnstormed across the country giving lectures in packed halls, Mark Twain recognized that many of his audience members didn't believe his tall tales.

Twain told his crowds that his stem winders were full of facts, but "expected everybody to discount those facts 95 percent." Nonetheless, he maintained, "all through my life, my facts have had a substratum of truth."

The American public's thirst for discounting facts has led to a seismic shift in its politics over the past decade – an era in which I worked as a reporter and columnist documenting the slide into a culture of "alternative facts."

This book is a compilation of the wild events of the past ten years (give or take) as I wrote them down. (Sadly, Mötley Crüe stole "A Decade of Decadence" for their greatest hits album, so you're stuck with this title.)

Contained within are columns and essays about the rise of the Tea Party on the political right, the wild days of the public sector protests that roiled the country in the early 2010s, the re-election of President Barack Obama, the emergence of Donald Trump as a political force, and all the cultural baggage that came with the transformation of a party to which I once belonged.

The last decade had become what I deemed in 2016 be the "Golden Era of Anti-Knowledge," where influencers are better off sticking to an absurd position than showing weakness by backing down and accepting a moderate one. It's basically the Enlightenment if John Locke and David Hume settled their disputes by punching each other in the testicles.

The last decade has seen a presidential candidate boast about the size of his junk during a nationally televised debate. (And he won because of it, not in spite of it.) It has seen a U.S. president cajole a throng of his supporters into attacking Congress and threatening to hang the Vice President – and the president not only faced no consequences for his actions, he remains the favorite to win his party's nomination in 2024.

The last ten years has seen a global pandemic that has cost (at this writing) 700,000 American lives, yet a sizeable portion of the U.S. population has lined up in solidarity with the deadly virus. It has seen facts that exist only in the minds of deranged ideologues become a mainstream part of the national discourse, such as when Republicans claimed the 2020 election was stolen from their nominee.

And there have been seismic cultural shifts in the past decade that came on so swift and so strong that it is difficult to imagine a world before them. Same-sex marriage is the law of the land. Marijuana is legal in large swaths of the nation. Newspapers as we knew them have all but ceased to exist; people overwhelmingly get their news from social media platforms.

And I have had the honor of documenting it all.

I don't even know how I became a writer, but it was mostly out of sheer desperation. After a brief career as an anonymous blogger while working in the Wisconsin Legislature, I had to shift to writing after Republicans lost control of the Senate in 2006 and I was out of a job. Previously, I had spent a brief time as a reporter at a local paper as I worked my way through graduate school, and I was editor-in-chief of my high school newspaper, but that hardly signals a fruitful career as a national political writer.

Nonetheless, finding employment at a conservative think tank, I began writing about matters both political and policy-related. My work eventually caught the eye of National Review, which gave me a space to hold court on issues increasing the temperature of the Midwest. From there, I was offered the chance to be a conservative columnist at the Milwaukee Journal Sentinel, where I stayed until they mothballed the opinion page in 2018. (It has recently been revived, featuring a liberal TikTok activist. This is not a joke. I never thought I would lose a job as a columnist because I was an insufficient dancer.)

Nevertheless, my writing found its way into the pages of the New York Times, the Wall Street Journal, the Washington Post, and many other publications I pretend to read in order to seem smart. You may be asking yourself: Why am I holding a compilation from a columnist who isn't on Meet the Press regularly? Who is Christian Schneider? Where am I? What is that smell?

Assuming you are not on fire (please check before moving forward), I will try to answer.

For one, these are my favorite pieces from the past ten years or so. You will like them!

Secondly, as a writer working today, it is often impossible to find your work in a single place. The columns and stories in this book were strewn throughout the web (both dark and light), and they finally have found a home together. Seriously, finding the recipe for methamphetamine online is easier than stumbling on some of my earlier work.

And by putting it in a book, it guarantees a sort of permanence. I have no idea whether some of these sites are going to survive into the next decade, so I thought it was important for my life in writing to be represented with paper and ink, on a shelf somewhere for people 100 years from now to find. And if they do find it, they will obtain complete world knowledge (minus around 95 percent) of the zeitgeist that was the second decade of the 21st century.

(It will also help me remember what I once wrote. As Twain said, "When I was younger I could remember anything, whether it had happened or not; but my faculties are decaying, now, and soon I shall be so I cannot remember any but the latter.")

Each chapter represents a different aspect of public life from the last ten years. First ("For the Culture,") I discuss our cultural markers, from popular entertainment, to monkeys bringing lawsuits, to proper punching etiquette. The second chapter ("Intrigues") reflects on the giant political issues of the era, from health care, to immigration, to the drug war, to abortion, and so on.

Subsequent chapters contain works about the executive branch (including the rise of a singular unfit president), the Congress (with a number of exclusive features about former Speaker of the House Paul Ryan, whose rise and fall reflects the age of politics on the right), plus chapters on the courts and the illiberalism of the American university system.

Given I cut my teeth writing in Wisconsin, there's a chapter for the cheeseheads, detailing everything from Gov. Scott Walker's fights with public employees to the state's colorful third party candidates.

There's also a chapter full of silly stuff I've written (and which, to my eternal surprise, people actually published.)

Finally, the book ends with a previously unpublished short nonfiction piece I wrote about an entertaining 1973 teachers' strike in tiny Hortonville, Wisconsin, which ripped the state apart and made it all the way to the U.S. Supreme Court.

There is a hint of sadness in collecting all these columns and articles together, almost as if I am saying goodbye to them. The job of "columnist" these days is very different from when I grew up reading compilation books from the greats like George F. Will and H.L. Mencken. (I very much wanted to steal the name of Mencken's compilation – "A Mencken Chrestomathy" – but it seems one's book title shouldn't send potential readers to a dictionary. Also, my last name is not Mencken, so that may have been problematic.)

In the old days of writing columns, a staff writer could simply write what he wanted (and yes, they were almost always "he's") without worrying about his opinions overlapping with those of columnists around the country. But with the advent of the internet, every column, whether it's written in Walla Walla, Washington or New York City, is a national column. The convenience the internet provides in finding new things about which to write is overtaken by the difficulty in finding a new angle that nobody else has covered.

And yet, I made this my goal with everything I wrote – and continue to write. Hopefully in this volume you will read takes you didn't consider and metaphors that make my ideas more vivid. (One pre-emptive apology – given my love of Oscar Wilde, I rely on him quite often for quotes - sometimes the same quote more than once. I couldn't help myself.)

In pulling together the pieces for this book, I retroactively stumbled upon my greatest regret as a columnist. In looking back, I realized I spent entirely too many columns writing about the Donald Trump outrage of the day. Between 2015 and 2021, I penned well over a hundred pieces about Trump and the damage he has done to America. In retrospect, I wish I had spent far more time writing about all the other fragrant issues of the past half-decade. (Mercifully, I tried to limit the number of these Trump columns in this book.)

Chesterton observed that when Shakespeare wanted to write a ridiculous page, he sat down and did it without further ado. He enjoyed the process of pushing the boundaries of his creativity – if he didn't know his limits, how could he fulfill his potential?

On the other hand, as Jorge Luis Borges has noted, a mediocre poet might not have any very bad poems. He might not have them because he is conscious of his mediocrity, because he is constantly keeping watch on himself.

"I think a poet should be judged by his best pages," Borges said.

This book contains my best pages. Judge at will.

Christian Schneider, November 2021

CHAPTER ONE:

FOR THE CULTURE

THE GOLDEN ERA OF ANTI-KNOWLEDGE

December 30, 2016

Shortly before his death in 1983, eccentric futurist Buckminster Fuller introduced what he called the "knowledge-doubling curve" to describe the rapid acceleration of human knowledge. Fuller estimated that before 1900, humanity's cognitive database doubled every century; after World War II, the doubling of knowledge occurred after every 25 years. But with technological advances, recent studies suggest the total knowledge base is now doubling every 11 hours.

That is, until the year 2016, which seems to have drastically reversed this trend. This past year appears to be the first year in human history that actually extracted knowledge from the human database. We now know less than we did before the year began 12 months ago.

Clearly, we now have no idea what it takes to run a successful presidential campaign. The staid, mostly-serious affairs of the past were jettisoned in favor of a freewheeling, fact-deficient performance art piece that at one point featured the eventual U.S. president bragging about the size of the content of his pants. (A boast that had media fact-checkers calling in sick en masse the next morning.)

President-elect Donald Trump laid waste to political consulting, pollsters, fact-checkers, and general good taste with his tornado of blight, grabbing the American electorate's previously hidden parts and not letting go.

In victory, Trump dismantled our finely-honed perception of the seriousness of the American presidency. An office once held by Abraham Lincoln and Thomas Jefferson is now inhabited by a man who believes George W. Bush had knowledge of the September 11, 2001 attacks before they happened, led the charge to prove President Barack Obama wasn't born in the United States, accused a competitor's father of helping assassinate John F. Kennedy, mocked a disabled reporter, and flirted with the idea that Supreme Court Justice Antonin Scalia was murdered. It was a year that a contestant on The Bachelor who declared "deep intellectual things are just my jam" may have proven herself too much of a philosophical elitist for the American electorate.

Further, on Trump's way to the presidency, we learned about the balsa wood structure that undergirds the conservative movement. Faced with a candidate that was neither conservative nor Republican, the American right raced to see which member could offer the most embarrassing capitulation to Trumpism. Whereas years of experience had taught us that the "religious right" spoke for morality and decency, that impression has

3

evaporated. Perhaps the newest printing of the Bible will be updated to warn us that "a man with tiny hands and a large Twitter following shall lead you."

This year also rolled back whatever perception Americans had of Bill and Hillary Clinton as a political dynasty. In losing to Trump, Hillary Clinton exposed herself as one of history's worst presidential candidates, unable to inspire those on the left who remained loyal to socialist septuagenarian Bernie Sanders following the primary. In the May obituary for Mary Anne Noland of Richmond, Virginia, her loved ones noted that when "Faced with the prospect of voting for either Donald Trump or Hillary Clinton," Noland chose, instead, "to pass into the eternal love of God on Sunday."

For those who thought the peaceful transfer of power from one individual to the next was an accepted American tradition, 2016 was also a jarring experience. Upon Trump's election, therapists began seeing patients for Trump-related "fear, anxiety, and depression" disorders. Women began shedding their long tresses, no longer wanting to fit in to an America where Trump's election represented "an attack on minorities, women, and marginalized people in general." One distraught Washington Post writer claimed Trump's election sapped her of any desire to find a lover.

Yet politics wasn't the only area in which Americans were faced with a choice between two historically inept competitors. A week before the election, as the Chicago Cubs fell behind the Cleveland Indians by a three games to one deficit, the prognostication website FiveThirtyEight highlighted the Cubs' long odds with a post entitled, "The Cubs Have A Smaller Chance Of Winning Than Trump Does."

In other previously-inconceivable sports news, the words "Cleveland" and "championship" met together in a sentence for the first time in over a half-century as the Cavaliers won the NBA title. U.S. Olympic gold medalist swimmer Katie Ledecky shattered what we thought we knew about how fast humans could move through water, as it seemed she was on a flight back to America right around the time her competitors were finishing.

2016 was also a tough year for those who believed in the power of everlasting love. America's celebrity royalty, Brad Pitt and Angelina Jolie, finally called it quits after 12 years as a couple. Pitt was once engaged to noted scientist Gwyneth Paltrow, who this year declared that negative words and sounds can hurt water's feelings. Paltrow was following the lead of Japanese scientist Masaru Emoto, who believed that shouting at rice can spoil it.

Following the election, traditional media outlets blamed Trump's victory on the spread of "fake news." As if visited by the gods of irony, after printing a lengthy piece exposing the nefarious reach of such disinformation, The Washington Post issued a correction admitting their article had, in fact, relied on information from suspect news sources.

Yet the greatest threat to humanity's collective intelligence in 2016 happened to be the spread of actual news. In Wisconsin, "Pastafarians" gained the right to wear colanders on their heads in their drivers' license photos. In Washington, three people sued Chipotle over the restaurant chain's labeling of a 300-calorie burrito, claiming it made them "excessively full" (perhaps because it may contain more than 300 calories). In September, a 21-year old Australian man was bitten on his penis by a poisonous spider — for the second time.

In August, an 18-year old correctional center escapee contacted police on the department's Facebook page to request they use a better photo of her in their "wanted" alerts; she was quickly captured. In November, the New York Review of Books called the Beach Boys' song catalog "problematic" because their songs relied heavily on "beach privilege." Yet society saved its most biting criticism for those who thought "Lady Ghostbusters" was pretty good.

It's possible that the greatest subtraction of brainpower will be felt with the passing of genius over the year. The deaths of Scalia, David Bowie, John Glenn, Pat Summitt, Muhammad Ali and countless others have left a permanent hole that can't be filled. Sadly, when God buys a ticket to a personal Prince show, humanity is left significantly less sexy.

It is unclear whether this golden era of anti-knowledge will continue unabated. Perhaps an optimist would look at 2016 and claim we did learn something. Much like the realization that you're stupid almost makes you smarter, we can only hope learning that we don't know anything will be a valuable lesson in 2017.

Milwaukee Journal Sentinel

TRUMP AND CHURCHILL: MAGA FEVER DREAM

June 6, 2020

The title of Nick Adams's new book, Trump and Churchill: Defenders of Western Civilization, has it half right: Trump is very much like Churchill.

Just not Winston Churchill.

Instead, Trump very much resembles Winston's father, Lord Randolph Churchill. The elder Churchill was born into privilege, reached high office, and was prone to caustic, unhinged outbursts as he battled a brain ravaged by syphilis.

Near the end of his life, according to biographer William Manchester, Randolph would stand in Parliament, "denouncing the government in the crudest language members had ever heard there." At times, Churchill "could not engage in a coherent conversation," having entered what his friend Frank Harris called the "malignant monkey" stage of insanity.

Adams's book, however, makes the preposterous case that President Donald Trump is better for Western civilization than even the man who rescued the world from Nazism and Socialism. The very title, to quote Churchill himself, "defends itself against the risk of it being read."

It's such a ridiculous proposition that making the comparison hadn't occurred to Newt Gingrich, author of the book's foreword.

"As a longtime student of Prime Minister Winston Churchill and a supporter of President Trump, I have to confess that until I read Nick's book it had never occurred to me to join the two as historic phenomenon," Gingrich writes. And this is a man who authored a Trump hagiography so adoring its foreword was provided by Trump's son, Eric.

But the comparison made perfect sense to Trump himself, who tweeted congratulations to Adams for "the @simonschuster publication" of the book. "Certainly a great honor to be compared, in any way, to Winston Churchill," Trump wrote.

On Wednesday, the White House made the connection even more explicit, comparing Trump's staged Monday photo-op in front of St. John's Episcopal Church to Churchill inspecting the rubble in bombed-out London during WWII. Famously, Churchill did not have to tear-gas his own citizens to make way for his inspections, as Trump did.

I checked with Simon and Schuster, and they disassociated themselves from the book. The corporate office told me they sometimes distribute books from other publishers on their website. Adams's actual publisher is Post Hill Press, upon whose website one can purchase Adams's Donald Trump coloring book.

Trump and Churchill, on the other hand, is not for children—it is pure pornography for the Red Hat crowd, so much so that it should be delivered in a brown paper wrapper.

Of course, to any sentient human, comparing Donald Trump to Winston Churchill will invoke aneurysm-inducing bouts of laughter. And indeed, Trump and Churchill is, unintentionally, the funniest book I have read this year. It almost seems unfair to call it "garbage," because most actual garbage at some point had some value to someone.

Before we actually dive into Trump's new favorite tome, let's just tick off some of the obvious ways Trump and Churchill are barely members of the same genus:

Churchill was a man of great personal courage, as he volunteered to serve in the Second Boer War, was captured, and escaped. (Leading to his famous declaration, "There is nothing more exhilarating than to be shot at without result.")

As a young man, Trump dodged military service, saying at one point that avoiding sexually transmitted diseases was his "Vietnam."

Churchill was one of the grandest orators of the 20th century, inspiring millions of people to be courageous while displaying a brilliant wit.

Trump is a witless crank who elicits laughs from his followers by simply saying things that are beneath the dignity of a world leader to say. In doing so, he encourages people to be nasty and brutish to one another. He is not inspiring, he is de-spiring. ("One was a great orator; the other is a great tweeter," Adams writes in trying to compare the two.)

During the Blitz, Churchill used to stand on rooftops, at great personal risk, to watch the German bombs fall on London. During weekend protests by American citizens over police violence, Trump retreated to a White House bunker.

Oh, and another minor point—Churchill stared down both Hitler and Stalin, saving the world from catastrophe and sparing millions of lives.

Trump, on the other hand, has stared down Rosie O'Donnell and Stormy Daniels. Meanwhile, his bromances with dictators like Putin and Kim Jong-un have become legendary.

But let us suspend reality and briefly take Adams's book semi-seriously. In the introduction (which seems to take up at least one-third of the book), Adams says if there were two people in history with whom he could chat on a park bench for an hour, it would be Trump and Churchill.

Which is fine, but seems to be a thin reed on which to ascribe a comparison from one to the other. (For my park-bench interlocutors, I would choose Ronald Reagan and Lady Gaga, but I'm not sure that makes Gaga a great world leader—although, in fairness, I haven't heard her thoughts on the Marshall Plan.)

What Adams attempts to do is to construct one vague principle —"Western civilization"—and assert that Trump is superior to Churchill in defending it. This is not a Kissinger-level analysis of America and the world order, no, "Western civilization" as Adams characterizes it is no more than an abstraction and weaponization of socially conservative scruples.

7

"I never thought I would see in my lifetime a political figure who was even close to Churchill," Adams writes. "I didn't think it was possible. Then along came the political candidacy and leadership of Donald Trump. He was the leader I had been waiting to see."

According to Adams, a recent Australian immigrant to America, defending "Western civilization," means preventing transgender people from using bathrooms that are different from their biological sex—he mentions this example over and over again, as if Stalin's political prisoners were primarily worried about having to pee next to a drag queen.

Another of the characteristic values of Western civilization, according to Adams, is the "right to the freedom of speech, including the right to criticize or praise one's government; to write books, pamphlets, or on social media about one's views on any issue." Serendipitously, the day I read this passage, Donald Trump was crafting an executive order threatening to regulate Twitter for adding a further explanation tag to his tweets. Free speech, indeed.

Yet Adams remains undeterred.

"President Donald J. Trump will end up in the history books as a greater defender of Western civilization than even Prime Minister Winston Churchill, a man who deserves enormous credit for defeating Nazi Germany and protecting Great Britain, and Europe at large, from being perpetually ruled by fascists," he writes.

While obviously not intended to be a serious work of history, Adams's knowledge of Churchill's life and politics are akin to an eighth-grader frantically googling "who won world war two" the night before a paper is due. At one point, he identifies the great William Manchester as the author of Defender of the Realm, the third volume in Manchester's The Last Lion trilogy about Churchill, but as anyone who has read the book knows, it was almost entirely written by Paul Reid after Manchester was afflicted by multiple strokes and then died.

Adams compares the literary output of both Churchill, who wrote volumes of high-level war accounts and biographies, to Trump, who Adams says is "himself is a prolific writer and one of the best." Clearly, nobody has told Adams that virtually all of Trump's books have been ghostwritten.

In fact, the book is padded with long passages from both Churchill and Trump, attempting to compare the two. In one chapter, Adams—and I am not kidding—compares Churchill's legendary "We Shall Fight on the Beaches" speech following Dunkirk to Trump's inaugural address.

The book unloads a deluge of howlers, including these observations, which were evidently written by an actual human being:

"President Trump's slogan is 'Make America Great Again,' like Churchill made England great again."

"In fact, while Churchill may have had his disputes with other European leaders and President Roosevelt, those people were more or less on his side." (Hitler and Mussolini were unavailable for comment.)

"It has been a habit now for almost twenty years that whenever I visit England, I seek out Churchill locations such as Chartwell and the Cabinet War Rooms. In the U.S., I've even made the trek to Fulton, Missouri, where Churchill delivered his much famed 'Iron Curtain' speech—the greatest address by a foreigner on American soil—with President Truman watching. Similarly, when I find myself in New York; Chicago; Washington, D.C.; or Las Vegas, I always seek out the local Trump Hotel."

After noting Churchill's willingness to "go it alone" in warning about the Nazis, the book says, "President Trump has often had to go at it alone, including venturing further into the real estate game in New York than his father did."

"And though the high-stakes game of New York real estate is still not as pressure-filled as trying to defeat Nazi Germany, Trump's skills in real estate helped make him a great leader to defeat radical Islam."

There's a story that Jean Cocteau could entertain friends at parties by stripping naked, lying back on a table, and bringing himself to orgasm solely by using the power of his mind. As it turns out, Cocteau's imaginative powers prove to be far less vivid than those of a typical Trump supporter, who believes a man who overcomes problems he, himself creates and an ambiguous cloud of conspiracy are comparable to a singular leader who beat back an existential evil that landed on his doorstep.

The Bulwark

AMERICA'S MOST BELOVED LIBERTARIAN

Dec. 17, 2013

When the NBC show "Parks and Recreation" began in 2009, it was pretty clear that the character of Ron Swanson was destined to be a one-joke running gag. Swanson, played by the stocky, mustachioed actor Nick Offerman, was supposed to elicit laughter because he was an anti-government enthusiast who ran the city parks department.

"I don't believe in government," Swanson says in the pilot episode. "I think that all government is a waste of taxpayer money. My dream is to have the parks system privatized and run entirely for profit by corporations."

9

The show's co-creator, Michael Schur, has said the Swanson character was based on a real-life libertarian woman he befriended in Burbank, Calif. "I don't really believe in the mission of my job," she told him. "I'm aware of the irony."

But during the show's five-plus year run, Swanson has undergone a transformation, becoming one of the most popular characters on television. In 2011, Paste Magazine named him the second-best television character in America. In fact, Swanson may be the most popular conservative in America, period.

Interestingly, "Parks and Recreation" is a show with a liberal temperament that claims a fairly strong left-of-center viewing audience. A 2011 study showed the sitcom was the fifth-most-popular show among liberals, behind overtly progressive political shows such as "The Daily Show" and "The Colbert Report." (In recent episodes, the show has mocked people who oppose governmental limits on soda sizes and has lampooned constitutional originalists as delusional tea partyers who wear tricorn hats.)

So how is it possible that the greatest right-wing character in television history (sorry, Alex P. Keaton) has emerged on a show so beloved by the left?

For one, the writing is some of the most entertaining on TV, and Offerman's droll delivery is a master class in deadpan comedy.

But the show also tackles political issues in ways you won't see on other network sitcoms. In one episode, a fourth-grader named Lauren comes to the office to learn about why government matters. Swanson befriends the girl, explaining how taxes work by taking a large bite of the sandwich she had packed for lunch.

"And that, Lauren, is how FDR ruined this country," Swanson tells her, before handing her a land mine and telling her to use it to "protect your property."

And sometimes, the show's writers even let Swanson be right. In one episode, he opposes a city bailout of a local video store, believing that doing so would turn the town into a "socialist hellscape." After the bailout passes, the store starts selling only adult videos, thereby creating taxpayer-subsidized porn. "The government should not prop up a failed business," Swanson tells Leslie Knope, played by Amy Poehler. "That would be like giving food to a mortally wounded animal instead of slitting its throat and properly utilizing its meat and pelt."

In fact, despite being a fictional character, Swanson's popularity might actually hold a lesson for today's conservatives. While Republicans are perpetually tarred as the party of the rich (see: Romney, Mitt), Swanson is simply a regular guy who wants the government to leave him alone. (Schur describes him as a 19th-century rugged individualist.)

Swanson loves drinking scotch ("clear alcohols are for rich women on diets"), is an unapologetic gun owner and hunter and eschews exercise. He eats primarily breakfast foods and steaks, builds furniture in his wood shop and occasionally moonlights as saxophone player Duke Silver.

In this way, Swanson taps into a rich "live and let live" philosophy that the right could once again reclaim. He isn't lobbying on behalf of corporations, and it seems he's not particularly interested in imposing any kind of religious values on anyone. He's a guy who believes liberty is found in individual rights and freedoms, as summed up in his mantra, "I live the way I live, I eat the way I eat and I will die the way I die."

Granted, it may be treacherous to learn lessons from a fictitious character who initially was intended to mock conservatives. But Swanson's rise in popularity among both the left and right seems to suggest that a strong individualistic strain still runs through our culture.

If the GOP is looking for a successful 2016 presidential candidate, it should look for someone who can make the uniquely American brand of liberty appealing again. For as Ron Swanson said, "History began July 4th, 1776. Anything before that was a mistake."

Milwaukee Journal Sentinel

NOBODY CARES THAT YOU'RE SAD ABOUT PRINCE

April 26, 2016

[Ed. note: This column provoked more hate mail than any other I've written.]

In 2016, when a celebrity dies, it is best to turn off your computer, slowly back away and proceed with the rest of your day as if you were a grown human adult.

Doing so will spare you all the attention-chasing histrionics that now accompany any death of every famous person. Soon, your Twitter feed will be full of people posting selfies of themselves "ugly crying" over Prince's death, sharing phony stories about how they saw "Purple Rain" in the theater even though they were 11 years old when the movie came out (we can do the math), and how the last 55 seconds of Prince's "Let's Pretend We're Married" made them the person they are. These are the same people who believed they had insights into the Paris shootings because they stayed in a hostel there once.

It is now a requirement that people grieve in public, and in a way that lets everyone know they were much more of a fan than anyone else. The important thing isn't the person's death and the hole it leaves in the world; the true effect of a celebrity death is how it affects you.

And thus people construct elaborate scenarios in which they are somehow the aggrieved party when a great musician is found dead in an elevator far before his time. Consider it the "verbal selfie."

Sure, recognitions of the immense talent of Prince or David Bowie or Antonin Scalia or whoever else are fine. Their passings are all newsworthy, and their achievements deserve recognition. And people who actually met these people and have stories to share, then fine.

But such honest remembrances often quickly turn into insufferable narcissistic bromides about how Prince "made me the person I am," or some such nonsense. Writing in the Independent Journal Review, Kate Bennett offers up this stomach-turning bit of prose: "For the next three decades, I quite openly let Prince's music teach me other things, about the world, about life, sexuality, compassion, individuality, lust, and funk."

Good grief. First of all, there's a 95% chance none of you mourning Prince's death had listened to anything he recorded in the past quarter of a century. When he played at halftime of the Super Bowl in 2007, you said to yourself, "Hey, he used to be great!"

And no, Prince did not make you the person you are today. You know no more about sex or life or the color purple than if he had never existed. If you learned about "compassion" from a guy who reportedly didn't allow employees to look at him in the eyes, perhaps some counseling is in order. (The only lasting effect Prince had on preteen boys in 1984 was forcing them to daydream about the feminine wonders to be found in Lake Minnetonka.)

But the compulsion to grieve so publicly is simply too much for people today to resist. It's almost as if there is some government bureau taking note of who expressed sadness over Prince's passing and who didn't. It's not like saying "so sad Prince died!" on Twitter goes into your compassion bank, to be cashed in at a later date. You won't be on trial, and the judge says, "Well, he did steal that car and ram it into that hospital for puppies, but then again, he also seemed pretty shaken up about Bowie's death."

That doesn't prevent the most acrid modern death phenomenon, the "celebrity reaction" tweets. "Today is the worst day ever. Prince R.I.P. I am crying!" said erstwhile celebrity Boy George. "Prince was the greatest live performer I ever saw," said Piers Morgan, adding that he admired Prince's "astounding, sexually charged energy." (I apologize for ruining whatever you were just eating.)

Even politicians get in on the grievance parade, thinking there may be "purple primary" voters out there willing to set aside their views on abortion, taxes, ISIS and immigration and say, "well what did he think about 'Lovesexy?'"

Sure, we all grieve in different ways, but it would be great if you didn't do it by making a spectacle of yourself. Just keep in mind — people who live lives of quiet desperation are typically doing everyone else a favor.

Milwaukee Journal Sentinel

WE DON'T NEED A CONSERVATIVE SNL, WE NEED CONSERVATIVES ON SNL

June 14, 2018

"I think a lot of young people don't just watch comedy shows to stay informed," comedian Tina Fey told journalist Eric Spitznagel in a 2003 interview about the politics of Saturday Night Live. "They also want to be guided on how they're supposed to feel," Fey added. "I guess that's what we do, to some extent. We have a liberal bias, obviously, and that's very much the tone of (Weekend) Update."

In the subsequent 15 years, little has changed. The show continues to target the progressive funny bone, rarely turning the tables and scorching Democrats. In one of the most embarrassing bits ever aired on national broadcast television, one January 2017 episode actually ended with two cast members mournfully singing goodbye to President Barack Obama. It looked as if it belonged on "Saturday Night North Korea."

It's SNL's bias that led TownHall.com columnist Mike LaChance to pen a widely mocked column suggesting conservatives start their own "Saturday Night Live," set in America's "heartland." (He points to Omaha, Neb., as "ideal.")

LaChance offered some ideas for sketches, including "Very Deep Thoughts from Joe Biden," "Lifestyles of the Rich and Democrat," and "Bernie Sanders hosts a radio show where he can't explain the historical failures of socialism to a single caller." He even suggests the show's first five hosts: James Woods, Ann Coulter, Greg Gutfeld, Sarah Palin, and Adam Baldwin.

In other words, LaChance wants a show that's about as funny as juvenile diabetes. This might be the first time in history a pitch for a TV show is funnier than the show itself.

For one, Omaha isn't particularly Republican: it was one of two Nebraska counties Hillary Clinton won in 2016.

Further, pushing a political agenda above all else isn't how comedy works. The jokes come first; if they're not funny and rooted in truth (and SNL's jokes often miss the mark), the show will be a disaster. Not to mention that sketch comedy writers are like NFL quarterbacks — there are only a handful in the world that are any good. If SNL has the top talent every year, and its skits are still shaky, where would that leave "Live in Omaha?"

But in order to see more balance in sketch comedy, conservatives don't need their own SNL. SNL needs more conservatives. They do exist — SNL's greatest political writer, Jim Downey, is a Republican, and the show does occasionally take a swipe at liberal totems, such as when it repeatedly needled African-Americans for their infallible support for Barack Obama.

Yet instead of "going Galt" and starting their own doomed-from-the-start shows, conservatives should try to make inroads in places where they wouldn't normally be welcome. Don't try "separate but unequal" comedy, have the guts to succeed in the big leagues. If right-wingers face barriers in popular entertainment because of ideology, they just have to be better than everyone else. Funny is funny, and there is room on any comedy show for someone who can consistently make people laugh.

This is a conversation conservatives are forced to have when trying to break into progressive-dominated fields. Many conservatives, frustrated with liberal dominance in academia, argue in favor of starting universities oriented to the political right. They see more value in places such as Michigan's Hillsdale College than in lefty strongholds like Harvard or Yale.

But as National Review's Jonah Goldberg frequently argues, conservatives don't need their own universities, they need more representation in the established ones. Similarly, while conservative newspapers offer valuable insight, the right also needs representation in America's legacy newsrooms. Simply splitting our national institutions into "left" and "right" harms both the producers and consumers of news and entertainment.

LaChance says his SNL-for-Trumpists show would "meet the left on their turf," "beat them at their own game," and "devastate their narrative." He concludes, "As they say with the lottery, you can't win if you don't play."

But conservatives separating themselves and refusing to compete in the only relevant arena isn't "playing," it is "conceding." Instead of grinding out a painful mediocrity of a show, we just need to hone our skills and compete on the progressives' turf.

Because, as SNL's Stuart Smalley once said, "only the mediocre are always at their best."

Milwaukee Journal Sentinel

SEARCHING FOR THE NEXT STEVE MARTIN

July 30, 2018

To a young person in 2018, a Steve Martin comedy album from the late-1970s is likely perplexing. Martin's most riotous bits merely involved him firing off catch phrases—audiences howled with laughter as he blurted lines like "excuuuuuuuuse me!" and "I'm a wild and crazy guy!" His signature prop was a magic shop-style arrow through the head. He would often coax audiences into hysterics simply by shifting into a silly voice or wildly flailing his arms and feet.

In a vacuum, a young person may wonder how any of that is actually funny. But the key to understanding any national phenomenon is to understand its context. While his act was impossibly silly, Martin knew exactly what he was doing. By the mid-1970s, he felt America's fatigue with the caustic, left-wing political comedy of the Vietnam Era and sensed comedy lovers wanted something new.

"The political scene was exhausting," Martin writes about the early 1970s in his memoir, Born Standing Up. He notes that in the late-1960s, with the ubiquity of political comics like George Carlin and the Smothers Brothers, "Silliness was just not appropriate for hip culture."

"And many people, including me, were alienated from government ... Change was imminent."

Martin sought to be that change, dropping the political content from his act and stitching together an act of avant garde absurdism. "To politics I was saying, 'I'll get along without you very well. It's time to be funny,'" Martin writes. "Overnight, I was no longer at the tail end of an old movement but at the front end of a new one."

The transformation wasn't immediately successful—he produced a number of cringeworthy television appearances, such as one bit where he attempted to tell jokes to an audience of dogs on The Tonight Show. But by the end of the decade, Martin was America's most recognizable entertainer, moving millions of records and selling out shows in 20,000-seat arenas.

Martin's era-specific act is a reminder that huge cultural shifts don't happen on their own: They are part of a chain of events that occurs both before and after. For instance, historian H.W. Brands, who has written biographies about both Franklin Delano Roosevelt and Ronald Reagan, once told me that Reagan could not have happened without Roosevelt; the excesses of the New Deal led to an eventual backlash captained by the conservative savior.

Similarly, while the Donald Trump presidency may be an anomaly in American history, Trump was elected as a reaction to a cultural shift that had been evolving years before the 2016 election. Citizens who supported his candidacy saw political correctness taking over college campuses, racial unrest in America's cities, and a loss of control over their own destinies. They chose a dramatic course correction in casting their ballots for Trump.

Putting events in context explains much of the inexplicable in American history, especially in the world of entertainment. In the early-1990s, grunge music became a way for America to wash away the excesses of the late-1980s hair band fad. By the mid-1990s, having tired of the stream of Seattle-based gloominess defining music, the public lurched back to Britney Spears and boy bands.

This boomerang effect happens time and again in American comedy, too. The original political correctness era on college campuses in the late-1980s sparked a resistance that included coarse comedy from vulgarians like Andrew Dice Clay and Sam Kinison. Soon, Adam Sandler's dopey films reigned supreme at the box office, signifying a proud middle finger to cultural elites.

America seems to be on the back end of a similar cultural wave in 2018. Comedy fans are intimately familiar by now with the humorous beats and rhythms of the liberals sitting behind an "anchor desk" grouching about Donald Trump. They've seen the "stupid Republican" video clips that cut back to the host making a face expressing disgust. They've heard the hosts use comedic metaphors enhanced with absurdist graphics. They've seen the earnest "field reporters" saying insensitive things supposedly believed by conservatives, and the joke is—get this— they don't actually mean what they say!

Not only is the satirical news blueprint stale, the comedy itself on these shows has become lazy and uninspired. Shows like Jon Oliver's Last Week Tonight and Samantha Bee's Full Frontal have all but ditched any guise of speaking truth to power, relying instead on microwaved progressive applause lines. Memorably, Bee recently roiled conservatives by calling Ivanka Trump a "feckless c--t." Yet the primary news to emerge from Bee's transgression was not her use of the vulgarity, it was essentially that she had retired from doing actual comedy.

What Jon Stewart's acolytes seemingly don't understand is that people laugh the hardest when they're laughing at something they shouldn't find hilarious. The best comedy challenges conventions, not reinforces them. Shows like Stephen Colbert's Late Show simply serve up comfort and predictability for those afraid of having holes poked in their ideology.

This monolithic dedication to liberalism in humor has now spawned a new genre of stand-up comedy, in which the performer doesn't attempt to be funny, a brand of entertainment about as pointless as alcohol-free scotch. In Hannah Gadsby's recent stand-up special "Nanette," Gadsby talks in detail about her life as a queer woman and shares stories of being raped. Saturday Night Live co-head writer Michael Che has criticized this new brand of anti-comedy as "stand-up tragedy," adding that "you still need a punchline ... can't just walkout and say, 'the holocaust. good night.'"

Soon, the days of left-wing hectoring will burn out and give way to something more provocative and profound. Big-name comedians are already challenging liberal dogma and earning praise for doing so: Dave Chappelle's recent Netflix specials have addressed transgender pronouns and the #MeToo movement; Chris Rock's most recent concert condemns pornography, explains why some kids need bullying, and mocks the idea of telling kids in his daughters' school they can be anything they want. "Maybe four of them can be anything they want to be," he jokes. "But the other 2,000 better learn how to weld."

Chappelle and Rock, of course, are established comedians with rabid followings. It will be more exciting to see what creative direction the younger members of the upcoming backlash will take. Will they be as silly as Steve Martin making balloon animals? Let's hope so. Will they be puzzling and inventive? We should demand it.

Most importantly, they should keep giving voice to the things we all think but can't say out loud. As cultural mores push us one way, comedians should push us back.

Presumably, one day, this backlash will fade and itself face its own backlash. And then, 40 years later, we will all look back in amazement that we spent a decade paying large sums of money for white liberals to harangue us on a nightly basis.

The Weekly Standard

MOVIES HOLLYWOOD ISN'T LIKELY TO MAKE

March 1, 2014

If the old adage that "politics is show business for ugly people" is true, then so is the converse. Show business is also politics for those who have won the genetic lottery.

Yet while ugliness is an affliction that demonstrates no partisanship, one must be of the right ideological stripe to take part in the politics of show business. The stereotype of Hollywood as the playground for rich liberals is pretty well-ingrained; but simply because something is a stereotype doesn't mean it's not demonstrably true.

This diamond-studded progressivism will be on display Sunday at the 86th annual Academy Awards, where the glitterati get together to celebrate themselves and allow the rubes in flyover country to watch. There is no way to guarantee an Oscar win, but there is certainly a way to guarantee a loss: Make a movie with a conservative theme.

Every year, there are movies Hollywood deems to have the "right" message. And that message is almost always ripped from the headlines of the Huffington Post. (Merely saying "Academy Award winner Michael Moore" is like gargling battery acid.)

In 2006, Al Gore became an Oscar winner with his hysterical global warming documentary, An Inconvenient Truth. Four years later, the same director, Davis Guggenheim, made a transformative film about the pitfalls of public teacher unionization ("Waiting for 'Superman'") and got shut out of a nomination altogether.

After Meryl Streep won a Best Actress Oscar in 2011 for her role in The Iron Lady, her acceptance speech was lacking two very important words: "Margaret" and "Thatcher." (A year later, Julianne Moore was showered with awards for playing Sarah Palin as a buffoon in the HBO movie Game Change; voters were evidently unaware that the movie was terrible.)

Awards aside, having a liberal point of view can be enough just to get a movie made. The Lorax featured a little orange-mustached CGI monster hectoring people about global warming. Same thing with Best Picture Oscar nominee Avatar, except the characters are blue. There Will Be Blood is an allegory for greedy oilmen. In Elysium, Matt Damon turns into a robot so people can get Obamacare. Not even the Muppets are sacred — in the last Muppet movie, Kermit and friends take on a big oil tycoon named Tex Richman.

Thus, in order to appeal to the other half of the country, I am offering Hollywood some ideas for movies with conservative themes. Any of these film ideas can be bought from me for either $100,000 or by letting me meet Alison Brie:

"Blue Life Special": Amy Adams stars in a stirring role as a single mother who develops breast cancer but is able to get top-notch treatment from the health plan she receives as a Walmart employee. After the local city council shuts down the store through zoning regulations, Adams loses her health care and ends up paying five to nine times as much for less coverage on the Obamacare exchanges. (This also marks the end of the "Amy Adams has stopped wearing makeup" portion of her career.)

"Disorganized Labor": Shia LaBeouf returns to respectable acting as a fiery union leader who organizes employees against their company in search of higher wages. Soon, the factory closes and moves all of its jobs to China. LaBeouf then renews his career mobilizing people to action in Yelp comments online.

"Third-World Super-Size Me": A Burundi family eats McDonald's every day for a month and immediately declares America to be the greatest nation on Earth for producing so much low-cost, delicious food.

"Divine and Conquer": A Southern Christian family somehow manages to be deeply religious without speaking in tongues, handling snakes or murdering anyone. While volunteering at a local shelter, they meet a homeless pregnant teenager and vow to help her turn her life around. When they bring her to church, somehow there are no rich old women fanning themselves, giving her the stink-eye and clucking their disapproval.

"The Best Medicine": In this avant-garde art film starring Johnny Depp, the U.S. government bravely caps the cost of prescription drugs, so pharmaceutical companies can't invest in research and development into new medicines. The entire four-hour movie is one shot of Depp's character laying there, dying. (The New York Times raves, "it is definitely a series of moving pictures!")

"Finding Nemo II": Nemo's school of fish closes down after his teachers go on strike to protest paying into their own pensions.

OK, maybe these could use a little work. (I will thereby downgrade my demands to $10,000 and Gabe Kaplan.) But it is clear Hollywood folks are leaving a lot of money on the table; perhaps they should give the occasional nod to the free-market policies that made them all millionaires in the first place.

Milwaukee Journal Sentinel

WHEN PUNCHING PEOPLE, FOLLOW PROPER ETIQUETTE

January 24, 2017

Common sense would dictate that any time a Nazi gets punched in the face, an American soldier gets a medal.

On the streets of Washington, D.C., last Friday, this theory was put to the test, as racist, anti-immigrant, anti-Semite Richard Spencer was punched in the head from behind while being filmed giving an interview shortly after President Donald Trump's inauguration.

Immediately, the attack on the "alt-right" leader ricocheted gleefully through the Internet, with some social media users setting the haymaker to patriotic music. Both political left and right cheered as the incident left one fewer Nazi face unpunched.

Upon reflection, however, there emerged detractors of this brand of vigilante justice. Charles C.W. Cooke of National Review argued against assaulting Nazis on constitutional grounds, reasonably claiming that "a great test of any free country is how it treats its dissenters." (Although it would seem people prone to punching other people would tend not to be steeped in history, unless that person is Indiana Jones.)

America always has had a love affair with people punching each other in the face. There is something dignified about a man being willing to defend his own honor with his fists.

And certainly, there are situations where punching someone else is acceptable. In sports, rows break out all the time that end up with blows being rained down on the participants' heads, and no criminal charges are ever brought. In "Captain America: The First Avenger," the hero stages a play where he literally punches Adolf Hitler in the face (in Milwaukee!) to cheering crowds. Is there a more cathartic scene than the one at the end of "Die Hard" when Holly McClane punches the reporter that aired video of her children?

But even though none of us lacks sufficient reason to pop someone in the face, there must be rules for doing so.

Obviously, hitting someone is acceptable in the case of self-defense. If you are a man, hitting a woman is never acceptable, and if justice serves, reasonably should lead to you being pummeled yourself. And of course, excessive punching that endangers someone's life is never allowed. ("Assault: how much is too much?")

Otherwise, punching should be limited to those engaged in a consensual fight. Upon calculating the risks, if two people agree that "taking it outside" is the best way to solve things, that choice is one each is entitled to make. This is in keeping with the long American tradition of dueling — some states still even have clauses that bar state employment for those having participated in a duel. (Presumably, like old times, most bar fights begin with a declaration like, "Good day, sir, I believe you have dishonored me — I therefore challenge you to engage me in fisticuffs!")

A subset of those engaging in consensual fights is those who find themselves engaged in a fight by ignoring prior warnings. Suppose you're on a plane and hear "stop playing that tuba or I am going to punch you in the face." If you ignore this warning and continue to play your tuba, you have unwillingly entered a verbal contract and therefore consent to being beaten with your brass instrument.

That brings us to the second major category of punch recipients — those who are unaware they are about to be punched. For these people, the anti-violence enthusiasts have it right; we cannot have a society where people just take the punching laws into their own fists and start clocking people with whom they disagree.

But even though you shouldn't hit Nazis, that doesn't mean there isn't a good reason to. As James Madison said (probably), free speech doesn't mean freedom from ass-beatings.

Thus, if you are a racist and stand on a Washington, D.C. street corner and proselytize white supremacy, you have to understand the chance of you finding yourself amid a fist blizzard is dangerously high. Call people the n-word or unironically refer to someone using the gay-related f-word and it is unlikely they will quickly check the statute books to determine whether to allow you to keep your teeth.

Most important, if you do find yourself in a situation where you have to hit someone, keep in mind that you are risking damaging yourself more than the other person. Movie-style fights where one person wails on another are fiction; punching someone in the face actually feels a lot like punching a bowling ball. If you swing at someone's head, you better have a really good reason, as you might be wearing a cast for a while.

Just to be clear, hitting people who don't consent to being punched is always wrong and you shouldn't do it. It's just that in some cases... we understand.

Milwaukee Journal Sentinel

THE CATS COME TO WESTMINSTER

February 3, 2017

If an American citizen from early 2016 jumped into a time-hopping Delorean and skipped ahead to today, he or she may not even recognize the country he or she once inhabited. Universities are removing portraits of Shakespeare because he doesn't represent "diversity." The Chicago Cubs won the World Series. Average American citizens now cower in fear that the U.S. president might call them a "turd burglar" on Twitter.

But, soon, an event is occurring that should cause all Americans to, in the words of William F. Buckley, stand athwart history and yell "Stop!" Next week, cats will be featured at the Westminster Kennel Club Dog Show.

In the words of noted fictional ectoplasmologist Peter Venkman, cats and dogs living together is the very definition of "mass hysteria." And the outrage of allowing cats to share the stage with dogs at the Westminster Dog Show is the latest unmistakable sign that the world is coming unmoored from its safe harbor of common sense.

The cats will be part of a showcase at the show called "Meet and Compete," which is supposed to teach "responsible pet ownership." (One of the cats taking part in the show is a Bengal named "Jungletrax Abiding Ovation," suggesting he is likely in the feline witness protection program for involvement in the Cat Mafia.)

And even though the cats won't be out running around and being judged with the dogs, this is how societal decay begins. Some might consider this "progress" — and while societal progress often can mean righting historical wrongs, measures of "progress" are often defined by those just looking to get something they want.

And cats have some very high-profile defenders. Leonardo da Vinci believed that "the smallest feline is a masterpiece." Sigmund Freud once said that "time spent with cats is never wasted," although given his self-medication regimen, Freud could have easily replaced the word "cats" with "cocaine."

Yet if "progress" simply means eroding tradition and social norms, it isn't always something worth pursuing. Respect for order and history are admirable aims in and of themselves, and blurring societally agreed upon mores can lead to catastrophe.

It is unclear what wrong this unspeakable intermingling of cats and dogs is supposed to right. Cats already are the most entitled of animal species — through their mind tricks, they have already convinced humans that they should be allowed to defecate indoors. Are we granting them special privilege for Donald Trump threatening to grab them during the campaign? (I think that's what that was about — my memory is hazy.)

Allowing cats at the world's most famous dog show perhaps would be more tolerable if cats weren't so awful. Even feline enthusiasts have to admit, if cats had opposable thumbs, humans would be living in caves underground. No one will be able to convince me that cats aren't waiting for the just right time to make us all their servants. I'd be willing to block all cat adoption from animal shelters until we can, in the words of Donald Trump, "figure out what is going on."

That doesn't, of course, absolve the dog show itself of being a cauldron of weirdness. When Shih Tzus sport pedicures expensive enough to feed a third-world child for a year, perhaps some perspective is in order. And if dogs could read history books, they might recognize that judging others by the purity of their genetic bloodlines doesn't end particularly well.

But change for the sake of change isn't always "progress." The Westminster Dog Show has been gloriously cat-free for 141 years; let cats have their own shows. Allowing them to crash one of America's favorite institutions is an idea that deserves exactly zero lives.

Milwaukee Journal Sentinel

LITIGIOUS MONKEYS

April 27, 2018

In one installment of the "Brevity" comic strip, a dog sits in a witness chair as he is being grilled by a prosecutor.

"If you didn't eat the homework, why did the arresting officer say he smelled geometry on your breath?" the attorney asks.

"I had just eaten a square meal!" said the dog.

As it turns out "animals in court" is a pretty familiar trope among cartoonists.

Anthropomorphizing animals into plaintiffs and defendants is a evidently a bottomless resource for laughs. (Another "Brevity" cartoon features two small oysters staring at each other, with one threatening to take the other to "Small Clams Court.")

Yet last Monday, the prospect of litigious lemurs got a lot less funny when the U.S. 9th Circuit Court of Appeals ruled that animals actually have a constitutional right to file lawsuits against humans.

It all began back in 2011, when wildlife photographer David Slater was taking photographs in Indonesia. Slater, seeing a 7-year-old crested macaque monkey, left his camera alone in the jungle, hoping the primate would begin taking pictures of himself. Sure enough, the monkey, later named Naruto, began snapping "selfies," which Slater then brought back to the U.S. and published as a book. (Naruto, of course, now has several Twitter accounts dedicated to him.)

In 2015, People for the Ethical Treatment of Animals filed suit against Slater while naming Naruto (a name they gave to the monkey) as a plaintiff, arguing Naruto took the pictures, and was thus entitled to the book's revenues. In filing on behalf of a primate, PETA invoked "next friend" status, which is typically used for groups who sue on behalf of someone who are unable, such as those with disabilities. Last October, PETA and Slater settled the lawsuit, with the cameraman agreeing to donate 25% of the book's earnings to "protect the habitat of Naruto and other crested macaques in Indonesia."

But the lawsuit didn't end there. The court rendered a judgment anyway, slamming PETA for taking advantage of Naruto to further its own goals, and suggested Naruto could even sue the animal rights group for using him as an "unwitting pawn in its ideological goals."

But while PETA lost the battle, it may have won the war. While the court ruled Naruto didn't fit the requirements to sue under the U.S. intellectual property statutes, animals still have general standing to sue under Article III of the U.S. Constitution. This means that in the 9th circuit, animals are free to bring lawsuits. (Keep in mind, this is a monkey currently residing in Indonesia, whereabouts unknown.)

While it sounds ridiculous, this is a breakthrough for animal rights groups, who have been seeking to sue on behalf of animals for years. PETA and other groups are gaining traction in their quest to flood animal industries with lawsuits, tangling them up in court and draining them of revenues.

Imagine, for a moment, the lawsuits that could be brought against the University of Wisconsin's research arm, which uses animals in laboratory testing. Recent biological research being done at the UW-Madison includes trials to create an Ebola vaccine, experiments to help women create estrogen to aid in their fertility, and cell-editing research to combat cancer — all of which involve animal testing. Tying this research up in courts could not only cost lives, it could put taxpayers on the hook for legal fees to fight the tsunami.

And make no mistake, the lawsuits would be coming if animals were granted legal personhood, followed by aggressive lawyers seeking to cash in on obnoxious litigation. While it may seem funny to envision a giraffe in a tie sitting on a witness stand, the reality of animal rights lawsuits will be to stifle valuable research and hurt America's food and apparel industries.

And then the 9th circuit will truly become a kangaroo court.

Milwaukee Journal Sentinel

YOU HAVE A RIGHT TO BE OFFENDED

May 20, 2014

On Friday night, Grammy Award-winning rapper Macklemore found himself on the hot seat after he appeared onstage in Seattle wearing a disguise some believed incorporated traditional Jewish stereotypes. It immediately became the most offensive thing about Macklemore, at least to those who haven't actually heard his music.

The whole controversy pitted America's two most odious internal threats against one another: white rappers vs. the perpetually aggrieved. It is simply impossible to pick sides in such a conflict.

Fortunately, there's only one Macklemore. Conversely, there are growing armies of people who wake up every morning intent on being offended by some aspect of their immediate world.

This has become the case in universities across America, where a movement is afoot to label classic literature with "trigger warnings" to prevent students from stumbling upon a passage that might make them uncomfortable. The movement, as reported by The New York Times, has its basis in feminist ideology; at Oberlin College, students suggested that a course's syllabus should flag anything that might "disrupt a student's learning" and "cause trauma," such as passages including "racism, classism, sexism, heterosexism, cissexism, ableism and other issues of privilege and oppression."

If the professionally aggrieved get their way, our children's delicate psyches won't be sullied — as 130 years of young readers' have — by reading classics such as Mark Twain's "The Adventures of Huckleberry Finn," which deals with racism in the stark language used in 1884. Or Shakespeare's "Merchant of Venice," which treats the Jewish character of Shylock historically appropriately. These texts are historically invaluable, as they remind students what the world once was; in that sense, they serve the same purpose as modern films such as "12 Years a Slave."

Of course, the very process of learning consists of coming into contact with ideas that cajole, discomfort and challenge. Much of the acrimony in modern politics is likely traceable to the inability of people to learn to handle opposing viewpoints; sheltering students from challenging literature out of a sense of "sensitivity" is ensuring they will remain ill-prepared when they spring forth from the womb of campus. As Greg Lukianoff of the Foundation for Individual Rights in Education told The Times, "There is a real important and serious value to being offended."

Gone are the days when campuses served as places where unpopular ideas could be given voice; now, universities purge ideas from the public square if they don't fit their infantilizing sensitivity models.

Take, for example, Rutgers University, which recently threw former Secretary of State Condoleezza Rice overboard when students protested her invitation to be commencement speaker. Or universities around the country that harangue students about the role "white privilege" plays in their success, as if skin color usurps their hard work in getting ahead. Or the U.S. Justice Department and the Department of Education's Office of Civil Rights, which jointly have issued new regulations for universities that include restrictions on vague "sexually harassing speech."

Naturally, sensitivity nonsense isn't limited to campuses. This week, when The World's Largest Brat Fest, based in Madison, invited a motivational Christian speaker, the city's sensitivity police sprang into action. Madison Ald. Lisa Subeck objected and soon organizers capitulated and disinvited the speaker.

Given that the U.S. Supreme Court has yet to affirm the separation of church and sausage, Brat Fest organizers could have stuck to their guns. But Subeck evidently can't fathom the idea of eating encased meats while others listen to a faith-based message, so she supports denying others the right to witness it.

In Madison and on university campuses, where liberals reign, the left has begun to eat its own. Some would say that on the right, the tea party is a reaction to the toothlessness of the GOP over the past 20 years; similarly, the fringe left has gotten restless and demands more influence in the places liberals wholly control.

In the early 20th century, British journalist Hannen Swaffer observed that "freedom of the press in Britain is freedom to print such of the proprietor's prejudices as the advertisers don't object to."

This is where we appear to be in America at this point, with a small cadre of speech police protecting us from uncomfortable concepts. In fact, under the left's own standard, students should be given a trigger warning to shield them from the violence being perpetrated upon the free exchange of ideas.

Milwaukee Journal Sentinel

PERFORMATIVE GLUTTONY

July 22, 2018

English author and historian James Laver once wrote of the late 20th century in Britain as a time where social status served as a source of inspiration rather than revulsion. Laver remembered "the Edwardian age was probably the last period in history when the fortunate thought they could give pleasure to others by displaying their good fortune before them."

This phenomenon didn't particularly take hold in America, where status was far more egalitarian. American reporter Richard Harding Davis, writing from England, noted, "In America we hate uniforms because they have been twisted into meaning badges of servitude; our housemaids will not wear caps, nor will our coachmen shave their mustaches." Davis noted that "this tends to make every class of citizen more or less alike.

In modern America, it is still considered gauche to rub everyone's face in your wealth; it is why famous actors typically favor dressing like hobos. But like early 20th century England, it seems America has developed a mechanism for delighting its downtrodden with vulgar displays of gluttony.

I am talking, of course, of hot dog eating competitions.

Americans appear to be fond of gathering in front of large stages and watching human beings endure caloric Armageddon while thrusting encased meats down their gullets. This typically happens on the Fourth of July, where America's independence from England has become intertwined with the nation's dependence on heart disease.

Yet the popularity of eating contests continues to spread like sauerkraut over a bratwurst. At fairs all across America, audiences delight in watching sweaty contestants jam their cheeks with regional delicacies, many of which remain regional for a reason. Soon, undisputed hot dog champion Joey Chestnut will appear at the Wisconsin State Fair to ingest cheese curds, an appearance for which he is being feted in local media as if he were the ghost of Abraham Lincoln.

There are many fronts on which to wage this war against stomach sports. First, let us quickly dispense with the complaints of animal rights groups, who object to the morality of so many animals being eaten in so little time. Suppose our culinary tastes are, indeed, being judged by some sort of supreme being — clearly the best evidence for the existence of God is bacon.

Others argue competitive eating is an affront to people who don't have any food to eat. There is merit in this claim, although the evidence suggest America's poorest residents are actually more prone to obesity than those on the upper-income scale. Taken to its logical conclusion, this argument would pre-empt anyone from purchasing anything nice because someone else can't afford it.

On a world stage, however, competitive eating is truly a stick in the eye to nations who suffer from a lack of food. If citizens in 90 percent of the countries of the world watched a hot dog eating competition, they'd automatically assume the winner was the wealthiest man or woman in America.

Yet the primary arguments against competitive eating are the twin prongs of decency and propriety. Somehow, loading one's mouth with food has become symbolic of freedom and self-determination, a bold defiance of rules laid down by society and the government. (Who can forget Patrick Henry's declaration to "give me liberty or give me 25 pounds of jalapeno poppers?")

But freedom from needless regulation (eating contests have now become the antidote to Obamacare) doesn't grant one a license to engage in grotesque excess. Freedom demands responsibility, not deep-fried vulgarity. Subjecting one's self to an arterial Gettysburg only proves one's independence from fear of diabetes.

In the interest of full disclosure, I am not innocent of the charges I am bringing. In fifth grade, I participated in — and won — a pie eating contest in order to impress classmate Mary Beth Hammond. I was so proud of my achievement, I theatrically wore the blueberry pie filling and whipped cream on my cheeks the rest of the afternoon to drive home the point.

Needless to say, I had overplayed my hand, and my love for Mary Beth was never to be returned in kind. But she turned out to be the clear thinker in this equation. Americans should be more like her, expressing revulsion for the obesity Olympics. Jamming sausages into your belly isn't the sign of good fortune; it is simply an indication of terrible judgment.

Milwaukee Journal Sentinel

MARRIAGE EQUALITY A LONG TIME COMING

June 9, 2014

[Ed. note: This was my most widely read column at the Milwaukee Journal Sentinel. I heard from a number of progressives who complained that I was too late getting on the same-sex marriage bandwagon and that I only wrote the column because the issue was all but settled. And I heard from former Republican co-workers complaining that they always knew this was my position and I was just now trying to get attention for it. Just can't win.]

In 2006, actor Brad Pitt declared that he would only propose marriage to new girlfriend Angelina Jolie "when everyone else in the country who wants to be married is legally able."

At the time, this was an inspired work of genius. Every man around the country who was being nagged by his girlfriend to get married could now just say he was taking a principled stand on an important cultural issue.

Girlfriend: "When are you going to propose to me?"

Boyfriend (half asleep, face down on couch): "Yeah, I'm uh ... like, taking a stand in favor of gay marriage or something. We must remain vigilant, despite the long odds. Solidarity, sister."

Brad and Angelina didn't wait around; they were engaged in 2012. Clearly, they couldn't hold out any longer, because even a few years ago, it seemed as though "gay marriage" remained a cultural oxymoron.

It was no different locally. In 2006, Wisconsin voters overwhelmingly approved a constitutional amendment preventing gay people from wedding one another. Yet it was only a matter of time before the legality of the "one man, one woman" definition of marriage was decided in court.

That time came Friday, when U.S. District Judge Barbara Crabb overturned Wisconsin's ban on same-sex marriage. The further away 2006 looked in the rear-view mirror, the more likely Crabb's decision seemed; the U.S. Supreme Court has handed down several recent pro-same-sex marriage rulings, and President Barack Obama, recently an opponent of gay marriage, has switched his position to embrace marriage equality. Crabb's decision likely will be appealed, and either she or a federal court could issue a stay within the next few days.

My own experience with the gay marriage issue likely has mirrored that of many Americans. Raised in a Catholic household, I always viewed marriage as more of a religious institution than a government one. While I believed "marriage" to be the thing men and women did to have babies and raise them, I always thought gays and lesbians shouldn't be denied equal rights under the law.

If government conferred a benefit to heterosexuals, such as tax credits to married couples, then I thought it was unjust to deny it to those who I believed (along with Chief Justice Lady Gaga) were born differently. I did think, however, that such benefits could be conferred through domestic partnership laws, rather than "marriage."

Yet there is no doubt that I was publicly dismissive of opponents of Wisconsin's 2006 gay marriage ban. On my blog, I knocked them for what I considered to be eyeroll-inducing arguments. (In one post, I ripped a March 2006 Journal Sentinel guest column arguing against the amendment as being particularly odious, even though I said I was "generally on this guy's side.")

At one point, amendment opponents said the law would hurt Wisconsin's tourism economy, as gay fishermen would stop coming to the state to fish. They falsely argued that the amendment would prevent law enforcement from prosecuting domestic violence crimes between non-married adults. The day before the election in 2006, one anti-amendment group began running a confusing radio ad telling people to vote "no" on the amendment to preserve family values — a clear attempt to try to trick people into voting the "wrong" way.

In effect, my criticisms of the pro-gay marriage crowd weren't criticisms of their opposition to the amendment; it was just that as a conservative, I couldn't bring myself to admit that they were probably right. I couldn't reconcile the fact that these people, who wouldn't hesitate to throw me off a bridge if given the chance, held the more morally defensible ground. (I feel the same way about being anti-death penalty, which also means aligning oneself with a cadre of lefties.)

At the same time, I never bought the line that same-sex marriage somehow "devalued" traditional marriage. The six-month-long NBA playoffs has done more to harm my marriage than two guys getting hitched will ever do. At a time when supposed "legitimate" relationships are producing unwanted children in broken homes with single parents, I never considered going after other productive, loving partnerships to be really all that much of a priority.

Along with a great deal of Americans, I have come a long way in the past eight years. When gay couples rushed to the Dane County Courthouse on Friday night to finally legalize their marriages, my heart told me our state had gotten a little better. In the blink of a cultural eye, we had gone from Andrew Dice Clay mocking "trans-testicles" in his comedy act to legal marriage equality.

A few months ago, I recall reading a column arguing that we should be more "forgiving" of gays and lesbians. In a sense, I disagree. We should instead hope that gays and lesbians are more forgiving of us, given that some of us took so long to get to this point.

Milwaukee Journal Sentinel

'BUYCOTT' PRODUCTS AT YOUR OWN RISK

Aug. 26, 2014

Are you weighed down by a surplus of serenity in your life? Do your feelings of being well-adjusted activate pangs of guilt and remorse? Have your friends complained that you aren't sufficiently lecturing them on their consumer ethics?

Thankfully, we live in an age where there is an app for that.

You can demonstrate that you are a true citizen of the world by downloading "Buycott," a smartphone app that guarantees you will be insufferably outraged no matter where you are. Say you're at the grocery store — simply use the app to scan items with your phone, and you will get a message telling you whether you are ethically bound to boycott that product. Does Count Chocula utilize child labor to maintain his opulent castle? Now you'll know. Does Wonder Bread secretly funnel money to Third World despots? Wonder no more.

Given that I am a particularly compassionate person, I signed up for every one of the "campaigns" on the Buycott website. When an item is entered into your phone either manually or via scanner, the app will tell you how many of your campaigns the item triggers and makes a recommendation whether to avoid the product.

Naturally, there are some companies that trigger a lot more campaigns than others. If you enter the words "Koch brothers" into the app, you run the risk of your phone bursting into flames. It appears someone actually created a phony campaign to test the app, which he or she called "Test Please Delete." The one company the author chose to boycott for the trial run? Koch Industries.

The app has counseled me to boycott Hostess Zingers, as it conflicts with eight of my subscribed campaigns. One of those is "Save the Pigs," which is appropriate given that boycotting Hostess products will prevent me from resembling one. A scan of a box of Willy Wonka's Everlasting Gobstoppers turns up 38 campaigns, including "Demand Justice and Democracy in Bangladesh," "Say NO to the use of aborted fetal cells" and "stop cacao related child slavery." (Word has it that Oompa Loompas are also paid about 16% as much as real people.)

These may all be fine causes, but sometimes a jawbreaker is just a jawbreaker. Take Kraft Foods, which gets it from both sides. On the left, it takes heat for supposedly donating to the conservative American Legislative Exchange Council, for using artificial dyes in its food, for being owned by big tobacco and for supporting genetically modified foods. (There are dozens of anti-GM food campaigns.)

But some conservatives are also urging a Kraft boycott, as they believe the company supports pro-abortion causes.

And while most campaigns focus on national and worldwide issues, there is a campaign to boycott contributors to Wisconsin's Republican governor, Scott Walker. But this has been tried before; following the year of union unrest in the state, groups sent out lists of Walker donors to avoid.

This was, in a sense, retroactive protesting — the actual demonstrations accomplished nothing, so union loyalists wanted someone to pay after the fact.

And thus, in the wake of the Wisconsin political turbulence, eating a stick of Sargento string cheese became an act of political provocation. If you used an S.C. Johnson toilet bowl cleaner, it meant you were also flushing your union bargaining rights away.

Of course, none of these boycotts was effective. Even if they had managed to make a dent in these large companies, it only would have hurt the lower-wage workers at their factories. And unbeknownst to many of the pro-boycott folks, a great deal of their 401(k) and pension accounts are tied up in these corporations. Take them down and plan on working an extra year to make up for the smaller retirement checks.

Instead, maybe open a window and get some air. Go for a walk. Enjoy a bratwurst without thinking about what the pig in that delicious encased sausage would have thought about the human rights abuses in Egypt. Pour yourself a nice non-political beer. (And use the app I am developing, where you just push a button on your phone and an unlicensed individual shows up at your house and starts pouring beer into your mouth. I am calling it "Ubeer.")

But if you must use Buycott, make sure to take note of one product that it says must be avoided. It is a product that supports theocratic dictatorships, NSA wiretapping and somehow contributes to the abuse of bears in China.

That product? The Apple iPhone, for which the app was created.

Milwaukee Journal Sentinel

WHEN THE RADICAL RIGHT COMES FOR YOUR CULTURE

December 3, 2020

Since its founding, Black Rifle Coffee has branded itself as coffee for tough guys, associating itself with Second Amendment advocacy, pro-police activism, and veterans' issues.

"We develop our explosive roast profiles with the same mission focus we learned as military members serving this great country and are committed to supporting veterans, law enforcement, and first responders," promises the company's website.

The company, based in Salt Lake City, Utah, gained new visibility in 2017 when, after Fox News host Sean Hannity defended accused child molester (and GOP Senate candidate) Roy Moore, Keurig coffee pulled its advertisements from Hannity's show. This prompted Donald Trump Jr. to endorse Black Rifle on his Twitter account.

But those kinds of endorsements can work both ways. Black Rifle Coffee found itself the subject of unwanted attention recently when Kyle Rittenhouse was spotted wearing a T-shirt touting the brand. Rittenhouse had just posted bail; he'd been in jail since October 30 after being charged with killing two people and injuring one other when a protest in Kenosha, Wisconsin, turned violent last August.

BRCC tried to distance itself from Rittenhouse, making clear it had no business association with the teenager.

"We're not in the business of profiting from tragedy," CEO Evan Hafer said in a video message addressing the controversy. "We have zero interest in collecting one dollar from any of this—it is ethically inappropriate for us to do so or even give the perception," said Hafer.

But Hafer's attempt to distance the company from an alleged gunman earned him some new enemies: Rittenhouse supporters who believed the company was capitulating to political correctness. This included the right-wing paramilitary group the Proud Boys, who accused the company of trying to cater to "genderless college students."

Black Rifle Coffee's struggle is hardly unique. Other companies have experienced similar scenarios since the rise of the alt-right in the last five years. Just look at what happened to Depeche Mode.

In February 2017, white supremacist Richard Spencer had called Depeche Mode the "official band of the alt-right" while speaking outside of the Conservative Political Action Conference in Washington, D.C.

That was news to the bandmates.

"My phone kept ringing and ringing," lead singer Dave Gahan, told the New York Post. "I had to tell everyone, 'No, we're not the official band of the alt-right.'"

"I could understand some commie jumping on us because of our history and working-class background," Gahan told The Post. "But this was ridiculous."

The band soon issued a statement distancing itself from Spencer and denouncing his views. Spencer was unmoved by the rejection from one of his favorite bands, tweeting "Depeche Mode has already written all the anthems the #AltRight needs."

Therein lies the frustration for companies and public figures who find themselves involuntarily tied to controversial figures. Their denials and protestations often fall on deaf ears.

Pop icon Taylor Swift started getting the racist appropriation treatment as early as 2016, when alt-right website the Daily Stormer began featuring articles like "Aryan Goddess Taylor Swift: Nazi Avatar of the White European People," and "Taylor Swift, Avatar of European Imperialism."

In turn, a progressive publication called PopFront accused Swift's song "Look What You Made Me Do" of playing to a "subtle, quiet white support of a racial hierarchy."

Swift's attorneys got involved, drafting a letter calling PopFront's article "a malicious attack against Ms. Swift that goes to great lengths to portray Ms. Swift as some sort of white supremacist figurehead, which is a baseless fiction masquerading as fact and completely misrepresents Ms. Swift."

Sometimes, though, public figures actually do make politically tinged statements that bring endorsements from undesirable groups. That's what happened in 2017 when Papa John's CEO John Schnatter blamed national anthem protests by NFL players for sinking pizza sales — the Daily Stormer rushed to declare Papa John's "the official pizza of the alt-right."

The company was shocked by the endorsement and immediately tried to distance itself from it.

"We condemn racism in all forms and any and all hate groups that support it," Peter Collins, then-senior director of public relations at Papa John's, told the Louisville Courier-Journal. "We do not want these individuals or groups to buy our pizza."

A Papa John's spokesperson did not respond to a request to comment for this story.

In 2016, the Daily Stormer deemed New Balance the "Official Shoes of White People" after the company's VP of Public Affairs, Matt LeBretton, said "things are going to move in the right direction" during a Trump presidency. LeBretton has also said the Obama administration "turned a deaf ear" to New Balance in pursuing the Trans-Pacific Partnership, a free trade agreement that critics argued would hurt American companies.

Not only did neo-Nazis start to endorse New Balance, but Trump opponents also began filling their social media feeds with photos of New Balance shoes lit on fire or thrown in the trash.

The company quickly began to contain the damage, pointing out that LeBretton was simply discussing Trump's position on TPP. The company's opposition to TPP was shared by progressives like Sens. Bernie Sanders and Elizabeth Warren.

In a tweet, New Balance said the company "does not tolerate bigotry or hate in any form."

"As a 110-year old company with five factories in the U.S. and thousands of employees worldwide from all races, genders, cultures and sexual orientations, New Balance is a values-driven organization and culture that believes in humanity, integrity, community, and mutual respect for people around the world," the company wrote.

The first response to the apology tweet features two New Balance shoes with the "Ns" turned to represent the "N" and "Z" in "Nazi."

Representatives for New Balance did not respond to requests to comment.

Perhaps the most notable example of neo-Nazi brand appropriation took place when white supremacists adopted Pepe the Frog as their mascot.

In 2005, aspiring comic book writer Matt Furie created a character named Pepe the Frog as a part of his subversive Boy's Club series of comics. One frame of the comic featured Pepe urinating in a toilet with his pants all the way down to his ankles, the way a 3-year-old would. While relieving himself, Pepe utters the phrase "Feels good man."

Soon, Pepe made his way to the notorious website 4chan, where users would use the frog as a meme to describe their feelings, whether they "felt good" or felt sad. At one point, pop star Katy Perry tweeted a Pepe meme to express how tired she was after a trip to Australia.

But soon, the Pepe meme morphed into a way 4chan's anonymous users could repel "normies," whom they didn't want using the site. User-created images of Pepe as a Nazi or terrorist began flooding the site, attracting white supremacists, who soon claimed Furie's creation as their own. The Anti-Defamation League subsequently added Pepe to its list of white supremacists symbols.

The Pepe phenomenon was given a dose of steroids when the Trump campaign willfully associated itself with the offensive memes featuring the frog. In 2015, Trump himself tweeted a photo of Pepe wearing a Trump wig; in 2016, Donald Trump Jr. posted a photo of "The Deplorables" on Instagram, one of which was Pepe, right there next to his father. Spencer vigorously embraced Pepe as the alt-right's mascot. In a famous video of Spencer being punched in the face on Trump's inauguration day in 2017, Spencer had just begun explaining to a reporter what the special meaning of Pepe is to the white nationalist movement.

And as the transformation of Pepe took place, Furie looked on in horror.

In the beginning, "I was all proud of myself, strutting down the street," Furie told filmmaker Arthur Jones in the recently released documentary Feels Good Man. "Now I'm just slithering down the street in a pool of my own waste, or something. Just a slurping slimeball."

At one point, Furie purchased $45,000 worth of Pepe T-shirts to sell, but he can't even give them away to thrift stores because he is horrified at the prospect of white supremacists proudly wearing them. Unable to rehabilitate Pepe's image, Furie killed the frog off in a comic—but by that point, he'd effectively lost control of Pepe's image. Furie would go on to sue InfoWars' Alex Jones, who had been using a Pepe image to sell posters. (Jones used the lawsuit to increase the price of the posters—eventually, InfoWars settled with Furie.)

Furie's attorneys estimate they have issued between 75 and 100 successful legal challenges halting the unauthorized use of Pepe. But the damage remains: Despite his best efforts, Furie will forever be associated with a toxic symbol of white supremacy.

The ability of racist and extremist factions to infiltrate society through social media and other means has also spoiled actions that, until just years ago, nobody considered to be controversial.

For instance, as racial strife spread throughout America this spring and summer, an armed far-right anti-government group known as the Boogaloo Boys adopted Hawaiian shirts as their official uniform.

"As a fat guy I take this extremely personally," tweeted Washington Post reporter Dave Weigel at the news of the Hawaiian shirt takeover. "This is the shirt of my people."

In 2017, a Wisconsin-based company that made Tiki torches was forced to issue a statement distancing itself from the white supremacist-led marches in Charlottesville, Virginia, that summer. Some Americans are now afraid to wear the red baseball hats of their favorite Major League teams lest someone mistake it for a "Make America Great Again" cap.

Progressive activists are only too happy to pile on. In just the past few months, they have declared the following to be indicators of "white supremacy": Referring to classical music composers by their last names, modern architecture, Roman statues, being on time, Tom Brady's popularity, horse mascots, and the Kardashians.

With both extremes willingly taking part in this plot to stake out territory, it remains to be seen whether anything enjoyable will be left untainted by grievance politics. If this continues, we may eventually see brands actively trying to associate their competitors with white supremacists across the dark corners of the internet—if you see a 4chan user praising Pizza Hut's "supreme" toppings, there may be a Papa John's IP address behind it. It would be as if political campaign staffers crossed their fingers, praying for the day their opponent was endorsed by David Duke.

Until then, brands will have to prepare for the day that extremists commandeer their good names. Association with these groups can do lasting damage to historical and beloved U.S. institutions.

The Dispatch

LATTE LIBERALISM

March 22, 2015

For the past few years, one of the most popular bits on "Saturday Night Live" has been cast member Cecily Strong's depiction of "The Girl You Wish You Hadn't Started a Conversation With at a Party." In the sketches, Strong's airheaded character mangles condescending political platitudes while frequently checking her cellphone. For instance, she calls the Ebola crisis "uncomprehendable," says the commercialization of holidays is a "tragesty," and complains about all the homeless people out there "that can't even pay their mortgages."

Strong's clueless activist immediately came to mind when Starbucks recently announced its "Race Together" initiative, in which the coffee giant's employees will be encouraged to strike up discussions about race with unsuspecting latte enthusiasts.

According to Starbucks CEO Howard Schultz, the program is meant to "create a more empathetic and inclusive society - one conversation at a time." A brisk racial colloquy with your barista will make, as Schultz vows, a "significant difference as we go forward."

You may have seen the torrent of criticism this idea has gotten, and thought to yourself that maybe the idea doesn't deserve such public mockery. Well, you'd be right. It deserves far more.

Starbucks, of course, is the corporate behemoth that serves as a temple to under-caffeinated white people across America. And Schultz's preposterously tin-eared "Race Together" program is merely a chance for Caucasians to assuage their guilt in the wake of highly publicized racial unrest in places such as Ferguson, Mo.; Staten Island, N.Y.; and Milwaukee.

As Heather Wilhelm at RealClear Politics has pointed out, the recent shootings in Ferguson and Staten Island aren't attributable to the lack of racial conversations in their local Starbucks coffee shops. That's because the Starbucks nearest to Ferguson is 13 miles away in Richmond Heights - median income $69,681. Similarly, Eric Garner's Staten Island neighborhood had no Starbucks to help the community heal. These areas aren't suffering from a paucity of soy milk; their challenges run just a bit deeper.

Just imagine the horror felt by a Starbucks employee when a random customer picks up her Cinnamon Dolce Latte and wants to talk about racism. One imagines a typical barista would gladly take a hefty pay cut in order to avoid race discussions at all costs. I would happily take half minimum wage if it allowed me to dodge having to lecture anyone on race relations. One imagines underground colonies of baristas huddling together until this nightmare is over.

Perhaps Howard Schultz has never had a heartfelt discussion about race, so maybe he doesn't realize such conversations never take place between complete strangers. There has to be a builtin amount of trust between the interlocutors; almost as if one were talking to a doctor, lawyer or priest. If the Legislature has passed a law establishing a "barista-client" privilege, I am as of yet unaware of it.

Clearly, racial discussions are fraught with whole battlefields full of land mines. What if a barista, whose training may primarily consist of how to properly display scones, hears some racial opinions that he or she finds execrable? Is there training on how to handle belligerent customers who want to cause a scene?

The sensitive nature of racial discussions is why, before going on television to talk about anything race-related, I have often run my thoughts by a trusted African-American friend who will tell me how things I say might be interpreted. In a sense, she is my "racial adviser," and the conversations we have are far more edifying than any that will take place over an Iced Caramel Macchiatio at Starbucks. (This is also a lucrative career opportunity for African-American entrepreneurs; white people will pay good money to have their statements pre-authorized by a racial arbiter.)

And how is a Starbucks employee supposed to navigate electric issues for which centuries of debate haven't been led to answers? Go ask your barista why society thinks black men are far more influenced by their popular culture than other races. Or ask what effect the splintering of black families under slavery had on the current African-American family unit. You are likely to get a blank stare before the young man or woman hands you a cup with your misspelled name scrawled on it. If they are particularly bold, they might offer up wisdom like, "but there are people out there that are being racisted against!"

In essence, Starbucks is attempting to have the conversation about race everyone wants to have until we all start having it. If the company were to open a Ferguson franchise and hire an all-black staff, it would do more for race relations than any eyeroll-inducing "conversation" at any of its other stores.

Let's hope opportunities to have "serious" discussions about race get a lot more serious than this.

Milwaukee Journal Sentinel

JESTERS DO OFT MAKE PROPHETS

December 2, 2014

When the brilliant comedian Chris Rock was recently asked why he has stopped playing college campuses, he had a curious response. "The reason is because they're way too conservative," he told New York Magazine's Frank Rich.

This response immediately elicited guffaws from both conservatives and people who still guffaw. College campuses, after all, are carefully sealed bubbles of progressivism, where standard fare conservatism rarely gets a hearing. But Rock clarified:

"Not in their political views — not like they're voting Republican — but in their social views and their willingness not to offend anybody."

So Rock was essentially using "conservative" as a stand-in for "something I don't like." But, in fact, there's nothing particularly "conservative" — either socially or politically — about fostering a climate of perpetual offense, as college campuses do. In fact, it is the exact opposite.

And, thus, Rock stumbled upon an inconvenient truth for today's left, which dominates our university systems. Modern speech suppression is much more likely to come from progressives than right-wingers. The ideology that claims to value "tolerance" is, in fact, the most intolerant of differing views.

In fact, Rock was talking about a recent incident in which a student panel disinvited comedian Bill Maher from speaking at the University of California-Berkeley because of a series of statements he has made about Muslims. On his television show, Maher said that the Muslim world has too much in common with the terrorist Islamic State group, including the practice of female genital mutilation, and said that liberals should stand up for liberal ideals, such as gender equity.

The student action to disinvite Maher was overridden by a faculty panel, but it follows a recent trend of university groups canceling speakers under pressure from student and faculty groups. Conservative Washington Post columnist George Will recently was disinvited from speaking at Scripps College in Delaware because he questioned the veracity of sexual assault statistics on college campuses. Rutgers pulled an invitation from former Secretary of State Condoleezza Rice when student groups protested.

In fact, the Foundation for Individual Rights in Education has compiled a list showing over 263 campus disinvitations over the past 14 years. According to the study, university speaker disinvitations reached a 15-year high in 2013. There was a time when liberals went to the mat to preserve federal funding for an art project consisting of a crucifix encased in a jar of urine; now, the thought of listening to the thoughts of a female, African-American former secretary of state is evidently too much to endure.

The effect of the "heckler's veto" isn't to promote understanding or to facilitate discourse. It is to bully people into conformity. Now the only opinions that matter are those that belong to the hive mind. From speech codes to "trigger warnings," liberal-dominated campuses are at the forefront of viewpoint suppression.

And it isn't just campuses where left-wing mobs are out for scalps. Recently, an unknown congressional staffer named Elizabeth Lauten counseled President Barack Obama's daughters, Sasha and Malia, to "show a little class" during the annual pardoning of the Thanksgiving turkey ceremony. On Twitter, Lauten told the girls to ""Rise to the occasion," "Act like being in the White House matters to you," and "Dress like you deserve respect, not a spot at a bar."

The liberal bullies immediately descended on Lauten, and the story became national news. Soon, Lauten resigned.

Two weeks before the Lauten affair, scientist Matt Taylor appeared on a webcast celebrating a probe he worked on landing on a comet 310 million miles from Earth. Taylor wore a tacky bowling-style shirt that featured scantily clad women, for which he was forced by angry feminists to make a teary-eyed apology days later. And, thus, the story became about Taylor's shirt, not the fact that the guy helped land a probe on a comet 310 million miles away.

Modern progressivism can't handle speech it doesn't like. In fact, congressional Democrats like soon-to-be-ex-Senate Majority Harry Reid are pushing an effort to amend the First Amendment to limit political speech they'd rather not see.

Maybe using Rock's words to make a point about speech suppression is doing exactly what he's counseling us not to do — take comedians too seriously. But as Shakespeare counseled in King Lear, "Jesters do oft make prophets." And the liberal crackdown on free speech is no laughing matter.

Milwaukee Journal Sentinel

THE MAN WHO IS NEVER WRONG

October 18, 2015

Let us all sing in praise of The Man Who is Never Wrong.

This man has the internal fortitude to spend hours behind his keyboard, creating a custom reality known only to himself. Typically, his world knowledge would come from interacting with other human beings outside his home, but The Man Who is Never Wrong has no time for superfluous human contact - he has tweets to send.

Before the Internet, the world never knew that he was never wrong. But now he gets to broadcast it with machine-gun rapidity, poorly spelled tweet by poorly spelled tweet. Do not criticize his lack of grammar and punctuation, pedant - the common rules of grammar are mere shackles holding down his vigilante brand of passion.

Further, do not peer down your long nose at his virulent attacks on others. He has been wronged in his life, and previously had no avenue for retribution. For The Man Who is Never Wrong, feelings are a zero-sum game; if he can make you feel one point worse, he feels one point better. When he sees that you have blocked him, he puts down his burrito and gives a silent fist-pump; he knows he has infiltrated the recesses of your brain.

The Man Who is Never Wrong has no problem explaining to you how Republicans' primary choice for the job of speaker of the House is a weak-kneed liberal, despite that congressman being virtually alone in fighting for major social program reforms while The Man was still using a dial-up Internet connection.

The Man Who is Never Wrong has never put his own name on a ballot, volunteered for a campaign or taken part in any political engagement that occurs outside his front door; his expertise is merely in paying his broadband bill on time.

Typically, The Man Who is Never Wrong will inform you of his rightness in adverse proportion to how much he actually knows about a subject. He gets all the information he needs from professional controversialists who are looking to sell books or get ears trained on their radio shows; clearly, the most trusted voices in America are the ones who have a financial interest in setting themselves apart from common wisdom.

That is why our brave conversationalist is likely to revere the ultimate Man Who is Never Wrong, a billionaire with a hairdo more architecturally implausible than his 70-story high rises. This wealthy non-Republican is already this man's president; the bullying billionaire's ability to tell-it-like-it-never-will-be has granted millions of other Men Who are Never Wrong free license to tyrannize fellow Internet enthusiasts.

Within three mouse clicks, The Man Who is Never Wrong can find any graph or chart that verifies his position. Want a ridiculous chart showing that Republicans have become more ideological while Democrats have remained moderate? There's one floating around. But always being right means never checking the veracity of any graphic, even if it flies in the face of mountains of research that show both parties have become equally as ideologically driven.

In the world of The Man Who is Never Wrong, the world is perfectly right. In his universe of lurid websites, the women never say no. The pirated movies are always free. The shopping websites don't try to chat with him while he's purchasing embarrassing figurines meant for children. And, most often, nobody even knows his real name.

And this is why, sadly, it is difficult to identify these brave men and grant them the recognition they deserve. They walk among us, quietly filing away opinions that they can later unleash on their keyboards.

So we salute you, Man Who is Never Wrong, for ushering in the Golden Era of Anti-Knowledge. May you and your likeminded roving band of dis-informants soldier on, making enemies of facts and complete sentences.

Milwaukee Journal Sentinel

YOU CAN'T BAN STUPID

March 9, 2018

If modern America were to erect a statue in honor of a historical figure that most expresses the current zeitgeist, it could do no better than Lothrop Withington, Jr.

In 1939, the Harvard freshman boasted to his friends that he had once swallowed a live fish. They bet him $10 he couldn't do it again, a challenge he gleefully accepted. So on March 3, with incredulous classmates and a reporter on hand, Withington threw a three-inch goldfish into his mouth, chewed a couple of times, and swallowed.

As National Review magazine recently noted, Withington's stunt set off a national craze among college students. A University of Pennsylvania student swallowed 25 in one sitting; he was quickly outdone by an MIT student who gulped 42 fish, then a Clark University student who swallowed 89.

Proving stupidity has no expiration date, young people in the YouTube era revived the goldfish challenge, leading to thousands of videos of kids and adults engaging in imbecilic behavior that predated World War II.

Other "challenges" followed, including downing as much cinnamon as possible in one gulp and drinking a gallon of milk under an hour; some teens began lighting themselves on fire, trying to douse the flames before suffering horrifying burns.

Yet the most recent YouTube fad may be the most puzzling of all. In late 2017, young people and adults alike began posting videos of themselves biting into Tide laundry pods, allowing the contents to burst into their mouths. Likely instigated by media reports of this bizarre "trend," thousands of these videos began showing up in mid-January of 2018.

It is easy to blame "millennials" for such an aggressive modern level of stupidity, but America has a storied tradition of people doing dangerous things to get attention. It's been almost 20 years since the inception of the "Jackass" franchise, in which young men treat themselves as crash testicle dummies for laughs. One of television's top shows during the early 2000's featured women in bikinis eating live worms.

But perhaps the more embarrassing actions recently have been by politicians rushing to respond to the Tide Pod craze by seeking to legislate stupidity out of the populace. In New York, lawmakers introduced a bill requiring Tide's parent company, Procter & Gamble, to make its laundry pods look less...um...delicious and add warnings to each individually wrapped pod. "They are so alluring, they smell sweet and they look like gummy bears," said Democratic Sen. Brad Hoylman. "They might as well say 'bite me' on them."

(P&G has already implemented two of the changes sought by the bill, adding child-proof packaging and providing warning labels on their primary packaging.)

Of course, the last thing Tide wants is people eating their pods. But if devouring laundry detergent on an online video is the pinnacle of shameless exhibitionism, then trying to inject yourself into a national story by claiming to "do something" about the "trend" is a close second. In fact, lawmakers introducing knee-jerk legislation to "solve" an ephemeral issue is a time-honored tradition; even Massachusetts quickly made goldfish swallowing illegal following the craze in the early 1940s.

Take, for example, Republican Indiana lawmaker Milo Smith, who last year introduced a bill allowing Indianapolis Colts fans who felt disrespected by players kneeling for the National Anthem to claim a full refund for the cost of their ticket during the first quarter. Or 24-year-old Minnesota state Rep. Drew Christensen, who claims he is drafting a tongue-in-cheek bill to ban "The Bachelor" star Arie Luyendyk Jr. from the state for not choosing Becca Kufrin, a contestant who hailed from Prior Lake.

Perhaps the worst types of these attention-grabbing bills are ones named after individual people. Typically, when an individual is harmed or even killed, it is the result of a unique situation that can't be fixed with legislation. Hard cases make for bad law, and as Radley Balko has written, these proposals "play more to emotion than to reason." (I hereby propose a new bill banning the use of peoples' names in legislation, and I demand it be called "Christian's Law.")

As the saying goes, if you fear that government moves too slow, just wait until you see the damage wrought by a government that moves too fast. Legislation based on fleeting headlines is almost always a bad idea. Instead, we should offer politicians a new challenge: Post a video of yourselves resisting the temptation to grandstand.

Milwaukee Journal Sentinel

THE INTERNET'S ATTACK ON MEMORY

July 24, 2012

I can remember my first Milwaukee Brewers baseball game as clearly as if it were a week ago. It was 1981, and the heavily mustachioed Brew Crew were on their way to their first playoff appearance.

As I walked into County Stadium on that warm night, my eyes grew to the size of manhole covers - I had never been in a stadium packed to capacity before. Tommy John was on the mound for the hated New York Yankees; the Brewers' Gorman Thomas hit two home runs, and my dad and I went home as happy and worn out as if we had played the game ourselves.

There's only one problem with my fondest of memories: None of it is true. The only game John pitched in County Stadium in 1981 was on Sept. 14, and the Yankees hammered the Brewers, 10-2. The crowd that night was a tepid 17,545, and the temperature at game time was an unseasonably chilly 62. The only Brewers home run was hit by catcher Charlie Moore.

I was able to debunk this warm memory of mine within about three clicks of a mouse while surfing the Internet. I now wonder how many other formative elements of my childhood are out there in cyberspace, just waiting to tell me I'm someone different from who I thought I was.

Our country's oral history is rampant with exaggerated bromides about personal courage and individual achievement. Sometimes, hard facts are impediments to the enjoyment and instruction these stories can bring. And now, these facts are everywhere.

Take, for example, one of Wisconsin's most famous stories about its favorite son: Green Bay Packers coach Vince Lombardi. As the tale goes, when Lombardi found out in 1963 that center Jim Ringo had hired an agent to represent him during contract negotiations, Lombardi traded Ringo within five minutes. For decades, the story (often retold by Lombardi himself) buttressed how the coach's no-nonsense attitude led the Packers to glory.

Only the story was apocryphal. Ringo never dealt with Lombardi and later said he never hired an agent. It only served to reinforce Lombardi's tough-guy persona, which was already legendary. As the Italians say, se non e' vero, e' ben trovato (even if it isn't true, it is well-founded).

But this story could never fly in 2012, where not only is virtually everything verifiable, fact-checking can be done on a smartphone while eating dinner at a restaurant. As of now, it is no longer permissible to say, "I don't know" when asked a question - the answer is usually right there in your hand. Famous sports arguments hashed out over beers at a tavern now can be settled by one person with fast fingers and a 4G Internet connection. Armies of fact-checkers wait at their computers for politicians to misremember important facts, so they can whack them down a few notches.

With memories, perception is reality; a strong recollection, even if incorrect, has the force of fact. And while complete world knowledge at our fingertips can be a wonderful thing, it also can erode the fabled history and storytelling tradition that molds us. (Thankfully, Twitter didn't exist during the Civil War: Just saw lincon give some speech about freeing slaves - wassup with the hat!! Lol!)

My parents tell a great story about how they met. In third grade, my dad sat at the back of the school bus, while my mother sat at the front. When the bus went up a hill, my mom's lunch box slid to the back of the bus, where my dad picked it up and returned it to her, introducing himself for the first time. There's no way it actually happened, but for me, it will always be true. I hope there's no YouTube video to ruin it.

Milwaukee Journal Sentinel

'LINCOLN FREED US FOR THIS?'

January 12, 2013

Over the past decade, no institution has more vividly documented the continuing American moral decay than "reality" television.

One television show depicted women who didn't know they were pregnant and usually end up having their babies while sitting on a toilet. The TLC network show "My Strange Addiction" documented a 27-year old Arkansas man who was in a sexual relationship with his car. (Single Red Geo Prism seeks companionship; enjoys walks on the beach, oil changes.) After a typical season of "Jersey Shore," it is usually wise to get your television tested for a sexually transmitted disease. If that's not bad enough, sometimes cable television delves so low that it even broadcasts Congress.

Yet even amid this prurient morass, one new show stands alone for its ability to scrape the bottom of the barrel, then keep digging. The Oxygen Network has decided to move ahead with a show it is calling "All My Babies' Mamas," featuring an Atlanta-based rapper named Shawty Lo.

Presumably, hilarity will ensue when Mr. Lo, his 11 children and their 10 different mothers all move into the same house to learn valuable life lessons. Despite dealing with a sensitive issue such as fatherless children, the show demonstrates all the discretion you would expect, distilling the mothers down to characters like "Fighter Baby Mama," "No Drama Baby Mama" and "Shady Baby Mama."

Naturally, the show has endured heavy criticism, especially for its depiction of African-Americans. Columnist Clarence Page of the Chicago Tribune, who is African-American, asked, "Lincoln freed us for this?"

Given that more than 72% of African-American children are currently born to single mothers, there is certainly a temptation to discuss fatherlessness in terms of race. But in the past 50 years, single-parent births have increased among virtually all ethnicities in America. In 2012, for the first time in history, more than half the children in America born to women under 30 were born in single-parent households.

More recent scholarly work has focused more on class divisions in single parenthood than on racial divisions. It seems two-parent households are actually becoming a luxury item: Very few highly educated, wealthy women have out-of-wedlock children, while single parenthood in the middle and lower classes has increased significantly. Currently, 6% of babies born to highly educated women were born outside of marriage, compared to 44% of babies born to moderately educated single women and 54% to the least educated single mothers.

The class distinction is especially important, because having a child while single often begins a vicious cycle: Low-income women give birth to children that hamper their earning potential, making it even harder to climb up the economic ladder.

And, of course, a mountain of evidence demonstrates that children born to single mothers are more likely to have trouble in school, to have behavioral problems and to become involved in criminal activity. The more behavioral problems our kids see, the more costly it is for governments to have to rectify these problems in school or in the criminal justice system.

Naturally, there are exceptions to this rule. The past two Democratic U.S. presidents have essentially been raised by single women. Who knows - maybe Shawty Lo has spawned a team of scientists who will cure Alzheimer's disease (under the close tutelage of noted academic "Baby Mama From Hell").

But encouraging marriage is one of society's most intractable problems. Give people more economic benefits for getting married, and you're subsidizing people who are statistically more likely to succeed on their own. Take marriage benefits away, and people have an incentive to remain unmarried just to keep their government checks coming.

Some, such as sociologist Charles Murray, believe that America's only hope is for its elites to drop their "condescending nonjudgmentalism" toward those who have children out of wedlock. "Married, educated people who work hard and conscientiously raise their kids shouldn't hesitate to voice their disapproval of those who defy these norms," said Murray last year in The Wall Street Journal.

Murray is right. In essence, America's upper classes don't preach what they practice - rich people don't have babies in single-parent homes, but they have created a culture in which poor people doing so is permissible. It is this culture that led some producer in a boardroom to decide that "All My Babies' Mamas" was an acceptable idea. America's elites know the path to financial stability, but they're keeping it a secret, just for themselves.

And for those looking for decent reality television, stick to shows where people either pawn things or creepy Canadian twin brothers sneak into your house and renovate your kitchen while you're sleeping.

Milwaukee Journal Sentinel

WHAT COMICS CAN TELL US ABOUT POLITICS

May 07, 2013

One year ago, before facing a recall election, Republican Wisconsin Gov. Scott Walker traveled to Chicago to give a speech to the Illinois Policy Institute. Following his talk, Walker fielded a question from a woman who, citing a recent movie on education reform, asked whether Walker was the "Superman" she was waiting for. Walker chuckled, then said he was more partial to Batman.

With this admission, Walker stepped squarely into a debate that takes place exclusively in the dark corners of the Internet, where politics nerds and comic book dorks meet to clandestinely debate the political ideologies of superheroes. Which superhero a given politician idolizes may actually tell us a little bit about his or her political philosophy, given one undeniable fact:

Superman is a liberal, and Batman is a conservative.

As noted in Glen Weldon's superb new book "Superman: The Unauthorized Biography," the Man of Steel has deep roots in FDR's New Deal era. Just start with a comparison of the two heroes' professions: Superman's alter-ego, Clark Kent, is a member of the dreaded liberal mainstream media, and his father, Jor-El, was one of Krypton's most noted academics and scientists. Bruce Wayne is a Scarlet Pimpernel-esque billionaire playboy whose father made his money in the real estate market before the economy collapsed (sound familiar?) and whose company, Wayne Enterprises, manufactures military weapons. Superman hangs out with reporters; Batman's best buddy is a cop.

Even in 1938, Superman was taking on causes liberals would still be fighting for in 2013. In one of his first showdowns, Superman battles a crooked gun manufacturer named Norvell who has hired a sleazy lobbyist to create new markets for the company's munitions. Later, Superman exposes substandard prison conditions, busts a crooked brokerage firm for selling shares in a nonexistent oil well and threatens building companies for using cheap construction materials. If he didn't have X-ray vision, he might be running an organic food co-op in the Park Slope neighborhood of Brooklyn.

The early years demonstrate Superman's faith in both government and human redemption. After rounding up a group of delinquents, he blames their criminal activities on poor living conditions. "So the government rebuilds destroyed areas with modern cheap-rental apartments, eh?" he says before tearing down the slums with his hands. Later, they are replaced with "splendid housing conditions."

Sometimes, Superman gets directly involved in Democratic politics - in the early 1960s, he befriends President John F. Kennedy and trusts him enough to divulge his real identity. Kennedy goes so far as to disguise himself as Clark Kent to fool Lois Lane while Superman rushes off on a mission. (In 1986, Superman meets Ronald Reagan, but the storyline makes Reagan seem like a buffoon.)

Batman, on the other hand, is less of a believer in the inherent good of man. In the early Bob Kane comics, Batman was cruel, often mutilating his opponents before killing them.

And Batman's opponents are illustrative, too. Ra's al-Ghul is an environmentalist who wants to destroy humanity and its inherent decadence. By fighting him, Batman is essentially defending wealth and free markets. Other notable Batman foes include a who's who of lefty bad guys, including another tree hugger (Poison Ivy), a college professor (the Scarecrow) and an occupier with a respiratory problem (Bane).

The most recent slate of Batman movies from director Christopher Nolan are seen by many as sympathetic to Republican politics of the past decade. In "The Dark Knight," Batman is reviled by the public as he wages a "war on terror" to keep Gotham's citizens safe. (Nolan might as well have called the hero "Bat W. Man.")

In "The Dark Knight Rises," Batman takes on a gang of filthy hippies who occupy the stock exchange and fight for the "oppressed" against the 1%. We find out that Gotham fell into disrepair because Bruce Wayne's profits were down and he didn't have enough to spend on charitable activities to keep at-risk youths out of trouble. Batman cherishes order; his opponents relish revolution.

During campaigns, politicians are often slippery about where their ideological sympathies lie. They duck, they dodge, they obfuscate. It seems that there might be one question the press can ask to nail down how progressive or conservative they are:

"Red cape or black?"

Milwaukee Journal Sentinel

MY SPEECH TO THE GRADUATES

June 01, 2013

"More than any time in history," Woody Allen famously observed, "mankind faces a crossroads. One path leads to despair and utter hopelessness. The other to total extinction. Let us pray we have the wisdom to choose correctly."

I am slightly less pessimistic. I believe we as humans have the capacity to solve the mysteries that have plagued mankind for eternity: the mind's relation to the body, whether God exists and how nobody can tell Clark Kent is Superman just because he's wearing glasses.

It would seem I would be a questionable choice to offer any kind of counsel to graduates, as when I matriculated, my BAC was higher than my GPA. But as Kierkegaard noted, we are all condemned to live life forward and review it backward. I hope I can provide some reasonably sensible tips on how to navigate the sometimes confusing, often exciting journey you have in front of you.

First, find what you want to do and make it a job, even if it doesn't pay a lot right away. If money is all you ever want, it is all you will ever have. Take ownership of your own career — don't leave it in the hands of other people. Act as if nobody is thinking about you unless you are standing directly in front of them.

That person you're relying on to get you the job you want is actually sitting at his or her desk, gazing at a ham sandwich, wondering whatever happened to Tootie from "Facts of Life."

Be so outstanding that no employer can resist you. Don't measure your greatness by the relative success of those around you — measure it only by what you expect from yourself.

Take an interest in politics, and, regardless of your ideology, arrive at it honestly and with conviction. Be a well-rounded person with a political worldview, not an ideologue who sees everything through the lens of politics. Also, it's OK to be conservative — now that you're out of college, being a Republican is no longer an impediment to seeing a member of the opposite sex without his or her clothes on.

Remember that confidence is cyclical — if you don't have any, people will be able to tell, and they will therefore try to take advantage of you — which will cause you to have less confidence. The best thing to do is to have the courage to pretend you have confidence for a week or two, and then people will start treating you appropriately.

Make real friends — not the Facebook variety — and never let them go. As the late Christopher Hitchens sagely noted, one of the melancholy lessons of advancing years is the realization that you can't make old friends. The close friends you make as a young person will always be there to drag you up out of an emotional hole or cut you down to size when you need it.

If you find yourself in a fight with a friend, think ahead and weigh whether that short-term disagreement is worth sacrificing a life's worth of great memories with that person. It never is.

Take your younger years to question everything, like what the purpose of love is, the limits of human knowledge and why Dora the Explorer's parents would let her travel the Earth supervised by only a monkey. Because later in life, after you get married and have kids, you will only have time to question how a single tiny baby can produce so much poop.

Find art that stimulates you and pay for it. Reward the artists who make you see the world differently — as much as people create art for the love of the craft, many of them have to take crappy jobs to make a living (see the advice above on finding what you want to do and making it your job). They can spend more time making your life better if you don't feel entitled to getting everything for free.

Take the Bible's advice and "as you wish that others would do to you, do so to them." But men, please note — this does not mean you should plant a passionate kiss on random pretty women on the street. They will generally reciprocate with pepper spray and a restraining order.

Remember that your time on this planet is limited — the only way you can truly live forever is in the kind deeds you do for others.

Teaching selflessness and compassion are the easiest way to earn immortality. Your name may one day be forgotten, but your actions remain alive in those you affect positively.

Finally — and I cannot emphasize this enough — if you're at the mall and need to go to the bathroom, use the really nice one in Pottery Barn, not the public mall restroom, which is almost always gross.

George Bernard Shaw once said that youth is wasted on the young. It is now up to you to go forth and prove it untrue.

Milwaukee Journal Sentinel

WHICH PARTY IS 'ANTI-SCIENCE'?

July 02, 2013

Last week, Wendy Davis went viral. Late into the night, over 180,000 Internet viewers watched the Texas state senator stand and speak for 11 hours in an attempt to filibuster a bill banning abortions after 20 weeks. Eventually, a boisterous mob descended on the Texas Capitol, delaying a vote on the bill until after the session had ended, effectively killing the proposed law.

While Davis — who has since been deemed a national "folk hero" by NPR's Mara Liasson — commandeered the Senate floor, Republicans around the nation were subjected to the typical abortion taunts — that the GOP is "anti-science" and "anti-woman."

While abortion advocates claim to have science on their side, they conveniently ignore certain indisputable scientific truisms. Most important, late-term abortion ends a life — not of the mother but of the person growing inside her.

As National Review's Charles C.W. Cooke has ably noted, some scientific studies show that at 20 weeks of development, an unborn child can recognize the voice of its mother. By this time, the baby can have dreams. Teeth have begun to form, and the child can suck its thumb. By the fourth month, the baby can yawn, hiccup, stretch and make faces and has developed eyebrows, eyelashes, nails and reproductive organs. Even as early as two months, bones have developed, as well as facial features, ears, eyes, arms, legs, toes and fingers.

All these facts are brought to us by scientific discovery, but it is science that doesn't conform with the pro-abortion movement's agenda. Thus, it is locked away and ignored, scuttled in favor of the amorphous language of "choice." A typical press release issued by a liberal group regarding abortion resembles a lexical game of Sudoku, with each line having to contain some combination of the words "health," "care," "women" and "choice."

Teri Huyck, president and CEO of Planned Parenthood of Wisconsin, recently boasted that her organization provided "abortion care," an oxymoronic term that begs the question: care for whom? The child whose life is being terminated? Recently, Philadelphia abortionist Kermit Gosnell was sentenced to life in prison for killing babies born alive at 23 weeks in development; yet an abortionist just down the road from Gosnell in Maryland still performs legal, elective abortions at 28 weeks. The only difference between the two children is that one still happens to be inside the mother.

Consequently, it makes sense that those advocating for the availability of a procedure as barbaric as a third-trimester abortion want to change the subject. Abortion follows the old truism of American political rhetoric: If you can't defend the issue, ratchet up the language to create a diversion.

But while supporters of ending late-term abortions are derided as "extremists" and "anti-woman," the public has consistently sided with the pro-life side on the issue. According to Gallup, 80% of Americans believe abortion should be illegal in the third trimester. Even support for second-trimester abortions has historically topped out at 27%, while 62% of Texans supported the bill Davis tried to block.

The "Republicans are anti-science" attacks recently came to a head in Wisconsin when the Legislature approved a bill that generally requires a free ultrasound be performed on anyone seeking an abortion. (Under the law, it is up to the woman whether she wants to view the results of the ultrasound.) A Planned Parenthood representative called the bill "cruel," as if allowing a woman to see the baby growing inside her is more inhumane than terminating the life of an innocent human.

In fact, the bill merely provided women access to more scientific information that pro-abortion advocates would rather have withheld from the mother. One can legitimately argue the extent to which the Legislature should be micromanaging medical procedures, but one cannot oppose the bill on the grounds that it is "anti-science." Being able to see a child's development in the womb is a scientific miracle, developed over decades; but the stunning clarity with which a child can now be seen in utero is a significant setback for those continuing to advocate for abortion on demand.

It has been reported that Davis is considering a run for governor of Texas. Clearly, her celebrity status among those who purport to be "pro-science" has given her enough name identification to raise the funds needed for such a big endeavor.

But if she does embark on a longshot run, it will be one of the more macabre campaigns America has seen. The stench of a woman trying to ride a wave of death to the statehouse is palpable. Fortunately for her, the victims of her stance on late-term abortion will never get to cast a vote.

Milwaukee Journal Sentinel

A REVEREND'S OPTIMISM

Aug. 27, 2013

When the Rev. Martin Luther King Jr. stood on the steps of the Lincoln Memorial on Aug. 28, 1963, he had good reasons to be optimistic.

Nearly 10 years earlier, the U.S. Supreme Court had desegregated schools in the landmark Brown vs. Board of Education case. Hard-fought victories had been won over segregationists in Montgomery, Tallahassee, Little Rock and New Orleans.

And while King's speech that day was harshly critical of the state of the nation's blacks ("America has given the Negro people a bad check"), King's fundamental tone was one of unbridled optimism. He believed in America's founding principles and that one day those ideals could "lift our nation from the quicksands of racial injustice to the solid rock of brotherhood." But at the time, it remained only a dream.

King gave his landmark speech 100 years following the Emancipation Proclamation; it has now been a half a century since "I Have a Dream." Yet the state of blacks in America remains the most visible stain on the nation's character.

In the years following the March on Washington, King became more disenchanted, calling for "a radical redistribution of economic and political power." He openly supported a guaranteed income and expressed skepticism with capitalism. As historian David Halberstam wrote in 1967, "King has decided to represent the ghettoes; he will work in them and speak for them. But their voice is harsh and alienated. If King is to speak for them truly, then his voice must reflect theirs; it too must be alienated, and it is likely to increasingly be at odds with the rest of American society."

Yet regardless of the unpopularity of his remedies, King never wavered from his indefatigable optimism. In his final speech in Memphis on April 3, 1968, King revisited the positive vision he had for his country: "Let us move on in these powerful days, these days of challenge to make America what it ought to be. We have an opportunity to make America a better nation."

However, 50 years later, it seems King's dream of attaining a colorblind society died with him. As Derrick Bell, the first tenured African-American professor at Harvard, once said, "We have made progress in everything, yet nothing has changed."

That is because in 2013, discussions of race exist almost exclusively to tear political opponents down, rather than to honestly craft solutions to lift people up. Baseless charges are racism are now a cudgel used to punish political adversaries; those on the left consistently inject race into places it does not belong and conveniently scrub it from examples that make them uncomfortable.

MSNBC's Chris Matthews, for instance, has said that those who oppose Obamacare believe "the white race must rule." In the wake of the recent IRS scandal, the same network's Martin Bashir has said use of the term "IRS" is tantamount to using the "N-word." Even Bill Clinton, deemed "the first black president," caught the brunt of the racial industrial complex when he called Barack Obama's 2008 candidacy a "fairy tale." Serious black leaders took umbrage with the characterization, and Clinton had to quickly backtrack to avoid further damage to his wife's presidential campaign.

In 1849, Frederick Douglass wrote that "white and black must fall or flourish together." But it appears many Americans have given up on this goal, simply accepting the decay of our inner cities as a fait accompli. Implicit approval of society as it is means dodging the tough questions — such as asking why nearly 75% of all black children are born in single-family homes and how that relates to crime and income inequality. Or explaining why there are 2,500 black men in the University of Wisconsin System and 9,200 black men in the state prison system.

Asking those questions is widely seen as blaming the victims of poverty, so we pretend that personal choice and responsibility are only bit players in individuals' lives. There's always another government program down the road to save us from economic injustice. Yet despite the government's War on Poverty, poverty remains virtually undefeated.

Instead of doing the difficult work of addressing the underlying causes of inequality, we save our racial outrage for ephemeral issues, such as requiring photo ID to vote. (This despite evidence that African-American voting has increased in states such as Indiana and Georgia after they began requiring photo ID.) It is easy to find disgruntled victims of stop-and-frisk policing, but more difficult to find blacks and Latinos who have remained safe because of the proactive policing program. Meanwhile, African-

Americans in Milwaukee continue to be gunned down at an alarming rate.

King's boundless optimism can be revived. But this means asking hard questions and being ready to hear difficult answers. As African-America poet Carl Wendell Hines wrote about King's death, "it is easier to build monuments than to make a better world."

Milwaukee Journal Sentinel

JUST DON'T SAY IT.

August 6, 2013

A while back, I was having a discussion with an African-American friend that can only be had between two people who trust each other. It was the sort of "conversation on race" that the public always calls for but then recoils in horror when it actually occurs.

We were discussing whether there was any appropriate place for Caucasians to use the dreaded "N" word. I posited a situation where I was rapping along with a hip-hop album and the word came up. What should I do? Just blank out the word? Say something else? Surely, substituting the term "upstanding African-American" in place of the offending word would disrupt my legendarily ill flow.

He turned somber at my nonsense and spoke very slowly for my benefit. The discussion ended with him uttering four words.

"Just. Don't. Say. It."

It's an easy rule. There is a simple wisdom in urging people not to say the most poisonous and hurtful word in the English language. If you never say it at all, you never have to worry about saying it in a place where you have to defend its context. It is such a powerful word that even uttering it while committing a crime can reclassify your offense as a much more serious "hate crime." In 2007, the New York City Council symbolically banned the use of the word altogether.

But recently, several notable Caucasians have not adhered to my friend's rule. Famous chef Paula Deen, thinking racial epithets go down much more easily when doused in clarified butter, admitted she used the word decades ago. Philadelphia Eagles wide receiver Riley Cooper, who plays in a league in which 68% of the players are black, was caught offering to "fight every ('N' word)" at a Kenny Chesney concert in June.

Every time something like this happens, I shake my fist and yell "come on, white people," right before I return to listening to the latest Vampire Weekend album. But while Deen and Cooper could have benefited from the simple ban on use of the word, there are some interesting caveats in the use of the word today. Just never saying it might not be so simple.

For one, a version of the word is still in heavy use within the African-American community, primarily as a term of endearment. I, for one, never understood white people who thought it was "unfair" for blacks to be able to use the word or a version of the word in reference to one another.

Who are these white people dying to use a word that brings so much pain to people? As a male, I recognize that only women "get" to have children, but I've never considered this to be "unfair," and the idea of pulling a human being out of my body doesn't seem desirable in any way.

But the use of the word has been a debate that has raged within black culture for decades. In their 1993 song "Sucka Nigga," Tribe Called Quest make their case for using the "N" word, claiming they are "embracing adversity" by seizing the term back from white people. Black comedian Chris Rock, who frequently discusses the word's usage and etymology, claims the word is "poetry" in the right hands.

In the past week, CNN anchor Don Lemon, who is black, was heavily criticized for suggesting African-Americans should drop the word altogether. Hip-hop mogul Russell Simmons said it sounded like white people were "pulling (Lemon's) strings."

Further, the word lives on in historical texts created during a time when the term was more common. Dads today still have to determine how they will read Mark Twain's "Adventures of Huckleberry Finn" to their sons and daughters, as the classic book contains repeated use of the word. (And is sympathetic to the cause of black freedom.)

In the late 1930s, Louisiana Gov. Earl Long used the word while urging full voting rights for blacks. Last year's "Django Unchained," by Caucasian filmmaker Quentin Tarantino, contains 110 uses of the "N" word, as it tries to more accurately paint a disturbing picture of the slavery culture.

However, even if white people avoid using the word in question, that doesn't mean they are necessarily in the clear. Granted, there are entire grievance industries that fund themselves by accusing others — especially conservatives — of racism. But white people also have huge blind spots as to what minorities may consider racial topics. (For instance, any discussion of Milwaukee Public Schools is ostensibly a discussion of "black kids." Some even objected to the use of "Chicago" as a term for President Barack Obama's 2012 campaign, thinking it carried racial connotations.)

It is also not helpful for white people to use obscure racist words, such as when George Allen used the term "macaca" while running for U.S. Senate in Virginia in 2006. If you use a word to describe minorities that hasn't been used in 100 years, it's just creepy — like you've been holed up for months doing racist research.

So while it may be impossible to never utter the word, the instances when it is acceptable are extremely rare. The word is just as caustic to whites as it is to African-Americans, and it hurts just as much to hear people use it. So be warned: If you say it, the argument generally won't be over the nuances of the word; it will be over whether you're ever allowed to work at your job again.

Just don't say it.

Milwaukee Journal Sentinel

LEAVE THE KIDS ALONE

April 7, 2018

On Monday night, Villanova men's basketball star Donte DiVincenzo was basking in his team's second national championship in three years when he got a question he wasn't expecting. DiVincenzo, who had just poured in an unexpected 31 points to lead the Wildcats to victory, was asked about a tweet posted to his account seven years earlier, in which he quoted a song lyric from rapper Meek Mill that used the word "n***a."

"I didn't do that," said DiVincenzo, who is white. "It's my account, yes," he said. "But I never remember doing that."

So on the greatest night of his life, a 21-year old Final Four MVP was forced to answer questions about a tweet he allegedly wrote seven years ago, when he was 14 years old. (In subsequent days, more old tweets from DiVincenzo's account were unearthed, in which he discusses scatological topics and uses insensitive language about gays.)

The most disturbing part of the deep-dive into DiVincenzo's Twitter history isn't the use of the racially derisive song lyric he quoted when he was a child, which would seem to be an issue best worked out with his black teammates. In fact, comedian Chris Rock actually has a detailed bit about when white people can use the "n-word:" exemptions can be allowed only after checking with your "consulate" of black friends, and only if the word is being used in a hip-hop lyric. "It's got to be in the song, though," Rock warns.

The more depressing aspect of the tweet's exhumation is that it appears in the age of social media, children are now on the record all the time. Kids who express unfortunate thoughts while still figuring things out (or even thoughts acceptable at the time that become less acceptable over the years) are now being held to adult standards of appropriateness. And as they get older, they may never be able to escape things said as a juvenile. (There are apps that automatically delete old tweets, but few people use them, and even adults have figured out that anything on the internet is typically there forever.)

In just the last eight years, the number of Twitter users has increased more than tenfold, while the number of Facebook users has grown from 100 million in 2008 to over 2.1 billion at the end of 2017. The young teenagers who adopted these technologies early, thinking social media would be a good way to communicate with friends, are now leaving college and heading for the workplace, while their childhood musings remain in cyberspace for the world to see.

The potential damage this could cause was expertly predicted, as usual, by The Onion satirical newspaper, which in 2012 declared that "Due to Facebook, every potential candidate for the 2040 presidential race, no matter how smart or accomplished, is now completely unelectable." According to the gag, Democrats in need of a presidential candidate had begun searching basements and creepy backyard sheds for "Someone who was kidnapped at a young enough age that they have no online presence."

(This was, of course, before America elected a septuagenarian with a regrettable online presence.)

In fact, children's thoughts are typically so horrifying, a type of therapeutic entertainment has cropped up in which adults stand in front of a crowd and read embarrassing things they wrote as teenagers. A decade ago, I got in the act and posted a love letter on my blog that I wrote at age 16 after being dumped by a girl. Needless to say, the results are mortifying; if you simply read lines like "Just like I needed my brain to think or my lungs to breathe, I needed you," and "If not liking me was a crime, the entire female gender would be in prison," it should disavow you of any notion that juveniles should have the privilege of posting anything that can be read worldwide and embarrass them in perpetuity.

Of course, this runs counter to the prevailing idea that because of social media, children are more informed and sophisticated than kids who grew up just decades ago. People act as if Alexander Graham Bell, who changed the world with rudimentary tools like electricity and copper wire, was, in comparison, a rube because he was denied the pleasure of watching YouTube videos of grown men playing Fortnite for hours on end.

One of the great joys of childhood is being able to learn and grow without the glare of the public on you. To be able to find yourself and learn from your mistakes without subjecting yourself to bands of cackling jackals delighting in your mistakes.

Further, an even greater joy is to be able to shed the awkwardness and pain of your youth on your way to adulthood. Let's ease up on kids that tweet childish things, even after they grow into productive adults. Instead, let's save our enmity for the grown-ups who tweet juvenilia from the White House.

Milwaukee Journal Sentinel

TEA PARTY: EXHAUSTING BUT NECESSARY

September 27, 2013

The tea party's greatest strength is that before signing on to the cause, many of its members had never been involved in politics. The tea party's greatest weakness is that before signing on to the cause, many of its members had never been involved in politics.

Since the various "tea party" elements coagulated in 2009, the movement has been the heart of the Republican Party, if not always its head. The tea party has been able to draw public attention to issues that normally may have been neglected; its presence was certainly crucial to the Republican landslide of 2010. To Democrats, the tea party became like gluten; they don't really know what it is, but they obsessively yammer how terrible it is for everyone.

But the last two electoral cycles have demonstrated the inherent duality of the tea party movement; it is excellent at stocking the American marketplace with common-sense, market-based solutions. But it also ensures that the marketplace has a fully stocked fruits and nuts section.

Take some of the "tea party" candidates the movement has thrust upon America in the past three years. American voters love the idea of outsiders going to Washington to make change — but they expect a basic modicum of political polish and knowledge.

In 2010, the tea party missed two easy U.S. Senate layups in nominating the one woman in Nevada who couldn't beat Majority Leader Harry Reid and another woman who actually had to take to the airwaves to declare she was not a witch. In 2012, a couple of tea party boobs lost easy GOP pickups because they missed the day they taught "rape biology" at the school of common sense.

Then again, Republicans would never have been in a position to win as big as they did without the tea party consistently warning of the perils of big-government programs such as Obamacare. And while the public may not have a particularly high opinion of the tea party itself, it seems to be on board with its issues: Recent polling has shown that three in five Americans oppose Obamacare.

This American discontent with government-controlled health care became fertile ground for a recent tea party procedural misfire that has forced a nasty internecine split within the GOP. Newly elected U.S. Sen. Ted Cruz of Texas has urged the defunding of Obamacare (a terrible problem) by threatening a federal government shutdown (a terrible solution).

In a parliamentary stunt last week, Cruz stood on the Senate floor for 21 hours and spoke against funding Obamacare, weaving in stories about Nazis, Ashton Kutcher and reading from Dr. Seuss' "Green Eggs and Ham." Cruz took advantage of a Senate rule that basically allows a single senator to stand and speak on the floor until he or she collapses or has to urinate.

But Cruz's cause was never anything but a mathematical impossibility. His plan to defund Obamacare was never going to pass the Democratic-controlled Senate, and there was never any chance President Barack Obama was going to sign a bill gutting his signature accomplishment.

But according to Cruz and his supporters, the ability to count to 51 senators makes one a malodorous Occupier. (Hey — is that Paul Ryan over in that drum circle?) So Cruz charged at the Obamacare windmill, his primary accomplishment being to swell his e-mail list — one presumes being on that list will earn signatories the exciting chance to contribute money to Cruz's 2016 presidential campaign.

But as nakedly self-serving as Cruz's tea party catnip was, it focused the nation's collective eyeballs on the perils of Obamacare for 21 hours. Cruz and others are absolutely right — the "Affordable Care Act" is anything but; it will raise premiums on Wisconsinites and limit health care choices without holding down costs. It was passed using a procedural trick, wherein the House never actually voted on the Senate version of the bill. Portions of the bill were upheld by the U.S. Supreme Court using an argument (that the plan is a tax) that Obama himself staunchly denied leading up to the decision. Obama himself has delayed implementation of major portions of the bill using an authority that can't be found anywhere within the U.S. Constitution.

The Republican Party needs the tea party to make these points. In the mid-2000s, the GOP had become a corpulent shell of itself, funding things such as a massive prescription drug benefit and unpopular wars; the tea party dragged Republicans back to the safe haven of morally defensible conservatism. (Unfortunately for the party, it took Democratic wipe-outs in 2006 and 2008 for it to reform itself.)

But while folding all the energetic neophytes into the party has rejuvenated the GOP, at some point the party needs to show it is capable of governing. Cruz's grandstanding may have been good for Ted Cruz, but it was confusing to people who aren't fluent in parliamentary procedure. The American people want something better than Obamacare, but they want an antidote created by someone who's been in the U.S. Capitol long enough to know where the bathrooms are.

Milwaukee Journal Sentinel

POLITICS MAKE FOR SNUGGLY BEDFELLOWS

September 24, 2013

As weird as it sounds, I always thought George Orwell's 1984 was underrated as a romance novel. Amid the dystopia, Winston Smith and Julia surreptitiously find each other and their love flowers, leading to breathy passages like:

> "Almost as swiftly as he had imagined it, she had torn her clothes off, and when she flung them aside it was with that same magnificent gesture by which a whole civilization seemed to be annihilated. Her body gleamed white in the sun...
>
> Not merely the love of one person, but the animal instinct, the simple undifferentiated desire: that was the force that would tear the Party to pieces. He pressed her down against the grass, among the fallen bluebells. This time there was no difficulty."

Fifty Shades of Totalitarianism, indeed.

It seems like in many futuristic dystopian tales, the natural becomes the forbidden. (In the novel, Big Brother also oversees the Junior Anti-Sex League, to prevent such crimes of affection.) If they were caught, Julia and Winston could be "unpersoned" (killed) just for the act.

But with modern advances in technology, it now seems the natural has simply become the inconvenient. Things human beings used to do face-to-face can now be facilitated online, leaving people isolated and unable to interact on a personal basis. Meeting a girl used to mean awkwardly trying to make conversation while sweating profusely and feeling as if a cannonball was lodged in your stomach - now it merely means sending a friend request. And online you don't even have to be you - a funny profile picture can mean never having to horrify a girl with a pimple the size of a tractor.

These fond memories all came back to me this morning as I saw a website for an allegedly soon-to-be-opened business in Madison called "The Snuggle House." According to the site, for $60 you can pay for one of their employees to snuggle you, or you can fork over $110 for the much sought after "double snuggle." (These prices seem steep - I would try to strike a deal to only pay $30 for a one-armed snuggle.)

The website strongly reinforces that it is a snuggling-only zone: no nudity, sex or inappropriate language or behavior will be tolerated. It claims that "Security camera's [sic] and on-site security will be present during all operating hours," but given the lack of attention to punctuation detail in that sentence, I'm skeptical that a snuggling client wouldn't occasionally find themselves the victim of some - ahem - unwelcome affection. The world's newest profession (professional snuggler) could easily morph into the world's oldest profession ("snuggler-plus," as I believe the Romans called it.)

There seems to be a reasonable chance that this is a hoax - earlier this month, Capital Times reporter Jessie Opoien tried to contact someone to talk about the business, but her messages were not answered. (It's too bad, because Governor Scott Walker might make his 250,000 jobs created pledge if we can qualify "snuggling" as a real job.)

But even the fact that it might be real says a lot about the state of society today. I mean, it could happen and it would probably have its fair share of clients. (Especially if they start cross-promoting, like offering a free snuggle with a set of Michelin tires.) There are already legitimate Snuggle Huts in New York, and snuggle parties seem to be the rage in some circles.

But it's believable mostly because it is just one more example of humans not being able to do something that they traditionally have been able to do themselves. In this case, finding someone to snuggle by going out into the world and interacting with potential cuddlers. Now, not only do you not need to develop yourself into a desirable snuggler, you can get all the cuddling you need with the click of a mouse.

Soon, we'll have services you can pay for to experience all the wonders of life. Ten bucks to have a dog lick your face. Twenty bucks for a pretty girl to bump into you with a stack of papers, so you have to help her pick them all up. And as someone suggested on Facebook, it should be thirty bucks for an old guy dressed like your dad to show up at your house and play catch with you while saying "great arm, sport!"

Perhaps I'm just growing old and grumpy and I'm as fearful of change as I am of blinking lights and sports drinks. Two years ago, I bought a car that I didn't realize had this special feature that essentially cuts out your engine when your tires slip in the snow. Now, I am the world's best snow driver, and I don't need this stupid feature to navigate icy roads for me, so I end up yelling obscenities at it every time it kicks in. Who is ever going to learn to drive in the snow if your car does it for you? Who is ever going to learn to parallel park if your car's computer does it with cameras?

Clearly, this has turned into an Andy Rooney-style rant. Maybe I just need a hug.

If I only knew where to get one...

Milwaukee Journal Sentinel

DRUNK ON HISTORY

September 5, 2013

Quick - who was the North Korean ally that helped fight American troops during the Korean War?

If you answered "China," you know more about the conflict than 78% of high school seniors, according to the most recent report from the National Assessment of Educational Progress (NAEP) report. (38 percent responded "Russia," while 23 percent responded "Vietnam.")

According to the report, American schoolchildren are worse at U.S. History than any other subject taught in schools today. On the test, most fourth graders couldn't name why Abraham Lincoln was an important historical figure (aside from his vampire hunting prowess), and only 32 percent of eighth graders could name an advantage American colonists had over British soldiers when doing battle during the Revolutionary War. (If there's a silver lining in the overall scores, it is that students eighth grade and below seem to be improving, and minority students appear to slowly be catching up to white students.)

Clearly, getting America's young people interested in world history has been a challenge. But what if there were a way to make learning about history as fun and exciting as it should be? Certainly, any television show that could elbow its way into youth culture and teach young people historical events would be a valuable public service, right?

Well.....

Sort of. Last week, Comedy Central wrapped up the first season of a show called "Drunk History," which features individuals getting plastered and trying to tell the story of an important historical event. Their narratives are then earnestly acted out by a cadre of A-list Hollywood stars, who re-enact exactly what the inebriated storyteller is saying - even if, as in some cases, the narrator happens to be vomiting.

The show - which is based on a series of short web episodes - is eminently entertaining, and unexpectedly instructive. Its creator, 33-year old actor and comedian Derek Waters, says the show has a researcher and the stories are "100 percent true," but it certainly has the feel of someone getting loaded and spouting off random facts in the same way alcohol makes many people "liquid experts" in any number of topics.

For instance, an early web episode featured a woman named Jen Kirkman telling the touching story of Mary Todd Lincoln (played by Zooey Deschanel, sans Siri) gifting the late Abraham Lincoln's (Will Ferrell) walking stick to Frederick Douglass (Don Cheadle.) Douglass would later write to Mary Todd Lincoln to thank her, saying that the walking stick was not merely a memento, but is was an "inclination of his humane interest" in the "welfare of my whole race."

Of course, in Kirkman's wine-besotted telling, she breaks the action to wonder where her pants went. She refers to Lincoln as "President Clinton" at one point (which gets a nod in the re-enactment), calls Frederick Douglass "Richard Dreyfuss" (likely due to Douglass' stellar work in "Jaws"), and imagines the characters swearing at each other using very modern curse words.

But oddly, it all works - and if you didn't know anything about the story, now you're privy to an important historical event that may have been lost to the history books. Recent episodes have also included segments about The Alamo, the Scopes Monkey Trial (featuring Wisconsin native Bradley Whitford), the assassination of Abraham Lincoln, and Chicago's Haymarket Riot. (For me, the highlight of the season was Winona Ryder's portrayal of Mary Dyer, who fought religious persecution in Massachussetts. Again, language warning.)

The question, of course, is whether it is culturally healthy for society to teach history through a show that features people purposely drinking to the point of almost blacking out. Obviously, the lesson to the young folks would be - learn these great stories first: the drinking part is optional. Killing brain cells with alcohol almost surely offsets the gray matter strengthened by learning the nation's history. (Further, the show is pretty honest about the gross things that can happen when you are "overserved.")

Thankfully, the show isn't targeted towards children - it's meant for young people who like great stories and can relate to drinking culture. And if it teaches college-aged kids some lessons about our past that they previously wouldn't have taken the time to learn, well then that's knowledge they wouldn't have had before.

Interestingly, each episode focuses on the history of a specific city or area - Washington, D.C., Chicago, Boston, Detroit, and San Francisco have all been featured. I, for one, would like to volunteer myself for the Milwaukee edition, whenever it comes around. They wouldn't even have to get me drunk - they can just stop by my desk at any time during the work day.*

In fact, it could be argued that no city deserves the drunk treatment more than Milwaukee, which has a legendary alcoholic history. For instance, at the Milwaukee Journal offices, legendary editor Brownie Rowland used to tie a string to a telephone directory, and when reporters would pick it up off the floor, Rowland would yank the book out of their hands. If the reporter was able to figure out why the book kept slipping out of their hands, Rowland would declare the reporter sober enough to work that day.

(During Prohibition, Journal reporter Cap Manly used to frequent a speakeasy near the paper's offices. When the feds came in to bust the place one night, the quick-witted Manly yelled at the cops, saying he was working on an undercover story about the joint for weeks, and they just ruined it by taking the place down. He got off scot-free.)

The question is, which Milwaukee historical events would make the show? Jeffrey Dahmer? McCarthyism? Milwaukee's Socialist history? (Feel free to offer suggestions in the comments.)

As long as the show makes it clear that these people aren't getting in their car and driving anywhere, I see no problem with providing an edgy Trojan horse to provide people with historical knowledge. The more people know about history, the less likely we are to repeat it - the last thing we need is the Germans bombing Pearl Harbor again.

Note to employer - this is a joke.

Milwaukee Journal Sentinel

WHEN DEATH FINDS YOU FIRST

November 9, 2013

I have to be honest — before his death became news last week, I had never heard of Charlie Trotter.

The University of Wisconsin-Madison graduate who went on to revolutionize the Chicago restaurant scene is being remembered fondly, although many of his associates couch their praise in code words, saying he was "intense" or "stern." (For some reason, we accept "chef" as one of the few occupations in which being a raging egomaniac is not only acceptable but helpful.)

Despite my unfamiliarity with Trotter's work, I felt especially sad when I read the news reports of his demise. I was most affected by the headline:

"Charlie Trotter, famed Chicago chef, found dead in home."

Death is a distressing event no matter how it occurs. (Although death makes us sad more for the experiences we'll miss with the deceased, not because the dead person is sad — he or she is dead — or "in a better place," as people who have never been to Krispy Kreme early in the morning when the first batch of doughnuts rolls out like to say).

Yes, at some point, we all will pass on. Yet I still live in constant fear of being "found dead." Those two words are pregnant with issues that further complicate the dying process and could change how you are remembered for eternity.

Many of us would love to have the idyllic death we see in the movies, where we're lying in a hospital bed, surrounded by friends and family. Your brothers and sisters get to tell you how much they love you, and you get to reciprocate. You can pass on your deathbed wishes and utter "famous last words" for posterity.

But in most cases, you don't get to play chess with death, making plans along the way. It just finds you. And once it taps you on the shoulder, the painting that was your life is complete and open for interpretation by others. It stands alone as a work, without explanation.

Plus, the manner in which you are found can affect how your life is viewed (ask actor David Carradine). Generally, about 80% of the time, I don't want people to know where I am or what I'm up to. But if you drop dead doing something untoward, you are forever frozen in time as "the guy who died doing that thing."

This is why I always keep an unsigned $1 million check made out to my favorite charity in my pocket. If I ever feel like the Lord is calling me home, I will just pull the check out so it is in my hand when someone finds me.

I imagine the coroner saying, "Look, this upstanding, generous individual was about to give a million dollars to charity when he died!" (While the officer on the scene asks, "Then why was he wearing snow goggles, a fluorescent 10-gallon hat and leopard print pajamas?")

Not to mention the fact that I would really feel bad for the person who found me. Presumably, finding a dead body can really ruin someone's day. So if the person who eventually does stumble across my corpse is reading this right now, let me offer a pre-emptive apology.

I know we can't control when and how we go, but we can certainly control how we are remembered. It would seem that if you fill up your canvass with beauty and good deeds, it will leave friends and family with no choice but to view your life favorably. In the end, all we are is what people remember.

Further, it wouldn't kill us to tell each other what we think of our family and friends from time to time. The right time may never come; why not take all the mystery out of it and fill in all those blind spots?

Maybe Trotter was waiting for the right day to tell everyone who thought he was "difficult" that he couldn't have been successful without them. We'll never know.

To ease the public admiration process, my friend Stephen Thompson at National Public Radio has proposed "Appreciation Day," a single day out of the year when participants can tell anyone how much they mean to them without any awkwardness. Wouldn't it be nice to tell people how much you appreciate them without them thinking you're about to ask to borrow money or propose having sex with them?

Until Appreciation Day becomes a national holiday, however, I will stick to conventional means for managing my image in death. This includes keeping a case full of Miles Davis CDs in my car. Sure, I never listen to them, but if I'm in a fatal car crash, my obituary will note that I was the coolest millionaire philanthropist ever.

Milwaukee Journal Sentinel

GEORGE CLOONEY JUST MADE US ALL DUMBER

April 19, 2016

Hot off the presses, the reviews are in for George Clooney's appearance on last Sunday's "Meet the Press!"

"A blockbuster of banality!"

"A victory for vapidity!"

"A feast of fatuity!"

Clooney, whose primary skills involve not eating a lot and getting great haircuts, was given the first 12 minutes of America's cornerstone Sunday morning political show to hold court on a variety of political matters. During an interview with moderator Chuck Todd, Clooney forcefully decried the "obscene" amount of money in politics, just hours after holding a fund-raiser at his home that charged $353,000 per person to dine with Hillary Clinton.

If only there were something Clooney could do to keep money out of politics — like, maybe not raising a tsunami of dollars for candidates. As conservative columnist Jonah Goldberg put it on Twitter, "stop me before I fund-raise again!"

Yet Clooney's vacuity was just pulling out of the garage. He decried Citizens United as "one of the worst laws passed since I've been around." Of course, Citizens United was a Supreme Court decision, not a "law passed." A Democratic Congress and president didn't pass and sign the "Citizens United law of 2010."

In fact, the actual Citizens United decision centered on something Clooney probably can understand — an actual movie. In its decision, the U.S. Supreme Court struck down a federal law that would have barred a film critical of Hillary Clinton from being released in the months before the 2008 presidential election.

Perhaps Clooney might feel differently if one of his corporate-funded political thrillers — "The Ides of March," for instance — were banned by the government for framing Republicans in a negative light. One would think he'd have a different perspective, provided he actually knew what the decision meant.

Instead, Clooney just dished up empty bromides about "corporations" buying influence — you know, those same corporations that pay him millions of dollars so he could spend his single years changing supermodels about as often as most men change their socks. In fact, later in the interview, Clooney actually praised corporations for opposing the new North Carolina transgender bathroom law. So if you're keeping score at home — corporations influencing politics is good, as long as George Clooney agrees with the issue. Perhaps President Hillary Clinton will create the Clooney Free Speech Panel to decide who gets to exercise First Amendment rights and who doesn't.

Of course, celebrities talking about politics as if they just caught five minutes of John Oliver's latest show isn't anything new, nor is our fascination with their boobish observations. But in this election cycle, such dimwittery has been weaponized, as a reality television show star with only a tangential knowledge of fundamental political issues currently leads the Republican presidential contest.

Like Clooney, Donald Trump has been critical of Citizens United, and has even threatened to sue groups that have run unflattering television advertisements against him. And if that wasn't enough to convince Americans that Trump's relationship with the First Amendment is completely self-serving, last week Trump actually threatened to sue an artist who painted a nude picture of The Donald that suggested — uh, how to put this — that Trump Tower may be more of a duplex?

Recently, Clooney referred to Trump as a "xenophobic fascist," further accusing him of political "opportunism." But as one of Clooney's film protagonists might say of his enemy, "we're not unalike, you and me." They are both rich liberals pitching half-baked politics on a willing electorate, hoping their wealth and fame lends them gravitas. In the end, both Clooney and Trump are the same side of the same coin.

And they are willing to spend a lot of those coins to dupe the American people.

Milwaukee Journal Sentinel

LEFT OUT OF THE GENETIC HOUSE PARTY

May 18, 2016

I have an announcement: I am white. But I'm not any run-of-the-mill white guy — I am literally tied with several millions of other Caucasians as the whitest human on the planet. I am a walking human flashlight. Polar bears ask me what my secret is. Off-duty mimes throw money at me on the street. I could sue dry-erase boards for copyright infringement.

This information was recently delivered to me by the world of science. A few months ago, I took a DNA test to determine my ancestors' country of origin, and as it turns out, I am 100% European. The most eclectic my family lineage gets is my 0.6% Italian heritage, which is ironic, as 90% of the food I consume involves either pizza or pasta. That one Italian that sneaked into my bloodline must have been a pretty persuasive guy.

Here's how it works: You pay $200, a kit is sent to your house, and you spit into a tube until it fills up to a line — then you mail it back in. True story — in order to get enough saliva to fill the spit tube, I held a Big Mac in front of my face to get my mouth to water. I thought the test was going to show I had descended from McDonaldland, and Grimace was my third great-grandfather.

For weeks, I waited to see my results. And when they finally arrived, I experienced a completely unexpected sensation: I was really bummed out.

I admit, I was provoked to take the DNA test by the variety of ancestry shows that have cropped up over the past few years. On a show like "Finding Your Roots," a celebrity will typically take a DNA test, then find out their lineage is far more diverse than they expected, spanning multiple continents and ethnicities.

The lesson I've taken from these shows is that despite our racial differences, we are all genetically interconnected. We all share DNA with others we wouldn't expect to share DNA with, making us a complicated community of relatives. According to a 2014 study, the average African-American carries 24% European DNA; the average American Latino carries 18% Native American ancestry, 65.1% European ancestry (mostly from the Iberian Peninsula), and 6.2% African ancestry.

Granted, it is far less likely for self-described European Americans to share African DNA. Only about 4% of European Americans carry African DNA. But self-described European Americans also can find DNA from Asia, the Caucasus (Iran, Turkey, Armenia, etc.), from Native Americans, Hispanics and from Ashkenazi Jewish populations.

I got none of this. It's like America is holding a genetic party, and I'm standing outside while the bouncer taps his foot and glares.

I will concede that American minorities may have little sympathy for my plight. They would point out that being white in America is a pretty good gig. (Comedian Louis C.K. has a bit about how when time machines are invented, they will be solely a white privilege, as no African-American would choose to visit any time before 1980.)

On top of that, behind the genetic mixing I find admirable are some horrifying realities. African-Americans often carry a heavy load of European DNA because they were forced to procreate against their will. In Louisiana and South Carolina, heavy slave-trading states, more than 12% of European Americans have more than 1% African DNA, far higher than the rest of the nation. Further, of European Americans with at least 1% African ancestry, the African DNA is 15% more likely to be on the X chromosome, suggesting African female-European male relationships were far more common.

But among the disgraces of the past also live inspirational tales of strength and survival. And I want to be connected with the stories of those who endured such struggles. Whether it's those who survived slavery or fought against European settlers in the West or risked their lives on a makeshift raft to float here and experience the American dream, these are all strands in the American fabric

But I'm stuck holding one thread.

That's not to say my relatives always had it easy. Many of them came from Germany and Sweden on crowded boats in the 19th century, risking everything to make it here. My ninth great-grandmother is Mary Towne Esty, who was hanged in Salem for allegedly being a witch. (The evidence against her was that she had a wart, which was used as a "nipple" to "suckle the devil.")

But it does suggest that, historically, my relatives have lived segregated lives, away from anyone who didn't look like them. Maybe this was just a product of geography; maybe it was intentional.

This, naturally, leads any white person to ponder the awkward question of what his or her family thought about race relations. And it smacks a modern European American in the face with perhaps the most uncomfortable question of all: If it was you in that situation, what would your attitude about blacks have been?

And perhaps this is why I so wanted to be more genetically diverse; in a small way, maybe I thought it could inoculate me against such a segregated lineage. (Then again, if I did have African DNA, there is a chance a direct relative was a slaveholder and a rapist.)

Maybe the DNA test is wrong. I've always been skeptical. But if this report is right, in the future when genetic lines are even blurrier, I will be the "Caucasian" statue in the Smithsonian. Maybe the test was unnecessary; I did, after all just pay $200 for a ticket to see Radiohead.

Milwaukee Journal Sentinel

BLACK AMERICA'S GENEALOGY OF HOPE

December 15, 2016

There are plenty of ill-advised things people do after a few drinks. They talk to people they shouldn't. They divulge untoward personal details. They get in cars and drive.

My weakness? I offer to do genealogy for people.

This was the case a few weeks ago when, over drinks with my friend Brandon Mines, I volunteered my services to look up his family history. Had I known what I would find, I would likely have demurred.

Within a day, I found information that I realized would substantially change the way Mines, who is African-American, would view his family forever. As a confirmed Caucasian, it felt wrong knowing information about his lineage that he didn't; this wasn't my secret to tell. I texted him and asked him if he wanted to know. He said he did.

In 1855, Mines' great, great, great grandmother gave birth to a baby boy. She was a slave, owned by one of the largest slave owners in the state of Alabama. On later census forms, the boy was listed as "mulatto;" family histories I found confirmed that the boy was, in fact, the son of the white plantation owner and his black female slave. Between slave owners and slaves generally, these encounters were frequently non-consensual.

I found a slave schedule from 1860, listing a five-year old boy living on the plantation. He had no name, and no parents listed. He was a child stripped of all identity, whose lineage was almost certainly a shameful secret. Just looking at the entry in the document is an emotional experience.

Yet when the slaves were freed, the young boy was granted his own plot of land. (This wasn't atypical — slave owners would often grant land to children they had conceived with slaves.) Soon, he would marry a pretty mixed-race girl from nearby and they would have seven children together.

When he was granted his plot of land, he was the only black farmer in an entirely white Alabama town. And yet he farmed that land successfully until his death in 1936. One suspects he was a hardworking, driven man who demanded a lot of his children; soon, five of the seven would move to Chicago, bringing the Mines bloodline to the Midwest.

The story of the Mines family is notable for a few reasons. For one, it is an example of the amazing stories that are out there to be told, just hiding in Census forms and family histories. Had I not done this digging, it's possible that nobody would ever know of the hard work and perseverance my friend's family endured to rise from the depths of human depravity.

(The weirdest story actually comes from the white side of his family. When his four-times great grandfather joined the War of 1812, he only did so on the condition that if he died, his wife would marry his identical twin brother. He died, his wife swapped in the identical twin, and they had four more children together.)

Yet the story also serves as a lesson for those looking to help people of color make progress in America today. Current racial discussions are locked into an inescapable paradigm, with both sides talking past one another. Whites frequently cite personal responsibility as the salve for problems that ail minority communities, viewing African-Americans trapped in poor communities as "takers" and not "givers."

But my friend's history has made me far more optimistic that things can get better. The story shows people rising from the most oppressive period in American history to make better lives for their children. Of course we should never forget the horrors slavery wrought upon the country, but by equal measure we shouldn't forget the heroism of those who rose from those inhumane conditions to succeed. These people weren't super-human; they were simply regular folks who wanted to work hard to provide for their families.

It is this — especially in the Trump era — that should be the animating feature of American public policy. Instead of doubling down on programs that have failed to lift people out of poverty, lawmakers should emphasize programs that increase educational and job opportunities for those who want to better their lives. It can get better — we have seen progress, but the work is far from done.

I still think about Mines' three-times great-grandmother, who is now buried in a family slave cemetery on the plot of land she used to work. Her grave is marked only by a rock with her initials scrawled into it — nobody thought she even deserved a proper headstone. She would never find out that her great, great, great-grandson would become a successful doctor.

Hopefully, however, she can provide an inspirational lesson for those wanting a better chance at upward mobility. If we do this right, from the unspeakable, more can one day flourish.

USA Today

IT'S TIME FOR A GAY SUPERHERO

May 27, 2016

Responding to rumors about his sexuality, the late writer Christopher Hitchens once wrote that his looks had "declined to the point where only women would go to bed with me."

Yet there is a special class of American male whose looks never fade, who live eternal lives free of self-loathing, carbs and often the laws of gravity. They are our superheroes.

Perhaps it is their perennially marble chins that have led fans to argue that many notable superheroes are — or at least should be — gay. Most recently, Captain America's forlorn glances at his longtime pal Bucky Barnes in the movie "Captain America: Civil War" led Vanity Fair's Joanna Robinson to posit Cap's demonstration of heterosexuality the film's "one flaw." (The stars of the movie also have made a superhuman effort to avoid dissuading speculation that the two characters are a couple, fueling the rise of the #GiveCaptainAmericaABoyfriend hashtag on Twitter.)

Naturally, some comics purists are acting as if altering the sexuality of a foundational comic book hero is akin to writing the word "boobs" into the Declaration of Independence. But gay superheroes aren't a new thing: In 2012, DC Comics announced that Alan Scott, the original Green Lantern, was gay. (This led the group One Million Moms to accuse DC of "heavily influencing our youth by using children's superheroes to desensitize and brainwash them into thinking that a gay lifestyle choice is normal and desirable.")

And even if comic book characters aren't overtly gay, many have traditionally carried gay overtones. In his excellent new book, "The Caped Crusade: Batman and the Rise of Nerd Culture," National Public Radio comic book reviewer Glen Weldon details the gay panic of the 1940s and 1950s, when comics were routinely accused of trying to turn kids gay.

German-born psychiatrist Frederic Wertham even launched a personal crusade against comic books, and, following the scrutiny the industry received after Wertham's efforts, 24 publishers went out of business, leaving dozens of authors and artists without jobs. Wertham specifically targeted Batman, whose relationship with the young Robin, Wertham argued, injected the stories with a "subtle atmosphere of homoeroticism."

Yet society survived, even with gay themes — consciously or otherwise — being woven into the stories read by our youth. And now it is time for one of the big characters to come out of the phone booth, cave or wherever they live in silence.

This should not be controversial. For one, as Weldon expertly points out, superheroes are not static; they are constantly evolving. Adam West's campy Batman of the 1960s bears little resemblance to Christopher Nolan's dyspeptic Dark Knight of the 2000s. At some points in the Batman canon, the Caped Crusader has been both an obsessed loner and a violent, psychotic murderer; is that somehow less corrosive than the fact that Batman may enjoy Robin's soft embrace?

Further, comics companies often run different versions of characters on parallel tracks — Lego Batman, for instance, is different from comic book Batman, who is different from Ben Affleck's franchise-debilitating Batman. Would it be possible to take one of these multiple personas, give him an alternative lifestyle and leave the others intact? Seems worth a try.

Most important, a gay Superman, Captain America, Batman, Iron Man or other major character would send a signal to young, gay comic enthusiasts that they aren't the "others" anymore. They wouldn't have to be ashamed about their reasons for liking Captain America any more than a straight young boy should be ashamed of having a Kate Upton poster in his room. They would be fully a part of the comic community.

And when they're done with that, comic companies can start working on a fat superhero to represent us pudgy old guys.

Milwaukee Journal Sentinel

THE CONCERT-GOING CONSTITUTION

August 2, 2016

When Jean-Paul Sartre wrote that "hell is other people," he was almost certainly at a music festival.

That was the conclusion I reached after attending just one day of the Lollapalooza music festival in Chicago over the weekend. From Thursday through Sunday, downtown Grant Park was full of seas of the unfortunately dressed, dangerously inebriated, and tragically tattooed. Think of whatever the opposite of a job fair is, and you'd have Lollapalooza.

But this is all fine — humans have agency over themselves, and each individual is welcome to live their own truth. Where it crosses the line is when the freedom-afforded concertgoers begin to infringe on those who paid good money to actually enjoy the music acts. It's almost as if when writing The Federalist No. 10, James Madison sought to protect the individual rights of people who just wanted to hear LCD Soundsystem without someone talking for a half hour about how they're a Kraftwerk rip-off.

Therefore, it seems necessary to compile a list of simple rules everyone can follow in order to make the show-going experience pleasurable for all involved. Consider it the Concert Constitution.

Article I:

Nobody paid money to hear you sing.

On Friday, I paid more than $200 to see the greatest band working today, Radiohead. What I got to hear instead was a 6-foot-4 lummox screaming every lyric to every song at the top of his lungs. Even with the best sound systems, the audio can be sketchy in these large music festival fields. And especially during quiet songs, it can be impossible to ignore a guy three feet from you doing his best Thom Yorke impersonation. (Also, Thom Yorke is one of the greatest rock vocalists of our time, and this guy most likely works a desk job – if he sounded anything like he thinks he does, he'd be on one of those stages.)

This concept was taken to a whole new level when my friend Rob was listening to a quiet instrumental piece by the band Local Natives, and a girl behind him started free style rapping to the song. She was contributing an unsolicited guest verse!

Look, we know you lost your fantasy football league, and you need to show the world you are proficient in something. And that thing is knowing Radiohead lyrics, fine. But save the duets for long car rides.

Put the camera down, Tarantino.

Look, we all want to memorialize the time we saw Jane's Addiction do a face-melting performance of the Ritual de lo Habitual album, front-to-back. But there is no reason to record every song on your smart phone. You paid $200 to come see your favorite band — and now you're going to watch the whole thing through a two-inch by four-inch video screen? And what exactly to do you plan to do with this grainy, vertically-aligned video when you go home? Watch it over and over? Post it to YouTube along with all the other crappy user-submitted concert videos that are shaky and inaudible?

If you want to get a photo or two, or even a short video clip, then fine. But music shows are like other intimate moments – it's almost better for them to live on in your memory. Imagine meeting a boy one night and making out with him, only to have him pull out his smartphone and start recording the proceedings for posterity. Some things are best left as experiences to remember in your own way.

(Actually, in some cases, this rule conflicts with the first rule — if anyone is excessively filming, it is, in limited circumstances, OK to sing really loudly into his or her phone to memorialize both acts of obnoxiousness. Mutually assured musical destruction.)

Spare us the soliloquy.

The Unique thing about music festivals is that it brings people to see acts that they may not be all that interested in seeing. Maybe a young fan came to enjoy up-and-coming band Modern Baseball in the afternoon and just stuck around to see what this "Radiohead" was all about. Contrast this to normal shows, where you know everyone is there just to see their one favorite act.

But this leads to less interested festival fans having long, inane discussions while you're trying to hear your band play. All you want to do is hear this one song, but there's a tattooed Garrison Keillor behind you waxing nostalgic about he survived growing up in the pre-Snapchat era. He is simply a verbal vandal, defacing sound instead of bridge overpasses.

Your girlfriend is not a V.I.P.

I am, in most cases, opposed to the death penalty, but men who put their girlfriends on their shoulders deserve lethal injection or being forced to watch Bill Maher do stand-up for eternity. Man has not yet concocted an action that is more selfish than blocking the view of the people behind you just so your drunken lady friend can get a better perspective.

Maybe slow down on the alcohol and drugs?

Look, this one is a hard one for me. I am no Nancy Reagan. I have had my moments of catastrophic bacchanalia like everyone else. (Thankfully, most of it pre-Internet.)

But my appeal for self-control is strictly an economic one. It never made all that much sense to me to pay hundreds of dollars to go to a festival, only to not remember it at all. In a philosophical sense, the arts exist in the moment, then in your memories. If you don't even remember any of it, did it really happen at all? What is really the point of blacking out? You're better off saving the money and just staying home and watching shaky, grainy YouTube videos of it.

Also, you are far less likely to hit me with your backpack over and over while dancing like an idiot.

And finally. ...

Clean up your garbage.

This isn't a movie theater in the 1970s — you can't just throw your garbage wherever you want and expect people to clean up after you. Yet when everyone walked out, the field was covered in bottles, blankets, cans and whatever else people brought. Real people have to clean up after you — actual people with actual jobs. Maybe show them a little respect and take your trash to a local receptacle?

I am fully aware that part of the appeal of music is that it breaks all the rules — so a list of rules at a festival seems like an oxymoron. But unless you are actually making the music, you are a real person who has to share space with other real people. And we all deserve some R-E-S-P-E-C-T, too.

USA Today

NOSTALGIC FOR A LESS NOSTALGIC ERA

September 07, 2016

While recently rummaging through items in my basement, I ran across a ticket stub from when I saw a new band called the Foo Fighters at a small club in September of 1995. I immediately felt a sense of nostalgia wash over me. For one, I'm nostalgic for the era of ticket stubs, as many of them were art forms in themselves. Today, you download tickets to your smartphone and wave it at the bouncer on the way in. I miss dumping all my archived stubs out on a table and reliving the memories.

But I also felt nostalgia for that time. I was a senior in college, and it seemed like I was never going to get old. It felt like I'd be the same person, listening to the Foo Fighters for the rest of my life. (Wait, that second part actually happened.)

In reality, my life wasn't that great then. I was completely broke — often having to sell CDs to the local used music store just to afford tickets to shows. The job market for graduating seniors was terrible. I had no girlfriend and no real prospects. My GPA was lower than my average blood-alcohol level.

But nostalgia is a powerful impulse. We remember things more fondly before the pressures and obligations of adulthood come crashing down on us.

America is saturated with nostalgia. It permeates every aspect of our culture, from popular entertainment to politics. It's an impulse we should resist.

Take this summer's breakout series, Netflix's "Stranger Things," which serves as a faithful ode to the 1980s sci-fi films of Stephen Spielberg, George Lucas and Stephen King. While the writing is sensational, the series took off because it triggers a childlike wonderment from a supposedly simpler time. Who wouldn't want to be a kid in the '80s again, riding your bike around and getting in adventures?

But while "Stranger Things" trades in nostalgia, it isn't consumed by it. That is reserved for the out-and-out naked "reboots" we now see every year. Just this year, theaters have seen new Ghostbusters, Star Trek, Star Wars, X-Men, Alice in Wonderland, Tarzan, Captain America, Teenage Mutant Ninja Turtles, Batman and Superman franchises make returns. The film industry's primary standard for funding a film seems to be "have we heard of it before?"

But the nostalgia craze has even more thoroughly infected our politics. Donald Trump's slogan "Make America Great Again" is literally a call for a return to the past. Perhaps this is why, according to polls, the older you are, the more likely you are to support Trump. Maybe he reminds you of a past when people could say untoward things without setting off protests by the perpetually aggrieved (or when America had a much lighter skin tone.) Even Trump's conservative opponents use nostalgia against him, dreaming wistfully of a day when a candidate like Ronald Reagan would once again bring forth prosperity.

Hillary Clinton trades in it, too. Her whole existence as a candidate hinges on a return to the prosperity of the late 1990s, when the Internet boom helped fuel a robust economy with full employment. Her liberal supporters wax nostalgic about the days where unions ruled the workplace, of 80% top tax rates on the rich, and of FDR making it rain on the economy with that sweet, sweet New Deal money.

In a time of uncertainty, it makes sense people would retreat to the comfort of the past. We've seen that movie, and we know how it ends.

But overdependence on gauzy memories stifles creativity and innovation. We can learn the lessons of the past without having to replicate them. We missed a chance to nominate a major party candidate who could advocate for real change instead of a return to an outdated place in history.

I will never feel nostalgic for the time America was awash in nostalgia.

Milwaukee Journal Sentinel

THE GROWING CONSERVATIVE COUNTERCULTURE

November 25, 2016

Last December, when legendary composer Andrew Lloyd Webber was about to debut his new Broadway musical "School of Rock," he received an interesting request — then-presidential candidate Donald J. Trump wanted to attend the show's opening.

But the musical theater legend didn't want him there. "Actually I managed to persuade him not to come," Webber told a British talk show last week, saying he told Trump he was too famous and might overshadow the kids in the musical. (Which sounds exactly like the way you would get Trump to do something — by over-flattering him.)

Of course, this snub was merely the appetizer to last week's imbroglio in which conservative Vice President-Elect Mike Pence was booed at a performance of the universally praised Broadway show "Hamilton." After the show, the cast read a statement to Pence urging him to govern in the interest of all Americans. (Pence took the high road, saying the boos are "what freedom sounds like.")

It is unclear whether barring conservatives from Broadway is going to become a trend akin to what sexy astronauts has become for Hollywood. But there couldn't be a better tool to recruit young Republicans than having conservative theater goers singled out and lectured by self-satisfied Broadway actors.

Predictably, Donald Trump once again proved capable of learning exactly the wrong lesson from the exchange, calling the play "overrated" and saying the theater "must always be a safe and special place."

But Trump's ham-handed attempt to co-opt the jargon of the left has it backwards. The theater is a safe space — for progressives. We all just saw how threatened they became when an advocate of traditional marriage dared to enter their sacrosanct womb of smug self-approval.

In fact, "safe spaces" are actually anything but for conservatives. The chances of a right-winger being cracked on the dome for invading a progressive's "me time" are far higher than any threat a conservative poses by stumbling upon a "safe space." A year hasn't yet passed since University of Missouri journalism professor Melissa Click was charged with assault for confronting a student trying to take a picture of her public "safe space." (Click later dodged a formal assault conviction, but the video of her calling for "muscle" to remove the student photographer lives on forever.)

The truth is, conservatives neither need, nor want, a "safe space" to debate their ideas. We have spent our lifetimes being lectured to by popular entertainment figures who can't fathom our flyover-country ideals. As an independent music fan, I would frequently go to small shows in Madison during Gov. Scott Walker's battle with the public unions and have to sit through lectures about union rights and how the Koch brothers ran state government. Needless to say, I wasn't granted the opportunity for rebuttal.

But if the theater battles are a stand-in for a broader cultural phenomenon, it seems as if there is now a shift. In the past, elite liberals saw themselves as sticking up for the common person against corporatism and greed. Think of America as Tom Wolfe's "Radical Chic" writ large.

Yet for the past eight years, progressives have had control of the White House and a monopoly on smug, self-important entertainment figures. Americans are tired of being told John Oliver has "destroyed" something they hold dear and being lectured to by Amy Schumer in Budweiser ads.

And thus, the cultural shift: Liberals are now the establishment, and conservatism is now the counterculture. For many Americans, voting for Donald Trump was a punk rock-style single-digit salute to the existing power structure. Ordinary citizens are tired of safe spaces and vegans and being told they're racist.

The irony is, if the left does this right, we could see a golden age of anti-Trump art. If a Trump presidency provokes Radiohead to give us another "Hail to the Thief" or Green Day to write another "American Idiot," we'll all be better off.

But for now, Trump is the titular head of a movement to topple America's liberal elitism. Just don't look for this notable conquest to be reflected in a Broadway musical about his life 200 years from now.

Milwaukee Journal Sentinel

THE LAST AMERICAN HERO

December 13, 2016

"Could I ask for a show of hands how many are confident that they will come back from outer space?"

As Tom Wolfe noted in "The Right Stuff," this was a particularly awkward question to ask a group of astronauts, especially those who had yet to puncture the atmosphere in a space capsule. But at the 1959 press conference unveiling the Project Mercury astronauts, a reporter posed just that question.

Of course, not raising one's hand meant that he thought he was going to either be blown to bits on takeoff, cast adrift in space or roasted by the heat upon re-entry. So each of the astronauts raised his hand.

Near the end of the table, John Glenn raised both hands.

Glenn didn't have reason to be so confident. The Atlas rocket that soon would be thrusting him into the great beyond had a pesky habit of exploding in a fiery ball once it left the launch pad. Perhaps the Marine's 149 combat missions in World War II and Korea instilled a faux certainty that he was indestructible.

And while the human form of John Glenn left us last week, John Glenn the American Hero still lives on. In fact, Glenn's death at the age of 95 is a reminder that there may never be another figure like him in our country.

As Wolfe wrote in a later essay, "John Glenn, in 1962, was the last true national hero America has ever had."

Just months before Glenn became the first American to orbit the earth in a spacecraft, Soviet cosmonaut Gherman Titov had circled the Earth 17 times on the Vostok 2 capsule. The "space race" with the Soviet Union was an existential battle; any nation that controlled the heavens also controlled the weapons that could be fired from above.

Thus, Glenn's voyage on Friendship 7 wasn't merely notable because a man was willing to strap a missile between his legs and ride it into space, the future of the United States as a nation was believed to be at stake. Had the Atlas rocket exploded, it would have cost Glenn more than just his life — many Americans were afraid that such a failure would have granted the Soviets a near monopoly on space and put them in peril.

In modern times, the word "hero" has been devalued to the point of near irrelevance. Next time anyone hears of Beyonce's "heroic" Super Bowl halftime show, it might be worth taking some time to reflect on exactly how many American lives her dance moves saved.

It's also difficult to think of any modern figure who is as universally beloved as Glenn continues to be. As soon as any American figure gains notoriety, it is now a sport to see who can be the first to tear him or her apart. Even Americans who are above reproach are now subjected to parasitic websites whose sole agenda is to dole out buckets full of reproach. It seems that the only current American who enjoys 100% public approval is a dancing, rapping man-pixie who writes historical Broadway musicals.

Had modern media existed in 1962, it would have not gone unnoticed that all the Mercury Seven astronauts were white males. Or that they enjoyed fast cars and the teeming crowds of young, available women who descended on their training facilities. (Women to whom Wolfe applied the term "labial piping birds.")

It was actually Glenn, the deeply religious Presbyterian, who was able to get his fellow astronauts in line and succeed in suppressing stories about his colleagues' indiscretions.

Of course, in 2016, media manipulation for the greater good of the program would be an impossibility. Further, in the era of social media, one could fully expect a website to start digging around Glenn's church and exposing some of his faith's more "extreme" views.

Perhaps Glenn's most endearing characteristic, however, was the example he set for men and boys around the nation. He was a man's man – the sort of accessible superhero Hollywood still can't quite get right. (And is trying to manufacture more of, given the paucity of real-life heroes.)

But now we are constantly warned of the pernicious effects of "toxic masculinity" in America and how it perpetuates "patriarchy" and "male dominance." Duke University actually recently offered men on campus a "safe space" to contemplate their "toxic masculinity" — Glenn's mere presence on campus would have likely caused a collective fainting spell.

Sadly, with Glenn's passing, we may not ever know what a real hero is anymore. This is perhaps why America just elected a con man as president; dignity, virtue and personal courage now appear to be mere fetishes. And it now seems the Era of True American Heroes is as far distant as the time before man ventured into space.

Milwaukee Journal Sentinel

THE IDENTITY TRAP

December 27, 2016

"To get back one's youth," Lord Henry says in Oscar Wilde's "The Picture of Dorian Gray," "one has merely to repeat one's follies."

Henry's observation, however, deserves a modern update. In their search for eternal youth, adults now are pushing their follies on the young people of 2016. George Bernard Shaw thought youth was wasted on the young, but today's progressives see youth as an opportunity to cement their legacy of grievance and division.

Take, for example, a video released by MTV earlier this week that intends to provide New Year's resolutions "for white guys." Among the advice these teens provide is to "recognize that America was never 'great' for anyone who wasn't a white guy." A young man offers that "Blue Lives Matter isn't a thing," and a bespectacled young woman pleads with white men to "learn what mansplaining is and stop doing it."

It would be a shame for today's young people to ignore the "mansplaining" of white guys like Wilde, for instance. Wilde, of course, was gay — not in the "bake me a wedding cake or I'll file a federal lawsuit" way, but in the "you could spend the rest of your life in a 19th century prison" way. And the way he lived a life of independence from the domineering, restrictive mores of his time should be inspiration to young people of any era.

It just so happens that those restrictive voices are now those on the left, policing language and behavior in order to foist their grievances on everyone. Presumably, MTV isn't run by 16-year olds, so this is exactly what the adults at the channel are trying to do — imbue children with their same divisive ideals and biases.

MTV, of course, has been gasping for relevance ever since music fans realized they could get their songs and videos whenever they wanted on the Internet. The channel's target demographic has eroded from college students to young teens to people who can't find their remotes to change the channel. One of MTV's flagship shows, "Catfish," features literally the dumbest people left in America: teenagers who think they are dating supermodels online, only to realize they have been duped into sexting with large women who can pop the glass eyes out of their head.

In America's distant history, there actually was a time when young people strived to act older.

But if you're a teenager today, there's a cabal of grown-ups who want to make sure you stay frozen in your current mental state in perpetuity. When you're a child, they want to make it seem like conservatism is a mental problem, making it near impossible for you to get along with someone of a different political persuasion. When you get to college, they will make sure you never hear or see anything that might challenge the beliefs they injected in you as a high schooler. And when you're an adult, they'll expect you to show up and scream at Republican electors who try to cast their Electoral College ballots.

But for young people, it doesn't have to be like this. Take heed of Flannery O'Connor's advice to "push back against the age as hard as it pushes against you." (Bonus: she's a woman, so it's advice you're allowed to take!)

You may have noticed that in school, the most admirable kids are also the most subversive. In 2016, rejecting authority means tossing aside the divisive identity politics being fed to you and thinking for yourself.

As Wilde himself said, "everything popular is wrong." Reject the grievance fad, and you may not be popular, but you'll enjoy the benefit of being right.

Milwaukee Journal Sentinel

SACRILEGE BY PUNCTUATION

December 23, 2016

Earlier this year, I was interviewed for a news article about what it's like to be a conservative living among liberals. I made the point that at every neighborhood cookout, a local liberal would introduce himself or herself, then begin asking questions about what I did for a living.

"And it's like, 'Oh god, here we go,'" the story quoted me as saying.

The quote is accurate, except for one detail. I was referencing "God," not "god." The Lord. The Creator. The Holy Ghost. The Holy Spirit. Yahweh. Allah. The Dude in the Clouds.

It has become increasingly popular to use the lowercase "god" to refer to the singular deity central to so many faiths. Perhaps this is out of ignorance; maybe it's simply because we more heavily communicate with each other through the written word on social media. When we used to communicate verbally, capitalization wasn't an issue.

But it seems that, more often, not capitalizing "God" is a statement about the author. If one doesn't believe in God, he or she often will think it's fine to disrespect those who do by dropping the "G" to lowercase. Such a stylistic change is a small way of taking sides in a dispute that spanned centuries and caused much blood to be shed — and yet it now can be done not with a sword, but in comfortable pajamas.

But rules are rules. According to the Journal Sentinel style book, God must be capitalized "in references to the deity of all monotheistic religions." The lowercase "god" is only used in reference to gods and goddesses of polytheistic religions.

It is thus not in the power of a writer to determine whether "God" deserves capitalization or not. When you see someone on Twitter declare "Oh my god," they are almost certainly not adherents to Norse mythology. It may still happen, but we have yet to declare Thor's and Loki's birthdays to be national holidays.

No, when people punctuate an assertion with the word "god," they're talking about my guy. The notorious G-O-D. And when monotheistic believers named their deity, they called him "God."

And this reason alone justifies the capital "G," even if you believe a single deity to be fictional. "God" is a proper name, just like "Buzz Lightyear" or "Darth Vader." Even if I don't believe there's a singing jungle animal named Baloo, capitalizing his name remains a simple bare necessity.

Doing otherwise is simply a disrespectful finger in the eye of religious believers. As Richard Eskow noted last year in Salon — a website that is itself no bastion of right-wingery — refusing to capitalize "God" "makes the writer seem petty and silly, like those Republicans on Fox News who talk about the "Democrat" Party.

Undoubtedly, this phenomenon only will get worse as proper grammar and punctuation go the way of the folding map. Social media has developed an entirely new lexicon in which capitalization is optional.

It also will increase as people take religion less seriously. According to a 2014 Pew poll, Americans who consider themselves religiously unaffiliated jumped from 16% to 23% in the previous seven years. This split was starkest among age groups, as 67% of those age 60 and above considered religion an important part of their lives, while only 38% of those born after 1990 thought the same.

But even if you're not religious, if your goal is truly to "Coexist," then pay proper respect to the capital "G." And if you're looking to spice up your interjection, for the love of God, keep our deity out of it.

Milwaukee Journal Sentinel

OUR RIGHT TO SWEAR IS F---ING GOD-GIVEN

September 22, 2017

Attend any University of Wisconsin home football game, and you'll get to hear the ribald "cheer" that forced ESPN to begin muting the student section years ago. Translated into polite-speak, the cheer implores one section of Camp Randall Stadium to "dine on excrement," while another section is invited to "engage in intercourse." (It seems one of the sections comes out way ahead on this deal — in fact, Christopher Hitchens once expressed puzzlement at the "F--- you" insult, noting it confuses an amorous act with "an act of aggression.")

For years, athletic director Barry Alvarez and other campus administrators have implored students to end this cheer, given the number of children who attend Badger games. But while the chant might be tasteless and boorish, it certainly isn't criminal.

Yet the issue of whether profanity itself is speech protected under the First Amendment has found its way to the Wisconsin Supreme Court. The court must decide whether a mother can be criminally prosecuted for "disorderly conduct" for using profanity toward her own son in the privacy of their own home.

After Ginger Breitzman's son burned some popcorn, she went on an extended profane tirade against the 14-year old boy while he was on the phone with a friend, calling him a "f--- face," a "retard" and a "piece of s---." All the evidence against Breitzman suggests she is a terrible mother — she has done jail time for other child neglect charges, which she currently isn't disputing.

But the disorderly conduct charge is important as a matter of precedent — as a catch-all crime, it could effectively criminalize the use of profanity in the home. As Chief Justice Patience Roggensack noted during the oral argument on Wednesday, no disorderly conduct charge would have been brought against Breitzman had she told her son she was "disappointed in him," or that he had "been disrespectful," or that he was "behaving poorly." It was the specific profane words she used that landed her before the Supreme Court fighting a criminal charge.

In 1971, the U.S. Supreme Court visited the issue of public profanity, overturning 19-year-old Paul Robert Cohen's conviction for disturbing the peace by wearing a jacket that said "F--- the Draft" in a public courthouse. "To many, the immediate consequence of this freedom may often appear to be only verbal tumult, discord, and even offensive utterance," the court wrote, but "that the air may at times seem filled with verbal cacophony is, in this sense not a sign of weakness but of strength."

The court recognized that the First Amendment not only protects specific language but ideas expressed by that language. And it didn't want to be the referee determining which words could be used to further those ideas.

The fact is, people use profanity for a variety of reasons. It can be used to shock, offend, punctuate and berate. For some, profanity is an art form; a comedian like Dave Chappelle expertly commands the "F" word like Cézanne wielded an oil brush. Some believe profanity is a tool for the undereducated to overcompensate for their sub-optimal vocabularies; yet even American vice presidents like Dick Cheney take untold delight in urging combative senators to "go f--- themselves."

Are the courts going to determine what words are acceptable and which ones aren't? Can I escape prosecution if I refer to someone by the clinical name for a reproductive organ rather than the slang for it? Some words have different meanings given the context and community standards. Thus, setting out a hierarchy of filth would be impossible, given that, as the court recognized in the Cohen case, "one man's vulgarity is another's lyric."

It should be clear that while profanity is often unwelcome, it is constitutionally protected speech. Standing alone, dirty words don't fall within the classes of unprotected speech (incitements to violence, obscenity, libel, threats), so citizens shouldn't be prosecuted more harshly for using them in their own home.

Ginger Breitzman richly deserves prison time for her acts of cruelty against her son. But, for the sake of profanity-users everywhere, giving her extra time for swearing would be complete bull----.

Milwaukee Journal Sentinel

A HOSTILE ACT AGAINST GRAMMAR

May 29, 2018

One must give President Trump credit where it is due: Arguing he is innocent of obstructing justice by threatening to fire the investigator looking into whether he obstructed justice is a novel strategy. It would be like an accused arsonist ordering a judge to find him innocent or he'll burn her new car to the ground.

Yet while the president and investigators publicly wrangle over collusion, obstruction and "spying," Trump continues his assault on something as valuable as democracy itself: the English language. As the president makes daily pronouncements on Twitter, one only wishes he occasionally colluded with a dictionary.

Surely, Trump's supporters admire his willingness to defy convention. But when proper grammar, punctuation and spelling are treated with more enmity than Vladimir Putin, it weakens America's standing and undercuts the force of the president's words.

A recent Boston Globe report suggested aides who post tweets on Trump's behalf actually add garbled syntax, unnecessary exclamation points, and random capitalization to Trump's posts just to make them sound like the president of the United States. "Some staff members even relish the scoldings Trump gets from elites shocked by the Trumpian language they strive to imitate," says the Globe report, "believing that debates over presidential typos fortify the belief within his base that he has the common touch."

For one, the debate over "typos" isn't necessarily one about misspellings or awkward punctuation. It is a well-grounded concern that the most powerful man in the world often communicates to the world without any filter or prior review by his advisers. Certainly anyone on Twitter long enough will admit they have regretted sending certain tweets, but our inept postings likely won't lead to a Syrian village being vaporized.

And granted, while one is unlikely to hear the Queen's English being spoken at backyard cookouts across America this summer, the president's official statements should adhere to a basic standard of properness and decorum. If the president aspired to be a "drain the swamp"-style rabble-rouser, it would be more palatable if he demonstrated a fifth-grade proficiency in language.

That's not to say there wouldn't be times where the president couldn't defy language conventions, Tom Wolfe-style. But before one begins stuffing prose with extraneous exclamation points and random capitalization, they should at least master the basics first. International conflict is not the proper venue to feature Trump's off-the-cuff beat poetry.

Instead, Trump's tweets (or at least the ones he writes) portray an undisciplined, capricious mind prone to laziness and emotional outbursts. Take, for example, this gem from May 23, in which Trump tweeted:

"Look how things have turned around on the Criminal Deep State. They go after Phony Collusion with Russia, a made up Scam, and end up getting caught in a major SPY scandal the likes of which this country may never have seen before!"

One visualizes Trump breathlessly tapping the shift button on his phone to emphasize the words "Phony Collusion." The capital "P" and "C" are simply too much for him to resist; finally, he gives in to temptation, as if the eye-popping uppercase characters are a porn star at a golf outing. His Ivy League education (recall his declarations that he has the "best words" and "a very good brain") begs him to use his linguistic turn signals; but making letters bigger just feels ... oh so right.

In Aldous Huxley's The Doors of Perception, Huxley argues the role of the human brain is "eliminative:" the brain essentially serves as a referee, filtering all of the body's senses and desires to allow humans to function. In the same way, proper use of language further distills the base emotions in the brain into an orderly, understandable stream of communication.

The inability of the most powerful person in the world to adhere to even basic linguistic rules — and to brag about this lack of discipline! — should worry even Trump's most ardent supporters. His lexical lurches toward whatever is on his mind that very second are a window into his unpredictable temperament and capricious judgment.

With his game of syntactical bumper cars, Trump highlights both the best and the worst of the American system of government. On the one hand, it demonstrates anyone can be president. On the other hand, it demonstrates that anyone can be president. Let's just hope one day we find out he's had an undisclosed meeting with Merriam-Webster.

Milwaukee Journal Sentinel

TEAM MAGA'S WAR ON LITERACY

December 20, 2019

On the afternoon of December 11, freshman Republican Senator Josh Hawley was grilling Justice Department Inspector General Michael Horowitz about a recent DOJ report detailing the basis of an investigation into Russia's meddling in the 2016 election. In trying to make the case that domestic meddling in elections was worse than foreign meddling, Hawley pinpointed the real culprit in the report was the "Democrat National Committee."

In past years, such a political malapropism would be written off as a slip of the tongue. Hawley fancies himself a salt-of-the-earth Midwesterner who doesn't truck with fancy elites, but he did go to Stanford and then Yale Law. Surely he didn't mean to say "Democrat" when he clearly meant "Democratic," right?

Even the transcribers at C-Span gave Hawley the benefit of the doubt, recording that he had used the correct word. (He had not.)

Alas, Hawley's lexical toe-stub was not a mistake. It was intentional.

After appearing on Fox News the following day, Hawley issued a press release bragging that he had appeared on the network to argue that the "Democrat National Committee was essentially able to purchase a federal investigation of the Trump Campaign."

Using the term "Democrat" in place of "Democratic" has been a minor debate in Republican circles for some 60 years, but it has only recently become mainstream as the party has placed lib-owning at the top of its collective Maslow hierarchy.

Saying "Democrat" instead of "Democratic" has become a shibboleth—a verbal handshake to signal that you're on Team Red Hat. It's about as annoying as people rolling their "r's" when ordering a "burrito" to prove they once vacationed in Cozumel. But whatever. Triggering Democrats has become so important to Republicans that they're willing to assault the English language if the people who like good grammar are the Bad Guys.

Traditionally, right-wingers objecting to the use of "Democratic" were irritated because they imagined that the term allowed Democrats to claim they spoke for everyone. So in 1955, former GOP national chairman Leonard Hall took a page from Thomas E. Dewey's playbook and began referring to the "Democrat" Party.

"I think their claims that the represent the great mass of the people, and we don't, is just a lot of bunk," he explained.

American Speech magazine wrote that the Republicans' attempt to rebrand opponents was because, among other reasons, "Democrat Party" didn't roll of the tongue as easily.

"Whether they have meant to imply that the party was no longer democratic, or whether they banked on the harsher sound pattern of the new name; whether they wanted to strengthen the impression that they were speaking for a new Republican party by using a new name for the opposition, or whether they had other reasons, the fact remains that... highly influential speakers... used the shorter adjective," wrote Atcheson Hench.

In his political dictionary, the late William Safire offered that he thinks the "harsher sound pattern" refers to the "crat," which draws a parallel with unpopular words like "bureaucrat," "autocrat," and "aristocrat." In 1996, saying "the Democrat Party" actually became the official policy of Bob Dole's presidential campaign. George W. Bush routinely dropped the "-ic," a practice picked up by Rush Limbaugh and now embraced by the Republican cognoscenti.

Yet using "Democrat Party" doesn't make sense on any linguistic level. For one, "Democrat" is a noun and "Democratic" is an adjective—one should not use one in place of the other (such as when Trump says we need to get "tough on cyber" or he's not a fan of "the anal.")

On top of that, a political party should be free to call itself whatever it wants. This is a policy deeply ensconced in the Associated Press Stylebook, which specifically warns, "Don't use Democrat Party."

But low-key shittiness is now a rite of passage for calling yourself a Republican. And with a tidal wave of nonsense coming from the right on a daily basis, it's impossible to correct the micro-idiocies. And so, here we are.

Today, in order to consider yourself a "conservative," you don't need to study Hayek or spend time ruminating on the proper role of government intervention in our lives. You just have to publicly celebrate anti-knowledge. Because it drives the DemocRATS nuts!

All of which is why an Ivy Leaguer like Hawley must now play the role of lexical low-roader, winking to the MAGA-nistas. Don't be surprised if his plan to cinch the 2024 Republican presidential nomination will be declaring that gerund phrases are tools of the Deep State.

The Bulwark

MAKE PROFANITY GREAT AGAIN

September 12, 2020

In December of 1989, mourners flowed into the Great Hall at St Bartholomew's Hospital to hear former Monty Python group member and cancer victim Graham Chapman eulogized.

Yet, Chapman's longtime writing partner John Cleese offered more of a roast than a eulogy.

"Good riddance to him, the freeloading bastard, I hope he fries," Cleese deadpanned, claiming Chapman would have never forgiven him if he didn't take the opportunity to shock everyone on his behalf.

As he finished, Cleese imagined a discussion in which the late Chapman urged him "to become the first person ever at a British memorial service to say 'fuck.'"

One of the world's funniest people, Cleese understood the power in using a vulgar word in a staid context. When the profane clashed against the sacred, it helped everyone in the audience release the sadness and tension that had built.

Profanity similarly achieves the same goal in our lives. Obscenities can help us cope with extreme circumstances, can signal to others when we're being playful or serious, and can even help others know when we're telling the truth. Fewer things are as satisfying as conducting a symphony of swear words to provoke a reaction.

But what if the concept of profanity vanished?

In 2020, virtually all of the guardrails that have kept obscenity out of public life are gone. People watch television on streaming apps like Netflix, Hulu, Amazon Prime, and HBO Now, where profanity is de rigueur.

Even basic cable has lifted its language limits—audiences recently delighted as the 1990s-era Chicago Bulls brought locker room language to our living rooms in ESPN's "The Last Dance" documentary series. Fans who have watched televised NBA games without spectators in the seats have no doubt caught some fragrant words despite the networks' efforts to block them with delays and crowd noise.

Public debates take place on Twitter and Facebook, where regular people get to talk exactly how regular people talk. (HBO now owns exclusive rights to Sesame Street, where presumably Oscar the Grouch will one day graciously thank Big Bird for inviting him to "eat shit.")

Even legacy media outlets are getting in on the act, with bestseller lists including book titles like Mark Manson's The Subtle Art of Not Giving a F*ck, Gary John Bishop's Unf*ck Yourself, John Kim's I Used to Be a Miserable F*ck, and of course, the children's book parody Go the F**k to Sleep by Adam Mansbach.

Newscasts are also getting in on the action. During coverage of the George Floyd-related protests, cable news broadcasts made little effort to shield the public from fragrant language and graffiti. In February, former Illinois Gov. Rod Blagojevich tried to make the case that he was a "political prisoner" to CNN anchor Anderson Cooper. The normally composed Cooper declared Blagojevich's pleadings to be "bullshit."

And, of course, politicians have seized on the new era of public vulgarities, often uttering verboten words on the record.

President Donald Trump leads the pack in this regard, seasoning many of his statements with language befitting his Queens upbringing. Some newspapers have had to re-imagine their style guides during the Trump era to catch all the president's profanities. (The Washington Post, which printed the word "bullshit" five times in one day, compared Trump to President Camacho of the movie Idiocracy, who began his State of the Union Address by saying, "Shit. I know shit's bad right now.")

Trump's opponents have often tried to match his profane effluence. When a media outlet reported former Secretary of State John Kerry was considering a late entry to the 2020 Democratic presidential primary, Kerry responded with a tweet (later deleted) that said he was not getting in the race and that "any report otherwise is fucking (or categorically) false."

Current vice presidential candidate Kamala Harris referred to Trump's proposals as "bullshit." Failed Presidential candidate Tulsi Gabbard called Trump "Saudi Arabia's bitch."

And, of course, who could forget the Bard of Bravado, former presidential candidate Beto O'Rourke? When answering a question about a mass shooting in Odessa, Texas last year, O'Rourke said "We don't yet know what the motivation is ... but we do know this is fucked up."

After O'Rourke's utterance, columnist John McWhorter of The Atlantic took up the soon-to-be-ex-candidate's cause, arguing "fuck" as a public punctuation is no longer any worse than "damn" or "hell."

"The truth is that in 2019, using the F-word is quite commensurate with being clean of scrub," wrote McWhorter, arguing the word is "less obscene than salty." Shifting linguistic mores, he argued, have rendered the word "spicy, but hardly evil or taboo."

O'Rourke made no apology for his verbal habanero, as his campaign soon began selling t-shirts adorned with the words "THIS IS F★CKED UP." His continued use of the word on the campaign trail hinted his newfound love of public profanity was more of a media stunt than a sincere heat-of-the-moment expression of frustration.

Profanity is nothing new, and nor is widespread indifference to it. Throughout history, there have been eras when the rampant use of obscenities was commonplace. But those times were characterized by a broader cultural coarseness—the societal mores were so crude, "swearing" or "cursing" hardly seemed out of bounds.

Similarly, the current acceptance of profanity isn't causing cultural rot—it is merely a symptom of it.

Niggling over the president calling predominantly minority nations "shithole" countries or Congresswoman Rashida Tlaib promising to "impeach this motherfucker" is like watching pornography and getting upset when an actress curses. There have to be rules of propriety in play for something to offend —if society itself is vulgar, then obscenities no longer shock.

Further, the twin crises of the COVID-19 pandemic and the protests and riots following the death of George Floyd have demonstrated another historical trend: When society is under duress, policing language no longer takes priority.

Like John Cleese saying "fuck" in a church, the broader context is everything.

There may be no era of literature more bawdy and obscene than the medieval era. Chaucer's Canterbury Tales, written in 1386, features one character telling another that his rhyming is "not worth a turd," and features terms like "arse," and "coillons," a crude synonym for "testicles." Chaucer also generously uses anachronisms such as "dight" (screw) and "swive," a term interchangeable with "fuck." Chaucer referred to corrupt priests as "shitten shepherds."

Another mid-fifteenth century poem, A Talk of Ten Wives on Their Husbands Ware, features women discussing the size of their husbands' penises. One complaining her husband's "meat" is the size of a snail, one says his "ware" is the size of three beans, and one observes that when her husband's pants have a hole in them, his "penis peeps out of the hole like a maggot."

As author Melissa Mohr argues in her lively book Holy Sh*t: A Brief History of Swearing, the 15th and 16th centuries were a time when life for the average person was crude and indiscreet. The concept of a private restroom had not yet caught on, so after a big meal, someone might just walk over to the corner of the dining room and drop a deuce. Male and female servants often slept naked in the same room as their masters, leading one historian to remark that "the sight of total nakedness was the everyday rule up to the 16th century."

In other words, the medieval era made Game of Thrones look like Downton Abbey.

It wasn't until the late sixteenth century that architectural innovations began taking into account the unique notion that some people might actually want privacy. The idea began with the upper classes and then trickled down to the masses, who began walling themselves off from others in bedrooms and lavatories.

This physical separation and the rise of Protestantism coincided with a growth in the concept of shame.

"Privacy created what we've seen Elias call 'the invisible wall of affects,' and with it the embarrassment and shame at the sight or mention of bodily functions that medieval people lacked," writes Mohr.

"Sixteenth-century people were ashamed of more things than their medieval forebears, and ashamed in front of more people," Mohr writes. "It became more and more important to conceal these various shameful body parts and actions, in public life and in polite language."

The new emphasis on shame led some sixteenth century linguists to begin defining what words could be said and which ones were "obscenus." In 1587, a new Latin-English dictionary counsels that the "filthie, foule, uncleane, wanton, bawdie, unchast, ribauldrie, abhominable," and "dishonest" should be avoided.

Interestingly, these new rules of propriety did not apply to those whom had nothing for which to be ashamed—that is, people in positions of power. A lord, for instance, may talk about the size of his package in the presence of his inferiors—being tawdry and indecent was a power move meant to demonstrate one's social superiority. (According to journals kept by André Hurault, Queen Elizabeth was fond of baring her breasts in front of the

French ambassador to show her condescension—she was 64 years old at the time.)

Soon, indecent language was relegated to the commoners, who enjoyed "low" entertainment like the plays of Shakespeare. The Bard, of course, was filthy, but often cloaked his sexual content in euphemism and innuendo. (For instance, when Hamlet tells Ophelia, "Do you think I meant country matters?," he's discussing anatomy, not geography.)

According to Mohr, obscene words violated class norms during the eighteenth and nineteenth centuries.

"They were seen as the language of the lower classes, the uneducated—and accessed the deepest taboo of Augustan and Victorian society, the human body and its embarrassing desires, which had to be absolutely hidden away in swaths of fabric and disguised in euphemisms," she writes.

Consequently, many American families changed their names to avoid embarrassing connotations—for instance, Little Women author Louisa May Alcott's original family name was "Alcox."

Naturally, that didn't mean people denied themselves the delights of the occasional obscenity. The notoriously tawdry Benjamin Franklin, writing pseudonymously in Poor Richard's Almanack, zinged the upper classes with jibes like "The greatest monarch on the proudest throne is obliged to sit upon his own arse," and "Force shits upon reason's back."

Until modern times, however, profanity was largely kept out of the public record. Official writings and news accounts rarely reported obscene acts. In the course of writing a book about the year 1916, I read hundreds of news reports from that year—in one instance, a burglar stole an "iron man" from a sorority girl's dresser drawer. In another, a man and a woman were arrested for engaging in a "soul kiss" in an alley. A different man was arrested for soliciting a "commercialized hug." (The paper noted he "walked away in the arms of the law.") And so on.

Yet court records, which were obliged to transcribe testimony verbatim, suggest that common folk used profanity much in the same way we do now.

For example, in one 1836 case, a woman named Mary Hamilton was charged with public obscenity for walking behind a group of women and telling them to "go and fuck themselves"—the first recorded use of this phrase. (Why there is no statue of Mary Hamilton commemorating this milestone remains a mystery.)

And while courts and society alike have wrestled with the issues of profanity and indecency forever (insert obligatory George Carlin "seven words you can't say on television" reference here), the linguistic handcuffs are all but off in the internet era. The idea that one should be prohibited from swearing is a quaint one when censor-free quotes rocket around

Twitter and Facebook.

And it is social media that has contributed to the coarseness of political dialogue—"canceling" the insufficiently woke and "owning the libs" now rule the day, when angry retweets serve as rocket fuel for online platforms. One study estimates one in every 13 tweets contains a profanity, with "fuck" making up 34.7 percent of the obscenities used.

YouTube videos, streaming music apps, and podcasts are virtually unencumbered by language filters. According to the Wall Street Journal, 70 percent of children 10 years of age and under subscribe to TikTok, the preferred app for teenagers lip-syncing to profane hip-hop songs.

In an everything-goes culture in which the president is not only elected in spite of talking about the size of his junk during a debate, but instead because of it, policing the appropriateness of language is a lost cause. People wave off the indiscretions of a philandering, porn star-loving president who picks fights with war heroes because they feel it is necessary to teach the political cognoscenti a lesson.

Mohr told me she agrees that the "f-word" is becoming less powerful because its use is less taboo, but that it is being replaced by racial slurs and epithets. "I used to think eventually the racial slurs would lose their power too, and we'd come up with something else, but at least right now it's hard to see that happening," Mohr said.

Mohr said she didn't necessarily see the greater acceptance of swearing as a negative—she thinks it is more just a result of fewer societal limits on cursing. "I don't think decorum is dead," she said.

"Part of decorum is paying attention to other people and trying to not offend them," said Mohr. "If I was going to locate a point of cultural decline, I might do it there. Some people seem to think whatever they are feeling, it's important for them to express it at all times," she said.

But there is no longer a dividing line between what Mohr deems the "Holy"— the sense of propriety and religious conviction that polices language—and the "Shit"—the obscene. It is Trump, after all, that thrust the word "pussy" into our homes in 2016, and his behavior has actually devolved since then.

It is impossible to tarnish what is, by definition, tarnish.

This is not to argue that profanity isn't useful or necessary—quite the opposite. Profanity serves many crucial purposes that innocent euphemisms just can't deliver.

For one, swearing has physiological benefits—in one study, researchers showed subjects were able to keep their hand in cold water for a longer period of time when allowed to say the word "shit" instead of "shoot."

"I would advise people, if they hurt themselves, to swear," said the study's lead researcher, Richard Stephens.

Profanities are also easier to remember—throw one into a public utterance, and amygdalas light up, helping semi-attentive people recall what they heard. According to cognitive psychologist Steven Pinker, swearing triggers an electrophysical response "that emanates from the anterior cingulate cortex, a part of the limbic system involved in the monitoring of cognitive conflict"—alternately known as the "Oh Shit Wave."

Pinker also notes that hearing a profanity will often cause an individual to stop what they are doing and pay more attention. This is the thinking behind brands adopting names that sort-of sound like obscenities, such as the restaurant chain Fuddruckers. (At this point, we might as well finally fulfill the prophecy of the movie Idiocracy and resign ourselves to the fact there will one day be a restaurant called "Buttfuckers.")

Further, while profanities can lead to physical violence, they often serve as a substitute. On the scale of hurting another, swearing is about as violent as one can be without punching someone. In some venues, people who swear are even seen as more honest, as they are "the kind of person who would not mince words to spare someone's feelings or sense of decency."

Nor should anyone be thought of as less intelligent when they use profanity. It is an old canard that those who swear only do so because they can't think of a better word to describe something. In 1934, Cole Porter made this point, singing, "Good authors, too, who once knew better words / Now only use four-letter words / Writing prose, anything goes."

But sometimes, you just need the right goddamn word, regardless of social status. If I loudly deem Sean Hannity to be "replete with biosolids," it simply doesn't have the same rhetorical swag as if I opted for the crude alternative. (Spending time among the linguistically chaste Mormons in Utah, I picked up the term "footsacking" to use in place of "fucking," and it never made me feel better when McDonald's got my drive-thru order wrong.)

As history has shown us, there will always be things we can and can't say. Ironically, the political left, once the driving force behind comedian Lenny Bruce's right to offend with impunity, is hard at work policing what currently can be uttered in polite society. College campuses are awash in complaints against professors and students alike who commit the sins of misgendering individuals and referring to—but not using—the "n" word. (Interestingly, as Pinker notes, this public language regulation process has changed some words, like "queer," from good to bad, then back to good again.)

But breaking these taboos is far less satisfactory than swearing. When I can't find my car keys, I will not calmly explain something that might irritate someone's delicate sensibilities—I will need to commit a full-on act of macroaggression with unspeakable words said at maximum volume.

Soon, those words will be just like any other words. Sure, people aren't defecating in the streets like medieval times, but our cultural coarseness has rendered profanity a triviality.

"Swearing with panache has always been associated, in my mind at least, with a willingness to take risks, and not just linguistic ones," wrote author Gully Wells in 2014. "It's rebellion against convention and having the confidence not to care what people think," she wrote.

But there appear to be few conventions left to break and even fewer people who care.

And that is a fucking tragedy.

The Bulwark

THERE'S NOT SCREENS FULL OF 'GO TO HELL'

January 10, 2017

In 1993, CNN aired one of its first reports about a promising new technology called "Internet." The story, which is aptly now available online, brims with optimism about how much smarter this new connection of computers will make humanity, as it promises to "allow the high-tech flow of facts and figures between government, business, schools and citizens."

"One of its greatest achievements seems to be as an aid in scientific research," the report continues. "By tapping into Internet, scientists can share knowledge with another scientist at lightning speed."

At the time, Internet enthusiasm had even reached the White House. According to the CNN report, just days before, Vice President Al Gore said he could "foresee the day when a youngster just home from school, given a choice between Nintendo and the Encyclopedia Britannica, would choose to access the encyclopedia."

One can't blame Gore for being bullish on the prospects of such information being available with a couple strokes of the keyboard. Without the Internet, this column you're reading right now wouldn't be possible. And the scientific progress made in the era of the World Wide Web has been undeniable.

But rather than making the average American smarter, the Internet has instead allowed us to retreat back to our most base impulses. Whereas it once promised a high-minded world of boundless knowledge, interconnectivity has instead reinforced our flaws. We are now primarily roving packs of like-minded ideologues hell-bent on eviscerating dissent and demonstrating primacy within our own groups. (Who, when taking breaks, watch a lot of Netflix and porn.)

There is no more notable example of this than our incoming president, who has eliminated the phrase "I wonder what Donald Trump thinks of this issue" from our public nomenclature. No one ever need ask it again, whether the issue happens to be Korea's nuclear capabilities, Russia's interference in American elections, whether Twilight star Kristen Stewart's boyfriend should dump her, or why only fat people drink Diet Coke.

But Trump's reflexive musings also frequently attack others in the style of an anonymous troll. Opponents are "dishonest," "stiffs," "clowns," "overrated," or whatever happens to be careening through his cranium at the time. In doing so, the most powerful man in the world feeds the cultural decline only he thinks he can revive.

It didn't have to be this way. In an early Canadian news report, playwright and "Internet enthusiast" John Allen tells a reporter being online "feels a bit like every day human fellowship."

"There's an interesting kind of restraint that you find," Allen tells the CBC. "There's not a lot of cursing or swearing, there's not a lot of personal cuts, there's not a lot of put-downs that one would expect to find. There's not screens full of 'go to hell.'"

"One would think if you're anonymous, you'd do anything you want." But groups "have their own sense of community and what they can do."

But now that the Internet has grown, these groups have turned against one another, with often vulgar and tasteless results. Even within groups, Internet users are vilified for not being sufficiently wed to the cause; now whenever a celebrity dies, it is important to demonstrate how much deeper your appreciation of, say, Carrie Fisher, was than everyone else's.

According to the 1993 CNN report, Internet "critics" were afraid the web "could turn out to be an elitist system, one available only to people with a computer and a modem." But the problem isn't that we have become too "elite," it's that we've become too comfortable behaving like our actual selves.

Milwaukee Journal Sentinel

EVERYTHING THEY SAY ABOUT MILLENNIALS, THEY SAID ABOUT GEN-X

April 21, 2017

In 1749, a cantankerous Benjamin Franklin engaged in a tradition older than America itself: Throwing shade at a younger generation. Franklin, referring to the common complaint that the youth of America were not of "equal ability" to their predecessors, said that, "The best capacities require cultivation, it being truly with them, as with the best ground, which unless well tilled and sowed with profitable seed, produces only ranker weeds."

Imagine what Franklin would have had to say about Millennials.

One does not have to scan the news too vigorously to find endless condemnations of the latest crop of American youth. Children born from the mid-1980s to the early 2000s are now routinely derided as "snowflakes," as if each thinks he or she is a unique gift to the world. Raised in a culture of "trigger warnings" and "microaggressions," Millennials have been accused of fostering a culture of hypersensitivity, unable to connect with the naked realities of the real world.

Nowhere has this transition been more evident than on college campuses, which have taken racial and sexual balkanization to new extremes.

For instance, who can forget when the University of Minnesota banned the use of female cheerleaders, believing their routines fostered demeaning "sexual stereotypes?" Or when University of Wisconsin-Milwaukee officials distributed a list of 49 "Ways to Experience Diversity," including urging students to "Hold hands publicly with someone of a different race or someone of the same sex as you" and "Go to a toy store and investigate the availability of racially diverse dolls?" Or when the University of Connecticut banned "inappropriately directed laughter?"

You may think you saw these examples fly by on Twitter over the past few months. But they all actually took place in the late 1980s and early 1990s, when campuses were at the pinnacle of the first era of "political correctness." At one point, the University of Arizona instituted a "Diversity Action Plan" that banned discrimination on the grounds of things like age, color, ethnicity, race, religion, sexual orientation and "personal style." A campus "diversity specialist" clarified that "personal style" would include "nerds and people who dress differently." (All these examples can be found in Charlie Sykes' prescient book A Nation of Victims, released way back in 1992.)

Amid the modern tumult, it's easy to forget that we've been here before. And it's probably now safe to say that college students of my generation (I started school in 1991) made it through this era of progressive inculcation okay.

Generation X was literally known as the "slacker generation" — an ironically detached group of kids raised in the 1970s that couldn't be bothered to muster up enthusiasm for anything other than flannel shirts and Winona Ryder. A Washington Post headline from the early 1990s perfectly represented the enmity Baby Boomers felt against Gen Xers: "The Boring Twenties: Grow Up, Crybabies."

And yet Gen Xers — the neglected middle child between the Baby Boomers and the Millennials — have now inhabited the cultural and political positions of power they once disdained. Speaker of the House Paul Ryan is a Gen-Xer, as are United Nations Ambassador Nikki Haley and rising Senators Marco Rubio and Cory Booker. Among their members, Xers also count the founders of tech giants like Twitter and Google — tools which, ironically, can aid interested Millennials in finding out more about Gen X. (Suggested first search: "Who is Pauly Shore?")

Predictably, now it's Gen X's turn to heap disdain upon the younger generation. (As Michael Kinsley once quipped about Gen X, "These kids today. They're soft. They don't know how good they have it. Not only did they never have to fight in a war . . . they never even had to dodge one.")

It is true that Millennials differ from other generations in some important regards. A report released by the U.S. Census Bureau on Wednesday of this week demonstrated that today's young people are far more likely to live at home and delay getting married and having children. But Gen X is also heavily influenced by major demographic and cultural changes that took place during the 1970's — with more women in the workplace and increased access to birth control, Generation X is far smaller than the two generations that sandwich it on either side.

But while their styles are different — Gen X went out of its way to prove it didn't care about anything while Millennials seem to care way too much about everything — the two groups share a lot more in common other than the fact that Jennifer Aniston appears to not have aged during the transition.

For instance, both groups experienced a campus climate with an excruciating emphasis on identity politics. Perhaps most notable for the Gen Xers was the "speech code" enacted by the University of Wisconsin-Madison in the late 1980s. "The university is institutionally racist," declared Chancellor Donna Shalala at the time, adding that the campus simply reflected American society, which is "racist and sexist." Not surprisingly, conservative speakers at the state's other campuses were soon pelted with hard objects and shouted down — a scene that would become common once again in 2017.

In fact, the last few years on college campuses have become a virtual "I Love the '80s" of grievance and victimhood. A group of students at Pomona College recently wrote a letter to their school's administration claiming "the idea that there is a single truth . . . is a myth and white supremacy." Earlier this month, Rice University stopped using the term "master" to refer to the heads of its residential colleges, as they feared the term was too closely associated with slavery. And on and on.

Thankfully, the cyclical nature of the political correctness movement offers hope for the Millennial generation. For one, the mere process of growing up, becoming an adult, getting a job, having kids and paying taxes typically has the effect of grounding people in reality. It happens with every generation.

Further, if the PC movement of the late 1980s and early 1990s is any sort of blueprint, there will soon be a backlash to the modern buffoonery happening on campuses. Society typically has a way of finding its water level — the political correctness of decades ago was followed by cultural figures devoted to shattering that oversensitivity.

It was no coincidence that 1990 saw the rise in Andrew Dice Clay and 2 Live Crew — middling artists that reveled in tastelessness and taboo-shattering. Soon, Adam Sandler movies were making hundreds of millions of dollars. Culture eventually corrects itself. (That is not to say Clay or the 2 Live Crew made the world a better place, but there's always good money to be made in a well-timed backlash.)

Most importantly, we should have learned by now that dividing up individual people by birthdate is a wildly inaccurate way of judging a generation's relative quality. Every age group is going to have their leftist radicals and their religious conservatives. My generation managed to birth both Janeane Garofalo and Ted Cruz. Yet the internet is always going to devote more pixels to the attention-seekers shouting into bullhorns than the students putting their heads down and gritting their way through their studies.

During recent campus incidents in which conservative speakers were accosted by groups of protesters, the fact has been lost that a good number of students actually showed up at these events to see what the speakers had to say. In fact, there's ample evidence that campus activism might be provoking a silent backlash. While Millennials clearly do support "liberal" positions such as same-sex marriage, young people now are less likely than their parents to support legal abortion and at least as likely as older people in their support for gun rights.

Although new technology may seem like we're in unchartered territory, history tells us that the kids that scare us now will one day be just fine. Swap in Lena Dunham for Kurt Cobain, Lady Gaga for Madonna, and the cycle grinds on. And if we don't do enough to help Millennials to succeed, it will be the older generations that will have failed them, not the other way around.

USA Today

THERE REALLY IS NO ESCAPE

April 4, 2017

Since November of last year, if you were looking for "partisanship" in the dictionary, you wouldn't have to flip to the "p" section. Since Donald Trump's election, the folks running the social media accounts at Merriam-Webster have continuously trolled the Republican president, offering snarky responses to his ever-present malapropisms and his staff's often novel use of words.

One Merriam-Webster "Trend Watch" column took aim at Trump adviser Kellyanne Conway's use of the term "alternative facts." Other social media posts have poked at Trump's refugee travel ban, highlighted his staff barring reporters from a media "gaggle," and needled Speaker of the House Paul Ryan's use of the word "sycophant" to describe Julian Assange. On election day last year, the dictionary's Twitter feed changed its header to the German word "Götterdämmerung," or "a collapse (as of a society or regime) marked by catastrophic violence and disorder."

In a word, this is all "troublous." (And yes, that is a word.)

There is now no segment of American society to which one may retreat without being subjected to politics. Every corner of our lives is illuminated with talk of filibusters, health care strategy and minor cabinet appointees. It is as if the American economy now runs on demagoguery.

Remember when you could watch sports to escape from politics? No more. As The Ringer's Bryan Curtis argued in February, sports writing is now a liberal profession, having soaked up more of the left-wing flavor of the traditional media. With the advent of Twitter, both columnists and straight sportswriters alike often have little compunction about expressing their political views publicly, frequently explaining how intolerant or uninformed their own readers are.

Take, for example, a much-read New York Times article from last November that lavished praise on the Wisconsin Badgers men's basketball team for being "college basketball's most political locker room." The article highlighted, for instance, forward Nigel Hayes' support for the Black Lives Matter movement and guard Bronson Koenig's travels to protest the Dakota Access pipeline.

Does anyone actually believe the Times would have written such a tongue bath had the players been "political" on the right? What if they had been, for example, outspoken in opposition to gay marriage? Or if they marched against abortion? Would they be praised in one of America's most influential newspapers for "speaking their minds"?

Perhaps it is America's fault for electing an entertainer to the presidency, but politics has become indistinguishable from pop culture. Online magazines that once covered exclusively movies and music have now moved into lefty political punditry, leaving no conservative pop culture fan unlectured. There is no safe haven anymore — for a taste of what it's like, imagine being progressive and having Sean Hannity follow you around berating you while you're trying to listen to the "S-Town" podcast.

Even comedy, the last bastion of "tell-it-like-it-is-dom" has fallen into line. Virtually every late-night comedian thinks he or she has to do some sort of imitation of St. Jon Stewart to coax his or her liberal followers into sharing their rant on YouTube the next day. Sadly, the list of people who care about what Seth Meyers thinks about politics is exactly as long as the list of guys named "Gus" who own a yoga studio.

It works the other way as well: If any comedian expresses a sentiment that doesn't conform to the speech police, he or she can expect a swift flogging by thinkpiece. A few weeks back, comedian Dave Chappelle crossed swords with progressives when he released a pair of stand-up specials in which, among other retrograde observations, he questioned the need to use different pronouns for transgender men and women. He was immediately subjected to a torrent of online disapproval, calling him "sexist" and "transphobic."

Indeed, many of Chappelle's jokes would have seemed out of date even 20 years ago. But a comedian's first job is to be funny, not to mirror whatever cultural worldview an audience member might have. If that were the case, comedians wouldn't be able to make jokes about, for example, religious people — jokes Chappelle's new critics might applaud. All these people spent years defending Stewart's political activism by pretending his attacks on the right were fine because he was "just a comedian." Perhaps they should heed their own lesson.

From now on, there is no respite for the weary. You can run, but progressive condescension is going to find you. Politics get clicks, and clicks bring revenue. There is no incentive for all this new punditry to be accurate or fair.

Undoubtedly, Merriam-Webster has a bucketful of arcane words to describe the way politics has saturated our culture. But it is most aptly expressed by America's great philosopher, Donald J. Trump:

#Sad!

Milwaukee Journal Sentinel

THE SELLING OF LEFTY CULTURE AS 'CONSCIOUSNESS'

April 14, 2017

Anyone who hasn't had the opportunity to listen to pop songstress Katy Perry's recent song "Chained to the Rhythm" is missing one of the most awful pieces of music to ever be inflicted upon the American public. By the time you hear Perry warble, "So comfortable, we live in a bubble, a bubble/ So comfortable, we cannot see the trouble, the trouble," your ears will have filed for divorce.

Yet upon its release, this aural Antietam received positive reviews in large part because it reflected Perry's new "political activism." (Indeed, this must be true for, on her Twitter profile, Perry describes herself as an activist.)

"Perry's fed up with the complacency of the capitalist entertainment culture that she has thrived off," chirped The Atlantic, comparing the song's theme to that of Sinclair Lewis' classic political novel "Babbitt." (Lewis' novel won a Nobel Prize, despite the author evidently never having donned a cupcake bra.)

But rather than some foundational political anthem, Perry's song is simply a series of microwaved liberal bromides repackaged and sold back to liberals. It's a tried-and-true formula: Masquerade lefty culture as "consciousness," and you make your terrible art critic-proof.

Recently, liberals and conservatives alike roundly mocked an Internet ad produced by Pepsi that tried to cash in on today's left-wing protest culture. In the ad, which stars the inexplicably famous Kendall Jenner, a multicultural group of young, thin demonstrators march through city streets demanding ... something. (Perhaps Coke's secret recipe?)

Wielding peace signs and offers to "join the conversation," the marchers stare down a line of menacing police officers until Jenner offers a cop a Pepsi, at which point he seems to say to himself, "this 50-cent carbonated beverage has rendered my crowd control manual obsolete, and I, therefore, will not tear gas these morons."

Liberals recoiled at the ad, accusing it of stealing imagery from the Black Lives Matter movement and minimizing the issue of police brutality. Pepsi apologized and "pulled" the ad, whatever that means — it is still readily available online — and also apologized to Jenner.

But Pepsi's only crime is making the lame repurposing of progressivism so nakedly obvious.

Corporations always try to capture the zeitgeist and monetize it; ask any child of the "grunge" era who began to see ripped jeans and large flannel shirts in J.C. Penney catalogs. And when political issues bubble up, they take their place next to the Geico gecko and the Most Interesting Man in the World as tools to move product.

Take, for example, Audi's embarrassing Super Bowl ad this year that tried to tangentially relate selling cars to women being paid less in the workplace. In the spot, a father watches his daughter compete in a soapbox derby-type race, wondering whether he should have to tell her that no matter her qualifications, "she will automatically be valued as less than every man she ever meets." The ad ends by saying Audi of America is "committed to equal pay for equal work."

Evidently, no members of Audi's all-male Board of Management are aware that the "wage gap" is complete nonsense, having been debunked by scores of fact-checkers. While there is a disparity in pay among men and women, it is almost entirely the result of different choices the genders make in pursuit of their careers. Control for those factors and the gap all but disappears.

But Audi has cars to sell to women, so they just slap a new coat of paint on those old talking points and get them back on the road.

Of course, progressives didn't protest this pandering, as it aided their larger cause. They were conveniently unconcerned that a corporation was stealing their platform to sell cars — Audi furthered the narrative, so they ate it up.

All the Hillary Clinton voters who railed against corporations having political free speech rights suddenly disappeared, likely hiding in the same underground bunker as all the lefties who voted for "Crash" as Best Picture in 2006 because they thought it would solve racism.

Democrats should be more concerned about the cynicism that propels such ads; these companies are taking caricatures of liberals and trying to get young consumers to buy them, just like any other commodity.

The Pepsi ad went too far because the caricature was too broad, but it's the same idea that has saturated advertising for decades: "Lefty activism is hot, so let's try to sell it to younger people who don't know better!" (This, incidentally, seemed to be the guiding principle behind the entire Bernie

Sanders presidential campaign — selling socialism to people too young to realize what a disaster it has been.)

Naturally, there's nothing wrong with using free-market capitalism to trick liberals into buying products. Anyone who bought a Coke in 1971 because a hippie sang them a nice song was helping the economy and creating jobs.

But the left should realize these ads are meant to trigger the same basic response in them that videos of Big Macs are supposed to trigger in hungry people. Just don't be surprised when Mayor McCheese starts wearing a pink knit hat.

Milwaukee Journal Sentinel

NO, THE ROCK SHOULDN'T BE PRESIDENT

May 19, 2017

Historians have long disagreed about which moment represents the high point of the U.S. presidency. Some say it was Abraham Lincoln's Gettysburg Address. Others argue it may have been FDR's New Deal or Ronald Reagan's victory over communism.

But most scholars concede it was the day the president single-handedly saved America from the scourge of terrorism. No one will ever forget the presidential press conference where reporters, after asking a series of awkward questions, ripped off their masks to reveal themselves as machine gun-wielding terrorists.

As everyone now knows from the Ken Burns documentary, the president leaped down from the podium, seized a machine gun and mowed down the ethically ambiguous enemy. Just as the president ripped the arms from one of the insurgents and began beating him with his own limbs, the president noticed a helicopter leaving the Rose Garden. The president ran out, grabbed hold of the helicopter's landing gear, and climbed inside while it flew 2,000 feet above the ground.

Upon noticing the terrorists were trying to steal the U.S. Constitution, the president fought the pilot, finally commandeering the aircraft while kissing his biceps for the crowd gathered below.

Of course, the preceding passage wasn't from Donald Trump's personal diary during his short tenure as president. It is from a history book written in 2068 about the long reign of President Dwayne "The Rock" Johnson, who, as the one dollar bill will one day reflect, saved America in the post-Trump era. (Following his White House heroics, the Washington Post declared President The Rock to be "AMERICA'S POUNDING FATHER.")

Or at least this is the vision of those in modern times pushing for The Rock to run for president. Lest anyone believe the idea of America's top-grossing movie star running for president is mere fancy, consider that The Rock himself recently considered a run "a real possibility."

This has set America — particular conservatives dissatisfied with Donald Trump — afire. "At this time in American life, we need points of agreement," wrote David French in the conservative National Review, "and right now tens of millions of Americans on both sides of the political divide agree on The Rock."

It's not just Republicans whose reaction to a Rock run has been – ahem – fast and furious. A poll released last week suggests that The Rock would beat Donald Trump heads-up by a 42% to 37% margin, leading to unintentionally hilarious headlines like, "Dwayne Johnson calls presidential support 'flattering' and 'Baywatch' role 'daunting.'" While some obviously support a Rock candidacy with tongue firmly in cheek, plenty of people do so with their tongues resting comfortably under a fist load of movie popcorn.

But voter enthusiasm for The Rock is mostly the byproduct of the damage Donald Trump has done to the American presidency. People are now looking for a savior, whether their heroics are genuine or CGI-produced.

Yet Trump also shattered the ceiling for celebrities looking to run for the nation's highest office. If a reality show star can win the presidency, how can any famous person be ruled out? Last year, Kanye West suggested he was going to run for president, provoking boisterous laughter among those possessing sanity. But after the last election, is anyone laughing now?

The fascination with electing people simply because we've heard their names is simply proof that we refuse to learn. How can anyone look at the problems a political neophyte like Donald Trump has had (to put it as generously as possible) and think the solution is someone with even less experience?

Policy-wise, how do we even know what The Rock stands for? The only real-life aggressor he has fought off appears to be carbohydrates. Re-arming the military doesn't mean wearing a sleeveless shirt. How would it necessarily help school children that their president was the only one to win People Magazine's "Sexiest Man Alive" award? (Famously, Franklin Pierce finished second.)

The intermixing of politics and celebrity has to stop. We should enjoy celebrities because of the work that they do that actually made them famous without immediately declaring them presidential material. Fame is a terrible qualification for the nation's top office; we're much better off having someone boring and competent.

Just ask Vice President Gaga.

Milwaukee Journal Sentinel

FOR THE LOVE OF GOD DO NOT LET YOUR EMPLOYER MICROCHIP YOU

August 4, 2017

Imagine talking to someone from the 1980s and telling them the type of behaviors human beings would be engaging in just 30 years later.

Tell them that everyone would carry devices with them that had access to all the world's information base, and yet would use these miraculous devices to send each other pictures that never should be viewed outside their urologist's office. Or that on trips, people would stay in total strangers' houses, reassured solely by the fact that the homeowner has the same app on his or her phone. Or even weirder, imagine explaining Donald Trump was elected president.

But we have now reached the most inexplicable modern "advancement": businesses implanting microchips into their employees, allowing those businesses to track these workers' movements and purchases.

Three Square Market, a Western Wisconsin company that specializes in vending machine technology, has offered employees the chance to voluntarily have the chips implanted under their skin, which would allow them to access certain areas of the building and pay for items with the swipe of their hands. Unbelievably, around 50 employees have agreed that being constantly monitored by their employer seems like a pretty swell idea.

Of course, any type of new technology is bound to provoke some "the government is turning our frogs gay with chemicals" style of conspiracy theories. But the whole idea of humans being implanted with a chip to control their behavior has been the stuff of cautionary science fiction for decades. Way back in 1966, Philip K. Dick wrote a short story about a man with a chip implanted in his head that the government used to turn him into a trained assassin without his knowledge. And I don't want to become a trained assassin, as it sounds exhausting and it rarely comes with dental coverage.

Naturally, Three Square Market has assured its employees that the information stored within the microchip will be used only for the powers of good. But while the technology of the chips may remain the same, the technology in the world around them may change rapidly.

Who's to say some rogue company won't develop a chip reader of its own to scan people as they walk down the street? What if a big box store starts reading you and mailing you coupons based on what section of the store you spent the most time in? What if your employer wants to monitor how much time you spend in the bathroom, or at lunch? Ninety percent of the time I'd rather people not know where I am — I have no desire to live within The Matrix.

Employees who have had the chip implanted delight at the "convenience" of it all — imagine being able to purchase snacks at the company cafeteria by simply waving your hand! But have we really regressed to the point where the process of extracting a wallet from your trousers to exchange currency has become too much of a burden for common workers? Has anyone complained to their daughter, "Sorry, sweetheart, I'm not going to be able to make it to your piano recital tonight, I'm going to be busy picking up some Combos from the work vending machine"?

Yet employees still insist they're willing to go along with it because they think they're simply riding the unavoidable wave of time. Soon, those of us who find the practice horrific are going to be cast into the lot of retro fetishists, like people who currently buy records, go to movie theaters and talk to their children in person.

"In the next five to 10 years, this is going to be something that isn't scoffed at so much, or is more normal," software engineer Sam Bengtson told the New York Times. "So I like to jump on the bandwagon with these kind of things early, just to say that I have it."

But I subscribe to the immortal words of Robert Frost, who counseled:
"Ah, when to the heart of man
Was it ever less than a treason
To go with the drift of things..."

And thus, someone is going to have to implant a microchip in me over my dead body. (Which will probably be caused by a microchipped government assassin.)

Milwaukee Journal Sentinel

JUDGING GOD'S FLOW

May 30, 2017

None of us really enjoys feeling judged. Typically, if you're a person who frequently says things like, "Only God can judge me," other actual human beings have probably already judged you to be a nuisance.

Certainly, God's aggressiveness in judging the actions of members of his flock has been a theological question as long as humans have worshiped him. Many believe Christianity allows for both a graceful, forgiving God and the one who, speaking through Samuel L. Jackson in Pulp Fiction, promises to execute vengeance upon evildoers.

But the conflict between gracious God and wrathful God — a debate that has taken place among religious scholars and philosophers for centuries — has suddenly been rekindled in modern hip-hop music made by America's two foremost artists.

As writer Miguelito at the website DJBooth noticed, recent albums by hip-hop titans Kendrick Lamar and Chance the Rapper seem to be in direct contradiction with one another over the role God plays in shaping behavior.

While Chicago's Chance — an electric rubber band of optimism — uses his album Coloring Book to describe the suffering around him, he also praises God as the source of all of his blessings. Chance has been praised as a pioneer of "gospel rap," which explains why seeing him perform his exhortations about God's love in person is such a joyous experience.

Contrast that with Kendrick Lamar, whose recent album DAMN. portrays a God that imposes dire consequences for not following His teachings. Lamar's God is like the IRS — He's always watching, and punishment might be heading your way when He decides you need an audit.

"Our God is a loving God," Lamar told DJBooth in an email. "Yes. He's a merciful God. Yes. But he's even more so a God of DISCIPLE. OBEDIENCE. A JEALOUS God."

"And for every conscious choice of sin, will be corrected through his discipline," Lamar continues. "Whether physical or mental. Direct or indirect. Through your sufferings, or someone that's close to [sic] ken. It will be corrected."

Not exactly a slogan one will find on a coffee mug at Target. But as Miguelito notes, Chance and Kendrick are "two sides of one coin, illustrating two separate but necessary ways for the religious believer to move through the world."

While that may be true, Lamar's conception of God is by far the more useful. Typically, people break down into three categories: those who don't believe in God, those who believe the Lord will punish you for your sins, and those who believe God is laid back, kind of like a divine camp counselor.

But what is the point in devoting your life to serving God if you just think His beliefs merely happen to track along with yours? Do you support the death penalty? Well, then God probably does, too. Think the Lord is cool with you abandoning your children? He probably wouldn't want you to feel bad about it! Do you secretly believe La La Land was better than Moonlight? Then so does God! (Just kidding — even a super chill God couldn't stand being lectured about jazz by Ryan Gosling.)

The main benefit of religious belief is to compel people to serve themselves and others. Worshiping a higher power is supposed to make you do things you normally wouldn't do. Without some sort of need to follow God's orders, you turn into one of those insufferable "spiritual but not religious" hippies that hopefully God is saving for lightning bolt practice.

The idea of a harsh, demanding God has a long tradition in American gospel music, particularly among the African-American Pentecostals of the early twentieth century — many of whom survived slavery.

"Yes, He killed the rich and poor / And He's going to kill more / If you don't turn away from your shame," sings Elder David R. Curry and his congregation in the 1930 song Memphis Flu. God's vengeance is always lurking in songs like Reverend Sister Mary Nelson's Judgment, which counsels, "Well, all you hypocrite members / You wasting your time away / My God's calling for workmens / And you had better obey." As Matt Labash once wrote about Pentecostal hymns, "Holiness types didn't play around."

We have seen that when religious belief recedes, everyone else is left to pick up the pieces. In the early 1970s, nearly 70% of American adults were members of a church or synagogue; today that number has fallen to 55%. And when people stop practicing religion, government necessarily has to step in. Today, it is incumbent on public schools to feed kids and police officers to raise them. Less charitable church work for the disabled and poor causes more stress on public services. Even those who don't particularly care for religious people should be wishing we had more of them.

Of course, people can go too far in the name of religious extremism, and should be condemned when they do. But God isn't Donna from Parks and Recreation, constantly urging you to "Treat yo self." And while He may be merciful and forgiving, that doesn't mean there won't be consequences for your actions. You're free to believe in God or not, but if you're just looking for someone to agree with your every decision, you're better off buying a cactus.

Milwaukee Journal Sentinel

HOLLYWOOD'S LIBERALS THINK YOU'RE AN IDIOT

October 31, 2017

Listing all the things wrong with actor Kevin Spacey's recent statement announcing he is gay is too much to ask of a single column. On Sunday, responding to accusations that he had made a sexual advance towards a 14-year-old boy 31 years ago, Spacey said he did not remember the encounter, suggested he may have been drunk, and apologized, adding that now he chooses to live his life "as a gay man."

It was a stunning statement in its obtuseness. In a few words, Spacey was able to reinforce the most negative stereotype about gay men — that they are pedophiles who prey on children. It's as if he was doing public relations for the Westboro Baptist Church.

Spacey used the announcement of his sexual identity to draw attention away from the accusation of sexual assault. He assumed liberals in the media would dedicate more pixels to that shiny diversion than the charge he was facing. Just weeks ago, disgraced movie producer Harvey Weinstein tried the same gambit by vowing to fight the National Rifle Association in a statement in which he essentially acknowledged sexually harassing women. Basically, Weinstein's argument was, "Hey guys, I'm liberal, so maybe let this slide?"

These recent escape strategies hatched by Hollywood's most powerful names answer an important question for those on the left: Just how stupid do the party's "elites" think rank-and-file Democrats are?

In the wake of the Republican Party's crackup, much has been written about the battle between the GOP's philosophically conservative eggheads and its Trump-inspired populist wing. But Democrats face similar battles within progressivism — namely, wealthy elites who view the rubes in flyover country as valuable only to the extent that they serve the interests of the party's politically connected.

It is this disconnection that likely caused Hillary Clinton, the patron saint of progressive elitism, to unexpectedly lose blue-collar states such as Wisconsin, Michigan and Pennsylvania. While Trump made outlandish promises to turn low-income workers' lives around, Clinton deftly floated above the rust belt, deeming many of its inhabitants "deplorables." Had she shown more interest in the working class, Clinton might not have lost white voters without college degrees by a whopping 39 percentage points.

The party's coastal elites sneer at hardworking Democrats in the heart of the country. Hollywood mocks their traditional cultural views while pretending the entertainment industry isn't a snake pit of degradation. Americans are now learning that the actions of Weinstein, Spacey and other notable men have been an "open secret" in Hollywood for years. We should all look forward to the year 2030, when we learn what the "open secrets" were way back in 2017.

The split between working-class and coastal Democrats is longstanding. In 2008, presidential candidate Barack Obama tried to explain rival Hillary Clinton's support in rural Pennsylvania by asserting that "bitter" rural voters "cling to guns or religion." Keep in mind, Obama wasn't talking about right-wingers; he was referring to non-urban Democrats he thought favored his opponent.

When a supporter told Adlai Stevenson, who twice lost as a Democrat running for president, that the "thinking people" supported him, he is reported to have answered, "Yes, but I need to win a majority." For Democrats to succeed nationally, they need to wrest the voters they once appealed to away from Donald Trump, and that means respecting their intelligence and opinions when they're not also asking them to buy tickets to a movie.

Milwaukee Journal Sentinel

JOHN MCCAIN: KEEPING FAITH WITH THE FAMILY CREED

October 26, 2017

"There was no curtain, no retirement," wrote Lord Rosebery of Winston Churchill's father, Randolph. "He died by inches in public."

If Arizona Sen. John McCain's diagnosis of aggressive brain cancer proves to be accurate, McCain's inches will soon become yards, and those yards will become miles. It was 50 years ago Thursday that McCain was shot down over North Vietnam, and it now seems probable that glioblastoma will do what a fall from the heavens and subsequent torture by Vietnamese soldiers couldn't do — deprive America of McCain's singularly heroic life.

Since the diagnosis, which McCain has called "very, very serious," the longtime senator has drawn the ire of fellow Republicans for dramatically casting the deciding vote against a major GOP effort to scale back former president Barack Obama's signature health care law. In recent months, McCain has leveled numerous criticisms at President Trump, including condemning Trump's policy in Syria, his attempts to draw a moral equivalence between white supremacist marchers and counter-protesters in Charlottesville, Va., Trump's calling the media "the enemy," and his attempts to set transgender military policy through Twitter.

Predictably, McCain's unwillingness to genuflect to Trump has made him an enemy of those not fit to wash his underwear. This includes a president who claimed McCain was not "a war hero" because he was shot down and captured. "I like people that weren't captured," said candidate Donald Trump, who received five deferments to avoid service in Vietnam, the final one for having "bone spurs" in his feet.

McCain, however, requested to go to Vietnam, as both his father and grandfather had served honorably in the U.S. Navy. As he said in his first memoir, McCain wanted to serve his country "to keep faith with the family creed."

On Oct. 26,1967, McCain found his A-4 fighter hurtling towards the ground at 550 miles per hour. His plane had been hit by Vietnamese ground forces during his bombing run over Hanoi; knowing he had only seconds to live, McCain ejected from his cockpit, hitting the plane on the way oon the way out and breaking his left arm, his right arm in three places, and his right knee.

Knocked unconscious in the fall, McCain came to when he hit the waters of Truc Bach Lake. But he was quickly dragged out by a large group of Vietnamese, who kicked him, struck him, and spit on him. As a prisoner nursing grievous wounds, he was still tortured endlessly in hopes of extracting information about U.S. operations. Pressed for information, he gave the names of the Green Bay Packers' offensive line as members of his squadron.

All told, McCain spent nearly five years in solitary confinement, communicating primarily with other prisoners through a complex code delivered by tapping on the thick cell walls. His injuries from the poor medical care he received have stayed with him for the remainder of his life.

And it is a life any of us should have been honored to lead. From soldier to senator to presidential candidate, McCain has always been his own man. While his forays into limiting campaign speech and, more recently, his crusade against gerrymandering are often infuriating to conservatives, his independence was not negotiable. (And he wasn't shy about saying so in front of a camera or microphone, which once compelled MSNBC's Chris Matthews to note that "The press loves McCain. We're his base.")

One can only dream of living a life in which the worst thing that can be said of it is that it was insufficiently ideological. Especially when, in McCain's case, the best that can be said is that he has been a model of American greatness, strength and valor. Despite sacrificing five torturous years of his life in service of a war he would later criticize, McCain has never missed an opportunity to extol the virtues of American exceptionalism. It is a voice we will all miss when the time comes.

When told that a sailor's life was miserable, Samuel Johnson once responded that "the profession of sailors and soldiers has the dignity of danger. All men feel ashamed at not having been at sea or in battle."

John McCain willingly conquered the dangers of battle, and rose to prominence with dignity. It is a path many of his critics should be ashamed not to celebrate.

Milwaukee Journal Sentinel

MEN ARE COMPLICIT IN THE HARVEY WEINSTEIN SCANDAL AS ENABLERS AND ABUSERS

October 14, 2017

When you read the stories, the voltage of the actresses' names illuminates the screen. Gwyneth Paltrow. Angelina Jolie. Mira Sorvino. All share more in common than having won Academy Awards: They have all recently spoken about being sexually accosted by Hollywood career-maker Harvey Weinstein.

Hopefully the stories being told by these women and many others are an important start towards progress. But as eye-catching as these women's names are, the broader issue is about men — men who both commit and enable the ecosystems of horror inhabited by creatures like Weinstein.

They are the menacing, sad men lounging around hotel rooms in bathrobes, waiting for obeisant staff to push young actresses through their doors as a zoo employee tosses meat into a lion's cage. They collect unearned conquests as currency; perhaps their whole motivation towards wealth would be to one day wield enough power to churn through scared young actresses afraid of losing their big break.

As youths, maybe they took inspiration in fictional film producer Jack Woltz from The Godfather movie, who brags about his conquests with innocent young women all over the world. But in the far less cinematic real world, they use their influence to abuse women, casting them off with broken dreams and emotional scars, knowing there are always more just pulling into town.

Then there are the men who enable such behavior, knowing what's happening and still saying nothing. They could be male employees of Weinstein's company afraid to blow the whistle for fear of losing their jobs, or notable actors who knew of Weinstein's actions but remained silent.

Dozens of women presumably could have helped by exposing Weinstein decades ago; but as long as the juicy roles and giant checks kept coming, many men likely felt it was necessary to protect Hollywood's most notorious predator. Of course, it is a victim's decision to tell her (or his) own story; but a conspiracy of silence only enables monsters to keep offending. Naturally, a flood of male actors will now come forward and condemn Weinstein; but they were all absent when they were needed the most.

There are the men who try to purchase good will by writing checks to progressive women's causes; they're always ready with a hefty check for Planned Parenthood, or willing to accuse the bumpkins in flyover country of waging a "war on women." They're simply a wealthier version of the college guy who tells girls in bars that he volunteers for the Sierra Club during the summers, hoping to score a deeply emotional one-night relationship. Only turning the rich guy down can come with career-ending consequences.

The Weinstein story is also about the men in law enforcement who knew of Weinstein's assaults and sat idly by. Men like Manhattan District Attorney Cyrus Vance, Jr., who held in his hands a recording of Weinstein admitting to past sexual assaults, and yet chose to do nothing. The crime Weinstein could have been charged with — misdemeanor third-degree sexual abuse — only carried a maximum of three months in jail, and thus probably didn't seem worth the trouble. But it likely would have shone a light on Weinstein's alleged crimes well before today.

No one seriously believes that Weinstein is the only powerful man in America who uses his influence to harass and even assault women. In the words of a man who was elected president of the United States less than a year ago, "When you're a star, they let you do it. You can do anything."

That's why the consequences of what powerful men do to women (and men) reverberate throughout society. Gargoyles like Weinstein are why women have to have their heads on swivels, not always sure of the situation they may be in. It's why they can't be sure if a one-on-one meeting with a male colleague is just for business, or whether a first date is with a nice guy or someone who might try to attack them later that night.

Men like Weinstein and his enablers harm women, but their actions also sully other men and complicate the relationships they have with women. We all need to listen to the stories women are telling now; but we should also pay equal attention to the deafening silence from men all along.

Milwaukee Journal Sentinel

THE ARTISTIC DEATH PENALTY

December 15, 2017

In my early teens, I picked up a dog-eared copy of Woody Allen's book Side Effects and immediately imagined a future as a writer. I would spend long afternoons reading and rereading Allen's short stories, admiring how he wove complicated philosophical references together with silly gags I could actually understand. (Sample joke: "The government is unresponsive to the little man. Under 5'7, it is impossible to get your congressman on the phone.")

I couldn't have known what moral compromises I would have to make in the years ahead to remain a Woody Allen fan. What we knew publicly about him was unsettling enough. The man would marry his longtime partner Mia Farrow's adopted daughter. That was unsettling. Accusations by his own adopted daughter Dylan Farrow, that he sexually assaulted her at age 7, rise to a completely different level of horror. If they had been proven true, Allen's name would be erased from polite society and his years of comic genius would fade away. (A prosecutor said there was "probable cause" to believe Allen molested his daughter, but he wanted to spare the child a trial; Allen has forcefully denied all the accusations against him.)

Now, in an era where accusations and evidence of sexual assault are rightfully taking down famous men and providing justice for women, fans are left wondering whether it is, indeed, possible to separate the art from the artist. If Woody Allen is guilty as alleged, can I still recognize his brilliance, even if it was the result of a deranged mind? Do Louis C.K.'s timely observations about relationships still hold true now that he has admitted to sexual deviancy?

Some media companies, trying to shed themselves of the justifiable outrage over these stars' activities, are beginning to throw their work down the memory hole. Kevin Spacey was wiped out of the soon-to-be released movie All the Money in the World, replaced by veteran actor Christopher Plummer. Minnesota Public Radio announced it would stop rebroadcasting episodes of its cornerstone Prairie Home Companion after host Garrison Keillor was accused of "inappropriate behavior" for placing his hand on a woman's bare back. HBO has pulled Louis C.K.'s stand-up specials and his defunct television show, Lucky Louie, from its on-demand service. (Although several of C.K.'s stand-up specials are still available on Netflix.)

But ridding the world of the works of morally compromised individuals leaves us poorer as a culture. For example, during World War II the great writer P.G. Wodehouse was taken prisoner by the Nazis while living in the

French countryside; after months of imprisonment, Wodehouse recorded some brief radio essays for the Germans that were used as pro-Nazi propaganda, earning him worldwide opprobrium. But if his Works were banished as a result, the world would be missing the novels of the greatest English language humorist of the past century. (Wodehouse apologized for his inexplicable mistake, saying the ordeal caused him "a great deal of mental pain.")

USA Today

EVERYTHING IS POSSIBLE BUT NOTHING IS REAL

June 8, 2018

If you blink, you might miss one of the most astonishing moments in American cinematic history. Near the end of Buster Keaton's short film "Cops," Keaton runs towards the camera while attempting to evade a mob of police officers. Reaching the end of an alleyway, he then nonchalantly throws his arm out and grabs hold of a speeding car, which immediately lifts him parallel to the ground and pulls him out of the frame.

There were no special effects used to film the scene; it was simply another example of Keaton's supernatural athleticism and unique bravery.

Modern films are full of special effects and imagery that far surpass anything Keaton could have conceived in the 1920s. Anything is now possible on the screen, down to bringing deceased actors back to life to put words in their mouths.

But for all the science fiction universes filled with spaceships and CGI superheroes and digital explosions, each seems antiseptic when compared to a human actor doing something beautiful or legitimately dangerous. (In 2014, "The Amazing Spider-Man 2" recreated Keaton's truck-grabbing stunt, claiming no special effects were used.)

The great effect of technology is to allow us to witness images and events that we once thought impossible. But the downside has been to eliminate the human element in virtually every aspect of our lives. Vivid, descriptive writing has fallen prey to instant video; painting a picture with words now seems antiquated when the thing being described is likely a few clicks away on YouTube.

The cornerstone of major movie studio budgets are now CGI-saturated franchises, crowding out quirky human interest stories. A small film like last year's "Lady Bird" likely cost as much to produce as about 10 seconds of screen time for Digital Yoda.

But the further digitization of our lives has more dire consequences beyond Americans' mere entertainment choices. With more reliance on online interactions, we lose the humanity we gain when we speak to another living person on the phone or in person. We treat each other not as people, but as caricatures and enemies useful only for well-crafted Twitter burn. We now grow impatient any time we have to have a conversation in which we don't want to take part, as if there should be a real-world "mute" button.

Much like the pixelated landscapes in movies, digital outrage is no longer real. Feigned offense exists to demonstrate moral superiority over people you've never met. It appears everyone hates you until proven otherwise. Your online "friends" are people you don't know on any level deeper than exchanging a few messages.

That is why an early May study conducted by Cigna showed the youngest Americans — those most likely to use social media — are the loneliest people in the nation. "I have students who tell me they have 500 'friends,' but when they're in need, there's no one," Jagdish Khubchandani, a health science professor at Ball State University in Muncie, Ind., told USA TODAY after the report's release.

Khubchandani added online socialization is often the result of time spent alone on computers in peoples' homes, leading them to gain weight and shun face-to-face interaction. According to a 2017 Boston Globe report, loneliness among older men is increased their risk of cardiovascular disease, stroke, and the progression of Alzheimer's.

Despite the promise of "social media" to bring people together, it is making us demonstrably more unsocial. In both entertainment and our personal lives, technology is robbing us of our humanity.

So instead of using your phone to check Twitter, use it to actually make phone calls. Meet and talk to people in person. As the "Unbreakable Kimmy Schmidt" counsels us in an episode this season, eye contact is "the handshake of the face."

(Of course, that show is on Netflix, so maybe all technology isn't bad.)

Milwaukee Journal Sentinel

A GAY AMNESTY PLAN

May 8, 2018

As a child, my friends and I would often kill time playing a game called "Smear the Queer." One kid — dubbed the "queer" — would hold a ball, only then to be chased down and thrown to the ground while all the other kids piled on top of him. In the 1980s, kids' cardiovascular fitness was often proportional the robustness of their homophobia.

It has only been in the past few years that large swaths of society have begun to realize how horrifying our attitudes towards gays and lesbians were for all of human history. People with different sexual orientations were one of the last groups it was socially acceptable to mock — I think I first learned the anti-gay slur that begins with the word "F" from listening to Eddie Murphy comedy albums. Soon, I heard it casually used in the John Hughes movie Sixteen Candles. The Beastie Boys famously wanted to name their first major-label rap album "Don't Be a F----t." And so on

All these examples seem painfully archaic, given public opinion's drastic shift over the past handful of years. According to the Pew tracking poll, support for gay marriage jumped from 37% in 2007 to 62% in 2017, with Democrats and Republican support increasing in tandem during that time.

Unfortunately, in the internet era, there will always be easily accessible evidence of who we were before this positive societal shift. Take MSNBC anchor Joy Reid, who has spent a week trying to distance herself from a series of "hateful" (her word) posts about the lesbian, gay, transgender, queer (LGBTQ) community dating back to 2009 that appeared on her blog. At first, Reid cooked up a preposterous conspiracy theory that someone had hacked an off-site archive of her blog to make her look bad, even asking the FBI to look into the matter. Yet her theory wasn't backed up by cybersecurity experts, as it was less plausible than a Nicolas Cage movie in which he tries to steal the U.S. Constitution.

Despite her lack of evidence, Reid dug in and maintained she hadn't written the posts, nonetheless apologizing for some similar posts she confessed to have written. Despite her ridiculous and almost certainly dishonest machinations, Reid's coworkers and fans universally supported her, and she is evidently now allowed back on the air to continue demagoguing conservatives for being culturally insensitive.

But Reid should have been spared this humiliation in the first place. As she said herself, "the person I am now is not the person I was then." And that goes for those on the right just as much as it does for those on the left.

I would propose, then, that the straight people of the world throw ourselves on the mercy of the LGBTQ community and ask for an amnesty of sorts. We promise to be better today if they agree to ignore anything said by any straight person before 2012, the year which former president Barack Obama finally announced his support of same-sex marriage.

In order to make progress, society has to molt, shedding its old skin in favor of a new one. Problem is, Google always gives us access to the old skin, which can be used to further drive us apart as we try to move forward. It's important to remember where were once were, but equally important to recognize that we've all changed a great deal in a very short amount of time.

Milwaukee Journal Sentinel

REPUBLICANS NEED NEW CELEBRITIES

May 30, 2018

Aside from the fact that the world would never see any more of his stunning works, the recent passing of author Tom Wolfe represented a deeper cultural shift. While he didn't consider himself a political "conservative," Wolfe reached the top of the American literary world by exposing liberal snobbery through wit and erudition, as opposed to many of today's right-leaning "celebrities" who traffic in crass insults. Upon his death, he was feted by conservatives and liberals alike, as his skill was undeniable and his targets timeless.

Yet gone is the day where "conservatives" like Wolfe or P.G. Wodehouse or T.S. Eliot can sit atop the world of popular entertainment and be judged by the quality of their work and not its political content. Today's famous conservatives are almost always famous for being conservative, with their talents considered only secondarily.

Which brings us to Roseanne Barr.

Barr's self-immolation this week was even more predictable than a Cleveland Cavaliers-Golden State Warriors NBA finals. When the newest iteration of her Trump-friendly television show debuted in March and the "Roseannaissance" was officially underway, it was merely a question of "when" she would say something to earn the show's cancellation, not "if."

That finally happened this week, when Barr issued a Twitter post saying African-American former Obama advisor Valerie Jarrett was a product of the Muslim Brotherhood and "Planet of the Apes." With one Ambien-fueled declaration of racism, Barr sent her top-rated ABC show to the guillotine, leaving the show's other actors and crew jobless. (If ABC wanted ironic justice, they should have simply killed Roseanne's character off in an episode where she refuses to sign up for Obamacare and contracts a terminal disease.)

It is less than helpful to the cause of Republicans when the first show hailed as an honest look at Trump supporters (Trump himself praised the show) is cancelled because its star compares black people to monkeys. But all the signs were there: Perhaps the photo shoot in which Barr dressed as Hitler and placed cookie "Jews" in an oven may have been a tip-off. There is nary a crazy conspiracy theory Barr has failed to endorse, from 9/11 being an "inside job" to the Boston Marathon bombing being a "false flag" operation.

However, the primary fault here doesn't lie with Barr — people suffering from her brand of derangement can be found hanging around any of your city's finer coin-op laundromats. The real culprit is conservatives who embrace insane famous people, hoping to bring the GOP a modicum of cultural cache.

When liberal stars gather to support progressive causes and candidates, the condemnation from Republicans is universal: "What does Scarlett Johansson know about Obamacare?" "Who is Mark Ruffalo to lecture me on immigration?" And so on.

That is, of course, until a celebrity lets slip even a sliver of conservatism, in which case they are suddenly imbued with the wisdom of Solomon. Conservatives once called Barack Obama the Kim Kardashian of presidents; yet they remain silent when Trump is praised by Kim Kardashian's husband, Kanye West.

And the hunt is always on for new examples of celebrities that make us feel more a part of the cultural conversation. As Republicans, we huddle in clandestine groups, trying to solve the riddle of which actors we might call our own. We use the Ronald Reagan Memorial Decoder Ring to parse anodyne public statements:

"Chris Pratt said he loves God! He's one of us!"

"Brad Pitt has been a proud gun owner since kindergarten! PITT 2024!"

"John Krasinski was in a Benghazi movie!"

But like Wolfe's liberals making common cause with destructive forces like the Black Panthers, so, too are Republicans now mau mau'ing any unstable celebrity that dares bat his or her lashes at President Trump. If you think the Barr imbroglio is bad, just wait until Kanye West needs to sell more albums and publicly renounces his Trump affair to garner more attention.

The antidote to this stench of desperation is for conservatives to stick to their original principle: Celebrities don't have any special insight into foreign or domestic affairs. Often times, when famous actors speak up in service of a liberal cause it does their crusade more harm than good. Trust the people to make that determination.

Secondly, if Republicans absolutely need celebrities to help make their arguments, make new celebrities that deserve the adulation. Search out right-leaning authors or academics or military heroes that can explain conservatism in interesting ways without resorting to simply "triggering the libs." This is the beauty of America — if we don't like the celebrities we have, we can always make new ones. (Further, contra Laura Ingraham's assertion that athletes should just "shut up and dribble," sports are actually full of conservative athletes: Sports is darn near Hollywood for Republicans.)

But conservatives should refrain from playing the movie star sweepstakes with Democrats; we will be outgunned every time. Instead, our spokespeople should be determined by merit, class and dignity — spokespeople who can effectively ridicule the vulgar celebritization of politics many Americans abhor.

Milwaukee Journal Sentinel

LEAVE DEAD PEOPLE ALONE

August 23, 2018

On the most recent season of HBO's Westworld, one of the Native American characters offers a rumination on immortality. "You live only as long as the last person who remembers you," counsels Akecheta, a Ghost Nation elder.

There has always been a romance to living forever, even after one's physical body dies. Artists, authors, actors, and athletes all strive for immortality, hoping their words and deeds live on to influence people in the future.

But new technology is now making a mixed bag out of the concept of life after death. Late last month, it was announced that audiences across America will soon be entertained by a hologram of singer Roy Orbison, whose touring career has been cut short by the inconvenient fact that he has been dead for three decades. Cyber-Orbison, who plays sixteen songs backed by a live orchestra, will soon embark on a 28-city tour beginning in October. It goes without saying that "Oh, Pretty Woman" will be pretty creepy.

Such hologram technology is just the latest example of using computers to exhume dead people, forcing them to dance like marionettes to suit our tastes. Until now, having assumed room temperature meant your story was over — whatever reputation you earned while alive was cast in stone and your carefully cultivated image remained yours.

However, in the era of CGI and holograms, the persona a celebrity or historical figure spent a lifetime perfecting immediately falls into the hands of advertisers and computer programmers. The quality of these likenesses are getting to the point where human actors in movies may become superfluous — in the Star Wars-based "Rogue One" movie, actor Peter Cushing, who died 24 years ago, was recreated from scratch. The same film used CGI to portray a young Carrie Fisher as Princess Leia; after Fisher's death in 2016, rumors swirled that the actress would be digitally recreated in future Star Wars movies (Disney has since said that option is off the table.)

Let's say, for the sake of argument, Fisher were revivified for the upcoming films. Are we sure the character would say things Carrie Fisher would allow her character to say? Do we know the filmmaker would make choices the real Fisher could accept to protect her public persona?

Of course, a celebrity's image is often the property of that famous person's estate or family members, and public figures can try to legally restrict the use of their image upon death. But what if the person being recreated isn't necessarily famous and doesn't have a team of attorneys? Or what if their family members use their posthumous likeness as an ATM, selling out to whomever writes them a gargantuan check?

For instance, in 2013, CGI Audrey Hepburn appeared in a television ad for Galaxy brand chocolate bars. A mid-1990's commercial featured Fred Astaire dancing with a Dirt Devil vacuum cleaner. Digital Marilyn Monroe can be found in commercials hawking perfume. Would any of these celebrities have consented to these recreations? Would we be cool with Paul McCartney gathering together some digital Beatles for a reunion tour, or Martin Luther King, Jr. yelling "Make America Great Again!" in a Donald Trump campaign ad?

Just because society can do something doesn't mean it should. If you're fortunate enough to be remembered well beyond your death, you should be remembered by the way you chose to live your life, not the way keyboard-banging ghouls want you to be memorialized. Presumably, dead people have already had a rough time of it — we should all leave them alone.

Instead, let's leave CGI for its most enlightened purpose – to make dogs crack flatulence jokes in movies.

Milwaukee Journal Sentinel

WHY I LOVE BEING OLD

January 25, 2016

"Youth," Oscar Wilde once said, "is the one thing worth having."

As I exited my youth and aged into my thirties, and now forties, I felt much the same. How nice it would be to once again get out of bed without my ankles shooting pain through my legs. My belly button has begun to flee my abdomen as if it had just robbed a bank. At age 42, a good bit of every day is devoted simply to being a human in the world – exercising, trying to eat well, finding new places I need to shave – all things one takes for granted in the prime of youth. I feel like they should build a statue of me outside my house every time I successfully get my socks on.

But while most of our culture is geared towards making me feel terrible about succumbing to the horrors of aging, I'm starting to feel good about getting old. In fact, I wouldn't swap being 42 for being 21 for anything in the world.

So I thought I'd jot down some of the benefits of being a near-senior citizen. Y'know, before I forget them all.

Having Money

Most of my early 20's were spent with all my possessions in the back of my car, and all my money paper-clipped together in an envelope. I worked primarily as a waiter, stuffing dollar bills in my back pocket after a shift. I had no credit, no bank account, and couldn't afford to pay attention. The extent of my money management skills was knowing it was better to bounce one big check rather than a series of smaller checks, since you only have to pay the one-time bad check fee.

When you're old, those days have passed – you typically have savings, can afford to eat, and can pay for a stable roof over your head. I can buy the car I want, rather than my dad paying the neighbors $200 for a rusted-out 1981 Chevette with a bumper sticker that says "I Brake for Unicorns."

And, of course, having money leads to...

Drinking Better Alcohol

There's a reason I perfected the art of bonging cheap beer in college – because it was typically terrible, and I wanted to get it in my stomach with as little interaction with my taste buds as possible.

But when you're old, you have no time for bad alcohol. (That is, unless you are trying to be an Ironic Drinker, in which case the worse the beer, the higher your stature.)

The secret of "old drinking" is that the more expensive the booze you buy, the less of a hangover you end up with. Drink all the 12-year old scotch you want – a couple of ibuprofen before you go to bed, and you wake up ready to wrestle an alligator. If college students figured this out, it would bankrupt them all.

Old drinking is also preferable because people don't judge you nearly as much for engaging in it. If you drink a lot when you're young, people worry about its long-term effects; it could cost you jobs, relationships, and keep you from reaching your potential.

However, once everyone sees you've pretty much maxed out on the potential scale, you're free to pickle yourself as you see fit. When you're young, you drink to make new memories. When you're old, you drink to forget the memories you've made.

Once you hit 40, drinking at home isn't a sign of loneliness, it's an adorable personality quirk that doesn't really hurt anyone. People aren't like, "aw, now poor Christian's never going to be an astronaut," they're more like, "yeah, seems about right."

Aristotle once said that "young people are in a condition like permanent intoxication." Clearly he said that before he turned 40 and he was in a state of actual permanent intoxication.

Knowing Things

Whenever I go back and read a column I wrote just a week earlier, I think of all the things I learned in the days since it was published. And it feels like someone else entirely wrote the column. I picture myself just a week earlier, being naïve about how the world works and not really knowing what I was talking about.

Now multiply this by a thousand weeks, and you get a sense of how much I feel I've learned in the past 20 years. Would I give up all the things I've seen, all the events I've experienced, and the books I've read just to be young again? Of course not. To surrender my experiences would be to entirely change who I am now, which is way too risky of a proposition.

That's not to suggest young people don't know things. I'm just partial to the things that I know.

The Wooderson Effect

Everyone remember the famous Wooderson line from Dazed and Confused – "That's what I love about these high school girls, man – I get older, they stay the same age."

What Matthew McConaughey's creepy-but-still-cool character doesn't realize at the time is that his own perception of the opposite sex will change as he gets older.

When you're a young man, you're obviously attracted to girls your own age – older women seem out of reach. (This seems different for young women, who are more open to dating older men.) If you're a 25 year old guy who prefers 40-year old women, you're viewed as kind of a weirdo. But as you age, you begin to find women your own age attractive – your preferences grow older along with you.

So when you get to your 40s, more people are attractive. Younger women are attractive, older women are attractive. Part of it is, the older you get and the more flaws you recognize in yourself, the more accepting of other peoples' flaws you become. Plus, who wouldn't want to live in a world where "My Cousin Vinny" Marisa Tomei and "The Wrestler" Marisa Tomei can exist in harmony?

No Wasting Time

In my 20s, I spent a lot of time experimenting with things out of my comfort zone. I listened to all the music I could get my hands on, no matter how avant garde; at one point in college, I found myself listening to a CD of a German band who made music by banging on shopping carts with spoons.

When you're old, you no longer need to pretend to be into things you're not. You are free to do what you wish with the few remaining years you have on this earth. If all your young hipster friends demand that you like The National, you just shrug, and say "not for me" and move on. Your time left on this mortal coil is too valuable to dabble in ephemera. And especially not when "The Bachelor" is on.

Kids

When you're older, you get to have children. And the wonder of having kids narrowly cancels out the glory of not having them.

People generally think that having and raising children is a selfless act. But it's the exact opposite – having children is the ultimate act of vanity. For old people, making children is the eternal selfie; you're cementing your legacy for eternity with little people who look just like you.

Further, having kids immediately brings clarity and focus to your life. No matter how disjointed or scattered your life was up to that point, once a child emerges, you know exactly what the purpose of your life is. From then on, you cease to be the author of your own biography – your life story is being written by a 10-pound human. And your only reason for existing is to take care of that mini-you. You could pay a life coach a million dollars and they wouldn't convince you to get your shit together like a baby does.

Feigning Ignorance of Technology

Even if you're old and technologically savvy, you can always use your age to get you out of uncomfortable situations. If someone from work texts you with immediate instructions, take your time – you can always say something like, "all these blinking lights confuse me!" or "what's this internet I read about in the newspaper?"

People Listen to You

For some reason, when you're old, people automatically assume you know what you're talking about.

It is true, that when you age, you have perspective. If any one emotion characterizes youth, it is the belief that one is the axis upon which the universe turns. But the older you get, the more you see the world around you and grasp your relative insignificance. It's nice knowing that fads will come and go, and the world will not cease to exist. You just sip your expensive alcohol and enjoy the ride.

Connection to a Specific Time

127

Perhaps this one is more personal, but not only do I like being old, I like being old exactly at this time in history. It means I got to be in college during a revolutionary era in popular entertainment – the "grunge" era – when artistry and skill was actually valued. I wouldn't trade the experience of being body passed to Jane's Addiction at the first Lollapalooza for Mumford, his Sons, or his Grandsons.

I love that I grew up before the internet, so I know what it's like to not have to feel like I'm missing out on every news story, joke or meme. I can find my way to places without using GPS, and I can have arguments without having to dive into my iPhone for information to back me up. I love that when I was ten, my parents would kick me out of the house with instructions only to be back by dinner time – a practice that led to a great deal of tree climbing, garter snake handling, fort building, and basketball shooting.

Christopher Hitchens wrote that "A melancholy lesson of advancing years is the realisation that you can't make old friends." It is true, nobody will know you like the friends that you had when you were kids. They've seen you at your best and your worst, and kept you around for all of it.

But being older and having a strong connection to a specific era with someone else is actually a pretty decent stand-in for long-term friendship. Meeting someone your age and realizing they, too, thought Pearl Jam was overrated is a solid foundation for future friendship; and the older you are, the more cultural touchstones you are able to share with other people.

So yeah, being old is good, but being old in 2016 is even better.

George Bernard Shaw is often credited with saying something along the lines of, "youth is wasted on the young." But I, for one, refuse to accept this as my fate. The young can have their youth – I have my memories. If only I could remember them.

BOOK END: IMAGINE A WORLD WITHOUT THE PRINTED PAGE

April 16, 2012

A few days ago, I stood in the local big box electronics store for 20 minutes, gazing at the array of e-book readers lined up on the counter. I felt myself aging ten years per second as I navigated between Nooks and Kindles, gigabytes and dual core processers. In the end, I decided I couldn't take part in euthanizing the book industry, in which I one day hope to be a participant.

My stolid on-site review of these devices led to an instantaneous reflection on the role of good, old-fashioned books in our lives. The cultural influence of the printed page is impossible to measure; once ink becomes a relic, the unintended consequences could be severe.

Consider, for example, the obvious physical footprint books have on our topography. Some of our largest, most ornate buildings exist solely to house books; at some point, these libraries, bookstores and archives will simply serve as empty, cavernous remnants of the pre-digital era.

When books vanish, no longer will you be able to dazzle dinner guests with your imposing bookshelves full of mahogany-bound Russian poetry. A computer hard drive is a much less exciting conversation piece, and certainly a more difficult item about which to brag. (I always keep a book of poetry in my car, in hopes that if I die in a car accident, the headline will read "Area Man, Lover of Yeats, Decapitated in Horrible Flaming Wreck.")

On a personal level, many readers will miss the tactile sensation of leafing through books. Devout bibliophiles even like the pain they feel in their necks after perusing bookstore shelves with their heads cranked to the side in order to read the vertically oriented spines. They buy books they will never read, but feel better about having them on their shelves at home. They relish finding hidden treasures left in used books, whether they're notes scribbled in the margins or clues to the previous book's owner on a slip of paper used as a bookmark.

The move towards digital books will also likely bring about the same type of information egalitarianism we've seen with the internet. In the days of the printed word, publishing was more or less a meritocracy; if a publisher was willing to back a book with the type of cash it takes to print a few thousand copies, it meant it was at least a professional product. (Those that want to point out that a publisher actually issued a book penned by The Jersey Shore's "Snooki" may have their say at this point.) It will be much more difficult sorting through texts that don't bear a publisher's imprimatur, since all one needs to be considered an "author" now is to be able to turn on a computer.

Perhaps most importantly, physical books also provide a cultural permanency that would go missing if everything were stored on digital files. Right now, it doesn't matter how arcane the issue is about which one might want to learn; somewhere, there's a physical book that contains that information. Sometimes, the value of certain texts aren't apparent within the same decade they are written. Yet if the value of historical information was left up to the capriciousness of e-book readers, it could all vanish with a few keystrokes. (Undoubtedly, had the U.S. Constitution been written on an iPad, it would have contained a few more references to Rebecca Black's "Friday" video.)

Similarly, physical books grant authors eternal life. The literary world is replete with names of writers who received lukewarm reviews during their lives (Nietzsche, Blake, Thoreau), but who became posthumously indispensable. Emily Dickinson's first compilation of works wasn't published until four years after her death, when her sister found her secret stash of nearly 1,800 poems. Yet authors in the digital age are just a few "delete" button presses away from eternal extinction.

It seems unlikely that there will be a day where books disappear completely. As long as there are wealthy people, rare books will be sold as commodities and held as investments. Middlebrow texts will become the realm of book fetishists, much as vinyl records are today. But once our cultural mores are untethered from the book standard, we could be set adrift in an age when everything is possible, but nothing is real.

Of course, the primary beneficiaries of the new digital age are the stately trees and critters that live amongst them, who will not be sacrificed to the paper mills. But next time you see a squirrel, see if he can get Tom Wolfe to sign your Kindle.

SATURDAY NIGHT LIVE'S PREDICTABLE POLITICS

January 18, 2015

When conservatives tuned in to Saturday Night Live on the evening of November 22, they likely had to check their channel guides to make sure they were watching the right channel. The show opened with a skit that took a blowtorch to President Barack Obama's recently announced executive action to grant amnesty to nearly 5 million illegal immigrants in America. The skit featured cast member Kenan Thompson dressed as the famous Schoolhouse Rock character "Bill" from Capitol Hill, whom Obama repeatedly throws down the Capitol steps. Each time, Bill provides an explicit description of the painful fall.

Saturday Night Live, now in its 40th year, has been influencing the way Americans think about the political process and their elected leaders for longer than many up-and-coming political figures have been alive. Yet, despite its age, the show still has the ability to affect the public debate. After the Obama-amnesty sketch, the Washington Post immediately leapt to Obama's defense and fact-checked it, declaring constitutional challenges to Obama's actions to be "dubious." (Perhaps for their next project, they will allow Henny Youngman's wife a long-awaited rebuttal or will interview someone who respects Rodney Dangerfield.)

Over the past four decades, no American institution has provided a more consistent or effective brand of political humor than SNL. Ever since Chevy Chase first appeared as President Gerald Ford in 1975, few politicians have evaded the point of the show's satirical rapier. But the depth of the wound is often predicated on the target's political party. "We have a liberal bias, obviously," former SNL star Tina fey has said.

Of course, political satire is nothing new. Comedians have been ridiculing politicians since the dawn of the American republic. But nothing in modern America has attained the breadth or depth of SNL's reach into the public consciousness; the national lexicon is replete with SNL political references.

The show debuted in the post-Watergate era, when politicians were viewed with heightened distrust, and was initially given its political conscience by Lorne Michaels, a young left-wing Canadian. "I think coming on right after Watergate was crucial," Michaels would say later in an interview. "I was 30. We'd just lived through all that, and because of that and Vietnam, politics was something everyone knew and talked about. I think we defined ourselves as a generation in that way."

In the nearly 40 years that have followed, the show has saddled many political figures with public personae they would rather shake. Chase's Ford impression showed him as a bumbling buffoon, constantly falling and injuring himself. Privately, Chase made it clear that he hoped Ford would lose in 1976, and three days before the Carter–Ford election, the show replayed the speech in which Ford announced he would be pardoning Richard Nixon. Michaels later listed this as one of his proudest moments as the show's producer.

Few other political figures were spared. The show took a while to find a suitable take on Ronald Reagan (it tended to be non-political in the early 1980s), but in 1986, the late Phil Hartman devised a portrayal of the president as a tactical genius hiding behind a simpleton's façade. Perhaps the most lasting cultural memory of George H. W. Bush's single term in office is Dana Carvey's affected "Nah ga do it" and "Wouldn't be prudent" lines. Hartman's portrayal of Bill Clinton as a regular guy, unable to control his voracious appetite for women and eating, presaged the troubles that would eventually drag Clinton down.

With the election of George W. Bush in 2000, the show adopted a more aggressive tone, mercilessly lampooning the new president. As "Weekend Update" anchor, Fey regularly savaged Bush, zeroing in on the president's alleged history of drug use and his repeated recourse to capital punishment as Texas governor. (Sample joke: Bush kept his drunk-driving arrest secret from his daughters because he would rather they see him as a "failed businessman who executes people.")

Cast member Will Ferrell's Bush impersonation wasn't any more charitable. It was less an impression of his mannerisms than an interpretation of his character and intelligence, incorporating his malapropisms and lampooning his self-regard. Ferrell's portrayal of Bush involved manufactured words like "strategery," which reportedly became actual terms of art within Bush's inner circle: His strategists got to be known within the White House as the "Department of Strategery."

In SNL's long history of political takedowns, one stands out among the rest.

Shortly before 11:30 p.m. on September 13, 2008, Senator John McCain's presidential campaign couldn't have known that it was experiencing its high point. When the lights went up, Tina Fey, dressed as newly minted vice-presidential candidate Sarah Palin, began the most memorable and effective skewering of a public figure in modern political history.

Fey's mockery of Palin was so thorough that it became popular in academic circles to measure the "Fey Effect" on the 2008 presidential election. In one 2012 study, researchers from East Carolina University determined that Fey's impression of Palin did change how voters viewed the Alaska governor.

According to the study, which surveyed 1,755 respondents, subjects who saw Fey's Palin spoof had an 8.5 percent probability of approving McCain's selection of Palin, while 75.7 percent disapproved. Of those who hadn't seen the spoof, 16.1 percent approved of McCain's choice and 60.1 percent disapproved. Among those who watched a skit lampooning the vice-presidential debate between Joe Biden and Sarah Palin, 45.4 percent said they were less likely to vote for the McCain–Palin ticket; of the respondents who saw only the actual debate, only 34 percent said Palin's selection would make them less likely to support McCain.

After McCain announced Palin as his running mate, the race to cast her public image was on – and Fey won it. After Fey's multiple appearances caricaturing Palin, a Zogby poll found that 86.9 percent of respondents believed that Palin had actually said, "I can see Russia from my house," the show's 10 million regular viewers no doubt contributing to that finding. (ABC's Charles Gibson had earlier asked Palin what she had learned from her state's proximity to Russia. "They're our next-door neighbors, and you can actually see Russia from land here in Alaska, from an island in Alaska," she responded.)

SNL is different from most popular political humor in that its characters actually dress up and inhabit the roles of the people they aim to mock. The Daily Show, The Colbert Report, and other late-night talk shows are full of jokes about political figures; SNL enacts the jokes with characters saying the lines themselves.

"I don't think it's a crazy thing to say that SNL was one of the things that influenced voters in the 2000 election," said SNL writer Jim Downey after George W. Bush took office. (Downey, a Republican, is widely credited with being the show's best political writer.) During the 2000 campaign cycle, Al Gore and his aides studied SNL's parody of a debate in an effort to understand where Gore had gone wrong.

The length of the typical skit on SNL – between six and ten minutes – almost always exceeds the length of time nightly news programs spend on political coverage. When politicians are quoted on news shows, their sound clips last, on average, eight seconds. And newscasts have begun incorporating SNL clips into their programming. The Internet – through such websites as YouTube, Hulu, Yahoo!, and the show's website – then exposes SNL's parodies to millions more than see the original broadcast.

This constant mockery hasn't kept important political figures, including Gerald Ford, from appearing on the show: The president once taped a short segment at the White House that involved his saying, "I'm Gerald Ford, and you're not." Michaels later said that, at the outset, Ford was getting it all wrong. To loosen Ford up, he quipped, "Mr. President, if this works out, who knows where it will lead?" According to Michaels, this joke was completely lost on Ford.

The show's portrayal of Ford was in keeping with its take on Republicans. Generally, GOP politicians lampooned on SNL fall into a few categories: stupid (Sarah Palin, George W. Bush, Dan Quayle), old and evil (Dick Cheney, Ronald Reagan), old and clueless (George H. W. Bush, Bob Dole), and just clueless (Romney). By contrast, the show regularly depicts Democrats as too brainy (Jimmy Carter, Michael Dukakis, Al Gore).

Given the show's liberal predispositions, mocking Obama has proven to be a challenge. During the 2012 presidential election, the show clung to an unfair portrayal of Mitt Romney as a Bidenesque, gaffe-prone windbag, but Jason Sudeikis's imitation never really rang true. (In the summer of 2014, in his ice-bucket-challenge video to benefit ALS research, Romney challenged only two people to take it themselves – his wife and Sudeikis.)

Conversely, the show has never even tried to find Obama's "thing," an attribute it could present as an overarching theme. In one interview, former head writer Seth Meyers suggested that Obama might be portrayed as hopelessly under the thumb of his wife, Michelle, but dismissed the idea as a one-show type of joke.

Yet the events since Obama's reelection in 2012 have proven to be too juicy for SNL to ignore. It has ridiculed the president on issues from Obamacare to Ebola to immigration. Kenan Thompson regularly lampoons Al Sharpton's scattershot MSNBC show, and SNL often jabs African Americans for their unshakable support of the president.

Many a bettor would have lost money predicting the demise of SNL over the past four decades. Every few seasons the show hits a lull that seems to spell its downfall, then rises again with new cast members and new characters. Sometimes, the show is shocked out of torpor by political events that simply seem to be gifts from the heavens.

As President Obama transitions into the lame-duck phase of his presidency, the problems that have dogged his administration don't seem to be going away. The worst of Obamacare is likely yet to come, the courts have yet to weigh in on his amnesty plan, and Republicans who now control Congress are certainly going to force him into some politically embarrassing vetoes. When all is said and done, the president may have added one accomplishment to his résumé — he may have become the first president to force SNL to give Republicans a fair hearing.

National Review Online

CHAPTER TWO:

INTRIGUES

WHY LOYALTY TO TRUMP COULD PAY DIVIDENDS FOR GOP ASPIRANTS

January 22, 2020

In early August 1973, Paul Harvey used his nationally syndicated column to defend President Richard Nixon as impeachment proceedings began in Congress.

Harvey, a conservative who had previously been critical of Nixon for extending the war in Vietnam, laughed at the charge that Nixon had been involved in "political chicanery," noting that he had seen far worse behavior among politicians.

"Election after election I've watched machine politicians play the game the way the city's electorate expects," Harvey wrote of his native Chicago. He said he had seen local party officials "tilt the voting machines; vote winos for four bits and dead people for free; lose enough ballot boxes to reverse a defeat," adding that the "pomposity and sanctimony of some politicians in this present instance make me sick!"

Yet like many others in the conservative movement, Harvey's cringeworthy paean to Watergate whataboutism would not affect his future career prospects. Within three years, he would launch his "Rest of the Story," radio feature, spinning avuncular, folksy tales of cultural oddities.

Like Harvey, many prominent Republicans would go on to enjoy successful post-Watergate careers, easily sidestepping the possible taint from their vigorous Nixon defenses. And some of Nixon's critics within the GOP would quickly vaporize, their presidential aspirations vanishing under charges of disloyalty.

Among Nixon's other defenders was California Gov. Ronald Reagan, who at a banquet in November 1973 said Nixon had been the target of a "concerted effort in Washington to undermine him and make it appear he is not fit to govern."

"There are some who would destroy a man in order to destroy a mandate of all the people," argued Reagan, who claimed Nixon had done nothing wrong and the Watergate burglars were not "criminals at heart."

At a meeting of the Southern GOP Conference in December, Republican National Committee chairman George H.W. Bush told the group there was "no real pressure" for Nixon to resign and that calls for impeachment had been "orchestrated" by consumer advocate Ralph Nader and labor leaders.

"Get off his back and let the man do the job he was elected to do!" Bush told the crowd in Atlanta.

(In a Trumpian rhetorical flourish, Bush mocked impeachment talk from "that zany voice from under that big, floppy hat," referring to New York feminist congresswoman Bella Abzug.)

At the time of both the Reagan and Bush defenses, the House had already conducted impeachment hearings, where White House lawyer John Dean had testified the president was involved in a cover-up of the Democratic National Committee headquarters burglary. Nixon had recently declined to turn over his taped White House conversations to special prosecutor Archibald Cox, had fired Cox in the "Saturday Night Massacre," and had uttered his memorable "I am not a crook" defense.

And yet, as the summer of 1973 ended, more than 60 percent of Americans still opposed impeachment. This fact was not lost on GOP leaders, who continued to dig in on behalf of their president.

Such loyalty is a historical lesson heeded by some current conservatives, whose contortions in backing President Donald Trump are simultaneously baffling and laughable. Senators who once bitterly opposed Trump now trample others to get in front of cameras to defend him. Former Trump administration officials who once gave speeches warning against the impulse to govern by triggering Democrats have now commenced what can only be called an "owning the libs" world tour in defense of Trump.

As Trump's defenders have learned, America is forever making more past. As more news stories roll in, the Trump era will soon seem like a quirky relic from the past, their unconscionable defenses dissipating.

But as in the case with Watergate, those who cross Trump may forever feel the effects in a party that has succumbed to the president's will.

Take the case of moderate Republican Illinois Sen. Charles Percy, who in 1973 appeared to be on the fast track to the White House. A Harris poll conducted in June of that year placed Percy ahead of every other candidate, including Sen. Ted Kennedy, Vice President Spiro Agnew (who would soon resign independent of the Watergate scandal), and Ronald Reagan.

William F. Buckley, who remained unimpressed with Percy, called him "the lushest bloom of the medium-to-left spectrum of the Republican Party," but predicted Percy's opposition to Nixon "could remove him from the fallout that, before Watergate is finally over, could poison those who were nourished under Mr. Nixon's mushroom cloud."

In October 1973, Percy, no doubt with an eye on the White House, defended Nixon, saying it was time for "Republicans to stand together." In February, during a Chicago banquet at which he expressed his interest in running for president, Percy said the Nixon administration should be praised for everything but the "tragic excesses of Watergate."

But by March, Percy was telling the Republican Party to disassociate itself from the Watergate scandal, suggesting the party would be better off if Nixon resigned.

"I think it is important that we deal with the real world, with the political facts of life if we are to avoid political disaster and achieve, instead, victory at the polls," Percy told the Midwest GOP Leadership Conference in Chicago. Percy warned the Republican Party was on its way to becoming the "Avis" of political parties, referring to the rental car company's "We're No. 2" advertising campaign at the time.

Nixon, of course, had no particular love for Percy, with whom he had battled for years. During a Cabinet meeting with senior White House aides in mid-1973, Nixon said Percy would never be president "as long as I have anything to say about it."

Nixon was right.

Soon, the content of Nixon's audio tapes was released, Republican Party leaders turned against him, and Nixon resigned. Vice President Gerald Ford took over the presidency on August 9, forcing Percy to run against Ford in a Republican primary if he sought the presidency.

In announcing his decision not to run, Percy bitterly criticized Ford's decision to pardon Nixon, saying it "reinforces the cynicisms of millions of Americans," especially young persons. Rather than healing the wounds of Watergate, Percy said the pardon "exacerbated those wounds."

Nevertheless, Percy's star dimmed quickly, while Ronald Reagan's profile increased. As Reagan ran against Ford in the 1976 primary, he only sporadically addressed Watergate. In March of that year, George Will noted that "if prior to August 9, 1974, Mr. Reagan came to believe that Mr. Nixon had done something unpardonable, Mr. Reagan was not boisterous in advertising that belief."

"Mr. Reagan has never been what you would call obsessed with Watergate," Will wrote.

It was, in part, Reagan's feigned lack of interest in Watergate that kept his political future alive within the Republican party. His refusal to openly condemn Nixon comforted the base of the GOP that always believed Nixon got a raw deal—even late into 1974 the bitter-enders flooded editorial boards blaming Nixon's downfall on the hypocritical liberal media.

But it serves as a lesson to any Republican in 2020 who has political aspirations: At some point, today will be yesterday. And yesterday will be last month. And last month will be years ago.

It is why many Republicans in the Senate bite hard and pretend Donald Trump is a fit president. As Heraclitus noted, no man steps in the same river twice—in the future, it will be a different river, with different currents. The goal of Trump's defenders is to avoid drowning in that river before they get the chance to swim in more welcoming waters in the future.

And who will take control of the future of the party by being sufficiently obeisant to Trump? That, of course, is the rest of the story.

The Dispatch

AMERICA'S SELF-INFLICTED MISSING PERSONS CRISIS

September 23, 2016

Early in the morning of July 4, 1977, I remember my father shaking me awake. He had burst into our camper to pull me out while wind and rain swirled around the Flambeau River State Forest in northern Wisconsin, where our family had been camping. He ran with me in his arms and threw me in the back of the family car as a tornado ripped through the campground. I was 4 years old.

It wasn't until we returned to our home in Milwaukee that they sat me down and explained to me that my sister, one year older than me, wasn't returning from the trip. A tree had fallen on our camper, breaking her back and killing her. She had been sleeping just feet from me.

At 4 years old, I wasn't exactly sure what that meant. And we didn't talk about it. But as I grew older, I started to realize that the family was missing someone. It was as if we had a phantom limb. I was constantly thinking, "there should be someone else here." I was aware of her absence just about as much as I would have been aware of her presence.

As I grew to adulthood and became more tuned into politics, this feeling of missing a human life clearly colored my views on social issues. For one, I couldn't understand how anyone could abandon a child, either before or after its birth. And I especially couldn't understand why anyone would terminate their baby's life before it was born. I yearned to spend more time with my sister; and yet people were choosing to end their children's lives before they ever got a chance to experience the world.

Obviously, the politics of abortion have been litigated in public for decades, and few minds have been changed. My side argues that a human fetus is a life deserving protection, your side argues it's a woman's right to choose whatever "health care" she wants, yelling ensues, and we end up right back where we started.

But aside from the traditional arguments we have, I've never been able to shake my childhood feeling that people are missing. In every grocery aisle in America, there could be someone there that isn't. On university campuses, there is valuable research that isn't being done because the student wasn't wanted before birth. History tells us that children born under the most dire circumstances often rise to greatness; but now there's a 54-million person hole in society where those people would be.

The answer to this problem, of course, would be to encourage policies that dissuade abortion and promote childbirth. There's good news on this front: According to an Associated Press report last year, abortions dropped 12% nationwide since 2010, due largely to the decline in teen pregnancy rates over that time. Research has shown that millennials are now more likely to be pro-life than their parents, even if they reject the "pro-life" label.

But there's more that can be done. For one, we can help make sure pregnancy doesn't occur in the first place, whether that means increased access to birth control or expanded programs teaching personal responsibility to both boys and girls.

And steps can be taken to make childbirth a more attractive option for women faced with that decision. Expanding adoption services can help children find homes where they'll be loved. Technology can help single mothers continue on with their lives while still in their homes; more jobs can be done remotely, and college classes can be taken over the Internet. If we make a conscious effort to help women raising children alone, more will be able to move on to successful careers.

There is rarely a day that goes by that I don't think about my sister. We still have old family movies of us playing together as children. I often wonder how different my life would have been had she survived —would we have fought non-stop? Would she have bought me beer before I was of age? Would she have teased me mercilessly about girls I liked in high school? Would I now be a cool uncle to her kids?

I'd give anything to know the answer.

USA Today

NAGGING US BACK TO HEALTH

May 11, 2018

In their 1983 punk rock ode to gluttony "I Like Food," Descendents' lead singer Milo Aukerman yelps that he's "gonna turn dining back into eating!"

Thirty-five years later, the federal government has stepped in to do just that. This week, a new federal rule went into effect mandating virtually all businesses that serve food prominently display the calorie count for the items they sell. Advocates of the new rule, passed in 2010 as a part of the Obamacare healthcare bill, say calorie labeling will allow consumers to make healthier choices. Food and Drug Administration Commissioner Dr. Scott Gottlieb believes mandatory calorie counts will have "a profound and generational impact on human health," helping to reduce the instances of cancer, diabetes and heart disease.

Yet with the new rule, the federal government is taking away the delight of enjoying restaurant food, reducing every bite to an antiseptic caloric transaction. Gone is the romance of diving into a plate of tortellini and worrying about the consequences later — the federal government has mandated every decadent bite be seasoned with a heavy dose of guilt.

Presumably, the rule exists for the fictional American who is unaware that eating an apple at home is healthier than slamming back some Denny's "Moons Over My Hammy" after a night out drinking. Sadly, even the National Restaurant Association (which is also badly in need of an acronym change) has gone along with this attempt to nag the American population into health, calling the rule "a huge win for everyone," and saying it "represents a powerful example of government and industry working together to benefit those we serve."

Yet it seems the Restaurant Association may be suffering from a bit of Stockholm Syndrome. (And if that made you think of meatballs, shame on you — go choke down some celery.) In the absence of a federal mandate, restaurants were perfectly free to provide nutritional information for their menu items, and many did. If consumers truly appreciated feeling guilty about ordering food they already knew was less healthy, no government involvement would have been necessary.

In fact, a heaping ladle full of studies have demonstrated that menu labeling makes little difference in what people order — it will simply make them feel worse for ordering it. One study by researchers at Carnegie Mellon found that consumers still ordered high-calorie menu items even when those items were placed in the context of how many calories one should eat during a meal or for a whole day.

In 2015, the New York Times deemed menu calorie counts a "failure," noting that at some point, customers begin to ignore the nutritional labels. "At no time did the labels lead to a reduction in the calories of what diners ordered," noted Aaron E. Carroll, a professor of pediatrics at Indiana University School of Medicine writing for the Times.

Clearly, Americans don't want a government bureaucrat standing in between them and their queso burritos. Yet feeling the need to "do something," Congress swooped in and passed the new law, which has been proven to be costly to restaurants and retailers alike. According to the National Association of Convenience Stores, the total compliance cost for the entire food industry is expected to be $300 million per year, a sum that will most likely be passed on to consumers.

The law doesn't even allow restaurants to satisfy the nutritional reporting requirement through lower-cost measures, such as posting calorie counts on a website for consumers to peruse. Those who really wanted to know what they were eating could simply reference that information on their phones. In fact, anyone who has tried to lose weight already knows the market is already saturated with mobile applications that will tell you a lot more about restaurant offerings than simply calorie count, which is only one of many measures to determine whether food is healthy.

Eating food is a magical process, irreducible to numbers or statistics. A great meal is often a mystery that unfolds as one savors each bite after another. To demagogue people about a meal's contents with crass nanny-state caloric warnings is an insult both the to diner and the food.

"After a good dinner one can forgive anybody, even one's own relations," said Oscar Wilde. Yet no meal is good enough for us to forgive Congress for this pointless, condescending intrusion on our ability to eat in peace.

USA Today

SUCKING THE LIFE OUT OF BEVERAGES

July 27, 2018

For years, a cornerstone of America's progressive canon has been that the nation's jails are packed with an inordinate number of nonviolent offenders. Prison, the argument goes, should be reserved only for those who pose an immediate threat to other citizens.

Last week, some on the left have identified just the type of criminal that needs to do hard time to ensure our safety. I'm speaking, of course, about restaurant employees that hand out straws to customers.

Last week, the city of Santa Barbara, Calif., passed a new ordinance that could result in up to six months in jail or a $1,000 fine for restaurants who hand out plastic straws to patrons. Those penalties, which kick on a second violation of the ordinance, are cumulative — so handing out four straws to a single table could mean two years in jail for a restaurant owner who practices their own vigilante brand of drink justice.

Santa Barbara's ban is just the latest in the long tale of eco-nonsense that frequently grips America. Efforts to ban plastic straws have either been successful or are underway in all the predictable areas — Seattle, Portland, New York, San Francisco, Washington, D.C. — with the Santa Barbara ban being the most restrictive. When Seattle banned plastic straws, it allowed an exemption for compostable plastic, but Santa Barbara went even further, allowing only straws made from paper, bamboo, or metal.

Environmentalists argue that 500 million plastic straws per day are polluting our oceans, a number that appears to have come from a phone survey conducted by a 9-year old Vermont boy. In fact, studies estimate straws make up only about 0.02% of the plastic waste that makes it into the ocean or to coastlines. Further, the United States is only accountable for around 1% of the world's marine plastic waste, far behind China at 28%.

But of course, these types of meaningless bans aren't about actually saving wildlife; they are simply the latest weapon in an arms race of smug self-regard. We saw this charade a decade ago when municipalities began to ban plastic bags out of environmental concern. As Reason Magazine reminds us, 10 states (including Wisconsin) had to deal with customer backlash by banning municipalities from banning plastic bags.

That doesn't mean businesses can't ban straws on their own, or "straw shame" customers by forcing them to ask for a straw on their own. If they don't want me to ever to go their restaurant again, they are more than welcome to set their own rules and ditch straws altogether. One tip, though — businesses should probably keep some straws on hand for either disabled people who can't drink directly from a cup or to aid servers who don't want to spend time cleaning up spilled drinks from children.

But using the power of government to enforce an obnoxious eco-fad is another story. This would simply be creating a black market for plastic straws; adults who find it revolting to put their mouth on a glass that someone else's gross lips were on just minutes before would huddle around in bathrooms trying to get one last straw hit before returning to their tables. Pablo Escobar wouldn't have to import cocaine to America, he could make his billions smuggling in plastic cutlery. At restaurants, undesirables would roll up dollar bills and use them to suck down that sweet Mountain Dew before the police bolted in and slapped the cuffs on them.

All plastic straw bans will achieve will be to increase costs on consumers (paper straws are far more expensive) or to irritate customers to the point where they stay home. The only people who could honestly advocate for such a policy would be drive-through customers who enjoy wearing their beverages to the office.

Let's leave our laws for those who pose a threat — handing someone a drinking implement shouldn't be a one-way ticket to Shawshank. Ironically, in this case, it's the people who enjoy using straws that don't suck.

USA Today

SOCIALISM AS A TALKING POINT

February 7, 2014

In 1891, before the world began to experience the brutal work of the Bolsheviks and other revolutionaries, socialism was still very much a plausible concept. It was that year that Oscar Wilde, one of the world's great novelists and playwrights, wrote a compelling defense of the nascent movement known as socialism, arguing that eliminating private property would free men to realize their full selves.

"Socialism itself will be of value simply because it will lead to individualism," wrote Wilde, arguing that being freed from work would allow men to become poets, artists and philosophers. Elimination of private property would allow a man to "realize the perfection of what was in him, to his own incomparable gain and to the incomparable and lasting gain of the whole world."

In arguing that socialism necessarily begets freedom, Wilde's ideas closely reflected those of none other than Karl Marx, who three decades earlier had argued that reducing the reliance of labor in society "corresponds to the artistic, scientific, etc. development of the individuals in the time set free."

Given that the language of modern progressivism is hopelessly rooted in the past, it's no surprise Democrats exhumed this calcified nugget of wisdom last week. In response to a Congressional Budget Office report that estimated Obamacare could effectively reduce the number of American workers by 2.5 million over the next decade, Democrats immediately began explaining how much better off workers will be when they are freed from the suffocating shackles of employment.

The day the CBO report was issued, White House press secretary Jay Carney argued that Americans "would no longer be trapped in a job just to provide coverage for their families, and would have the opportunity to pursue their dreams." Wisconsin Democratic Rep. Mark Pocan explained that when jobless, a former worker "might be able to tuck their child in bed at night, and read a bed-time story, or go to an activity. Which means they're better off." Even before the bill's passage, then-House Speaker Nancy Pelosi called the Affordable Care Act "an entrepreneurial bill, a bill that says to someone, if you want to be creative and be a musician or whatever, you can leave your work, focus on your talent, your skill, your passion."

These excuses are so absurd they would probably elicit a guffaw from even the most committed old Trotskyite. (And Chairman Mao wasn't exactly known for his facility with sidesplitting one-liners.)

Just try some of these out on your loved ones:

"Oh, your wife just left you for her yoga instructor? You'll never have to hand over the remote control again!"

"What's that? Aaron Rodgers just cracked his collarbone? Just think of the great draft pick the Packers will get next year!"

Say these to your friends, and you might be freed from the shackles of having an unbroken nose.

Of course, as oppressive socialist regimes rose in the 20th century, "freedom" often meant freedom from life on Earth. The collectivism of agriculture in Russia in the early 1900s led to the murder and starvation of tens of millions of peasants. Later, under more benevolent socialist regimes, the death toll was reduced to tens of thousands. If you equate "freedom" with standing in line for half a day for toilet paper, then perhaps socialism is for you.

Obviously, this is not to say Obamacare is pure, uncut socialism or that the president himself is a socialist. (Although the health plan does move America more toward the diet socialism found in much of Europe today.)

But the CBO report demonstrates what happens when the government begins to micromanage private markets; low-income individuals are now incentivized to work less, and are denied the upward mobility regular employment brings.

Obamacare's "unforeseen consequences" were perfectly foreseen by people such as U.S. Rep. Paul Ryan (R-Wis.), who said government is now better at "inducing the person not to work who was on the low-income scale, not to get on the ladder of life, to begin working, getting the dignity of work, getting more opportunities, raising their income, joining the middle class." According to Ryan, Obamacare means "fewer people will do that."

In just one week, Democrats shifted from being the party of workers to the party of "work is for suckers." Currently, about 138 million Americans are being oppressed by their jobs; if the left has its way, the country will be better off when that number is much lower. And if those people want to return to the workforce, they can interview by explaining their lack of computer skills through the timeless art of interpretive dance.

Milwaukee Journal Sentinel

HOW TO TALK TO WHITE PEOPLE ABOUT VOTER ID

Aug. 1, 2014

Any time the state Supreme Court issues a major decision, things in the state get a little sensitive. Feelings are hurt, egos are bruised and political charges are leveled.

Chances are, you have a white, liberal friend who will want to talk about Thursday's decisions in which the court upheld the state's law requiring photo identification to vote. This has the potential to be unpleasant, but following just a few simple tips will make this inevitable conversation go much smoother.

First, approach your white friend slowly, making no sudden movements to scare him or her. Sit down at your favorite bar or coffee house, order him a chai latte and calmly mention something interesting you found while digging around in the bowels of this May's Marquette University Law School poll. Tell him you thought it was interesting that 58.5% of white poll respondents favored imposing a photo ID requirement. But that it was even more interesting that 67.2% of African-American respondents supported photo ID, and you noticed that this number tracks with a lot of national polls.

Upon hearing this information, your friend will have a confused look on his face, as he has been told that imposition of a photo ID law is akin to the reinstitution of separate water fountains for different races. He will tell you he's pretty sure the black guy he knows is against it.

In fact, the idea that blacks support voter ID more than whites will be particularly puzzling, because there's nothing white people like more than telling African-Americans what they should think. You may point out that this used to be called "racial paternalism," where whites set the standards to which blacks were expected to conform.

At this point, your white friend likely will show visible signs of irritation and become more animated. You may calm him down by mentioning "The Wire," a show white people revere because sympathizing with drug dealers in inner city Baltimore absolves them of their racial guilt. (As a backup, you also may use Ken Burns' documentary series about jazz.)

When you resume the voter ID discussion, your friend will use terms such as "poll tax" and will say, as Chief Justice Shirley Abrahamson wrote in a dissent, that voter ID moves us closer to the Jim Crow era. You may remark at how amazing it is that nearly 70% of the state's African-Americans want to return to the era when they were systematically denied the right to vote.

(Note: At this point, in order to reassure himself of his superiority, your white friend reflexively will think you are a racist, but he will not say so to your face — he will log in to his anonymous Twitter account and broadcast the revelation to his six followers.)

You may now tell your friend about studies showing that black voter participation has increased in states that have introduced photo ID. And that the Wisconsin Supreme Court eliminated the "poll tax" concerns by virtually eliminating the financial requirements for obtaining a valid government ID. Feel free to point out that voting now is easier than ever with the advent of the "motor voter" law, same-day registration and absentee voting.

If your friend hasn't left yet, his retort will almost certainly not be on topic and will include the words "Koch brothers." Do not panic. In fact, build a bond with him by mentioning how great it is that in 2012 Wisconsin had the highest turnout rate in the nation, a ridiculous 73% of eligible voters.

But then mention that, as studies have shown, turnout increases in races where there's a lot of spending, so when independent groups dump buckets of Benjamins on a state like Wisconsin during the recall, it educates voters and gets them more motivated to vote. If you are feeling comfortable, you may make a joke about Gov. Scott Walker being "The Great Enfranchiser." (Warning: Saying this out loud could result in a locally sourced kale wrap being hurled at your head.)

If all else fails, console your friend by telling her or him that the state Supreme Court's ruling is not in effect, as the issue has been commandeered by the federal courts. However, you might want to buy him a stiff artisanal microbrew before you mention that the appeal is currently before the 7th Circuit U.S. Court of Appeals, the same court that upheld Indiana's photo ID requirement, which then was upheld by the U.S. Supreme Court.

This may bring your friend a modicum of comfort. He will say he hopes the U.S. Supreme Court finally gets some justices that show respect for African-Americans, unlike that "Uncle Tom" Clarence Thomas.

And if you are at a bar, before you go home, make sure you order as many drinks as you can on your buddy's tab. Just give the mixologist your friend's name — no identification necessary.

Milwaukee Journal Sentinel

FDA RULES GRATE CHEESE MAKERS

September 9, 2014

At first blush, it would seem as if outlawing a certain type of cheese in Wisconsin would be like banning giant hats in Vatican City. The Dairy State currently makes more cheese than any state in the nation, providing one-quarter of the country's cheese supply.

But recent uncertainty by the U.S. Food and Drug Administration is causing one artisanal cheesemaker in western Wisconsin to halt production of one of his farm's signature cheeses. Andy Hatch, owner of Uplands Cheese, announced in August that he wouldn't be producing this fall's run of Rush Creek Reserve, a soft cheese popular during the holidays.

"Food safety officials have been unpredictable, at best, in their recent treatment of soft, raw-milk cheeses, and until our industry is given clear and consistent guidance, we are forced to stop making these cheeses," Hatch wrote in an email to fellow cheesemongers and distributors in late August. This uncertainty has forced Hatch to halt production of his signature cheese, as he doesn't want to begin aging his product only to have it outlawed at the whim of the FDA months later.

In an Aug. 29 letter to the American Cheese Society, the FDA announced that it would be changing its testing protocol for non-pathogenic bacteria in cheese and admitted that it had made some mistakes in its raw milk cheese testing procedures. But according to Hatch, "It's really not a meaningful enough shift to change the way I'm thinking about the regulatory climate."

The FDA letter "just serves to reinforce the impression that I have that this is not especially organized and not well thought-out," Hatch told me. "The fact that they're changing horses midstream again only adds to the impression that we don't know what to expect next," he said.

It appears that not only is the FDA behind the times, it might be lagging the science of raw milk cheese by centuries. People have been making cheese from unpasteurized milk for many hundreds of years.

The FDA's current rule, in place since 1949, mandates that cheese containing raw milk has to be aged for 60 days. But according to Hatch, the FDA has since discovered that the 60-day requirement is not the proper way to regulate cheese containing raw milk. For instance, now we know certain pathogens can survive for more than 60 days, which is why the FDA has been scrambling to write new rules.

But Hatch has never gotten a single report of anyone getting sick from any of his cheeses. "We test every batch of cheese that leaves this building, and our cheese has always tested fine," he said. Hatch points out that the decision to halt Rush Creek Reserve wasn't based on a problem at their farm; it was because of the FDA's ability "to move the goal posts without warning."

Instead of a capricious age limit, Hatch suggests batch testing as the new standard. He supports "testing the product itself, proving it's uncontaminated and using that as the basis."

Part of the problem is that the public often conflates fluid raw milk with raw milk cheese, which is a completely different product. For one, fluid raw milk is regulated on the state level, while cheese is regulated by the FDA. Cheese-making is meant to preserve milk in a safe way — it has a number of safeguards in the process that fluid raw milk doesn't have. Plus, there's time to test cheese, whereas milk needs to be consumed fresh.

It's also not as though consumers don't know what they are buying. Given the cost of the cheese (I paid nearly $10 for a small slice to sample — it is delicious), it's not as though people are going to be accidentally buying it and putting it on burgers. (At my local grocery store, a whole wheel of the company's Pleasant Ridge Reserve is $263.80, which is more than I've paid for four wheels on my car.)

Hatch pays attention to politics "quite a bit," and politicians from both sides have reached out to him on this issue – U.S. Rep. Ron Kind (D-Wis.), Democratic Sen. Tammy Baldwin and Republican Sen. Ron Johnson all have contacted him to help. Democratic gubernatorial candidate Mary Burke has toured his farm, and U.S. Rep. Paul Ryan (R-Wis.) has been using him to demonstrate the hazards of regulatory overreach.

But Hatch says that he's not against regulation; he just wants the rules to be clear and predictable in how they are enforced. "Having a safe, well-regulated food industry is part of what makes us a first-world country," he said, adding that as long as the new rules are science-based and recognize that raw milk cheese can be made safely, "I'll be OK with that."

Milwaukee Journal Sentinel

NO WINNERS IN FERGUSON

November 25, 2014

In the wake of events in Ferguson, Mo., Monday night, I imagined what it must have been like to have been a juror being asked to weigh the evidence against police officer Darren Wilson.

Even if you were convinced that Wilson was justified in shooting and killing unarmed, 18-year-old Michael Brown, would you be willing to decide that one man's innocence was worth risking the businesses — and potentially the lives — of other dismayed Ferguson residents once your decision was announced? After months of demonstrating in the streets, the prospect of riots, looting and property damage was almost a certainty; would you be confident that the evidence you saw justified the violence to come as a result?

For grand jurors, the answer was "yes." Despite the immense pressure put on them both nationally and locally to indict the white officer for shooting the African-American teenager, jurors spent 25 days listening to testimony from 60 witnesses before concluding charges against Wilson were not warranted. According to documents released Monday, many of the original eyewitness accounts of the shooting were flawed, as some Ferguson residents had testified to things they had never seen. Instead, St. Louis County Prosecutor Robert McCulloch noted the grand jurors relied on forensic evidence, which "does not change because of public pressure or personal agenda."

In the end, the grand jury clearly thought the account Wilson gave regarding the events of Aug. 9 was backed up by physical evidence. Wilson says that, riding alone in his squad car, he pulled up next to Brown and his friend Dorian Johnson and asked them to move to the sidewalk. Wilson says Brown came at him through the driver's side window, punching him several times.

During the struggle, Wilson was able to grab his firearm, which he believed Brown was trying to take from him. After Wilson fired two shots, Brown retreated and Wilson gave chase on foot. According to Wilson, Brown then turned and charged at him, ignoring orders to get on the ground. Wilson then allegedly fired three sets of gunshots, eventually shooting Brown in the head when he was eight to 10 feet away.

Of course, the shooting of a black teenager by a white cop has inflamed the usual racial tensions seen in high-crime, police-heavy areas. (Although, as McCulloch noted, all the witnesses who said they saw Brown "charge" at Wilson were African-American.)

But political opportunists would have us believe that one's feelings about the Brown case are an either/or proposition: as if believing that the facts are in Wilson's favor means that you're also unaware of the very justified distrust African-Americans have of police and the legal system. In fact, both can be true and valid.

In his statement Monday night, President Barack Obama perfectly struck this tone. He noted that "nobody needs good policing more than poor communities with higher crime rates." Indeed, areas of high crime are the ones most likely to be flooded with police, and therefore more confrontations between citizens and officers are likely. Obama suggested that having more officers that demographically represent the neighborhoods will help; but while it sounds good on its face, at least in the Brown case, one would have to know whether a black cop would've acted differently than Wilson did.

But Obama also noted that while the rule of law should be respected, communities of color "aren't just making these problems up." And in Ferguson, aside from a history of racial tension, the police made plenty of mistakes to help foment the anger we saw Monday. On the day of the shooting, Brown's body was left in the street for hours. McCulloch passed the prosecutorial buck to a grand jury, which it seems was meant to insulate himself and opened up charges that Wilson was getting a special deal. And announcing the grand jury decision at 8 p.m. couldn't have been worse.

Nevertheless, now that the evidence is available, trying to paint the broader issue of law enforcement race relations on the narrow canvas of the Brown shooting is perilous. The two can be mutually exclusive.

Of course, facts in the case mean nothing to the contingent in Ferguson hell-bent on destroying the city. In the wake of Martin Luther King Jr.'s assassination in 1968, the Milwaukee Journal printed thousands of photos of King for businesses to put in their windows to keep rocks from flying through them. Similarly, businesses in Ferguson, many owned by African-Americans, boarded up windows and adorned them with "hands up, don't shoot" posters to demonstrate solidarity with protesters. Yet businesses were indiscriminately looted and set on fire.

And thus, Monday night's victims were law-abiding residents who only sought to make their city better. But after seeing their city in flames, the only change has been for the worse. And again the spiral begins; while the nation had a brief moment to improve race relations, the Ferguson riots will only set them back.

Milwaukee Journal Sentinel

CURRENCY NEEDS DIVERSITY OF EXPERIENCE

June 25, 2015

Walk into any state capitol in America, and you're likely to get a glimpse of the high regard in which government holds itself. Soaring columns, majestic domes, marble floors and gold paint are de rigueur for statehouses, which are often among the most ornate buildings in a given state. Government's selfadmiration is also evident in its currency. Every national historical figure memorialized on U.S. paper money is someone who served in a governmental capacity.

Only Ben Franklin and Alexander Hamilton never served as president, and at least two (Ulysses S. Grant, Andrew Jackson) aren't universally recognized as being particularly good chief executives.

Last week, Treasury Secretary Jack Lew announced that Hamilton was being demoted on the $10 bill in favor of a woman. This set off a round of objections from Hamilton fans, who think Jackson should be the one getting the boot from his privileged perch on the $20 bill. (In actuality, the true currency crime is that Thomas Jefferson is still slumming it on the $2 bill, which is only utilized by grandmothers wary of sending $5 through the mail.)

Immediately after Lew's announcement, the Hamilton replacement guessing game began. (Lew said the new woman and Hamilton may be featured together on the bill, hopefully in a hot tub.)

Public sentiment seems to be in favor of Harriet Tubman, and for good reason. Not only does Tubman represent the experiences of both African-Americans and women, throughout her life she showed great personal courage and bravery in helping slaves escape via the Underground Railroad.

But Harriet Tubman also would be an inspired choice because she represents another previously unrecognized demographic: Americans who didn't work for the federal government.

Granted, having Founding Fathers on the paper currency helps us remember the nation's original principles - but that doesn't mean we can't freshen up our money from time to time. The most recent living human being on a paper bill is Grant, who died in 1885. Surely, there are American non-presidents who have acted in ways worthy of recognition since then.

Instead of yanking Founding Fathers off the currency, several options come to mind.

First, bills have two sides - the Treasury Department can keep the current inhabitant on one side, but pay tribute to, say, Rosa Parks, Clara Barton, Jackie Robinson or Mark Twain on the reverse side. (In honor of McDonald's dollar menu, the one dollar bill could feature George Washington on the front and Ray A. Kroc on the back - the man not only figured out how to feed billions of people inexpensively, he spawned an entire documentary film industry to make poor people feel terrible about it.)

Perhaps we could start diversifying the denominations and adding Americans who changed the world without the benefit of having been president. Martin Luther King Jr. goes on the $25 bill. Jonas Salk, who certainly saved millions of lives by eradicating polio, gets the $40 bill.

Thomas Edison gets the $75 bill.

Coins are another option, and traditionally have been more welcoming to non-Founding Fathers. When each state designed its own quarter, coins became the minor leagues for governmental recognition; names such as Duke Ellington, Helen Keller, John Muir and the Wright brothers began popping up.

But those are boutique coins - the standard ones still feature visages of presidents and revolutionaries. So let's open up the field and disqualify anyone on paper currency from being on a coin. Sorry, Abe, you get the $5 bill or the penny, not both.

Perhaps this is all folly. Soon, with the advent of technology, the only people who use paper money are going to be husbands who don't want their wives to know what they bought.

But in the meantime, if we want more diversity on our money, it should mean diversity of experience, too.

Milwaukee Journal Sentinel

RATINGS AGENCIES GET A LOW GRADE

July 6, 2013

The Wall Street bad guys who sent the American economy into a tailspin in 2008 were a lot like the bad guys in a zombie movie. There were thousands of them, they moved deliberately and operated in broad daylight, and yet they still managed to devour everything in sight.

Foremost among the greedy actors that tanked the American financial system were the large security rating agencies, which repeatedly granted risky securities flawless ratings. The imprimatur of the main three agencies — Moody's, Fitch Ratings and Standard and Poor's (S&P) — led investors to sink billions of dollars into these securities, unaware of how risky they were.

But as we know now — and even knew at the time — the rating agencies are caught in an inherent conflict of interest, as the financial institutions that issue products such as collateralized debt obligations and residential mortgage-backed securities pay the agencies to rate their products. This would be like the Green Bay Packers being allowed to hire the referees for home games. One face mask penalty against Clay Matthews, no matter how justified, could lead to that referee never being hired again. Rating agencies need to keep churning out positive grades to keep business headed their way.

153

Decades ago, it was investors who paid rating agencies to assess risk and assign a grade to securities, which made sense because individual investors need accurate information to make decisions about where to put their money. But in the 1970s, the banks themselves began paying for the ratings in an attempt to garner higher grades and therefore lure investors to their products. In the ensuing years, Congress has made sporadic efforts to rein in the agencies, but its warnings have essentially boiled down to "stop, or we'll send you a sternly worded letter telling you to stop again."

This mutual backscratching can lead to embarrassing — and dangerous — results. Before the collapse, the Nationally Recognized Statistical Rating Organizations (NRSOs) rated tens of thousands of financial products. A majority of these securities received AAA and other investment-grade ratings, despite obvious red flags that should have sent investors fleeing as if the zombie apocalypse was upon them. For instance, Moody's mortgage security model didn't incorporate any information about an individual borrower's debt-to-income ratio, which is one of the strongest predictors of default.

We know how this ended. Traditionally, securities that carry the vaunted AAA rating have less than a 1% chance of default. But more than 90% of the subprime mortgage-backed securities that received AAA ratings in 2006 and 2007 were eventually downgraded to junk status.

In fact, Fannie Mae, the quasi-governmental lender that became the nation's largest issuer of subprime home loans, had an especially cozy relationship with S&P, which it paid handsomely to rate its questionable securities. As detailed in New York Times reporter Gretchen Morgenson's book with Joshua Rosner, "Reckless Endangerment: How Outsized Ambition, Greed and Corruption Led to Economic Armageddon," S&P consistently protected Fannie from congressional Republicans seeking more transparency from the lender. In fact, it was only on Aug. 11, 2008, three weeks before the federal government had to take over the bankrupt lender, that S&P downgraded Fannie's risk-to-the-government rating, all the way from A+ to A.

Congressional efforts to break up this financial old boys' network have fallen short. Sen. Al Franken (D-Minn.) proposed an amendment to the 2010 Dodd-Frank bill that would have essentially created a government-run ratings clearinghouse: Each bank would contribute to a fund for ratings services, but wouldn't be able to choose which agency was hired to grade its securities. Yet in negotiations between the Senate and House, Franken's proposal was watered down to merely require study of the issue.

Finally, in December of last year, the Securities and Exchange Commission issued its study, which concluded that the agency needed to study the issue in more detail. (Dodd-Frank did implement penalties for agencies that handed out inflated grades, but the SEC is still writing the rules, and it is unclear whether any actual punishments will be included.)

Perhaps Franken's proposal isn't the single shot to the head that will keep you from becoming a savory zombie hoagie, but it is a step in the right direction. The conflict of interest between banks and the rating agencies still exists, and with Americans having lost $3.4 trillion in retirement savings, the full bill for the financial collapse has yet to come due.

Regulatory freedom in the financial markets is essential to job creation and economic growth — but when investment decisions are made on a rotten foundation, reform is the responsible course of action.

Milwaukee Journal Sentinel

BRINGING MEDICARE BACK TO LIFE

August 18, 2012

The other day, I ran across the first cellphone I ever bought. In 1999, it cost about $200, and carrying it around must have been like hiding a toaster in my pants. It's so old, the numbers only go up to six. I'm fairly certain it's gasoline-powered and has to be kick-started to make a call.

Yet the antiquated way health care is delivered through the nation's Medicare program makes my phone look like something from the Jetsons. A growing retirement class, new and expensive medical treatments and rapidly rising health care costs have put Medicare on the brink of insolvency. According to the Congressional Budget Office, the Medicare trust fund is scheduled to run out of money a decade from now.

This is, in large part, because of the perverse incentives built into the Medicare program that drive up the program's costs. In 1960, health care spending made up 5.6% of America's economy; today, health care spending makes up a whopping 17.9% of the U.S. economy.

The basic framework of the Medicare program encourages high health care cost increases. Under the current fee-for-service arrangement, a Medicare recipient goes to see a doctor; that doctor then bills the government for the medical service, no questions asked. The doctor is then reimbursed for the service using taxpayer funds and borrowed money - the patient is completely disconnected from the cost of the service because you and I are paying the bill.

It's not difficult to see how this program can go wrong. The incentive for health care providers to offer the best care at an affordable price is extremely low. And since Medicare is an entitlement program, taxpayers are on the hook for these services, whether they are satisfactory or not.

A bipartisan contingent of budget experts and lawmakers, most notably vice presidential candidate Rep. Paul Ryan (R-Wis.), has offered a "premium support" plan to rectify these perverse incentives. Ryan's plan, which doesn't apply to anyone over the age of 55, would give future Medicare recipients the chance to pick from a list of health plans that fit them the best.

Under the plan, nobody can be denied because of a pre-existing condition, and poorer seniors receive more aid than the wealthy. Once insurance companies have to compete for business, costs will drop and quality will increase.

For a look at what competition does to service quality, consider the cellphone example. With wireless companies doggedly fighting for business, costs have gone down and technology has improved immeasurably.

Remember the stone ages when your favorite NFL quarterback had to send you pictures of himself naked via the postal service? Or when you had to pay for cellphone calls by the minute? Now I can call Natalie Portman six times a day and still have plenty of bail money left over.

So, while Democrats portray Ryan's plan to save Medicare as a "cut," that simply isn't true. (Aside from the fact that the changes are optional; if a future senior prefers the current fee-for-service arrangement, he or she can keep it.) Ryan's plan saves money by reducing the overall cost of health care, not by underfunding it.

On the other hand, President Barack Obama's health care law takes a different route. Rather than using patient choice as a way of keeping costs down, the Affordable Care Act empowers 15 unelected bureaucrats to decide which services Medicare will cover and how much doctors will be reimbursed. Like a sumo wrestler wearing spandex, it simply tries to cram a growing program into a smaller window, which can only lead to service cuts and care rationing.

My cellphone is so old, I might be able to use it to call the 1989 Packers to urge them not to draft Tony Mandarich. But my second call (priorities, people) would be to Americans of the past, urging them to elect leaders who were serious about keeping our entitlement programs solvent for future generations.

Milwaukee Journal Sentinel

OBAMACARE'S DISAPPEARING INK

Aug. 17, 2013

On the day President Barack Obama signed the Affordable Care Act into law, he was overflowing with confidence. "Today we are affirming that essential truth," Obama said, "a truth every generation is called to rediscover for itself, that we are not a nation that scales back its aspirations."

Yet since that day in March 2010, Obama has done a great deal of scaling back aspirations, as if the 22 pens he used to sign Obamacare were filled with disappearing ink. In the past three years, Obama's Health and Human Services Secretary Kathleen Sebelius has granted hundreds of waivers to well-connected unions and special interests, allowing them to escape Obamacare's tight grip.

Soon after the law began to unravel, the president unilaterally suspended a portion of the law that required most businesses to purchase health insurance for their employees. This followed a decision to suspend a cap on out-of-pocket expenses, which the administration feared would drive premiums upward. The administration also delayed implementation of a plan to verify program eligibility, instead trusting enrollees to sign up via the "honor system."

All these changes begat perhaps Obama's most egregious edict, which was to provide a 70% insurance subsidy for members of Congress and their staffs — many of which rake in over $100,000 per year.

Thus, through executive fiat, the bill now looks very different than the one Obama signed three years ago. In a recent press conference, the president said he had to circumvent the legislative process to make these changes because we aren't in a "normal political environment."

But the U.S. Constitution does not say the president can shirk his duty to take care "that the laws be faithfully executed" whenever the "political environment" might be uncomfortable. We never hear wedding vows that allow a man to take a woman "for better or for worse, in sickness and in health, to love and to cherish; until death do us part, or until she gets too fat or a better option comes along."

Further, the law — which it was clear nobody fully understood at the time of its passage — is now a fundamentally different law than Congress passed in 2010. There are a lot of Democratic senators and representatives who were swept out of office in the anti-Obamacare election of 2010, which gave control of the House of Representatives back to Republicans. With Obama backpedaling so quickly on his signature piece of legislation, how does Russ Feingold feel now, knowing he's no longer in the Senate because he stuck his neck out in favor of a bill that the president doesn't even support anymore?

But perhaps the most corrosive effect of Obama's unilateral dismantling of his law is on the legislative process itself. Now it appears all new laws that are passed are provisional until the president can adequately feel out the "political environment." Why spend days, months and years working on passing bills, when, even if they earn the president's signature, they can still be gutted by executive decree based on whether it will make him or her look bad in the next election.

If there's one thing of which the American people have grown weary, it is the constant interjection of unserious politics into the serious business of writing laws. But Obama now has conflated the two — if presidents can nullify congressional actions, laws are only as good as the next election tells us they should be.

Obama will get a pass from Democrats, as they will argue that the law contains a great deal of executive flexibility in the rules process. (Also, it puts Republicans in the weird position of complaining about rolling back Obamacare's major tenets, which they would normally rush to support.)

But Obama shouldn't get any more slack just because it is his own law he is undercutting. The next logical step is for presidents to stop enforcing laws passed by previous congresses and signed by different executives. In fact, Obama has done just that, with his Attorney General, Eric Holder, ordering U.S. attorneys to stop charging nonviolent, non-gang related defendants with crimes that carry mandatory minimum sentences. The Obama administration also announced that they would cease enforcing immigration laws as they pertain to young illegal immigrants brought to this country by their parents.

Of course, the Obamacare disaster could all have been avoided. Instead of ramming through enormous, complicated bills (and, according to then-Speaker Nancy Pelosi, learning what is in the bill by passing it), Congress should take the time to vet legislation that fundamentally changes our lives. It is clear the administration didn't know how all the widgets of this bill fit together, and it is now up to Obama's eraser to change things.

Just in time for the 2014 elections.

Milwaukee Journal Sentinel

YES, THE GOP HAS A PLAN

December 7, 2013

For most Americans, the last two months of even-numbered years are a time to exhale and enjoy the peace and quiet after campaign season. We apply a pleasing exfoliating scrub to our brains in order to forget all the muck we just witnessed during the November elections.

But while most campaign shenanigans are worth blocking from memory, some are discarded too quickly. For instance, hardly anyone can remember the health plan Sen. John McCain pushed during his 2008 campaign against future-President Barack Obama. Had McCain won, his plan would have provided a more common-sense, consumer-based alternative to the disaster that has become Obamacare. But instead, it has been cast into the dust bin of history.

Yet the erstwhile "McCaincare" does still serve a useful purpose: It exposes the fraudulence of the Democrats' most recent talking point, that Republicans have "no alternate plan" to the Affordable Care Act.

On CNN, Democratic strategist Donna Brazile recently said that Republicans were "not offering an alternative," adding that, "They're not giving people who are desperately seeking health care an option to even enroll in something that they can afford." Washington Post columnist Kathleen Parker said Republicans "appear to be rooting only for failure."

The "GOP doesn't have a plan" argument by the left is doubly obnoxious. First, even if it were true, Democrats would never support a plan Republicans came up with. So they feign outrage that the GOP doesn't have a plan they would oppose anyway.

Second, Republicans do have plans. Plenty of them. And they talk about them a lot. Anyone pushing the narrative that the GOP is devoid of alternatives generally has run out of ways to defend Obamacare. In fact, Democrats would have the public believe Obamacare was passed because Republicans wake up in the morning craving to deny people health care, and the GOP would have gotten away with killing reform if it weren't for that meddling Obama. (Picture U.S. Rep. Paul Ryan in his office, shaking his fist and yelling "outsmarted again!")

But in contrast to the ACA's government control and individual mandates, McCain's plan would have created a larger national insurance market and pushed health care decisions into the hands of consumers. It would have taxed employer health care plans as income, then granted individuals a $2,500 federal tax rebate ($5,000 for families) to purchase insurance in the private market where plans have to compete. This would incentivize individuals to move to low-premium, high-deductible plans that tend to be less expensive.

These fundamentals of McCain's plan have made their way into an Obamacare alternative plan currently being circulated in the House of Representatives. In its current iteration, the plan would give a $7,500 tax deduction to each individual and a $20,000 deduction to each family to purchase insurance in the private market. (I would argue that this should instead be a refundable tax credit, in order to help low-income individuals who may not have enough income to use the full deduction.)

Further, the plan would provide federal assistance for high-risk pools to cover individuals with pre-existing conditions and decouple health insurance from employment. According to an analysis of a similar plan, this option would cover 8 million more Americans than the Affordable Care Act does by 2015.

Naturally, liberals bristle at the notion that health care can be treated like any other product in the free market. But Obama himself has insisted that the ACA uses those very free-market forces to keep costs down. In a Nov. 14 speech, Obama said the health insurance exchange "marketplaces" would create "a place where people can shop and through competition get a better deal for the health insurance that their families need."

The current GOP proposal actually could work well in concert with Ryan's "premium support" plan, which would grant seniors a sum-certain amount to choose from a variety of health plans based on their needs. The program is means-tested, meaning the lowest-income seniors get the largest benefit.

Ironically, Democrats have spent years attacking Ryan for his health care reform plan, while now complaining that Republicans have no plan. Perhaps their television ad featuring Ryan pushing a wheelchair-bound elderly woman off a cliff was merely a mirage.

In next year's midterm elections, it might just be enough for Republicans to remind voters how toxic Obamacare is. After all, simply putting the brakes on a catastrophic plan seems to be a pretty good plan in and of itself.

But it also would be wise for the GOP to emphasize its own plan, which actually holds care costs down before providing a generous subsidy. Obamacare's failures will suck up a lot of the wattage next fall, but the GOP has a chance to promote a good campaign plan that people might actually remember.

Milwaukee Journal Sentinel

A BROKEN CAMPAIGN PROMISE ON OBAMACARE REPEAL

March 10, 2017

Humorist P.J. O'Rourke once summed up a typical American politician's slate of campaign promises: "Vote for me, folks, and you'll be farting through silk."

If American voters were feeling particularly gassy in 2016, it was because of the steady diet of nonsense being fed to them by the presidential hopefuls. Hillary Clinton thought gender politics was enough to carry her to the White House. Poor Bernie Sanders supporters thought revolution was afoot and we were only a few Sanders spittle-infused arm waves from universal health care and free college.

But the huevos rancheros of all candidates was eventual winner Donald Trump, whose unceasing stream of impossible promises put all others to shame. He was going to be the one to ameliorate any problem any working American had. In fact, Trump was particularly effusive in his desire to scuttle the Affordable Care Act, which he called a "disaster" and a "disgrace."

"It should be repealed and replaced, and if I'm elected we're going to repeal it, replace it with something much better, much better and much less expensive," Trump promised two weeks before the election. In doing so, he was simply recycling the overblown rhetoric of the Republican primary, in which candidates such as Ted Cruz promised to "repeal every word of Obamacare." (A truly savvy GOP candidate would have promised to "burn the original bill, melt down the pen Barack Obama used to sign it, and shoot the press used to print it into outer space.")

Yet when the House Republican plan was revealed this week, it looked far more like a standard pair of tighty whiteys than a pair of fine silk boxers. The plan leaves in place large swaths of the Obamacare framework, including retaining the requirement employers provide health care, the mandate that health plans must cover pre-existing conditions and the provision allowing children up to 26 years old to stay on their parents' health plans. It is a plan with no ideological underpinning that appears to have been stitched together by committee. Republicans appear to be willing to settle for "repair and replace."

On Thursday, House Speaker Paul Ryan held one of his famous PowerPoint-style presentations in an effort to explain the plan. Ryan remarked that the "American Health Care Act" is "the closest we will ever get to repealing and replacing Obamacare," citing the Senate as a major restraint on what the House could expect to enact in the bill.

This is where the hot rhetoric of campaign season meets the cold water of legislative procedure. As Ramesh Ponnuru notes at National Review Online, the need to craft a plan that could pass the Senate heavily influenced the bill, including the mandatory surcharge of 30% for those who drop insurance and attempt to re-enroll when they need it.

Obviously, every bill is influenced by legislative procedure. But this isn't what America signed up for, nor is it what Trump and others promised. For years, Republicans have expounded the need for portable health care untethered to one's job. They've explained how competition within the health care system was necessary to keep costs low and that private insurance is preferable to government dependency — yet this bill incentivizes states to sign up more people for Medicaid over the next three years.

For months, Ryan has had to wake up and eat a bowl of broken glass sent to him by Trump just so he could rewrite Obamacare; now his argument is essentially "it's the best we could do." It is the lesson that Americans will seemingly never learn — digesting legislative reality quickly turns an overblown campaign promise into a great deal of hot air.

Milwaukee Journal Sentinel

TOKE THE HIGH ROAD ON MARIJUANA

December 1, 2012

Traditionally, the truism about marijuana legalization is that if you think it's ever going to happen, you've almost certainly just sampled some yourself.

But with Colorado and Washington having recently legalized marijuana for recreational use, it might be time to re-examine our relationship with the drug and whether the federal government should be dictating marijuana policy to the states where citizens support legalization.

It's difficult to see exactly how different the world would be if states were allowed to dictate their own marijuana policy; it's not like the nation would be overrun by the guy from your dorm who played his guitar at 3 a.m. Currently, marijuana policy represents a facsimile of a world that we'd like to see, not the one that currently exists.

The people who want the drug right now can generally get their hands on it; some cities, such as Madison, have decriminalized "casual" possession in private places. Public possession amounts to a fine of only $100 and isn't considered a crime - you're likely to receive a larger fine for having a Scott Walker bumper sticker on your car. Yet people in Madison still get up, go to work, march on the Capitol and generally manage their lives.

It's difficult to condemn smoking weed when even the current president was once a card-carrying pothead. Back in his Hawaii high school, Barack Obama was part the self-described "Choom Gang," which believed in the doctrine of "Total Absorption" - blazing up in a car with the windows rolled up so you get the benefit of secondhand smoke. What's the lesson to kids here? Smoke weed and you'll only be elected to the presidency twice?

So far, 18 states have legalized medical marijuana, recognizing the need for compassion for the sick. But individual rights shouldn't begin simply because someone contracts a disease; freedom of choice should be extended to everyone. Plus, full legalization would end the ridiculous charade of people pretending they're sick to obtain phony "prescriptions." Generally, these people simply suffer from headaches brought on by lack of awesome weed. (Possible Surgeon General's warning: COULD CAUSE DANCING IN PUBLIC.)

There's actually a very good reason to outlaw most controlled substances - people addicted to them cause significant damage to others. For instance, there's no such thing as a "responsible heroin user." If you live next to someone on methamphetamine, enjoy your new flat screen television, because it'll be gone in a week.

But marijuana is different, especially when compared with Wisconsin's state pastime: drinking. Humorist John Hodgman once imagined society without alcohol: "All the unbroken homes! All of the highway nonfatalities! All of the well-considered tattoos and planned pregnancies and books unwritten by Charles Bukowski!" By contrast, marijuana users generally remain sedentary - and if you've seen some of the heaviest users, it's in society's interest to keep them at home (If only to spare us from speeches about how George Washington grew hemp.)

But even conservatives that might object to legalization of any kind can find refuge in the argument that states should be allowed to decide how best to cater to their own citizens. In 2005, the U.S. Supreme Court decided that California couldn't allow homegrown medical marijuana, deeming it a violation of the broadly interpreted Commerce Clause.

But Justice Clarence Thomas dissented, convincingly writing that our federalist system "allows California and a growing number of other States to decide for themselves how to safeguard the health and welfare of their citizens." Like the death penalty - which actually kills people - if you don't like marijuana, you're free to live in a state that doesn't allow it, or convince your local legislators to change it.

I get it - for social conservatives, starting to legalize drugs is just one more step toward a Gomorrah-like existence with which we are unfamiliar. Suddenly smoking weed isn't a crime, bread is actually bad for you and dudes are marrying other dudes in churches. But for those who are suffering from the angst of progress, come a little closer. I might have something that will take the edge off.

Milwaukee Journal Sentinel

MARIJUANA AS PROHIBITION

January 6, 2018

In 1932, when Supreme Court Justice Louis Brandeis deemed U.S. states "laboratories" for democracy, he couldn't have known that those labs would one day be filled with hydroponic weed.

This week, federalism and marijuana once again found themselves trapped in the same smoke-filled van as U.S. Attorney General Jeff Sessions rescinded a number of Obama-era policies that turned a blind eye as states legalized weed for recreational purposes. During the 2016 presidential campaign, candidate Donald Trump said marijuana enforcement should be left to the states; but on Thursday, White House press secretary Sarah Huckabee Sanders said Trump believes "that we should enforce federal law."

Federal law, of course, bans marijuana sale and use. It is that very restriction to which voters in states all over the country are now objecting. According to an October Gallup poll, 64% of Americans currently believe marijuana should be legalized, up from only 48% as recently as 2012. Amazingly, 51% of Republicans now believe in legalization, up a whopping 9% over just last year. Who knows whether that spike is a cause or effect of the Trump presidency.

In any case, Sessions' edict isn't supposed to be how this all works. Whether a guy can come home from work, fire up a bong, and watch Season Four of Black Mirror shouldn't be dependent on who happens to be president of the United States at any given time. Laws are on the books for a reason – the Attorney General shouldn't be able to just wave a capricious wand and deem things legal or illegal based on his or her mood on any given day

Such a system leaves us where we are right now – with thousands of marijuana farms and weed enthusiasts in a state of legal limbo, not knowing whether they're hardened criminals or productive taxpayers.

That's why lawmakers in states that have legalized recreational marijuana have been fighting Sessions' order. Republican Colorado Sen. Cory Gardner, who initially opposed legalization in his state, has vowed to hold up Department of Justice nominations if Sessions carried out his edict. Gardner said the Attorney General's actions have "trampled on the will of the voters in Colorado and other states."

The most palatable option would be for Congress to pass a law taking marijuana off the federal drug schedule, leaving the legalization choice up to voters in individual states. Democratic New Jersey Sen. Cory Booker has introduced a bill that would repeal the federal ban on weed, but has made it virtually impossible to pass in a Republican Congress by loading it up with trial lawyer-friendly provisions encouraging lawsuits against states that retain their anti-marijuana laws.

The more likely solution is what is happening now, with individual states and local governments rebelling against the federal order. With the quickly changing public perception of pot, it seems certain the courts will have to referee this clash between levels of government.

As recently as 2005, the U.S. Supreme Court decided that California couldn't allow homegrown medical marijuana, deeming it a violation of the broadly interpreted Commerce Clause. But in dissent, Justice Clarence Thomas appeared to see what was on the horizon, writing that the federalist system "allows California and a growing number of other States to decide for themselves how to safeguard the health and welfare of their citizens."

And it appears voters in states all over the nation agree. Currently, 29 states and the District of Columbia have laws legalizing marijuana in some form. On January 1 of this year, recreational pot became legal in California, which may have precipitated Sessions' new order.

Ironically, Sessions' new "law and order" plan may achieve just the opposite effect, driving marijuana sales back underground where they were primarily controlled by illegal cartels and other black market agents. It's as if we have learned nothing from the Prohibition Era, where underground liquor made with paint thinner and other dangerous chemicals killed thousands of Americans.

Similarly, if Sessions' goal is to keep young people from getting high, evidence shows that legalization is the way to do it. In Colorado, teen marijuana use dropped sharply after legalization, suggesting the drug's allure may be inversely proportional to the chance mom and dad are allowed to do it.

Unfortunately for marijuana activists, Congress is likely to take longer than a killer drum solo to make any changes in the federal law. Until that happens, it will be up to voters in the states to defy an attorney general who, with the stroke of a pen, just turned them into criminals. Jeff Sessions made the order – now let him try to enforce it.

USA Today

THE BENEFIT OF GUNS THAT AREN'T FIRED

Jan. 08, 2013

In January 1883, Lucius W. Nieman sat in the office of his brand new publication, the Milwaukee Daily Journal, when an angry acting troupe stormed into his office. The Journal had been writing extensively about the Jan. 10 Newhall House fire and had been critical of the hotel's owners for ignoring warnings that the building was a fire hazard. In an editorial, Nieman suggested the actors discontinue their show to allow the families of the fire's victims to mourn.

The actors asked Nieman who wrote the editorial suggesting their play be shut down.

"I did," replied Nieman.

"You'd better write another saying you've changed your mind," responded one of the actors.

"But, gentlemen, I haven't changed my mind," replied Nieman.

"Then we'll take it out of your hide," was the reply, as the actors moved closer to the editor's desk. Nieman reached into his drawer and pulled out what he would later call a "horse pistol" and began waving it around. The gun wasn't loaded, but the actors turned tail and fled the office. The paper, just several months old, was saved.

Historically, the newspaper business and guns have been inextricably intertwined. During World War I, the Milwaukee Journal received daily threats from some of the city's German residents, who thought the paper was too anti-German in its coverage. (Many believed the paper was receiving direct gold payments from Lord Northcliffe, founder of the London Daily Mail.)

Steel gratings were placed over windows at the Journal's headquarters to discourage bomb throwers, and most executives began keeping loaded revolvers in their desks. After taking a shortcut through an alley to get to work one day, a young copy editor named Alfred E. Pahlke was almost shot by one of the riflemen hired to protect the building.

Yet even with armed reporters, executives and guards, the paper remained safe. It is this paper that you now hold in your hands or read on your iPad (or, best-case scenario, have read to you while your servants feed you grapes). Without the protection guns provided, the paper may never have survived - yet nary a shot had to be fired.

We often hear about guns when they are involved in a horrific tragedy, such as Sandy Hook or Aurora. As a Second Amendment supporter, it sickens me to have to defend guns under such heartbreaking circumstances. But that's just the nature of news. We hear about all the terrible things guns do when tragedy strikes, but there's little attention paid to the benefit of firearms that aren't used at all.

We'd see those benefits if America's gun owners were to engage in a little test. Suppose everyone with a gun in his or her home decided to put a blue ribbon on the front door to indicate there was a firearm inside. It is almost certain that plenty of people without guns would be right there, pasting up blue ribbons, in order to prevent their homes from becoming a late-night fire sale for burglars.

In New York's upscale Westchester and Rockland counties, the local newspaper recently lent credence to this hypothetical. The Journal News published an interactive map showing where people with gun licenses lived, which, of course, put a neon "open for business" sign outside any home that wasn't listed. As pointed out to Fox News by Walter T. Shaw, an ex-burglar whom the FBI blames for more than 3,000 break-ins: "Having a list of who has a gun is like gold - why rob that house when you can hit the one next door, where there are no guns?"

Clearly, the best kind of gun is one that never has to be fired. In the early 1900s, gang-style wars broke out in cities such as Chicago when newsboys claimed certain city corners to sell papers from competing publications. On occasion, some paperboys were kidnapped and murdered over turf disputes in what became known as Chicago's "circulation wars."

And while those sad episodes are the ones that catch our attention, we also should remember the dog that isn't barking. During the quiet times in between tragic shootings, the mere specter of firearms keeps us safe from the bad guys. We just need to work to make sure those quiet times last much longer.

Milwaukee Journal Sentinel

THE TEA PARTY IS IN NEED OF A MAKEOVER

July 3, 2014

If I were a betting man, I would wager that Project Runway fashion guru Tim Gunn isn't a conservative. But if the tea party wants to, as Gunn would say, "make it work," it should give him a call.

Now nearing five years old, the tea party is desperately in need of a makeover. But it's going to need more than power-clashing ties and skinny jeans to turn the public's opinion around. In the most recent Marquette University Law School poll, only 23% of Wisconsinites said they had a favorable view of the tea party, with 47% saying they viewed the tea party unfavorably.

This fact is remarkable given that respondents overwhelmingly supported tea party positions on issues such as opposition to Obamacare, photo identification for voting, state debt and mistrust of government.

This is why Democrats now try to taint fairly standard Republican candidates with the "tea party" label. For instance, note how often U.S. Sen. Ron Johnson (R-Wis.) is labeled a "tea party" senator — despite the fact that during his 2010 campaign, Johnson often had a combative relationship with tea party groups that supported his primary opponent.

The first step in tea party rebranding should be changing the movement's name. Sure, we get the connection to the Boston Tea Party of 1773, when the Sons of Liberty protested a new British-enacted tax by dumping 342 chests of tea into Boston Harbor. But it may not be the best idea to name your 21st-century anti-tax movement after a singular event that occurred back when it was still legal to, say, own other human beings.

The "tea party" moniker makes the movement appear as if it is hopelessly stuck in the distant past. Sure, the principles of the Founding Fathers are important, and reminding everyone of their intent is a useful public service. But there has to be a more culturally relevant way to make those points. To modern Americans, the tea party conjures images of men dressing up in tricorn hats and yelling about what James Madison would think about mandatory birth control.

(And look, I'm all for Founding Father cosplay, just as I fully respect people who dress up at science fiction conventions to demonstrate their enthusiasm — but I'm not sure I would want some guy dressed like R2-D2 in charge of my Social Security.)

Instead, the tea party should rename itself with something more modern, stylish and popular. Pick up on a current buzz phrase and call itself the "Locally Sourced" party. Or instill fear in the left by calling itself something like the "Laser Sharks" party. Or cash in on something universally beloved and just rename itself "Tim Howard." ("Swatting away tax increases!")

It's not as though a name change is unprecedented. Years ago, the left eschewed the "liberal" label in favor of "progressive." And not only would a new name rebrand the right, it would prevent liberals from using "tea" in their typical vulgar epithet for the movement. (Personal side note: Tea is gross.)

Part two of the tea party makeover would be to lose some weight. Mostly, this includes the poundage represented by members hatching schemes such as urging states to secede from the union and trying to call a new constitutional convention.

Further, the movement's leaders should be quick to condemn members that engage in distasteful and counterproductive rhetoric.

Granted, the tea party exists as a counter to the party's "establishment." It is the right wing's incorrigible little brother, helping to drag conservatives out of their moderate Bush-era funk. And it should continue to be insurance against the GOP once again lapsing into a big-government malaise.

But there are limits to how far it should go in pushing around the right-wing establishment. Simply being louder and more ardent doesn't earn you points with the public. Sure, I could go stand outside the Capitol, sing at the top of my lungs and offend the "people with ears" establishment, but it probably won't earn me any converts.

Of course, much of the bad publicity the tea party garners is due to the Democrats' constant demonization of the movement. That's not going to stop.

As a counter, the tea party could go the other way, and take on a role similar to that of the heel in professional wrestling. It could recognize its unpopularity and dramatically milk it for the media attention. (Suggestion: Every tea party rally should feature a guy in the background with a stack of fanned-out $100 bills like Virgil used to do for the "Million Dollar Man" Ted DiBiase.)

Then again, professional wrestling might take exception to being compared with a system as dishonest as the federal government.

Milwaukee Journal Sentinel

BORN THIS WAY

Jan. 01, 2013

When Lady Gaga released the ubiquitous song "Born this Way" in 2011, it was immediately adopted as the official anthem of the gay and lesbian movement. The song's uplifting message tells people of all ages to be proud of who they are, because "he" (the song recognizes the existence of God and that "he" is a "him") made you "perfect."

Channeling his inner Gaga, future Republican vice presidential nominee Paul Ryan echoed this sentiment on the LGBT community, saying, "It's just who they are. They were just created that way."

Despite being a big dance hit, the song actually wades into some pretty contentious territory regarding what is learned and what is innate (the whole "nature" vs. "nurture" argument.) For instance, can the concept of being "born this way" also be applied to . . . conservatives?

A growing body of scientific research says yes. In 2005, a group of university researchers released a study indicating that between one-third and one-half of an individual's political orientation is hereditary. Whether a child grows up in a conservative or liberal household accounts for much less of their political ideology than simply genetics.

The researchers looked at sets of identical twins (who share all their genes and usually their childhood environments) vs. fraternal twins (who share half their genes and usually their childhood environments) and found that identical twins are much more likely to share ideologies, even if they grew up in different households (separated by, for instance, adoption).

If the childhood environment has less to do with the formation of political ideology, it would explain the difference between me (a conservative) and my dear younger sister (a college professor who is just to the left of Trotsky). We grew up two years apart, in the same house, with the same parents, watching the same crappy TV shows, going to the same schools with the same teachers. Yet we couldn't be more different politically.

The idea that one's political philosophy is hereditary is problematic to people with strong ideologies on both sides. We all like to think we came to our well-considered opinions about politics by staying up all night, drinking scotch, stroking our beards and reading Burke and Hobbes. Reasoning your way into a political position gives it a greater weight than if it were just implanted there genetically.

In fact, the idea that traits are heritable at all has been a great point of contention in psychology for decades. The idea fell out of vogue in the social sciences in the late 20th century, as it opened the door for some to argue that a specific race or sex could be innately inferior to another. (See the controversy caused by former Harvard president Larry Summers in 2005, when he suggested that innate differences between men and women may be why fewer females enter the fields of math and science. Some believe this comment alone hastened Summers' exit from his presidency.)

But more recently, the role of genetics in behavior has freed itself from such political correctness. University of Virginia psychologist Eric Turkheimer stated that "All human behavioral traits are heritable," that "the empirical facts are in" and that they are "no longer a matter of serious controversy."

But how does genetics inform someone's position on abortion or fracking or gun control or the merits of Big Bird? For one, studies have shown that conservatives and liberals have different brains - they react differently to different circumstances. Liberal brains emit glutamate, serotonin and dopamine differently that conservative brains when confronted with certain hypothetical situations.

It is this basic foundation that may cause those with conservative genes to seek out a life path that confirms their ideals, including surrounding themselves with like-minded people who help cultivate their specific opinions on any number of political issues. Same goes with progressives.

And, of course, just because genes may play a strong part in ideology, it doesn't mean it plays the entire part - personal experience is certainly in the mix, as well. As University of Virginia psychologist Jonathan Haidt says in his outstanding book, "The Righteous Mind: Why Good People are Divided by Politics and Religion," genetics are merely a "first draft" of human development.

But if ideology is truly hereditary, it has all sorts of political and policy implications for the nation. If conservatives want to take back the White House, the answer may not be in attracting new voters - it may be to simply make more new conservatives than the left. Time to light some candles and get to work, right-wing lovers.

Milwaukee Journal Sentinel

CAR WARS

May 28, 2013

Near my house, an obscenely large grocery store just opened. Its vulgar size marks it as a temple to the calorie — a tater tot Taj Mahal, if you will. (It even has an actual bar within the store, so you can pick up some dates in the fruit and vegetable aisle before you walk over and try to pick up some dates of the human variety.)

Given the store's recent grand opening, navigating the parking lot has been tricky, especially since a number of spots are set aside for those needing special assistance. The disabled, of course, are allotted their share of spots by city ordinance. Some stores have been setting aside spots for senior citizens. Others even reserve prime spots for expectant mothers.

But this new grocery store has reserved a good number of its best spots for a group wholly undeserving of such a designation. When cruising through the parking aisles, one can see empty spots marked "LEV" — or "low emission vehicle." In essence, the store is trying to encourage people to drive their electric or hybrid cars to the store, in order to promote the façade that they are a "green" business.

Of course, setting aside special spots for the disabled, elderly and pregnant is a really nice thing to do. One doesn't get to go home and stop being disabled for a little while; making it easier for handicapped shoppers to get in and out of the store is simply compassionate.

But exactly what hardship are we ameliorating by giving prime parking to Toyota Priuses? Are hybrid drivers oppressed by having to buy half as much gas as the rest of us? They already carry around the self-satisfaction of saving the environment (just ask them, they'll tell you) — being given front-row parking is just an extra ego boost. (It's particularly ironic that these people use energy-efficient vehicles to shop at a store that uses as much gas and electricity as Luxembourg.)

Further, when we talk about "low-emission vehicles," you have to ask: low-emission compared to what? Any car manufactured in the past decade is infinitely more fuel-efficient and burns cleaner than the environmental widowmakers of the 1950s. I'm pretty sure that in the 1970s, in his car that got roughly a half-mile per gallon, my dad had to stop for gas on the way to get gas.

Simply driving an LEV doesn't necessarily equate to having a smaller carbon footprint. With the existence of these parking spots, an electric car driver who spends the rest of his day pouring motor oil into sewers or on the Internet purchasing cowboy hats made out of baby seals gets better parking than those who try to live sensibly.

In many cases, it's not certain that these spots will make any difference at all in the environment. Let's say enough people decide that the store's General Tso's chicken is so delicious, they have to drive three miles to get it. Even if those people have cars that burn half as much gas, they will still burn more fuel than people who drive a normal car and live a mile away. (Please put down your pencils, the exam is over.) The more successful the store, the more fossil fuels will be burned, period.

Wisconsin has seen a green car parking backlash before. In 2009, a tin-eared University of Wisconsin-Fox Valley campus dean suggested that more spots be set aside for hybrids. The students revolted, noting that parking at the commuter campus was scarce, and few of them could afford fancy LEVs that ran between $22,000 and $50,000 apiece. Essentially, the campus' do-gooderism was going to price some students out of being able to park at the campus where they already forked over boatloads for tuition.

And there still appears to be a question about whether the city can even impose fines for parking in a spot reserved for a green car. According to the Madison police, a business has to call and complain before a $30 private parking citation can be issued — as opposed to handicapped spots, which police can issue "on sight" because such spots are mandated by city ordinance. Madison's parking enforcement supervisor, Stefanie Nielsen, told the Wisconsin State Journal that the city has never gotten a single complaint for unauthorized parking in a spot designated for an LEV.

I can think of a dozen classifications of people I would give preferred parking to over electric car owners: veterans, single moms, people who don't pay for groceries with checks, those who refuse to wear sandals with socks, etc. But further segregating the parking lot based upon which among us are worthy is an exercise in parking eugenics — the unwashed are forced to trudge long distances to buy their microwave mac and cheese. Soon, it will be like "Game of Thrones," with each group going to war to claim their territories within the asphalt expanse of the parking lot.

Of course, the store is free to do what it wants. If businesses want to give their parking spots to cars that run on wheat grass and bongwater, that's fine. But it doesn't mean I have to shop there.

Milwaukee Journal Sentinel

IMMIGRATION REFORM ISN'T 'AMNESTY'

May 21, 2013

If, as the saying goes, "words are the clothes that thoughts wear," American politics has become a full-fledged masquerade ball.

Clothes, after all, can hide people's true identity, in the same way words can cloak their true intent. This is why political adversaries choose their language carefully — the words one uses can make all the difference in framing an issue for a malleable public.

For instance, supporters of government funding for children to attend private schools couch their side in the language of "choice," while opponents opt for the less popular term "vouchers." Opponents of Gov. Scott Walker's plan to virtually eliminate public-sector collective bargaining decried their loss of bargaining "rights," knowing that the public was less likely to support revocation of a "right" than a "privilege." The language of "pro-choice" vs. "pro-life" has become a pillar of American political discourse.

Recently, the word "amnesty" has become a shibboleth for those opposing efforts to create a pathway to citizenship for the 12 million immigrants in America illegally. While Republicans such as Sen. Marco Rubio of Florida and Rep. Paul Ryan of Wisconsin have supported a framework to bring illegal immigrants into the nation's workforce, other conservatives have derided their efforts as granting "amnesty" to those who entered the country illegally.

Most notably, a recent report by the conservative Heritage Foundation referred to the proposed legalization process as "amnesty," while estimating the Rubio plan would cost over $6.3 trillion to implement. One of the report's authors, Jason Richwine, recently resigned after it came to light that he previously had made comments suggesting that Hispanic people have lower IQs than white people.

Yet Rubio's plan isn't "amnesty" in any sense of the word. The government will not just wave a magic wand and grant citizenship to those who have not earned it. The so-called Gang of Eight bill requires undocumented workers to pay penalties, then go through a process in order to be granted legal status. Under the plan, it will take a typical illegal immigrant 13 years to become a full U.S. citizen and blocks those who have committed a felony or three or more misdemeanors. Further, the "Registered Provisional Immigrant" program only begins once a number of border security requirements have been satisfied.

Despite the best efforts of those opposed to the plan, Americans seem to be on board with a program allowing earned legalization. One recent poll found that 71% of all voters, including 74% of conservative Republicans and 78% of liberal Democrats, supported a plan similar to the Gang of Eight proposal.

Arguments against immigration reform aren't without merit. Such a plan would reward those who came here illegally, and the federal government hasn't shown it is serious about shoring up the Mexican border.

But the anti-"amnesty" crowd can never answer perhaps the most important question of all: What do we do with the 12 million illegal immigrants currently living in America? Suddenly, a federal government incapable of treating tax-exempt organizations equitably is going to be able to surgically round up 12 million people and extract them from the country?

Perhaps we were too lax in allowing illegal immigrants here in the first place; but are we going to continue to relegate them to second-class status, especially once they have given birth to children who are U.S. citizens? Will they continue to exist in the shadows like apparitions? Here but not really here?

This is another fatal flaw with the Heritage study: it assumes once the legalization process begins, that immigrants will remain destitute, and therefore dependent on social services, rather than creating economic activity through better jobs. A recent letter to Ryan from the Congressional Budget Office estimates that enacting immigration reform will increase the nation's Gross Domestic Product once implemented. In a statement, Ryan said that "a proper accounting of immigration reform should take into account these dynamic effects."

Just as I will continue to wear shirts that try to obfuscate my belly's inexorable march outward, immigration reform opponents will continue to confuse the issue by using misleading words to characterize the problem. Opposing a pathway to citizenship is a legitimate position, but the linguistic battle should be fought on even ground. Consequently, we should not grant amnesty to those who insist on using the word "amnesty."

Milwaukee Journal Sentinel

KEEP FOREIGN BRAINPOWER IN AMERICA

September 24, 2013

In the mid-1990s, one of my Asian-American friends — a pretty ingenious guy — began applying for medical schools; but, alas, he was denied entry into some schools in the Northwest that he really wanted to attend.

Later, he told me one school sent him a letter telling him he wasn't granted admission because it wasn't "accepting any more international students." Never mind the fact that despite his Vietnamese name, he was raised in Madison from the age of 1 — he's as American as Harley-Davidson, baseball and naked lady truck mudflaps.

Set aside, for a moment, the idiocy of trying to divine someone's nationality based on his or her name alone. Equally as questionable is the university's quota system, which alerted it to the idea that it had "too many" international students. Apparently, diversity is important, unless too many qualified students from overseas want an education.

Yet universities likely take their cue from the U.S. government, which has a similarly backward "catch and release" policy with regard to international students. Brilliant scholars come from around the globe to study in American colleges, then head home, victims of a restrictive immigration policy. According to studies, nearly 47% of foreign-born students return to their home countries after receiving an American college education.

Currently, the United States only grants a maximum of 140,000 employment-related green cards per year. (Other green cards can be earned by winning the ominously named "diversity lottery," which even George Orwell might find unsettling.) Green cards generally allow college graduates to stay in the country as long as they are gainfully employed. Each country, no matter the size, can receive a maximum of 7% of green cards. Unbelievably, Chinese citizens are granted as many cards as, say, citizens of a tiny island country.

Ideally, these green cards would be granted to bright international students who want to stay in the U.S. and make a go at creating American-style economic activity. But the nation's colleges crank out roughly a million international students per year; as columnist George Will has noted, the government could add a zero to the end of "140,000," and it still may not be enough green cards to satisfy the demand of international students.

Several years ago, George Lightbourn and Sammis White authored a paper for the Wisconsin Policy Research Institute that demonstrated the positive impact keeping foreign students in Milwaukee could have on the region. According to their data, Milwaukee has lagged other large cities in attracting foreign-born college graduates; in 2006, only 0.7% of metro Milwaukee's college-educated population moved from abroad — approximately half of the attraction rate of Chicago (1.4%) and Minneapolis (1.2%) and less than one-third of the attraction rate of Austin and Seattle.

Further, 44% of the population of foreign-born college graduates in America were Asian and more likely to be found working in science, engineering or computer-related occupations — areas with fantastic growth potential. A full two-thirds of doctoral candidates in engineering and science in America are foreign-born, destined to realize their potential overseas.

Recognizing the opportunity the U.S. green card limits affords them, several European countries have implemented a "blue card" system to attract all the international brainpower America is throwing overboard. The expedited application process allows countries such as Germany, France and Italy to siphon off talent trained — often at taxpayer expense — in America.

Much of the debate surrounding immigration in America these days deals with the front end: how we keep unskilled illegal immigrants from flooding into the country and taking the jobs Americans won't do. But equally important is a discussion about immigration on the back end: how we keep bright, college-educated immigrants in the country who will do the jobs most American's can't do.

Not only should America be encouraging more foreign students in its universities; its federal government should be ensuring more students stay here and realize the real potential our country offers.

In recent years, "green card" has become a pejorative term; it is reserved as a linguistic shiv, meant to discredit someone as a "real American." But "real Americans" need "real jobs," and the brainpower held by international students, trained in our own universities, can go a long way to restoring the "American" way of life.

Milwaukee Journal Sentinel

IMMIGRANTS AS ALLIES

March 14, 2017

In the early 1750s, Benjamin Franklin was distressed at how many criminals England was shipping across the Atlantic to America's shores. In fact, as payback for this practice, Franklin proposed a reward to any American citizen who rounded up a boatload of rattlesnakes, sailed them over to England, and deposited them in the gardens of the members of Parliament.

Yet Franklin didn't even consider this to be an even trade. "The Rattlesnake gives warning before he attempts his mischief, which the convict does not," he noted.

It is unclear whether President Trump is aware of Franklin's strategy (or if he even knows who Franklin is — "Ben Franklin, great guy, been getting recognized more and more"), but Trump's immigration strategy tracks closely with that of Franklin. Trump is, after all, the candidate who said Mexico was "forcing" criminals and rapists into America. It is why Trump has tried to rally support for his two travel bans by warning of the terrorist element trying to infiltrate the country.

Or, as Franklin put it, "Oh, what a fearful thing it is to have so many thousands of unruly and brazen sinners come into this free air and unfenced country!"

There is a difference, of course, because the immigrants Trump is concerned about have a distinctly different skin tone as those Franklin warned about. For instance, Americans aren't staying up at night worrying about the infiltration of Canadians into their culture, even though Seth Rogen almost started a nuclear war with North Korea.

(Franklin actually mostly disdained the Germans, as he thought German women were too unsightly — he once actually proposed a government subsidy to induce English men to marry German women, in order to dilute the German ugly gene pool.)

Rather, for Trump's supporters, the "criminals washing up on our shores" argument appears mostly to be a Trojan Horse for another argument – that immigrants are costing America its traditions and identity.

This case has been made explicitly by Trump senior advisor Steve Bannon, who has openly described his "alt-right" movement as "nationalist" and who has publicly complained that there's too much legal immigration to America going on. In an interview in March of last year, Bannon noted that 20% of Americans are immigrants, and deemed that fact to be a "massive problem." Later, Bannon would complain that "two-thirds or three-quarters" of Silicon Valley CEOs are Asian, adding that "a country is more than an economy. We're a civic society."

It seems unlikely that Asian billionaires are out prowling the streets threatening to break into our homes, so it's clear what's at work here. A large segment of Trump supporters yearn for a more traditional America — one in which people went to church with their neighbors, where couples stayed married and raised kids, and where a working class job could provide for a whole family.

Clearly, the nationalists see people with different skin color as a code for a changing world that they don't recognize or understand. And they see immigrants as watering down the America they once knew, contributing to the fact that Trump beat Hillary Clinton among voters over 65 by eight percentage points.

It's not necessarily bad to wistfully remember America of decades past. And Trump is certainly within his rights to limit who enters the country — big, beautiful wall and all.

But the answer to Making America Great Again isn't stigmatization, it is assimilation. It is misguided to believe that new immigrants don't share in that desire for tradition or family or work. Many of them have strong family bonds, go to difficult jobs every day, and obey the law. (Numerous studies have concluded immigrants are less likely to commit crimes than native-born Americans.)

The arguments people make against these immigrants are the same ones that have been made against Italians, Germans, Jews, the Irish and others for more than a century: they're uneducated, they steal American jobs, they have too many babies, etc. But ultimately they all assimilated and, ironically, it is now their descendants who are demanding America return to some imaginary golden age of purity.

The "nationalists" should not ignore immigrants and minorities and write them off as combatants in a cultural war. Instead, the new conservative "America first" crowd should support policies that make immigrants just as proud to be American as they are. Demonstrate to them that lower taxes and less regulation can lead to better jobs and higher pay. Give them more options to educate their kids through school choice programs. Let them freely practice their religion without government interference.

Progress will only be made when conservatives engage and persuade immigrants and other minorities that being traditional doesn't mean living in the past. Republicans have a potential cultural partner waiting for them; they should resist the temptation to fear immigrants like a bucket of Ben Franklin's snakes.

USA Today

TAYLOR SWIFT'S IMMIGRATION POLICY

September 6, 2017

To date, President Donald Trump's relationship with Congress has played out in public with the same diplomacy and subtlety as a Taylor Swift song. Like the delightfully vengeful pop queen, Trump can't help but use his megaphone to settle old scores - earlier in August, he even used a presidential signing statement attached to a bill relating to Russia sanctions to throw shade at the legislature, saying "Congress could not even negotiate a health care bill after seven years of talking."

(Or as noted political philosopher Swift recently put it, "I don't like your little games / Don't like your tilted stage / The role you made me play / Of the fool, no, I don't like you.")

Of course, Trump's dig at House and Senate leaders was to distance himself from the disastrous health care reform collapse that happened on his watch. The American president, perhaps unaware he was speaking aloud, actually said that when Obamacare collapsed, he wouldn't "own it."

But despite believing Congress to be too inept to pass a health care bill he sought "on day one," Trump suddenly has a new task for the House and Senate: take the heat off of him for repealing the Deferred Action for Childhood Arrivals, or DACA, program.

On Tuesday, Attorney General Jeff Sessions announced Trump's plans to rescind DACA, a program that protects children of illegal immigrants brought to the U.S. as children. But Trump's proposal leaves DACA in place for six months, pushing the responsibility off on congressional Republicans to find a solution during that grace period. If they don't,

Trump can then blame Congress for throwing innocent children out of the country, as he invokes the Taylor Swift principle of governance: "Look What You Made Me Do."

It's obvious why Trump would suddenly trust a legislative body that he clearly believes is a pack of inept jackanapes; the president is dumping the issue squarely in Congress' lap so he can keep his campaign promise to rescind the program, but so he can also eventually sign something that saves him from that same promise. (Of course, he's already tweeted that he might not mean it.)

But if Trump's ultimatum to Congress gets the House and Senate to approve a legal framework for determining who stays and who goes, it actually will have been a success.

The DACA program itself was created by an executive order by President Barack Obama back in 2012, without any input from Congress. Now Democrats are learning that an executive order's greatest strength is also its primary weakness — when a president writes sweeping immigration reform on his own, the next executive can just as easily rescind it. In a sense, Obama's actions on DACA are akin to the U.S. Supreme Court decreeing same-sex marriage to be the law of the land; it's a positive outcome from a deeply flawed process.

Yet if Congress remains constipated and can't produce an immigration reform bill, Trump will have made a tremendous mistake. In conservative circles, the entire backbone of the pro-life community relies on the idea that pre-born children are "innocent" — the same presumption of innocence should be applied to young children who have been born and then carted to America by their undocumented parents. These children are in many ways completely indistinguishable from any other children who grow up in America, and banishing them to countries they have never known would be unconscionable.

But if the prospect of the deportation of innocents provokes Congress into passing a bill that protects the status of so-called "DREAMers," then Trump's bluff will have been worth the temporary national indigestion it caused.

It is often said that in 1895, the state of Ohio had only two cars, and they crashed into each other; under similar odds, it appears Donald Trump may have collided with an idea for good governance. Of course, Trump's move is political — but there's no rule that says decisions made for political purposes also can't be the right ones.

USA Today

WHEN ANTI-BIAS PROGRAMS BACKFIRE

May 4, 2013

"Racist," said the late, great essayist Christopher Hitchens, "is an accusation that must be made good upon, or fully retracted."

But in modern America, there appears to be a caveat: Even if there is no evidence of actual racism, the charge may remain in force as long as there's a hefty payday at the end of the line.

Recent revelations about the Obama administration's Justice and Agriculture departments confirm this unfortunate fact. So far, the two departments have committed $1.33 billion in awards to supposedly rectify past discrimination against African-American, Hispanic and female farmers - including thousands of individuals who never actually claimed racial bias in court.

In 1997, the federal government faced a complaint from 91 black farmers who claimed they had been denied loans from biased federal officers. In what is now known as the "Pigford" lawsuit, there was virtually no evidence of any discrimination, and the farmers were eventually rebuffed by the U.S. Supreme Court. Yet the litigants didn't drop their cause, and in 2010, the Obama administration began handing out $50,000 awards to black farmers - a framework that eventually became a magnet for fraud.

When enterprising attorneys got wind of the cash awards, some began combing impoverished areas and rounding up potential claimants, including some who had never planted a single seed in the ground (these came to be known as "attempted farmers"). According to The New York Times, the program saw applicants who were 4 and 5 years old; in some cases, every single member of a family would apply. One woman told the paper she received an award in the name of her dead father. Thirty percent of all payments, or $290 million, went to urban counties where there are virtually no farms.

While there are only 18,000 black farmers in America, the awards eventually yielded 100,000 claimants. Attorneys for these individuals, whose claims total over $4.4 billion, stand to make more than $130 million in fees representing them.

The Pigford scandal would be shocking enough if there wasn't ample precedent for taking fraudulent government programs and cloaking them as racial do-gooderism.

In 1992, the Boston Federal Reserve released a report indicating that minority applicants were nearly three times as likely as whites to be denied home loans. Groups such as the Association of Community Organizations for Reform Now (ACORN) took the study and began pushing for relaxed home lending requirements, despite many academics demonstrating that the Boston Fed report was wildly inaccurate.

Soon, quasi-governmental agencies such as Fannie Mae were buying up billions of dollars in questionable home loans, supposedly meant to help low-income, minority populations. The implied governmental backing and sweetheart terms Fannie Mae enjoyed helped increase the number of subprime mortgages from $40 billion in 1994 to $160 billion five years later. Of course, these loans trapped millions of people, many of them minorities, in loans they couldn't afford.

Whenever Congress attempted to rein in Fannie Mae's largesse, the company would call out its cadre of community organizers to paint the reformers as racists. Many of these minority leaders were beneficiaries of the company's funds. For instance, Fannie Mae contributed millions to the Congressional Black and Hispanic caucuses, and its members routinely blocked actions to regulate the lender.

The history books tell us what eventually happened. Unscrupulous private lenders - many of whom only existed because they knew they could pawn their bad loan bundles off on Fannie and Freddie - started going under, as did the banks that underwrote their scams. With trillions of dollars of junk home loans going bad, the economy went bust in 2008.

Meanwhile, low-income and minority neighborhoods, including many in Milwaukee, were devastated by the collapse. In the end, minorities were laid low by the very fraudulent programs that were supposed to help them - while banks walked off with record profits before going belly-up.

Obviously, anyone who doesn't believe racism still exists in America is living on another planet. But even unproven accusations carry a punishing stick, and are therefore sometimes leveraged into lucrative money-making opportunities by nefarious actors. These frivolous accusations not only dilute attempts to counter actual racism, they often end up harming the very minority groups they intend to aid.

Milwaukee Journal Sentinel

DYING TO SAVE THE ENVIRONMENT

April 9, 2013

With the aging of the baby boomer generation, the American implant and prosthetics sectors are becoming more lucrative. According to the Journal of the American Medical Association, more than 280,000 hip replacement surgeries are performed in the U.S. every year. Among Medicare recipients between 2000 and 2006, hip replacements increased 15%, while shoulder replacements increased 67% and knee replacements increased 48%.

But there are also some unexpected - and macabre - business opportunities to be had with so many seniors lugging around so much hardware. Services are cropping up around the country that will actually recycle the metal used in implants and prosthetics once their owner has died. Cobalt chromium, titanium, and stainless steel could all be reused in new patients (and will come in handy if the gates of Heaven are now equipped with metal detectors.)

"We propose to lead our industry toward more environmentally focused and responsible actions," said Paul Rahill, the environmental and technical adviser for the Cremation Association of North America in a 2011 interview. "This includes the handling of prosthetic implants from the human remains that are cremated."

This is just a small segment of the "green death" industry. More seniors are now opting to decompose directly into the earth, rather than be embalmed and laid to rest in a casket. The Green Burial Council, an advocacy group promoting environmentally responsible burials, has even been formed to encourage post-mortem conservation (although one would expect their client list isn't particularly vocal.) The Council certifies burial grounds as "natural." There are 22 such cemeteries now, up from just one in 2006.

None of these innovative eco-friendly practices were dreamed up by governments or elected officials; they arose - ahem - organically, from individuals who wanted to do the right thing for the environment.

Yet many still don't seem to realize that most of the benefits to the environment in the past few decades haven't occurred because of government mandates or elected officials funding pet initiatives; America is getting cleaner because customers are demanding it.

Nobody in the government told car companies that they should start making gas-electric hybrids; citizens wanted them because they wanted to buy less gas and feel like they were making a difference. Cab companies now incorporate "green" cars into their fleets because they feel they'll attract more customers, not because any government mandate told them they had to.

And yet we still see billions of dollars dumped into "green" companies, dozens of which have either gone belly up or are nearing bankruptcy. Last year, the Heritage Foundation fingered 34 companies that received a portion of the $80 billion set aside in the 2009 federal stimulus bill that were either bankrupt or economically troubled. President Barack Obama, the great stockbroker-in-chief, has done such a poor job of investing in companies, it's only a matter of time before we see Uncle Sam on "Pawn Stars" hocking the Declaration of Independence for 50 bucks.

Wisconsin's state government hasn't fared much better. In 1993, the state set up the Recycling Market Development Board, which was supposed to create markets for recycled products. The program was a flop: In 2004, it was repealed after shelling out $26.6 million in loans and grants, much of which went to private nonprofits whose job was to advise businesses on recycling practices. Many businesses found virgin materials to be cheaper and more reliable, and the markets never developed in the way state government had foreseen.

State government wasn't done, though. In 1998, it created the "Renewable Portfolio Standard," which mandated that a certain percentage of electricity in the state come from wind and solar sources. A recent study issued by the Wisconsin Policy Research Institute demonstrated that this mandate will cost consumers $788 million between now and 2017, while providing little benefit.

In the future, nobody knows where the next eco-innovations will come from. Years ago, the idea of biodegradable caskets and urns would be laughable - now, when I'm pushing up daisies, I kind of want them to be chemical-free.

What is certain is that it won't be government that drives innovation - it will be the demands of the consumers that do so. Whether those consumers are above ground or below it.

Milwaukee Journal Sentinel

'SO, YOU KNOW HOW YOU FELT ON 9-11? YEAH, THAT'S HOW WE FEEL WHEN IT COMES TO RACE'

July 16, 2013

Late Saturday, after a Florida jury declared George Zimmerman not guilty of second-degree murder in the shooting death of 17-year-old Trayvon Martin, the kabuki dance began. Both sides of the political spectrum entrenched themselves safely in their own corners, hoping to graft their pet national issue onto a night-time altercation between a Hispanic man and an African-American boy that turned violent.

The usual cadre of African-American "spokesmen" took to the airwaves. The Rev. Al Sharpton called the verdict an "atrocity." Georgetown University professor and MSNBC contributor Michael Eric Dyson said that in order to understand how African-Americans felt about the verdict, one had to think about terrorism. "So, you know how you felt on 9-11? Yeah, that's how we feel when it comes to race," Dyson said. PBS host Tavis Smiley proclaimed that in America, "color will get you killed."

On the other side, the deification of Zimmerman had begun. His supporters wailed that an innocent man, defending himself, should never even have been subjected to a trial. They complain that Zimmerman's life is now ruined and that he will live in fear of threats against his life. But they use the verdict as a cudgel to bash liberals who oppose gun laws and foment racial discord.

Coverage of the trial and the verdict has been woefully predictable. (We see Tom Wolfe's "Bonfire of the Vanities" performed on a real-life national stage every few years, although admittedly, it is better than the 1990 film adaptation.) The media has to take each extreme and pit them against one another in order to create a contrast and thus a story. Then people say ridiculous things in response to one another, further perpetuating the conflict and filling up column inches (or pixels). The story continues to feed itself.

But in this instance, it feels as if the standard practice of choosing up "teams" is out of step with the way the public actually views the verdict. An individual can hold a number of differing opinions about the case, none of which are necessarily mutually exclusive.

For instance, it appears that the prosecution never had a chance to convict Zimmerman of anything. Its evidence was weak, and the state's self-defense statute is strong. It wouldn't have mattered if Zimmerman had provoked a confrontation with Martin, or for what reason — once fisticuffs ensued, Zimmerman had a right under the law to protect himself. If the shooter had been black, hopefully the same lack of evidence would have led to the same result.

But that doesn't mean Zimmerman shouldn't be condemned for his actions. Just because he was found not guilty of murder doesn't mean he is innocent of stupidity. Whatever the reason for his physical engagement with Martin, it seems it could have been avoided — most people seem to be successful at avoiding such physical confrontations on a daily basis.

Further, it's not outrageous that this case went to trial, as some have suggested. When a boy ends up dead, it's not asking too much to find out exactly what happened. In this case, the shooting of a boy may have been legal, but given the factors that preceded the tragic event, that doesn't mean Martin's shooting wasn't wrong.

Zimmerman is no hero, and there are few salient political points to be scored off the tragedy. (To borrow a line from comedian Chris Rock, every day I look in my mail for my George Zimmerman prize, and nothing's come yet.)

The Trayvon Martin story will soon fade, and the conflict industrial complex will go into hibernation until it's needed following the next tragedy. But the bottom line is, there are no winners and losers in this sad tale. There is only a family without a son and an overzealous neighborhood watch volunteer who has to live with the consequences of his actions.

Milwaukee Journal Sentinel

PROPOSING THE BONEHEAD RULE

September 13, 2013

Recently, Virginia Tech English professor Steven Salaita stopped at a convenience store to buy $1.82 worth of mozzarella sticks for his fussy 16-month-old son. He paid with two $1 bills; the clerk asked him if he'd like to donate the remaining 18 cents to "support the troops." He said no thanks.

Yet the seemingly innocuous transaction didn't stop there. It provoked Salaita into writing a column for Salon.com in which he argued we should "stop saying 'support the troops,'" because the phrase is "trite and tiresome."

Around the same time as Salaita's transformative purchase, Iowa Rep. Steve King appeared on television to hold court on the issue of illegal immigration. A staunch immigration reform opponent, King said undocumented immigrants are primarily "130 pounds" with "calves the size of cantaloupes because they've been hauling 75 pounds of marijuana across the desert."

In the past, when newspaper column inches and network television time were at a premium, boneheaded statements such as the ones above would barely cause a ripple in the public attention span. Yet the modern news monster — fueled by social media and cable television — is always hungry for news, no matter how bizarre or inconsequential. Thus, both stories "went national," allegedly representing what each political ideology thinks about American troops and illegal immigrants.

And while these were just knuckleheaded things said by single individuals (granted, King's were probably worse because people elect him to spout such absurdities), they become talking points in the ongoing ideological war. Lefties hate the troops. Righties hate immigrants. That is, until some other inconsequential public figure says something boneheaded that social media sucks up to bludgeon the other side on another topic. (One of Gov. Scott Walker's campaign staffers once joked to me that the easiest way to get a promotion was to do or say something really stupid — then the media immediately refers to you as one of Walker's "key" employees.)

The "bonehead effect" leads to perhaps the most obnoxious campaign tactic: trying to tie someone important to statements made by someone wholly unimportant. As if a candidate who fails to condemn something crazy said by someone who supports the candidate means the candidate endorses those comments completely.

For instance, last February, Walker addressed a meeting of the National Rifle Association in Wausau. Among the reams of literature distributed at the conference was a flyer called "The Reality News," which called for secession and alluded to armed rebellion. In an unintentionally hilarious statement, Democratic Party of Wisconsin Chairman Mike Tate demanded that Walker "denounce any talk of secession." (Are we to believe that at the typical liberal gathering, there aren't groups there that even make true-blooded Democrats cringe?)

Perhaps we should follow a few simple rules on boneheads. First, if just one person says something intemperate, let's just consider it the incoherent rantings of a madman — if more people start saying the same thing, we can consider it a theme. We should also take into account the stature of the speaker; Vice President Joe Biden accusing Republicans of wanting to put African-Americans back in chains is much different than a cable television host doing the same.

Admittedly, these rules are somewhat self-serving, as the curse of the boneheads generally haunts conservatives more than liberals. When notable Democrats Anthony Weiner and Eliot Spitzer engage in untoward priapic misadventures, it is written off as individual glandular problems; when Republicans such as Rep. Mark Foley are caught in gay sexual harassment scandals, the media report it as if it is a plague of hypocrisy infecting the fabric of the entire GOP.

One need to look no further than the 2012 election season, when the undisputed King of the Boneheads, Missouri Rep. Todd Akin, essentially said a woman couldn't get pregnant from a rape, as a female victim's body "shuts that whole thing down." I have been involved in conservative politics for decades, but have never heard such a theory posited — but soon, Akin's comments not only cost him his race against vulnerable Democrat Claire McCaskill, they began to feed into the national storyline that the GOP was waging a "war on women." Congressman and vice presidential candidate Paul Ryan (R-Wis.) immediately denounced Akin's comments, but that didn't keep David Axelrod, President Barack Obama's chief strategist, from calling it the "Akin-Ryan" position on rape.

I offer this proposal: At each party's annual state convention, the party should be able to pick three people on its side who are granted "bonehead exceptions" for the next 12 months. These people can say whatever they want with immunity from criticism from the other party. If conservative author Ann Coulter refers to John Edwards using a homophobic slur, we all ignore it. If liberal buffoon Alec Baldwin lashes out on Twitter calling a male reporter a "toxic little queen," we don't burn a week's worth of legitimate news talking about it.

And if Obama doesn't immediately condemn this proposal, we can all agree he supports it completely.

Milwaukee Journal Sentinel

DRUG PRICES NEED A DOSE OF THE FREE MARKET

February 5, 2016

The only explanation for Martin Shkreli's performance before Congress on Thursday is that he is engaging in some sort of long-form performance art piece to see how much vitriol America can collectively gather to detest a single individual. Speaking before a House committee, Shkreli mugged, smirked and laughed while the "imbeciles" in Congress (as he put it in a later tweet) asked him questions about his now-famous scheme to prey on the sick.

Shkreli is the kindergarten capitalist who last year bought the rights to the lifesaving drug Daraprim and quickly jacked the price from $13.50 per pill to $750 per pill — a 50-fold increase. Shkreli's company, Turing Pharmaceuticals, has made a practice of buying orphaned generic drugs and increasing their price 20-fold or more. (Note the abject moral rot of running a company that denies medicine to AIDS patients and shares a name with gay mathematical pioneer Alan Turing.)

In the wake of Shkreli's unconscionable Daraprim price hike, some have called for tighter regulation of the pharmaceutical industry. Despite being the largest recipient of Big Pharma campaign contributions from either party, Hillary Clinton frequently has criticized drug company "predatory pricing." Citing Shkreli by name on her website, Clinton says she will use "every tool at my disposal to go after these companies that are doing this to people who need the help."

But while some blame the free market for Shkreli's actions, the opposite is true; Shkreli can get away with preposterous price hikes only because he found a loophole in a government regulation that allows him to do so.

As explained by blogger Derek Lowe at Science magazine, Daraprim is a generic formula; it could be made by any company that wanted to do so. Typically, when a drug is patented, the company that discovers it can charge high prices to recoup the cost of research and development; but when that patent expires, costs plummet as generic manufacturers jump in and begin competing for business.

However, the FDA will grant market exclusivity to certain companies that buy up existing generic formulas, as long as the company agrees to update the drug to its current regulatory framework. This is what Shkreli did for Daraprim, which was first approved by the FDA in 1953, and which sold for about $1 per pill several years ago. As pointed out by pharma blogger Alex Tabarrok, generic variations of the pill are widely available in Europe, and in India it sells for around five cents per pill.

The price of any good is essentially an unspoken contract between producer and consumer — when you buy a ticket to see "Star Wars," you're agreeing that the price is worth you paying for it. Naturally, the company wants that price to be as high as you can bear, so it makes more money. (And in the case of pharmaceuticals, much of that money is pumped right back in to research to produce more lifesaving cures.)

But that transaction doesn't work when someone is dying and needs medicine. And it's doubly worse when someone such as Shkreli has a monopoly and can soak sick people.

However, the answer isn't more government regulation, it's less. Eliminating the loophole Shkreli is exploiting will allow competition, and the price will fall back in line when other manufacturers are able to manufacture pyramethimine (Daraprim's generic name.)

Further, the FDA should consider allowing American customers to purchase pharmaceuticals from Europe and other countries, as long as those drugs have been previously approved in the United States. Typically, such reimportation schemes are a bad idea, as they deny American drug companies the revenue needed to create new drugs; but Shkreli's company does no research and development — it simply feeds on the carcasses of existing formulas. And for medicine that already has FDA approval, the competition will benefit sick consumers.

As long as the FDA grants monopolies to rent-seekers such as Turing Pharmaceuticals, we will see more abuse of the drug pricing system. In the end, government regulation isn't the cure for people like Shkreli; it's the affliction itself.

Milwaukee Journal Sentinel

DEMOCRATS HAVE A FOUR-LETTER WORD OBSESSION

February 12, 2016

In the canon of 2016 presidential election political pandering, one episode stands above the rest. In August of 2015, Democratic presidential aspirant Hillary Clinton invited her Twitter followers to explain their feelings about student loan debt to her. "Tell us in 3 emojis or less," she requested.

If you are a college student who communicates via emoji, the only appropriate emoji for you to be using is one of a diploma engulfed in flames. But as evidenced in last Thursday night's presidential debate in Milwaukee, Democrats' messaging hasn't gotten any more sophisticated.

Instead of three emoticons, both Hillary Clinton and Bernie Sanders can distill their campaign messages into four simple, traditional letters: "M-O-R-E."

While Republicans are earning the rap as being the "dumb party," Democratic campaigns continue on their mission to promise "more" things to "more" people. Running a Dem campaign is simple: If you think something is good, just say we need "more" of it. If we need expanded health care, let's spend more. If college students don't like paying tuition, let's give them more money to go to school.

During Thursday's two-hour debate, candidates used the word "more" over 40 times. Among the list of things we need "more" of, according to Clinton and Sanders: Families paying taxes to fund universal health care, people on government-run health care, information on fixing the criminal justice system, federal dollars in communities with persistent generational poverty, rich people paying taxes, money in the Social Security fund, government infrastructure jobs, and on and on. Both candidates agreed that America needs more of pretty much everything — they only disagreed about the degree to which government should control every aspect of our lives.

That's primarily because Sanders is the iron-fisted ruler of a kingdom that exists only between his ears. According to an analysis by The Wall Street Journal, Sanders' plans would cost taxpayers $18 trillion over a decade. There is no dollar in your pocket over which he doesn't salivate, as he believes higher taxes are the salve that cures all the nation's ills. From racism to criminal justice reform to higher education to income inequality, Sanders' knee-jerk invocation of "millionaires and billionaires" is repetitive enough to make Marco Rubio supporters cringe. (Number of times "Wall Street" was name-checked during the Democratic debate: 25.)

By reflexively promising "more," of everything, Democrats are emulating the arch-villain of overpromising, Republican Donald Trump. The New York billionaire titillates the lowest common denominator simply by offering "more" stuff and "better" leadership. Without even pretending to issue any specifics, Trump has promised everything from a more terrific military to classier health care to a tremendous economy to better-looking baristas. And as much thought is needed to generate these musings as there is to just mindlessly utter the word "more."

Indeed, at Thursday's debate, the candidates were asked to answer a Facebook question about whether there were any areas of government they'd like to reduce. Suddenly, the loquacious Sanders turned into Marcel Marceau, mumbling about general "waste and inefficiency" in bureaucracy. Sanders not offering a single specific was the equivalent of lighting his podium on fire and running off the stage, hoping nobody noticed. Out of the over 16,000 words spoken at the debate, the candidates spent 1.4% of them answering the question about ways to reduce government.

This is certainly conservatism's biggest handicap; explaining how smaller government and less regulation ultimately benefits citizens is more difficult than simply waving government's finger and decreeing things to be so. But if we want plausible, specific solutions from our politicians during this election season, we could use a lot less of "more."

Milwaukee Journal Sentinel

CLINTON'S BAD HISTORY ON REAGAN AND AIDS

March 18, 2016

When public figures are forced to issue a retraction for something they said, typically they're talking back an unfair criticism they've made of someone else. Perhaps they get overemotional and say something intemperate about an opponent, and subsequently have to apologize.

But man took a healthy bite out of dog last week when presidential candidate Hillary Clinton was forced to retract a compliment. On the day of former first lady Nancy Reagan's funeral, Clinton praised Reagan's efforts to combat the AIDS virus, saying, "because of both President and Mrs. Reagan — in particular, Mrs. Reagan — we started a national conversation, when before nobody would talk about it. Nobody wanted anything to do with it."

It was a human moment from the robotic Clinton, who often appears as she needs tears extracted from her eyes with a pair of pliers. But her praise of the Reagans with regards to AIDS and HIV sent her liberal backers running for paper bags into which to breathe.

Gawker called Clinton's comments "shocking, insulting and utterly inexplicable." Charles Kaiser, author of "The Gay Metropolis," said, "This is shameful, idiotic, false — and heartbreaking." On Twitter, Clinton claimed she "misspoke" about the Reagans and AIDS and quickly apologized.

But Clinton had nothing to apologize for.

It is part of the standard left-wing canon that Reagan was an anti-homosexual monster, based mainly on the fact that he never publicly mentioned AIDS until 1985. This, despite the fact that Reagan vocally opposed a late-1970s California ballot measure that would have barred gay men and women from teaching in public schools. When Reagan was asked during the 1980 presidential primary whether he thought gay people had the same civil rights as everyone else, Reagan replied, "I think they do and should."

But the "silence" charge seems like a bogus way to measure an administration's commitment to an issue; certainly, Barack Obama supports research projects that he doesn't mention in public speeches.

And Reagan's deeds outpaced his lack of words. As historian H.W. Brands put it, Reagan "quietly allowed money for AIDS research to be included in the federal budget, but he let others in the administration do what little talking executive branch officials did on the subject."

In a speech in 1987, Reagan noted that it was only in June of 1981 that five cases of AIDS appeared in California, and the AIDS virus was only detected in 1984. But between 1982 and 1986, Reagan's budgets spent over $500 million on AIDS research. When asked about it in 1985, Reagan answered that AIDS "has been one of the top priorities for us." He noted that the federal commitment to AIDS research in 1986 alone would be $126 million, saying, "Yes, there's no question about the seriousness of this and we need to find an answer." When Reagan sent his budget to Congress several months later, AIDS research funding was categorized as a "high priority" program.

Reagan also rejected the idea that AIDS was simply a gay disease, saying, "I don't want Americans to think AIDS simply affects only certain groups," adding, "It calls for compassion, not blame. And it calls for understanding, not ignorance."

Of course, Reagan's record on gay rights isn't perfect — he once noted that the Bible considered homosexuality an "abomination," but later backtracked, saying what people did in their own bedrooms was their own business. And for Republicans in the early 1980s — many of whom considered AIDS "God's judgment" on gays — Reagan's view was far more compassionate.

A more accurate accounting of Reagan's stance on AIDS exposes Hillary Clinton's weak-minded pandering to the edges of her party. On the day she praised the Reagans for their efforts on AIDS, I also complimented Clinton for her fairness and open-mindedness.

But as is now evidently custom, I have to publicly and vehemently retract that compliment.

Milwaukee Journal Sentinel

THE LIBERTARIAN MOMENT

May 25, 2016

For years, the Libertarian Party in America has been a dumping ground for the politically disaffected, ideologically homeless and conspiratorially inclined. But Libertarians may want to put on a tie, comb their hair and shine their shoes, because they may soon be getting the bright spotlight they've always wanted.

According to a new Wall Street Journal/NBC News poll, 47% of Americans would consider a third-party candidate in the 2016 presidential campaign. This is up from 40% in 2012 and 38% in 2008, owing much to the fact that for many voters, choosing between Hillary Clinton and Donald Trump is like deciding which eye they'd rather pour salt into.

The Libertarian Party is attractive to conservative Republicans who have been left without a freedom-minded soul mate to support. Enter former New Mexico Gov. Gary Johnson, the 2012 Libertarian presidential candidate and front-runner for that post in 2016 (there are currently 18 announced candidates, including one who was formerly on the run from Guatemalan and Belizean law enforcement who wanted him for questioning in the murder of his neighbor).

As his vice presidential choice, Johnson has tapped former Massachusetts Gov. William Weld. The Johnson/Weld pairing is polling upward of 10% in recent three-way presidential polls.

But Libertarians are still left having to fight the perception that they are a motley band of purist misfits, endlessly proselytizing about drug legalization, Ron Paul and the gold standard. Yet in its purest form, libertarianism can claim strong roots in America's founding and popular appeal in the modern electorate. In many ways, Libertarians reflect where many Americans are politically — fiscally conservative and socially liberal. The party's "live and let live" ethos is an attractive message against politicians who promise to be the salve for every one of our problems.

Wisconsin is an apt microcosm of both the Libertarian Party's successes and challenges. In 2002, Libertarian Ed Thompson won 10.5% of the vote in the gubernatorial election that year, leading many to believe he swung the election in favor of the victor, then-Attorney General Jim Doyle.

But Thompson was no doubt buoyed by his famous last name and relation to his brother, the popular former governor, Tommy Thompson. And Ed Thompson's strong showing wasn't exactly a victory for small "l" libertarianism. As mayor of Tomah, he governed as if he were any mayor of any small town in Wisconsin. His gubernatorial platform included more environmental regulation and more money for the University of Wisconsin System, and he complained about not receiving enough public tax money to run his campaign — a concept anathema to philosophical libertarians.

In 2008, former UW-Madison lecturer Kevin Barrett ran as a Libertarian for Congress against U.S. Rep. Ron Kind. Barrett caused an uproar in 2006 when he taught his UW class conspiracy theories asserting the 9/11 attacks were an "inside job" by the federal government. When he ran for Congress, Barrett promoted universal health care and expanded Social Security and Medicaid programs — things conscious Libertarians rail against.

And even when Wisconsin Libertarians do get a philosophical libertarian to run, things can quickly get supernaturally weird. Robert Burke, the party's 2014 gubernatorial candidate (who received 0.8% of the vote) now produces YouTube videos explaining how the federal government is withholding information about aliens.

It is perhaps ironic that the small government-centered Libertarian Party would get such a popularity boost from a pair of big-government candidates in Hillary Clinton and Donald Trump. But in order to take advantage of this newfound interest, the party needs to shake its reputation. If it does, it might incentivize more conservatives to come to the polls and save down-ticket Senate and House seats for the GOP.

The Onion once ran a story headlined, "Libertarian Reluctantly Calls Fire Department." It may be Republicans calling their oddball neighbors on the right to save their house.

Milwaukee Journal Sentinel

A BAD BET ON GERRYMANDERING CASE

November 22, 2016

It goes without saying that Donald Trump's victory in Wisconsin nearly two weeks ago was unexpected. But according to a three-judge federal panel who just declared Wisconsin's legislative maps unconstitutional, Trump's stunning victory would have been all but impossible.

In striking down maps passed in 2011 by state Republicans, the federal panel scoured the U.S. Constitution and created an entirely new protected class of voter: Democrats who think they should be represented by a Democrat. Even though the United States Supreme Court has previously looked at the issue of partisan redistricting and proactively denied the existence of such a category, these two judges have now spun a new standard out of whole cloth, upending a perfectly legal reapportionment process.

In breaking with settled law, the judges play the role of political prognosticators, determining that the outcome of too many Assembly districts is predetermined. But perhaps this would be news to Hillary Clinton, who appeared to be enjoying a six-point lead in the polls leading up to election day. In fact, if the entire state of Wisconsin were a legislative district, the judges would have considered it a safe Democratic seat in presidential election years, as no Republican had won it since 1984.

But people aren't computers, and their votes are often affected by a complex mix of candidate personalities, issues and national trends. As the Journal Sentinel's Craig Gilbert noted on the day after the election, 13 counties in Wisconsin have voted for Donald Trump, President Barack Obama twice, Gov. Scott Walker three times, Senate Democrat Tammy Baldwin in 2012 and Senate Republican Ron Johnson in 2016. This year, Trump won 22 counties that Barack Obama won just four years ago, completely undermining the court's contention that voters are set in stone.

In their lawsuit, Democrats complained that the number of seats they were winning in the Assembly was disproportional to the total statewide Democrat vs. Republican vote. For instance, they note that in 2012, Republicans received 48.6% of the two-party statewide vote share for Assembly candidates and won 60 of the 99 seats in the Wisconsin Assembly. In 2014, the Republican Party received 52% of the two-party statewide vote share and won 63 assembly seats.

But the idea that the number of legislative seats held by a political party has to be commensurate with the statewide vote is bad math, out of touch with reality and contradicts precedent.

For one, voters don't vote for Assembly seats with the statewide math in mind — they vote for the candidate who will best represent them in Madison.

Further, Democrats in Wisconsin are typically packed into dense geographic areas (Milwaukee, Madison), leading to many blowout wins. A good number of Democrats win large victories without a Republican challenger, which artificially inflates their share of the statewide vote. In

2012, Milwaukee saw historic voting levels, which distorted the math in their favor even more. If hard cases make bad law, historic turnouts make for even worse legislative maps.

In order to prove apportionment bias, Democrats brewed up a formula they called the "efficiency gap," which dissenting judge William Griesbach called an "unhelpful and dangerously misleading" metric for gauging actual electoral disparities.

Put simply, the "efficiency gap" measures how many votes a party "wastes" — in theory, the fewer votes a party "wastes," the easier it is for them to translate their votes into legislative seats. Democrats say Republicans enjoyed an efficiency gap advantage of 13% in 2012 and 10% in 2014.

But even their own standard fails to show anything nefarious was afoot. Democrats glide right by the fact that the maps in place in the previous decade — maps drawn by courts, not by partisans — produced an average efficiency gap of 7.6%, reaching a high of 11.8% in 2006. Yet, miraculously, no lawsuit was forthcoming until Republicans took full control of state government.

Were the 2011 maps drawn to help Republicans? Of course they were — as they always have been. But the U.S. Supreme Court has rarely been troubled by the fact that maps are drawn by politicians.

"The mere fact that a particular apportionment scheme makes it more difficult for a particular group in a particular district to elect the representatives of its choice does not render that scheme constitutionally infirm," the Supreme Court wrote 30 years ago in upholding an Indiana map even more aggressive than the one currently in place in Wisconsin. While the U.S. Constitution prevents the dilution of voting power based on race, there is simply no such protection for ideology.

And as the recent election shows, that ideology switches from election to election, from candidate to candidate. Which simply proves that judges make for bad political pundits.

Milwaukee Journal Sentinel

JUDGES AS PUNDITS

June 23, 2017

Think of the jobs you'd like to see fewer of in America. For instance, we clearly have way too many parking cops, dopes trying to squirt lotion on you as you walk through the mall, and "Instagram models."

A new case accepted by the U.S. Supreme Court on Monday, however, could be a boon for another of America's most overpopulated professions: political prognosticators. In a lawsuit that originated in Wisconsin, plaintiffs are arguing that the state's reapportionment following the 2010 census is too partisan, thus resulting in a distorted Republican majority in the state legislature.

Typically, courts have reviewed "gerrymandered" state legislative maps for evidence of racial discrimination. Throughout American history, white supremacists have abused the process to dilute the voting power of minority populations.

But these new maps are being challenged on partisan grounds, even though "these districts make Democrats sad" has never been the basis for a successful challenge in the U.S. Supreme Court. Allowing challenges to partisan apportionment demands that judges all over America suddenly become political pundits, determining which candidate should "rightfully" win each legislative seat in every state.

It's not as if gerrymandering is a new practice; according to some accounts, it predated even the American Revolution. Partisan apportionment was known to the nation's founding fathers — it is rumored that Patrick Henry actually attempted, unsuccessfully, to gerrymander James Madison out of the First Congress. (Which, in my fan fiction describing the event, ended with an old-style caning to settle the dispute.)

But Democrats are now acting as if partisan gerrymandering is a recent development, and they are armed with misleading statistics to prove it. They note that in 2012, Republicans received 48.6% of the two-party statewide vote share for Assembly candidates yet won 60 of the 99 seats in the Wisconsin Assembly. In 2014, the Republican Party received 52% of the two-party statewide vote share and won 63 assembly seats.

Yet this is largely a product of geography, not greedy subterfuge. The cities of Milwaukee and Madison are highly populated Democratic strongholds where you're more likely to see a roller-skating dolphin than a red "Make America Great Again" hat. In the districts that represent these areas, Republicans often don't bother fielding candidates – and even when they do, they lose by margins that would impress Kim Jong Un.

Perhaps most laughable is the suggestion that Democrats wouldn't do exactly what Republicans did upon taking full control of the Wisconsin government. In 1982, the state's Democratic legislature and Republican governor, Lee Sherman Dreyfus, clashed over maps, leaving the matter to a three-judge panel. But that year Dreyfus lost, and in 1983, Democrats and new Gov. Tony Earl wiped the year-old maps clean and redrew them to their liking. It would be another 11 years before Republicans would hold

197

one of the houses of the legislature.

Of course districts have always been re-jiggered for partisan advantage by both sides. But that hasn't kept Democrats from blaming their recent struggles on reapportionment.

In a recent interview, former U.S. Attorney General Eric Holder said it's his job "to make redistricting sexy" for Democrats. So if your idea of "sexy" is poring over census data while Eric Holder lights a scented candle and gives you a foot rub, your dream is not out of reach. This is great news for horny geography nerds, but one warning — if Holder asks you to review his peninsula, best to double-check to make sure you heard him correctly.

Even with partisan redistricting, the voters that inhabit those districts are not static. They vote different ways on different issues and for different candidates. Thirteen of Wisconsin's 72 counties have voted for Donald Trump, President Barack Obama twice, Gov. Scott Walker three times, Senate Democrat Tammy Baldwin in 2012 and Senate Republican Ron Johnson in 2016.

Asking courts to play political prognosticator and guess who should rightly win these counties in any given year is a foolish endeavor. How is a court possibly supposed to set a standard at which admissible partisanship in redistricting suddenly becomes too much?

If traditional voting patterns used to draw districts were 100% reliable, then there's no way Donald Trump would have won Wisconsin, which last went Republican in 1984. Redistricting is no more than a "best guess" that is often rendered unpredictable by voters, candidates and issues. So we can either keep the locally-controlled system we have now or just give Justice Ruth Bader Ginsburg her own show on MSNBC to pick the members of Congress.

There's no doubt Democrats in swing states all over America are chafing at the districts drawn by their Republican counterparts. But the courts are not the place for Democrats to engage in group therapy. Given America's status as the land of useless professions, the Supreme Court should keep centuries of precedent and simply issue each Democrat a session with a professional snuggler.

USA Today

NEW GOP DEMONSTRATING NEED FOR OLD GOP

September 21, 2016

On the cold, windy night of March 20, 1854, at a small schoolhouse in Ripon, Wis., Alvan Earle Bovay gaveled in the first meeting of a new political party he was intent on creating. Bovay, a Whig, was disgusted by his party's inability to block Democrat Stephen A. Douglas' "Kansas-Nebraska Bill," which would organize two new territories, but also repeal antislavery provisions of the 1820 Missouri Compromise. Of perhaps even more concern to Wisconsinites was Douglas' measure that would deny voting rights to noncitizen immigrants — Wisconsin was a prime landing spot for European settlers.

For his new party, Bovay picked the name "Republican," largely because Thomas Jefferson had used the word for his party, and Bovay knew it would be held in reverence. But Bovay also favored the word because it suggested a more optimistic equality, that "you are as good as I," not the Democratic doctrine of "I am as good as you."

From this meeting sprung a Republican Party that was, as Bovay urged, "a champion and promulgator of liberty." Soon, Republicans were winning elections to Congress. President Abraham Lincoln joined the party in 1856. It eventually grew into a party for those who eschewed a strong central government, instead preferring to leave decisions up to local and state governments.

In 2016, the Republican Party nominated a presidential candidate that stands for exactly none of these foundational principles. In fact, Donald Trump will gladly tell anyone with a microphone that his rise to prominence within the party is due to his antagonism towards noncitizen immigrants. In 1854, immigrants fought for their right to vote; in 2016, Trump wants to rip families apart by deporting them altogether. If you're of the wrong religion, Trump wants to deny you entry altogether.

Further, small government Republicans have been duped into supporting a self-declared strongman who seeks to implement big government policy changes on the force of his personality alone.

During the course of the 2016 campaign, Trump has indicated an openness to universal health care ("Everybody's got to be covered. This is an un-Republican thing for me to say ..."), to micromanaging the nation's economy by restricting trade, to leaving Social Security alone as it bankrupts itself, to increasing the police force so that crime and violence "will soon come to an end." Just last week, Trump unveiled a plan to guarantee women six weeks of paid maternity leave, which the Washington Post characterized as "a striking departure from GOP orthodoxy." (Trump says the plan was crafted by his liberal-leaning daughter, Ivanka, whose primary policy argument was, "Daddy, Daddy we have to do this.")

For those conscious conservatives who reject both Trump's government-aggrandizing plans and attempts to drag the party towards European-style white nationalism, there's a special irony waiting around the corner. Last week, Republican National Committee chairman Reince

Priebus threatened Republicans that don't bow before Trump, hinting that the RNC might penalize future GOP candidates that didn't offer their endorsement in 2016.

So for those keeping score, the chairman of the party that seeks to prove top-down government doesn't work is attempting to muscle future local and national candidates into conformity. In a sense, Priebus disproved his own efficacy, becoming a laughingstock among establishment Republicans. "The idea of a greater purpose beyond oneself may be alien to political party bosses like Reince Priebus," wrote Ohio Gov. John Kasich adviser John Weaver in a statement, "but it is at the center of everything Governor Kasich does." Kasich is a notable Trump holdout, refusing to even attend a national convention in his home state.

Sadly, the party can no longer tell people "you are as good as I," as the Republican Party stands in direct opposition to the principles under which it was founded. The party was formed when Alvan Earl Bovay felt his party no longer spoke for him. Now, when the 2016 embarrassment stands adjourned, the party needs another Bovay to kill it and start anew. The new Republican Party is proving why the old Republican Party was so necessary.

Milwaukee Journal Sentinel

WEINER'S WRATH

October 31, 2016

During this eternal sojourn through the 2016 presidential campaign cycle, I've often had lefty friends ask me what it's like to have Donald Trump as my party's nominee. "Imagine if Anthony Weiner was your nominee," I'd tell them. "It's exactly like that."

Then last week happened.

It is true that Weiner, the former congressman whose inability to control his online libido has sent his life spiraling out of control, is not on the presidential ballot. But Weiner injected himself squarely into the presidential race on Friday when reports surfaced that his computer contained emails belonging to his wife, Hillary Clinton aide Huma Abedin. FBI director James Comey, who in July declined to file charges against Clinton for her use of a private email server during her tenure as secretary of state, sent a letter to congressional leaders on Friday telling them of the discovery of the new emails.

Certainly, there's not much about this presidential election that's worthy of celebration. But for conservatives, there's more than just a bit of Weinerfreude at work here.

For decades, every Republican sleazebag who makes news has been held up immediately as the new Face of the Party. When a GOP congressman solicits sex from young male Capitol pages, suddenly Republicans become the party of child predators and hemorrhage seats in the House of Representatives. When a Republican Senate candidate demonstrates a knowledge of the female reproductive system that appears to have been learned from reading Penthouse letters while chugging cough syrup, the GOP is suddenly complicit in a "war on women."

It is therefore refreshing to see the left finally have to answer for one of its own scabrous degenerates. For years now, Weiner has hovered on the periphery of Democratic politics, as he has continued to make headlines for his glandular excesses. Even after resigning his congressional seat in shame in 2011, Weiner again was caught in 2013 sexting a young woman under the pseudonym "Carlos Danger." In September of this year, Weiner was accused of sexting with a 15-year-old girl, which led to the investigation that reportedly uncovered his wife's emails on his computer.

And yet all along, Democrats have the luxury of laughing off Weiner's transgressions, even as he lived in the same home as their presidential candidate's closest adviser. They get to treat him as a rogue pervert, the party's distant relative with whom you wouldn't leave your children.

Yet had Weiner been a Republican, his name would have lit up Democratic talking points as they linked him to every GOP politician on the planet. Mitt Romney evidently had a problem with women because he had binders full of them that he wanted to hire for jobs — and yet a quick stroll through Weiner's binders of women would likely require a vigorous eyeball bleaching afterward.

The double standard on Republican scandals undoubtedly stems from the appearance of hypocrisy. The GOP is, after all, the party that espouses individual discipline and family values, and it makes for an irresistible news morsel when a right-winger falls short of his or her own standard.

Democrats, on the other hand, rarely make any public issue out of fidelity or morality. It's why Al Gore can allegedly demand a masseuse release his "second chakra" and still be the face of the Clintons' efforts to recruit millennials in 2016.

One of the great tragedies of this election year is that Republicans have chosen a nominee who appears to have learned his manners toward women at Weiner University. (Indeed, Trump has donated to Weiner's past congressional races, giving him the maximum amount legally allowable in 2007 and 2010.)

Democrats can survive sex scandals. Bill Clinton is still a major draw on the campaign circuit, and even back in 1998, voters punished congressional Republicans who took part in impeaching him. But Republicans rarely are allowed so much moral latitude. And the so-called "religious" wing of the GOP that now supports Trump has forfeited any moral authority to condemn such actions from Democrats in the future.

Nobody yet knows what's in the trove of materials on Weiner's computer. And one doesn't envy the poor FBI agent who has to review the unspeakable materials contained within.

But it's about time a Democratic punchline punched back at the party.

Milwaukee Journal Sentinel

DEMOCRATS SUDDENLY DISCOVER DANGERS OF PRESIDENTIAL OVERREACH

November 16, 2016

Ask any Midwestern liberal where to find Madison, and they will likely point to the progressive city that houses the Wisconsin Capitol.

Yet in the months after a Republican wins a presidential contest, suddenly liberals are able to find Madison in an entirely different place. When conservatives take over power, the left rediscovers James Madison, America's tent pole separation-of-powers enthusiast. (Predictably, the city of Madison features no statue of the city's namesake, but does feature a statue of former Wisconsin Badgers head football coach Barry Alvarez.)

It is accepted canon among progressives that there's no problem government can't solve as long as Democrats are in charge. Yet when Republicans gain control of the levers of government, liberals suddenly begin singing hymns of "checks and balances" and espousing the benefits of federalism. Under George W. Bush, the Patriot Act meant Dick Cheney slumped over a telephone listening in on your phone calls; under President Barack Obama, the Act suddenly became a necessary law enforcement tool to keep Americans safe.

It is appointment viewing to now watch the same Democrats who stuffed Barack Obama's presidency with as many powers as possible to deny that President-elect Trump has the same latitude. They evidently took no time to reflect on what would happen when their fiercest political opponents got hold of all the new powers they had gifted to the presidency.

Consider, for example, the 1 million undocumented immigrants who entered America as young children who turned over their personal information to the Obama administration in order to shield them from deportation. Now that the federal government has this information on the so-called "DREAMers," those same identifying details could be used to deport them. All President Trump would have to do is eliminate Obama's Deferred Action for Childhood Arrivals (DACA) program, which would mean eventually that the status of these immigrants would revert to illegal.

These new progressive guardians of gridlock should familiarize themselves with Madison's counsel that "In republican government, the legislative authority necessarily predominates." Madison knew that an unchecked executive could run roughshod over the rights of minority factions. (In today's parlance, Madison was the founding father that was most "woke.")

Of course, executive power is most widely executed through the federal government's bureaucracy, which has wide latitude to govern as its unelected appointees see fit. The nation's federal departments typically act with little oversight from Congress, enacting rules that are usually under no obligation to reflect public opinion.

One can only imagine the reaction if, for example, former presidential candidate and Trump surrogate Ben Carson carried out his plan to use the federal Department of Education to "monitor" universities for "political bias" and deny these same institutions federal funding if such "extreme bias" exists.

In recent years, progressives have mocked Republican efforts to rein in the Internal Revenue Service, which used its authority to crack down on conservative-leaning nonprofit groups. Think that was funny? Well, welcome to the new Trump IRS. If you run a group that was critical of the president-elect during the campaign, an investment in a good accountant might be wise.

If the prior year were less about Donald Trump's glandular exigencies and more about issues, voters would have heard more about House Speaker Paul Ryan's plan to rein in the executive rule-making process. In his "Better Way" proposal, Ryan has recognized that programs passed through the legislative process are not bound to the caprices of an individual president; once ensconced in law, programs — immigration regulations, for instance — cannot be waved away by the next chief executive. The lawmaking process is more open and transparent than the federal rule-making process, and those that vote for new programs are accountable to their voters.

Ryan's plan also recognizes the need for the legislature to pass laws that leave less leeway for federal regulators to act. Typically, Congress will pass vague legislation and leave the unpleasant details of implementing the new law up to rule-making bureaucrats. The result of such abdication is demonstrated in the wake of the Affordable Care Act, which has produced, at the very least, 10,000 new pages of federal regulations.

In fact, the government itself estimates that it takes about 11.5 billion hours annually for businesses and individuals to comply with regulatory record-keeping requirements alone. In the first six years of his presidency, Barack Obama implemented nearly 500 new regulations, frequently circumventing the legislative process to do so. Including Congress in rule implementation would bring many of these regulations back into contact with those who are most affected.

So for those looking to check Donald Trump's power, perhaps Ryan's plan is worth a look. It mitigates many of the problems created when you kick the regulatory can down the road, only to have Donald Trump there to one day pick it up.

Milwaukee Journal Sentinel

NBA ALL-STAR BOYCOTT HURT THE WRONG PEOPLE

February 22, 2017

Following his MVP performance in the nearly unwatchable NBA All-Star Game on Sunday, New Orleans Pelicans forward Anthony Davis had an admission: Before the game, he had actually lobbied his teammates to help him win the award.

"I stressed that, I think more than enough, to the guys in the locker room before the game that I wanted to get the MVP for this crowd, for this city, and I ended up doing it," said Davis, after shattering the All-Star Game scoring record with 52 points.

But Davis doesn't have his teammates to thank — nor should he thank his "opponents," who, in a game that featured not a whisper of defense, guarded Davis as if he had a bomb strapped to his chest. For playing in front of his home fans in New Orleans, Davis should send his game check to former North Carolina governor Pat McCrory.

Last year, the NBA moved the 2017 All-Star Game to New Orleans as a reaction to North Carolina's passage of a "bathroom bill" requiring citizens to use the restroom that corresponds with their biological gender. The game had been scheduled to take place in Charlotte, but NBA Commissioner Adam Silver moved it, costing the city an estimated $100 million in economic activity, according to the Charlotte Regional Visitors Authority.

Regardless of what one thinks of North Carolina's law, sports leagues blackmailing states to change regulations enacted by their legislatures is a pointless endeavor that serves to harm those who might be ideologically aligned with the cause. It was actually the city of Charlotte that enacted a pro-transgender rights ordinance; it was the state legislature that reacted by passing the now-infamous HB2, requiring citizens to use the bathroom associated with their biological gender.

What message does the NBA think it's sending, then, by punishing Charlotte? A great number of the people who are being hurt are the city's residents who love NBA basketball and oppose HB2. People in Charlotte could have marched every weekend in favor of repealing the state law, but business owners in the city still missed out on a good bit of revenue last weekend.

Suppose you're a dad in Charlotte who is not engaged in politics at all but wanted to take his kid to finally get a glimpse of Giannis Antetokounmpo. Or say you're an arena candy vendor sapped of a paycheck for the now non-existent All-Star weekend. How does it help the NBA to punish you for the actions of a few state lawmakers, especially when it has frequently held All-Star games in cities with no transgender protections? These boycotts are targeting the wrong people.

Of course, as a private business, the NBA has the right to put its special events wherever it wants. But whether it's wise to play politics is a different story. If the league had kept the All-Star Game in Charlotte, would people really have associated the NBA with bigotry and hate? Or could the NBA simply just have said it disagrees with the law and hope it is changed? (Most entertaining is the sudden realization of those on the left who, after arguing against the Citizens United court decision for years, are suddenly lauding a corporation's individual right to engage in political free speech.)

Further, exactly how is the league going to decide on which issues to take a stand? Are the 21 states with Religious Freedom Restoration Acts modeled after the federal law (and supported heavily by Democrats in the early 1990s) now on the boycott list? Lesbian, gay, bisexual and transgender rights groups oppose those laws as ardently as they do North Carolina's bathroom law.

As of this week, there had been 88 homicides and 468 shooting victims in Chicago this year. Would the NBA dare withhold a game there until the violence subsides, or is its cultural conscience reserved for people who crave urinal freedom?

Ultimately, change will come to North Carolina only when the state's voters elect different lawmakers — this process appears to be underway, as McCrory lost his re-election bid in November. Until that political realignment takes place, the NBA shouldn't pretend it's making any positive difference to anyone other than Anthony Davis. Before it solves discrimination in America, perhaps the league should get to work providing an All-Star Game that's watchable.

Milwaukee Journal Sentinel

THE PROGRESSIVE TROJAN HORSE

April 28, 2017

On June 3, 1916, tens of thousands of Chicagoans marched through the city's streets to support "preparedness," or the idea that the U.S. military should be ready for eventual engagement in the First World War. Official crowd counts put the number of parade participants at more than 130,000 — The Chicago Daily Tribune newspaper boasted that that made the parade the largest in American history. "Surely every one of the marchers went home last night a better American," noted the paper.

At the same time, preparedness marches were occurring all over America — but the Chicago parade was particularly of note, as it directly preceded the Republican National Convention that was about to kick off just blocks away from where the parade was held. And just days later, the first women's political party was formed, with a large march scheduled in Chicago's streets on the day the convention began. While 30,000 marchers were expected, only 5,000 showed up to demonstrate in the driving rain. (In order to recruit marchers, the suffragists hired a parrot that they trained to say things like "Polly's going to march" and "Polly wants a vote.")

These were the days when marching for a cause may have been at its most effective. The demonstrators pushed for a single, identifiable goal. They were organized and clear about their aims, and tried to persuade rather than insult. (Although dissent wasn't necessarily tolerated — several people on the preparedness parade route were arrested in their own homes for posting anti-war signs in their windows.)

Contrast those demonstrations with today's protests in which people march in favor of vague concepts like "women" and "science." In the past when protests were specific, people marched for things you could oppose, like preparing the military for war or granting voting rights to women (and many did.)

But the lexical shift towards generality now tries to put the theme of these events out of the reach of criticism. Who opposes "women?" Or denies that science is important? Or believes that black lives don't matter? If any local town held an "anti-women's" march, it would be a national public embarrassment (as well as a sub-optimal place to find a date.)

Of course, the whole purpose of naming these marches after amorphous concepts is to throw shade at your ideological opponents. Marching in favor of "science" presumes your political opponents don't believe in it. In the most passive-aggressive way possible, it tries to demonize non-participants while pretending to be pushing something universally accepted. If right-wingers held a "March for Economics," progressives would be justifiably peeved that the topic insinuated they are idiots. (Start building your John Maynard Keynes parade float, lefties.)

But the real reason to keep protest topics vague is to build a Trojan horse that allows the demonstration to smuggle in leftist politics under the guise of something more widely accepted. Clearly the "Women's March" was really all about abortion — women happily wore genitalia-themed headwear and pro-life groups were banned from being official partners in the event. If you are a woman who believes science tells us human life begins at conception, you were cordially invited to march elsewhere.

The same smugness infiltrated the March for Science, which was essentially a glorified climate change rally. The rally was headlined by television scientist Bill Nye, who is a scientist in the same way Bill Cosby is an obstetrician. Nye's recently released Netflix series features both a scene where Nye wonders aloud whether we should punish parents that have too many children and a song performed by TV star Rachel Bloom entitled My Sex Junk that encourages "butt stuff." (A scientific term first coined by Copernicus, I believe.)

It's fine if abortion enthusiasts or climate change congregants want to take to the streets to argue their respective cases. But they should stop identifying themselves as broad-based movements immune to counter-criticism.

And for those that agree, I'll see you all at the March for Better Marches.

Milwaukee Journal Sentinel

MAGICAL THINKING ON THE MINIMUM WAGE

July 14, 2017

Well before the preternaturally talented Lonzo Ball was taken with the second pick in the NBA draft last month, his loquacious father LaVar knew his son would end up playing for his hometown Los Angeles Lakers. "I'm going to speak it into existence," Ball promised. (And against all odds, he happened to be right.)

The ability to simply speak things into existence in the face of all evidence seems also to be a common political strategy on the left. Take, for example, the Democrats' indefatigable insistence on the economic benefits of increasing the minimum wage. Basic economics tells us that making employees more expensive leads to higher unemployment and reduced hours but progressives forge ahead, undaunted.

Perhaps now they'll realize they should be far more daunted.

A recent study by the University of Washington found that the City of Seattle's recent move to increase its citywide minimum wage to $15 has been detrimental to the very workers it was trying to help. According to the report, commissioned by the city itself and published by the National Bureau of Economic Research, the wage increase (only to $13 per hour now, but scheduled to hit $15 in a few years) actually decreased worker earnings by around $125 a month.

The conservative reaction? "Yeah, we know."

The news seemed to come as a shock to liberals, many of whom attacked the study's methodology and conclusions. Seattle's mayor even signed up for a new study from a team at the University of California-Berkeley that produced a study with results more to his liking.

This is entirely predictable, as the embarrassing results would undermine a core tenet of the left's agenda. During the presidential campaign, Hillary Clinton tied herself in knots explaining why she supported a $15 minimum wage. In April, Senators Bernie Sanders (I-Vt.) and Patty Murray (D-Wash.) introduced a bill to jack up the federal minimum wage to $15, and other bastions of progressivism such as Seattle, Minneapolis, New York, Washington, D.C., and the State of California already have done so. (In November, Milwaukee County passed an ordinance requiring a $15 "living wage" by 2021, but it only applies to county workers and those who do business with county government.)

But the University of Washington study, while not yet peer reviewed, includes the most detailed data set yet provided to minimum wage researchers. And the overwhelming majority of studies that have been conducted do show that higher minimum wages slow economic growth and cost low-income workers jobs. (Not surprisingly, anyone who questions the "scientific consensus" on climate change is labeled as a "denier," while those who ignore a similar consensus by economists on the minimum wage are simply seeking "economic justice.")

In this tradition, the Washington study tells us that once Seattle's minimum wage moved to $13 in 2016, the city lost 5,000 low-skilled workers, a reduction of 6.8%. Workers making less than $19 an hour lost nearly 3.5 million in work hours, a drop of 9.4%.

Naturally, the workers hardest hit weren't rich folks like Lonzo Ball. The study suggests that when the higher minimum wage hit, businesses would replace more lower-earning employees with fewer higher-earning ones to try to maximize productivity. This is in line with what we already knew — that minimum wage hikes are most detrimental to workers who are young, minority and low-income. (Thomas Sowell has written a great deal about how in the 1930s, minimum wage jobs were initially intended to squeeze black workers out of the workforce.)

Of course, none of this will affect progressive organized labor enthusiasts, who will continue to try to get theirs at the expense of other workers and the economy in general. They will ignore the fact that businesses that run on thin profit margins aren't piggy banks, and doubling their labor costs will throw people out into the street. They will keep holding rallies at which they will insist on speaking the benefits of minimum wage hikes into existence.

And when those rallies are over and they're feeling hungry, they can speak their order at McDonald's into a robot.

Milwaukee Journal Sentinel

DON'T TRY TO REGULATE 'FAKE NEWS'

October 20, 2017

In the 1500s, a new technology allowed for the mass distribution of information in a way the world had never seen. Suddenly, citizens of all continents had access to uniform sources of information, rather than depending on regional myths and customs.

That technology, of course, was the printing press.

The availability of cheap printing presses flooded the globe with books, treatises and pamphlets, exposing people in geographically distant lands to different ideas and soaking the global knowledge base with facts. But the wide distribution of knowledge came with a price; now that just about anyone could print up a pamphlet or book, sources of information became untrustworthy. Even printed materials as simple as maps were often wildly inaccurate; historian Daniel Boorstin once noted that "they were not so much maps of knowledge as maps of Scriptural dogma."

As America has seen recently with the promulgation of Internet-delivered "fake news," this new deluge of unverified information struck the world of politics, as well. "I thank God, there are no free schools nor printing," remarked William Berkeley, a 17th-century governor in colonial Virginia, "and I hope we shall never have these (for a) hundred years; for learning has brought disobedience, and heresy, and sects into the world, and printing has divulged them, and libels against the best government. God keep us from both!"

It appears the modern American public has taken Berkeley's side in the battle against "fake news:" A recent Economist/YouGov poll showed that only 20% of Americans opposed fining media outlets for "for publishing or broadcasting stories that are biased or inaccurate." Only 29% opposed shutting down media outlets for the same violation.

Ironically, despite the commonly-held belief that Internet-based "fake news" helped Donald Trump win the presidency in 2016, it is actually conservatives that want a crackdown on biased or incorrect reporting. Conditioned by decades of liberal media bias, 55% of Republicans want to see misleading news organizations fined, and 45% want to see news organizations forced to shut down.

This movement gained momentum last week when Trump suggested that "fake news" networks such as NBC should have their "licenses" pulled. "It is frankly disgusting the press is able to write whatever it wants to write," Trump said on Twitter.

Perhaps Trump has a keen sense of irony, as it is literally "fake news" to suggest anyone can "pull" NBC's license to report news.

But on the other end of the spectrum, Democrats are pushing new rules that would regulate whether foreigners can advertise on social media platforms such as Facebook during campaign season. Former Federal Elections Commission chair Ann Ravel has even suggested relaxing libel laws to go after social media sites that run "fake news," whether it's paid for or simply passed on after a five-second vetting session by that guy you worked with three jobs ago.

Of course, First Amendment protections aside, full-blown regulation of political discussions on Facebook is just as unfeasible as yanking broadcast licenses. For one, the spread of bogus stories will always outpace the regulators' ability to catch them. Further, who would be the one to determine what constitutes a "political" discussion? Do liberals really want to put Donald Trump in charge of policing their online chatter?

In fact, the evidence "fake news" made all that much difference is still very much in dispute. Of those who saw stories like "Trump Offering Free One-Way Tickets to Africa & Mexico for Those Who Wanna Leave America," how many actually either believed them or had planned to vote for Hillary Clinton and changed their mind as a result of seeing them?

And while Facebook admitted to accepting $100,000 in advertising from Russian sources, that number is almost infinitesimal in a race that saw $2.4 billion in spending, nonstop mainstream media coverage, three widely-watched debates, and two major party conventions. Anyone who has worked on campaigns knows how difficult it is to direct public opinion with spending and advertisements. As 2008 Hillary Clinton campaign chief strategist Mark Penn has noted, Clinton poured $6 million into Florida, Wisconsin, and Pennsylvania in the final weeks of the 2016 campaign. How did that turn out?

As was the case in the 16th century, the world will have to adapt to the influx of unreliable information. Hopefully, trusted sources will once again form to make sense of what's real and what's not. But if the mainstream media wants to accept the role of arbiter of truth, it should work harder to understand the half of the country that wouldn't object to seeing them vanish from the face of the Earth.

Milwaukee Journal Sentinel

THE POLITICS OF ENVY

December 5, 2017

As Republicans in the U.S. Senate passed tax reform legislation last week, a dark force swelled among liberals in America.

"America died tonight," tweeted Kurt Eichenwald of Vanity Fair, urging millennials to "move away if you can. USA is over. We killed it."

The next morning, comedian Patton Oswalt awoke and declared, "There's no America now," or at least "Not the one we knew."

Deep breath, guys.

It's. A. Tax. Cut.

The effect of the bill that has those on the left so worked up is the mistaken idea that the Republican plan raises taxes on lower income brackets and cuts taxes for America's wealthiest. If true, this would exacerbate "income inequality" in the U.S., requiring middle-class taxpayers to subsidize the rich.

But it's not true. According to an analysis by the liberal Tax Policy Center, under the bill, every income group would see an increase in after-tax incomes in 2019 and 2025. As Manhattan Institute economist Brian Riedl has noted, 75% of families will see a tax decrease, and the 12% that will see an increase are clustered among higher earners. The typical middle-income family will see a tax cut of about $850 per year until the year 2027.

Those pretending the bill increases taxes on the "little guy" focus on 2027 when the tax cuts expire. They cite tables showing taxes increasing disproportionately on lower incomes in the 10th year and scream the plan is a "tax increase," completely ignoring all the tax relief those families get in the first nine years of the plan and assuming Congress wouldn't re-authorize the cuts in the future.

Make no mistake: If Democrats killed this plan, middle-income taxpayers would pay nearly $7,000 in higher taxes over the next decade. And yet liberals believe Republicans are the ones vacuuming your pockets.

Progressives forge ahead with misleading statistics in service of their dedication to "fairness." The bill, they argue will exacerbate "income inequality," widening the gap between rich and poor.

But this is simply stoking resentment among taxpayers who will be better off because someone else might better off than they are. As Margaret Thatcher famously declared, the "income gap" has two ends. Taken to its logical conclusion, progressives would be happier with a smaller wage gap if the poor were poorer and the rich not so rich. This tax plan seeks the opposite — it tries to make everyone better off, regardless of the spread between rich and poor.

In fact, it would be virtually impossible to implement a meaningful tax cut without disproportionately benefiting the people who pay the most in taxes. Currently, the top 20% of taxpayers pay 88% of all federal income taxes; the lowest 40% of earners pay no income tax at all. If Congress determines it wants to let people keep their own money, it has to target those who contribute.

Instead of vilifying rich people, progressives should be in favor of creating more of them because, without high-earners, government programs would be gasping for cash. (Just imagine the Democrats' reaction if Republicans had made the cuts to government necessary to fund these tax cuts, rather than relying on $1 billion in new debt.)

Somewhere along the line, Americans on the left began thinking incomes were a zero-sum game; if someone was making more money, it meant they were making less. But the idea that your life would be better if someone else was worse off is antithetical to an opportunity society.

Envy may be a useful talking point, but as a general rule, deadly sins make for bad tax policy.

USA Today

TIME TO RETIRE SOCIAL SECURITY NUMBERS

January 9, 2018

On Dec. 1, 1936, government administrator Joe Fay walked over to a stack of cards in his Baltimore office, plucked the first piece of paper off the top, and made a historic announcement.

Written on the card was the name of John David Sweeney, a 23-year old shipping clerk from New Rochelle, N.Y. By having his name announced, Sweeney was the first record entered into a new government program called "Social Security."

Along with Sweeney's entrance into the program came an identifying number (055-09-0001) that would allow him to collect his Social Security benefits when he retired. Ironically, Sweeney was a Republican who didn't think much of President Roosevelt's New Deal programs, although he admitted he favored Social Security. But he would die in 1974 at age 61 without collecting any of the benefits he had accrued over the course of his working life.

From Sweeney on, Americans would be issued a unique number that would match them up with their Social Security benefits. But over the years, those Social Security numbers have morphed into something completely different; they have now essentially become every American's national identification number, wreaking havoc on personal security and privacy.

The dangers of using Social Security numbers as a unique identifier became clear last year when credit reporting giant Equifax was hacked, endangering the personal data of up to 145.5 million Americans. The Equifax disaster exposed individual Social Security numbers, which can now be used to apply for credit, set up checking accounts, apply for jobs, and to access personal financial information online. The leak of Social Security numbers and dates of birth are especially damaging, since, unlike passwords, those identifiers can't be changed once they've been stolen.

In the early days of paper record-keeping, Social Security numbers were reasonably secure; the number-holder held a card with a number known only to them printed on it. In the 1960s, banks began using the numbers to match names to bank accounts; soon, credit reporting agencies began using the numbers to authenticate individuals' identities. In 1972, the government stopped printing "Not for Identification" on Social Security cards.

But in the computer era, large swaths of these numbers can be stolen, transmitted, used to steal an individual's identity. This was never supposed to be the case; according to the Social Security Administration, the cards were "never intended to serve as a personal identification document."

Fortunately, both President Donald Trump's administration and congressional leaders are looking into ways to supplant Social Security numbers as Americans' primary personal identifier. Republican Congressman Patrick McHenry of North Carolina has introduced a bill requiring credit-reporting firms to phase out the use of Social Security numbers by 2020. White House cybersecurity coordinator Rob Joyce has floated the possibility of replacing the numbers with "cryptographic keys" that unlock an individual's private data. Joyce has noted "every time we use the Social Security number, we put it at risk."

Thus, while technology has rendered Social Security numbers obsolete, new advances may hold the key to replacing them. Anyone who's bought an iPhone in the past year can see how quickly biometrics have progressed; fingerprint and face recognition are now standard for unlocking electronic devices. Given last year's Equifax breach, your Instagram account currently appears to be more secure than your credit history.

With the enormous power credit-reporting agencies have over our personal information, Congress should move quickly to force agencies such as Equifax, Experian PLC and TransUnion to modernize their authentication procedures. America's government safety net record-keepers have done the hard work for these agencies for too long; now it's finally time for Social Security numbers to retire.

Milwaukee Journal Sentinel

I'M NOT TO BLAME FOR SAN BERNARDINO

December 9, 2015

Imagine my surprise last Wednesday when I found out I was complicit in a mass shooting.

Within hours of Syed Farook and Tashfeen Malik killing 14 people in San Bernardino last week, social media lit up with people blaming insufficient gun control measures for the massacre. Quite often, they were accompanied by a hastily penned platitude about how "we are all responsible" for the California bloodbath. Even as details still unfolded, the New Yorker's Adam Gopnik sprinted to his keyboard to bang out an essay titled "Our Shared Blame for the Shooting in San Bernardino."

But I have good news for those suffering from guilt over last week's events: You are in no way responsible for mass shootings. And neither am I. Not one damn bit.

Perhaps it brings solace to some to feel as if they are "citizens of the world," interconnected with every action that takes place in society. No one wants to be John Donne's proverbial island, entire of itself.

But the blame for any violent act resides solely with whoever carries it out. I'm no more responsible for someone who picks up a gun and shoots another human than I am for someone who drinks too much Wild Turkey and crashes a car into a school bus or someone else who posts racist comments online.

And, of course, the tenuous connection between gun control and the San Bernardino shootings evaporated almost immediately as authorities realized Farook and Malik were Islamic terrorists intent on eviscerating as many of their neighbors as possible. Guns were merely the medium they used for their act; had they not used their legally purchased firearms, they could have used the dozens of bombs they had assembled at home.

California already has the most restrictive gun laws in America; no new firearm law would have dissuaded any violent terrorist willing to die in the act of killing Americans. Malik was a mother who left behind her 6-month-old child before going on a suicidal killing spree; presumably, she hadn't spent a good deal of time combing through California's statute books.

In fact, in the past 30 years, gun laws have been liberalized to the point that every state now allows citizens to carry concealed weapons — and in that time, both the overall and violent crime rate has been cut nearly in half. Between 1993 and 2011, the gun homicide rate in America fell 49%. If causation is to be ascribed, Second Amendment enthusiasts should be getting credit rather than blame. A simple "thank you" would suffice.

But this all gives too much credit to the idea that by staying "silent," Americans are co-conspirators in gun violence. Gopnik even predictably invokes the Germans who stood by as the Nazis committed war crimes.

"We did not, at Nuremberg, find the German people guilty of war crimes; we found their generals and the S.S. apparatus guilty... But to talk of German responsibility for the crimes was legitimate and, indeed, essential," writes Gopnik. Never mind that opposing the SS apparatus in the 1930s could earn a German citizen a bullet to the head — in 2015, objecting to the National Rifle Association in America may earn a dissenter the horror of seeing NRA President Wayne LaPierre in a television ad.

The left often forgets that Democrats had full control of Congress and the presidency between 2009 and 2011. If one believes these proposals now being used to demagogue the GOP would have made any difference, why wouldn't the party that failed to enact them when they had full control of the government be more culpable?

That's because to liberals, saying all Americans "share" responsibility is a seemingly magnanimous way of pointing the finger at Republicans. If San Bernardino is about gun violence, the GOP is to blame; if it's about terrorism, President Barack Obama gets the criticism.

But when everyone is responsible, then nobody is to blame. Only those who fire guns at others are culpable for their actions. And for this reason, I find you not guilty.

Milwaukee Journal Sentinel

THE PUSH FOR MORE IMMATURITY IN POLICYMAKING

February 27, 2018

"Youth," wrote Oscar Wilde in "The Picture of Dorian Gray," "is the one thing worth having."

And in the days after the tragic school shooting in Parkland, Fla., commentators are proving that Wilde's words are prophetic — they are promoting the unbridled emotionalism of teenagers over the wisdom of their elders. Media appearances by students who survived the tragic shooting at Marjory Stoneman Douglas High School have cast a spell over adults smitten with the idea that children can be just as knowledgeable and politically active as their parents.

But this has led to some terrible ideas, including proposals to allow children under the age of 18 to vote. Writing in Bloomberg, Jonathan Bernstein argued the voting age should be as low as 13 or 14, calling voting the "training wheels of political participation." University of Kentucky law professor Joshua Douglas wrote in support of 16- and 17-year-olds voting, calling them "the real adults in the room."

This is on the heels of a fawning national media that realized children have political opinions the second they begin pushing for gun control. Curiously, thousands of teenagers take to the streets at the March for Life in Washington, D.C., every year but the major news outlets haven't rushed to praise their political involvement.

This newfound enthusiasm for children voting is all the odder because it contradicts the message being pushed by gun control advocates. At the same time we are supposed to believe 16-year-olds are mature enough to vote on matters of national importance, we are also being told that the minimum age to own a firearm should be raised to 21.

It's not as if immaturity is the one thing politics lacks. President Donald Trump's critics frequently shred him for acting like a "child," or behaving like a "teenager." If we desire more of the juvenilia dished up by Trump on a daily basis, there would be no better way than to let actual juveniles pick the president.

In the wake of the shooting, the passion displayed by some of the survivors has been admirable. But the idea of pushing children onto a national stage to discuss complex issues hasn't exactly been a success. One student, on national television, defended the school safety officer who refused to engage the shooter, blamed Florida Gov. Rick Scott for the failure of local law enforcement officials to enter the school during the shooting, and is trying to get vacationers to boycott Florida during spring break. (When the teenager realized the county sheriff was actually elected and not appointed by the governor, he backed off his criticism of Scott.)

These are the pitfalls of elevating regular kids to be policy experts simply because they were witness to a traumatic event. The public perception of politics has gotten so bad, it appears, that Americans are willing to give the opinions of anyone, even those not old enough to vote, equal weight. (The real lesson for these kids should be that their government — even if warned dozens of times — cannot always keep them safe. And that they should be wary of a bumbling government deciding how citizens should protect themselves when law enforcement fails.)

There are kids who are eloquent and smart and who impress us with their maturity. But not even the progressive fever swamps have granted the full franchise to voters under the age of 18. It is an idea historically rejected even by partisans who stand to gain the most.

While some progressives are telling us that college students are so delicate they must be protected from "microaggressions," they now seem to believe high school children are imbued with magical wisdom and worldly knowledge. It's an argument one would almost expect from a 16-year-old.

Milwaukee Journal Sentinel

THE KIDS AREN'T RIGHT

March 30, 2018

Have you ever looked at a photo of yourself from just a week ago and thought, "Man, I wish I knew then what I know now?" Have you remembered things you did ten years ago and felt like they were done by a completely different person? Do you have untold volumes of sage advice you would pass down to your high school self?

Now think about all the accumulated knowledge stored up in people who have lived two or three times as long as you have. If you're impressed by how much you've learned in the last week, start adding up week after week until it gets into the tens of thousands. As the saying goes, when an elderly person dies, it's like losing a library.

In the past month, however, America has decided it would rather steep itself in the nascent wisdom of a bunch of young people who have yet to graduate from high school. TIME Magazine has dubbed them the "school shooting generation," and they have been lionized with worldwide media coverage before, during and after national demonstrations.

Sure enough, there's an excitement to seeing a young generation of Americans get so involved in pressing issues of the day. (Although kids the age of the Parkland shooting survivors have been fighting in American wars going back to the nation's founding, and doing so without the gratification of having a Twitter hashtag named after them.)

The gun control kids are emotional, telegenic, and frequently wrong. But they're attractive because they represent the promise of new ideas and unexpected possibilities. Like the child rulers from centuries ago, they have been imbued with a magical ability to affect societal change before they're even allowed to go see "Get Out" in a movie theater.

Plenty has already been written about the wisdom of allowing children to speak with authority on complicated issues that intermingle history, society and government. It seems a better use of time to make a positive case for experience.

In other words, give me the old folks.

As Austrian novelist Marie von Ebner-Eschenbach said, "In youth we learn; in age we understand." Senior citizens not only have the benefit of being able to see what is happening in front of them, they are also able to put those events in context to gauge their relative importance.

The elderly have seen wars and assassinations. They have witnessed terrorist attacks and the spread of deadly diseases. They were around in the mid-1960's when Congress passed gun control and homicides increased. They remember that the "assault weapons" ban of the 1990s made little difference in the amount of gun crime in America.

But that is the appeal of using young people to push a political message; they don't remember any of these things, so their idealism is unmoored from history. They are free to adopt the attitude of Lord Henry from Oscar Wilde's "The Picture of Dorian Gray" — that "Experience was of no ethical value. It was merely the name men gave to their mistakes."

And thus, high schoolers have now become the first generation we are listening to because of their inexperience, not in spite of it. At last weekend's March for Our Lives, reporters scrambled to interview any baby-faced cherub walking with a sign, as if youth alone was a qualification for their point of view being taken seriously. During the march, no reporters were parked outside the retirement home interviewing seniors and simply identifying them as "Person Who Has Lived a Long Time."

Perhaps my affinity for the aged is rooted in the fact that they tend to be more conservative. Republicans almost always win voters over 65 by wide margins, presumably because of older voters' desire to "conserve" the world they have known since childhood. Younger voters, on the other hand, aren't wistful for the old days, and thus don't necessarily see any benefit in "conserving" traditional social mores. They believe their generation is the first one to have inhabited the earth and are unaware of the historical forces that have forged America pushing against them.

218

Of course there are plenty of seniors who support the aims of the Parkland survivors, just as there are plenty of elderly people who shouldn't ever be on TV expressing their unfortunate views on race and sexuality. But as a society, we have come to value emotion over experience, and youthful vigor over knowledge.

At some point in the future, many of the young people speaking out today are going to look back, see the video footage, and wonder if the fresh faces on the screen are even them. It is why, to quote Wilde again, "To get back one's youth, one has merely to repeat one's follies."

Milwaukee Journal Sentinel

IF THE NRA OWNS REPUBLICANS, PLANNED PARENTHOOD OWNS DEMOCRATS

February 26, 2018

In August 2015, Sen. Elizabeth Warren, D-Mass., took to the Senate floor to decry ongoing Republican attempts to defund Planned Parenthood. The vote was taking place after a summer in which the nation watched grisly undercover videos showing Planned Parenthood abortion doctors discussing the sale of fetal body parts to activists posing as researchers.

Naturally, there was a media outcry over Warren's speech, given that she had received more than $16,000 from Planned Parenthood during her 2012 campaign. Major newspapers were saturated with stories reminding us that the left was in the pocket of Big Abortion. Who can forget all the hours the news networks dedicated to blaming Democrats for the loss of millions of innocent lives after Planned Parenthood had spent nearly $50 million on elections and lobbying since 2012?

Of course, nobody can forget any of that because none of it ever happened. Instead, Democrats were showered with gushing mainstream news articles praising their fight for "women's health care" and their personal resolve in standing up to those who want to "take away a woman's right to control her own body."

Contrast that with coverage Republicans receive after any mass shooting in America. Suddenly, the National Rifle Association is unmasked as the GOP puppet master, blocking any and all "commonsense" legislation to cut down on gun violence.

Within hours of the shooting tragedy in Parkland, Fla., last week, The Washington Post had updated a page for readers to see how much money the NRA had given their member of Congress. After the Las Vegas shooting last October, The New York Times' editorial page ran a woefully misleading chart purporting to show which congressional Republicans had received the most help "from the NRA" while mocking the idea of sending "thoughts and prayers."

The double standard is clear: When Democrats work on behalf of a special interest that aborts millions of children, they are doing so from a place of conscience and ideological purity. When Republicans argue in favor of Second Amendment rights, it is because they have been bought off by a disfavored lobbying group looking to profit from carnage. (Or as comedian Jimmy Kimmel diplomatically put it, the NRA has the GOP's "balls in a money clip.")

Evidently, the NRA is the only special interest group that owns a testicular entrapment device. Rare are the stories exposing the money spent electing Democrats by unions, trial lawyers or environmental groups — all of which outspend the NRA year after year. In fact, since 2012, Planned Parenthood alone has donated virtually the same amount ($2.6 million) to individual candidates as the NRA ($2.7 million).

The NRA has, however, spent more in third-party independent ads that either criticize Democrats or support Republicans. But this highlights one of the most pervasive misunderstandings about the NRA's involvement in politics. Candidates actually "accept" very little money from gun-rights groups. Instead, almost all of the spending the NRA does is in the form of issue advertising independent of the candidates they support.

Though gun-control advocates may try to smear Sen. Marco Rubio, R-Fla., for having taken $3.3 million from the NRA, the reality is that the group has directly donated only about $5,000 to his campaigns.

The rest is in the form of its own spending, which the NRA would have every right to do even if Rubio told them to stop or if he disagreed with its message. And, of course, a direct contribution of a few thousand dollars is an almost infinitesimal amount when compared with a congressman's total fundraising.

Even so, the vilification of the NRA makes complete sense for gun-control advocates, as it depersonalizes the issues and makes it seem as if no reasonable individual person could oppose new gun laws. The NRA is powerful only because a lot of regular Americans agree with it; but slamming an evil, faceless monolith is easier than explaining why, unless it's right after a trauma like a mass shooting, half the country generally opposes most new gun control regulations, including reinstating a ban on "assault weapons."

In a Washington Post-ABC News poll released last week, 57% of respondents said mass shootings in America are more a reflection of problems with identifying and treating people with mental health problems, while only 28% blamed inadequate gun control laws. So statistically, if you support gun control to "solve" the recent spate of shootings, two of your neighbors don't think new regulations alone would have made any difference. Were they bought off by the NRA, too?

(That's not to mention Democrats, who controlled both Congress and the presidency from 2009 to 2011 and did nothing to tighten gun laws.)

From abortion to guns, special interest groups support candidates who most closely reflect their values. The constant need to tie a party's actions to these contributions is a cynical ploy that only devalues Congress in the voters' eyes. And it is especially destructive when applied only to one party.

If money equals votes, the solution for gun-control advocates should be easy — Kimmel and his pals should write a huge check to Republicans to get them to change their mind. Unfortunately for him, he'd find out the hard way that a money clip is a little harder to apply than he thought.

USA Today

FEDERALISM IN THE WOMB

July 10, 2018

In 1944, 14-year-old George Stinney stood less than 5 feet tall and weighed under 100 pounds. According to reports at the time, Stinney's small stature made it difficult for prison guards to strap his small arms into the electric chair. When his executioner finally flipped the switch, Stinney's convulsions knocked off the mask he was wearing, exposing his tearful face to onlookers.

Stinney, a young African-American boy living in South Carolina, had been found guilty of brutally beating two white girls to death with a railroad spike. The trial lasted two hours, and the jury deliberated for 10 minutes before sentencing Stinney to the electric chair.

In December of 2014, seven decades after his death, Stinney was exonerated.

In 2018, 31 states still utilize the death penalty to punish offenders. Across America for most crimes, state legislators ultimately decide the most fundamental questions about the value of human life.

Yet the system isn't perfect. According to the Innocence Project, 358 inmates have been freed since the first DNA exoneration took place in 1989; of these, 20 served time on death row. Without new technology, these inmates, like George Stinney, would likely be dead at the hands of their state or federal government.

It would seem that the government putting its own people to death would be a matter of grave public concern, yet anti-capital punishment protests are rare. The demonstrations that do occur are typically small and local. There are no rallies in Washington, D.C., featuring millions of marchers and celebrity speakers, even though polling currently suggests support for the death penalty has fallen to its lowest level (55%) since 1972.

The national reaction to the death penalty stands in stark contrast to the reaction to abortion, which still drives massive protests on both sides. Emotions are likely to become even more frayed, as President Donald Trump unveiled Judge Brett Kavanaugh to replace Justice Anthony Kennedy on the U.S. Supreme Court. Kavanaugh may hold the deciding vote to overturn the 1973 Roe v. Wade decision, which legalized abortion across the nation.

Before Roe, abortion was treated much as the death penalty continues to be — state voters and lawmakers were able to determine what their consciences could tolerate.

Roe and a number of other "reproductive rights" cases ripped the abortion issue from the hands of voters. Fueled by gender politics, the court instead conjured a then-unprecedented "right to privacy" that continues to have no basis in the U.S. Constitution.

So while state legislatures were once able to determine to whom all the rights and privileges of citizenship applied — even if they had yet to be born — the Supreme Court invalidated those laws in favor of its own will. This heavy-handed usurpation of representative democracy has driven the emotional debate for the last 45 years. Rather than lobby their state representatives and governors, activists on both sides have been driven to grand spectacles and extreme rhetoric to win the public relations battle.

This rhetoric includes pro-choice scaremongering about Trump's court pick. Groups such as Planned Parenthood and NARAL are busy ginning up theatrical hysteria, warning that abortion will be outlawed once Roe v. Wade is overturned. Before even knowing who would be nominated, pro-choice advocates were already deeming the next pick "extreme."

Yet in their most recent poll, Gallup found 53% of respondents believe abortion should either be "illegal in all circumstances" or "legal only in a few circumstances." This, of course, is around the same number of Americans who support the death penalty.

In one instance, citizens are empowered with matters of life and death and in another they are not — a dichotomy that has triggered decades of discontent. (In many states, a mother choosing to kill her unborn child is legal, while a man who kills that same unborn child without the mother's permission can himself be given the death penalty.)

A fifth conservative on the Supreme Court wouldn't necessarily render Roe a dead decision walking. But even if Roe were overturned, abortion wouldn't suddenly be banned — the issue would simply revert back to states or fall to Congress, where the democratic process would once again take hold.

As the late Justice Antonin Scalia once said, there is no longer any use "trying to persuade your fellow citizens one way or the other about the subject," as abortion has been "taken off the democratic stage."

Putting the issue back on the playbill will allow voters to make their own decisions about when life begins and when it ends. Citizens should be able to cast a ballot to protest the premature extinction of human life — whether or not that person has undergone the technicality of having been born.

Milwaukee Journal Sentinel

WHAT DEMOCRATS MEAN WHEN THEY TALK ABOUT SCIENCE

March 13, 2019

In the early 1900s, Dr. Arthur Reynolds served as a sort of Dr. Oz for American newspaper readers. Reynolds, the former health commissioner of Chicago, would write articles in American Magazine sharing the latest scientific breakthroughs with his readers. Papers across the country would run excerpts of his groundbreaking work, instructing millions on ways to change their lives for the better.

In July 1916, Reynolds released the results of a scientific study that showed men go bald because they wear hats. Hats caused baldness "by compressing the arteries, the veins, the lymphatics, and to some extent the nerves that supply and nourish the hair," Reynolds wrote. He acknowledged that women also wore hats, but women's hats "do not grip the head as men's hats do."

Reynolds had also argued that the key to having good skin complexion was to defecate the same weight of food from your body per day as you take in, and he once warned parents that children should go barefoot at all times during the summer and while indoors, as shoes "distort" children's feet and toes. At one point, Reynolds suggested drinking cocktails made one much more likely to contract pneumonia.

Needless to say, the science of 1916 was far different than the science of 2019. Yet because of such drastic changes over time, one might expect those citing modern science to use a little humility. But those people are not running for the Democratic presidential nomination.

In announcing her run for president, Kamala Harris said she had to act "on science fact, not science fiction." At her announcement, Amy Klobuchar insisted the facts were on her side because the people "believe in science."

And then there's Elizabeth Warren, who frequently swears blanket obeisance to science. Interesting, then, that science has proved her a fraud; DNA testing has demonstrated that Warren has almost no Native American genes, though she once touted her Indian heritage. It is clear she has descended from a rare group known as homo preposterus, human beings who take pleasure in stepping on rakes.

Of course, all these candidates are speaking about "science" simply as a lever to implement their preferred policies on climate control and to cast conservatives as retrograde mouth-breathers. It's not enough to believe the the earth is warming; those who are skeptical that the answer is to drink out of soggy paper straws are cast aside as heretics.

Because for progressives, at least in the case of climate change, the science is static. Never mind that such a belief demonstrates a hubris that doesn't recognize either the past or the future. Simply genuflecting to "science" assumes we'll always know exactly what we know now.

In fact, for those involved in politics, science has almost always been the slave of ideology. During Prohibition, "drys" frequently cited scientific studies that purported to show alcoholism could damage an individual's DNA (or "germ plasm"), and damage his offspring through heredity. One poster by the National Education Association, which favored alcohol prohibition, argued:

Laboratory experiments have taught us that even small doses of alcohol attack the most highly developed cells of the body—the brain, the nerves, the racial cells of procreation. These creative cells in alcoholic parents—if not completely destroyed—are degenerated and the child suffers the fatal consequences even before birth. The children of drinking parents show a strong tendency toward weakened mentality—there are more idiots and inferior individuals among them. It is even probable that the germ plasm itself —that vital spark which continues on thru countless centuries—is so affected by alcohol that the children for generations to come suffer from the sins of the fathers.

"Wets" argued this was nonsense. "If alcohol did cause feeble-mindedness," wrote Dr. Henry H. Goddard, "the number of the feeble-minded would be enormously greater than it now is." One Wisconsin congressman said he believed drinking cultures had been proven superior, crudely boasting of a "handful of beer and ale drinking Englishmen holding in subjection 300,000,000 Hindu teetotalers."

Yet the Prohibition enthusiasts—the great majority of whom were progressives who believed alcohol harmed the working class—used "science" simply as a means to achieve their broader goal, expanded government control over Americans' lives. None of this science was actually valid; it simply fit their purpose like a baldness-inducing fedora.

And control over our lives is simply what modern progressives are after. The Green New Deal has almost nothing to do with science and nearly everything to do with dictating how regular Americans travel, live, eat, and interact with one another. Alexandria Ocasio-Cortez, who believes science has told her the world is going to end in a dozen years, has actually raised the specter of population control, an idea taken whole cloth from the racist progressive eugenicists of the early 20th century.

Obviously, a great deal of science is real and produces demonstrable results. Just last week, scientists announced an HIV patient had been cured of the disease. Scientists are making significant progress in understanding how we age, and fighting cancer. Astronomers are finding new planets all the time, and even some that aren't so different from earth.

But "science" writ large is always changing, always churning. As Thomas Kuhn wrote in his classic 1962 book The Structure of Scientific Revolutions, what we know now will not always be the case. As we collect more information, paradigms shift and more creative theories come to light. "Science" is a process, not an immovable object—otherwise, every child in America would have mangled feet.

Around two years ago, I took a DNA test from a major testing service. When I received the results back, the report said I was twice as English (30 percent) as I was German (15 percent). Last week, I checked the results again, and those numbers have now switched to 25 percent and 26 percent, respectively. Every day I am getting more German—in two years, I might just be a giant bowl of sauerkraut.

Clearly, science is always changing. The question is whether as a society, we want to implement potentially damaging policies that could outlive the way we look at the world. Someday, obsessing over the warming climate might seem like tweeting from an abacus.

The Bulwark

SCENES FROM A NIGHT OF RIOTING IN MADISON

August 22, 2021

MADISON, Wisconsin—At midnight, standing where a statue commemorating women's suffrage was torn down just weeks earlier, a young woman with a bullhorn explained rioting etiquette.

"Make sure you stay with your buddy when the s--t goes down," she said, adding, "people who are alone get arrested."

She noted that when the violence actually began, anyone caught with their cell phone out taking pictures would be dealt with. "Pictures get people identified," she barked.

She then announced the group would then be headed to the Dane County Jail.

It was the second night in the most recent round of protesting in Madison following the shooting of Jacob Blake of nearby Kenosha. Blake is still in serious condition and is reportedly paralyzed from the waist down following the shooting.

Violent riots have engulfed Kenosha after Blake was shot seven times in the back by police—on Tuesday night, three people were shot and two died after an encounter between protesters and armed men at a gas station.

Madison, meanwhile, has been in protest mode almost continually since the death of George Floyd while in the custody of Minneapolis police. The fact that another act of police violence against a black man happened an hour's drive away renewed the penchant for property damage among Madison's youth.

On Monday night, Madison experienced what Fire Chief Steven Davis called "probably the most destruction and damage I've seen in this city as far as arson fires and attempted arson."

And so on Tuesday, Madison Police Chief Vic Wahl said property damage would not be tolerated.

"We are committed to preserving people's ability to protect their opinions, but property damage, starting fires, violence and things that put our community at risk is obviously the type of behavior we're not going to condone and will make us intervene," he said.

But at midnight, despite the protesters announcing where they were going to begin to damage property and how they planned to avoid arrest, law enforcement was nowhere to be found. On the off chance the crowd of about 200 people encountered a police car, the officer would courteously pull away and let the chanting marchers continue unabated.

Minutes after the blueprint for bedlam was given to the crowd— organizers explained that nobody can tell people of color how to express their pain because they suffer from "post traumatic slave syndrome"— young men started picking up small rocks and hurling them at glass windows in the courthouse. The structure has an enormous wall made up almost entirely of windows, and I often had to duck to make sure I wasn't hit by a rock thrown by the people five feet to my right.

The crowd then turned left on Carroll Street, where an enormous American flag had been draped on the street and lit on fire. The flag, however, was stubbornly flame-retardant, so protesters began spraying it with some sort of accelerant. Finally, one protester just dropped the whole pressurized spray can on the flag, and it exploded like a bomb going off.

The crowd stopped marching every few blocks for more speeches, but the violence didn't let up. Finally, a skinny man with what appeared to be a motorcycle's exhaust pipe began smashing in enormous windows belonging to a local poke bowl restaurant. They continued down the line, shattering windows to what appeared to be a condominium office next door. Some men crawled through the opening and danced inside.

When one protester suggested cleaning up the broken glass, another said "let the white people clean it up."

As this took place, almost out of nowhere, some men appeared with a dumpster full of flaming materials, rolling it out to the middle of University Avenue. Soon, other protesters cracked the window of a Papa John's pizza franchise as an irate employee looked on from inside, waving his arms in anger. Finally, a second wave of rioters finished the job and smashed the window completely out. Several other protesters stopped to help clean up the broken glass.

By this time, the flaming dumpster had become an afterthought, but upon looking back, I realized that it had erupted, with flames 20 feet high. The protesters had left it and were 100 yards down the street setting fire to another dumpster and smashing more windows.

The night had begun on a far different note. At about 9:30, a group of elected officials led by respected Boys and Girls Club CEO Michael Johnson gathered to urge nonviolence throughout the night. "We can't burn our city down," said Johnson. "When people come here and try to tear s--t down, we need to intervene," he said.

And for a while, his pleas worked. For two hours, the mass of people marched through the streets of the city, chanting, and sporadically stopping in front of large apartment buildings to urge the beer-drinking students on their patios to come out and join them.

Amid the occasional waft of marijuana smoke, the group, led by two young women with bullhorns, ran through a litany of chants. At one point, one of the women stopped to lecture the attendees for walking too fast down a hill. "You have to walk slowly down a hill!" she yelled, ending with "UNITY!"

At about 11 p.m., the mass of people stopped in front of Memorial Library on the University of Wisconsin campus. Several speeches were given, many with theatrical pauses and emotional notes. Bits of wisdom imparted on the crowd ranged from "without change, nothing happens" to "unless change comes, it's a problem."

But the primary speakers did give their demands to any lawmakers who might be listening. They want passage of a law banning no-knock warrants, such as the one used in the killing of Breonna Taylor by police in Louisville, Kentucky. They demanded passage of the "Hands Up, Don't Shoot" law, which would require the immediate arrest of any officer that kills an unarmed individual. And finally, they urged "community control" of the local police force, which would allow citizens to overrule law enforcement practices and decisions.

But in order to control the police force, they would have to find them first. With fires raging and broken glass littering the ground, officers in riot gear finally appeared at 1:20 a.m., late enough to allow those who smashed windows and started fires to vanish. With officers on horses and in squad cars, they eventually pushed everyone back to the Capitol where a number of arrests were reportedly made.

At 2 a.m., with the crowd dispersed, I began walking back to my car when I saw it was surrounded by police cars. To my right, I saw a young man run up beside me and throw what looked like a lit piece of dynamite at the cops. One officer yelled "incoming!" and an enormous explosion took place—it was the size of one of the fireworks they shoot into the air during the Fourth of July. I was just far away enough that I didn't get hit, but close enough that an officer would easily assume I was the one who threw it.

I quickly walked backward, ducked into an alley, and was able to work my way behind the police to my car. I was thankful I was alive and not in handcuffs.

But it was clear, after another night of violence and destruction, nobody was any closer to receiving justice.

The Dispatch

REMEMBER WHO THE ENEMY IS

April 22, 2021

Everyone knows that a drama is often most compelling when it has an identifiable villain. But in real life, it's not always easy to know who the bad guy is. Modern-day struggles often involve an evil that is invisible—carbon dioxide, pathogens, existential dread, etc.

This is the conundrum for the politically-minded in America right now— the COVID-19 virus doesn't have a face. It doesn't laugh maniacally. It doesn't tie you up, deliver an extended soliloquy about what its plans are, then leave you hanging over a pool of sharks while you wriggle to freedom. And there are consequences for using metaphors for medical circumstances.

Unable to vilify a microscopic organism, society's aspiring dramatists have turned against other humans as the cause of their woes.

The bad guys in MAGA-world are now America's governors, all of whom in some fashion have shut down schools, businesses, and socializing in the wake of what has now become America's leading cause of death—in little over a month.

Viruses don't have motives, so right-wingers have been happy to ascribe them to both Republican and Democratic governors. According to these self-appointed true patriots, governors are delighting in flexing their authoritarian muscles, robbing freedom-lovers of their constitutional rights. Had James Madison only known the joys of Outback Steakhouse, they argue, the nation's founding document would have protected an individual's right not to have to get a Bloomin' Onion via takeout.

Under this theory, governors across America are huddled with their staffs, calculating that the best way for them to achieve re-election is to shut down economic activity in their state, costing thousands of people jobs, and leaving schoolchildren uneducated. Naturally, this makes for a suboptimal yard sign come November.

"Aha!" Team Red Hat yells through their unmasked mouths in between coughs. "They are purposely trying to destroy the economy that President Donald Trump built in order to make him look bad during the election!" This is not an exaggeration:

This theory, however, would be news to Republican governors like Maryland's Larry Hogan and Ohio's Mike DeWine, both of whom took swift action to close their states down when the true threat of the coronavirus was known. Again, Republican and Democratic governors alike have taken strict actions to mandate social distancing; even the GOP-led states like Arkansas and South Dakota, while not issuing strict stay-at-home orders, have closed schools and requested businesses institute social distancing measures.

Partisan motives aside, it is insane to believe governors are exercising this authority because of a political agenda or that they "don't care" that their small businesses are suffering. Governors are keeping a close eye on their states' jobless claims—but they are paying more acute attention to their states' health statistics.

Governors care very much about their bars, restaurants, and salons—but they also care very much about their constituents dying. Hopefully, we will soon see states enact more aid programs to help stem the tragic loss of jobs we have seen—but a job can return. A human being, with one notable exception, cannot.

Sure, there are some governors who appear to be melting under the COVID-19 heat lamps. Michigan's Democratic Gov. Gretchen Whitmer has been issuing orders that reach way too far and make little sense, leaving the people of her state confused and angry.

The real tragedy of the overreaches by Whitmer and others is that they give the "open America now" crowd a straw to grasp. Now people in Ohio and Minnesota and Wisconsin are acting like their governors are one step away from instituting martial law.

Over the weekend, thousands of Americans gathered in public to protest the actions taken by their individual states. The same erstwhile Tea Partiers who once advocated for more local control rallied against federalism when Donald Trump is at the controls of the national government.

For more than a month, well-meaning Americans have voluntarily sacrificed and stayed indoors—but aspiring hot spot-based protesters are now trying to make sure all that effort is for naught. Protesting measures to prevent sickness by doing the thing most likely to get you sick is like protesting gun control by letting people shoot at you.

It's almost as if America is playing into the comic book trope where every superhero trying to save lives is vilified as a bad guy.

Just imagine if there were a governor who just reopened his or her state's elementary schools, college campuses, and restaurants by snapping their fingers, letting "herd immunity" run wild. They would over-night be the new darling of the MAGA Right—guaranteed to be named America's Awesomest Governor, holding concerts and baseball games and doorknob-licking contests.

But there's a reason nobody from the reddest to the bluest state has done it.

"Herd immunity," of course, has traditionally been known as "vaccination." But in the absence of a vaccine, it is best known as "let's let everyone get sick, and even though millions of people might die unnecessarily and our medical systems will be overwhelmed, at least we'll get it over with sooner."

And if you're looking for a governor's true motivation, it is to prevent exactly this from happening. Purposely killing grandmothers has traditionally been an unsuccessful election platform.

As John Barth wrote, "Everyone is necessarily the hero of their own story." And in order to be heroes, the "I need a haircut" crowd has made enemies of politicians that deserve a lot more credence.

The "hidden ulterior motive" for these executives is to keep Americans alive. Every governor in America is aware that these orders to stay home are going to anger their residents and ultimately might cost them their jobs.

But they will ultimately keep more people alive. Remember, body bags don't vote.

The Bulwark

THE LEFT MADE A SPECTACLE OF ITSELF IN 2011

December 29, 2011

In Wisconsin, 2011 came in like a lion and left like a lion fighting for its health benefits. Newly minted Gov. Scott Walker's proposal to require greater health and pension contributions from government employees, along with virtually removing public union collective bargaining, set off a cacophony of tumult that ricocheted through every corner of the state's borders.

The year began with an appeal for more civility in politics, in the wake of the shooting of Arizona Democratic Congresswoman Gabrielle Giffords. Yet when the Capitol explosion began in mid-February, Walker and legislators of both parties started receiving death threats. State Sen. Spencer Coggs called Walker's plan "legalized slavery," and state Sen. Lena Taylor (along with dozens of protesters) compared Walker to Adolf Hitler. A Democratic Assemblyman yelled "you're fucking dead" to a Republican colleague on the chamber floor following debate on Walker's plan. Protesters targeted Walker's children on Facebook, and Republican Rep. Robin Vos was assaulted with a flying pilsner.

So shocking was Walker's plan that President Barack Obama criticized the governor, deeming it an "assault" on unions. Yet if Walker was a first-time union assailant, Obama continues to be a serial offender - federal employees aren't allowed to collectively bargain for wages and benefits.

2011 was a year when unions said "it wasn't about the money," before many of them (including Madison city workers) rushed back to the bargaining table to "Walker-proof" their benefits before the new collective bargaining law went into effect. While statewide unions said they would accept the increases in health and pension contributions, many local unions clearly weren't reading from the same playbook.

Speaking of money, during the summer, unions spent over $20 million to unseat six Republican state senators who voted for Walker's plan. This exposed exactly why it's about the money. Government employees merely serve as conduits for taxpayer funds to work their way to the unions, who then spend money electing obeisant legislators to negotiate favorable contracts. Shockingly, lefty "good government" groups appear not to have a problem with this blatant purchase of favors.

It was a year that granted the definition of the word "democracy" a previously unimaginable elasticity. While bullhorns around the Capitol blared "this is what democracy looks like," 14 Democratic state senators fled to Illinois to prevent democracy from occurring. Later, a single Dane County judge would overturn Walker's law, which irony-deficient Assembly Minority Leader Peter Barca called "a huge win for democracy in Wisconsin." The law would later be reinstated by an incredulous state Supreme Court.

It was these same "democracy enthusiasts" who decided to use Wisconsin's 85-year-old recall law to cast a number of democratically elected Republicans from office. Since the law was passed in 1926, only two state elected officials had been recalled from office; in 2011, nine state senators faced that fate, demonstrating that this is what democracy has never looked like. Despite over $40 million being spent on the senate recalls, Republicans won four of the six contested seats and retained control of the state senate by a one-vote margin.

In some districts, Republicans won by more comfortable margins than they ever had before. Of the two GOP senators who lost, one was in a district Barack Obama carried by 18 percentage points. The other was embroiled in a personal scandal involving a 25-year-old mistress. Thus, after the rancorous recall process, the enduring lesson was: It's probably a bad idea to cheat on your wife.

It was a year where Madison teachers showed parents how much they valued their kids by walking out on them for a four-day sick-out. Some teachers even brought their pupils down to the Capitol to help them protest. When a group of Madison East high school students were asked why they were marching on the statehouse during a school day, one young man said he was "trying to stop whatever this dude is doing."

2011 was the year that public-sector bargaining became a fundamental human right, bestowed on the people of Wisconsin from the heavens. "We will not be denied our God-given right to join a real union," thundered Marty Beil, head of the Wisconsin State Employees Union, in February.

Yet God apparently first appeared in Wisconsin in 1959, when Democratic Gov. Gaylord Nelson signed the nation's first public-sector collective bargaining law. It was a shrewd political move - four years earlier, unions had financed 55% of unsuccessful Democrat William Proxmire's gubernatorial campaign. The year before Nelson created the law, Democrats had a $10,000 deficit in their state account; four years later, that had turned into a $50,000 surplus. At the time, it looked a lot less like a divine right and more like a naked political favor. (God has yet to visit 24 other states, which either have limited or no public-sector collective bargaining at all.)

Assuming Walker's reforms don't mean the end of public education in Wisconsin, school kids will one day look back at 2011 as the year the state motto changed from "Forward" to "Actually, We Like Things Quite the Way They Are, Thank You." It will be remembered as the moment in state history where "progressivism" came to mean "don't touch my damn benefits."

Isthmus

2012: THE YEAR IN REVIEW

Dec. 29, 2012

A college friend of mine once had a contrarian theory on how to find the best women to date. He believed you should always target women already in relationships. "If a girl has a boyfriend, you only have to be better than that one guy," he would say. "With single women, you have to be better than every other dude in the world."

In 2012, Gov. Scott Walker took this advice to heart as he staved off a bitter recall effort initiated by swarms of angry public-sector union members, whose ability to collectively bargain he had all but eliminated in 2011. One observer cleverly deemed the public unions' efforts in Wisconsin "frozen custard's last stand."

But Walker didn't have to defeat the concepts of "collective bargaining," or "unions." He simply had to beat the political corpse of Milwaukee Mayor Tom Barrett, who had lost two previous bids for governor, the last in 2010 to Walker himself.

The June 5 recall election fractured Wisconsin both at the state and individual level. On election day, a Chippewa Falls woman tried to drive to the polls to vote against Walker but was blocked by her estranged husband - so she ran him over. The recall inspired a Madison-area rapper with the unfortunate sobriquet "Dudu Stinks" to pen the "Walker Recall Anthem," which included the Beatle-esque lyric, "Get this power hungry man out of office and away we go. . . . this is larger than the current student-teacher ratio." Inexplicably, the voting public failed to heed Mr. Stinks' plea and re-elected Walker by a larger margin than he had garnered against the somnambulistic Barrett merely two years earlier.

Similarly, President Barack Obama benefited by only having to defeat one person. Even with a flagging economy and high unemployment, the talented Republican stable of attractive candidates decided to sit this election out, and Mitt Romney emerged from a GOP primary that had begun to resemble the Creature Cantina in "Star Wars."

As one Iowa caucus voter surveyed the Republican deck of cards, he mused that there wasn't "a face card among them." Among the competitors Romney vanquished in New Hampshire was a white-bearded man who wore a boot as a hat, called himself "Vermin Supreme" and advocated a mandatory toothbrushing law in order to prevent America's rapid "moral and oral decay."

Yet in the land of the blind, the one-eyed man is king, and Romney emerged, eventually choosing Wisconsin congressman Paul Ryan as his running mate. While the congenial Ryan had spent 14 years in Congress finely tuning his message of fiscal restraint and lower taxes, the top Google search relating to the congressman during the campaign was "Paul Ryan shirtless." Clearly the female electorate supported his right to bare arms.

But even Ryan's popularity at home wasn't enough to close Obama's 14-point margin of victory in Wisconsin four years ago. Obama won the state by seven percentage points, helping carry Madison's Tammy Baldwin, perhaps the most liberal member of Congress, to the U.S. Senate. In the span of five months, Wisconsin went from being the Republicans' Great Hope to forcing the GOP to smell its dairy air.

Even beyond electoral politics, Wisconsin continued to make national news. During the Miss America pageant, Miss Wisconsin, Laura Kaeppeler, confided that her secret dream was to swim with dolphins. The good news is, she became Miss America - the bad news? Now the dolphins know.

In Madison, a young man named Beezow Doo-Doo Zopittybop-Bop-Bop was hauled to jail for the least surprising drug arrest in recorded history. Weeks later at a Madison Denny's, a man posing as the restaurant's new manager was arrested after he walked into the kitchen and began cooking himself a burger and fries. In February, Kaukauna's Stephanie Teatek was named America's fastest grocery bagger. In May, a Thiensville man picketed outside a local restaurant after, he says, they stopped serving him on all-you-can-eat fish fry night.

After a 15-1 regular season, the Green Bay Packers became conscientious objectors to the barbaric practice of tackling and lost to the New York Giants in the NFL playoffs. Milwaukee Brewers outfielder Ryan Braun became the first player to beat Major League Baseball's performance-enhancing drug testing rules. On the positive side, Braun went on to have another MVP-type season - although at one point he had to announce publicly that he had never contracted a sexually transmitted disease.

In fact, the biggest accomplishment in Wisconsin sports may have occurred when veteran Packers wide receiver Donald Driver won the nationally televised "Dancing with the Stars" competition in May. Conversely, Wisconsin sports' sweetheart, Olympic runner Suzy Favor Hamilton, admitted she had been working as a high-priced Las Vegas call girl for the past year.

And, thus, with the nation headed to the precipice of a fiscal cliff, with 2012's slate of gun violence from coast to coast, and with Wisconsin's summer of discontent behind it, 2013 has a very low bar for success. It doesn't have to be better than most years; it only has to be better than 2012 to be a considered a winner.

Milwaukee Journal Sentinel

2013: AMERICA TAKES A SELFIE

Dec. 28, 2013

The year 2013 began with all the pomp and circumstance of a presidential inauguration — albeit one that featured the incongruous image of Congressman Paul Ryan (R-Wis.) standing next to rapper Jay-Z and his wife Beyonce. And then things got weird.

In fact, the year was capped by another image, of the American sorority-girl-in-chief Barack Obama squishing his face next to Denmark's comely prime minister for a cell phone picture at Nelson Mandela's December funeral. Obama's breach of the Mandela event's solemnity thrust the word "selfie" into the nation's lexical spotlight, and more important for him, appeared to draw the ire of the First Lady.

Yet in 2013, Obama was more than willing to Photoshop himself out of whatever tough spot the White House found itself in. When his National Security Agency was found to have collected data on millions of personal phone calls, the president maintained he wasn't in the loop. Ditto for when the Internal Revenue Service was caught auditing conservative organizations in an aggressive manner that suggested political payback. And when the website enabling his signature accomplishment — Obamacare — was in the midst of a catastrophic rollout, Obama claimed he was in the dark about what millions of Americans already knew: that the website wasn't even good enough for the proverbial government work.

Clearly, Obama had more pressing issues to deal with, such as calling former NBA player Jason Collins in April within hours of Collins' bravely announcing he is gay. Unfortunately, it appears that Collins, a marginal player near the end of his career, may never play in the NBA again — although the positive response he received after coming out may have paved the way for an athlete to do so while still playing.

As it turns out, 2013 was a big step forward for LGBT causes. The U.S. Supreme Court negated the federal Defense of Marriage Act and overturned California's Proposition 8, a 2008 law banning same-sex marriage. Phil Robertson, star of the highly rated show Duck Dynasty, lost his job for making anti-gay statements; future historians will look back and see that for much of December 2013, the biggest story in America was essentially "Louisiana man thinks gay sex is gross."

Even the new pope, picked in March, showed a softer side toward gays, insisting that the church must "always consider the person." Pope Francis proved to be savvy in the public relations arts, saying the Catholic Church "cannot insist only on issues related to abortion, gay marriage and the use of contraceptive methods."

Yet even the pope's media relations sensibility paled to that of Miley Cyrus, whose grotesque dancing foisted the word "twerking" on an unsuspecting American public. Cyrus' hip gyrations were covered like they were the assassination of Archduke Ferdinand, proving Oscar Wilde's adage that the only thing in the world worse than being talked about is not being talked about.

In sports, the oft-banged up Green Bay Packers finally suffered the one injury they couldn't sustain. After Aaron Rodgers broke his collarbone in November, a four-game winning streak turned into a five-game winless streak as the Packers rotated a gaggle of journeymen through the starting quarterback spot. It quickly became clear that the Packers without Rodgers are like *NSync without Justin Timberlake.

Rodgers' buddy, Milwaukee Brewer Ryan Braun, ended up serving a 65-game suspension after finally admitting he used performance-enhancing drugs. Ironically, the Brookfield restaurant Braun formerly co-owned with Rodgers promised "all natural beef" — a standard the owner couldn't even maintain for himself. The season was cursed from the start, as the team's Italian racing sausage, Guido, was stolen in April; the costume was presumably recovered after the suspects were thoroughly grilled.

Keeping Braun off the front pages, however, was the complete immolation of former New York Congressman Anthony Weiner, whose bid to become New York mayor was effectively ended by revelations that he had trolled for young girls online using the sobriquet "Carlos Danger."

It seems unlikely that such ribald allegations will taint next year's Wisconsin gubernatorial race, in which Republican Scott Walker will try to claim a second term. In March, Walker was cleared of any wrongdoing in a "John Doe" investigation that his opponents had used to dog him for years. While the budget Walker signed this year expanded the school choice program statewide, it was otherwise not very controversial; clearly it was the type of plan he thinks he can sell in a re-election effort and possibly beyond.

This year saw the end of the critically acclaimed television series "Breaking Bad" and with Democratic control of the U.S. Senate in peril because of the Obamacare collapse, Obama should recognize the words of the show's protagonist, Walter White: "I am not in danger, I am the danger." That is, of course, unless President Selfie can once again convince the public that he is totes adorbs.

Milwaukee Journal Sentinel

2014: THE YEAR OF THE NARRATIVE, TRUE OR NOT

Dec. 28, 2014

When Mark Twain gave one of his fantastical lectures, he was keenly aware that many in the audience didn't believe his wild stories. He bragged that his long speeches contained many facts, but that he "expected everybody to discount those facts 95%." Nonetheless, he maintained, "all through my life, my facts have had a substratum of truth."

The year 2014 was a year in which the truth lay beneath the surface, not in facts, but in "narrative." It was a year in which political activists frequently relied on the Italian maxim, "se non e' vero, e' ben trovato" — while it may not be true, it is well-founded.

Perhaps the most prevalent narrative of the year was found in a mere gesture. Following the August death of African-American teenager Michael Brown at the hands of a white Ferguson, Mo., police officer, protesters adopted the "hands up, don't shoot" gesture, adopting the narrative that Brown was attempting to surrender when he was shot. Yet the evidence overwhelmingly demonstrated that Brown attacked officer Darren Wilson in his squad car, then charged at Wilson in a second altercation before Wilson shot Brown to death.

Nonetheless, narrative trumped facts, and looters set Ferguson ablaze on the night the grand jury announced its decision to not charge Wilson with Brown's murder. Even after all the forensics and testimony were made available, the "hands up, don't shoot" gesture lived on in protests around the country. In essence, "hands up, don't shoot" became a stand-in for

African-American distrust of police departments around the country; distrust intensified by the officer-instigated deaths of Eric Garner in New York, Tamir Rice in Cleveland and Dontre Hamilton in Milwaukee.

Yet poor areas weren't the only place where the wish became the father of the facts. On college campuses, feminists pushed the "rape culture" narrative, trying to convince Americans that sexual assault on elite campuses was more prevalent than in violent Third World nations. President Barack Obama himself cited an extremely wobbly statistic that claims 20% of women on campus are victims of sexual assault; near the end of the year, the U.S Department of Justice reported that the number was more like 0.6%, and women were actually safer on college campuses than in society at large.

But the need for the campus rape narrative to be true was so intense that journalistic standards sometimes placed a distant second. In November, Rolling Stone published a widely praised article that claimed a grisly gang rape took place at a University of Virginia fraternity, causing the university to shut down all fraternity activity on campus. Soon, the story unraveled, but the narrative marched on.

Feminists set fire to the straw men who criticized the story because they believe "rape doesn't happen." One Washington Post contributor wrote a column claiming that we should automatically believe rape claims, evidently believing "To Kill a Mockingbird" was a guidebook to ornithology.

Of course, electoral politics are often nothing but narrative, and the 2014 elections brought America an ample dose of it. Democrats centered many of their campaigns on the idea that Republicans are misogynistic perverts, united in their quest to keep female pay down and fertility up. The "War on Women" backfired, sending historic numbers of Republicans to Congress and statehouses across America. But the anti-women meme will surely return; following the end of times, the only survivors will be cockroaches and the myth that the GOP doesn't want women to have birth control.

As Keats wrote, "Beauty is truth, truth beauty — that is all Ye know on Earth, and all ye need to know." There wasn't much truth in 2014 — let's all hope next year is heavier on the beauty.

Milwaukee Journal Sentinel

2015: A LOOK AT THE YEAR IN PREVIEW

January 4, 2015

There's a memorable scene in Rocky III where a reporter asks Clubber Lang, played by Mr. T, for a prediction regarding his imminent fight with Rocky Balboa. "Prediction?" Lang asks. He then breaks the fourth wall, turns directly to the camera and growls, "Pain."

Such a prediction would have been right on for the year 2014. If Republicans and Democrats can agree on one thing, it is that last year is better off left in everyone's rear view mirror.

So while 2015 might not be the year of "pain" its predecessor was, it still promises to be one of action. Here's a quick glimpse of things that are likely to happen in the next 12 months.

In January, the U.S. Supreme Court declares all same-sex marriages to be valid. In a simple one-line decision, the Court says, "Charles Manson can get married, but gay people can't? C'mon."

In February, Gov. Scott Walker introduces his new state budget, but is slightly embarrassed when his plan for big income tax cuts in Iowa and New Hampshire are rejected by the Wisconsin Legislature.

As part of his image makeover, Walker begins wearing a toupee to cover his bald spot. Without any news to cover, three statewide daily newspapers just run blank pages for a week, and two more go out of business.

Stinging from criticism that reporters didn't properly investigate gubernatorial candidate Mary Burke's past, the state media suffers further embarrassment when it is discovered Burke was actually a sweet potato.

The Detroit Lions make it to the NFC Championship Game in Green Bay after Ndamukong Suh eats both Tony Romo and Russell Wilson during their games against the Cowboys and Seahawks. The league fines Suh $25 for each offense. In their game with the Lions, Aaron Rodgers evades Suh by disguising himself as a vegetable.

In a naked Academy Award grab, Twentieth Century Fox releases a sequel to "12 Years a Slave." In the film, through a crazy coincidence, Solomon Northup is once again captured before Brad Pitt manages to singlehandedly end slavery for a second time. North Korean dictator Kim Jong Un calls it "the feel good hit of the summer!" and allows it to be played in American theaters.

In June, state Democratic Party chair Mike Tate tenders his resignation. State Republicans beg him to reconsider.

Suffering from record low-approval ratings, President Barack Obama seeks to align himself with someone more popular than he is and appoints Bill Cosby as vice president.

In July, Hank the Dog accidentally gets into a Fed Ex box meant for Ryan Braun. As a result, Hank ends up starting at third base for the National League in the All-Star game. Given the declining state of spelling and grammar on social media, lexicographers throw their hands up and replace the English language with a series of grunts, emoticons and pictures of people pointing at hamburgers.

Taking the "affirmative consent" movement one step further, the University of Wisconsin-Madison also imposes a "negative consent" policy. From now on, every woman on campus must tell each man she meets that she will definitely never, ever have sex with him under any condition. I am called as an expert witness, as the new policy eerily mirrors my freshman year in college.

Wisconsin Rep. Jim Sensenbrenner announces this will be his final term as a representative, setting off a 74-way Republican primary for his seat. When the primary election finally does roll around, State Rep. Dale Kooyenga of Brookfield wins in a landslide, garnering 3% of the vote.

In a news conference, Milwaukee Mayor Tom Barrett continues to argue that Republicans are trying to ruin the city. When a reporter mentions that Democrats have dominated city government for decades, Barrett flips the table over and sprints out of the room.

The feminist website Jezebel builds a new wing on its headquarters based on the new revenue they earn by covering new Wisconsin Rep. Glenn Grothman.

Democratic Massachusetts Senator Elizabeth Warren keeps denying she's running for president. People grow skeptical, however, when she continues to deny it in her Iowa and New Hampshire primary victory speeches.

Finally, U.S. Rep. Paul Ryan decides not to run for president, citing a desire to spend more time with his biceps.

Here's wishing everyone a happy and healthy 2015. Let's all agree to try to keep the pain to a minimum.

Milwaukee Journal Sentinel

CHAPTER THREE:

"SAVE THE PRESIDENCY FROM THE PRESIDENT."

POLITICS WILL NEVER BE THE SAME

October 21, 2020

As America careened toward the 2016 presidential election, Hillary Clinton's supporters could not stop crowing about the "historic" nature of her impending presidency. Like Barack Obama before her, Clinton's ascendance to the White House would mark an important "first"—she would be the nation's only female president.

Unspoken at the time was that if Clinton's opponent were somehow elected, he would represent an even more unprecedented break from historical practice. Sure, Donald Trump was an old white guy—but never before had the nation given its most cherished position of public trust to someone so erratic and ill-equipped to handle it.

We have seen women run major democracies before. But we had never seen a game show host whose claim to fame was fake-firing singer Meat Loaf ascend to the world's most powerful position.

Thus, with Trump's tradition-breaking election, it follows that other practices deeply ingrained in American democracy would also fall. As his first term comes to a close, Trump has transformed U.S. politics in ways we never could have imagined—and even if he loses in November, these changes aren't likely to ever revert back to the old days.

For instance:

The (political) party's over.

Before Trump, political parties served an important purpose—they tried to convince as many voters as possible to join their side by using the "party line," or arguments why their vision of America was better.

Over the years, campaign finance laws have served to weaken the parties, allowing independent lobbying groups to gain power in crafting campaign messages and helping candidates. As a result, the old-fashioned political parties have stopped even pretending they stand for any policy agenda—their only unbreakable position is that they should be in power, even if it means dropping their positions faster than Subway dropped Jared Fogle as its sandwich spokesman.

The Republican Party openly admitted this permanent change when it declined to even offer a party platform during the Republican National Convention this summer. The GOP's only platform is whatever Trump wants. And now there's little reason to believe any argument they make in the future isn't simply a naked power play.

Politics is no longer local.

Trump's singular guiding principle is that all news should be about him at all times. It is why he wakes every morning, reaches for his phone, and fires off a tweet that will have Americans chattering away until he does the very same thing the next morning.

The nation simply doesn't have the attention span to keep up with his daily scandals and also pay attention to local politics. State and local races are now mere afterthoughts, with Americans believing everything good or bad in the country emanates from the White House, and candidates for city council and council commissioner ape his style and attitude.

Even local stories now become national referenda on Trump—no account of a police shooting or minor story about voter fraud or wackadoodle conspiracy theories stay within the communities in which they happen. They rattle around Twitter before they make their way to Trump, who passes public judgment without knowing any of the details.

This is no doubt exacerbated by the decline of local newspapers (more on that below), which in so many towns and cities are too understaffed to do consistent in-depth reporting on local issues. As a result, fewer people know anything about the events around them or the people who represent them locally—the people who have the most influence on their daily lives.

Lowering the bar on negative campaigning.

Before Trump, entire industries were built around the "dark arts" of campaigning—opposition researchers dug through old voting records, personal documents, and tax filings trying to find dirt on candidates of the other party.

But Trump's ascendance appears to be, in large part, because of his wretched behavior, and not in spite of it. "He fights!" remains the rallying cry of those who defend Trump's unwillingness to release his taxes or his mockery of American soldiers or his mistreatment of women.

So, if Trump can succeed with an entire landfill of dirty laundry out in the public, who's going to care if a local or state candidate has some indiscretions on their record? Oh—you've heard Senator So-and-So took a $100 contribution from a millionaire who made his fortune turning baby seals into iPhone cases? Well the president won just weeks after a video was released in which he encouraged sexually assaulting women by grabbing their genitals.

Burning down the House (and Senate).

Congress has effectively ceased to legislate. Instead of winning political arguments on the floor of the House of Representatives, members see their primary duty as "clapping back at the haters," a process notably un-referenced in Article I of the Constitution. (James Madison was famously more of an Instagram guy.)

This legislative flaccidity has affected other branches. Building consensus and passing laws through both houses of Congress can be arduous—which is why elected officials are far more likely to kick their desired changes over to the U.S. Supreme Court, where issues can be demagogued on social media without ever having to take a tough vote.

This shift in the power between the branches is why America now devolves into a holy war every time there is an opening on the Supreme Court—as the federal judiciary takes on more of a legislative role, voters are going to treat justices with the same vitriol and partisan rancor as they do members of the House and Senate.

It is the Senate that has most recently demonstrated how weak it truly is. Only one Republican senator, Mitt Romney, voted to impeach and remove Trump from office after the president effectively blackmailed Ukraine to get dirt on a domestic political opponent. It is a sign that moving forward, no president will ever be removed from office as long as his or her party controls the Senate.

The media are now a footnote.

Trump was the first president to circumvent the media to get his message out to his supporters, but he won't be the last. Future politicians will simply take their message straight to the voters, spreading falsehoods portraying an alternate reality.

Of course, Trump's critique of "fake news" didn't come out of nowhere—for decades, conservatives have known the mainstream media was tilted against them, and Trump exploited this distrust to turn irritation with the "lamestream media" into outright contempt.

The best Americans can ask for at this point is for media organizations to serve as arbiters of what's true and what is not—an endeavor at which they often fail miserably. Further, these messages won't penetrate the large portion of Americans who get their news from conspiracy websites or aspiring movement "stars" who have a financial incentive to mislead them.

The only question is whether there will be enough reporters left to tell the story of their own demise.

A requiem for "conservatism."

Since Trump won the GOP primary in 2016, the word "conservatism" has morphed from "free market, individual rights, and low taxes enthusiast" to "Trump fan."

Out is the principled conservatism that stressed free speech and fought market regulation—in is a "conservatism" that thinks private social media companies should be regulated if they don't meet Trump's definition of "fairness." Wave goodbye to the conservatism that stressed local control—

welcome the new conservatism that thinks the federal government should mandate "patriotism curriculum" in local school districts. And so on.

Get used to stories like "conservatives oppose wearing masks in public," "conservatives think Kamala Harris wasn't born in the United States and isn't eligible to be Vice President" and "conservatives think Tom Hanks, Hillary Clinton, and Ellen DeGeneres are stealing children to drink their essence."

Even if Donald Trump loses in November, the office will have been distorted to fit his unique presidency. Hopefully, some of his more grotesque impressions will one day snap back—demonization of immigrants, overriding scientific experts, sowing distrust in election results, and the like.

But any desire for "normalcy" must recognize that "normal" now means something completely different. And we may just be at the beginning.

The Dispatch

'THERE'S A CULTURAL WAR GOING ON AND ONLY ONE SIDE IS FIGHTING.'

August 27, 2020

The list of super PACs supporting President Donald Trump in 2020 reads like verbal Sudoku: There's Great America, Make America Great Again, Americans for Greatness, the Committee to Restore America's Greatness, Make America Number 1, and America is Winning Again. So much greatness.

But one group stands out in both its mission and its fundraising prowess. That group is Black Americans to Re-Elect the President, which has raised nearly $2.8 million since it began accepting contributions in May 2018. According to OpenSecrets.org, Black Americans to Re-Elect the President has raised more more money during the 2020 presidential cycle than any other pro-Trump SuperPAC other than America First Action, Trump's "official" super PAC, which has raised $46 million.

The mastermind behind the group is Vernon Robinson, a pugnacious controversialist and serial fundraiser who once dubbed himself the "Black Jesse Helms." Robinson, 65, a graduate of the Air Force Academy and former officer, has spent years in North Carolina running dozens of (mostly) unsuccessful campaigns for local and national office.

Robinson's most controversial campaign took place in 2006, where the incendiary accusations he leveled against his opponent were similar in tone, if not exactly the same in content, as something ripped from the Trump playbook.

At the time, he relentlessly accused his opponent, North Carolina Democratic Rep. Brad Miller of being gay. "If Miller had his way, America would be nothing but one big fiesta for illegal aliens and homosexuals," a Robinson radio ad said.

In one flyer, Robinson emphasized Miller was "childless" and had "gotten into bed" with a male blogger from San Francisco. (Miller had contributed to the Daily Kos, run by Markos Moulitsas.)

Unbeknown to the public, Miller and his wife, Esther Hall, were unable to have children because she had a hysterectomy 20 years prior.

"To be clear, the gay stuff didn't bother me even then," Miller told me. "I was inclined to make a joke of it and say that it was true that I kind of liked show tunes but otherwise I was straight, but my consultants said I had to be outraged."

"Many of his attacks had some weird sexual insinuation," said Miller. "He ran an ad that I voted to study masturbation by old men and sexual stimulation in teenage girls because I voted for the NIH budget. NIH spends a good deal more to study cancer and heart disease."

Robinson told me he never called Miller gay. He said he simply used the term "political bedfellows" and "that was the case."

"The left is going to lie, like they always do," he said.

Miller beat Robinson by a nearly 2-to-1 margin.

But Robinson's attacks have often been aimed at Republicans whom he deemed insufficiently conservative. In a 2004 congressional primary, Robinson compared his opponent, conservative Republican Virginia Foxx, to then-Sen. Hillary Clinton, attempting to portray her as a left-wing feminist. (During the campaign, Robinson was condemned by Jack Kemp but praised by Pat Buchanan.)

Robinson called Foxx a "political cross-dresser" who accepted money from "radical homosexuals."

That specific race featured a Robinson campaign ad that eerily intoned, "The aliens are here, but they didn't come in a spaceship. ...They sponge off the American taxpayers. ...They've even taken over the DMV. These aliens commit heinous crimes."

And In one 1997 city council race, Robinson accused his Republican opponent of being a nudist. ("Yep - like nekkid - like no clothes," read one campaign mailing.)

Despite his often unseemly tactics, Robinson hasn't lost all his campaigns. He won a seat on the Winston-Salem city council, but lost his re-election bid in 2005 after he paid $2,000 for a one-ton monument of the Ten Commandments to be moved to the steps in front of City Hall. That very day, the mayor forced city workers to remove it.

Robinson said the Ten Commandments stunt was inspired by Judge Roy Moore in Alabama, writing that more religion was needed in public spaces to keep the left from overturning the Boy Scouts' policy of "keeping atheist pedophiles out of pup tents with our 13-year-old sons."

And that thing about America becoming a "fiesta for immigrants and homosexuals"?

"It has become that," Robinson told me.

Now Robinson is betting that his confrontational style will win Trump more black voters, hoping anti-immigrant and anti-gay sentiment will shift African Americans toward the president. He is buoyed by his preternatural ability to raise campaign money: Since 2004, he has set up a total of five campaign committees and super PACs, raising more than $26 million for himself and other candidates.

His messaging relies heavily on the notion that Democrats have failed black voters. He frequently cites problems in inner cities that have long been run by Democrats and tries to convince African Americans that Democrats are the real racists.

"Antifa—or KLANtifa, as I call them—is the modern face of the Democratic Party," Robinson tells me in one of his extended monologues during our discussion. "It is easier to survive a nuclear bomb than it is to survive 70 years of Democrats running your city into the ground," says Robinson. (The internet meme he mentions with this fact actually cites Hiroshima, and its veracity is in question.)

Robinson believes with his help, Trump will get more than 20 percent of the African American vote in November of this year—two and a half times greater than the 8 percent Trump received in 2016. He argues Democrats are creating "faux racial crises" to try to gin up turnout, calling it "despicable politics."

"Most people believe the Democratic Party is strong in the black community," Robinson tells me, adding he thinks Democrats have a "significant and exploitable strategic weakness, to have to have a high turnout and 90 percent of the [black] vote in order to win."

In 2018, he began testing his theory. He used $4,400 to purchase an ad on black radio in Little Rock, Arkansas, that warned the city's black residents that "white Democrats will be lynching black folk again" if they regained control of the House of Representatives.

This is a real radio ad currently running in Arkansas in support of Republican Congressman French Hill on radio stations targeted to the African American community. I don't even have words to describe it.

The ad, which ran as the U.S. Senate debated Brett Kavanaugh's nomination to the Supreme Court, featured two African American women discussing the committee's actions. In the script, one woman muses that if Democrats can bring "a presumption of guilt" to the accusations against Kavanaugh, "What will happen to our husbands, our fathers, or our sons when a white girl lies on them?"

The woman ends the ad by saying, "We can't afford to let white Democrats take us back to bad old days of race verdicts, life sentences and lynching when a white girl screams rape." Robinson ran similar ads on contemporary urban radio in Missouri, Tennessee, Michigan, and Mississippi.

Rep. French Hill, the Arkansas Republican the spot was ostensibly meant to help, was horrified.

"I condemn the ad in the strongest terms," tweeted Hill, adding, "I do not support that message, and there is no place in Arkansas for this nonsense." Hill ended up winning the election.

"The congressman (Hill) has to run his own campaign," Robinson said at the time. "My obligation is to communicate with black voters about the president's agenda," he said.

"In spite of the party's lack of interest in communicating with black voters, those ads are very effective," Robinson told me, "because when black voters hear, in many cases for the first time, that the candidates they have been voting for support Planned Parenthood and the holocaust of 21 million dead black babies and the selling of body parts, that has an arresting influence on their enthusiasm."

Robinson considers his most successful effort to date his campaign to draft Ben Carson to run for president. He started a super PAC in 2013 that eventually raised more than $17 million.

Most of the funds were used to pay fundraisers and mail vendors. In 2014, the prodigious fundraising of the Draft Ben Carson super PAC raised eyebrows at the Washington Post, which noted most of the group's money was going to two vendors, Omega List and Campaign Funding Direct.

Bruce Eberle, the founder of both vendors, began a test solicitation on behalf of Carson on August 16, 2013. When the donations began pouring in, Eberle sunk even more money into fundraising. By the end of 2013, Draft Ben Carson raised $1.2 million, with more than 75 percent going to pay for fundraising through services and lists tied to Eberle himself.

Aside from paying vendors to raise the money, not all the expenditures were directed toward coaxing Ben Carson to run; during the 2014 election cycle, Robinson spent more than $500,000 to help defeat Democratic Sen.

Mary Landrieu in Louisiana and to boost Republican Thom Tillis in his successful Senate race against North Carolina Sen. Kay Hagan.

Carson actually credited the group with convincing him to get in the race, citing their success in fundraising as a factor. Nonetheless, a phone call to Carson may have been more cost-effective.

Carson eventually dropped out of the race in March 2016.

Meanwhile, Eberle paired with his wife to give Black Americans to Re-Elect the President $50,000 in late June of this year. It has been a solid investment for him—the super PAC has paid Campaign Funding Direct and Omega List a total of $351,000 during the 2020 cycle. Eberle and Robinson have even authored a book together called Coming Home: How Black Americans Will Re-Elect Trump.

In 2016, FEC commissioners Ellen Weintraub and Ann Ravel issued a letter warning about the proliferation of what they deemed "scam PACs" during the 2020 election cycle. In order to spot scams, wrote the commissioners, one should look for political committees that "collect political contributions, frequently using the name of a candidate, but which spend little to none of the proceeds on political activity benefitting that candidate."

Further, they warn that common characteristics of scam PACs are "high operating expenses and/or large disbursements to entities associated with the managers of the PACs." Recently, Democratic Rep. Katie Porter of California and Republican Rep. Dan Crenshaw of Texas introduced a House bill to more tightly regulate alleged "scam" PACs.

Other PACs have used the names of potential candidates to raise money, including committees to elect former Rep. Allen West, talk show host Laura Ingraham, and former Milwaukee Sheriff David Clarke. All used the names and likenesses of these individuals without their consent. But the FEC has frequently dismissed such complaints, claiming nobody is being defrauded when such a PAC operates.

University of Wisconsin-Madison political science professor Kenneth Mayer, who studies campaign finance law, told me there's really no way to separate these unauthorized campaign committees from "legitimate" PACS.

"This is one of the things I think you can attribute to Citizens United," Mayer told me, noting PACs participating in political activities before the landmark Supreme Court case were bound by a $5,000 contribution limit. "That limited the scope of these kinds of things because it takes a lot of work to raise that kind of money in $5,000 chunks," said Mayer.

"The problem is, how do you write down a rule that says 'this is the line?'" Mayer said, noting the difficulty in deciding which super PACs operate within the spirit of the law. "Who's going to decide?"

Regardless of who's benefiting from his spending, Robinson's style may earn him more donors and more mainstream acceptance. In 2017, Trump-friendly Newsmax ranked him as the nation's 18th most influential African American Republican.

Robinson does have some mainstream conservative positions he thinks will draw African Americans to the polls, including support for school choice, vouchers, and charter schools.

Robinson, who has run unsuccessfully for North Carolina School Superintendent twice (in 1992 and 1996) told me he's going to run a school choice ad against Biden because "almost all Democrats send their kids to private school, then deny poor kids school choice because they have to pay off the union." And he sounded downright giddy when reciting a line in his jobs and wealth creation ad: "The only private sector job that Joe Biden has ever created was one for his son in the Ukraine."

"My ads tend to be tough," he said, adding his abortion ads will end with "every time Joe Biden asks for your vote, ask him why he doesn't want our children."

Robinson said when black voters hear ads like that, two things happen—they either stay home or more of the black voters that do go to the polls vote for Republicans.

But even if there are issues on which African Americans lean conservative, two big issues threaten to drive black voters away from him: The protests that followed George Floyd's death, and Trump's handling of the pandemic, which has affected blacks disproportionately. In regards to the latter, Robinson blames Democrats and their leadership for poor black health. "If you're in a single-parent household, you're going to have all sorts of medical problems associated with poverty," he said, while claiming that Black Lives Matter wants to get rid of the patriarchal nuclear family altogether.

It didn't take long after Biden announced Kamala Harris as his running mate for Robinson to start making plans for his messaging. "How did she move from first Indian American senator to first black Veep qua Presidential nominee? [I say] presidential because Biden has dementia and while his wife would like to do a Wilson and run the country, those pulling his strings have decided that after 25th Amendment removal, Harris would be the best president."

Never mind that Trump supporters howled when critics raised the idea of removing him from office via the 25th Amendment. Robinson is pulling no punches. And he's frustrated by those who do.

"There's a cultural war going on and only one side is fighting. Republicans are still in this dreamland that they're back in the days of Tip O'Neill having a scotch with Ronald Reagan," he said."

The Dispatch

END IOWA'S CAUCUS MONOPOLY

March 19, 2015

[Ed. note: After I wrote this, I talked with a producer from The Daily Show about doing an interview. It never panned out. They seem to prefer people who have no idea what The Daily Show is.]

In the American Midwest, there exists a magical land where one isn't tethered to his or her problematic past. It is a land of rejuvenation, where past actions and positions all melt away in favor of a newer, fresher persona. The residents are all savvy enough to direct the course of the world, and are given that power through the American electoral process.

I am talking, of course, about the utopia we call "Iowa."

On a quadrennial basis, candidates descend upon our neighbor to the southwest to lavish its caucus voters with talking points that they crave to hear. Any previous strongly held position vanishes to wherever Hillary Clinton is keeping her emails; dissent from the corn cob canon is not tolerated.

Take Gov. Scott Walker's recent bout of pander-monium while surging to the lead in Iowa. The most blatant example occurred earlier this month when Walker pledged to support the federal ethanol mandate, a windfall to the state's agricultural mafia. In fact, the mandate may only exist because of Iowa's special place in the presidential nominating process. Nonetheless, Walker backtracked from his previous opposition to the mandate, having rightly derided it during his short-lived 2006 gubernatorial campaign as "central planning" and "big government."

This position reversal obviously wasn't enough for Iowa's caucus voters. Walker also reversed his position on immigration, defenestrating his previous defense of a "pathway to citizenship" for the 12 million immigrants currently in America illegally. Instead, Walker now offers a calorie-free word salad that sprinkles in terms such as "amnesty," "Obama," and "secure the border," while the governor prays for the interviewer's next question.

251

Walker's denouement came this week, however, when campaign consultant Liz Mair resigned (read: invited to not work for Walker anymore) shortly after being hired. Some Iowa Republicans had complained about Mair's previous comments criticizing the caucus process and ethanol subsidies.

Of course, l'affaire Mair is most important to a small cadre of conservative writers and consultants but it seems to prolong a troubling trend. On the stump, Walker has made his toughness a centerpiece of his campaign, frequently invoking his fight against protesters in Wisconsin to advertise his thick skin. But if Walker can't stand up to a handful of moody Iowans, how is he going to stave off Russia or Iran? What's next -- will he put Iowa, Iowa State and Northern Iowa in his Final Four bracket out of duty?

While Walker tries to narrow the Mississippi River and pull Iowa closer to Wisconsin, it's not even clear a victory there means that much. As Sean Davis at The Federalist has pointed out, the winner of the last seven competitive GOP Iowa caucuses has won the presidency only once. Further, Iowa has only supported a Republican presidential candidate once in the last 30 years.

On primary election night 55 years ago, Sen. John F. Kennedy sat not far from where my desk currently sits at the Journal Sentinel office, waiting for Wisconsin's election returns to roll in. At the time, Wisconsin was the second primary, and a strong test for whether Kennedy's Catholicism would play in a national election.

And maybe if Wisconsin's primary were first now, I'd be defending it. But having a different state go first every time would be a truer test of a candidate's fitness for office, as he or she would have to navigate something other than the same, tired, agricultural/evangelical maze embedded in Iowa every four years. The only challenge that exists in Iowa is finding enough Chapstick for politicians to smooch every posterior in the state.

Milwaukee Journal Sentinel

FORGOTTEN BUT NOT GONE

February 14, 2008

As I approached the Concourse Hotel in Madison this morning, I noticed something strange. Parking spots. A major presidential candidate was speaking here this morning, and there were empty parking spots right across the street. There may have been even more had the Huckabus not been taking up three of them.

Huckabee faces an impossible road in the Republican primary. John McCain will be the GOP nominee, yet Huckabee soldiers on with little money and no chance. As the Robbie Fulks song says, he's "forgotten but not gone."

Yet one of the reasons Huckabee is still standing is his preternatural speaking ability – which is why I was excited to go see him. The hotel banquet room at the Concourse is about half full when I roll in. I eyeball the crowd and put it between 150 and 200 people. (Later, Wispolitics.com would estimate the crowd at 500, which I think is wildly overstated.)

A couple of Huckabee's campaign workers circle the room. Having worked dozens of campaigns myself, it's easy to spot a campaign worker. They always have an ill-fitting suit that probably actually looked good when the campaign started – yet months of late nights and junk food have shrunk it two sizes. They have sunken eyes, the complexion of chalk, and no will to live.

Some unidentifiable country music begins to play in the background. Country music and Republican politics now, unfortunately, go hand-in-hand like cheese curds and ranch dressing. After about two songs, I call my sister to make sure we're actually not married.

I ran into Steve Eggleston, who got some much-deserved national publicity for his post pointing out that McCain only needed 24 percent of the vote from here on out to win the nomination.

One of the things I notice about the event is the lack of security. There are a couple guys talking into their sleeves, but no pat downs or coat checks on the way in. I chat with a reporter and we agree that we shouldn't check the polls to see who's winning the race, we just need to figure out how many secret service people are assigned to each campaign. Huckabee's lack of security detail befitted his long-shot status.

One of the down sides of the New York Giants beating the New England Patriots in the Super Bowl is that it allows Huckabee to stand up and compare his situation to that of the underdog Giants. Apparently, Huckabee used this talking point in a Wisconsin speech yesterday, and it went over like a lead balloon. He had likely forgotten that the Giants had beaten the Packers in the NFC Championship game, which is still a sore subject in the Dairy State. He should have focused on a more pleasant topic, like incest.

Huckabee hits the stage, introduced by Tim Michels – who reportedly ran for something once. Apparently, there's evidence on the internet of this. Michels says that while talk radio has gone after Huckabee for not being conservative, Huckabee has been endorsed by the Minutemen. Well, that settles it.

Huckabee starts his speech with a smart move – by appealing to Wisconsin's desire for national press. He says that if McCain wins, Wisconsin will be forgotten – yet if Wisconsin goes to Huckabee, the national press will blather on about the Badger State ad nauseam. There's nothing Wisconsin residents crave more than positive press about their state. There seems to be a burning desire to be nationally relevant – and for reasons other than people having sex with corpses.

Huckabee went on to tell a story about singing the National Anthem at Lambeau Field during the 2004 Bush campaign. I stood near the back of the room, which made me feel suspiciously like Travis Bickle at a Palantine rally. Fortunately, my mohawk has grown back in.

He uses his big applause line about how he wants to get rid of the IRS (it might actually be easier to pass a bill through Congress that eliminates the letters "I," "R," and "S" from the English language). He indicates his support for a constitutional amendment to protect the unborn. When making a point about protecting life, he begins to cite the Declaration of Independence – obviously about to reference the guarantee of "life." On the way to that point, he says "We hold these truths to be self-evident..." and some woman begins clapping wildly by herself. Apparently, she was a big fan of Self-Evidence. Woo! Huckabee ignored her and made his way to the intended applause line.

When discussing valuing human life, Huckabee used an example that I thought was really good. He pointed out that in the field of battle, our soldiers go out of their way to save their wounded comrades, because we do value life so much. That contrasted nicely with his portrayal of militant Islam, who sends children out to die for the cause. I hadn't heard the whole sanctity of life argument posed that way before, and thought it was a nice touch.

Huckabee pointed out that he was the first male in his bloodline to graduate from high school. I never understood how this was an effective talking point. Should be give politicians credit for the fact that their family members are uneducated? Should I be ashamed that my father is a lawyer? Wait – don't answer that.

The applause dies down as Huckabee goes on, until he gets to immigration, which perks the crowd up. He then introduces a 14-year old kid who claims to have made 1,000 calls on Huckabee's behalf. The crowd oohs and ahhhs, while I cringe. How does this kid not have time to do regular 14-year old kid stuff? Buy that kid a Playstation. Obviously, his family didn't get the Sports Illustrated swimsuit edition this week – that little guy would have spent more time in the bathroom than on the phone.

The single most asked question of Huckabee these days is "why are you still in the race?" But when you see the flood of press that still follows him around, you can understand why. When is Mike Huckabee going to ever have a national stage like this again? Politicians like to be heard – why wouldn't Huckabee keep talking as long as the media are paying attention?

In closing, Huckabee has said he's staying around until the convention. Someone call Mitt Romney and ask how that promise went.

BILL CLINTON DOES MADTOWN

February 14, 2008

After seeing Mike Huckabee this morning, I was fired up to go see the First Black President (Bill Clinton), whose wife might actually lose the the presidency to the Second Black President (Barack Obama). Sure, Huckabee is a great speaker, but Bill Clinton is Bill Clinton. If you saw Mike Huckabee in a Denny's, you'd say to yourself "hey, there's Mike Huckabee," and go on eating your huevos rancheros. Bill Clinton is the former leader of the free world – for eight years, from what I understand.

I was interested in seeing how rough Clinton would get with Obama. In Wisconsin, Obama isn't a candidate – Obama is a way of life. It's clear Wisconsin is getting the South Carolina treatment from the Clintons – Hillary looks ahead to more favorable states, while Bill stays behind and takes shots at The Chosen One.

This morning, I told my 4-year old daughter (who first endorsed Obama, then Clinton, now McCain) that I was going to see Hillary's husband. I then threw in, as an afterthought, "oh yeah, he used to be president, too." Then I realized how crazy that must sound to a 4-year old. She probably thinks there's a pool of, like, three people that are allowed to run for president. It doesn't help that Hillary's husband was sandwiched by a father and son. Nuts.

Clinton's speech was held in a barn. Literally. The Stock Pavilion on the campus of the University of Wisconsin-Madison is a campus building where livestock shows are held. When I showed up at 12:30 (show time was 1:30, so I thought I'd get there early so I didn't get Obama'd), there were probably 50 to 100 people in line. It became clear to me, however, that the wait to get in was going to be outside in the 25 degree weather. I thought I'd tough it out, just to get a real sense of what attending one of these events is for the regular folk. I mean, any press person can hop from event to event – it takes determination to stick it out in freezing cold weather.

In front of me in line was a group of giggling college girls, not all of them Clinton supporters. One of them actually had a Barack Obama ringtone on her phone. When she got a call, her phone boomed, "YES WE CAN! YES WE

CAN!" The girls struck up an interesting political conversation. One said she thought McCain was creepy, and didn't like him "because he'd probably die." She said she might vote for him if he picked Condoleezza Rice as his running mate. Another girl, excited to see Bill Clinton, said "what if I get to touch him?" No joke really necessary there.

The wait went on and on, as did the freezing cold. After about 45 minutes, I felt like the muscles in my legs had the texture of beef jerky. The line grew to about 100 yards long, although dozens of people cut in line right up to the front. These people were easy to spot – they'd start out in the street, sizing up the line. They would then flip open their cell phone and pretend to call someone at the front of the line. Finally, they would start waving to their supposed "friend," and begin working their way through the crowd. At least 20 people pulled the same maneuver, causing a bit of friction among the people who had been freezing there for an hour.

As we waited in line outside, several Hillary volunteers began canvassing the crowd with clipboards to get people to "sign in." They implied that you had to sign up to get in to the event, which I knew was complete nonsense. Yet it seemed that hundreds of people complied, so best of luck to them getting off that mailing list.

Finally, the Clinton campaign provided some much-needed hope. A front door flew open, and with it the smell of cow manure from the pavilion. This was the most welcome cow manure smell ever – but also likely served as a harbinger for the speech we were about to hear inside. (I'll be here all week, folks.)

As I walked in the door and got patted down, I noticed that the sign up tables were being staffed primarily by attractive, thin, well-dressed young women. I felt ashamed of myself for immediately assuming they were from out of town. One of them slapped a Hillary sticker on my chest, which I didn't necessarily mind. I'm probably third in line to being the next Hillary Clinton campaign manager, anyway. When in the Stock Pavilion, do as the cows do, as they say...

Once inside, I got a good look at the almost-empty pavilion. I was told it seats about 2,000 people. The gray, concrete seats form a disinviting bowl around the livestock area. I guess if your clientele is mainly livestock, there's really no need to go for aesthetic charm in a barn. The floor, naturally, is all dirt. The aluminum ceiling is painted black, with large metal beams holding it up. The press area is roped off in the middle of the dirt area, and ten cameras are already set up on a large platform.

As the people file in, it is clear that one of the most important jobs for Hillary's staff is to get the right people behind the podium, in camera range. It appears that one of the best strategies for placement behind

Clinton is to be in a group wearing similarly-colored t-shirts. AFSCME union workers wearing their signature green shirts were all herded up to the front. The red t-shirt wearing "non-partisan" AARP of Wisconsin members were seated to the lower right behind the podium. I'm 100% sure I could start a group demanding thicker and fuller mustaches, get some friends to wear the same purple t-shirt, and we'd be plopped right behind the podium at the next Hillary event. Viva la Mustache!

Aside from the t-shirt wearers, there appears to be a hierarchy of who gets to be human wallpaper at these events. The pecking order of who gets to sit up front behind the podium for Democratic events seems to be: 1. Veteran wearing a hat; 2. Anyone in a wheelchair; 3. People wearing similarly-colored t-shirts; 4. Anyone wearing some kind of ethnic clothing.

With regard to #4: A young man wearing a Puerto Rico shirt was shuffled up to the front by one of Hillary's staffers. As a test, I think people should start showing up to these events in over-the-top ethnic attire. You'd watch one of Bill Clinton's speeches and see an Italian guy with a big curly mustache flipping a pizza, some people wearing lederhosen gulping beer, and some samurai warriors eating egg rolls.

Up in the crowd, a cute girl wearing a tight t-shirt is holding a heart-shaped sign that says "BILL, WILL YOU BE MY VALENTINE?" This is EXACTLY what Clinton needs at one of his rallies. This would be like an Obama supporter showing up at an Obama rally with a sign that said "Hey, Barack – WANNA DO SOME BLOW?"

Some of the young crowd members around me start to chatter about politics. One Hillary supporter actually says he doesn't mind McCain because he thinks given McCain's POW experience, that he won't rush the U.S. into war – since he knows first-hand the toll it takes on soldiers. I almost had to pinch myself to see if I actually was at a political rally. Certainly the last place you expected to hear a level-headed comment. It's like seeing the Pope in a strip club.

The girl behind me said she was going to call her sister and brag, because her sister is a huge Bill Clinton fan. In fact, she's such a fan, her sister named her cat "Clinton." Again, the jokes write themselves.

Finally, some unidentified woman got up on stage to remind us that in addition to today being Valentine's Day, tomorrow is a day that's equally as important – Susan B. Anthony's birthday! If I now have to go buy my wife some Susan B. Anthony candy and flowers, me and that broad are going to fight.

She went on to say how much Hillary had fought for "kids' issues." I started wondering what these "kids' issues" might be. The biggest issue my son seems to have is not being able to get Mr. Potato Head's nose on straight. If Hillary can come over and do that for him, she might get his vote. She also remarked how successful Hillary has been at "strengthening women." Presumably, this was in Hillary's brief career as a personal trainer.

This woman, whose name I will likely never know, said that while George W. Bush had promised to "invest" in renewable fuels, Hillary had promised to "re-invest" in renewable fuels. So for those of you at home who need to update your liberal language dictionaries, the order of commitment to expanded government programs is now:

1. "Re-investing"
2. "Investing"

On came Congresswoman Hilda Solis of California, who was supposed to impress us because... she came all the way from California! This point is made about five times during the speeches. But I can guarantee no part of Hilda Solis' trip to Wisconsin was as unpleasant as the time I just spent waiting outside the pavilion. The crowd remains unimpressed, and provides milquetoast applause.

Solis recalled a time long ago in 1992, when Hillary Clinton came to her Congressional district to help her win her first election. "I said to myself then," said Solis, "that this woman was going somewhere." Of course, Hillary was about to become the first lady, as her husband was running for President. Thanks, Nostradamus.

Solis pushed the fact that Hillary is going to fight "climate change." It was wise of her not to say Hillary's going to fight "global warming" to a crowd that had just spent freezing their asses off for more than an hour outside. "Climate change" lets Democrats claim that any time the needle moves, something's wrong.

Finally, Solis took a shot at "Milwaukee right wing radio," saying that "some host" told people the Clinton event in Waukesha was postponed. Without knowing what had happened, I immediately knew who she was talking about, and how likely her charge was to be completely made up. As it turns out, it was.

Before Solis exited, she demanded a "big round of applause for Dane County Executive Kathleen Falk!" The crowd immediately groaned, and Falk, over on the side of the podium, cracked a big smile. "...and President Bill Clinton!" added Solis. The crowd stood and cheered their rock star.

Falk approached the podium, and began talking about Hillary. She said Hillary Clinton was the "first presidential candidate to have a plan for the economy," which made me chuckle. As if Barack Obama was sitting around a month ago, turned to his advisors and said "Hillary keeps talking about 'the economy.' What's all that 'economy' talk about?"

Falk introduces Bill Clinton, who cuts a radiant figure on stage. He is thin, tan, and appears energetic. He launches into a criticism of Republicans' health care policies. "Raise your hand if you know someone who doesn't have health care," he implores the crowd. Nearly everyone does. He reiterates his support for universal health care. Later, he will likely be surprised to realize that he was actually President for 8 years, and never enacted universal health care. No need to point that out now, though – he's on a roll.

Knowing he has to be extremely subtle in his attacks against Obama, Clinton gingerly rolls out the newest talking point. "Solutions are better than speeches," he says, intimating that while Obama is a great speaker, he's short on accomplishments. Much of his talk focuses on this point. (The full speech will likely be available on the internet soon, so there's no need to go into great detail about its content.)

Clinton's speech rambles on for a while, and the crowd begins to lose a little air. The guy behind the podium who was inexplicably waving a copy of Clinton's autobiography in the air for the first 20 minutes of the speech has ceased. Clinton says Hillary is going to help the "victims" of the subprime lending crisis. He says one of his wife's basic tenets is that we should make the world better "for our grandchildren." Finally, someone has the guts to look out for the grandkids. He tries to peddle the line that New York State is actually very Republican, and Hillary helps those people anyway. He says the way to turn the economy around is through a better environment. (On the way out of the speech, I ask a squirrel for a job, and he hands me a business card and tells me he'll get back to me.)

At one point, Clinton looks like he's going to make a personal concession. "Full disclosure..." he says. Now when someone says "full disclosure," they're generally about to tell you something that conflicts with their eventual point. Something like "full disclosure – I have bought several Michael Bolton albums, but I think he doesn't have any talent." Something like that. Instead, Clinton's point is something like, "full disclosure – Hillary thinks we should take care of veterans." And that's it. Somewhere, the devious anti-veteran interest groups are shaking their fists.

Clinton closed his speech out by bragging about the $13 million Hillary has raised since Super Tuesday two weeks ago. Obama has raised $32 million in the last month. He said that was enough "to make this a contest." Obviously, Clinton is pitching his wife as a large underdog – a claim the polls tend to bear out. He ends his speech by saying Hillary is "a problem solver." I'll be sure to call her with questions about my Algebra homework.

At this point, I had been standing for four hours. Clinton descended on my side of the barrier, where I was only about three people deep. He reached into the crowd, which surged forward to meet him. His hand actually swung right by my head. I reached up, shook his hand, and bolted.

I walked 20 minutes in the snow back to my car, only to find that I had become the "victim" of a parking ticket. Time to call Hillary Clinton for help.

ONE NATION, DIMINISHED EXPECTATIONS

September 29, 2012

At home and at work, there is one inviolable rule to getting out of things you don't want to do: Don't perform the task well, otherwise you'll get stuck doing it forever. For instance, I once complained to a friend that my wife was making me do all our family's laundry. He laughed and said, "Just do it wrong once, and she'll never make you go near the washing machine again."

This method of lowering expectations has worked well for President Barack Obama. Last week, Obama told a Univision television audience that during his presidency, he has learned "you can't change Washington from the inside." He routinely blames the George W. Bush administration for the nation's terrible economic state without explaining how a single Bush policy caused the 2008 economic meltdown - or that Democrats held large majorities in Congress when mortgages and banks entered a free fall. For Obama, "Yes We Can" has become "At Least It's Not Worse."

And Obama has good reason to try to persuade the public to expect less of him. Three million more people are now in poverty than when Obama took office, and individual incomes have shrunk by 8%. America has suffered through 43 straight months of unemployment over 8%. While the president once charmed us with bromides about "hope," his re-election is only plausible because so many people have given it up; if 8 million people hadn't quit looking for jobs since the "recovery" began, the unemployment rate currently would be 11.2%.

Yet the polls still show Obama with a slight lead over Mitt Romney. In an odd sense, Obama might actually be benefiting from the fact that the economy has been so terrible for so long. Americans' expectations have been lowered to the point that they've settled into complacency. It has been so long since they've seen what a good economy looks like, Americans may have forgotten the good times and adjusted their lives accordingly. Prodded to accept less, we appear to have acquiesced.

Of course, Romney hasn't been much more inspiring. Despite the fact that no president has been re-elected with an unemployment rate over 7.2%, Romney has failed to convince Americans that he can deliver a brighter future. There's still time, but he can no longer simply posit himself as "better than the other guy." Romney needs to paint a picture depicting how life will be better under his presidency not just for business owners but for those remaining who still refuse to accept a lower standard of living.

Sadly, the fact that we are willing to accept less tells us a lot about our diminished opinion of ourselves. In high school, I was a happy guy any time a girl with two eyes and a full set of teeth would speak to me. But that's because I was a loser. On the world stage, America deserves to date only the prettiest girls. We can no longer simply be content with not getting worse - the United States has to once again show the planet why it is worthy of its place as the world's lone superpower.

It wasn't long ago that America used to be the place where expectations had no ceiling. It provided wealth and opportunity, the freedom to speak and to practice religion. And all Americans asked in return was for citizens to do their best and take responsibility for their lives. High expectations were the bond that everyone shared.

Yet now, as we limp toward the November election, we are being asked to recalibrate what we expect of our nation's leaders. As Stuart Smalley once said on "Saturday Night Live," "only the mediocre are always at their best" - and Obama is trying to impress us by leaping over that one-inch-high hurdle.

It just remains to be seen if we're willing to let him near our laundry again.

Milwaukee Journal Sentinel

INSULTING VOTERS MAY NOT BE A STRONG STRATEGY

September 18, 2012

In late April 2010, British Prime Minister Gordon Brown was engaging in some staged pre-parliamentary election retail politics when something unexpected happened: He met an actual voter.

Walking down the streets of Rochdale and flanked by television cameras, Brown bumped into widowed grandmother Gillian Duffy, who gave the prime minister an earful on issues such as immigration and government debt. Whisked away in his car while still wearing his wireless microphone, Brown was caught calling the meeting a "disaster" and referring to Duffy as "a bigoted woman." Days later, Brown's Labor Party would lose 91 seats, and he would resign as prime minister.

Traditionally, insulting voters hasn't been a solid electoral strategy. When a supporter told Adlai Stevenson, the losing Democratic presidential candidate in 1952 and 1956, that the "thinking people" supported him, he is reported to have answered, "yes, but I need to win a majority."

On Monday, video surfaced of Republican presidential candidate Mitt Romney speaking at a May fundraiser in which Romney indicates that 47% of the electorate won't support him because they pay no income taxes and receive too many government benefits. Romney followed that he would not "worry about those people," adding he would "never convince them they should take personal responsibility and care for their lives."

Romney's comments were reminiscent of when Barack Obama in 2008 tried to explain opponent Hillary Clinton's support in rural Pennsylvania by asserting that "bitter" rural voters "cling to guns or religion." (Oddly enough, Obama was talking about rural Democrats - his feelings about Republicans might make the author of "50 Shades of Grey" blush.)

Coincidentally, both Romney's and Obama's remarks were delivered at fundraisers, where they thought they were out of the public eye. For some reason, American politicians are like pole dancers: You flash them a little cash, and they reveal way too much.

Romney was right in that the growth of the welfare state has been staggering; 49% of all Americans currently receive some form of government assistance, up from 30% just three decades ago. Further, the idea that democracies are unduly influenced by a class of lazy moochers is nothing new.

In 1857, Thomas Babington Macaulay, writing about the new democracy in France, warned that the country soon would go bankrupt due to "a ruinous load of taxation laid on the rich for the purpose of supporting the poor in idleness." Macaulay worried that the "poorest and most ignorant part of society" would "plunder the rich, and civilization would perish."

But Romney's comments are ill-advised for two reasons: They reinforce the stereotype that he is detached from the experience of working people, and his claims are misleading. It is true that 47% of Americans don't pay income taxes - for years, Rep. Paul Ryan has been warning of the tipping point between at which society's "makers" join the ranks of the "takers." But many of those who don't make enough to pay income taxes do pay payroll taxes (for entitlements such as Social Security and Medicare). When payroll taxes are figured in, only about 18.1% of U.S. households pay no tax at all.

Furthermore, voters are more complicated than Romney would suggest - if seniors were computers that simply voted on the basis of Social Security and Medicare funding, Republicans wouldn't hold a single federal office. Instead, some polls currently have Romney up on Obama by nearly 20 percentage points among those 65 and older.

In fact, a good number of the 47% who don't earn enough to pay income taxes might even vote for Romney if he'd stop unfairly stereotyping them as vapid, brainless Obama minions. According to a recent Gallup poll, one in three voters who make less than $24,000 a year support Romney - a sign he might not want to throw them overboard.

During this election season, Republicans have rightfully been criticizing Obama for fomenting class warfare against the wealthy. But Romney's statements about the 47% push all the same buttons, just in the opposite direction. Romney is merely replacing disdain for people who make a lot of money with disdain for those who don't. And in the next few weeks, he needs to explain to the latter how he can help them become members of the former.

Milwaukee Journal Sentinel

ROMNEY'S CHARITABILITY

September 25, 2012

While running for president in 2000, George W. Bush created a new term that he thought would recast Republicans as the party of charity. He called it "compassionate conservatism," and it was noteworthy because it ran counter to the perception that the GOP was made up of Mr. Burns-style misers who are all too eager to release the hounds on the poor.

That was a perception buttressed last week when a video of Mitt Romney surfaced in which he noted that 47% of Americans who pay no income taxes would never vote for him because of their self-interested reliance on government. Put most generously, it was an inartful comment, for which Romney took a great deal of grief (from yours truly included).

But while Romney's words were clumsy, they were just that - words. Late last week, Romney released his 2011 tax returns, which cast his commitment to the poor in a very different light. Last year, Romney donated over $4 million to charity, or nearly 30% of his income. In addition, Romney only took $2.25 million worth of tax deductions on this charitable giving, meaning he paid more in taxes that he was obligated to. (In 2010 and 2011, Romney paid nearly $5 million in taxes to the federal government - so by President Barack Obama's reasoning, "you didn't build that" . . . Mitt Romney probably did.)

Of course, the left will give Romney very little credit for his charitable giving. To Democrats, compassion only counts when filtered through the government. While conservatives favor private charity to the causes with which they feel the most comfortable, liberals argue that people should be compelled through taxation to support causes with which they might disagree.

But when government expands, private charity contracts. According to the Charities Aid Foundation, America is the most charitable developed country in the world, giving more than double the amount of the second most compassionate country, the United Kingdom. The study placed American giving at 1.67% of gross domestic product, with the French dead last among the nations at 0.14% of GDP. By that measure, Americans are 12 times as charitable as the French.

Even within America, there is a sharp divide between those who contribute and those who don't. According to Arthur Brooks of the American Enterprise Institute, who wrote a book on the topic of charity, "people who favor government income redistribution are significantly less likely to behave charitably than those who do not." In other words, liberals who believe in equalizing economic outcomes see less need for private charity, as they believe that power should rest with the government. As Ralph Nader said, "A society that has more justice is a society that needs less charity."

This divide is borne out by data. Brooks found that in 2000, households headed by a conservative gave, on average, 30% more to charity than those headed by a liberal ($1,600 to $1,227). This discrepancy existed despite the fact that liberal households earned, on average, 6% more than conservative households. According to poll respondents, 77% of liberals believed the government could do more to redistribute wealth, while only 24% of conservatives felt the same way - which is why "heartless" right-wingers are more likely to volunteer, give blood and write charitable checks.

This is why conservatives favor contributing to organizations with low overhead, where donors are comfortable knowing the funds will get to the people who need them. As was seen in the collective bargaining fight in Wisconsin, a large part of government funds is diverted toward pensions and benefits, not to the people who are ultimately meant to benefit. And those forced to pay taxes have no choice but to play along.

Some conservatives bristle at the "compassionate conservative" label. Conservatism is by definition compassionate, they say, just in a way that isn't necessarily measured by government aid. And while Romney may mangle a speech now and then, his actions - both as governor of

Massachusetts and in his private life - do more speaking than he probably should.

Milwaukee Journal Sentinel

LOOK FOR THE UNSEEN

September 15, 2012

Picture the next big political Hollywood blockbuster: A single mother's 9-year-old son develops a tumor, and the mother's health plan, paid for by her corporate employer, pays for the child's surgery and he lives a happy, productive life.

By movie standards, it's not a very compelling story. Chances are, it would make its way to the bargain DVD bin quicker than "Rock of Ages." But in real life, similar scenarios play out every day. And because they lack all the drama of an uninsured patient fighting for coverage, these stories slip by our consciousness.

In most cases, our attention is weighted toward what we can see vs. what we can't. It's just human nature - we tend to recognize those tangible things that are right in front of our noses and ignore the hypothetical.

Here's a test: One day, come home and brag to your wife about all the women whom you managed not to have sex with that day. There's a 100% chance you will quickly find yourself on a list of "men who did not avoid a concussion" that day.

Our bias toward what we can see was put in economic terms by the great French philosopher Frederic Bastiat in 1850, when he observed that of the effects created by law, "the first alone is immediate; it appears simultaneously with its cause; it is seen. The other effects emerge only subsequently; they are not seen."

In other words, for example, nobody shows up to work thankful that the minimum wage isn't higher because nobody knows who would lose his or her job if it were increased. We know exactly how much we spend on the U.S. military (the seen) but have no idea how many lives it saves (the unseen).

A good many of the seen/unseen paradox examples break down along traditional conservative/liberal ideological lines. Liberals see an immediate action as the most desirable: When the president says he can create "shovel ready" government jobs, he just signs a bill to do so. In this sense, liberals have a huge advantage - it's much simpler to say "we need to fund government jobs," as the jobs are created immediately.

Conversely, pitching the conservative counterargument involves invoking all the people who could have jobs if government would get out of the way and let people spend their money on the productive sector. Terms such as "unintended consequences" and "Laffer curve" will be thrown around. Soon, you have to call vice presidential candidate Paul Ryan over to your house with his graphs and charts, your kids have fallen asleep and your husband has slowly shuffled over to the television to watch "Pawn Stars."

In fact, the bias in favor of the seen certainly has relevance to the presidential race. Ryan's plans to reform entitlements are fairly new and, therefore, unseen - which is why Democrats are inaccurately trying to make Ryan's plans seem as if they affect current Medicare and Social Security recipients.

On the flip side, President Barack Obama would be further ahead if everyone couldn't see how terrible the economy is - his primary challenge is to sell the unseen premise that more people would be without jobs if he hadn't signed the stimulus bill.

There are plenty of other scripts that never will be read by a movie producer. A power plant adheres to environmental regulations and puts up a transmission line that makes no one sick but provides power to thousands of lower-class individuals who need basic amenities. A person willingly pays for his prescription drugs because he knows pharmaceutical companies have to plow millions of dollars into research to create pills that will save his life. A college student happily takes on debt in order to pay for college, knowing it is an investment in her future earning potential.

It is this group of people who don't need government aid and who remain out of public sight - and, therefore, out of lawmakers' minds. On the other hand, it is a small but intense group of people dependent on government funds who tries to make its cause more comparatively visible (this is what the Wisconsin public employee protests of the past two years have been all about). The dog that doesn't bark never gets a bone, which is why government never gets credit for the things it funds - only blame from the people who want more.

Milwaukee Journal Sentinel

CATFISHED BY OBAMA

January 22, 2013

Every few years, a new generation of America's youth takes part in an activity that their parents are certain will bring about global Armageddon. Over the years, older generations have decried listening to vulgar music, smoking marijuana, wearing baggy pants and getting tattoos (or as I call all the above, "Thursday").

The latest entrant in the implosion of culture is the practice of "catfishing," or creating a fake online profile to cruelly lure unwilling participants into thinking they're in an amorous relationship. For instance, a comely bikini-clad blonde will send a Facebook friend request to a lonely teenage boy and fire up his already raging concupiscence - only in real life, the blonde will most likely resemble an NFL offensive lineman in either stature or gender.

This dishonest practice recently made the news when Notre Dame linebacker Manti Te'o apparently fell prey to a catfishing scheme. Te'o claims he had an online relationship with a woman who later died of leukemia, only to find out that it was a hoax. A new popular show on MTV documents young people who finally meet their online lovers, only to be willingly devastated on camera when they find out they have been had.

It may seem odd that so many people refuse to do even the most rudimentary research on someone with whom they claim to be in a relationship. In most cases, there isn't enough fabric in America to make enough red flags for these fake profiles. People just want to believe in someone who makes them feel good about themselves.

Yet following the contentious 2012 presidential election, it appears America itself might have been catfished by the contest's eventual winner.

On Monday, President Barack Obama gave his second inaugural speech. Gone is the profile Obama once showed us as a centrist and a pragmatist; with electoral politics behind him, he is now a Woodrow Wilson-style liberal, unapologetic for his belief in government as the unifying order in society.

When Obama sent us his first friend request in 2008, he was using a Bill Clinton avatar he apparently downloaded from the White House web page. He offered generous helpings of "hope" and "change," yet relied almost exclusively on blaming the George W. Bush administration for the nation's economic ills.

We still were hopeful that the young president could unlock the potential of the private sector and protect the middle class when he said it would be unwise to raise taxes during a recession. Yet the recent "fiscal cliff" not only raised taxes; it did so on the very people Obama said he would exempt. According to the Tax Policy Center (a project of the liberal-leaning Brookings Institution), 77% of American households are now paying higher taxes because the fiscal cliff deal failed to extend a payroll tax reduction passed as part of the 2009 stimulus bill.

We were hopeful that Obama would begin to emphasize jobs, given that at 7.8%, the unemployment rate is exactly where it was when he took office four years ago, and hundreds of thousands of Americans have stopped looking for work altogether. Yet during his inaugural address Monday, he made almost no mention of the economy or jobs, instead ticking off the grocery list of liberal projects highlighted during the Democratic National Convention last year.

The Obama we saw was one who pledged cooperation with people of different political ideologies - one who transcended "red" and "blue" America, as he was so fond of reminding voters. In fact, during his speech, he decried "name-calling" in politics - before going on to portray his adversaries as climate-change-denying, homophobic cave men who don't want women to make a livable wage.

Apparently, Obama believes in a profile of Republicans that is as phony as the one he has been trying to get the country to buy for the past four years. (Or in modern parlance, the dreaded "double-catfish," where two parties are completely fooled about the other.) This week, he began revealing to America who he really is; if he continues to dig in and offer more of the microwaved agenda that has held us back for the past four years, America will certainly not be LOL'ing.

Milwaukee Journal Sentinel

OBAMA CREATING MORE GOVERNMENT CYNICS

May 14, 2013

It was less than two weeks ago that President Barack Obama stood before the matriculating students at Ohio State University, urging them to have unwavering faith in their government. "(Y)ou'll hear voices that incessantly warn of government as nothing more than some separate, sinister entity that's the root of all our problems, even as they do their best to gum up the works, or that tyranny always lurks just around the corner," Obama told the graduating class in Columbus. "You should reject these voices," he said, "because what they suggest is that our brave, creative, unique experiment in self-rule is just a sham with which we can't be trusted."

But in the past week, Obama may have created more cynics than a hundred Ohio State Universities could possibly churn out. A string of scandals perpetrated by his administration have managed to buttress the wildest caricatures of government posited by right-wing groups. And many of these stories are still in their nascent stages.

Last week, the Internal Revenue Service, either showing it is devoid of irony or has a great sense of humor, admitted that it used its governmental power to target groups wary of governmental power. The IRS, using code words such as "patriot" and "tea party" to flag conservative groups, subjected Obama's political opponents to audits and denials of tax-exempt status. When asked about the selective audits this week, Obama said "if" they happened, it would be "outrageous."

But the president was well behind his administration — the audits or conservative groups did happen. The IRS admitted it and apologized. In couching it as a hypothetical, the president tried to make it seem as though he hadn't gotten the news because his cellphone had fallen between his couch cushions. Further, Obama's spokesperson tried to blame the IRS debacle on some rogue yokels in the Cincinnati office, but that city is where the Tax Exempt and Government Entities Division office is housed; such a scandal couldn't have happened anywhere else. Plus, officials in Washington, D.C., were actively involved in the audits, often sending queries to conservative groups asking for lists of members, donors and expenses.

The IRS scandal broke on the heels of heightened scrutiny of the Obama administration's public statements following an attack in Benghazi, Libya, on Sept. 11, 2012, that killed four Americans. Immediately following the attack, the CIA, the highest-ranking American diplomat on the scene and the Libyan government all told the administration that it was a terrorist attack. Yet for weeks, the administration misled the American people by claiming the attack was a response to an anti-Muslim YouTube video.

During Senate hearings on Benghazi, Sen. Ron Johnson (R-Wis.) was excoriated as a knuckle-dragger for grilling then-Secretary of State Hillary Clinton as to why the State Department consistently blamed the video for the attack — which happens to remain the central question to this day. Obama maintains that the day after the attack, he called it an "act of terrorism," an embarrassing falsehood that his administration still clings to, despite weeks' worth of video of the president blaming the video. Recent reports show that despite being told Benghazi was a terrorist attack the day after the event, the administration scrubbed the talking points of any reference to terror, instead going with the YouTube narrative.

If that wasn't enough, The Associated Press reported on Monday that the Department of Justice had been monitoring their reporters' phone calls in an attempt to gather information on possible leaks within the administration. Again, Obama's spokesmen threw the DOJ under the bus, claiming the president had no knowledge of any such monitoring — in the next few days, it won't be surprising if Obama claims he doesn't know what

"Department," "Justice," or "of" mean.

When describing one politician he knew, H.L. Mencken observed that "he has been in public life a long while, and has not been caught yet." Obama has now been caught. And in doing so, he has lent credence to those wary of the use of government as a tool of vengeance.

The man who ran for president utilizing gassy bromides such as "what Washington needs is adult supervision" and "there is not a liberal America and a conservative America" has been exposed as a petty party activist, bent on using government to mislead the public and punish his political opponents. In the end, Obama's primary achievement may have been to create a whole new class of cynics.

Milwaukee Journal Sentinel

BIDEN IS THE PERFECT VP

February 22, 2013

In the history of American television and cinema, many actors - and some actresses - of consequence have played the role of the president of the United States. The role has presented some of our greatest film actors with a chance to display strength and gravitas and, in the case of Harrison Ford, the chance to throw terrorists off of a plane while cracking wise.

The vice president, however, is almost always portrayed as either a simpleminded dunderhead or as secretly evil, plotting either his own takeover of the White House or plotting some subterfuge with another country. This is why it is rare to see an "A" list star take on one of these buffoonish roles.

Sometimes, there is a delicious confluence between the real life vice president and the cartoonish portrayal movies provide. In fact, in Joe Biden, America is currently witnessing a vice president who is almost too ridiculous to appear in film.

In real life, there's a reason vice presidents rarely ascend to the presidency. (And the last one to do so, George Herbert Walker Bush, only served one term before Bill Clinton defeated him in 1992.) Being vice president means you are a special breed - someone willing to do little of consequence for four, or even eight, years in order to one day convince the American public that you have much more to offer than your primary duty during the previous president's term, which was basically just to remain breathing. (President Millard Fillmore once actually turned down an honorary degree at Oxford University, saying that previously he had only been vice president, so nobody actually knew who he was.)

Biden's most recent struggles came when the White House asked him to be its point man on a very serious issue: gun control. Last week, Biden waded into the issue with the delicacy and thoughtfulness with which he has become known - which is to say, none at all.

Last week, in an online chat sponsored by Parents magazine, Biden tried to explain to women why they don't need high-powered rifles to protect their homes, instead suggesting repeatedly that they "buy a shotgun." The vice president suggested that semiautomatic weapons such as the AR-15 are harder to aim and harder to shoot - despite studies that show just the opposite.

Biden went on to advise women to "Have the shells in the 12-gauge shotgun. And I promise you . . . as I told my wife . . . we live in an area that's in the woods and somewhat secluded. I said, 'Jill, if there's ever a problem, just walk out on the balcony here, walk out and put that double-barrel shotgun and fire two blasts outside the house. I promise you whoever is coming in is not going to.' "

In short, Biden's plan for women to protect themselves is: Fire a shotgun into the air, then wait patiently while you are robbed, as you have no more ammunition.

As it turns out, the hypothetical advice Biden would give to his wife is actually illegal. A sergeant with the Wilmington, Del., Police Department told U.S. News and World Report that it is illegal to discharge a firearm on your private property unless you feel your life is being threatened.

Americans have figured out that this is par for the course for Biden, he of the "put y'all back in chains" quip, the advice to Americans not to fly because of the swine flu and his suggestion that most Indian-Americans own convenience stores.

Sure, Biden may not be as bad as Vice President Noah Daniels on the Fox show "24," who tried to wrest control of the presidency away from Wayne Palmer so he could start a nuclear war, or Vice President William Walden on Showtime's "Homeland," who attacked children with unmanned drones.

And as far as we can tell, he hasn't hatched a plot to take over the presidency like Vice President Ted Matthews in "My Fellow Americans." So if Biden is interested in becoming president, he'll have to do it without hatching an underhanded plot. He will also have to make sure the public has an extremely short-term memory.

Milwaukee Journal Sentinel

THE 'NOBLE LIE'

April 12, 2014

Since the beginning of time, people have been telling lies that they believe are justifiable. For instance, it's worth preserving family comity by telling your mom you love her meatloaf as it sprouts legs and walks away from you on the table. Any day now, explorers are going to discover a drawing scrawled on the wall of a prehistoric cave that loosely translates to "those pants don't make your butt look big."

It was Plato who brought the idea of the "noble lie" into political philosophy. In "The Republic," Plato describes Socrates' telling of the "three metals" lie in order to maintain the social stratification of society. According to Socrates, God had put gold, silver and iron into each individual's soul, and which metal a person had in his soul determined his lot in life, without exception. (So, in modern parlance, Socrates was essentially the Paula Deen of ancient Greece.)

Plato argued that feeding the masses such a fable helps keep them happy where they are and would short-circuit any big ideas they get about staging a revolution to gain a better life. He argued that the people generally weren't bright enough to handle their own affairs and, as a result, society should be ruled by a handful of enlightened leaders.

America's enlightened leader of today, President Barack Obama, appears to embrace the "noble lie" construct in order to feed the populace whatever he may be selling. Obama keeps reeling off the howlers, one by one, hoping that even though what he says isn't true, the public will side with him because it should be true.

We saw this last week with the "celebration" of Equal Pay Day, a quasi-holiday based on a fictional statistic. We might as well have a holiday celebrating Spider-Man's birthday. The idea that women make 77 cents for every dollar a man makes, a "fact" trotted out by Obama in his State of the Union address, takes into account none of the factors why the illusionary disparity exists.

For instance, while the Census Bureau statistic compares full-time workers, "full time" means different things in different workplaces. As Mark Perry and Andrew Biggs of the American Enterprise Institute have found, men are almost twice as likely as women to work more than 40 hours a week and women almost twice as likely to work only 35 to 39 hours per week.

The statistic also doesn't take into account marriage and family decisions women make. Children often take women out of the workplace, leaving them with less experience when they re-enter the workforce later in life. According to the Bureau of Labor Statistics, single women who have never married earned 96% of men's earnings in 2012.

White House economist Betsey Stevenson even conceded that the administration's go-to was misleading when she told MSNBC, "I agree that the 77 cents on the dollar is not all due to discrimination. No one is trying to say that it is. But you have to point to some number in order for people to understand the facts."

There you have it. It isn't true, but it seems like it should be true. This explains why, miraculously, women seem to make a lot less money during election years in which Democrats are on the ropes.

Of course, that doesn't mean women shouldn't make as much as men for equal work or that workplace discrimination isn't a problem. But these are nuanced questions that deserve debate, not the club-over-the-head approach Obama uses when he compares paying women less to "adding an extra six miles to a marathon."

Other mistruths fall out of the White House like salt from a shaker. Perhaps you remember "If you like your health care plan, you will be able to keep your health care plan. Period. No one will take it away. No matter what." The statement that became PolitFact's "Lie of the Year" in 2013.

Or Obama's contention that under the Affordable Care Act, health insurance companies will no longer be able to drop policyholders. In fact, since 1996, all insurance companies have been legally forbidden from dropping an individual policyholder who developed a chronic illness and have been prevented from raising anyone's rates as a result of a new malady.

These lies were told in service to a noble goal — to get more people signed up for health care. Obama seems to have embraced the Nietzschean belief that it is better to give "life-giving delusion" than to offer "deadly truth."

But while politicians typically stretch the facts to their liking, most of Obama's fabrications were never true from the time he uttered them. And while he may believe his ends more than justify his means, it is time we recognize his lies as simply ignoble.

Milwaukee Journal Sentinel

TIME TO GET TOUGH WITH TRUMP

September 13, 2015

[Ed. note: They did not.]

Donald Trump is an immodest man with much to be modest about. Yet he has had one accomplishment of which to be proud: He is single-handedly keeping about 10 other candidates in the presidential race.

Currently, Trump is garnering around 30% support in Republican primary polls - yet no other candidates actually believe he eventually will be the party's nominee. So the Huckabees and Santorums and Grahams sit and wait, thinking those Trump votes eventually will be available for their taking. They yearn for Trump's 30% as Echo yearned for Narcissus, and are biding their time while their polling shows them with lower support than paper cuts.

In any other year, the bottom dwellers would take the hint - but not this year, when Trump's votes give them all hope. Thus, Trump's continued inclusion in the race ensures a joyless march to elect the candidate we find least objectionable, as we endure debates with more characters than "Game of Thrones."

The Catch-22, of course, is that in order for the moribund candidates to actually jump in and swipe Trump's votes, they have to start wresting them from him. Some candidates have tried to emulate Trump; it would be shocking if Sen. Ted Cruz hasn't taken to wearing Trump's signature cologne in order to complete the transformation. (Yes, "Donald Trump the Fragrance" is a real thing.) In this vein, earlier this week, the alwaysinsightful Sean Davis of The Federalist suggested that other candidates should be "sympathetic" toward Trump, and that his challengers should feel "empathy" for him.

But this is exactly wrong. Trump appeasement is corroding the Republican Party, and the first candidate to eviscerate him on a debate stage will see his or her stock rise among voters.

Undoubtedly, part of Trump's appeal is that he's willing to fight. But if a legitimate candidate were to show just a sliver of that pugilistic spirit in shooting down Trump's nonsense, it could have much the same appeal as Trump's irascibility.

And by using Trump's own tactics against him, it wouldn't be as if a candidate is betraying conservative principles. Trump is a tax-hike loving, gun-controlling, single-payer health care admiring, Hillary Clinton-donating abortion enthusiast. If Trump's appeal is due to his predilection to "tell it like it is," other candidates shouldn't be afraid to, in turn, "tell it like it is" about Trump. If you lay into him, it's not exactly like taking down Margaret Thatcher.

The criticism, however, should not veer into the ad hominem. In an attempt to gain traction, Louisiana Gov. Bobby Jindal, recently mocked Trump's hair, saying it "looks like he's got a squirrel sitting on his head." This is an example of using Trump's worst traits against him - the kind of traits that lead him to criticize Carly Fiorina's looks, for instance.

It could be argued that much of Trump's appeal has more to do with the Democrats than Republicans. When the front-running Democratic candidate seems to have just as much chance of occupying a jail cell as she does the Oval Office, it would seem to be a prime opportunity for the GOP.

Thus, as Clinton's popularity falls in the polls, many Republicans likely see now as the time for the party to take a chance on a "nontraditional" candidate. But there's a reason Trump is "nontraditional" - Americans don't typically elect hot-tempered, misogynistic carnival barkers to oversee our nuclear arsenal.

As Christopher Hitchens once said of Jerry Fallwell, if Donald Trump were given an enema, he could be buried in a matchbox. But by keeping so many lifeless candidates alive, he's doing the work of 10 soon-to-be-out-of-work campaign managers. Sadly, too many candidates are being kept in the race by the one man who has the least business being in it.

Milwaukee Journal Sentinel

BEST AND BRIGHTEST

January 27, 2016

Last March, I appeared on a local Madison political show to discuss the upcoming Republican presidential race. At the time, a fringe candidate was making rumblings that he was going to get in the race. In the past, Donald Trump had started rumors that he was going to run for president in 1988, 2004 and 2012, and actually ran as a Reform Party candidate in 2000. In every case, his name dissipated before any real action began.

It was for this reason I went on television and dismissed him as a serious candidate. I said something to the effect of, "don't worry, we won't be talking about him in a couple of months."

The very existence of this column you're reading right now is evidence of how wrong I was. I certainly wasn't alone — virtually all of us media "elites" couldn't contemplate a scenario where a coarse, flip-flopping vulgarian would rise to the top of a party that he had only recently discovered. (And anyone that considers me an "elite" at anything hasn't seen me lying on my couch, covered in empty beef jerky bags, watching "The Bachelor.")

So what did we miss? How did conservative commentators so misread the electorate we've spent years presumably speaking for?

The most generous explanation is that Trump supporters aren't Republicans; they are a loose band of disaffected, unaffiliated voters who have migrated to the GOP simply because of his presence within it. Ironically, a decade ago, when Republicans were getting slaughtered in election after election, the party's focus was about "broadening the base" and becoming a "big tent" party. And now that they've seen who's bought tickets to the circus, it might be best for them to start booting people out of the tent.

But it's also possible that us eggheads, sitting behind our glowing screens philosophizing about voter behavior, stopped actually going out and talking to real voters. Just as modern technology allows members of each party to live in their own virtual reality — a conservative can now go the entire day without reading or hearing a dissenting viewpoint — that same technology can cause internecine fractures within parties themselves.

For instance, a conservative who listens to talk show radio hosts such as Rush Limbaugh, Mark Levin or Sean Hannity likely has a far different assessment of the Republican Party than those who curl up with copies of National Review or the Weekly Standard, or even my regular column. While ostensibly working for the same goals, these groups might not even recognize each other if they walked by each other on the street.

Further, the nerd pundit class underestimated the extent to which campaigns have become about personality. Those of us who pore over tax rates and immigration plans and game theory in international relations may simply be counting our pennies while someone else robs the bank. What matters is that people feel alienated and disenfranchised, and they want someone who is going to do something — whether it adheres to their ideological philosophy or not.

This is even evident on the Democratic side, where self-described socialist Bernie Sanders is catching up to Hillary Clinton. Are the majority of Democratic voters socialists? Of course not. But in Sanders, primary voters see someone who tells it like it is and who they think will fight for them.

Writing in The New Republic in 1922, Walter Lippmann argued that the supreme qualification for high office is temperament, not intellect. Ninety-four years later, we're seeing Lippmann's theory swallow the election whole. When the voting starts, the nominees likely will be picked based on what part of their body voters listen to — their head or their gut.

Milwaukee Journal Sentinel

DOES TRUMP THINK AMERICA IS WORTH SAVING?

January 29, 2016

Donald Trump's candidacy is one wholly defined by its contradictions. He is the candidate of strength, but runs shrieking when confronted by the possibility of answering a question from Fox anchor Megyn Kelly. He claims he is the best candidate to defeat Hillary Clinton, but spent years supporting her both financially and rhetorically. Trump shouts that he will revive America's economy but his companies have filed for bankruptcy four times.

Yet there is one overriding paradox that colors Trump's run. If his supporters, as their rallying cry so succinctly states, are so serious about "Making America Great Again," why are they so effusive in backing an unserious candidate?

Try to think of the presidents his supporters likely think are great — Lincoln, Reagan, etc. — mocking disabled people, banning specific religions and getting mixed up in juvenile public spats. (It's actually a little known fact that Thomas Jefferson's early drafts of the Declaration of Independence guaranteed the "right to life, liberty and the pursuit of not getting schlonged.")

Perhaps the slogan itself provides a window into what really bothers Trump's army. "Make America Great Again" presumes that America is not currently great — that the country has devolved into a place unrecognizable to older Americans, who support Trump at a rate twice that of younger voters.

It's possible these disaffected voters view America as a lost cause. They see gay people getting married and transgender people accepting awards. They are afraid illegal immigrants are stealing jobs. They watch protesters run riot in their own cities to protest legitimate police action. They dread college campus-style political correctness spilling over into their own lives.

When all these things are taken into account, they likely see an America not even worth saving. The Trump candidacy essentially is a funeral for the life they fear now will only exist in history books — and soon, those history books will be written by transgendered Mexicans.

Even Bernie Sanders — a Socialist for goodness sakes — is running a deeply moving ad extolling our country's wonders. As a backdrop, the TV spot uses Simon and Garfunkel's song "America," which is about the journey to find the country's virtues, not mourning their passing.

That's not to say there isn't plenty about which to be cantankerous. One doesn't have to be an avowed member of the religious right to be horrified at the selling of aborted baby parts. But it is disconcerting to see many people of faith being driven into the arms of Trump, a thrice-married supporter of partial-birth abortion with a relationship history that, in the words of Morrissey, might make Caligula blush.

But Trump's people have watched the stature of the office of president shrink before their eyes during the last seven years. They blame a feckless Congress for not having improved their lives in any measurable way. Since they're pretty sure it doesn't matter who they elect to office, why not vote for a pompous windbag who is at least going to keep things entertaining?

As the campaign grinds on, we'll hear more informed candidates talk about what happens in Middle East countries when their leaders are deposed; often, dictatorial megalomaniacs rush in to fill the vacuum when there's an absence of leadership. But with the rise of the Trump nihilists, countries such as Syria and Libya may start to worry about us.

Perhaps relying on people who revel in shoveling dirt on America's grave will be enough to get Trump through a few primary states. But in the long term, it is poison to a party that is typically powered by optimism. Trump's unserious, dyspeptic platform appeals strictly to a shrinking bloc of voters and, if successful, will mean the end of the GOP as a functional party. Republicans need to persuade their disaffected brethren that America's strength isn't in its president, but in the people who elect him.

Milwaukee Journal Sentinel

CRUZ SHOULD BLAME HIMSELF FOR TRUMP

March 29, 2016

In early September of 2015, GOP presidential candidate Ted Cruz was set to attend a Capitol Hill rally to protest President Barack Obama's then-proposed Iran deal. But before he showed up, Cruz extended an invitation to another Republican candidate with whom he thought it was important to share the stage: Donald Trump.

In fact, for the first six months of the presidential campaign, Cruz dutifully shined Trump's shoes, embracing him in ways not yet even envisioned by the Kama Sutra. Right about the time of the Iran rally, I joked that Cruz likely went home smelling of Trump's signature name-brand cologne.

Even though Trump's toxic burrito of racism, misogyny and vulgarity were well known at the time, Cruz knew that, tactically, he had to appeal to the same voters Trump was speaking to. Early in the race, Rick Perry had called Trump a "cancer" on conservatism, and Jeb Bush had derided Trump's immigration position as "ugly" and "divisive." Even after Trump began spreading ridiculous rumors about Cruz not being eligible for the presidency because he was born in Canada, Cruz still couldn't quit The Donald.

"An awful lot of presidential candidates," Cruz said at the time, "have gone out of their way to take a stick to Donald Trump."

"I am not one of them."

It turned out to be a shrewd calculation — the candidates who criticized Trump early all have one thing in common; they are now all ex-candidates. Instead, Cruz behaved like a mouse stuck in an aquarium with a ball python; he was happy to kick all the other mice to the head of the line to be devoured one by one, hoping by the time the snake got to him, the python might have indigestion.

But now Cruz and the python are the only ones left in the tank, and the snake has turned its gaze squarely on the Texas senator. The bromance seemed to end officially when Trump tweeted an unflattering photo of Cruz's wife Heidi, comparing her to Trump's wife Melania, a former model. This set off Cruz, and, in a controlled tirade that almost approximated an actual human moment, Cruz called Trump a "sniveling coward," telling Trump to "leave Heidi the hell alone."

But in so many ways, Trump is Cruz's Frankenstein monster who has now turned on the villagers. With his self-aggrandizing antics in the U.S. Senate, Cruz pandered to low-information voters who had a tenuous grasp of how Congress works. Cruz created a class of Republicans who thought GOP legislators could get Barack Obama to repeal a law known as "Obamacare" if the Republicans simply wanted it badly enough. Cruz's government shutdown accomplished nothing but furthering the Golden Era of Anti-Information in which we now find ourselves.

"What he did was stood up for Ted and threw the Republican Party under the bus," said Sen. Lindsey Graham (R-S.C.) in the years since Cruz's shutdown gambit.

Little did Cruz know that this angry cabal of dyspeptic voters then would be commandeered by a billionaire reality TV show star. Hillary Clinton, of all people, actually put her finger on this in a speech she gave at the University of Wisconsin-Madison last Monday. Clinton criticized how Cruz's shutdowns wrote checks to voters he couldn't possibly cash. And, "Once you make the extreme normal, you open the door to even worse," she said.

Now, Cruz is stuck trying to convince Wisconsin voters that he's more than just the only mathematically plausible "anti-Trump" candidate left standing. One gets the feeling from Wisconsin voters that their newfound affinity for Cruz ("Encruziasm"?) isn't because he's a sensational candidate, but because he's their last hope of derailing Cruz's former BFF. Cruz's

Wisconsin motto might as well be, "Vote Cruz, I Guess."

But Cruz's appeasement of Trump will continue to haunt this race well beyond the Wisconsin primary. Ted Cruz made this electoral bed; now he and Trump are stuck sleeping in it together.

Milwaukee Journal Sentinel

R.I.P., GOP

May 3, 2016

[Ed. note: In the subsequent years, a number of columnists began using the "R.I.P., GOP formulation. As far as I can tell, I was the first.]

'If my dad, who died in 1995, came back right now, and I said 'Hillary Clinton vs. Donald Trump," said Milwaukeean Chris Stolarski on Twitter Tuesday night, 'he'd re-die.'

There's no doubt Stolarski's father wouldn't recognize the Republican Party of 2016, which all but handed its nomination to Trump after the business mogul's victory in the Indiana primary Tuesday. In one campaign, Trump has managed to negate every bit of political work put in by conservative activists for the last four years; all the phone calls made, columns written, literature dropped and Facebook posts by Republicans meant to spread the conservative message have gone the way of the compact disc, having been rendered obsolete at the presidential level.

And thus, with voters drawn to Trump's bombast, the Republican Party has ceased to be the national home for conscientious conservatives. Trump's vulgar populism is unmoored from any tenets of the liberty movement. And as a result, the GOP has ceased to be Grand, is certainly Old, and may no longer be a Party.

This is why, on a night when a major party candidate essentially clinched the nomination, large swaths of Republicans were disconsolate. Because they know, as former NBA star Latrell Sprewell counsels in a current commercial, 'success is just failure that hasn't happened yet.'

Despite Trump's proclamations of electoral prowess, he will be a historic drag on down-ticket races Republicans could win any other year. Trump will be the most unpopular nominee polling has ever measured; the only American politician in recent decades who approaches Trump's unpopularity is Richard Nixon after the Watergate scandal. Trump as the party's standard-bearer will have roughly the same effect as amending the party platform to ban women from obtaining driver's licenses.

As the Washington Post's Chris Cillizza pointed out this week, even with a popular candidate Republicans would have an uphill battle on their hands in the 2016 presidential race. If Hillary Clinton were to simply add

Florida (where she currently holds a double-digit lead over Trump) to 19 other states that Democrats have won every year since 1992, the presidential race is over. And that currently represents the rosiest set of glasses Republicans can wear.

As Republicans wave goodbye to the presidency, they also can bid adieu to control of the U.S. Senate and the Supreme Court. Many of the Republican senators who rode in on the anti-Obamacare wave of 2010 will ride right back out on the self-inflicted anti-Trump wave of 2016. With Trump at the top of the ticket, if there's no third-party candidate that conservatives can show up at the polls to support without wearing a disguise, the only campaign expense many of these vulnerable GOP senators will need is a new set of golf clubs.

Of course, there still will be something called the 'Republican Party,' but it will look fundamentally different from the party we now know. Instead of being a national political force, Republicans will need to make their case locally. There are still 31 GOP governors who can demonstrate the efficacy of conservatism at the state and local level, serving as a check against the Democratic-dominated Congress, presidency and Supreme Court.

But on the national level, Republicans are a laughingstock, having validated every liberal stereotype of xenophobia, racism and sexism that has been hurled at conservatives for decades. Donald Trump is a political vampire; he sucked all the life from the Republican Party, leaving it animate but devoid of a heartbeat.

When a party meets at its quadrennial national convention, it is typically a celebration to show the nation's voters what the party has to offer them in the future. This year, Republicans can only crow about their past conservative accomplishments, not the incomprehensible ramblings of their presumptive nominee. In that sense, Cleveland will be less like a party and more like a funeral.

Milwaukee Journal Sentinel

RYAN CAN'T GIVE IN

May 10, 2016

Last week, Paul Ryan took control of the Republican wing of the Republican Party.

On Thursday, the Speaker of the House appeared on CNN, telling host Jake Tapper that he couldn't "yet" support presumptive GOP nominee Donald Trump. But Ryan held out hope that he could one day back Trump. "I hope to, though, and I want to," Ryan told Tapper.

But Ryan's olive branch to Trump was overly magnanimous. He should not hope, nor ever want to back Donald Trump. To do so would be to betray his conscience, his decency, and his principles.

Those believing obeisance to the Republican Party is paramount are holding out hope that Ryan's meeting with Trump this Thursday will bring GOP unity. But Ryan had already downplayed the theatrical powwow, saying he doesn't have "huge expectations" for the meeting. It seems unlikely that an hour of eating a sandwich with Donald Trump will be enough to undo a lifetime of promoting a conservative philosophy.

Further, there's nothing to suggest that a meeting with Ryan will do anything to moderate Trump's outrageous behavior. Trump, who has a historically low thought-to-word ratio, spent the day he clinched the GOP nomination dabbling in a conspiracy theory that posited Ted Cruz' father was complicit in John F. Kennedy's assassination. Later, Trump lied about receiving a congratulatory call from Ryan on the eve of Trump's New York primary win — Ryan said no call ever took place. Just weeks ago, Trump held a press conference to sell Americans hypothetical meat products.

These examples don't even speak to the chasm between Trump's positions — whatever they may be at the time — and conservative tenets. In the past week, Trump renounced his own tax plan, supported raising the minimum wage, and proposed to default on the U.S debt, saying, "I would borrow knowing that if the economy crashed, you could make a deal."

The truly amazing thing isn't that Ryan has kept Trump at a distance, but how many conservative Republicans have vowed to support Trump the Insult Comic Candidate. The history books should forever stain any conservative who has capitulated to this big government vulgarian.

To his credit, Ryan may already be contemplating a long-term split. Earlier this week, he told me he would relinquish his duties as chairman of the Republican National Convention in July if Trump asked him to. It almost seemed like Ryan was offering an invitation for Trump to offer a dis-invitation. As Chicago-based writer Emily Zanotti observed, Ryan was essentially declaring, "Not my circus, not my monkeys."

Instead, Ryan should be giving cover to House members who can't stomach standing on a stage with Trump during their upcoming campaigns. Those in Congress looking to run on a positive, issues-related platform shouldn't be forced to respond every time Trump declares his love of Hispanics by tweeting a picture of him downing a taco bowl. Somewhere, the 60% of Republican voters who rejected Trump during primary season deserve a voice.

And one of those House candidates needing cover is Ryan himself, who is facing a primary challenge from a Sarah Palin-endorsed Trump supporter named Paul Nehlen. So with neck-breaking speed, Ryan's critics went from ripping him for being insufficiently conservative to slamming him for not supporting a presidential candidate who isn't conservative at all. When I asked Ryan what his Trump-infused opponents actually sought to achieve, he merely threw his hands up and said, "you'd have to ask them."

But what they seek is something Ryan can't possibly offer – his dignity. And when he finally sits face to face with Trump, he shouldn't negotiate away his conscience. As Neville Chamberlain once told Soviet ambassador Ivan Maisky, "If only we could sit down at a table with the Germans and run through all their complaints and claims with a pencil, this would greatly relieve all tensions." Any negotiation with Trump would be equally feckless.

This is why, in order to keep conservatism alive, Ryan should resist all of Trump's overtures. As Winston Churchill said, "When a snake wants to eat his victims he first covers them with saliva." In this instance, it should be the conservatives on the attack.

Milwaukee Journal Sentinel

RYAN GAVE IN

June 03, 2016

In William Shakespeare's Othello, Cassio warns of the dangers of alcohol, saying he "would not put a thief in my mouth to steal my brains."

Evidently Speaker of the House Paul Ryan drank too much Trump Vodka on Thursday, as The Donald absconded with Ryan's reputation as one of the few remaining conservatives of principle. Ryan ended his holdout and finally endorsed Donald Trump for president, citing the need for party "unity" going into the fall election.

Perhaps this endorsement was inevitable but it was jarring to see the sellout executed for free. Trump today is just as unfit to hold public office as he was when Ryan announced his pyrite protest. Perhaps Trump is the master negotiator he claims to be — he actually made Ryan tear down the wall between them, and Republicans are ultimately going to pay for it.

During Ryan's holdout, Trump made no progress toward the goals Ryan said he needed to see from the presumptive GOP nominee — in fact, just in the past week, Trump has floated discredited conspiracy theories about former Clinton adviser Vince Foster's death and attacked the ethnicity of a judge overseeing the Trump University case. Are these what pushed Ryan toward capitulation?

Now Ryan becomes like San Francisco Giants fans who cheered on Barry Bonds during his desecration of America's pastime. Normally sane fans defended Bonds simply because he wore the right color jersey.

Now that Trump is wearing the Republican jersey — one that still has the price tag on it, incidentally — conscious conservatives are losing their minds defending someone who is uniquely unqualified to lead the nation. If there existed an organization called "People Named Donald Trump," Trump wouldn't be cognitively stable enough to serve as its president.

And there will be a long-term price to pay. Any time Ryan stands before reporters detailing his positive agenda steeped in conservative principles, the podium should feature a giant asterisk — that is, House Republicans believe in the pillars of conservatism right up until the point when a puzzlingly hirsute man-baby decides to mock women, minorities and the handicapped. When Ryan espouses political civility, ask him about his endorsement of America's most prominent Obama birther. We now know that no person exists who is so disgusting that he is below Republican appeasement.

In fact, it is this complete lack of political conviction that is driving people away from conventional politicians and toward a bottom-feeding vulgarian such as Donald Trump. We all know the stereotype of the typical politician who believes in issues only as deeply as it allows him or her to further their career; Trump, on the other hand, seems authentic — he has convictions, even if they are about items of national security such as whether certain women truly can ever be "10s."

But now Republicans are hoping that supporting Trump is like breaking the speed limit — if everyone does it, nobody will ultimately get busted. Sure, Republicans may say their ultimate goal is to stop Hillary Clinton, but to replace her with what? A Hillary Clinton donor who opposes reforming Social Security and has publicly waxed poetic about single-payer health care? As president, Trump is just as likely to hold a news conference to sell Trump Tangy Barbecue Sauce as he is to announce a plan to rein in government.

And exactly what was the ultimate purpose of Ryan's several-week non-endorsement period? Why were we glued to our televisions as cameras buzzed around the Ryan-Trump summit a few weeks ago as if a high-level hostage negotiation was taking place? (Especially when we now know Ryan was the hostage all along?)

Ryan's holdout wasn't even long enough to earn him credit in the footnotes of future history books — he'll earn plaudits for delaying his Trump endorsement in the same way an arsonist will get credit for waiting three weeks to burn down a library out of respect for the Dewey Decimal System.

In 1984, George Orwell writes that in his dystopia, "Nothing was your own except the few cubic centimetres inside your skull." Conservatives were hoping Ryan would continue to own his own gray matter in the Era of Trump, but that dream has been incinerated — Trump is now the proud owner of the Republican Party's great minds.

Let's just hope he kept the receipt so he can return them to their rightful owners after his November decimation.

Milwaukee Journal Sentinel

THAT MAN IS POISON

June 07, 2016

Imagine a time when you were jumping out of your skin in anticipation of a first date. You take the other person to a swank restaurant, sit down, and order your drinks. But when your libations arrive, there appears to be a large cockroach lounging in your glass.

"Um, waiter, there appears to be an insect in my Manhattan," you protest. So the waiter reaches in, plucks the roach out of your drink with his fingers, and hurls it toward the kitchen.

"Salud," he says, sliding the drink back to you.

If you are a Republican in 2016, it would make total sense for you to gulp it down, as if a filthy hexapod had never been vacationing in your cocktail. That's because the Republican Party has its own cockroach to deal with: the short-fingered Trumpus Americanus, an indestructible pest who happens to be its presidential nominee.

Ever since endorsing Trump, GOP politicians have climbed on top of one another to disavow his pronouncement that Mexican-American and Muslim-American judges are ethnically incapable of doing their jobs. Trump has repeatedly said he thought federal Judge Gonzalo Curiel had a conflict of interest in a fraud case against Trump University because Curiel was "a Mexican." As it turns out, Curiel was born in the exotic nation known as Indiana, the same place that birthed Mexican NBA legend Larry Bird.

After Trump demonstrated such overt racism, his Republican supporters immediate renounced their endorsements, thereby saving the soul of the party and their own personal dignity. Hah! Just kidding, that didn't happen at all.

House Speaker Paul Ryan, who endorsed Trump late last week, called Trump's comments "textbook" racism, but vowed to continue supporting him. New Hampshire Sen. Kelly Ayotte, who is in a tough fight to retain her seat, said Trump's comments were "offensive and wrong," and urged him to retract them, but is continuing to support Trump. Wisconsin Gov. Scott Walker said that endorsing Trump over Hillary Clinton "doesn't mean I embrace all the things that he says or all the ways that he says it."

But one cannot simply compartmentalize Trump's odious statements, picking and choosing which ones with which to agree. His racist, intemperate ramblings poison any other positions he may take or any promises he may make to appoint a conservative to the Supreme Court. Escaping culpability for endorsing Trump is like being caught watching The Bachelorette and explaining you watch it for the interior decorating tips.

This blind obeisance to party is particularly puzzling, given that nobody can explain why deference to Trump is all that important. If a leading Republican politician were to say, "Trump is a vulgar racist lout who also happens to stand against everything conservatives have fought for decades to achieve," would GOP voters hold that against him or her in the next election? It seems the damage being done to the Republican Party right now still could be offset by the goodwill such a conservative leader would engender by being the voice of sanity.

Keep in mind that Trump is arguing Curiel is biased against positions Trump has taken on Mexican immigration. Trump's argument appears to be that he should be able to influence the outcome of a pending case against him by slandering the judge overseeing the proceedings — we always knew Trump was a racial simpleton, but judge-tampering adds a new, fresh layer to his abhorrence.

Certainly, not all Trump supporters are white supremacists — but you can bet that white supremacists will all be voting for Trump. It's simply unacceptable for the Republican Party to be in the position of defending a candidate by saying, "Well, he's not racist most of the time."

And if Republicans continue to allow Trump to befoul the party, The Donald, like the tenacious cockroach, will outlive the GOP altogether.

Milwaukee Journal Sentinel

TRUMP KNOWS ONE THING

June 14, 2016

"The fox knows many things," Greek poet Archilochus told us 2,600 years ago, "but the hedgehog knows one big thing."

Since America's inception, politicians have been foxes; candidates for office know a little bit about a great number of issues. When they hit the stump, they are expected to pirouette between questions about nuclear proliferation, when life begins and why their kids' school lunches are so greasy.

Donald Trump, on the other hand, may be our first hedgehog candidate. He knows one big thing — the campaign is about him and only him. He is the flaming gaseous ball around which all other planets circle. His positions aren't the story; he is. Details are for sissies.

This is why, in the hours following the horrific massacre in Orlando early Sunday morning, Trump kept the focus where he believed it belonged — on Donald Trump.

"Appreciate the congrats for being right on radical Islamic terrorism," Trump tweeted Sunday morning. "I don't want congrats, I want toughness & vigilance. We must be smart!"

Shoveling the fertilizer out of this 23-word statement requires a Hazmat suit, but for the sake of the historical record, let's dig in.

For one, who are these people congratulating Trump after the deadliest shooting in American history? If you woke up on Sunday morning, saw the atrocity that had been committed, and your first reaction was "Man, I should praise Donald Trump for predicting this," you are a terrible human.

And exactly what did Trump think he deserved congratulations for? Because he predicted there would be another deadly attack on American soil at the hands of someone inspired by ISIS? Did any adult in America think otherwise?

But perhaps most offensive is Trump's tone, which seems to suggest that the attack wouldn't have happened if he was in charge. This is truly the lowest form of political opportunism and a slander against the men and women of law enforcement who work to keep us safe.

And as for working "smarter"? Well, Trump naturally used the tragedy to push his ban on Muslims entering the country. In a follow-up tweet, Trump said he "called" the attack and "asked for the ban," adding that we "Must be tough."

One small problem with Trump's ingenious plan, though: the Orlando shooter was born in America and lived here his entire life — he wasn't an "Afghan," as Trump would later mistakenly claim. No ban on entering America would have prevented the tragedy, and the U.S. government can't deport American citizens. If anything, we need to stop the migration of Trump's bigotry from his brain to his mouth.

On Monday, Trump doubled down in a rambling, incoherent speech he gave under the guise of "national security." The same morning, on Fox News, Trump pitched a conspiracy theory positing that President Barack Obama may be sympathetic to the radical Islamist who gunned down 49 clubgoers in Orlando.

"He doesn't get it, or he gets it better than anybody understands," Trump said of Obama. "It's one or the other." Trump later went further, saying the president "is not tough, not smart — or he's got something else in mind."

To his supporters, Trump's primary appeal is that he will shake up the status quo in Washington. But the process of honoring the dead after a mass tragedy didn't need shaking up. And neither did the tradition of waiting until all the victims had been removed from the crime scene before accusing the sitting president of being sympathetic to the terrorist who committed the slaughter.

But Trump will continue to corrode politics in America, because he knows the one big thing. And the bigger that thing gets, the smaller he becomes.

Milwaukee Journal Sentinel

REFRESHING DISHONESTY

June 17, 2016

When a Russian hacker broke in to the Democratic National Committee computer system last week and stole the DNC's opposition research file on Donald Trump, the public got a glimpse at how Democrats would attack the GOP nominee. The very first point the secret document raises against Trump is that he "has no core," and that he will "say anything and do anything to get what he wants."

But this attack seems to be completely the opposite of the story Democrats should be pushing about Trump. It's not that he has no core — it's that the core we have seen is rotten. It's not that Trump doesn't believe anything — it's that what he believes is repulsive. As comedian Conan O'Brien recently tweeted, "It's tough this year. I'm worried Hillary's a liar, and I'm worried Trump's not."

Indeed, it is actually Hillary Clinton who is best known for her positional malleability. In a recent fake commentary in The Onion, Clinton declares, "If I Could Be Just Completely Honest For A Second, I Believe Exactly What You Believe."

In fact, it may be Clinton's history of political opportunism that helps her pick off a few Republican votes against the corpulent orange hair tornado. Sure, she has a long history of pushing left-wing plans — but she also has spent her adult political life running in Democratic primaries that have sent her careening to the left. Notably, she had to out-liberal a socialist over the past year.

What we haven't seen yet is Clinton try to appeal to conservatives and moderates, as she's never really had to. But the GOP nominee isn't conservative and is only tangentially Republican. This race is between two philosophical Democrats — and if Clinton can comfort enough voters on the right, she can steal a number of those whose consciences won't allow them to vote for Trump.

There's evidence Clinton, like her husband, can pivot and make a convincing appeal to right wingers that currently feel homeless. A self-described former "Goldwater Republican," she traditionally has been pro-free trade and pro-traditional marriage (she only recognized a constitutional right to same sex marriage in 2014.) She served as first lady while her husband passed welfare reform and tough crime bills. As governor of Arkansas, Bill Clinton staked his claim as the leader of the moderate New Democrats; even in 2013, Clinton was giving speeches in which he warned those on the left against "looking down your nose" at pro-gun voters.

Of course, none of these points will mollify those who have spent the past quarter-century convinced Hillary Clinton is the very portrait of deviltry. And the current FBI investigation into her email server has justifiably buttressed those arguments against her.

But unless Cleveland next month joins Medjugorje as the city of miracles and tosses Trump as the GOP nominee, Clinton and Trump are the only realistic candidates left. And yes, Clinton is a Democrat, but she is a Democrat in the traditional American political sense. Unless 2016 is a complete wipeout for Republicans, she will fight with the GOP-led House of Representatives, and maybe they can find deals to be struck.

But Trump is a Democrat in a sense that we've never seen. He works outside the traditional system, which is appealing to his followers — but Trump is more likely to convert the White House into a casino than he is to keep us safe from international threats. We have had Democrats like Clinton as president before, and the Union has remained intact. We have never had one like Trump.

Yes, it is sad that voters are forced to choose between the devil we know and the one we don't. In that scenario, both choices are the devil.

But given Hillary Clinton's history of issue-based malleability, the devil we think we know the best may turn out to be one that disgruntled Republicans can swallow. Perhaps now that Clinton is in an election in which she needs conservatives, she'll throw us a life raft. #NeverTrump may be a long way from #ImWithHer, but they should at least be #Let'sWaitAndSee.

Milwaukee Journal Sentinel

AMBITION BEFORE DIGNITY

July 8, 2016

Donald Trump is a "pathological liar" who "doesn't know the difference between truth and lies." Trump "lies practically every word that comes out of his mouth." Trump is "utterly amoral" and "will betray his supporters on every issue."

Remember the great orator who heaped such calumny upon The Donald? It wasn't Hillary Clinton or Bernie Sanders or President Barack Obama. It was Republican Texas Sen. Ted Cruz, shortly after Trump both accused Cruz's father of being complicit in the assassination of President John F. Kennedy and mocked Cruz's wife's looks.

That also would be the same Ted Cruz who, on Thursday of this week, agreed to speak at the Republican convention in Cleveland later this month. The very convention that will in all likelihood nominate Donald Trump. (As Business Insider's Josh Barro tweeted, "Ted Cruz did draw the line at Trump's demand that Heidi wear a paper bag over her head during the convention.")

Cruz's agreement to be in Cleveland to support Trump's coronation is exactly the reason people hate politicians. Sure, the image of the duplicitous politician is burned in the American psyche — citizens have accused elected representatives of being oleaginous weasels as long as they've been casting ballots. But watching conservative politicians capitulate to Trump's strong-arm tactics has quickly turned the knob to "11."

Even the GOP's once-most promising members have gotten in on the act. Louisiana Gov. Bobby Jindal called Trump a "narcissist," and an "egomaniacal madman" who had no principles — months later, Jindal endorsed Trump. Sen. Marco Rubio was once Trump's harshest critic, at one point saying Trump shouldn't be given access to the nation's nuclear codes. In May, Rubio endorsed Trump. (One wonders how we can trust Trump with the nation's nuclear football when we couldn't even trust him with the USFL.)

But in politics, we are once again finding out that almost all deeply held positions are situational. Politicians are willing to take courageous stands right up until the moment the usefulness of those beliefs expire.

Yet there is one politician who refuses to alter his positions for political expediency. And that is likely why he is the presumptive Republican nominee. Trump is the flip side of the weak-of-conscience opponents he defenestrated during the GOP primary; He will cling to his positions, no matter how obnoxious or detrimental.

And that is why it made sense for voters to pick a reality television star as a major party nominee; for many Americans, politics is now simply a television show that bears little resemblance to their own lives. They see backstabbing, screaming, narcissism and scheming, while nothing of substance ever gets done. Call this show "The Real House Members of Washington, D.C."

Much of the media coverage of the presidential race foments this idea of the whole thing as an empty spectacle. Right now, CNN is running a commercial that literally looks exactly like a movie trailer, promising "a race like no other" — as if that in and of itself were a selling point. If one of the candidates gave stump speeches while operating a ventriloquist dummy, it would certainly be a race like no other, but not in any way that was particularly edifying.

(Further feeding the politics-as-entertainment machine this week was Eric Trump, who suggested his sister Ivanka would be a terrific vice president because "she's got the beautiful looks." Evidently he's forgotten Dick Cheney's raw sexuality.)

So there in Cleveland will be a handful of Trump's vanquished foes, laying down to a candidate that bullied and intimidated them into submission. They will be there putting their party in front of their dignity, hoping to maintain in good standing with the party for future elections. It would no doubt serve members of the party of the elephant well to have much longer memories.

USA Today

OFF-BRAND REPUBLICANISM

July 22, 2016

On Thursday night, Americans saw the Republican Party officially become the generic Brand X party in American politics. The conservative active ingredient having been stripped from the party, the GOP is now canned populism wrapped in white packaging, emblazoned with the word 'PARTY' on the label in bold black letters. If it were an alcohol, it would be of a lower proof than Trump Vodka.

Ninety percent of Donald Trump's dour acceptance speech to the Republican National Convention on Thursday could have been delivered to any convention of any party. For 75 minutes, Trump ran through all the problems plaguing America, promising to fix each one simply by talking about them very loudly.

There was once a time that Republicans nominated Republicans to be their presidential candidate. But Trump is his own party, unshackled by the constraints of freedom and liberty. His policy preferences — when he can explain them at all — typically involve heavy-handed action from an all-powerful leader, who will micromanage America back to prosperity.

In fact, for all the hand-wringing about how combative and unprecedented Trump's campaign antics have been, his governing philosophy is fairly boring: whenever he declares something 'Bad!', it must be ended.

For instance, take Trump's insistence that companies shouldn't be able to move jobs overseas without 'consequences.' This is a line one likely will hear in abundance at next week's Democratic convention. What those 'consequences' might be are anyone's guess — but someone with a conservative world view might suggest providing companies with incentives to stay as the better option. (Trump has signaled an openness to raising the minimum wage to $15 an hour, which would send even more jobs overseas, causing him to punish even more employers.)

Often, having an ideology is looked down upon: conservatives or progressives are chided for being 'biased' or having closed minds. But a defensible view of the role of government, be it on the right or left, is a signal to voters of what they might be getting in a candidate. A governing philosophy is the nutritional information on the outside of the candidate's cereal box.

But Trump's motivating philosophy comes not from Madison, Jefferson or Locke, but from a simple belief that whatever he touches is going to be the most terrific success in the history of humanity. Early on in Thursday night's speech, Trump promised that 'the crime and violence that today afflicts our nation will soon come to an end.' He offered no specifics, only that he would make it happen by sheer force of his personality — as if nobody had ever thought of reducing violent crime before. (Also, violent crime is at a record low, suggesting Trump is creating a work of fiction of which he is the only hero.)

The only real tangential relationship Trump has to Republicanism is that he opposes Hillary Clinton. But simply criticizing a liberal does not a conservative make. Trump's primary digs at Clinton are based on her trustworthiness, her foreign policy and her lack of desire to fight the war against terrorism.

Yet none of these are particularly right-wing positions; had a Republican secretary of state used a private server and imperiled American intelligence, you can bet Democrats would be dedicating a full night to it at their convention.

And, of course, Trump continues to play the strongman by promising 'the biggest, most beautiful wall' between the United States and Mexico. Again, this isn't particularly a conservative issue — certainly, those on the right typically favor more stringent illegal immigration reforms but so do many on the left. You won't be hearing much about it at the Democratic Convention next week, but blue-collar unions always have been wary of illegal immigrants crossing the border and taking union jobs away from them.

Sure, Trump's speech provided a few minutes' worth of lines about tax cuts and conservative judicial philosophy, but these almost seemed obligatory, like when he is forced to mention the lesser Trump children. While lower taxes, less regulation and more personal freedom previously would have been at the center of a Republican convention, these concepts have been pushed to the fringes, leaving only conservative pundits to weep in despair.

If your recipe for Republican success calls for reheated Nixonian fear-mongering and leftover Bernie Sanders-style populism, Trump is definitely for you. But those who value the conservative principles of liberty and freedom are going to keep on shopping.

USA Today

POLITICS IN THE DARKEST TIMELINE

November 3, 2016

[Ed. note: If there was ever evidence that I lost my mind by the end of the 2016 campaign, this column is it. I began seriously contemplating whether we were living in an alternate dimension.]

In his recent book "But What If We're Wrong?," pop culture author Chuck Klosterman dips briefly into a novel philosophical theory that seeks to explain humanity's existence.

Citing the work of Swedish philosopher Nick Bostrom (currently at the University of Oxford), Klosterman lays out the case for the "simulation hypothesis," which posits that we all simply may be part of a computer simulation run by hyper-intelligent beings in the future. As the theory goes, super-beings of the future master technology to the point where it's so realistic, we can't actually tell we don't really exist. Our universe is Grand Theft Auto with characters who think they're real.

Normally, this is stuff typically reserved for late-night smoke-filled dorm rooms. But given the 2016 presidential election cycle, even the most far-fetched theories might be worth a second look.

Just consider what has recently transpired in the U.S. presidential campaign. A former congressman named Anthony Weiner had to resign his seat after sending pictures of his... uh... namesake... to women across America.

Just coincidentally, this man happens to be married to the closest adviser to the Democratic nominee for president. Following an unsuccessful run for mayor of America's largest city, he was then accused of having an inappropriate relationship with an underage girl. This transgression led the FBI to search his computer, finding emails from his wife that could potentially imperil the candidacy of the presumptive winner, Hillary Clinton.

This is no doubt evidence that we are experiencing a glitch in the system. This couldn't actually be happening if world events were simply random and affected by individuals with free will. I mean, the Cubs just won the World Series. There's obviously a software malfunction happening here. Someone needs to hit CTRL+ALT+DELETE on this election, and fast.

Consider that Republicans have nominated an individual who brags about sexually assaulting women, who frequently donated large amounts of money to his Democratic opponent and who shares almost none of their philosophy. It's almost as if a frustrated super-brain writer of the future pitched this election as a "Law and Order" episode, had it turned down for sheer implausibility, and decided to drop it in his simulation just to see what chaos he could create.

Obviously, discussions about humans' place in the universe have vexed philosophers even before Descartes boldly declared his own existence. But there still are some supernatural phenomena that we have never figured out. Consider the "glitches" that we've all learned to live with, like, what are dreams, and how can they be so vivid? Why do we get feelings of déjà vu? Why is Lena Dunham famous? Truly the unsolvable mysteries of all time — are they evidence of hiccups in the software?

And, of course, it follows that if we're all currently in a simulation, there also are thousands of concurrent simulations running at the same time. Somewhere, there's a competing simulation where in January President Paul Ryan is being sworn in, Antonin Scalia lives to be 250 years old and exercise makes you fat. If anyone figures out a way to buy a secret passport to that simulation, I'll put in a good word with Chief Justice Lady Gaga for you when I get there.

This theory, naturally, is not without its flaws. For one, it relies on a presumption that the living beings of the future will be some new breed of super-intelligent hyper-geniuses capable of creating a cyber-world so realistic the people in it think they have free will. Keep in mind that nearly half the country is about to vote for a guy who once spent an entire press conference trying to sell Americans invisible vacuum-packed meat. The trend isn't exactly towards cognitive superiority, here — if anything, we're heading toward a day where medical degrees will be conferred on anyone who can distinguish a human head from a roast beef sandwich. (And what if the beings doing the simulations are themselves simulations? Here's a towel to clean up the part of your mind I just blew.)

At some point recently, America went from "I can't believe what's happening" to "this can be explained only by a deep fracture in the space-time continuum." So if you're as distraught about the election as I am, take heart — this may not all be real. Let's just make a pact that in the event that we are just caught in a computer simulation, we should be hesitant to refer to the introduction of the Donald Trump character as "Artificial Intelligence."

Milwaukee Journal Sentinel

AN APOLOGY TO AMERICANS OF THE FUTURE

November 11, 2016

[Ed. note: You are now a person of the future, so this is addressed to you NOW.]

Dear People of the Future:

We're sorry.

Here in 2016, with the fate of the world at stake, we treated the whole process of electing a president with about as much seriousness as we take our news about Kanye West's children. In a Two Minutes Hate that stretched for a year and a half, Americans managed to nominate a gaseous septuagenarian toddler with no chance of winning, thereby clearing the path for a craven political lifer whose primary qualification is that she dodged a criminal conviction threedays before the election.

No doubt, in the decades since 2016, the abject lunacy of that year has been studied, examined and picked apart in every way imaginable. But for the sake of historical accuracy, it's important to document what it was like for those of us who were actually here, and to offer our regrets for our behavior.

At this point, nobody can really say with any certainty how we got to this point. Donald Trump and Hillary Clinton are polar opposites — Trump is a vulgar political ignoramus who has spent about as much time learning about national issues as the average American spends staring at their Netflix queue before determining there's nothing on. (No doubt hipsters of the future watch Netflix ironically, right?)

Thomasson: After all this, things in Washington unlikely to change

On the other hand, Hillary Clinton is a consummate insider who knows the levers of government all too well, and pulls them for her own aggrandizement. To voters, Clinton was unforgettable only because she refused to ever go away.

Ironically, while the Trump candidacy grew in the year and a half before the 2016 election, the phenomenon was foretold nearly 150 years beforehand by English poet Robert Browning. In his poem "Mr. Sludge, the Medium," Browning tells the story of a spiritual charlatan who earns credibility by simply telling people what they want to hear. Browning notes that those who fell victim to Mr. Sludge's lies were, in effect, his accomplices — by willfully closing their eyes and allowing themselves to be conned, they were just as complicit in the deception.

And that is why we, as Americans, owe future generations a sincere apology. This year, we had the opportunity to elect a serious candidate who didn't foment racial and class resentment. We could have selected a leader with a clear vision for America's place in the world, who understood the principles of liberty and self-governance. Instead, we ended up with two statist candidates so power-hungry they would have made Hobbes blush.

We are sorry for the fracture in the Republican Party that left America with a weakened voice for individual freedom and upward mobility. For years after the election, any time a Republican politician tried to make a serious, reflective point about public policy, Democrats would simply point, and say, "Yes, but you endorsed Donald Trump." This effect nearly wiped out a generation of talented GOP leaders who put party before principle, thereby splitting Republicans into warring factions.

In fact, before the election, some conservatives were actually hoping the party would be routed in the 2016 elections, thereby forcing wholesale changes in the party's governance — kind of like rooting against your favorite football team in the hopes they fire their head coach. ("Football" was a sport played in the 20th and early 21st centuries that involved millions of fans rooting for athletes to concuss one another.)

It was this split that forced the Republican Party to become the loyal opposition party for the next decade, good only for blocking the Democrats' bad ideas.

But the 2016 election also prevented Republicans from taking positive actions. So we are sorry Medicare and Medicaid went bankrupt; during the campaign, the issue was pushed aside like the lesser Trump children. We apologize for Social Security going belly-up; at some point, we just couldn't borrow enough money from China to keep these programs alive.

And we're sorry about what happened to the Supreme Court after the election. Remember just a week before the election when Texas Sen. Ted Cruz suggested the Senate could just stop confirming Supreme Court justices in order to block liberal control of the court? If there are still "history books" in your time, they surely will reflect Cruz's early support of Donald Trump — certainly, people of the future are having a good laugh watching Cruz look like a buffoon trying to fix a constitutional problem he created.

So, future being, be aware that in 2016, we knew full well we had our chance to save the American Idea and we blew it. In 2016, Donald Trump's mantra was that he wanted to "Make America Great Again" — little did he know that the best evidence America needed fixing was found in the fact that nearly half the country supported him.

Milwaukee Journal Sentinel

ILLEGITIMATE MAN, LEGITIMATE PRESIDENCY

January 7, 2017

House Speaker Paul Ryan stood stone-faced behind House Minority Leader Nancy Pelosi as she addressed the new 115th Congress. Before handing him the gavel, she tossed a Molotov cocktail at the GOP — saying our democracy cannot be "subverted by the dark operations of a foreign regime."

Pelosi was referring, of course, to reports that Russia had attempted to influence the American election in favor of Donald Trump, who it is believed is friendlier to the Russian regime. Just days before U.S. intelligence agencies released findings to that effect, she was surfing a wave of stories like one in the New York Times that bore the headline "Obama Strikes Back at Russia for Election Hacking."

This tapestry of vagueness has led to confusion about what exactly happened during the election. According to a recent YouGov poll, 52% of Democrats think the Russians "definitely" or "probably" tampered with vote tallies to help Trump's election.

Yet there is no evidence of any kind that this type of "hacking" took place. There is, however, strong evidence that Russian agents gained access to emails from the Democratic National Committee and other notable

Democrats and released them prior to Election Day. According to reports, many of these emails were compromised because of Democrats that fell victim to phony emails urging them to divulge their passwords.

There's scant evidence that even publication of these emails made any difference. Intelligence officials have said that is not possible to measure. Perhaps the most impactful national secret now out in the open is Clinton campaign chair John Podesta's recipe for creamy risotto.

But Pelosi is not interested in nuance. Her job is to feed the wing of her party that seeks to delegitimize the Trump presidency, even if she has to take the solemn first day of the new Congress to spin her conspiracy fantasies. And she is not alone — outgoing Senate Democratic leader Harry Reid opined that Russian interference in the election was "as big as" the attacks of 9/11 or Watergate.

In doing so, Pelosi is trafficking in a modern warhead of ideological weaponry: the idea that a new president of the opposite party is not only wrong, but that he or she actually holds the presidency illegitimately.

Certainly, Americans have always argued that ideologically opposite politicians are wrong, or perhaps unqualified. (And on these counts, I have argued Trump is both.) But the idea that the presidency was gained through trickery or subterfuge keeps gaining momentum.

It began most notably following the 2000 election, when Democrats convinced themselves George W. Bush actually lost Florida, and thus the election. Even though an extensive review of the vote by multiple news groups (including USA TODAY) in 2001 confirmed that Bush would have won almost any recount, liberals still hang on to this fantasy even in 2017

Of course, this is by no means a partisan phenomenon. Throughout Barack Obama's presidency, fringe Republicans pushed the idea that Obama was not born in the United States, and thus was ineligible to hold office. Ironically, one of the primary reasons Trump is unqualified for the presidency is that he gave life to the moronic "birther" movement.

And now the pendulum has swung back to the Democrats, who credit Russian skullduggery for Trump's win. This, of course, relieves them of the burden of reflecting on the awfulness of their own candidate. Ironically, near the end of the campaign, Clinton tweeted that not respecting the results of the campaign would be a "direct threat to our democracy." She likely has not responded to Pelosi's attempts to undermine the election results because she is wandering the woods of New York State looking for Eleven from Netflix's Stranger Things.

If the reporting on this so far is correct, what the Russians did was essentially add more information to the public knowledge base about the candidates. They simply put information out and let the public digest it, which is far less nefarious than the actual hacking of vote machines. In fact, on Election Day, there were few voters that didn't know Russia was trying to influence the election through the release of the emails. (I wrote about it in June.)

That doesn't, of course, mean that Trump's policies toward Russia shouldn't be under heavy scrutiny. If the president were anyone other than Donald Trump, a misguided desire to have friendlier relations with an adversarial power like Russia would be a foreign policy at least worth debating. But the contents of Trump's brain are often between him and his Twitter feed, and crediting him with a coherent view of the world appears to be presumptuous.

What's indisputable is that Trump is the properly elected president. At the very most, it appears the Russians disseminated information that was moderately embarrassing for a presidential candidate. But if this is now the new standard, the biggest danger for the American electoral system is Trump's own mouth.

USA Today

RECOGNIZING HONOR DISHONORABLY

March 1, 2017

Carryn Owens is a brave woman. Her late husband, Navy SEAL Ryan Owens, who was killed during a January commando raid ordered by President Trump, is an American hero. The widow's willingness to stand and be recognized while fighting back tears at Trump's address to the joint session of Congress is a testament to her strength.

She was also taken advantage of by a politician starving to appear presidential during the most important speech of his life. A politician who sent her husband on a mission in Yemen beset with errors, for which Trump has received wide condemnation — including from Ryan Owens' father. On the morning of Trump's speech to Congress, the president tried to dodge responsibility for the death, blaming it on "the generals."

"They lost Ryan," Trump told Fox News.

Both these preceding characterizations of his recognition of Carryn Owens can be — and are — true. By praising her husband, Trump cemented the soldier's legacy for all of history. But Trump clearly sought to wrap himself in the heroism the soldier displayed, a ploy to protect himself from further criticism over the unsuccessful mission.

Sadly, the point-at-the-gallery moments have become an all too common gimmick in major addresses. By inviting soldiers and military widows, presidents can attempt to imbue themselves with secondhand heroism. They simply hope that any association with people willing to risk their lives in defense of the country rubs off on them, and they're willing to use grieving human props to make their point.

For instance, in 2014, President Obama used a portion of his State of the Union Address to praise Army Ranger Cory Remsburg, who was nearly killed in a roadside bomb in Afghanistan in 2009. Naturally, Obama skipped any mention of the fact that Remsburg was in Afghanistan because Obama tripled U.S. forces stationed there.

And let us not forget Hillary Clinton's generous use of Khizr and Ghazala Khan, Gold Star parents whose son was killed in Iraq in 2004. Notably, Trump insulted the Khan family's speech at last year's Democratic National Convention; it seems soldiers who die under his watch are far more deserving of honor.

Of course, that's not to say presidents shouldn't honor the heroism of America's soldiers. Trump could just as easily have praised Ryan Owens without an excruciating made-for-TV moment where Carryn stood in the gallery crying for two minutes.

But one can honor soldiers without turning their widows' grief into a self-serving ratings-grabbing moment. Take Ronald Reagan, perhaps the most media-savvy president America has had, who was able to honor the dead with words, not exploitative gestures. In his very first inaugural address, Reagan famously told the tale of World War I soldier Martin Treptow, who was killed while serving in France.

"We're told that on his body was found a diary," Reagan began. "On the flyleaf under the heading, 'My Pledge,' he had written these words: 'America must win this war. Therefore I will work, I will save, I will sacrifice, I will endure, I will fight cheerfully and do my utmost, as if the issue of the whole struggle depended on me alone.' "

Reagan was able to honor military sacrifice with words, not with self-aggrandizement. He didn't appear to be, as Shakespeare sneered in Richard III, "merely a politician, and studied only in his own ends."

Undoubtedly, the temptation for Trump to wrap himself in the valor of a recently deceased soldier was too much to resist. Actors frequently win awards by playing historical figures who risked their lives in service of a cause, and yet the actor still benefits from the residual goodwill — despite being paid millions of dollars to dress up like someone who displayed actual bravery. Call it "dignity by proxy."

But simply exhuming culture does not create culture, just as recognizing honor does not, by extension, make one honorable. Secondhand compassion is not a thing, but it doesn't mean people won't try.

Ryan Owens died on a mission trying to aid America's fight against al-Qaeda. Let's hope the president didn't summon his widow to Congress on a mission to aid Trump's fight against sagging approval ratings.

USA Today

OBAMA'S OVERRATED ORATION

March 16, 2017

In critiquing President Woodrow Wilson's empty rhetorical style, polemicist H.L. Mencken noted Wilson's "ludicrous strutting and bombast," his "heavy dependence on greasy and meaningless words," and Wilson's "frequent descents to mere sound and fury, signifying nothing."

According to Mencken, Wilson knew "how to arrest and enchant the boobery with words that were simply words, and nothing else."

Sadly, Mencken would never live to see the presidency of Barack Obama, whose rhetorical style could be carved in precisely the same way. As Obama's fans craft his legacy, the former president's oratorical skills will no doubt be prominently featured as a primary strength. Writing for The Huffington Post, Richard Greene declared Obama the third greatest presidential orator in the modern era, just behind John F. Kennedy and Franklin Delano Roosevelt. (Ronald Reagan is listed behind Obama; of course, Reagan gave America a conservative revolution — Obama gifted America a reality star windbag.)

There's no doubt Obama's speaking style was top-notch. As John McWhorter recently noted, Obama often adopted the "preacherly cadence" to lend his speeches gravitas. His speeches were music — familiar and aurally pleasing — but the lyrics were frequently laughable. Never have so many words been sacrificed in the service of so little.

Cadence aside, can most people remember anything Obama actually said? Where were the memorable lines, the clever turns-of-phrase? In a preposterous Obama tongue bath by The New York Times' Michiko Kakutani in January, Obama was praised as the president "most fundamentally shaped ... by reading and writing" since Abraham Lincoln. (Unavailable for comment — Woodrow Wilson, a college professor and university president, or even poor George W. Bush, who reportedly read up to two books a week.)

Yet despite being a repository of literary brilliance, Obama's best-known passages are those worthy of ridicule. Remember his universally praised 2008 Democratic convention speech, when he was already reminiscing about his future administration as the time "the rise of the oceans began to slow and our planet began to heal?" Evidently, the oceans missed the speech.

In fact, Obama's most quotable lines are the ones Republicans used to run against him. Remember when he told those who had businesses that "you didn't build that"? Or when he declared, "If you like your health care plan, you can keep it?" That went on to become Politifact's "Lie of the Year," demonstrating that Obama was trading in "alternative facts" well before President Donald Trump.

It was actually the Affordable Care Act that best demonstrated Obama's lack of rhetorical alacrity. When the law was passed around Christmas of 2009, polls showed the public disfavored the new health care law. In revolt, Massachusetts voters even elected Republican Scott Brown to the Senate seat once held by liberal lion Edward Kennedy.

Once Obama hit the road in a series of speeches to defend the law, public approval dropped even lower. If Obama believed his superior rhetorical skills could turn America into Obamacare fans, he was sorely mistaken. According to the RealClear Politics poll tracker, the law never has been favored by a majority of the American public. And despite Obama's flood of speeches supporting his signature legislation, the law has produced Republican landslides in three of the last four national elections.

Yet Obama's oratorical legacy likely will get a boost from the speaking styles of the presidents sandwiching him on either side. George W. Bush is legendary for his clumsy malapropisms, from "Rarely is the question asked: Is our children learning?" to "Families is where our nation finds hope, where wings take dream."

And, of course, Donald Trump treats proper grammar as if it is a prisoner in Guantanamo Bay. Compared with Trump, Obama is Churchillian. While Obama sometimes could be inspirational with his style of speech, Trump's speeches are most likely to inspire Americans traveling abroad to tell people they're Canadian.

Despite the disparate styles, Trump's guttural meanderings are what Americans have decided they want in a commander-in-chief. Clearly, they will take Trump's lively verbal pugilism over Obama's sonorous snoozefests.

The problem, of course, was not how Obama said things, but what he actually said. His run-of-the-mill liberalism was treated by media elites as novel political thought culled from decades of deep reflection. Regular Americans saw it as microwaved New Dealism dressed up in a cool package. History should reflect that Obama was essentially Jimmy Carter with Jay-Z on speed dial.

Milwaukee Journal Sentinel

XI AND THE MAR-A-LAGO DREAM

April 6, 2017

Oh, how delectable the food on Air Force One must be these days!

President Trump, after all, has come to expect a certain quality of meal over the course of his life. Perhaps the family members all feast on well-done Trump Steaks doused with ketchup, then wash it all down with some Trump spring water. As Fox News buzzes away in the background, they all laugh the night away, taking turns regaling the president with tales of his preternatural wisdom and uncommon stamina. How lucky we all are to have bathed in the same river of time as this great man!

As James Laver once noted, Britain's Edwardian age was "probably the last period in history when the fortunate thought they could give pleasure to others by displaying their good fortune before them." But what of the new Trump lifestyle, which demonstrates to the world, and this week to the president of China, the glorious buffet of riches that awaits all Americans?

All Trump asks of us in exchange for this enticing representation of the American dream is the low sum of $3 million every other weekend so he can fly the first family to his Mar-a-Lago resort in Florida. Who cares if his Florida trips to date, six of them counting the meeting with President Xi Jinping, could fund the annual salaries of more than 400 elementary school teachers in America — without those teachers, those students will never be able to do the math! Problem solved!

The Trump version of the American dream probably is not quite the one running through the head of an elderly black man sleeping in a chair at the Milwaukee Greyhound station, warm inside on a cold morning. His head is resting at an impossible angle propped up on his arm, while a black hood is pulled down over his brow.

The bus station sits almost directly underneath one of the interstate highways. It is as if the city swept it under a carpet to avoid visitors from noticing it. The bus terminal shares a long, high-ceilinged waiting room with Amtrak rail. The terminal, like the city itself, is all but segregated: The crowds loading onto buses are almost exclusively black, while the groups exiting the trains are virtually all white.

When America's poorest residents need to visit a sick loved one or an out-of-town child, they are rarely afforded a personal, taxpayer-funded flight; instead, they ride the bus. Less than $100 will get a traveler as far as Cleveland, but the ride lasts 12 hours. Most riders on Wednesday morning are first bound for Chicago, a trip that can be purchased for $8-$10, depending on the time of day. The only actual security that exists is a sign near the terminal that tells bus riders to report anything they see that might

303

be suspicious, as if intuition were a plausible substitute for a metal detector.

Security is high at the "Winter White House," however, where Trump hosts world leaders under the careful watch of a mobile Secret Service detail. These expensive agents must be there to monitor Trump's golf outings with visitors such as Japanese Prime Minister Shinzo Abe; for that game Trump used a gold driver that Abe gifted him after the election.

Oh, to be present at the late night talks at Mar-a-Lago, where the men retreat to the cigar room! Presumably, the Trump vodka runs free while the locker room talk keeps everyone in stitches. "Shinzo, baby! I noticed you're bailing out on your short putts! Not good! Not good!"

Yet his swanky Florida resort is undoubtedly where Trump does all his deep thinking about how to fix depressed inner cities such as Milwaukee's. Coincidentally, it was in the outer Milwaukee suburb of West Bend last August where candidate Trump announced his plans to fix all that ailed African Americans.

"To every voter in Milwaukee, to every voter living in the inner city or every forgotten stretch of our society, I'm running to offer you a much better future, a much better job," Trump said at a rally in Washington County (black population: 1.2%).

The grandeur of Trump's recurring jet-fueled vacation obscenity has yet to trickle down to the young woman in the Milwaukee bus station trying to manage three children who all appear to be under age 3. Near the unceasing low buzz of the vending machines, she bottle-feeds the youngest child, while the other two girls, both wearing flower-print jackets, take turns dropping their water bottles on the floor.

When boarding is called, the woman stands, baby in her arms, while her two daughters dutifully line up like ducklings behind her. They are off to see America, where everywhere must seem as far away as a golf resort for billionaires.

USA Today

WHAT IS A 'CONSERVATIVE?'

July 25, 2017

As popular Republican president Dwight Eisenhower cruised to re-election in 1956, one young conservative magazine publisher remained unimpressed. In his new publication, National Review, William F. Buckley complained that Eisenhower only won because his opponent, Democrat Adlai Stevenson, was even worse than the incumbent was.

As a conservative, Buckley was appalled by Eisenhower's evident acceptance of New Deal statism, calling the president's domestic plans "measured socialism." Later, Buckley would hammer away at Eisenhower for not taking the Soviet Union and its attempts to spread Communism seriously enough. He called Eisenhower's political philosophy "incoherent" and called on the Republican Party to "repudiate" him.

Intending to prove the past is prologue, President Trump has found himself to be just as unpopular with the conservative movement as Ike was, and for many of the same reasons.

Only this time, conservatism evidently can't escape its association with Trump. For one, Trump's supporters argue vehemently (in the pages of National Review, no less) that the president is a rock-ribbed conservative, despite a lifetime of actions to the contrary. Further, when news outlets like Breitbart News or Fox News interview Trump, they are identified as "conservative" media.

It has thus become the case that the terms "conservative" and "pro-Trump" have largely been mixed together into the same cocktail. Trump supporters are often referred to as "conservatives" and vice versa, as if the terms are interchangeable.

And while Trump is supported by a great number of conservatives, being "conservative" and being "pro-Trump" are two completely different things. One describes allegiance to a philosophy; the other to a man.

But if Trump has grabbed control of the word "conservative" as if it were an unsuspecting Miss Universe contestant, it may be time for conservatives to consider a new word — especially if the term has become wholly uninstructive in describing someone's views on individual freedom and the powers of government. Years ago, the left wriggled out of the term "liberal" for their now-preferred "progressive." Conservatives should consider doing the same.

Conservatism was split in the 1950s when Wisconsin Sen. Joseph McCarthy's virulent anti-Communist crusade took hold. At the time, conservative professor Peter Viereck deemed right-wing support for McCarthy "a vengeful expression" of the "radical Populist lunatic-fringers against the eastern, educated Anglicized elite." Conservative author Ralph de Toledano wrote that the 1950s right was mired in "rootlessness and opportunism," and "bound more by frustration than by doctrine."

It is once again so that "conservatism" has come to be defined by what it is against (news media, liberals, microaggressions, intersectionality, Lena Dunham), not what it is for. And aside from its negative association with Trump, the word "conservative" also isn't particularly instructive. Long ago, Abraham Lincoln once observed conservatism is the "adherence to the old and tried, against the new and untried."

But the world has flipped. "Conservatives" are now the ones pushing innovative ideas, while "progressives," equally ironically, often defend the status quo. The left would rather not see any "progress" on Obamacare or abortion or public education, thank you very much.

Conservatism, on the other hand, is the ideology of bettering schools through competition, cracking open markets to unleash the sharing economy and utilizing personal choice to drive down health care costs. Right wingers don't want to "conserve" the regulatory monolith Democrats have built, they want to dismantle it.

Given that modern conservatism is still a campus that hosts a lot of majors, picking a replacement for the word would be tricky. Right-wingers still believe government closest to the voters is best, so reviving the "federalist" label might be a winner. And if there's one thing that brings the right together, it's the agreement on judicial adherence to the Constitution, so "constitutionalist" should be on the table. (Although in the Twitter era, who can spare 17 characters?) Perhaps, in the ultimate act of political jujutsu, the right can return the word "liberal" back to its rightful owners now that progressives have scrapped it.

Obviously, modern conservatives still hold some traditions sacred: intact families, the dignity of work, free markets and religious freedom come to mind. But as long as "Donald Trump" and "conservatism" remain synonymous, the term will continue to take on the substantial weight of the president's baggage. Every one of the president's grotesque utterances soils the memory of all the members of the freedom movement that worked so hard to make conservatism a mainstream ideology.

As a philosophy, conservatism will remain strong. But as a word, it should escape the damage the president continues to do to it.

USA Today

A SICKENING FETISH FOR CRUELTY

August 5, 2017

It isn't very often that the public gets to see a man's soul die inside his body. To see his dignity immolated. His manhood ripped from his bones.

And to have it captured all in one picture. Oh, the picture.

Late last November, President-elect Donald Trump and former Republican nominee Mitt Romney settled into a four-course dinner at New York's Jean-Georges restaurant, dining on frog legs and diver scallops. Over the previous year, Romney had been bitterly critical of Trump, calling him "con man" and "a fraud" — yet upon winning, Trump dangled the possibility of naming Romney to the position of secretary of State, leading to what would soon become Romney's Last Supper.

In a chilling photograph of the dinner, Romney has turned to the camera with the look of a man that would much prefer to be dining with the Grim Reaper. As Trump glowers at the camera with a mischievous grin, Romney's eyes yearn for a foregone era when he stood in resistance to the vulgarian in chief, a time before he was made to kiss the ring in exchange for serving his country as secretary of State. The only thing missing from the photo is a Sarah McLachlan song playing in the background and a phone number to call to stop the abuse.

Of course, two weeks later, Trump picked oil executive Rex Tillerson to be his secretary of State, ending Romney's parade of public humiliation. But Trump got exactly what he wanted: After the dinner, Romney told reporters that Trump "continues with a message of inclusion and bringing people together," and that his "vision is something which obviously connected with the American people in a very powerful way." Romney became another well-coiffed head for Trump's trophy case.

It wasn't the first time Trump stripped a conquered foe naked and paraded him in the public square, Game of Thrones-style. (And just like the citizens of Westeros, the #MAGA crowd evidently has plenty of time to take off work to spit and yell "shame" at Trump's vanquished opponents.)

Who can forget Trump holding an enormous umbrella and yet still forcing sycophantic Gov. Chris Christie of New Jersey to walk in the pouring rain? Or Trump mocking Christie to his face as he forced Christie to stand behind him on stage like a hostage?

One can even forgive the American public being "Little Marco'ed," "Lyin' Ted'ed" and "Crooked Hillary'ed" to exhaustion during the election. This is something entirely new — Trump clearly is a sadist who enjoys humiliating his opponents after he has already won.

Simply ask the third participant in the November dinner, White House Chief of Staff Reince Priebus. After months of harming his own reputation defending Trump's indefensible actions, Priebus was not only pushed out but done so in the most embarrassing way possible. As if to emphasize Priebus' "weakness," Trump brought in tough guy flesh-and-bone absurdity Anthony Scaramucci to show Priebus the door. Then "The Mooch" was dumped himself days later in his own whirlpool of humiliation.

Or ask Attorney General Jeff Sessions, whom Trump shreds on a daily basis because the president doesn't have the stomach to fire him. Or former FBI director James Comey, whose decision to decline Trump's request for a "loyalty pledge" led to a firing surgically engineered to ruin Comey's name.

These are not the actions of a well-adjusted person. Trump clearly has a maudlin fetish for cruelty. Given his pattern of humiliating both friend and foe, the president's brain is occupied with little else than Electoral College results and revenge fantasies. Trump is basically a 71-year old kid cackling in delight as he melts ants under his magnifying glass. Only these ants are attorneys general, senators, FBI directors and governors.

Naturally, Trump's supporters think toying with people's dignity is a show of strength — but it is the exact opposite. He's a weak leader who wastes what little political capital he has settling personal scores. With apologies to Winston Churchill, Trump remains an immodest man with much to be modest about.

And it's just a matter of time before he's under Vladimir Putin's magnifying glass.

USA Today

IS THE GOP CONDEMNATION OF TRUMP EVER COMING?

August 18, 2017

[Ed. note: It was not.]

In late June of 2015, then South Carolina Gov. Nikki Haley said what few Republicans would. In the wake of the Charleston church massacre, in which 21-year old Dylann Roof gunned down nine members of an African-American church, Haley called for the Confederate flag to be removed from the statehouse grounds.

"This flag, while an integral part of our past," Haley said, "does not represent the future of our great state."

In the weeks prior to Haley's declaration, 2016 Republican presidential hopefuls had waffled on the Confederate flag issue. Needing South Carolina's valuable delegates, candidates such as Jeb Bush and John Kasich hedged their bets, claiming that it was a local issue for South Carolinians to sort out.

But once Haley made her stand, the dam broke, and all the GOP candidates lined up behind her.

It took one leader to give the party permission to take the morally correct position.

It's the sort of leadership lacking among Republicans dealing with America's first toddler president. In what has become a tiresome cycle, Donald Trump again last week appealed to the worst elements of the American public and again escaped any condemnation from party leaders.

If one were to believe the words of its current standard bearer, the Republican Party now believes that "good people" attend Nazi marches and a white supremacist killing a woman while allegedly driving a car into a crowd of anti-racist protesters is the fault of "both sides." On Thursday, Trump used a false historical story about venerated former U.S. General John Pershing — circulated primarily in chain e-mails — to defend the shooting of defenseless Muslims in the war on terror.

Certainly, some rank-and-file Republicans have taken the president to task for his unconscionable comments. Freshman Wisconsin Rep. Mike Gallagher said the president "needs to be crystal clear that hatred has no place in our society," and that Trump is currently "failing at it." On Friday, former GOP presidential nominee Mitt Romney called on Trump to apologize for his comments.

But the party's actual leaders are falling short. House Speaker Paul Ryan released another anodyne statement merely condemning white supremacy as "repulsive," but not providing any context for why he made it. If only we could find the mysterious person who made Ryan's statement necessary!

Sadly, for leaders such as Ryan and Senate Majority Leader Mitch McConnell (R-Ky.), being stuck with Trump is like being trapped in a cross country car trip with a wolverine. They can't escape.

But Trump is killing whatever positive agenda they are trying to achieve. Every day, poor Paul Ryan has to walk in front of the press and show them the little birdhouse he built while there's a skyscraper on fire next to him. Just last year, Ryan said Trump's attack against Judge Gonzalo Curiel was an example of "textbook racism," so it's not as if Trump's appalling recent behavior comes as a surprise.

Yet even though the party's leaders are dealing with an erratic, vindictive juvenile, they believe they need to stay in Trump's good graces. But is passing tax reform really worth this? And can such a damaged president shepherd meaningful conservative reforms through Congress? Even if the Republican Congress is able to adopt some of its favored policies, what does it mean if America is ablaze with racial animus and hatred? As they like to say on "Game of Thrones," conservatives would merely be "kings of the ashes."

Hopefully, when the GOP cognoscenti finally decide Trump is of no use to them, their condemnation will be swift and strong. But that time may have already passed; the history books won't be kind to Trump appeasers.

A few years back, Republicans were obsessed with the idea of pulling new voters into the conservative coalition. But unless their leaders take action against Trump for his racist comments, the GOP will have quickly transformed from a big tent party to a big hood party.

Milwaukee Journal Sentinel

PROFANING OLD GLORY

September 29, 2017

"There are a lot of killers, we've got a lot of killers. What, you think (America) is so innocent?"

These words were not spoken by a Russian agent trying to tar America's standing in the world. They weren't uttered by a recent Antifa recruit on campus in Berkeley. They were famously said by the president of the United States during a February interview with Fox News' Bill O'Reilly that aired — as if the gods of irony needed a hearty chuckle — during the 2017 Super Bowl.

Last weekend and seemingly all week long, Donald Trump, America's self-styled national patriotism referee, harangued NFL players for insufficiently loving America, a country that Trump had just months before, and during its most-viewed NFL game, accused of engaging in Vladimir Putin-style political executions. At an Alabama campaign rally last Friday, Trump said NFL owners should fire players who kneel during the national anthem, prompting dozens more players to kneel in protest during the weekend's games.

It was another example of Trump using patriotism as a wedge in a cultural war that his supporters are more than willing to wage. According to a new Reuters/Ipsos poll, 85% of Americans say they stand during the National Anthem, yet 57% of respondents said they don't believe players should be fired for kneeling during the Anthem. Naturally, only 29% of Republicans disagreed with Trump's comments about firing football players, and the president is counting on the remainder who agree with him to enlist as soldiers to fight in the Great Battle of White Resentment.

Yet while Trump has now fashioned himself the protector of America's military honor, he has a history of slandering America and those who have given all to defend it. For instance, in 2015, Trump famously belittled Arizona Sen. John McCain, R-Ariz., saying the former prisoner of war in Vietnam was "not a war hero," explaining, "I like people who weren't captured."

A year later, Trump mocked the parents of Muslim U.S. soldier Humayun Khan, who died in 2004 while trying to save the lives of other troops in Iraq. To Trump, Khan's Gold Star parents had committed a sin worthy of a future president questioning their patriotism: They supported Hillary Clinton.

Trump, of course, never had the chance to be captured by any enemy, as he avoided service in Vietnam with a total of five deferments. The final deferment was accompanied by a note from his doctor claiming he had bone spurs in his feet, a condition that evidently healed quickly. ("I had a doctor that gave me a letter — a very strong letter on the heels," he would say later.)

McCain, as Americans would all come to know, was confined to a cell in Hanoi with two broken arms and a broken leg, beaten and tortured for five years. Conversely, Trump would later claim that avoiding sexually transmitted diseases while dating "is my personal Vietnam," adding that he felt like a "great and very brave soldier."

Perhaps Trump should think a bit more about America's honor when he personally leaks highly classified information to high-ranking Russian officials. Or when he endangers America in juvenile late-night tweets by threatening to eradicate North Korea. Or when he foments racial discord by giving comfort to Nazis marching on American cities.

It goes without saying that had any of Trump's adversaries done so much to disrespect America and its claims of moral exceptionalism, Trump's supporters would howl with disapproval. And yet they congratulate the president by claiming his contempt for American traditions is the very thing making America great again. When Trump speaks ill of America, his followers grant him the hero status that they deny others for protesting things like racial injustice and police brutality. In fact, the original meaning of the NFL protests are now all but lost — instead, kneeling players are more likely to be protesting the fact that Trump is — in the words of North Korea — a dotard.

Americans clearly back Trump in his belief that players should stand during the National Anthem. But it is also evident that Trump has hardly spent any time reflecting over what patriotism means. Given his tireless work to lower America's moral standing around the world, perhaps it should be Trump that kneels in front of the flag — in order to ask its forgiveness.

USA Today

WHAT GOP POLITICIANS SHOULD SAY ABOUT TRUMP

August 24, 2018

[Ed. note: This was my final column for the Milwaukee Journal Sentinel.]

As the midterm elections move closer, everyone seems to be wondering whether the elections are going to be about education or health care or roads or taxes. In fact, voters are likely to make their mind up on state and local races based on one factor — the individual currently occupying the West Wing of the White House.

Given Republican candidates' difficulty in trying to embrace certain parts of Trumpism while, at the same time, distancing themselves from its worst aspects, I have put together a sample speech for any GOP congressional candidate to use in the upcoming few months. (And all for the low cost of free-ninety-nine!)

Welcome, everyone, and thank you for that humbling introduction. I'm honored to be here at the (insert parade, festival, bingo party) — I remember my old (insert name of potentially fictional relative) telling me how much he enjoyed his days here as a child.

I know you all have questions about the elections coming up. Certainly, you're all concerned about the primary issue that hangs over this campaign season: "Am I going to get to meet Kim Kardashian if Kayne West campaigns here?"

But seriously, I know a lot of you are Donald Trump fans. I know you're fed up with the way things have been run in Washington, D.C., and you wanted someone who was going to drop a truth bomb on the government establishment. And if you wanted someone to shake things up, you certainly got more than you expected.

Of course, Donald Trump has been good in some very important respects. We all know about his appointment of rock-solid conservative Supreme Court justices. You probably have more money in your pocket because of the tax cuts he signed into law. Quite often, he takes down insufferable people in a cathartic way we would all like to.

But any honest Republican would have to admit that there has been a downside to Trump. I know other conservative candidates have been afraid to talk about these things, worried about being labeled "disloyal." But we can't continue to fix what's wrong unless we give Americans a look at how good things can be when they're going right.

In terms of policy, Trump has certainly been better than Hillary Clinton would have been. But candidates ignoring blatant mistakes made by members of their own party is a big reason why people no longer trust politicians — what's wrong is wrong no matter who does it.

It is this hypocrisy that is crippling our political system. When Barack Obama increased tariffs on foreign goods, Republicans howled — now, many of us are praising Trump for similar job-killing policies. For decades, the GOP was defined by its opposition to Russian strongmen like Vladimir Putin; now, criticizing Trump for taking Putin's side over American intelligence agents is seen as un-American.

As your (congressman, senator), I will support our president when he deserves it and try to push him to be a bit better when I can. I will adhere to a positive vision of conservatism, one in which every American has the freedom to live his or her life according to their own wishes. Presidents aren't what makes America great — it's the people who live here that do.

That is why it is time we get government out of the lives of those people to allow them to unlock their potential. Yes, we always need to care for those incapable of taking care of themselves — but the best way to lift people out of poverty is a free-market system that gives individuals the agency to move themselves up the social ladder with hard work and ingenuity, and allows them to pass down the fruits of their labor to future generations. Hopefully, everyone in this room is going to be around well after Donald Trump's presidency ends — we need policies that will make sure we are free no matter what presidents come and go.

More than loyalty to individuals, our system requires loyalty to principles. And those principles, as once explained by Margaret Thatcher, are that "the individual is more important than the system" and that "individual enterprise is the mainspring of all progress."

In order to make America great again, we can't rely on The System, or a single politician — we can only rely on ourselves. Let's get to work.

That's all my time.

Thank you for listening.

Milwaukee Journal Sentinel

DEFENESTRATE CLINTON

March 16, 2018

If you think about it, being a losing presidential candidate is one of the best jobs in America. No matter what you say, you come off way better than your opponent's portrayal of you as a bloodthirsty gargoyle. You go on late night talk shows and ham it up with hosts who set you up to be self-deprecating and winsome. People still take you seriously, but you can finally say exactly what you want.

And as an added bonus to all this, you don't have to actually be president.

Since the 2016 campaign ended, Hillary Clinton has demonstrated herself to be a singularly extraordinary former presidential candidate — "extraordinary" only in the sense that no ex-candidate has ever been worse.

At a recent conference in Mumbai, India, Clinton further cast aside her presidential façade and told the world what she really thought of "middle America." She boasted that she had won "the places that are optimistic, diverse, dynamic," and "moving-forward," and noted she did best in "places that represent two-thirds of America's gross domestic product."

She suggested President Donald Trump's appeal was mostly to white men who "didn't like black people getting rights," who disapproved of "women getting jobs," and who begrudged Indian-Americans for their success. As a final ingredient to her toxic bouillabaisse, Clinton added that white women often voted for Trump because of "ongoing pressure to vote the way that your husband, your boss, your son, whoever, believes you should."

If there were a Hall of Fame for irony, Clinton would have it named after her. In accusing weak-minded white women of blindly voting the way men told them to, she was proving exactly why white women were wise not to vote for her. It is a significant reason she has now had to play the role of failed presidential candidate twice.

Set aside, for the moment, the wisdom of airing one's bitter grievances against the American electorate on foreign soil. The timing of her Rancorpalooza couldn't have been worse for Democrats, who are actually trying to appeal to those very "deplorables" Clinton clearly reviles.

Take a place like Michigan, for example, which Clinton would have won if just 0.12% of voters switched their vote from Trump to her. Or Wisconsin, which she would have carried if only 11,400 voters marked "Clinton" instead. Had she overcome either of those infinitesimal margins, suddenly she would have shifted them from her "half-off coupon for marrying your cousin" category to her "forward-moving dynamic utopia" column.

These rust-belt voters are the ones to whom Democrats must ingratiate themselves in the 2018 midterm elections, but they still find themselves the victims of Clinton's condescension. Any wise Democrat running in the Midwest would wear garlic around their neck to keep Hillary Clinton away from their state.

But her personal horribleness also comes at a bad time for Democrats trying to undermine Trump. At the same time Congressional Democrats are trying to argue the Russians interfered in the 2016 election, Clinton seems dead-set on proving that it was her own acridity that cost her the election. Further, she is pumping oxygen to the jackals at Fox News desperate to thrust her into their nightly headlines. Right now, Donald Trump couldn't name a better 2020 campaign manager than Hillary Clinton; she's a human campaign ad for the other guy.

In both 2008 and 2016, America's voters filed a restraining order against Hillary Clinton. If they want to win future elections, it's time for Democrats to do the same.

USA Today

FATTY FALLS UP

May 16, 2019

In crafting his famous "Matt Foley, Motivational Speaker" sketch for Saturday Night Live, Chris Farley stumbled—literally—onto a name for his style of comedy. The portly actor, who combined a graceful athleticism with a preternatural ability to crash through things, explained his popularity succinctly: "Everybody laughs when fatty falls down."

In crafting his famous "Matt Foley, Motivational Speaker" sketch for Saturday Night Live, Chris Farley stumbled—literally—onto a name for his style of comedy. The portly actor, who combined a graceful athleticism with a preternatural ability to crash through things, explained his popularity succinctly: "Everybody laughs when fatty falls down."

Farley's lithe but bruising style is just one of the many comedic strategies available to people who want to make us laugh. There are lots and lots of pathways to humor: the relatable anecdote, the classic misdirection, the well-timed callback, the insightful metaphor. Some comedians roar, some whisper—some use props, others mine their own emotions for laughs accompanied by unease.

Attempting to delight his own fans, America's Comedian-in-Chief Donald Trump has committed to his own style of humor, melding insult comedy with groan-inducing inappropriateness.

It seems to be working for Trump. His rallies are often accompanied by howls of laughter from the #MAGA-heads in attendance. During a recent hour-and-a-half speech in Green Bay, right-wing talk show host Michael Knowles asked whether we've ever had a president as funny as Trump:

Set aside, for a moment, whether comedic "chops" are in the top ten (or 50) traits the citizenry should want in a president. (My own list would probably go (1) preventing a bomb from being dropped on me; (2) not raising my taxes in the name of a phony trade war, then spending more of my tax money to placate farmers hurt by said trade war; and (3) not obstructing justice. Your mileage may vary.) But Knowles' point isn't even right on the merits: Reagan kept notebooks full of witty one-liners scrawled to himself during his times thinking alone in his office. They're almost all superior to Trump's flaccid quips.

Trump's humor is largely dependent on the shock value of him saying things unbecoming of a U.S. president. Or, for that matter, a normal, well-adjusted adult. His sick burns are obvious, often juvenile nicknames he gives to people who are clearly renting space in his head: "Sleepy Joe," "Crooked Hillary," "Crazy Bernie," "Pocahontas," "Lyin' Ted." Over the weekend, he dubbed Pete Buttigieg "Alfred E. Neuman," which does nothing but remind people how very old the president is.

And as for Trump's non-insult laugh lines, most of them elicit more applause than actual laughter—they're much closer to the conservative version of clapter. And the lines that aren't call-outs to his fans are only funny in the sense of being out of place in what's supposed to be a semi-serious setting. Kind of like when a speaker at an insurance conference can turn into Jerry Seinfeld by making a joke about how he found out his "umbrella" insurance policy only covered being stabbed by an actual umbrella.

Get it? UMBRELLA!

None of Trump's one-liners display clever turns-of-phrase or sharp insights. Instead, his biggest laugh lines—his insults—are sledgehammers, notable only in an "Oh my God, I can't believe he said that" sort of way. Such stream-of-consciousness observations take exactly zero talent; 13-year old boys are currently doing better routines at middle schools across the country.

Take, for instance, an aside during his Green Bay speech when Trump discussed the difference between his motto—"Make America Great Again"—and Ronald Reagan's "Let's Make America Great Again" slogan. Trump explained to the sea of red hats why he didn't want to use the word "let's," saying, "You don't want the apostrophe, it's too complicated."

Do you hear that sound? It's not the sound of funny.

Certainly, there's a role for "I can't believe he said that" humor—some of the best comedians working today are the ones who break the silence on topical issues. (See: Dave Chappelle on transgenderism, Chris Rock on the value of bullies, etc.)

And insults can be fun, especially when accompanied by lacerating wit. My favorite, for example, is Christopher Hitchens' takedown of Jerry Falwell: "If you gave Falwell an enema, he'd be buried in a matchbox."

But the only time Trump is truly funny is when he's trying to be deadly serious. Watching him try to explain U.S. trade deficits with China is as adorable as viewing a rat on the New York City streets try to drag a piece of pizza up a flight of stairs. It's funny because we're not laughing with him; we're laughing at him.

Chris Farley was once criticized for engaging in dopey humor that appealed to the lowest-common-denominator. But the truth is, his act took immeasurable skill and timing. Watch him work and it's clear that he's a technician.

Trump's show, on the other hand, is only notable because it lacks any sign of talent other than a willingness to be embarrassed in public.

You might call Trump's style "fatty falls up."

The Bulwark

THE COL. JESSUP PRESIDENCY

October 8, 2019

The very day it came to light that President Donald Trump had withheld $400 million in military funds to Ukraine in advance of asking that country to investigate the Biden family for "corruption," the script was written.

"I did not make a statement that you have to do this or I won't give you aid," he said on September 24. "I didn't put any pressure on them whatsoever."

He then added: "I think it would probably, possibly have been OK if I did."

Either Trump was oblivious to the seriousness of what he was being accused of, or he was telegraphing his strategy to deal with it. The plan would soon metastasize into the president of the United States standing outside of the White House last Thursday, openly pleading with foreign governments to help him dig up dirt on his 2020 opponents.

"China should start an investigation into the Bidens," he said. "What happened in China is just about as bad as what happened with Ukraine."

Clearly Trump's strategy is to go full Colonel Jessup.

By belligerently admitting his lawbreaking in public—and then doing more of it—Trump is hoping his followers see him as a strongman doing what he pleases and not a confused weakling who didn't actually realize what he was doing.

You want me on that wall!

You need me on that wall!

And Mexico's going to pay for it!

But, of course, Trump won't be able to get away with it without coaxing other elected Republicans into his vortex of nonsense. Through Twitter bullying, he must mold an army of useful idiots afraid that he might say something unflattering about him.

In fact, the current U.S. Senate reminds me of another movie. There's a scene in (the criminally underrated) Billy Madison where Adam Sandler's character tries to convince the kids on a field trip that all the cool kids pee in their pants. Because if everyone does it, nobody will be embarrassed.

On Sunday morning, Wisconsin' obeisant Sen. Ron Johnson showed up on Meet the Press with a full bladder, anxious to relieve himself on command. A combative Johnson proclaimed he didn't trust U.S. intelligence agencies and pitched nutball conspiracy theories to exasperated host Chuck Todd, who rightly observed that the senator was just trying to placate America's most powerful TV viewer.

Sure enough, later in the day, Johnson's humiliating lapdog routine paid off, earning him a tweet of approval from the president:

Sleepy Eyes Chuck Todd of "Meet the Press" had a total meltdown in his interview with highly reaspected Senator @RonJohnsonWI. Seems that a not very bright Chuck just wasn't getting the answers he was looking for in order to make me look as bad as possible. I did NOTHING wrong!

— Donald J. Trump (@realDonaldTrump) October 6, 2019

So we now know the price of a Republican senator's dignity. It's exactly 278 characters.

Earlier in the week, Johnson had told Wisconsin reporters that he thought it was perfectly okay if Trump had solicited the Chinese for campaign help. Simultaneously he said that he doesn't trust China "any farther than I can throw them."

"I look at that transcript and I go, it's Trump being Trump," Johnson told a town hall last week, echoing the type of logic that kept Michael Jackson in polite company for 20 years. "I know he's got a thing for sleepovers with kids, but that's just Michael being Michael."

Johnson has had plenty of company. When asked about Trump's China comments, Marco Rubio said he didn't think Trump was making a "real request," telling reporters "I think he did it to provoke you to ask me and others and get outraged by it." Well, okay. Are you outraged by it, Beautiful Marco?

A week ago, after being confronted by a television anchor who pointed out that the facts in the CIA whistleblower's account against Trump had been verified, South Carolina senator Lindsey Graham told her "you've got an opinion and I've got an opinion," which is about as convincing as Ron Burgundy's offer to "agree to disagree" over the founding of San Diego.

This cowardice serves to aid Trump as he floods the media with outright lies. And it to normalizes his overtly criminal actions. A whole generation of young people is growing up to believe the GOP is populated only by maniacal narcissists and gutless opportunists who care only for their own careers. No, really: 62 percent of voters between 18 and 34 approve of the impeachment inquiry and 58 percent of that cohort say they believe Trump has committed crimes as president.

How do Johnson, Rubio, and Graham think this is going to work out for their party in the long run?

It's funny to think that one day when the history of the implosion of the Republican party is written, historians will note that the calmest period of Trump's tenure were the two weeks during which he drew on map with a sharpie in an attempt to convince people that Alabama really had been in the path of a hurricane.

As the saying (frequently misattributed to Winston Churchill) goes, "if you're going through hell, keep going." But that assumes there's another side from which to emerge. Trump's lawless boasting simply drags members of Congress and the American people further into hell. And if you need proof, consider that scotch now costs 25 percent more because of Trump's tariffs.

At the moment we need it most.

The Bulwark

THE REPUBLICAN VOTE FRAUD HOAX

November 11, 2020

Comedian Dave Attell has an old line about watching a notoriously ribald "Girls Gone Wild" video: I like to play it backward, because then it looks like the girls have learned their lesson.

Similarly, if Americans were to watch last week's election returns in reverse, they'd also learn a valuable lesson — that for months, the Republican plan has been to sow the exact sort of doubt in the election results they're fraudulently pushing now.

As everyone knows by now, voting during the COVID-19 pandemic took place in two distinct ways based on ideology — Republicans largely voted in person on Election Day, while Democrats rushed to vote early and by mail.

In many of the most hotly contested states, the Election Day votes were counted first, making it appear President Donald Trump had surged to insurmountable leads in states like Pennsylvania, Michigan and Wisconsin. But then the early votes started to be counted, and former Vice President Joe Biden managed to eclipse Trump in all three crucial states (although Pennsylvania is a commonwealth, as those of us glued to our televisions for days on end were constantly reminded).

In fact, the only reason the election looks close for some people is because of the mechanics of how the votes are being counted. Because the votes cast first were counted last, it appeared as if Democrats were making a last-ditch effort to rob Trump of his prodigious leads. But if the tape were rewound and the early and mail-in ballots were counted first, it would have looked like Biden had destroyed Trump and the incumbent was making a valiant comeback.

This would be the model in Ohio, where the early votes were counted first. Early on Tuesday night, it appeared Biden would run away with the state, carrying an 11 percentage point lead with half the votes in. Then the Election Day vote poured in, and Trump ended up carrying the state by 8 points. (You will not be surprised to learn that the Trump team is not alleging any vote fraud in the overwhelmingly Democratic-leaning early vote in Ohio.)

But now, because Trump is prone to boisterous tantrums, Republicans are forced to pretend the late surges in Biden votes are the result of nefarious machinations by Democrats — a plot so complex that liberals were able to steal the presidency from Trump but still contemporaneously hand House and Senate Republicans better-than-expected showings.

It is, of course, all nonsense. The votes cast are the votes cast, no matter what order in which they are counted. A peanut butter and jelly sandwich is still a peanut butter and jelly sandwich regardless of whether you correctly apply the peanut butter first, or whether you're a psychopath who dirties the knife with jelly first.

Clearly, the plot by Republicans all along was to force the early votes to be counted last and to try to portray the mail-in ballots as illegitimate. For months, Trump had been fomenting distrust in voting by mail, even though he had done it himself and a number of states conducted their elections almost entirely by mail with no fraud.

When asked in September whether he would commit to a peaceful transfer of power, Trump said, "Get rid of the ballots" and there would be a "very peaceful ... continuation."

"We want to make sure the election is honest, and I'm not sure that it can be," he later said. "I don't know that it can be with this whole situation — unsolicited ballots. They're unsolicited; millions being sent to everybody. And we'll see."

Republicans in places like Wisconsin and Pennsylvania responded by filing lawsuits trying to prevent mail-in ballots that didn't reach clerks by Election Day from being counted. And Trump's team of attorneys, who evidently don't know the difference between a fancy hotel and a landscaping company, are out carrying through on the whole fraud, alleging voting irregularities with zero evidence.

A number of Trump legal challenges have already been laughed out of court, and Attorney General William Barr has now authorized U.S. attorneys to investigate allegations of voting irregularities — a bonfire of taxpayer money that will no doubt be cheered on by "conservatives."

Of course, this is all to allay the fractured ego of a petulant president who thinks it is more important to drag America through a phony legal process than hand power over with dignity. It was his plan all along, and now it's just a cash grab to fund Trump Inc. when the Secret Service eventually drags him out of the White House.

For Trump's supporters, this money would be better spent on an old "Girls Gone Wild" videotape — they can probably be found at the sex shop next to Four Seasons Total Landscaping in Philadelphia.

USA Today

CHAPTER FOUR:

"LET US REPURIFY IT."

THE REAL THREAT TO CIVIC KNOWLEDGE

October 15, 2020

As senators began their opening statements prior to the first hearing for Judge Amy Coney Barrett's nomination to the U.S. Supreme Court, Democratic Hawaii Sen. Mazie Hirono was flanked by large posters featuring photographs of individuals with serious diseases. Hirono said that in nominating Barrett, President Donald Trump was using a "hypocritical and illegitimate process" in "keeping his promise" to install the "deciding vote to take health care away from millions of people."

Minutes later, New Jersey Sen. Cory Booker speculated that in Barrett's America, women who had miscarriages would be investigated to make sure they didn't have abortions. Democratic vice presidential nominee Sen. Kamala Harris defended the Supreme Court's legalization on same-sex marriage by saying "love is love," a legal principle conspicuously missing from the Federalist Papers.

The entire spectacle—of senators peppering a conservative nominee with questions about whether she would take health care from people or make it harder for minorities to vote—distorts the public perception of the proper role of the legislative and judicial branches. The conflation of judicial opinions with policy preferences is why every Supreme Court nomination fight now resembles the intensity of a presidential election crammed into a few tense weeks.

And most of this disinformation isn't spread by blogs, or bad social studies teachers, or even Russian Twitter bots. It is spread primarily by elected officials trying to wring votes out of a malleable electorate. In doing so, they are bleeding the public of basic civic knowledge.

In other words, to crib a popular formulation, those who pay little attention to politics are uninformed, but those who listen to politicians are misinformed.

It is this steady stream of misinformation from elected officials that leads to people embarrassing themselves by loudly declaring Barrett's nomination as "court packing." It foments a culture where online political observers high-five one another for suggesting Barrett can't be an "originalist" because she's a woman and females couldn't vote at the time of America's founding. (This sick burn only works if these people assume conservatives are as dim as they are: In reality, the late Justice Antonin Scalia frequently urged the use of constitutional amendments, which is exactly how women earned the right to vote 100 years ago.)

Sadly, the practice of grandstanding elected officials making Americans dumber isn't limited to matters of the judiciary. After the passage of the ACA, Republican Sen. Ted Cruz of Texas pandered to low-information voters by convincing them he could intimidate President Barack Obama into repealing Obamacare if the Senate shut the government down. Cruz's contention was that previous senators couldn't get Obama to repeal a massive bill bearing his name simply because other Republicans didn't want it enough.

"What he did was stood up for Ted and threw the Republican Party under the bus," said Sen. Lindsey Graham (R-South Carolina) after Cruz's efforts failed.

What Cruz's efforts did spawn, however, was the idea that someone with a forceful enough personality could get Obamacare repealed, legislative process be damned. And that person was businessman Donald Trump, a reality television show star who loudly declared he alone could fix what ailed America, as if the Constitution would cower under the weight of his taunts.

Alas, Trump's bellicosity was no match for Sen. John McCain's disdainful thumbs down, and efforts to repeal the ACA were unsuccessful.

But Trump has permanently changed public perception of the role of the executive. He has many of his acolytes believing a president's attempts to obstruct justice are legal as long as they call it a "hoax" frequently enough. He convinced all but one Republican U.S. senator that trading away American foreign policy to obtain dirt on a domestic political rival isn't grounds for impeachment and removal.

As for the judiciary, Trump has done his part to obfuscate the role of the Supreme Court, saying he would appoint only justices who would vote to strike down Obamacare—a statement Barrett has been fending off throughout her hearings this week.

But Trump's opponents are also writing checks their constitutional powers simply can't cash. Democratic candidate Joe Biden has declared proudly that on "day one" he would begin to address systemic racism in America, begin removing Trump's tax cuts, and ameliorating the effects of the coronavirus. Biden himself has called for a national mask mandate, something the president does not have the power to do.

All of this misinformation is laid at the feet of a credulous public that already has a tenuous grasp of American civics. According to a long-running Annenberg poll, only 39 percent of Americans in 2019 could name all three branches of government. Only 55 percent knew Democrats controlled the U.S. House of Representatives and 61 percent knew Republicans controlled the Senate. Barely more than half (55 percent) of

Americans knew that a narrow 5-4 Supreme Court ruling must be followed anyway.

As Amy Coney Barrett sits in front of hostile Democrats who insist on pretending a judge's only role is to uphold desirable policies, millions of American children are sitting at home in quarantine in front of computers. Parents are worried these children will suffer long-term knowledge loss if they can't soon return to their classrooms. But if these parents want to ensure their children are learning civics, the best thing they can do is keep their kids from watching the Barrett hearings.

The Dispatch

REBEL WITHOUT A PAUSE

July, 2010

Wisconsin Congressman Paul Ryan is a verbal machine gun. Silence is the only thing he attacks with more ferocity than government-run health care. But when the topic turns to him, he hesitates.

"Being recognized in public isn't something I ever really wanted," Ryan says to me as he takes a sip from his Singha beer. We're at Washington D.C.'s Talay Thai restaurant, which Ryan can see from his Capitol office window. "It's really weird to have someone write about your life – it just seems so boring to me," he says as he picks at his plate of drunken noodles.

"I'm not trying to sell myself as a star," he says. I note that we could wallpaper the Capitol with the portraits of representatives whose names will never cross the lips of another human being. Ryan says he can only handle 10% of the 50-to-60 press inquiries he receives each day. So why is he getting so much attention?

"I think there's a vacuum of leadership," he says. "The Bush-Cheney generation of leaders is gone, and people are hungry for the next generation. They're hungry for what I call conviction politicians – people who believe in something, stand for it, and are able to articulate it," he adds.

Ryan has become the ultimate political oxymoron – a Republican national media darling. To conservatives, this is akin to seeing Sasquatch roller skating down the street smoking a pipe. It simply doesn't happen.

And yet there is Paul Ryan, on a CNBC panel out-nerding all the high-paid TV financial analysts. And there is Paul Ryan on the Sunday network talk shows explaining how America is in the midst of a slow-motion federal entitlement catastrophe. And there is Paul Ryan dismantling the health care bill at President Obama's sham "summit," while the president glares at him as if Ryan just told the Obama kids there's no tooth fairy.

Ryan is a throwback; he could easily have been a conservative politician in the era before cable news. He has risen to national stardom by taking the path least traveled by modern politicians: He knows a lot of stuff.

Few members of Congress have attained Ryan's mind-boggling velocity. Elected to Congress in 1998 at the tender age of 28, he is on everyone's watch list. Fortune has anointed Ryan as President Obama's foremost adversary. Conservative patriarch George Will has Ryan all but penciled in as the GOP vice presidential nominee in 2012. America's Cougar-in-Chief, Sarah Palin, listed Ryan as her favorite presidential candidate in 2012. The London Daily Telegraph ranked Ryan as America's ninth most influential conservative, ahead of Mitt Romney, George W. Bush and Supreme Court Chief Justice John Roberts.

In fact, rarely does Wisconsin's fiscal dreamboat give an interview these days when he's not asked if he's running for president in 2012; he steadfastly maintains that he will not. But why are people so suddenly so excited by a congressman from Janesville, Wisconsin? In other words...

What's so damn special about Paul Ryan?

At dinner, I mention to Ryan that he has essentially become a talisman for Republicans: On the campaign trail, uttering the name "Paul Ryan," immediately brands you as a serious thinker. Candidates like Senate hopeful Marco Rubio of Florida play up the connection.

"It's not about me, or my name, it's about the ideas that I'm pushing," Ryan protests.

"What I say is what I do, and it's backed up with the numbers. I feel like it's a race against time to change the trajectory of the country.

He explains: "If we don't turn this thing around really fast, we're going to be a big welfare state. We will lose the American Idea in a nanosecond relative to history if we don't step up fast and get the American people to help us take this thing back."

After dinner, we walk back to Ryan's office to begin a "telephone town hall" with constituents in Rock and Walworth counties. Basically, Ryan stares at a computer that randomly auto-dials numbers and fields any questions the responders have. People can either ask him something or listen to others grill the congressman.

At 8:07 pm, with the Longworth House Office Building virtually empty, he sits down at his desk and slides on his headset. "Good evening, this is Congressman Paul Ryan," he greets callers, instructing them to hold on the line if they have a question. I wonder if I would even have a question ready if my congresswoman called me. Apparently plenty of people do.

Ryan rolls through calls, one by one, speaking at lightning speed. It's almost as if he's invented a way of breathing while speaking, to eliminate wasteful pauses. All the callers are polite. The final one, who identifies himself as a union worker, urges Ryan to run for president. Ryan answers with his pat answer: "My head isn't big enough and my kids are too small." (Ryan and wife Janna have three children – Liza, 8; Charlie, 6; and Sam, 5.)

When Ryan finishes, the computer says 5,895 constituents have participated. Many callers ask him about his pet issues. Several mention their concern about the national debt. One asks about the looming specter of inflation. It seems far-fetched that these issues are of concern to regular people, unless those regular people have the Prime Minister of the Congressional Nerd Brigade as their representative.

On the day Paul Davis Ryan was born in 1970, President Richard Nixon unveiled his record-setting $200.8 billion federal budget proposal for the upcoming year – a budget that included a large increase in Social Security payments.

Ryan was raised as a fifth-generation Janesville resident. His father practiced law in the same building as future U.S. Senator Russ Feingold's father. To differentiate Young Paul from Paul Sr., Ryan was nicknamed "P.D." People often mistook this moniker for "Petey," which caused Paul to recoil.

One day as a 16 year old, Ryan came upon the lifeless body of his father. Paul Ryan, Sr. had died of a heart attack at age 55, leaving the Janesville Craig High School 10th grader, his three older brothers and sisters and his mother alone. It was Paul who told the family of his father's death.

With his father's passing, young Paul collected Social Security benefits until age 18, which he put away for college. To make ends meet, Paul's mother returned to school to study interior design. His siblings were off at college. Ryan remembers this difficult time bringing him and his mother closer.

Within months, Paul's maternal grandmother moved into the house. She suffered from Alzheimer's, and it often fell on young Paul to care for her, including brushing and braiding her hair. Ryan credits his father's death and the care of his grandmother as giving him first-hand experience as to how social service programs work.

Ryan excelled at school and was voted class president his junior year. He also served as Craig's school board representative. He ran track and played soccer, but wasn't good enough to make the Craig basketball team, so he played Catholic league hoops.

Upon graduation, he headed to Oxford, Ohio, to attend Miami University. (Twenty three years later, he would return to give the commencement speech.) His junior year, Ryan took an internship with Wisconsin Sen. Bob Kasten's foreign affairs advisor. Ryan says he spent more time opening mail than working on the study of Soviet containment, but it got his foot in the door when a real internship with Kasten's small-business committee opened up over the summer.

Ryan returned to classes in the fall for his senior year. Two weeks in, he got a call from Cesar Conda, Kasten's staff director. Conda confided that the committee's staff economist was leaving the following May. Would Ryan take the job after he graduated for one-third of the salary?

Ryan wasn't sure...until Betty Ryan gave him a tongue-lashing. She feared her son was destined to become a ski bum. The Kasten post led Ryan to a job with two of the GOP smartest thinkers, Jack Kemp and Bill Bennett, at Empower America, then as Senator Sam Brownback's legislative director.

Ryan cites his time with Kemp and Bennett as the formative years that shaped his political outlook. However, he was homesick most of the time. He wanted to get back home, and he wanted to hunt more.

In 1998, Ryan's hometown representative, Mark Neumann, was gearing up to challenge Sen. Russ Feingold. He approached Ryan about running for his congressional seat. Ryan wasn't sure. At 27, even he thought he was too young. For advice, he turned to Bennett, who urged him to take the plunge. "I wanted to see if my running for Congress passed the laugh test," Ryan remembers.

At 9 on Wednesday morning, Ryan comes bounding into his office like a Labrador. He's wearing his ever-present iPod earbuds, which never leave his head during the five minutes he's here. A warning to reporters: If Ryan doesn't know you well, don't ask what he's listening to – he'll tell you with a straight face, John Tesh.

Highly disciplined, Ryan was up at the crack of dawn performing a grueling fitness routine that requires 200 push-ups. Then, he joined a congressional Bible study group that meets on Wednesday mornings.

At 9:30, Ryan is off to a Fiscal Commission working group that is addressing discretionary spending. He has volunteered to serve on President Obama's newly formed commission to manage government spending and debt, and today is the first meeting.

Back in the Ryan office, his staff fields phone calls and attends to constituents who visit unexpectedly. Tom and Janice of New Berlin drop in, and ask to see "the next president." Since Ryan is still at his meeting, they are given tickets to a Capitol tour and merrily go on their way.

Earlier in the day, I had showed Ryan's staff a copy of their boss' birth announcement that I had found in the Janesville Gazette. They tell me that they gave Ryan a copy, and that he was impressed. "And that was before he even had a press secretary," one of his staffers cracked.

Ryan returns at 11:30 and heads into his office to make phone calls before his Ways and Means Committee meeting at noon. At 11:36, he bolts from his office and hands me a sheet of paper. It's a breaking-news report from Politico.com that liberal Wisconsin Congressman David Obey has decided to retire.

Obey was first elected to Congress in April 1969 – nine months before Paul Ryan was born. But facing an energetic campaign from Ashland County district attorney and former "Real World" star Sean Duffy, the irascible Obey has decided to call it quits. Later, Ryan would tell me that he heard a rumor two weeks earlier about Obey retiring, but dismissed it as nonsense.

Ryan's press team huddled briefly to discuss what their boss should say regarding Obey's retirement. Regardless of political party affiliation, Wisconsin's congressional delegation is duty-bound to say something about Obey's interminable tenure in the House. I suggest they issue a simple one-line statement: "Dave Obey has a beard." I am ignored.

I duck into the Obey press conference to hear him declare that his district ready for a new representative "who won't use an actor's ability to hide the fact that he is willing to gut and privatize Social Security and Medicare and abandon working people to the arbitrary power of America's corporate and economic elite."

Clearly, an unsubtle shot at both Sean Duffy and Paul Ryan.

Eleven days after his 28th birthday, Paul Ryan announced he was running for Congress in Wisconsin's 1st District. He began as a heavy underdog to Democrat Lydia Spottswood, who had narrowly lost to Neumann two years before. But Ryan cruised to victory, winning 57.2% of the vote. It would be the last time anyone got that close to Ryan--he won his next five elections averaging almost two-thirds of the vote.

Thinking back on his first election, Ryan believes Wisconsin voters prefer young politicians. "You just can't come across as an arrogant young know-it-all," he says. He tells me that back in those days he made a conscious effort to be overly lugubrious during speeches and debates, to counteract his youthful looks.

Ryan can turn on the humor behind the scenes. An ex-staffer told me of a gift exchange Ryan conducts with cantankerous Wisconsin Congressman Jim Sensenbrenner, who is considered only humorous when compared to an amputation. One year, Sensenbrenner bought Ryan a reindeer that defecated candy – Ryan returned the favor with a pair of nose hair trimmers packed in a Tiffany's box. Sensenbrenner then purchased Ryan some men's hair coloring gel. And on and on it went.

In early 2000, Ryan announced he was engaged to Washington attorney Janna Little, whom he had been dating for a little more than a year. The engagement notice in the local newspaper identified Ryan as a Congressman, but also pointed out that he was "an avid hunter and fisherman who does his own skinning and butchering and makes his own Polish sausage and bratwurst."

Ryan began to garner national attention in 2003, during the debate over President Bush's proposal to expand prescription drug benefits to seniors through Medicare. Ryan is proud of the free market programs he inserted into the final bill (Medicare Advantage, Health Saving Accounts), and believes those are the "seeds" to a future overhaul of federal entitlement programs.

When Ryan gave a well-received speech to the 2004 Republican Convention in New York, the "P" word began popping up. Milwaukee Journal Sentinel reporter Katherine Skiba compared Ryan, then 34, favorably to John F. Kennedy. When asked about Ryan in 2004, Bill Bennett, said, "I keep telling him, 'Run for president, run for Senate. Start the plan.'" (Ryan maintains Bennett was joking.)

In 2006, Ryan got another boost when Republicans were hammered at the polls, losing both the U.S. Senate and House. A testy Ryan believed the Republican brand was damaged because of the "bad apples" in his party. "We don't need a feather duster; we need a fire hose," he said about purging the party of those unwilling to advance the Republican Party's core ideals.

Arguing for change, Ryan campaigned among his fellow Republicans to be named the ranking member of the House Budget Committee. He won, beating out a dozen members with more seniority. "If we were going to just keep promoting the next person in line, then what's the point?" he said.

After his promotion, he began codifying his thinking in a policy manifesto called the Roadmap for America's Future, saying it took nearly a year and a half to get all the numbers right. His plan boldly calls for reforming the income tax code and would reconfigure two of the sacrosanct programs in American politics--Social Security and Medicare.

It was this plan that President Obama waved over his head on Ryan's 40th birthday, at a House Republican Conference retreat in January. Obama said that he had read Ryan's plan and called it "a serious proposal."

However, Ryan is certain Obama shone the spotlight on his plan only as "a straw man that he could then knock down." He said he fully expects Democrats to use the Roadmap as a "demagogic weapon" during the 2010 campaign season.

Ryan's most dramatic tête-à-tête with Obama came at the famous "Blair House" health care summit, where both Republican and Democratic members of Congress convened around a table before a national television audience to debate Obama's proposed health plan. With Obama presiding, Democrats attempted to minimize the differences between the two parties, trying to leave the impression that agreement was close.

By the time Ryan was scheduled to speak, he remembers he had gotten very upset with the Democrats' attempts to portray the two sides as nearly identical. "They kept rattling off all these incorrect numbers and bogus stuff," Ryan says. "I think we knew the bill a lot better than they did themselves."

So when cameras turned to Ryan, he began systematically dismantling the Democrats' rosy cost estimates. He pointed out that much of the cost was hidden, as it raised taxes for ten years to pay for six years' worth of spending. He exposed the fact that the $371 billion "doc fix" (a plan to reimburse doctors more through Medicare) had been separated from the bill and considered as standalone legislation to keep the price tag down. "Hiding spending does not reduce spending," he said.

As Ryan spoke, the cameras would occasionally make their way back to President Obama, who was glaring icily at Ryan.

"I wanted to throw a match on this thing," Ryan remembers thinking.

There are plenty of reasons to suspect that Ryan's future may not be as bright as his boosters think. For one, Ryan is essentially Patient Zero when it comes to entitlement reform. No one really knows how a national audience would treat his bold proposals.

Ryan's critics have been hammering at a provision of his Roadmap that would fundamentally alter Medicare by injecting market forces into the program. Ryan would provide individuals under the age of 55 with a voucher worth $11,000 per year when fully phased in. The voucher would then be indexed to inflation and be increased for those with lower incomes.

White House budget director Peter Orszag, while acknowledging Ryan's plan would address the nation's long-term fiscal problem, argues that health care costs will rise faster than the value of the voucher. Saying Ryan's plan only saves money by "shifting a lot of the risk and expected cost onto individuals and their families," Orszag believes too many policymakers—Republicans as well as Democrats--will find that solution objectionable.

Ryan calls this the most "fair and accurate" criticism of his plan, but says that it's impossible to keep funding health care expenditures at the current rate of increase. He says the Obama plan deals with the problem by rationing care. "My plan gives individuals control to put market pressure on providers to compete," he says.

Unrestrained health care spending, he warns, will "kill our economy – it crashes the system." So the choice, he says, is either "the Obama method of rationing care down, or doing a...consumer-directed system."

Given how suspicious seniors are to any changes in Medicare and Social Security, this is a politically risky idea for Ryan to advance. We already know how rank-and-file Republicans react to Ryan's plan – and it's not entirely positive.

When President Obama made an issue of the Roadmap, Republican House Minority Leader John Boehner emerged from his tanning bed long enough to deny he had ever heard of this "Paul Ryan" fellow.

Furthermore, so far the Roadmap only has 12 House co-sponsors – all from below the Mason-Dixon line, save for Rep. Cynthia Lummis from Wyoming. No Senate companion bill has been offered. It is clear that most Republicans believe that to explain Paul Ryan's plan, you actually have to be Paul Ryan.

Ryan has also caught flak from the right on some high-profile votes. Ryan voted "yes" on such toxic bills as the bank and auto bailouts. He defends these votes by saying they prevented an economic collapse, which in turn would have prompted even more heavy-handed government regulation.

Whatever Ryan's problems are with Republicans, he more than makes up for in crossover appeal with Democrats. In many ways, Ryan's tenure in the House has mirrored that of his mentor, Jack Kemp.

Kemp represented the blue-collar southtown area near Buffalo; Ryan's district includes heavily unionized Janesville, Racine and Kenosha. In 2008, while Obama was pulling 66% of the vote in Kenosha, 67% in Janesville, and 70% in Racine, Ryan received a solid 52%, 59%, and 45%, respectively, in those same cities.

The conventional wisdom holds that a member of the House doesn't have enough stature to make a serious run at the presidency. But the conventional wisdom also held that voters would never elect an African-American president. Now it seems anything is possible.

How can you rule out a well-liked 42-year old candidate from the House? Can anyone say with certainty that the next president isn't currently a member of the Black Eyed Peas? I can't. I won't.

During Obey's retirement speech, Ryan met with a Republican study committee, spent an hour with constituents in his office, and then caucused with Republican House leadership. At 4:15, he's scheduled to conduct a live interview with MSNBC's Dylan Ratigan.

I'm sitting on the stage with Ryan's 25-year-old press secretary, Kevin Seifert, who has handed Ryan's personal earpiece to the cameraman. Ryan supplies his own TV earpiece, as the ones the networks provide generally fall out mid-interview.

Without a second to spare, Ryan darts into the media room and sits down in front of the camera. Ratigan, the interviewer, is in the MSNBC studio – we can see the show as it progresses on one of the large televisions behind us. Ryan plugs his earpiece in and seems legitimately thrilled that Mötley Crüe is now playing in his left ear. With about ten seconds before the interview starts, he looks at Seifert and says – "what's the topic?"

The topic happens to be the debt crisis in Greece, where government spending cuts have sparked deadly riots. He breezes through the interview. His appearance is flawless, although viewers with HDTVs can probably tell he's developed the hint of a five o'clock shadow. His hair is perfect.

And oh, the hair! Some would consider it Ryan's most recognizable feature. It is an astounding feat of modern architecture, with hairs taking off on one side of his head and landing safely on the other in perfect synchronicity. It often varies in length, but never lacks in durability.

Soon, the clock hits 6:15, and Ryan has to make his way to a conference of investment bankers at the Newseum, which is the print media's new monument to its former glory. On the way out the door, Ryan looks at staffer Sarah Peer and growls about being hungry. "Do I get to eat?" he asks. "It's not on the schedule," she curtly replies.

Ryan drives himself, Seifert and me to the speech. We get to the Newseum and meet up with a group of the hosts, who show us to the sixth floor, where a packed conference room awaits.

Veteran politicians see crowds like this at hundreds of events. Different people each time, but in a way they all act the same. They hover, waiting for the right time to step in and shake Ryan's hand. Finally, they get their 60 seconds to make an impression on one of politics' rising stars – and then they're gone, back to making small talk over stuffed mushrooms.

Neither Ryan nor his staff has prepared any talking points, but Ryan dazzles the financiers with honeyed pentameter about capitalism and free markets. After the speech, we dart back to the car. I ask Ryan how it is he can be "on" 24 hours a day? (When I meet new people, I usually want to take my shoe off and start hitting them with it.) He shrugs and says, "I don't really have any alternative."

We return to his office, and while we scarf down Thai noodles for the second straight night, I present him my theory on why "The Dark Knight," the latest Batman movie, is essentially the story of his own tenure in Congress. It's about one vigilante fighting against a corrupt political machine for the betterment of the public, whether or not the public knows it, or even wants it. The movie ends with Commissioner Gordon noting that Batman isn't "the hero we want, but the hero we need."

Ryan immediately begins systematically dismantling my argument, finishing by noting that Batman ended up the movie as the bad guy. I fully expected him to pull out a Congressional Budget Office chart comparing his budget deficit reduction plan to that of the caped crusader. I immediately regret bringing Batman up.

After he finishes eating, Ryan sighs. It's time to start another telephone town hall meeting, this time with the people of Racine County. He cracks a can of Miller Lite, ambles over to his desk, and slides his headset on. His computer screen lights up.

"Good evening, this is Congressman Paul Ryan..."

Forty years ago, on the day Paul Ryan was born, the Janesville Gazette ran a cartoon mocking President Nixon's handling of the economy. The cartoon shows Nixon in the passenger seat of a car dangling perilously off the side of a mountain, while telling the driver "now, put it in first gear and go ahead very slowly..."

Four decades later, Paul Ryan is facing the same predicament. He earnestly believes he has a plan to get America's economy off that cliff and back on the road to prosperity. All that's left to be settled is whether he will try to bring that change from a seat in Congress or from the Oval Office in the White House.

While we eat our second straight night of Thai food, the discussion turns to Ryan's fans continually demanding he run for president. I recount Act I, Scene II of Shakespeare's Julius Caesar – in which Caesar refuses the crown three times before his adoring fans force him to accept it.

Ryan smiles, pauses, and says, "And how'd that work out for him?"

Wisconsin Interest

MR. RYAN GOES TO WASHINGTON

April 21, 2011

Famous chronicler of presidential campaigns Ted White once described the snow in Wisconsin as representing a rudimentary form of economic justice. "Under the snow, it is impossible to tell the poor farm from the rich farm. . . . The snow gives a white uniformity to the landscape," he wrote.

There is still snow on the ground in late April as Congressman Paul Ryan drives the roads of Wisconsin to pitch his own brand of economic justice. After unveiling his 2012 federal budget two weeks ago, the chairman of the House Budget Committee has returned to his district to conduct 19 town-hall-style meetings.

It is a welcome return home for Ryan, who has seen his "Path to Prosperity" plan endlessly demagogued in the nation's capital. His bold budget, which gradually reduces America's debt largely by reforming Medicare and Medicaid, was most recently skewered by President Obama, who described Ryan's plan as "un-American." Without naming Ryan, the president said the "Path to Prosperity" endangered kids with autism and Down's syndrome in favor of "millionaires and billionaires." Later, at a Democratic fundraiser, Obama said Ryan wasn't "on the level," criticizing his congressional voting record with a specificity usually reserved for high-school boys who've been stalking their ex-girlfriends on Facebook.

Ryan's plan rolls federal spending back to 2008 levels and freezes it there for five years. For those under age 55, Ryan changes Medicare to a "premium support" system that allows beneficiaries to pick among a number of plans offered by private companies. He turns Medicaid into a block-grant program, sending a fixed amount of money to states and giving those states the flexibility to serve their citizens as they see fit. Failing to fix these deficit-driving programs, he says, "would rank among history's most infamous episodes of political malpractice."

He is taking this message to his district for the next two weeks. His staff says he enjoys doing town-hall events, as it allows him to "work out the kinks" in his PowerPoint presentation. He also expects better, more informed questions than the ones he gets from D.C. insiders.

As Ryan climbs into his car, he pulls out his iPad to check his e-mail. He has gotten a message from a gastroenterologist in his district who has vowed to give Ryan and his family free colonoscopies for life if he decides to run for president in 2012. "That seals it," he deadpans.

His first obligation is to speak at a luncheon in Madison for the website Wispolitics.com. Madison is still teeming with protesters left over from Governor Walker's fight with the public-sector unions, and many of them make their way to the sidewalk outside the Madison Club to protest Ryan's speech. A young man on a microphone barks about Ryan's budget returning America to the era of the "18th-century robber barons." One scruffy young man tries to "rickroll" Ryan's speech, barging in with a boombox playing Rick Astley's execrable hit "Never Gonna Give You Up" at full blast.

At the luncheon, Ryan provides an hour-long extemporaneous description of his plan. The moderator, Jeff Mayers, asks Ryan if he's going to run for president. "I feel like I can do a better job where I am right now, focused on these economic and budget issues," Ryan answers. "And I can do it while being in D.C. for four days a week and Janesville three days a week, and that's how I like my priorities," he adds.

In the car on the way to his first listening session, Ryan multitasks while his chief of staff, Andy Speth, drives. Ryan throws on a ridiculous pair of futuristic sunglasses that can't possibly have been bought for him — he looks like an extra from a Fast and Furious movie. On a staffer's tiny BlackBerry screen, he reads the newly released Standard and Poor's report downgrading U.S. debt from "stable" to "negative."

From the passenger's seat, Ryan holds court on a wildly disparate set of issues. He expresses his disappointment at the president's speech criticizing the House Republican budget, and specifically bristles at being called un-American. "I just don't think he knows what's in the plan — I don't think he's been well-briefed," he says. "I think [the president] is bigger than that speech," he continues, pointing out that many of the provisions in the "Path for Prosperity" come from Obama's own Fiscal Commission report. "I think that puts the president on the extreme left flank," he says.

The president's criticism, however, might actually be a positive sign. Woodrow Wilson once wrote that you should "never murder someone who is committing suicide," and Obama evidently sees Ryan as worthy of political murder. That is, in Obama's judgment, it may not be suicidal to reform entitlements.

Soon, Ryan is discussing a trip he took to his wife's home in Oklahoma, where he took part in some traditional hand-fishing. "Noodling," as it is called, involves sneaking up on a giant catfish, sticking your hand into the dark hole where it lives, and punching it in the face while wrestling it into submission with your bare hands. Ryan recalls catching a 40-pound catfish this way (the first fact of the day he didn't back up with a chart from the Congressional Budget Office), but complained that the fish bit him halfway up the forearm.

Years ago, Ryan's wedding announcement in the local paper mentioned he was a congressman who "does his own skinning and butchering and makes his own Polish sausage and bratwurst." But in the over 500 town halls he has held over the past decade, he has tirelessly educated his constituents about the impending debt crisis. He has grown from "Paul, the scrawny congressman" to "Paul, the slightly less scrawny national fiscal rock star."

As he walks into the packed community room at the North Prairie village hall, Ryan is greeted with a standing ovation from the 172 citizens in attendance. Many are made to stand in a hallway, where they can't even see Ryan. He breezes through his PowerPoint presentation, which is replete with graphical demonstrations of the fiscal apocalypse. Many of the slides bring audible gasps from the audience, which comprises, overwhelmingly, senior citizens.

Most of the questions he answers are critical of his budget; later, he says that's typical of town-hall meetings. Even if 95 percent of the room is on your side (as was the case in North Prairie), most of the questions you will get are from the skeptics. Ryan answers his challengers by referring back to slides in his presentation to demonstrate the crushing burden on the economy that the status quo represents.

At one point, a woman stands up and begins reading from a piece of paper. Voice quivering, hands shaking, and eyes fixed on her printed remarks, she implores Ryan to run for president in 2012, eliciting a loud ovation from the crowd. She says she understands his concern for his own kids, but notes that the lives of everyone else's kids are at stake. Ryan doesn't respond directly, except to point at her and jokingly say "that's not my mother." Then she calls Obama "the enemy of America," drawing howls of protest from another woman sitting near the front.

In the car afterward, Ryan huddles with staffer Joyce Meyer to discuss ways to make the slideshow better. One questioner had challenged Ryan's assertion that higher taxes slow down the economy. He's certain he's seen a chart that shows GDP slowing down as taxes increased, and wants to have that slide ready for future town halls.

On the drive to the next town hall in the Village of Mukwonago, Ryan collects his thoughts while listening to Led Zeppelin's "Hey, Hey, What Can I Do." In these town halls, he has been test-driving a new, more populist line of argument with regard to business taxes. Ryan has pointed out how unfair the tax-deduction system is — decrying the fact that the top 1 percent of income earners use over 90 percent of deductions. When he cites the unfairness of General Electric's making billions of dollars in profit and paying no taxes, his constituents, Republican and Democrat alike, all nod their head in agreement.

Ryan's plan would eliminate most tax deductions while lowering the top individual and corporate tax brackets from 35 percent to 25 percent. Not only would lowering the rate make America more internationally competitive, he argues, but eliminating deductions would broaden the tax base and end the system of "crony capitalism" that favors some businesses over others.

Ryan gives this pitch for economic justice in front of about 100 constituents in Mukwonago. Again the room is at capacity, and the police have to send people home rather than risk a fire hazard. (Ryan's office will conduct a telephone town hall for the residents who couldn't get in.)

At the end of the presentation, following the mandatory citizen question about running for president (and subsequent applause), Ryan ducks out and heads to his car with a police escort. A young man who is sporting a lower-lip ring and representing the group One eludes the police and hands Ryan piece of paper and a white bracelet. "Say hi to Bono for me," Ryan cracks. (The Irish musician is the organization's spokesman.)

Before he can get in his car, Ryan is besieged by television cameras and holds an impromptu press conference. An elderly woman hangs back, waiting to give him what looks like a T-shirt she made for him. He ducks into the car while television cameras press up to the windshield, celebrity-paparazzi-style, filming him driving away. Ryan grants them a cautious wave.

Two town halls down, 17 to go.

Ryan's budget plan will continue to be debated in congressional office buildings, at family barbeques, and on street corners. But if there is one weakness in the recent public rollout for the "Path to Prosperity," it is that it is a singular document tied to a singular man — one with a preternatural ability to explain it. In order to sell Paul Ryan's plan, you have to be Paul Ryan.

Thus, if the consequences for the nation are as dire as Ryan predicts, it may not be hyperbolic to say the weight of the world rests on his shoulders. Without his dogged determination, the desire within Congress to avert fiscal Armageddon simply wouldn't exist. And if Ryan were to be caught in some kind of scandal, his plan would likely never cross the lips of another member of Congress.

But it is his willingness to be the nation's fiscal whistleblower that has catapulted Ryan into the political stratosphere. He is now the nation's foremost Obama nemesis — and although he's eight years younger than the president, Ryan looks more and more like the adult in the relationship. In a presidential debate, Ryan would be the last candidate Obama would want to see walking across the stage to shake his hand.

Which is why Ryan's constituents still think there's a chance he'll run for president. They believe that if the path the nation is on is as dire as he says it is, Ryan has an obligation to run. Allowing Obama to veto all his good ideas until 2016 belies the budgetary urgency Ryan has been pitching indefatigably since being made budget chairman.

And if he wins, he can invite Bono over to the White House and say hello himself.

National Review Online

RYAN'S LESSONS

June 18, 2013

Our republican robe is soiled, and trailed in the dust," Abraham Lincoln said in 1859. "Let us re-purify it."

Lincoln, of course, was talking about "republican" with a little "r" — the system of government put forth by the nation's founders. But in modern times, the passage works perfectly for big "R" Republicanism — a political party desperately in need of some rehabilitation.

Yet Rep. Paul Ryan (R-Wis.) thinks he has the salve to cure the GOP's ills. Since presidential candidate Mitt Romney picked Ryan as his running mate in the summer of 2012, Ryan has been frequently giving speeches about issues such as poverty in America, the benefits of community and the need to appeal to political moderates — topics generally reserved for liberals.

This week, he agreed that it was time for conservatives to reclaim those issues rhetorically commandeered by the left. "I think (Republicans) have ceded the moral high ground on critical issues facing people of this country, like upward mobility, and that's unfortunate because our principles lead to better outcomes," Ryan told me this week. "And if we can show how we apply our core principles to the big problems vexing society like poverty and economic mobility, which is the American idea, you can make something of yourself."

Ryan said he believes "conservatism has a much fuller, richer view of American life," and that "we have not done as good a job of communicating that as we could. I think the left in some ways has been successful at trying to portray us in a caricature that is not accurate, but nonetheless has set in. And we cannot be complicit with the caricature in which they have placed us."

"Big government is encouraging people to disavow themselves of the responsibilities we have with one another in a free society," Ryan said. "And I think that's a part of conservatism that has been lost and that we need to rekindle."

Ryan disagrees, however, that the party needs to soften its position on social issues in order to attract young voters, the overwhelming majority of whom support things such as same-sex marriage. "I personally don't see a big change in social issues needed," he said. "I see an emphasis in economic issues needed."

"We are the party of equality of opportunity, of natural rights, of upward mobility — and that means we have good ideas and answers and solutions to everybody no matter what station of life they are in and no matter where they come from," Ryan argued. "Those are the things, I think, that matter the most — and I don't think it means we all of a sudden have to change our positions on social issues, I think it's these economic issues that speak more to our problems."

In the past, Ryan hasn't been shy about criticizing his own party. After the GOP took a pounding in the 2006 elections, a terse Ryan believed the Republican brand was damaged because of the "bad apples" in his party. "We don't need a feather duster; we need a fire hose," he said about purging the party of those damaging the brand.

Further, Ryan spent years dragging the party to a point where it could talk openly of entitlement reform. For the better part of the past decade, Ryan was almost alone in calling for changes to Social Security and Medicare — now, such discussions are part of political debates.

Which is why Ryan is a little surprised that he has critics on the right shredding him for his support of a version of immigration reform that would provide a pathway to citizenship for the 11 million undocumented immigrants in America today. Ryan vehemently disagreed that such a program represents "amnesty" for illegal immigrants.

"You pay a fine, you're on probation, you secure the border, you get the employer verification system up and running, you're at the back of the line, you can't receive any government benefits during this time, be it Obamacare, food stamps or welfare, and your status changes after everyone else has been dealt with in front of you," Ryan said, describing the House version of the immigration bill. "That's what we're talking about. That's not amnesty. You earn your way toward a legal status just like a judge puts someone on probation who has to earn their way toward a legal status by fulfilling the requirements of their probation."

Ryan agrees that Republicans need to take their message to parts of America "that have never seen an alternative to the dysfunctional social welfare state that we have today that has been offered by modern liberalism." He specifically singles out poor rural communities and poor inner city minority communities as areas where conservative voices are most needed.

And if the GOP is successful in reaching out to people in areas that normally don't hear conservative voices, that "R" in "Republican" can get a lot bigger.

Milwaukee Journal Sentinel

PAUL RYAN WROTE A BOOK

August 22, 2014

On the day Paul Davis Ryan was born, the small town of Janesville was abuzz with activity. Mrs. Ellen Thieler of Milton was awarded $51 by her weekly TOPS weight loss group for having lost 51.5 pounds during the year. (She was granted a maroon cape, bouquet of roses and, of course, a three-tiered foam rubber cake.)

The same day, a meeting of 25 men was held at a neighboring county's sheriff's department to deliberate setting up a Big Brother program. They noted that the year before, Janesville residents had donated $6,000 to start a program to help fatherless young men. (Participation was limited to men over 21 with "general moral character" and "stability.") Later that night, the Rotary Club met to hear a presentation on a slate of new federal tax changes that recently had taken effect.

It was this tight, interconnected community that formed Ryan's idyllic childhood in Janesville. In his recently released book, "The Way Forward: Renewing the American Idea," Ryan, now the Republican congressman from his hometown, argues that the tapestry of these associations — Kiwanis clubs, Rotarians, Big Brothers, weight loss groups — form the basis of "civil society." Citing Harvard sociologist Robert Putnam, Ryan posits that renewing this type of "social capital," whereby people look out for each other in their own communities, is the most effective way to help lift people out of dire poverty.

To spread his anti-poverty message, Ryan kicked off his book tour last week, with Thursday stops in Milwaukee and Chicago. At a noon luncheon at Milwaukee's downtown Intercontinental Hotel, Ryan spoke to a group of 100 Republican loyalists, arguing that the mélange of federal programs aimed to help the poor is focused more on "poverty management and not poverty eradication."

On the drive to Chicago, I ask Ryan why, after other Republicans have abandoned poverty as a primary issue, he thinks he's the one to carry the message for the party.

"By now, people know that if I dedicate myself to an issue, I stick with it," he says. "I just believe that the promise of the American Idea isn't fulfilled if we leave a whole generation of people behind."

"I believe there's a lot of good out there, and a lot of effort, but it has to be more effective," he says, adding that the focus should be on changing America's poverty fighting to outcome-based strategies, rather than ones that simply measure how much government is spending.

During the two-hour car ride, Ryan frequently taps away at his phone, utilizing an app that lets him gauge the density of the traffic ahead. "Who would ever say 'yes' to push notifications?" he asks.

When I suggest people may be skeptical that he has discovered poverty as an issue after nearly 16 years in Congress, he says his experience of traveling the country as his party's 2012 vice presidential nominee allowed him to "see the potential" of America.

"I've always had these issues in my heart. It's not like I just popped into this in 2013," he says. But while his focus had famously been on the budget and deficits, he began to recognize that he wasn't going to be able to get a handle on the nation's debt problem with President Barack Obama in control. "I've always cared about (poverty), always studied this issue, but I decided to throw myself into it more fully given that it was clear I wasn't going to be writing a massive budget agreement to fix the country's fiscal problems for a while."

Ryan hopes focusing on helping the poor increases the appeal of his party. As Republicans, "we can't just sit in an echo chamber and talk to each other," he says. "If we're going to realize our ideas and put our principles in place, we're going to have to get some converts."

"I'm trying to expand the appeal of our principles," he adds. "It doesn't mean a whole lot if we can't win the Electoral College and actually put these ideas in place. We have to resell conservatism in a way that is inclusive, attractive and majoritarian."

Ryan says he wrote a lot of his book at home, "pecking away" at his computer at night after his kids went to bed. He started with an outline and put a deadline on himself to complete each chapter. In all, he estimates it took him about six months to write. "I missed a lot of workouts," he complains.

The book, which is largely autobiographical, provides a point-by-point counter to virtually everything critical said about him in recent years. For instance, he regrets using terms such as "makers" and "takers" to describe Americans who pay taxes and receive benefits. He's embarrassed that he misstated his marathon time from college. He only voted for the expensive Medicare prescription drug bill and the auto bailout because each vote was the best option among a slate of bad choices.

"I've always been defined by other things and other people and other moves and other votes — I wanted to finally define myself for myself. You never get a chance to do that," he says, calling writing the book "cathartic."

In the book, he also defends his support of a "probationary" period for illegal immigrants, which has riled many to his right. "When you talk to a conservative about what I'm specifically suggesting, they agree. They're afraid of labels — they're afraid of being attacked. It's fear masquerading as principle."

The subtext of much of "The Way Forward" is that Ryan was the tea party before the movement had a name. In 2008, the National Republican Campaign Committee urged its members to ignore Ryan's entitlement plans, deeming them too politically toxic. But Ryan, after much contemplation in a deer hunting stand, decided to forge ahead on principle. (According to the book, Ryan makes most of his major life decisions while sitting in tree stands.) And now, the tea party criticizes him regularly, such as when he was excoriated for striking a budget deal with Democratic Sen. Patty Murray of Washington last year.

I show him a printout of an alternate book cover a liberal group called The Agenda Project is urging people to print out and put on his book in bookstores. The cover resembles the original book jacket, but features Ryan pushing a scared elderly woman in a wheelchair. (The group was also responsible for the famous 2012 television ad featuring Ryan pushing the same woman off a cliff.)

He laughs and says those types of tactics actually provide him encouragement. "It's a way of saying, in my opinion, that the left is intellectually exhausted, when all they can resort to is caricature and baseless attacks," he says.

When Ryan reaches Chicago, he gets news that Mitt Romney's plane is late arriving, leaving Ryan time to cause mischief in his hotel room.

Ryan spends time concocting an entertaining way to douse Romney with a bucket of ice, which is scheduled for later in the evening. When the idea is floated that Ryan should mock Romney's perfectly groomed head of hair by making him wear a shower cap during his ALS Ice Bucket Challenge, a frantic search of the hotel room is conducted. Unfortunately, no shower cap is found, and the plot is foiled.

After an hour's worth of posing for photos with book purchasers, Romney and Ryan take their seats in front of a packed crowd of 450 diners in a ballroom at the Union League Club of Chicago. Romney opens with a few jokes about running for president, then tells Ryan "you wouldn't be a bad president yourself," to a round of applause.

It is a unique characteristic of American politics that the first requirement of running for president is pretending that you don't want to run for president. Politicians have perfected Oscar-worthy performances in denying their desire to seek the presidency, and Ryan is now their Daniel Day Lewis. Despite the release of a book, a national tour and Iowa polls ranking him the most likable GOP candidate, Ryan convincingly says that he will make up his mind in 2015 about whether he's going to run in 2016.

At the very least, he is doing what he needs to do in order to be in a position to make the decision.

One thing is for sure, though. If he does decide to run for president, it will be a deer deep in the Wisconsin woods that knows it first.

Milwaukee Journal Sentinel

RYAN SHOULD RUN – AWAY FROM SPEAKER

October 13, 2015

In January of 1916, former president of the Milwaukee City Club F.C. Morehouse sat down with the local newspaper to explain his bold new reform to rid city government of corruption.

Morehouse, an active player in city government, explained a plan by which "the office picks the man." Instead of ambitious individuals running for office, a committee would appoint respected people from around the community to serve. "The present method by which every candidate advertises his own virtues does not result in the selection of the best material," Morehouse told The Milwaukee Journal. "We must make it possible for the voters to obtain desirable candidates, so as to avoid the results of a system which gives the advantage to the self-exploiter, who most frequently is the least fitted man for the office."

While this sounds admirable in practice, one can only imagine a local accountant being thrown in the back of a van and being forced to serve out his term as alderman while being handcuffed to his desk. Don't want the job? Sorry, the office picked you.

With U.S. House Republicans desperate for a speaker, this appears to be the conundrum in which Rep. Paul Ryan (R-Wis.) finds himself. The Janesville Republican has stated repeatedly that he has no interest in the job. Yet House members, convinced there is nobody else who can plausibly lead them, are close to throwing him in a burlap sack and locking him in John Boehner's old office.

Ryan should continue to resist their overtures. Columnist George Will once said that the sport of football combines the two worst aspects of American life: violence compounded with committee meetings, otherwise known as huddles. In his current job as chair of the House Ways and Means Committee, Ryan gets to take part in the active part of that equation; he's the quarterback - he can get out, run around and make things happen.

As speaker, Ryan would subject himself to the drudgery of nothing but huddles. The job is primarily administrative, comprised of meetings, travel and fund raising. In essence, Republicans would be taking their Aaron

345

Rodgers and putting him on the coaching staff.

Further, as speaker, Ryan would have to cater to a group of Republicans who are invested in seeing that he fails. The House "Freedom Caucus" is made up of tea party members who gained office by revolting against the establishment, and they have enough members to hold the next speaker hostage to their demands.

The Freedom Caucus believes that Republicans can run government from the House of Representatives, even with a Democratic president and a less-than-filibuster-proof majority in the Senate. Despite being Constitution-huggers, they tend to ignore the troublesome separation-of-powers bit. For these members, a new issue comes along every 10 minutes that justifies shutting down the government.

And for them, Ryan is anathema - a conservative who believes in governing. Ryan has typically followed the Ronald Reagan approach to public service: Fight like hell for conservative values, but then settle for the best deal you can get. Ironically, it was Ryan's bold reforms to Social Security and Medicare that helped birth the tea party. Now that they've all grown up, they have turned on him.

This is why Ryan is likely to say no. Any politician who can turn down a presidential race that he'd probably be leading is certainly able to reject the chance to train monkeys in the House. And he knows that speakerships rarely end well; by taking the job, he would likely be ending any future chance at higher office.

While Ryan is certainly the most appealing speaker candidate, it is an insult to Republicans to suggest that he is the only GOP House member capable of doing the job. And chaining him to a desk in Washington, D.C., strips the party's brightest talent of what he does best. In fact, the recent speaker sideshow only strengthens P.J. O'Rourke's maxim that "Republicans are the party that says government doesn't work, and then they get elected and prove it."

Milwaukee Journal Sentinel

SOME POLICIES DESERVE BETTER POLITICS

March 28, 2017

On the morning of May 27, 1995, the legislative director for U.S. Rep. Sam Brownback made his first appearance on C-Span's "Washington Saturday Journal" cable television show. Fielding phone calls from viewers early on a Saturday morning, the 25-year-old Republican staffer passionately argued in favor of a free-market solution for America's health care system as he fired off budget numbers like a Gatling gun.

"We would like to offer more choices to health care recipients," he nervously told viewers. "We would like to instill private sector forces such as choice," he said, adding that seniors should be able to both choose their own doctor and "have an incentive to go and save some money in the health care market."

Nearly 22 years later, Paul Ryan stood in front of the nation as speaker of the House explaining why his dream of market-oriented health reform was dead. Just two weeks earlier, Ryan had delivered a PowerPoint presentation explaining that his recently introduced bill was "the closest we will ever get to repealing and replacing Obamacare."

But last Friday, after the Obamacare "repeal and replace" bill fell short, Ryan struggled to explain why. "We were a 10-year opposition party," he said, "where being against things was easy to do. You just had to be against it. Now, in three months' time, we tried to go to a governing party where we actually had to get 216 people to agree with each other on how we do things."

It was a catastrophe for the Republican Party in general and for Ryan in particular. The GOP didn't become a "governing party" in three months — it had seven years to come up with a plan that both moderates and conservatives could accept. In the next election cycle, voters will have reason to be skeptical that Republican candidates up and down the ballot will do what they promise.

It didn't help Ryan that his negotiating partner was a president with virtually no knowledge of the changes he sought to make and who was unpersuasive to recalcitrant representatives.

But even Ryan's biggest fans have to concede that the strategy on the health bill was bungled. House leadership thought it could introduce new health care legislation the same way Beyoncé drops new albums, surprising America and skipping the critical review period. But Congress has no Beyhive, and none of the major conservative groups that would normally cheer Obamacare's repeal roared in approval when the secret bill was made public.

And rather than staking out a negotiating position on the right, the bill attempted to thread the needle between free-market solutions and keeping as much of Obamacare as possible. This angered conservatives and moderates, and both pulled on the plan. Had Ryan proposed something more conservative, he could have negotiated his way back to the middle.

This week, liberal magazine The New Republic declared the health care fiasco to be "The Death of Paul Ryan, Policy Genius," further deriding the speaker as more" con artist than wonk." But this analysis has it exactly backward; since his days as a legislative staffer, few have had a more thorough grasp on policy than Ryan. It was only Ryan's expertise in budget matters that made it possible to discuss reforming entitlement programs in polite company.

He routinely turned down chances to run for president because he enjoyed crafting sweeping proposals to right America's fiscal ship. (Among them, the "Path to Prosperity," the "Roadmap for America's Future," the "Tollway to Tax Cuts," and "the "Boulevard to Balanced Budgets." Note – I may have made a couple of those up.)

Crafting common sense proposals and herding members of Congress into voting for them are two different things — especially when your proposals are rescinding a benefit granted by a previous administration. The talents needed for writing legislation and strategizing its passage are often in conflict; it is as if the Green Bay Packers ordered Aaron Rodgers to play linebacker just because he's a football player.

In January of 2014, amid rumors he was in line to become speaker of the House, Ryan firmly denied his interest. "I'm more of a policy person," he told a gathering in San Antonio, Texas. "I prefer spending my days on policy and my weekends at home with my family."

Maybe it's time we started believing him.

Milwaukee Journal Sentinel

COCAINE MITCH, STONE-COLD LEGISLATIVE ASSASSIN

January 30, 2018

In March of 2014, America first became aware of a practice soon come to be known as "McConnelling" — candidates posting hokey stock videos of themselves online that Super PACs could then pilfer and use in their own ads. At the time, Senate Minority Leader Mitch McConnell of Kentucky uploaded an awkward reel of himself accomplishing several mundane tasks, including giving speeches, hanging out with his wife and flashing a million-dollar smile while staring deeply into voters' souls.

Now the Senate Majority leader, McConnell's updated video should portray him in a much more forceful light. Given his recent mastery of the Senate, the new "McConnelling" reel should feature clips of him walking slowly away from an explosion while flexing his biceps, swallowing dozens of Tide Pods with no adverse effect, and running for a touchdown while stiff-arming Democrats along the way — all ending with a celebratory display of twerking.

Amid the chaos of the Donald Trump presidency, McConnell has emerged as the one man able to channel the cacophony into tangible results. While Trump is certain his excessive use of insults makes him a tough guy, the avian-visaged McConnell is actually a genuine, stone-cold legislative assassin.

It was McConnell that fended off public pressure to replace the late Justice Antonin Scalia with Barack Obama-appointed Judge Merrick Garland, leaving the seat open for Trump to appoint originalist dreamboat Neil Gorsuch. After a humiliating defeat on Obamacare repeal, it was McConnell who stitched together the thinnest of margins to pass an increasingly popular tax cut, which included repeal of Obamacare's provision forcing people to buy insurance they didn't want or couldn't afford.

And it was McConnell this week who stood firm on a continuing resolution to fund the government while theatrically aggrieved Democrats shut the government down, thinking the public would blame the GOP. Senate Minority Leader Chuck Schumer, D-N.Y., bet heavily that Americans would approve of shutting down the federal government until the Senate voted on a plan to provide relief to undocumented young people brought here as children.

But on Monday, Schumer quickly reversed himself and the government re-opened, a humiliating defeat at the hands of McConnell and the Republicans. Saturday Night Live has a recurring segment in which liberal Supreme Court Justice Ruth Bader Ginsburg counsels people they have been "Ginsburned." If the show had any ideological balance, it would inform viewers that Democrats just got themselves "Mitch-Slapped."

Oddly, McConnell's most vocal foes of late haven't even been his liberal opponents; they've been members of his own party who see him as a weak-chinned sell-out. The alt-right bible Breitbart.com has made a sport of hammering McConnell, setting him up as everything wrong with the Republican "establishment."

Former Breitbart overlord Steve Bannon has publicly feuded with McConnell, saying that any Bannon-backed Senate candidate would have to vow to vote against McConnell as Republican leader. The feud exploded after accused pedophile Roy Moore, Bannon's candidate, lost in Alabama. "The political genius on display throwing away a seat in the reddest state in America is hard to ignore," McConnell fumed.

Even Trump and McConnell have had their spats, with the president slamming McConnell on Twitter for failing to repeal Obamacare and the majority leader wondering privately whether Trump will be able to salvage his presidency. Yet, ironically, McConnell's work has done the most to keep Trump afloat. Gorsuch, the tax cut bill and the recent six-year extension of the children's health program, each making Trump briefly look plausible, are all primarily McConnell productions (with a nod to House Speaker

Paul Ryan, who enjoys a much wider margin in his chamber).

As Republicans rolled through the presidential primaries in 2015 and 2016, there was much consternation about who could eventually overtake Trump and represent true conservatism in the federal government. But with a "very stable genius" now in office who doesn't appear to have much interest in policy or procedure, it appears the true primary winner may have been under our noses all along.

He was the guy sitting at his Senate office desk, looking at a camera and flashing that Kentucky smile for an uncomfortable amount of time.

USA Today

CONGRESS MEETING OUR LOW EXPECTATIONS

January 5, 2013

In The Federalist 10, James Madison made the case for why America needed representatives elected from the general populace. Madison believed that "men" elected to Congress should have all the noble traits found among America's citizens, "whose wisdom may best discern the true interest of their country, and whose patriotism and love of justice will be least likely to sacrifice it to temporary or partial considerations."

It is true that 224 years later, America has a Congress that represents the characteristics of the populace - only now, it tends to represent the worst in us, not the best. The U.S. Congress can only be characterized by its fealty to "temporary" and "partial" considerations and its willingness to spend beyond its means reflects the increasing consumer debt Americans continue to accumulate. Indeed, the typical member of Congress may have a good number of the traits of the average American, but those traits are now among the worst of our vices: procrastination, secrecy and shortsightedness.

The recent "fiscal cliff" negotiations are a perfect example of how we now get the government we deserve. It's not as if Congress was unaware the "cliff" was coming - its members wrote the law that allowed the Bush-era tax cuts to expire after the 2012 election, and it had been an issue during last year's campaigns. But the way it was handled was a toxic bouillabaisse of deceit and misinformation.

It began with both sides petulantly accusing each other of holding up a deal to avoid tax rates ballooning on Jan. 1 of this year (after all, they only had nine years' notice to get something done). When a deal was finally reached, the Senate passed it late on New Year's Eve, when the nation's inebriated were busy figuring out who would be most willing to smooch with them at midnight. Then, the final deal failed to address the nation's entitlement crisis, impending debt problem or government overspending. It kicked not one but three giant cans down the road - the debt ceiling will have to be addressed in just a couple of months.

The fiscal cliff bill obviously isn't the first time Congress has timed its schedule to avoid scrutiny. The U.S. Senate passed the highly controversial Obamacare health plan on Christmas Eve of 2009, as many Americans were busy trying on new socks given to them by the nation's aunts. The 2008 bank bailout and "stimulus" bills only passed after years of warnings of impending economic doom.

But Congress' behavior simply mirrors what lawmakers see among the people who elect them. Since 2000, outstanding revolving consumer credit (mostly credit cards) in America has jumped by 40%, despite years of economic malaise. Even with the housing crash in 2008, the amount of nonrevolving credit outstanding (mortgages, car loans) has doubled in that time period. While income and employment in America have fallen, it appears our willingness to take on debt to keep spending hasn't waned.

In fact, it was Americans' insatiable desire to own homes beyond their means that led to the 2008 economic collapse. Granted, a lot of banks were offering attractive subprime loans to attract lenders, but cheap and easy money only aided homebuyers in overextending themselves. Either they didn't know, or didn't care, that their payments would eventually jump, causing them to default en masse, leading to the banks' collapse.

Currently, Congress has about a 10% approval rating - slightly higher than the approval rating of gangrene. But in the kung fu movie tradition, the student has become the teacher - Congress' procedural tricks have been learned whole cloth from the people it represents.

As H.L. Mencken once famously observed, "Democracy is the theory that the common people know what they want and deserve to get it good and hard." As long as we continue to expect so little of Congress, it will continue to meet those expectations spectacularly.

Milwaukee Journal Sentinel

LINCOLN GOT THE FARMERS RIGHT

June 25, 2013

During my time working in the state Capitol, I often had occasion to meet with groups of farmers who were there to push for pro-agriculture legislation. Most farmers don't necessarily adhere to the stereotype of the slick, well-dressed lobbyist; they wear their decades of sun exposure on their faces and proudly wear overalls unironically. In some cases, I would be in a room with three farmers, but only nine limbs were present.

Clearly, despite technological advances, farming is still really difficult and dangerous work. And it is this public respect for farmers that is baked into the federal farm bill every five years, when Congress recertifies its national agricultural programs.

But respect for farmers also can serve as a shield against questionable programs slipped into the massive farm bill. The most recent incarnation of the bill included a new insurance program that would have required all dairy farmers who sign up for a specific insurance program to participate in a companion Dairy Market Stabilization Program, which would have limited the milk supply in order to raise farm milk prices.

Under the current Milk Income Loss program, payments are made to dairy farmers when prices fall below a certain level; but those payments are capped and apply primarily to farmers with smaller herds. Recently, those caps were lifted, making large dairy farms eligible for expensive subsidies under the guise of a dairy insurance program. Enter the Dairy Market Stabilization Program, which would have limited those subsidies, instead limiting milk production and driving up prices in order to benefit large dairy farms.

The program was the pet project of U.S. Rep. Collin Peterson (D-Minn.), who presumably was looking after his state's Land O'Lakes co-op. But America is a net exporter of dairy products, making new aid programs seem excessive. U.S. Rep. Paul Ryan (R-Wis.) said he opposed the bill because of the "corporate welfare" it contained, telling MSNBC that the farm program shouldn't be "subsidizing people earning hundreds of thousands of dollars a year."

Republican leadership rightfully rejected the new program. House Speaker John Boehner (R-Ohio) said the program was "Soviet-style" government intrusion into the free market. In a rare instance, the International Brotherhood of Teamsters agreed with Republicans, noting that the higher milk prices would squeeze workers out of jobs in industries that deal with dairy products.

When the farm bill hit the floor of the House last week, Reps. Bob Goodlatte (R-Va.) and David Scott (D-Ga.) offered an amendment to strip it of both the Dairy Market Stabilization Program and the new insurance program for large farms. According to the Congressional Budget Office, the Goodlatte-Scott version would cost $15 million less than the farm bill as originally drafted. The Goodlatte-Scott plan passed, 291-135.

Even with the stabilization program scuttled, the House still voted down the farm bill. Republicans were upset that the cuts to food stamps were not large enough; Democrats thought the cuts were too large. The Senate version cut $1.7 billion in food stamps over the next five years; the

House bill increased the cut to $9.6 billion. But given that the Department of Agriculture is slated to spend $394 billion on the Supplemental Nutritional Assistance Program over the next five years, either number is, according to Christine Harbin of Americans for Prosperity, "barely a haircut."

The food stamp component is usually a payoff for urban legislators to support the bill. Consequently, farm legislation usually sails through. Now, Congress has the option of extending the current farm bill (which is actually an extension of the 2008 farm bill). Yet an extension would simply recodify the corpulent status quo with regard to ag programs in America.

In a famous 1859 speech delivered in Milwaukee, Abraham Lincoln warned against the deification of the "class" of farmers. "My opinion of them is that, in proportion to numbers, they are neither better nor worse than other people," said the soon-to-be president. "I believe there really are more attempts at flattering them than any other; the reason of which I cannot perceive, unless it be that they can cast more votes than any other," Lincoln added.

Despite his misgivings about the ag community's political clout, Lincoln would go on to create the Department of Agriculture as president three years later. Since then, farm programs have ballooned to levels he couldn't have imagined. There have been times farmers needed help; but in modern days, limiting milk production would only serve to emancipate more consumers from money in their pockets.

Milwaukee Journal Sentinel

POLITICIANS MAKE BAD MOVIE CRITICS

August 13, 2013

Usually, if you keep your name off a government list, it's a sign that you're doing things right. Yet there's one government list that people are desperate to join.

In the mid-1980s, billionaire mogul Ted Turner bought up the rights to the entire pre-1986 Metro Goldwyn Mayer film catalog. Turner famously began using new technology to colorize old black and white titles, enraging film purists, who believed the films should not be tampered with. In 1988, Congress stepped in and created the National Film Registry, a list of films of "culturally, historically, or aesthetically significant" value that the government would aid in preserving with the help of the Library of Congress.

Pursuant to the National Film Preservation Act, up to 25 films per year are eligible for inclusion on the list, which first began adding titles in 1989. A movie must be at least 10 years old to be considered, and not only feature-length films are considered. The registry, which now boasts over 600 titles, includes propaganda films, shorts, workplace safety videos and music videos. (Legislation re-authorizing the registry was subsequently passed in 1992, 1996, 2005 and 2008, which shows there is a bipartisan desire to have Woody Allen testify before Congress.)

Of course, it is appropriate to question the necessity of government stepping in to create a list of America's most indispensable films. It seems like the job of creating a list of America's most culturally important movies is a job the private sector can handle. If there's any area in which Hollywood consistently excels, it is in paying tribute to itself.

Further, with the explosion of digital technology available, it seems less necessary that the Library of Congress would need to "preserve" films. There are surely backlogs of old film in vaults that need restoration, but anything made today will likely live on forever on hard drives. (Although Johnny Depp is probably busy working on a computer virus to destroy every copy of "The Lone Ranger.") And even if movies are "preserved," there are millions of people with digital editing software on their home computers able to remix and edit whatever films they want.

But as long as there is a list, it seems fair game to complain about both the films that are on it and those that aren't. That, in the end, is what these dopey lists are for, right?

The first class of films, added in 1989, hit all the no-brainers. You've got "Gone with the Wind," "Citizen Kane," "Casablanca" and Buster Keaton's epic "The General." But after 24 years of inductions, the choices are growing more suspect.

For instance, despite being eligible, 1994's "Pulp Fiction" — perhaps the most emulated movie of the past 20 years — is not on the list. Stanley Kubrick's "Full Metal Jacket" hasn't made the cut, nor has "Glengarry Glen Ross," a movie that is referenced in every office building in America at least once a week. No "Shawshank Redemption," "Grease" or "My Fair Lady" — a classic musical that won eight Academy Awards.

Yet the omission of the 1986 teen classic "Ferris Bueller's Day Off" is inarguably the most glaring hole in the list. Unbelievably, John Hughes, one of the most influential writers and directors of the 1980s, is completely shut out from the registry. Hughes' run in the '80s ("Sixteen Candles," "The Breakfast Club," "Pretty in Pink") rivaled that of any American director of his era. He provided the blueprint for how teen movies would be produced in the future, and his films still have a near-religious following to this day.

Instead, the films recently selected to the registry rely more on their politically correct subject matter than their quality. Take "A League of their Own," which isn't a great movie but has a pro-feminist message about female baseball players. Or "Stand and Deliver," about famous inner city educator Jaime Escalante. Inspiring story, so-so movie. Does anyone believe "Sex, Lies and Videotape" (added in 2006) has anywhere near the cultural imprint as any of Hughes' brat pack films? Who's picking these movies, the IRS?

There's an old adage that politicians want to be movie stars and movie stars want to be politicians. Maybe the government's desire to play Roger Ebert is harmless, but there's a reason Thomas Jefferson didn't codify the right to "Life, Liberty, and the ability to watch 'Harold and Kumar go to White Castle'" in the Declaration of Independence.

Milwaukee Journal Sentinel

'IT FORCES YOU TO MAKE BAD DECISIONS'

May 9, 2017

Throughout his life, progressive paragon Woodrow Wilson sneered at a system of government that vested so much power with Congress. Wilson, who enjoyed pointing out that the president was the only person elected by all the people of America, was frustrated by this disequilibrium. "The Senate always has the last word," he complained.

A century later, Wilson's enthusiasm for consolidation of power within the presidency has a powerful new fan. Last week, President Trump offered a Wilsonesque critique of the U.S. Senate, arguing he should be given more authority because he's "a closer."

"You look at the rules of the Senate, even the rules of the House, but the rule of the Senate and some of the things you have to go through, it's really a bad thing for the country in my opinion," Trump told Fox News on April 28.

Trump further argued for "tak[ing] those rules on" such as the Senate filibuster "because for the good of the nation things are going to have to be different." He added, "You can't go through a process like this. It's not fair, it forces you to make bad decisions."

Naturally, in the Trump vernacular, any decision he gets to make unilaterally is necessarily a "good" one, and every proposal slowed by a deliberative body is, by definition, "bad." In this way, the current Republican shares the Progressive Era's lack of constitutional humility.

355

But while Wilson's antipathy for the separation of powers was derived from years of scholarship (as an undergraduate he proposed allowing the president to choose his cabinet from among members of Congress, British Parliament-style), Trump's latest position seems to be crafted only upon visiting Washington, D.C. on the days he can get away from Mar-a-Lago.

Ironically, Trump's lack of knowledge of how Congress works actually makes the case of why Congress is now more important than ever. As he learns history on the job (sample tidbit about Abraham Lincoln from a March speech: "Great president. Most people don't even know he was a Republican, right?"), the legislative branch can provide him a valuable constitutional lesson by asserting its rightful authority.

Clearly in Trump's years in the private sector, his view of politicians took on a cartoonish bent, most likely informed by cable news and television dramas. During Republican presidential debates, the eventual GOP winner openly bragged about buying off politicians (mostly Democrats), arguing — incredibly — that his own corrupt practices were proof that only he could fix such a "broken system." (This recalls the time on Cheers when Norm derided the sad, pathetic people who sat next to him at the bar hour after hour, day after day.)

No doubt in Trump's New York City politicians were simply a procedural hurdle to be overcome when a building needed to be built — salt the city with a few dollars here and there and city council members would one day earn a ride in one of his golden elevators.

But Congress can now prove that it's not simply a beagle eager to have its belly scratched. For instance, Congress should take the advice of TV star Trump when he asserted that Congress should approve military operations in Syria, even if President Trump disagrees. The House and Senate should craft responsible infrastructure and health care plans independent of Trump's capricious Twitter meanderings. Trump wants billions in taxpayer funding for a southern border wall? Senate Majority Leader Mitch McConnell should send over a copy of The Federalist 51, a golden shovel, and tell the president to start digging.

It's not as if presidents haven't always felt dyspepsia about the role of Congress. When President Andrew Johnson faced impeachment in 1868, one of the articles against him charged that he had plotted to "excite the odium and resentment of all good people of the United States against Congress" and that he had used, "with a loud voice, certain intemperate, inflammatory and scandalous harangues, and therein utter loud threats and bitter menaces." These are phrases that should be emblazoned on the china in the Trump White House dining room.

"The office (of president)," Woodrow Wilson once observed, "is so much greater than any man could honestly imagine himself to be that the most he can do is to look grave enough and self-possessed enough to seem to fill it." Last week, Wilson's philosophical descendant, Donald Trump, similarly noted that he thought being president "would be easier" than it has been during his first 100 days.

Undoubtedly, the two presidents could learn much from each other. Perhaps one of these days Trump will pick up the phone and invite Wilson and Frederick Douglass to dinner.

Milwaukee Journal Sentinel

SLOGANEERING

July 25, 2017

SCENE: Democratic National Committee headquarters, early July, 2017. HOUSE MINORITY LEADER NANCY PELOSI, SENATE MINORITY LEADER CHARLES SCHUMER and DNC CHAIRMAN TOM PEREZ sit around a table to discuss the Democratic Party's future.

PELOSI: Glad you guys could both make it.

SCHUMER: I was told there would be nachos.

PELOSI: We'll work on that. But in the meantime, as we all know, the Democratic Party is being held back by just one thing — the lack of a catchy slogan.

PEREZ: It's true. Voters in the rust belt list "inadequate hashtags" as their primary concern, right between immigrants taking their jobs and the opioid epidemic.

PELOSI: I know, right? Our otherwise flawless presidential candidate would be in the Oval Office right now had she employed a catchphrase like, "Build the Wall" or "Lock Her Up." Chuck, get off your phone and please pay attention.

SCHUMER: Do you think my Bitmoji looks like me?

PELOSI: So we've been kicking around some slogan ideas. (Turns to DNC intern.) Can you read the winning idea off your computer?

INTERN, SPEAKING IN THICK RUSSIAN ACCENT: I just need password.

PEREZ: It's "password," duh. By the way, who are you, again? I've never seen you.

INTERN: I am lazy American teenager. "Fidget spinners. Pokemon Go." See? Also, winning slogan is "Better Deal."

SCHUMER: Wait — that's what we spent months workshopping? "A Better Deal?"

PELOSI: Isn't it great? As progressives, that's what we do. We propose "deals." Teddy Roosevelt's "Square Deal." FDR's "New Deal." Adlai Stevenson's "Pretty Good Deal." Hubert Humphrey's "Groovy Deal."

PEREZ: I feel like some of those aren't real.

PELOSI: They're right here on Wikipedia.

SCHUMER: Isn't literally Donald Trump's whole thing that he makes the "best deals?" Isn't "better deal" slightly short of "best?" Aren't we promising a worse deal than the president?

PEREZ: He literally wrote a book called the "Art of the Deal."

PELOSI: But the whole "Deal" trick for our side is 120 years old — that's what the kids want now. They want retro, century-old progressivism. It's the Bernie Sanders of slogans.

SCHUMER: Also, didn't we just control the presidency for eight years? What are we offering them a "better deal" from? The Obama era? And where are those nachos?

PELOSI: Look, we took a poll and that's what the people liked. I know House Republicans gained a record majority during my tenure as the Democrats' leader, but I assure you this one's the golden ticket.

PEREZ: I still like it. Even if it beat out my suggestion, "Republicans Don't Give a S--- About People."

SCHUMER: How about a mission statement that good old "Eddie Punchclock" can understand? Like this, here: "If you work your butt off and pay taxes, you should be able to easily understand and navigate the laws, tax codes, health care and anything else the government puts in place that affects us all."

PELOSI: Chuck, I think you're looking at a statement Kid Rock just issued. God, he's going to take the Michigan senate seat from us, isn't he?

SCHUMER: He sure is. (Sadly dips corn chip into guacamole.)

INTERN: Can you please say that louder into stuffed bear?

USA Today

AMERICANS FOR HIGHER TAXES

December 19, 2017

At this point, Republicans couldn't sell a toupee to John Travolta.

Only 26% of Americans favor a new tax-cut bill working its way through Congress, with 47% of respondents opposing the bill, according to a Monmouth poll released Monday. In only a matter of months, Republicans have sullied the primary reason Republicans have been getting elected for decades. If the Monmouth poll is right, about 5% more Americans favor keeping their own money than believe a UFO crashed in

Roswell, N.M., in 1947.

Undoubtedly, the tax bill's unpopularity is tied to the sagging public opinion of the GOP. In the public's eyes, the Republican Party makes apologies for people accused of child molestation, dismisses sexual assault claims and craves power over principle. Over the past year, the GOP's motto has become, "If you ignore everything we do or say, we're the party looking out for you."

Of course, it is difficult for members of Congress to explain a major tax overhaul when they are constantly responding to the daily tumult created by the nation's histrionic president. Questions such as, "How does this tax cut benefit the middle class?" have been shoved aside in favor of ones like, "Would it be OK for Donald Trump to fire the man investigating whether he broke the law by firing the man who was investigating him?"

Although Trump had little to do with formulating the tax bill, the proposal wears his name like a pair of cement shoes. According to a CNN poll released Tuesday, only 35% of American voters approve of the job Trump is doing — by far the worst showing of any president at this point in his term. As good as the tax bill is, it's like selling the public a diaper-scented candle.

And while Democrats in Congress are frequently wrong, they are not stupid. They see Trump's weaknesses and know that with the 2018 elections coming up, they must #resist at all times, lest they become tainted by complicity in Trumpism. All the major tax cuts of the past 50 years, from John F. Kennedy's marginal-rate cuts to Ronald Reagan's cuts in 1986 to Bill Clinton's capital-gains rate cut in 1997, had significant Democratic involvement. Even President Barack Obama once called for lowering the corporate tax rate from 35% to 28% in order to make U.S. businesses more competitive. But in 2017, Democrats are acting as if a corporate tax cut will have us all riding Mastodons to work by next week.

Predictably, the Democrats' newfound talking points against providing middle-class tax relief have been happily scooped up by a press determined to distort the bill beyond recognition. According to the Monmouth poll, 50% of Americans believe their taxes will actually go up under the bill, while only 14% believe the bill will cut their taxes. According to the left-leaning Tax Policy Center, more than 80% of taxpayers will receive a tax cut in 2018 (averaging $2,140), while less than 5% will see their taxes increase.

This mismatch of perception and reality is a result of commentators on the left claiming taxes will go up once the bill expires, and yet ignoring all the money families save while the cuts are in effect.

It hasn't helped that Republicans can't seem to explain the need for the bill.

The most effective conservative politicians can take even small issues and explain them in a broader context. A tax cut isn't merely more money in your pocket; it represents a retreat from government control and influence over your life. Even if taxpayers don't feel they need tax relief, do they believe the federal government will spend that money more wisely?

A federal government headed by Donald Trump, no less?

Milwaukee Journal Sentinel

WHAT MEMBERS OF CONGRESS WISH THEY COULD SAY

March 2, 2018

Perhaps you've noticed that members of Congress have had a hard time explaining their own agenda amid the media vacuum created by President Donald Trump. To rectify this, I have drafted a sample form letter every Republican congressperson can send to his or her constituents to explain what they really think.

Dear [INSERT CONSTITUENT NAME],

It's just a few months until the [LOCAL AGRICULTURAL ITEM OTHER AMERICANS FIND INEDIBLE] festival!

By now, you'll most likely be seeing more money in your check, thanks to the big tax cut bill passed last year. You know what has two thumbs and made that happen? THIS [GUY OR WOMAN].

Just think of all the things you will be able to purchase with all your new money! You can pay your phone bill, get a gym membership, or offset the cost of your kids' braces. In fact, if you are desperate to find a place to spend that cash, I have paid you the honor of adding you to my fundraising list!

I know you probably don't like a lot of things President Donald Trump says. Trust me, [BROTHER OR SISTER], I hear you. Do you know how humiliating it is for me to show up on Fox News every week pretending our nation isn't being led by a bath salt-eating baboon?

Take just this week, when President Trump said we could cut down on gun violence if we just "Take the guns first," and "go through due process second." Of course, if Barack Obama was president and suggested confiscating guns without due process, I would have immediately issued a call for his impeachment. But I hope you realize I can't say anything now, on the off chance I will need our very emotional president to sign one of my bills into law. [STRIKE THIS PARAGRAPH IF YOU ARE NEBRASKA SEN. BEN SASSE, THE ONE MEMBER OF CONGRESS

TO SPEAK OUT AGAINST TRUMP'S DECLARATION.]

Trust me — Donald Trump can't do anything too catastrophic without Congress, so I've got your back. Except, of course, when I voted for a spending-cap busting budget a couple of weeks ago. Or when Trump proposed new taxes on imports and I took a nap and let him do it. Or when the president went behind Republicans' backs and negotiated a debt limit deal with Democratic leadership a few months back. (Actually, now that I wrote these all down, they seem a lot worse.)

After all this, you may wonder why you should continue to elect Republicans to Congress. Because we INVESTIGATE DEMOCRATS! Yes, I have heard rumors the president paid $130,000 to a porn star to keep her quiet during the 2016 election, but those stories came from an unreliable source — the president's own attorney. If you keep electing Republicans, we will drain the swamp and make sure Hillary Clinton suffers even more embarrassment in her quest to win in 2016!

Since it's just me and you talkin' here, let's be honest. The tax cuts you're now enjoying will last far longer than Donald Trump. The good judges he puts on the Supreme Court will last far longer than Donald Trump, as will any conservative bills we can sneak through while he's watching television in bed.

Those of us in Congress aren't stupid; we know Donald Trump is a mere pimple in our nation's process of becoming an adult. Consider your tax cut our payment for having to deal with him. Just take your money, go see "Lady Bird" and forget whatever preposterous thing he may have said that day.

Thirty years from now, we'll all be able to look back and laugh at the Trump years as a grotesque anomaly, while some of the important things we passed will still be there in the law books in black-and-white. Just know that in 2018, we are just as embarrassed for ourselves as you are for us.

Go [ENTER NAME OF LOCAL SPORTS TEAM]!

Sincerely, [YOUR CONGRESSPERSON].

Milwaukee Journal Sentinel

SENATE REPUBLICANS CAN'T RUN AND HIDE

September 26, 2019

If you're a savvy investor, you might want to buy stock in fake mustache companies over the next few weeks as Republicans in Congress attempt to avoid detection.

Even if you are lucky enough to spot any GOP members of Congress, they will likely scurry away rather than face questions about the impeachment investigation against Donald Trump that Nancy Pelosi announced on Tuesday. If things really get bad, Senate Republicans might have to disappear to a place where they know they won't be seen by anyone, like giving speeches at the Emmy Awards.

National Review's Jim Geraghty has supplied these shy representatives with an easy out. Sayeth Geraghty:

Congressional Republicans will have an easy lay-up: "While I find the description of the president's actions troubling, we are just months away from the election. I believe this is a matter best left for the American people to judge at the ballot box."

If only it were that simple.

Even after Pelosi's announcement of an inquiry, and even after Trump released the memo detailing his conversation with Ukraine President Zelensky, it seems that we are still far removed from a formal impeachment by the House and even further from Trump's potential removal by the Senate. Much like football announcers reminding us that calls need indisputable visual evidence to be overturned, we are about to be constantly reminded that "impeachment" by the House is not the same as removal by the Senate.

But what if the Senate did determine that Trump outsourced American political muckraking to Ukraine and held back hundreds of millions of dollars in aid to get it done? Let's say, hypothetically, that evidence uncovered during the House's impeachment inquiry really uncovers bright-line lawbreaking.

If that is the case, the Senate couldn't simply just wave off the evidence by citing the upcoming election. That's because when removing a president, the Senate has two determinations to make: Whether the president should go, and whether he or she should ever be allowed to hold office again.

Article I, Section 3 of the Constitution says:

Judgment in cases of impeachment shall not extend further than to removal from office, and disqualification to hold and enjoy any office of honor, trust or profit under the United States: but the party convicted shall nevertheless be liable and subject to indictment, trial, judgment and punishment, according to law.

The Founders determined that an impeachment trial not only decides whether a president should continue to hold office, but whether they are eligible to "enjoy any office of honor, trust or profit under the United States."

This is why the Senate likely couldn't duck the question if the House votes to impeach Trump. The question wouldn't be whether voters should support Trump in the next election, the question would be whether he could even run for election.

If the House does impeach Trump, Senators may see evidence that they can't unsee and vote him out. Or, in a more crass calculation, they may decide running for their own seats on a ticket with a badly damaged president might cost them their own careers and remove him just for that.

But in doing so, they would have to make a dual judgment – should Trump go, and should he be allowed to run again?

It is unclear whether the Senate would somehow be able to divide those questions (the issue came up twice following convictions of impeached judges), but doing so would set up a ridiculous charade. If senators somehow removed Trump from office but declined to bar him from holding future office, it could set up the unprecedented prospect of a president who has been removed from office running for election just months after his ouster.

As Amber Phillips writes in the Washington Post, "we'd probably all be armchair-interpreting the Constitution to figure that one out."

No, if the House sends an impeachment recommendation to the Senate, the decision won't be to "let the people decide." The public doesn't get to vote on whether they think, for instance, Martha Stewart should go to prison – the process determines the outcome when someone has broken the law. This isn't an episode of America's Got Corruption.

Thus, the Senate will have to make a determination whether the law means anything – if they let Trump's transgressions go, they will be just as guilty as he is.

If the Senate ends up with an impeachment in its lap, it sets up a binary choice. Senators can either ignore the recommendation, infecting themselves with the poisonous corruption Trump has foisted upon politics, or they can permanently remove him from office, casting the electoral system into an unprecedented chaos.

Let us pray they choose wisely.

The Bulwark

CRUZ AND HAWLEY: JUDGES IN THEIR OWN TRIAL

February 9, 2021

Imagine sitting in a courtroom awaiting a trial of a man arrested for assaulting your mother. It was a robbery gone wrong — he merely tried to spook her into giving him some money, but in the process, he became enraged and knocked her over, breaking her hip.

The judge lets the jurors into the room and as they settle in, you see a familiar face. The driver of the getaway car is on the jury! He gives the defendant a thumbs-up and you realize the fix is in.

The impeachment of a U.S. president isn't strictly a legal procedure — it is primarily a political one. But when the Senate trial of former President Donald Trump begins this week, his co-conspirators will actually be sitting in judgment of his actions. And the fix is in — for some senators, to find Trump guilty will be to convict themselves.

For weeks after the election, Republican U.S. senators such as Josh Hawley of Missouri and Ted Cruz of Texas buttressed Trump's dangerous lie that the November election had been stolen from him via massive voter fraud.

Even after Trump and his allies had lost over 60 straight court cases, Hawley, Cruz and others promoted the cockamamie theory that by objecting to the Electoral College results in the Senate, the vice president could somehow reverse the election and grant Trump the victory he very clearly had not won.

On Dec. 30, Hawley announced that he'd object to affirming the results, fueling the lies about voter fraud. "Millions of voters concerned about election integrity deserve to be heard," Hawley wrote, adding, "Somebody has to stand up."

A few days later, Cruz announced that he and 10 other senators would "reject the electors from disputed states," calling instead for a 10-day audit of the results.

Both men sent fundraising letters boasting of their efforts. It was these lies, coupled with Trump's weeks of goading, that landed thousands of violent extremists at the U.S. Capitol on Jan. 6, when they then charged the building and left five dead. Before the "Stop the Steal" crowd attacked the Capitol, Hawley famously saluted them with a raised fist.

Yet even after the bloodshed of that afternoon, Hawley, Cruz and a handful of other senators continued their charade and voted to object the election results.

Now, with Trump on trial, it will be Hawley, Cruz and others who spent weeks telling delusional MAGA enthusiasts that the election had been stolen who will be sitting in judgment of Trump. In any normal jury selection process, they would not only be struck from the jury, they'd also be given a one-way plane ticket to Peru to keep them as far away as possible from the trial.

At the constitutional convention in 1787, the nation's Founding Fathers wrestled with how to structure impeachment so it wasn't merely a tool used by opposition parties to remove a president they don't like. But the structure they implemented (impeachment by the House of Representatives, conviction by two-thirds of the Senate) didn't consider that it could be too difficult to impeach a president for obvious crimes against the United States if a significant portion of the Senate was actually driving the getaway car.

Essentially, the president's sycophants are being asked to declare his actions a crime, which would immediately make them accessories to that crime. It would be like a defendant trying to get out of a bribery charge by handing the judge a bag full of money.

Further, the history books will never see another more blatant example of juror intimidation than this "trial." Senators who vote to convict Trump can almost guarantee themselves primary opposition, most likely led by the impeached president himself. For those who think they're presidential timbre in 2024, crossing Trump at this point will effectively be dropping out of the race.

There is a Latin phrase — "nemo iudex in causa sua" — that has been a foundational legal principle for centuries. It directs that "no one is judge in his own cause."

Similarly, in the case of the sham Trump impeachment trial, no one should be a juror in their own cause, either.

USA Today

THE DEMOCRATS' FAKE MUSTACHE

February 9, 2018

"Western societies have long acknowledged that facial hair is evidently a sort of performance," wrote historian of masculinity Christopher Oldstone-Moore in the Journal of Social History in 2011. "It has been recognized as a choice, a display, and even a mask intended either to disguise flaws or assert a character type."

Enter hirsute Randy Bryce, Democratic candidate for Wisconsin's 1st Congressional District and notable cookie duster enthusiast. Bryce, who has dubbed himself "Iron Stache," has gained national attention in his quest to knock off Republican House speaker Paul Ryan. By emphasizing his robust lip sweater, Bryce has tried to imbue his image with all of the positive connotations mustaches confer—that he's an authentic, working-class champion of the little guy.

Bryce, a 53-year-old former union ironworker and Army veteran, is trying to parlay this blue-collar aesthetic into electoral success—and given the titan he's trying to unseat, his efforts are getting plenty of attention. Writer Anthony Breznican tweeted that Bryce was "genetically engineered from Bruce Springsteen songs." The wry American Mustache Institute nominated him for their 2017-18 Robert Goulet award for "Mustached American of the Year."

But it was a heartstring-plucking YouTube video Bryce released last June that began his rapid rise to national prominence and saw him featured in the pages of virtually every prominent left-wing publication in America. In fact, Bryce's rise was too sudden—soon after his announcement, the vaunted Iron Stache appeared on CNN and looked lost in the bright lights. The media rookie stammered his way into endorsing a $32 trillion tax increase to pay for single-payer health care as incredulous hosts John Berman and Poppy Harlow tried to lead him to a cogent answer; clearly, he had less than an iron-clad grip on his talking points.

Nevertheless, Bryce began to gain attention from the Hollywood set desperate to reestablish contact with America's working-class voters. Sex and the City star Cynthia Nixon showed up at a Bryce fundraiser held at a Manhattan cocktail bar. Whoopi Goldberg name-checked him on The View. Cringe-inducing interviews with comedians Samantha Bee and Sarah Silverman soon followed.

(Sample Silverman question: "You're a dad, a union leader, you're Polish and you're Mexican and your sister's a teacher and your dad's a cop, you're a cancer survivor and you're adopted and you're a veteran—how do we get more good people like you to run?" Frost-Nixon it was not.)

Yet it has been Bryce's relationship with one of America's most prominent public inebriates, comedian Chelsea Handler, that has brought him the most attention. Handler jumped on the Iron Stache bandwagon and last September posted a group photo of herself and actresses Aisha Tyler and Mary McCormack posing with Bryce, each woman sporting a fake mustache. Since then, Handler has tweeted in support of Bryce to her nearly nine million followers dozens of times; on his website, Bryce ran a contest offering entrants the chance to get a beer with Handler and Iron Stache.

On January 31, Handler was scheduled to attend a $25-per-head public fundraiser for Bryce at a music theater in liberal Madison, well outside the district for which he is running. But after Handler posted a profane tweet attacking Sen. Lindsey Graham's sexuality, the event was quietly canceled and converted to a $500-per-person event at the private home of a Madison-area tech executive.

What Bryce has not yet grasped is that his big-money Hollywood friends are using him far more than he's using them. His savvy working-man image has allowed coastal elites to take a guy who has lost three local elections—one of them a Democratic primary—and use him to burnish their own blue-collar-friendly credentials. He is simply a walk-on performer in their community theater production of Democracy, the Musical. (Prior to her adoption of Iron Stache, Handler's most notable cause was posting topless pictures of herself on Instagram to push the "#FreeTheNipple" movement.)

Bryce is nationally known because of who he's running against, and celebrities want everyone to know they're taking an active role in #Resisting Paul Ryan. Much like the white supremacist Paul Nehlen, who parlayed his quixotic GOP primary challenges to Ryan into national notoriety, Bryce is earning fame more as a tribute to his opponent's political prowess than to his own.

In fact, it's not even certain Ryan is running again, having yet to commit to being a candidate in 2018. Recent reports that the speaker was thinking about quitting prompted Bryce to issue a series of groan-inducing tweets suggesting that the power of his mustache was the impetus for Ryan's indecision.

What no collection of comedians and starlets can paper over is the fact that Bryce is, at best, a third-tier candidate in a district Ryan has never won by less than double-digits. It's not even clear he will make it out of the Democratic primary against high school English teacher Cathy Myers. His fame is simply the triumph of marketing over substance; the Democrats' mustache is made of astroturf.

After months of uniformly positive media following Bryce's announcement video, Milwaukee Journal Sentinel reporter Daniel Bice began looking into the candidate's personal finances. Bice found that in 2015, the state had placed a lien on Bryce's property for failing to pay child support for the 11-year-old son he featured prominently in his first video advertisement. Bryce didn't fully pay off the $1,257 owed to his ex-wife until two months after he had declared his candidacy.

Weeks later, Bryce paid off another $4,200 loan that had been delinquent for 15 years. In 2004, Bryce borrowed nearly $1,800 from his then-girlfriend in order to buy a car. But he stiffed her, leading to a court judgment against him that he only recently paid back with interest.

Last weekend, Bryce's name popped up in a New York Times article listing notable people who, attempting to seem more popular than they are, had purchased Twitter followers from a shady online vendor. Bryce's spokesperson conceded that before he became a candidate, he had paid "about $10-20" to buy "1,000 to 1,500" followers," as he was "trying out blogging at the time."

It was just another example of how the Randy Bryce mystique has been built on a foundation of mustache wax. Bryce frequently rips Ryan for being a tool of his "wealthy donors" but has himself raised nearly seven times as much money from New York and California as he has from Wisconsin; on the night of Donald Trump's first State of the Union address, Bryce even paid $1,500 to run a television advertisement in Seattle and San Francisco, far from the southern Wisconsin district where he's running. (Bryce has defended this course because "that's where a lot of money comes in from.")

In the months following Donald Trump's 2016 general election win, Democrats began plotting new strategies to win back voters in America's heartland who live check-to-check. Randy Bryce is the Frankenstein monster of those strategy meetings; if he appears to be straight out of central casting, it's because he is. Bryce is simply an empty mustache cast in Nancy Pelosi's Hardhat Revue.

Give the Democrats credit—it is actually bold to hang a candidate's aura on his flavor saver, an adornment so out of favor politically that no major party presidential nominee has sported one since Thomas E. Dewey in 1948. But one must look no further than the president to recognize that these are unprecedented times, and the left clearly thinks they have manufactured the perfect Trump antidote.

Even if it's obvious Randy Bryce is just a disguise.

The Weekly Standard

CHAPTER FIVE:
JUDICIAL ARGLE-BARGLE

THE MOST LIKELY FRIENDSHIP

February 16, 2016

Following the death of conservative Supreme Court titan Antonin Scalia, progressives largely stuck to the Latin maxim de mortuis nil nisi bonum, or "Of the dead, nothing unless good." (There were, sadly, some predictable exceptions.)

Finding difficulty singing the praise of such an ardent opponent of, say, racial preferences, the left instead found goodness in Scalia's relationship with other progressives. Most notably, stories about Scalia's longtime relationship with fellow Justice Ruth Bader Ginsburg were retold, coloring the conservative with a humanity the left often found lacking in his withering dissents.

After the shocking news of Scalia's death spread, CNN, the New York Daily News, Yahoo, BuzzFeed, and the Daily Mail quickly posted stories about how "unlikely" Ginsburg and Scalia's friendship was.

True, Scalia once called the duo of New Yorkers the "oddest of couples." But for those on the outside, there's nothing at all "unlikely" about a friendship that spans ideological differences. If someone thinks having a dear friend of a different political persuasion renders that relationship "unlikely," that person would be best served to go out and make some new friends.

Ginsburg herself has said her relationship with Scalia was often difficult. Following a 2004 death penalty case in which Scalia savaged the Court majority in a typically aggressive dissent, Ginsburg said, "I love him. But sometimes I'd like to strangle him."

Most of us have people in our lives that we'd often like to pile-drive, but who we deeply revere. That doesn't make our relationships at all "unlikely," it makes them the norm. Granted, there may be added stress on ideological opponents whose job it is to publicly take the bark off one another in written opinions. But this newspaper's editorial board often writes pieces that make my eyes roll out of my head - and yet there has never been a terse word spoken between us.

I certainly don't want to hold myself up as any kind of standard of purity on this measure, however — I often fall short of this bipartisanship standard. Sometimes, I'll hear an acquaintance say something so backward, so outright false, that I mutter to myself, "how can I ever be friends with someone who believes something like that?"

Clearly, Ginsburg wrestled with this in her relationship with Scalia. "I was fascinated by him because he was so intelligent and so amusing," she once said. "You could still resist his position, but you just had to like him."

That doesn't mean one has to adhere to this standard when others aren't being intelligent or amusing. When I heard of Scalia's death, I was at one of my kids' basketball games, and when I let the nearby parents know, one pumped his fist and yelled, "this is great!" The news already had me feeling like I had been punched in the stomach — his antics made me want to reciprocate the sensation.

I'd like to think, however, the parent's celebration was a matter of personal boorishness and not ideology. Just last week, Madison's Capital Times ran a story about what it's like being a conservative in heavily liberal Madison, and how people frequently adapt their relationships to preserve comity. In anonymous corners of cities all over America, Scalia-Ginsburg relationships blossom without the glare of media coverage.

The bottom line is, as real people wandering around and bumping into each other in the world, we share about 98% of the experience of being humans. If the remaining political two percent forces you out of a friendship, then you are the one that's poorer as a result.

Milwaukee Journal Sentinel

'JUSTICE SCALIA ATE ALL THE OTHERS.'

February 17, 2016

"There is hardly a political question in the United States which does not sooner or later turn into a judicial one," wrote Alexis de Tocqueville in 1835. Nearly two centuries later, it is a statement that informs the upcoming fight to replace recently deceased Supreme Court Justice Antonin Scalia.

The existential battle over whether he should be replaced with a year left in President Barack Obama's term would likely have horrified Scalia, as he perpetually rued the expanded scope of authority the court had seized in recent years. As judges more frequently substituted personal preference for textual interpretation, the Supreme Court began to look more like a legislature, and thus more a part of the political end of the lawmaking process.

"Now, something very fundamental has changed," Scalia said in 2005. "What we originalists...have been saying...for a long time is that you cannot adopt a theory that the Constitution is evolving and the Supreme Court will tell you what it means from age to age. You cannot do that without causing the Supreme Court to become a very political institution."

It is this politicization that has landed America in the spot in which it is now mired. Following Scalia's death last week, U.S. Senate Republicans have vowed to block any replacement Obama might send to them for their advice and consent.

Democrats, pretending that they wouldn't do exactly the same thing if it were a Republican president making a nomination to fill the seat of one of the nation's most legendary progressive justices, have feigned outrage. Senate Minority Leader Harry Reid has risibly implored Republicans to stop their "nakedly partisan obstruction," perhaps forgetting, for instance, Democratic attempts to filibuster the nomination of Justice Samuel Alito in 2006.

In fact, historically, only 124 of the 160 nominations made by presidents have been approved by the Senate. Of the 36 who didn't make it, 25 never received any confirmation vote at all. Democrats are fond of pointing out that Justice Anthony Kennedy was approved in a presidential election year, but fail to mention Kennedy was only nominated after Democrats put the eminently qualified Judge Robert Bork through a wood chipper for four months.

But this battle to the death only exists because as the court has evolved, Tocqueville's observation has become more intensely true. Who sits on the Supreme Court often determines who will live or die, who can own guns, who can speak during political campaigns, who can marry and who is allowed to be born.

There are few nooks and crannies in which courts now refuse to stick their noses. And the more justices untether themselves from the original meaning of the text of the Constitution, the more crucial they become to the political process. "The question, 'What does society want?' Is not a lawyer's question," Scalia once said. "It is a legislator's question."

And there is a cost to the court soaking up so many disputes that belong in legislatures, not in courtrooms. Arguments that should be had between voters and lawmakers are now co-opted by the courts, leaving the public less engaged and more poorly informed.

Following a speech at Louisiana State University a few years ago, a student approached Scalia and told him he had named a pet fish after the justice. "Oh, you've named him 'Nino,'" said Scalia, citing his lifelong nickname.

"No," said the student. "I've named him 'Justice Scalia.'"

Another law professor interjected, asking the student, "Do you have other fish named after all the justices?"

"No," said the student. "Justice Scalia ate all the others."

In death, as in life, Scalia continues to dominate the public debate, both with his words and his prescience. He would have loved nothing more than for the nomination of his replacement to avoid becoming a political war. And it wouldn't be if more fundamental questions were left to politics, where he always knew they belonged.

Milwaukee Journal Sentinel

THE SECRET PERSON WHO COULD UNITE THE GOP

July 20, 2016

[Ed. note: This was written from the 2016 Republican National Convention in Cleveland.]

It is perhaps serendipitous that the city in which a divided Republican Party is holding its national convention was once called "Cleaveland." Founded in 1796, the city of Cleveland was named after land surveyor Moses Cleaveland, a man for whom there is no known likeness. Paintings of Cleaveland exist, but they are all based on written descriptions of his appearance.

It is apt that another person is dominating the RNC this week for whom no likeness exists. While Donald Trump commands most of the headlines, there is a secret, unknown man or woman out there who is profoundly affecting the presidential race. In fact, this person is so unknown, he or she doesn't even know they are altering the course of American politics.

That person is, of course, whomever President Donald Trump might eventually appoint to the U.S. Supreme Court. And that person's profile looms heavy at the RNC — it seems the most important person to the convention isn't actually in Cleveland. He or she has been mentioned frequently in convention speeches; on Tuesday night, Ben Carson warned that Clinton "would appoint Supreme Court justices, she would appoint federal judges, and that would have a deleterious effect on what happens for generations to come." Senate Majority Leader Mitch McConnell urged voters to let Republicans "put justices on the Supreme Court who cherish our Constitution."

Of course, courts have featured heavily in the past. In the tumultuous 1968 campaign, Richard Nixon openly criticized the excesses of the liberal Warren Court, believing the court too often sided with society's "criminal forces" against its "peace forces." Nixon sought more conservative justices, which would see "their duty as interpreting law and not making law" and not serve as "superlegislators with a free hand to impose their social and political viewpoints upon the American people."

But 2016 is perhaps even more urgent than 1968. With a tenuous 4-4 conservative-liberal split (depending on how many energy drinks moderate conservative Anthony Kennedy has had on any given day), the American people will be voting on the direction of the Supreme Court when they pick their president. And they won't be deciding how they want their court to operate in some undefined future — they will shape the court right now.

And despite the rampant dyspepsia at the RNC about Trump as the nominee, there is one thing upon which every attendee can agree: Even if America can tolerate four years of Hillary Clinton as commander-in-chief, the nation cannot bear a progressive Supreme Court for the next quarter-century.

Forget the seat vacated by Justice Antonin Scalia's death; three other justices are nearly 80 years old or older. The next president could be picking four new justices during his or her next term.

That is not to suggest, however, that we know anything about who Trump might appoint to the nation's highest court. In May, Trump released a list of possible candidates he would consider for the Supreme Court, likely an attempt to allay the fears of conservatives who would welcome a judge such as Diane Sykes of the 7th Circuit Court of Appeals. But given that the list also included names of jurists who had also openly mocked Trump on social media, it is worth a pause to wonder how deeply researched the list may have been.

Further, it was Trump who earlier this year said judges "sign bills," and who called into question the impartiality of a judge overseeing his Trump University case because of the judge's Mexican heritage. As the joke goes, it seems Trump's primary knowledge of the judiciary has come from his experience in divorce and bankruptcy courts.

If Trump wants to make the Supreme Court an issue, he has to hope two conflicting ideas merge. He has to hope that a nation serious enough to care about its judicial branch is also unserious enough to elect Donald Trump to lead its executive one.

Milwaukee Journal Sentinel

NOBODY IS SCALIA

February 17, 2017

The day President Trump nominated appeals court Judge Neil Gorsuch to the United States Supreme Court, The New York Times offered that Trump "has chosen a judge who not only admires the justice he would replace but also in many ways resembles him." The paper added that Gorsuch "shares Justice Scalia's legal philosophy, talent for vivid writing and love of the outdoors."

In related news, I share much with actor Ryan Gosling; we are both Caucasian males, both over 35 years old, and neither of us can sing.

Drawing comparisons between the old guard and tantalizing new talent is understandable; it imputes the new arrival with a set of characteristics that it would take far too long to explain individually. It's why Bruno Mars has to answer questions about being the "new Michael Jackson" (to which he rightfully shudders), and why dozens of otherwise talented NBA players have disappointed fans by failing to be the "next Michael Jordan.

That's because when making comparisons, it's important to understand time and context. Indeed, there have been plenty of conscientious folk warblers in the past few decades, but you can only do Bob Dylan once. His poetry and countercultural politics can only be understood in the context of the early Vietnam War and civil rights era. Young music fans of today can go to any number of coffee shops to see a solo artist with an acoustic guitar, but in Greenwich Village in 1961, it was a revolutionary act.

This is why comparisons to Antonin Scalia fall short. When "Nino" took the bench in 1986, he ushered in a new era of judicial conservatism, almost single-handedly dragging the court system to his view of "originalism." For conservatives, Scalia was the Ronald Reagan of the judiciary, shaking America out of its decades-long affair with New Deal-ism. And he did so with equal parts genius, bombast and panache.

In other words, you can only do Scalia once.

Naturally, all new conservatives will be declared the heir to Scalia's originalist throne. During his confirmation hearings in 2005, Samuel Alito was derisively coined "Scalito" by his opponents. And nary a profile shows up that doesn't mention Gorsuch's admiration of Scalia's originalist temperament.

But in the terms following three decades of the liberal Warren Court and only slightly less liberal Burger Court, Scalia's adherence to judicial originalism was seen as a legalistic parlor trick. "It is a view that feigns self-effacing deference to the specific judgments of those who forged our original social compact," sneered Justice William Brennan in 1985, adding, "But in truth it is little more than arrogance cloaked as humility."

Even Scalia knew how controversial his philosophy was. He once said originalism was such a minority position in academia and the legal profession that he was often asked when he became an originalist "as though it is some kind of weird affliction that seizes some people." He suggested the tone of these questions was the same as if he had been asked, "When did you start eating human flesh?"

But after 30 years on the Court, Scalia's insistence that laws be interpreted as they were intended at the time of enactment became the dominant ideology among the Court's justices. This adherence to original intent is now a requirement for Republican-nominated judges, who must denounce justices who "make law" rather than interpret it.

At a roundtable discussion honoring Scalia's life in September of 2016, even Justice Elena Kagan — a judicial progressive — conceded that Scalia should have "declared victory" for changing the Court's philosophy towards statutory interpretation. Nowadays, "Nobody on the court— left or right — could think you could write a decision that didn't really even mention the statutory text," Kagan said, noting the modern Court's diminishing reliance on legislative records and bill histories.

"Nobody on the Court would just think it was enough to say, 'Well, this kind of makes sense as we see it,'" Kagan added, saying that change was made in the prior decades "because of Justice Scalia."

Beyond changing the central temperament of the Court, Scalia did so with an erudite writing style that was rarely matched in the history of the judiciary. His critics often point to his withering dissents as examples of mean-spirited bitterness, but they were often when he was at his stylistic best. His confrontational writing style was the secret sauce that propelled him into the upper echelon of memorable justices; Scalia without his curmudgeonly demeanor is like a calorie-free donut – good in theory, but lacking what makes it best.

So while more recent conservative appointees may believe in originalism or have "lively" writing styles, nobody is Antonin Scalia. They may all be wearing the same ideological robes, but they are of a material Scalia crafted himself.

Milwaukee Journal Sentinel

JUDICIAL HYSTERICS ARE NOW THE STANDARD

February 1, 2017

On July 23, 1990, in front of a half-empty White House briefing room, President George H.W. Bush announced his pick to replace Justice William Brennan on the Supreme Court. Bush said David Souter, a little known New Hampshire state Supreme Court judge and former state attorney general, was "committed to interpreting, not making the law."

"He recognizes the proper role of judges in upholding the democratic choices of the people through their elected representatives, with constitutional constraints," Bush continued.

Before the news media's flash bulbs had cooled, the professional outrage machine was out for blood. The liberal People for the American Way unearthed a document written by Souter in which he referred to abortion as "the killing of unborn children," which prompted the president of the National Organization for Women, Molly Yard, to describe Souter as "almost Neanderthal."

"For the first time in history, the Supreme Court is on the brink of taking away a fundamental right: the right to choose," said Kate Michelman, executive director of the National Abortion Rights Action League.

The desperate attempts to torpedo the Souter nomination often veered into the absurd. Liberal groups assailed Souter for once arguing, unsuccessfully, that it was constitutionally permissible to fly the American flag at half-staff on Good Friday and that New Hampshire could force residents to carry the state slogan, "Live Free or Die," on their license plates.

One doesn't need to be steeped in Supreme Court arcana to know how this story ended. Souter couldn't have been more sympathetic to progressive legal causes, writing decisions as if wearing a pink knit hat. Barely two years after his confirmation, Souter authored the most prominent abortion decision since Roe v. Wade, 1992's Planned Parenthood v. Casey. In that case, the majority opinion found that regulations on abortion would be unconstitutional if they imposed an "undue burden" on a woman's right to an abortion. In that opinion, Souter wrote, "Our adoption of the undue burden analysis does not disturb the central holding of Roe v. Wade, and we reaffirm that holding."

Proving once again that the seriousness of political rhetoric is inversely proportionate to the gravity of the office an individual seeks, the detached left has once again dusted off the Supreme Court obstruction manual. Following President Trump's pick of U.S. Court of Appeals Judge Neil Gorsuch to replace the irreplaceable Justice Antonin Scalia, House Minority Leader Nancy Pelosi leaped into action, calling the Gorsuch nomination "a very hostile appointment" and "a very bad decision, well outside the mainstream of American legal thought."

"If you breathe air, drink water, eat food, take medicine, or in any other way interact with the courts, this is a very bad decision," Pelosi said during a CNN town hall held after the announcement.

But the real action is in the Senate, which has the duty of approving Trump's pick. Democrats, projecting a mirage that they can somehow thwart the process, have vowed to subject Gorsuch to unprecedented scrutiny in the upcoming months. Democratic leader Charles Schumer of New York, who served in the Senate when Gorsuch was approved without opposition to the federal bench in 2006, said the burden is on Gorsuch to "prove himself to be within the legal mainstream."

But even before Gorsuch has had a single meeting with a U.S. senator, other Democrats were less measured. According to stalwart progressive Wisconsin Sen. Tammy Baldwin, Trump has "made it clear he has no interest in being a president for all Americans, and that he is intent on creating more division in our country." She cited Gorsuch's "deeply troubling record," particularly his rulings "against disabled students, against workers and against women's reproductive health care."

Of course, feigned outrage over Gorsuch's "divisiveness" is a stand-in for frustrations Democrats are feeling over Senate Republicans' decision to block President Obama's nomination of Judge Merrick Garland nearly a year ago. Garland was approved to the District of Columbia circuit court in 1997 by a 76 to 23 vote and was seen as a concession to Republicans, who nonetheless held the seat open for Gorsuch to eventually fill.

Few Democrats are willing to concede their opposition to Gorsuch is simply political payback; they must then engineer opposition to him by backfilling his record with well-traveled attacks. For instance, his primary ruling against "women's reproductive health care" came in the famous Hobby Lobby case, in which both Gorsuch's 10th Circuit and the Supreme Court decided that a closely held family business couldn't be forced to provide certain types of birth control to their employees if it violated the business owners' religious beliefs.

This would all be more compelling if the unhinged hysteria over Supreme Court picks weren't so predictable. During the nomination hearings for Bush appointee Samuel Alito in 2006, Alito was even quizzed about magazines to which he might have subscribed, as if his philosophy on affirmative action would somehow be swayed by an article in Cat Fancy.

In 2005, NARAL Pro-Choice America aired a television ad insinuating that Bush nominee John Roberts was somehow complicit in a 1998 abortion clinic bombing, a slander that forced it to pull the commercial off the air. Of course, Roberts would go on to uphold the central tenets of the Affordable Care Act, applying justifications for the law that Obama himself had rejected.

Even among liberals who have worked with Gorsuch, he is considered a well-respected, mainstream jurist. He even has a tart sense of humor, such as when he once dissented by quoting Charles Dickens' observation that often enough, the law can be "a ass — a idiot."

One wonders whether he thinks the same could be said for those trying to defeat his nomination before it was even announced.

Milwaukee Journal Sentinel

THE CULTURE WARS, FOUGHT ONE BAKED GOOD AT A TIME

June 5, 2018

In any traditional kitchen, the mixture of sugar, eggs, and flour means something good is about to happen. But those same ingredients have produced a great deal of consternation in America's judicial system.

In a 7-2 decision released on Monday, the U.S. Supreme Court sided with Colorado baker Jack Phillips, who in 2012, citing religious objections, refused to provide a cake for a gay wedding in the state. At the time, Colorado did not recognize same-sex marriages, and the Supreme Court had not yet issued its landmark opinion essentially legalizing same-sex marriages across America.

Monday's Masterpiece Cakeshop decision is the mirror image of the Court's 2015 Obergefell decision that overturned state and federal anti-gay marriage laws. Obergefell was a bad decision that produced a good result; conversely, this week's ruling was a legally sound decision that, at least in this Colorado instance, could lead to gay couples having to go elsewhere to get their wedding cakes made.

At first glance, the case looked like a textbook example of two rights butting heads: The right of the gay couple to be free from discrimination and the First Amendment right of the baker not to be compelled to express himself in violation of his religious principles.

But rather than address the broad array of religious freedom claims that have been percolating across the nation (many of them gay wedding-related), the majority ruled very narrowly, excoriating the Colorado Civil Rights Commission for mocking Phillips' religious beliefs. One commissioner commented that "religion has been used to justify all kinds of discrimination throughout history," citing slavery and the Holocaust as examples. This commissioner deemed it "despicable" for people "to use their religion to hurt others."

The court's decision, written by Justice Anthony Kennedy, rightly condemned the commission for denigrating Phillips' sincerely held Christian beliefs. Kennedy noted the inappropriateness of that sentiment given the commission is charged "with the solemn responsibility of fair and neutral enforcement of Colorado's anti-discrimination law — a law that protects discrimination on the basis of religion as well as sexual orientation."

As the court noted, Phillips' case lines up nicely with another contemporaneous case that had been before the Civil Rights Commission in which a customer named William Jack had, citing his religion, tried to hire three bakeries to make him a cake with a message denigrating gay persons and gay marriage. In each case, the bakeries had declined to do so, believing the message to be offensive and distasteful. The commission upheld the right of the three bakeries in refusing to bake a cake they found abhorrent, even though the customer complained it was an infringement on his religious beliefs.

In his concurring opinion, Justice Neil Gorsuch argued the faulty logic in allowing bakers to refuse to serve Jack but forcing Phillips to bake one for a same-sex couple. "Only by adjusting the dials just right — fine-tuning the level of generality up or down for each case based solely on the identity of the parties and the substance of their views," wrote Gorsuch, "can you engineer the commission's outcome, handing a win to Mr. Jack's bakers but delivering a loss to Mr. Phillips."

While the decision is a victory for religious liberty, it is likely a short-lived one. Having been decided on such a narrow thread (hence the unexpected 7-2 margin), the more expansive issue of religious freedom is almost certain to come before the court as more states see their Religious Freedom Restoration Acts challenged.

For those who believe in the right to practice one's religion without government interference, let's hope this week's decision is merely an appetizer and not itself a dessert.

Milwaukee Journal Sentinel

GOOD RESULT; BAD OPINION

July 2, 2015

Oh, to possess the mind of a progressive jurist. Unburdened by conflict, untethered to precedent, liberal minds sleep well knowing justice has been served, regardless of how it was attained.

Unfortunately for us cantankerous conservatives, even if we consider the outcome of a case to be desirable, how the outcome was reached continues to be the pea underneath our stack of mattresses.

Yet ask progressives whether a U.S. Supreme Court decision was "good," and they will simply tell you whether they agree with its outcome. On the left, saying a case that was wrongly decided had a favorable outcome is like saying you had a bad meal that tasted great; the end result is really the only point.

This was very much the case last week, when the Supreme Court invalidated state laws barring gay couples from being married. Plenty of conservatives - myself included - support full marriage equality, and would happily cast a ballot to make it happen. Laws passed through the democratic process, after all, have more standing in the court of public opinion than those imposed by the boot heel of the federal court system.

But five members of the court, lacking precedent and clear legal reasoning, declared same-sex marriage to be a "fundamental" right, thereby ending an argument that pro-gay marriage forces had been winning at a historic speed.

It is easy to praise the effect of the opinion: same sex marriages should be recognized as equal to opposite-sex marriages. But this so-called "fundamental" right that needed court intervention is being worked out in states across the nation; so far, 11 states and the District of Columbia have legalized gay marriage through the political process.

Justice Anthony Kennedy's majority opinion, aside from the fallacy of associating "marriage" with "freedom," rests on the thinnest of legal principles. While Kennedy claimed marriage was subject to the 14th Amendment's guarantee of equal protection, the Constitution makes no mention of marriage whatsoever. The court has previously prevented states from denying marriage to certain individuals (interracial couples, for instance), but last week's case was different in that it mandated the definition of "marriage" to states.

Dispensing with legal formalities, however, the court declared a right to be "fundamental" that the world hadn't really considered as recently as 15 years ago. President Barack Obama declared his support for same-sex marriage in 2012; presidential candidate Hillary Clinton discovered a constitutional right to gay marriage all the way back in April of 2015. Most notable among those gay marriage "deniers" was Justice Elena Kagan, who in 2009 declared that there "is no federal constitutional right to same-sex marriage." Kagan, of course, joined the majority opinion last week.

Of course, the dissents were immediately labeled "heartless." But if compassion were the only qualification needed to write a Supreme Court opinion, why do we bother appointing lawyers to the bench? It seems like changing one's Facebook profile picture to a rainbow flag would be a sufficient requirement.

Full legal recognition of same-sex marriages constitutes a meaningful step forward. But as long as the court continues to use "but the plaintiffs want it really bad" as a guiding legal philosophy, it will undermine the progress made on these issues.

Ripping the issue from the hands of the democratic process is merely the latest chapter in a dangerous trend. Gay marriage is worth celebrating; but as Chief Justice John Roberts says in the close of his dissent, citizens should celebrate the achievement of a desired goal, the opportunity for a new expression of commitment to a partner, and the availability of new benefits.

"But do not celebrate the Constitution," Roberts adds. "It had nothing to do with it."

Milwaukee Journal Sentinel

ROBERTS' TAXING HEALTH CARE DECISION

June 30, 2012

When the U.S. Supreme Court convened on March 27 to hear oral arguments challenging the constitutionality of the Affordable Care Act, all eyes were on mercurial Justice Anthony Kennedy. It was the moderate Kennedy who many thought was the swing vote as to whether President Barack Obama's health care plan violated the U.S. Constitution's commerce clause and, thus, whether it passed constitutional muster.

Thus, during oral arguments, it went relatively unnoticed when conservative Chief Justice John Roberts made a seemingly innocuous point about the crux of the act: whether the law's mandate that U.S. citizens had to purchase health care was enforced via a "penalty" or a "tax." "Whether you want to call it a penalty or tax just doesn't seem to make much sense. . . . what happens if you don't file the mandate on your tax return? And the answer is nothing," said Roberts.

Obama, wanting to duck the political grenade that comes with raising taxes, forcefully insisted the mandate's enforcement mechanism wasn't a tax increase. "For us to say that you've got to take a responsibility to get health insurance is absolutely not a tax increase," said Obama in 2009, comparing the act to state laws that impose penalties for not purchasing car insurance. "Nobody considers that a tax increase," said Obama.

Yet on Thursday, Roberts simultaneously rejected Obama's "tax" argument and handed the president a historic victory in upholding the constitutionality of the individual mandate. Circumventing the commerce clause concerns (whether someone engages in "commerce" by simply doing nothing), Roberts sneaked the mandate in through the doggy door - he deemed the "penalty" to be the functional equivalent of a "tax" and, therefore, upheld the law, based on Congress' constitutional authority to lay and collect taxes.

Yet in doing so, Roberts had to rewrite the ACA, making it something it was not. In passing the law, Congress could have easily classified the penalty as a "tax." Yet likely recognizing the political fallout that would follow, it actively chose not to.

Furthermore, the court has never used the concepts of "taxes" and "penalties" inter changeably; in fact, they are very different concepts. "(A) tax is an enforced contribution to provide for the support of government; a penalty . . . is an exaction imposed by statute as punishment for an unlawful act," wrote the court in 1931.

"So the question is, quite simply, whether the exaction here is imposed for violation of the law. It unquestionably is," concluded Justices Antonin Scalia, Samuel Alito, Clarence Thomas and Kennedy in their dissent Thursday.

But it was Roberts' recasting the penalty as a tax that allowed him to avoid striking down the individual mandate on commerce clause grounds, which four courts already had done (although they usually disagreed on how many other provisions of the law had to go along with the mandate). For conservatives, this is like getting away with robbing a bank, only to be sent to prison because the getaway car had expired license plates.

But in upholding the law, Roberts adhered to another precept of conservatism: that disagreements are best handled at the ballot box than in courts. Consequently, Obama's victory on Thursday might be Pyrrhic; casting his wildly unpopular health care bill as an even more wildly unpopular massive tax increase isn't exactly the good news his campaign needed. The last time Obamacare was a central campaign issue, Democrats were wiped off the map.

But whatever silver linings Roberts' opinion provided for conservatives, they are obscured by the massive dark cloud that Obamacare casts over the country. It is clear now that Congress has nearly unlimited power to manipulate our behavior and choices, as long as that power is enforced via the body's taxing power.

The bill itself, which raises taxes, changes individuals' health plans, forces large deficits and leaves health care decisions in the hands of 15 unelected bureaucrats, is now the law of the land unless conservative forces can rally to the polls.

Roberts upheld a law Congress didn't pass, using an argument many of the law's most important defenders said was flatly untrue. Thought presidential campaigns were wrought with acrimony before?

Milwaukee Journal Sentinel

FREE SPEECH PROHIBITION FUELS RHETORICAL GANGSTERS

September 10, 2013

As Al Capone neared the end of his criminal reign over Chicago, he was sanguine about his years of providing gambling, prostitutes and alcohol to the city's citizens. "Public service is my motto," Capone told a reporter in 1927, adding that he "never had to send out high pressure salesmen."

After his 1931 conviction on tax evasion, Capone was more reflective. "Prohibition has made nothing but trouble — trouble for all of us. Worst thing ever hit the country," he told a reporter in 1932.

Much of the trouble wrought by Prohibition was due to the effect it had on pushing liquor manufacture and consumption underground, where few knew who was making or drinking it. People weren't going to stop enjoying alcohol, so many people tried mixing drinks with paint thinner, leaving them blind or otherwise incapacitated. At the same time, gangsters like Capone controlled the "legitimate" liquor trade, leaving dead bodies in their wake.

One thinks that given the Prohibition example, we would have learned a lesson: Legally preventing people from doing what they will inevitably do merely drives control of that behavior into the hands of miscreants. Yet we treat political speech as if it were some poisonous hooch that needs to be shielded from polite society.

For years, so-called good government groups have been pushing to reduce the amount of money in politics. Money purchases ads and airtime and facilitates political speech. The U.S. Supreme Court has held consistently that money is functionally equivalent to speech, since limiting the amount people can donate or spend on politics curtails their ability to disseminate their political messages.

These groups have opposed a bill working its way through the Wisconsin Legislature that would double the amount state candidates can accept from individual donors. The caps, which haven't been changed in nearly 40 years, currently allow Assembly candidates to raise $500 per individual, Senate candidates $1,000 and gubernatorial candidates $10,000 per person. The bill passed the Assembly and awaits Senate action.

The liberal Wisconsin Democracy Campaign, joining with 14 other groups, believes the bill "couldn't be more out of touch with what the people want" and that it will "allow big money to further drown out the voices of state voters."

But the exact opposite is true. For years, groups like the WDC have complained about so-called third party groups spending millions during election season, running anonymous ads attacking politicians. It's the foundation of their virulent opposition to the Supreme Court's Citizens United decision that allowed corporations and unions to support or oppose candidates without disclosing their donors.

The bill in the Legislature would take more of that money out of the political speech "black market" and bring it out into the public, making it regulated and reportable.

In the recent past, efforts to suck money out of the political process have failed catastrophically. As was the case with Prohibition, unintended consequences immediately emerged.

For instance, the Bipartisan Campaign Reform Act of 2002 (known as McCain-Feingold), sought to ban corporations and unions from "electioneering communications" during campaign season — but instead drove money away from candidates and political parties and into the hands of shady third parties. The law did nothing to curtail spending in elections and only served to make sure less accountable sources were spending it.

These unaccountable groups have been active in Wisconsin. Take the left-wing Greater Wisconsin Committee, which in 2010 falsely charged that then-gubernatorial candidate Scott Walker had voted to "deny women mammograms." Later, the group tried to tie state Supreme Court Justice David Prosser to a child abuse scandal involving a priest that took place 33 years before Prosser's 2011 re-election bid — a last-minute smear tactic that appears to have backfired.

Rather than handing the right to political speech over to groups like GWC, the state should allow candidates to be more in charge of their own messages. Generally, candidates are more temperate when their names are attached to an advertisement; allowing them the ability to raise more transparent funds will lessen the influence of unaccountable third parties.

There will never be a way to keep money out of politics. Instead of curtailing free speech, we should push for more transparency and regulated money, rather than letting political Al Capones run roughshod.

Milwaukee Journal Sentinel

THANK GOD AMENDING THE CONSTITUTION IS HARD

October 8, 2013

In a recent interview with New York Magazine, conservative U.S. Supreme Court Justice Antonin Scalia offered an interesting answer when asked what he thought the "flaws" with the U.S. Constitution were. Scalia said he would amend the portion of the document that allows for its own amendment.

Scalia said the amendment process "was not originally a flaw," but the country has changed enough to render changing the Constitution virtually impossible. "With the divergence in size between California and Rhode Island — I figured it out once," Scalia said. "I think if you picked the smallest number necessary for a majority in the least populous states, something like less than 2% of the population can prevent a constitutional amendment."

Scalia's answer is an interesting one, because it softens a common conservative taunt: That is, if judicial liberals want something in the Constitution, they should pass an amendment rather than simply reading it into the document's text.

It is a safe challenge for conservatives to offer, primarily because amending the U.S. Constitution is so difficult. It takes the agreement of 290 members of the U.S. House of Representatives, 67 senators, and both houses of 38 state legislatures. Consequently, it has been 43 years since a constitutional amendment was ratified by both Houses of Congress and by a sufficient number of states. (The 27th Amendment was ratified by the magical 38th state in 1992, but was originally sent to the states for approval in 1791, when there were no time limits for ratification.)

In fact, the 43 years that has passed since ratification of the 26th Amendment is tied for the second longest period in American history without amending the Constitution. Between the 12th and 13th Amendments, 61 years passed, and an identical 43 years passed between the 15th and 16th Amendments. Yet there is no current plausible constitutional change as far as the eye can see, and it is entirely possible America could blow through the 61-year record 18 years from now.

Making changes to the Constitution more realistic does have appeal for judicial conservatives; it makes the challenge to enact public policy through amendment more than a rhetorical jab. If the Constitution could be amended more regularly, it would provide a pressure relief valve; judges wouldn't be forced to invent rights and privileges that aren't found in the original document — they could instead urge fundamental societal change through the democratic process, where it belongs.

In recent years, the court has operated under Charles Evans Hughes' blunt dictum in 1907 that, "the constitution is what the Supreme Court says it is." (Fortunately, the court has not deemed the Constitution to be a salami sandwich, although that would make the U.S. both the world's oldest and most delicious constitutional democracy.) Pushing more responsibility for saying what the Constitution is out of judicial chambers and into the hands of voters could foster a more robust debate when it is time to make fundamental changes.

But while it is true that the founders couldn't envision the current fractured state of the union, they obviously intended for the amendment process to be difficult. Only the most broadly accepted changes to our fundamental document should be allowed; it shouldn't be left to the whims of a capricious public. In fact, if anything, the fact that it has only been amended 27 times is a testament to the original Constitution's genius.

In fact, more lax state constitutional amendment processes show us what a mess it can be when constitutions simply act as enhanced statute books. In states such as California and Colorado, voters have enacted constitutional changes via public referendum that often conflict with one another, leaving the courts to sort out the confusion.

Here in Wisconsin, where a constitutional change must pass two successive legislatures and a public referendum, voters and lawmakers rushed to the polls in 2006 to codify a constitutional ban on gay marriage; only seven years later, that decision looks as antiquated as a Limp Bizkit tattoo.

(The only other option provided by Article V of the Constitution would be to hold a constitutional convention, if requested by the legislatures of at least 34 states — but rewriting an entirely new Constitution in 2013 would be an absolute freak show. "We will now hear testimony from a group asserting its right to squirt lotion on you as you walk through the mall.")

The key to counteracting judicial activism is to do exactly what Scalia does best; eruditely make the case for originalism and textualism in our courts. Anyone who thinks the public won't act capriciously if given more flexibility to amend the Constitution should be forced to drink booze made of paint thinner in a dank speakeasy.

Milwaukee Journal Sentinel

CHAPTER SIX:
PANIC IN THE IVORY TOWER

A YEAR OF DISCONTENT ON CAMPUS

February 6, 2020

When students settled in to a sociology class on the University of Wisconsin-Madison campus on September 14, 2018, the professor started describing certain theories he said he was eager to critique in a proposal that he was thinking of sending to the sociology department.

Yet, the professor added, some theories and beliefs couldn't be critiqued; he called them "sacred cows" within academia.

This statement angered one student, who complained to university administrators that use of the term "sacred cows" was inappropriate.

"The way he used this term was offensive to me, because in some cultures, cows are deemed to be sacred, and his employment of the term as a snarky rhetorical device demonstrates the lack of awareness or concern this person has towards future colleagues and students who might be from those countries," the student wrote.

"I grew up in India, and found his use of this terminology to be condescending and racist," the student added. "I would not feel safe around him, and feel that his confident lack of awareness perpetuates the unsafe white-centric and white-supremacist environment of UW-Madison."

The student filed this complaint using the university's "Bias or Hate" reporting website, which encourages campus community members to report any uncomfortable interaction they encounter on campus. Students may file behavior reports anonymously against other students for words uttered in private interactions, or may report professors for words said in front of a classroom. The site began taking reports at the school in 2016, at a cost of $60,000 per year.

During the 2018-19 school year, 107 bias and hate complaints were filed at UW-Madison, each of which I retrieved through a freedom of information request. While the information identifying students and professors was redacted, the breadth and scope of what campus community members are willing to report one another for is revealing.

UW-Madison isn't alone—In 2017, the Foundation for Individual Rights in Education found 232 American schools with Bias Response Teams. This number is almost certainly outdated—in 2020, it is difficult to find any major public university that doesn't have some sort of reporting structure, whether they call it a campus "climate," "bias," or "caring" system. And with students defining themselves both by their group affiliations and victim status, such structures allow them to portray their campuses as snakepits of hate and vituperation, where discrimination runs rampant.

The UW-Madison website itself offers an unwieldy, broad definition of "bias" incidents that should be reported to administrators.

"Bias," according to the school, comprises "Single or multiple acts toward an individual, group, or their property that are so severe, pervasive, and objectively offensive that they create an unreasonably intimidating, hostile, or offensive work, learning, or program environment, and that one could reasoNably conclude are based upon actual or perceived age, race, color, creed, religion, gender identity or expression, ethnicity, national origin, disability, veteran status, sexual orientation, political affiliation, marital status, spirituality, cultural, socio-economic status, or any combination of these or other related factors."

Of course, such a system lets individual students decide what violates their own feelings of propriety.

In some ways, Bias Response Teams are more stifling than the pernicious campus speech codes of the 1980s—they turn classrooms, dorms, and student unions into surveillance states, where thoughts expressed in private conversations can make their way into the hands of a university diversity administrator. The university is effectively imposing a nebulous speech code, then crowdsourcing its enforcement. In fact, at the UW-Madison, the campus Bias Response Advisory Board includes two members of the UW Police Department —making the board a literal "speech police."

"Our campus is home to students from a wide variety of backgrounds, identities and points of view—that provides opportunities for learning but also, sometimes, for misunderstanding and conflict," UW-Madison spokeswoman Meredith McGlone told me. "The bias response system is a resource for all students to talk through challenging situations they may encounter."

On September 4, 2018, a UW-Madison student was watching video of an online course being taken by her roommate. On the video, a professor was making the case that it is often difficult for students with disabilities to understand and process information—to hammer this point home, the professor began speaking "in a way that mimics those with differing mental abilities," according to the student.

"At first, my roommate believed this was how he was actually going to lecture, then, a pair of puppets are shown in the video describing how terrible this professor would be as a lecturer," the student reported. "He says, 'Oh no, this is terrible' and 'this is going to be awful' or 'can you imagine a whole semester with this guy?'"

"We were extremely offended as my roommate herself has a speech impediment, but also for any person living with a disability," the student added, writing the video "far surpasses the border of what is appropriate."

"The slowed speech, gestures he uses, and the fact that he later shows the contrast between what he presented and how he will actually present himself led me to believe this wasn't just a joke gone too far."

Also in September 2018, a student reported a flyer distributed by the school's Morgridge Center encouraging students to vote. The flyer for the "Big Ten Voting Challenge," in which the conference's schools compete for the highest Election Day turnout, featured a photo from a Wisconsin Badgers football game in which all the students are holding their arms forward and above their heads.

"It shows students for voting materials very nazi / hate group vibe," the student reported.

On September 27, an adviser for the Multicultural Learning Community Floor in a campus dorm noticed that some construction paper decorations taped to the office's front door had been rearranged in the shape of a penis.

"As a mentor, it is my responsibility to help the residents when they come across life's challenges," the advisor reported. "Up until last night, there was no physical evidence of vandalism, microaggression, or racism. However, now there is. ... This is not okay."

At the end of a class in October, a student asked a professor to acknowledge that it was Indigenous People's Day. The professor answered that it wasn't necessary because the class would be discussing the topic the following Thursday.

This answer was unsatisfactory for the student, who sarcastically noted, "As if our progression only exists in academic settings, and is not to be acknowledged when it is actually happening in real life."

"This class as a whole has been one of the only things preventing me from feeling fully mentally healthy because of the nature of the class and the lack of indigenous representation," the student reported.

"Native students are silenced by white professors and TAs in this American Indian Studies Department, and this is not addressed, especially because the Director of the program is a white anthropologist. ... These classrooms are not safe spaces for indigenous students."

In reading more than 1,000 bias complaints from over 20 public colleges in the past year, I found complaints about professors to be one of the most frequent reports filed. Typically, a student will hear something from a professor with which they disagree, then report them for failing to offer a trigger warning when discussing sexual assault, for engaging in transphobia for mixing up a student's pronouns, or for making comments the student deems to be racially insensitive.

At some universities, professors who are on the receiving end of these complaints are never notified there has been a report filed against them. Sometimes when a complaint is lodged, a public record is created of their transgression, which can lead to a letter being added to their file. These notations can hurt professors either seeking tenure or looking for jobs at more prestigious universities. Often, there is no appeal process, with the professors unable to tell their side of the story.

Advocates for bias teams argue the systems often have no investigative or enforcement mechanisms. In an article for Inside Higher Education last June, pro-bias response researchers wrote that BRTs "do not shut down free speech or charge into classrooms to stop offensive statements from faculty members or students."

But in many cases, bias teams do investigate alleged "hate" speech. A controversial statement at dinner with a fellow student can earn an undergraduate a visit from a diversity counselor. Students have been called to testify in front of panels or have been forced to attend diversity workshops for things they've said on campus. Complaints are recorded in public files that can be permanent.

All of this has the effect of chilling speech on campus, as students who are anti-abortion, support traditional marriage, or argue in favor of stricter immigration policy can find themselves reported to the administration for making campus "unsafe." Rather than being pulled before a diversity counselor, students are better off simply keeping quiet if their views do not comport to the day's accepted progressive canon.

These tools can also leave instructors in a nearly impossible position. In November 2018, at a Zumba class at UW-Madison, a female student left her place during the workout and sat down. When the instructor asked her what was wrong, she said she was too hot—so the instructor turned on a large fan at the front of the class.

This, however, made several of the women at the front of the class too cold, so they went to turn the fan off. The instructor yelled at them for doing so, which brought charges of racism.

"The fact that that one girl who was not feeling well was White, and that the three of us were Asian, has led me to think uneasily about whether the incident came from racism and made me uneasy," a student wrote in a complaint against the instructor.

"Even if it was not about race, what [name redacted] did was neither appropriate nor professional, for she had failed to pay equal attention to all her students, some of whom was White and the rest Asian."

Later that month, a female professor was teaching students a historical political example of a U.S. senator wanting to hinder the progress of people of color. The professor referred to a 1981 case in which a senator used the "n-word," saying the specific word out loud.

"She did not at any point address the impact of this word or the negativity of it or that she even said it," a student complained. "It was not necessary to read this word and it was not to make a point about the word at all," wrote the student, adding that it came off "as extremely offensive."

"This does not create a safe environment for ANY student and does NOT represent UW," a different student complained in a separate report made the same day. "If this instructor gets away with this then who knows what happens next? Death threats to students?"

And sometimes students are merely offended by a professor's opinion being different from theirs. For example, a nursing professor was reported for expressing a sentiment "that it was 'refreshing' to see a different political group (Republican majority) as the majority when students' [sic] presented political demographic statistics of a zip code."

"Although, this may seem like a simple comment and observation, this causes concern due to the current political climate and the policy initiatives of the Republican party," the student complained.

The student alleged the professor "creates a negative space to allow microaggressions and is a strong example of white fragility."

In December, a male professor was giving a lecture on policing. "Throughout the lecture I felt as though he was constantly giving policemen and woman in many cases of police brutality the benefit of the doubt," complained a student. "I feel as though his teaching style toward this specific lecture was very bias [sic] and hurtful."

"Personally, I feel as though he has regard for what other people have to say, but concerned about whether his opinion is right and justified," the student said.

Pushback against bias response teams has come most notably in the form of lawsuits filed by Speech First, a pro-free speech nonprofit organization that has gone to court a total of four times in the past two years in an effort to dismantle bias reporting systems.

In October 2019, the University of Michigan settled with Speech First, disbanding its "Bias Response Team" and eliminating penalties the BRT could previously administer for speech violations. Before the Speech First lawsuit, the Michigan speech code prohibited "harassment" and "bullying," and further increased the potential penalties if such actions were motivated by "bias." Under this code, a student could be subject to significant penalties, up to and including expulsion, if another student perceives their speech as "demeaning" or "bothersome."

"The most important indication of bias is your own feelings," read the school's website.

Per the settlement, the University of Michigan has instead replaced its Bias Response Team with a "Campus Climate Support" program that does not contact the subjects of complaints, only reporting parties.

Speech First has also filed lawsuits against bias teams at the University of Illinois, the University of Texas at Austin, and most recently at Iowa State University. All three of these lawsuits are ongoing. Each of the lawsuits argue that incentivizing students to inform on one another constitutes prior restraint on political speech that would otherwise be protected by the First Amendment to the U.S. Constitution.

"The primary purpose of our bias response system is not to investigate or punish but to provide support and promote educational conversations," Meredith McGlone, the UW-Madison spokeswoman, told me. "That is consistent with First Amendment protections."

McGlone argued Wisconsin's bias response system is different than Michigan's in that reports are handled by a professional staff member. She noted Wisconsin also has an advisory group that meets monthly to "discuss recent reports and broader issues and concerns."

"Our campus is home to students from a wide variety of backgrounds, identities and points of view—that provides opportunities for learning but also, sometimes, for misunderstanding and conflict," McGlone told me. "The bias response system is a resource for all students to talk through challenging situations they may encounter," she said.

In February, McGlone herself reported an incident to the Bias Response website. According to McGlone's report, some teenage boys visiting Madison for the state's high school championship wrestling tournament cat-called some college-aged women walking down the street. McGlone saw the women discussing the incident on Facebook and submitted their posts to school administrators.

"I am reporting this with the hope that campus officials will share this information with WIAA (the governing board for high school sports) and participating schools, make them aware this behavior is not acceptable and request that they specifically address appropriate conduct with tournament participants in future years," McGlone wrote in her complaint.

Accompanying her report, McGlone attached screen shots of the discussion, in which one student said someone yelled "nice ass" at her. Another punctuated a post with a laughing emoji. McGlone said she was not aware of whether any of the female students was contacted before sending their discussion to the bias team.

"Just like any staff member, I have an obligation to respond when I become aware of discrimination affecting students," McGlone told me. "The university passed along their concerns to WIAA and WIAA was very responsive. I don't know whether any of the female students were contacted directly."

In January, a class took a field trip during which a tour guide read from a historical text that referred to Native Americans as "savages."

After the field trip concluded a report was filed, noting "The professor did not intervene or clarify afterwards that native people are not savages."

"This incident communicated to me that a huge leader in the field thinks it is ok to call native people this demeaning slur," the report read.

Also in January, a student reported a botany professor for "dead-naming" transgender scientist Joan Roughgarden, mistakenly introducing her using her former name "John" in a lecture slide.

Several days later, a non-student citizen named Jim Estes reported the UW Police Department for a humorous social media post featuring a police officer wearing a short sleeved shirt with the caption "#sleevesmatter."

Estes claimed the posts were "offensive, as they are clearly making fun of #blacklivesmatter with the #sleevesmatter reference." He deemed the posts "not funny" and claimed "this is why they have community trust issues."

The same day, a student filed a report against a professor who had given his students the assignment of writing a brief essay on the relationship between Maurice Ravel's Ma Mere L'Oye Suite and a dance performance by Kansas-based youth company Ballet Midwest.

Several students took the opportunity during an in-class discussion to express concern over how various Asian cultures were depicted through the choreography.

According to the complaint filed against the professor, he "appeared to praise students who did not write about the dance's cultural insensitivity, expressing that he was 'glad [they] did not have a concern about the Asian motif.'"

The professor allegedly "criticized students whose essays included a discussion of how the choreography misrepresented various Asian cultures. He labeled these submissions as 'harsh assessments.'"

If diversity measures like Bias Response Teams are meant to give students from marginalized groups a more comfortable campus experience, it doesn't appear they have been successful. In 2017, UW-Madison released results of a "Campus Climate Survey," in which 81 percent of students overall reported they felt "welcome" on campus.

But numbers for minority groups lagged behind those of the general population. Only 69 percent of LGBTQ students, 67 percent of students with a disability, and 65 percent of students of color felt welcome on campus. At the bottom rung were transgender and non-binary students, 50 percent of whom responded that they felt welcome on campus.

It is possible that initiatives like BRTs are actually doing more harm than good, as they force students to be on high alert for racial and gender-based transgressions at all times. Encouraging students to report one another may be institutionalizing victimhood and teaching students that the university is responsible for ensuring every utterance they hear is non-confrontational.

It is worth noting that the rising accusations of bias are taking place in the most progressive enclaves of America—prestigious college campuses. In the past two decades, both public and private universities have stuffed themselves with "climate" and "diversity" administrators, crowing to students about their dedication to equality. Yet the campuses' fealty to diversity may be having the opposite effect—it may be convincing students discrimination is an inextricable aspect of campus life.

In 2014, sociologists Bradley Campbell and Jason Manning studied the effect so-called "microaggressions" have had on college campuses. According to Campbell and Manning, universities "increasingly lack the intimacy and cultural homogeneity that once characterized towns and suburbs, but in which organized authority and public opinion remain as powerful sanctions."

"Under such conditions complaint to third parties has supplanted both toleration and negotiation," Campbell and Manning argue. "People increasingly demand help from others, and advertise their oppression as evidence that they deserve respect and assistance. Thus we might call this moral culture a culture of victimhood ... the moral status of the victim, at its nadir in honor cultures, has risen to new heights."

Or, as put by Jonathan Haidt, social psychologist and co-author of The Coddling of the American Mind: How Good Intentions and Bad Ideas Are Setting Up a Generation for Failure, "victimhood culture causes a downward spiral of competitive victimhood."

"Young people on the left and the right get sucked into its vortex of grievance," wrote Haidt in 2015.

In February, a university art exhibit featured a provocative sculpture of an Alt-right protester carrying a tiki torch. The piece was titled The Root of Hate.

According to a student filing a report against the school for allowing the sculpture to be displayed, the statue featured "many other figures on it that were clearly trying to rationalize this despicable human action including a rather insensitive depiction of what could be construed as mother."

"It was offensive to look, and brought up terrible thoughts about the rally in Charleston. It was triggering." (Presumably the student meant "Charlottesville.")

In April, a group of students in the same dorm took to a Facebook Messenger chat to threaten a cisgender male student who was heard saying he "would not feel comfortable sexually engaging with another male who identifies as a trans woman."

According to screen shots of the chat, a man said he wouldn't want to have sex with a transgender woman "because she has a penis." The text of the chat suggests the straight, cisgender student was having a talk with a transgender individual and earnestly asking questions about transgenderism.

"At least he used the right pronouns but god kill him," wrote one student. "I'm going to stab him with a dick shaped knife," wrote another.

Another student reported the conversation on the threatened student's behalf.

In May, a student complained about a Facebook advertisement for an upcoming panel discussion at the UW Department of Pediatrics that featured all white, male doctors and was subtitled "Is There a Doctor In the House?"

"There are many amazing faculty of color doing grand rounds, and the school decided to highlight this one in particular is difficult to justify considering that the title might to be considered exclusionary," the student reported.

In 1905, former University of Wisconsin president Charles Van Hise announced the tenets of the "Wisconsin Idea," a philosophy in support of an activist campus that benefits the entire state.

"I shall never be content until the beneficent influence of the University reaches every family of the state," Van Hise declared.

But Van Hise's university has now become a factory of discontent, encouraging its students to report each other to authorities in what has become a race to learned helplessness.

Van Hise no doubt believed deeply society could be made a more vibrant, creative place with the production of more scholars. But when a university subverts its marketplace of ideas to exacerbate its grievance culture, it only creates more victims.

The Dispatch

'BIAS TEAMS' WELCOME THE CLASS OF 1984

August 5, 2019

Hundreds of American colleges have "bias-response teams" or similar mechanism for students or faculty to report bias incidents. These systems enforce political correctness and turn campuses into miniature surveillance states.

Through the Freedom of Information Act, I recently obtained and reviewed nearly 300 alleged bias incidents at 11 major public universities. The reports, which we asked to be scrubbed of identifying information for both the accusers and accused, reveal students who are perpetually offended and on the lookout for ideological heresy. Actual crimes such as vandalism or threats of physical violence are typically handled by campus police. In most bias reports, campus community members simply heard or saw something that made them mildly uncomfortable.

At the University of Utah, a male student was joking around with his friends in the library and complained that his computer battery was dying. His friend gave him a power cord, and, when it turned out to be incompatible with his computer, told the student to jam the cord into the power socket anyway. "That's rape," the accused student whispered loudly. "I'm not raping my computer." A female student overheard and filed a complaint.

Supporters of bias-response teams argue they are harmless, since they typically cannot formally discipline anyone. "They do not shut down free speech or charge into classrooms to stop offensive statements from faculty members or students," two professors, two administrators and a doctoral candidate argued in a June article for Inside Higher Education.

Yet schools often investigate the complaints, and the teams themselves can call the accused in to demand an explanation in front an administrator or a panel of "diversity" specialists. At the University of Illinois, law-enforcement officers sit on the bias-response board—making the body a literal speech police. Complaints go down in permanent, often public, records, which can affect future employment prospects. Most bias-response systems don't offer any process by which the accused can clear their names.

The reporting is often ideologically biased. A Michigan State University student reported his dorm roommate for watching a video of conservative commentator Ben Shapiro. When a University of Oregon professor defended Justice Brett Kavanaugh's nomination, a female student reported she was "deeply offended" by the "false, ignorant, biased commentary" that "completely discredited sexual assault survivors like myself and Dr. Christine Blasey Ford, among countless other women."

A Portland State student filed a complaint against a woman who jokingly described herself as sometimes being "schizophrenic." An Asian-American student at the University of Minnesota reported a food-service worker for saying hello in Japanese. At Indiana University a teaching assistant filed a case against a guest lecturer who tried to explain the role of the Federal Communications Commission by citing the Janet Jackson "Nipplegate" controversy at the 2004 Super Bowl. A 22-year-old female student at Utah reported a professor for assigning too many classic works on economics written by men. She claimed the selections created a "hostile learning environment."

People can be reported for simply giving the impression that they are not sufficiently progressive. A self-identified "trans feminine" student at Indiana reported a faculty member for giving a "rude look" to the student, who wore lipstick to class, and for saying something to someone else in the classroom that the student couldn't hear but suspected was about the student's failure to look "totally masculine."

"Students and faculty are afraid to have honest conversations—or even joke around with each other—out of fear of being reported for a faux pas," Portland State professor Peter Boghossian told me earlier this year. The result is a culture of mistrust and bad faith, in which everyone is a suspect. Now that's a hostile learning environment.

The Wall Street Journal

WHY DO COLLEGES OFFER SEX SEMINARS?

October 15, 2013

When students at New York's small, prestigious Hamilton College walked on campus this fall, math, science and languages weren't the only topics of which they could avail themselves. The university's Womyn's Center also provided an "orgasm workshop," which aimed to teach "everything from multiple orgasms to that mysterious G-spot."

Not to be outdone, the University of Maryland is teaming up with a local sex toy shop this weekend to host a seminar on how to buy more "environmentally friendly" sex aids. This comes as great news to non-single men, because if sex is bad for the environment, it makes every married guy an Erin Brockovich-style eco-warrior.

The idea that our universities are in the business of teaching students how to have sex with each other isn't particularly new. For years, the University of Wisconsin-Madison has used student fees to fund the Sex Out Loud program, which serves the purpose of providing "graphic workshops on how to give and receive sexual pleasure." Supporters of the program claim it's necessary, given how 80% of students ages 18 to 24 are having sex. (Apparently, the other 20% are women who dated me.)

In the next two years, Sex Out Loud is scheduled to receive $200,000 to teach seminars such as "Kink," "Pleasure" and "Advanced Pleasure" (which, I assume is pleasure coupled with eating a roast beef sandwich). This week, its website features "Five Ways to Have a Kinky Halloween," including dressing like King Tut and re-enacting your favorite horror movie.

Perhaps these programs allow a valuable chance to go back and re-examine why we have universities in the first place. Presumably when UW's forefathers encouraged "sifting and winnowing," they weren't doing so in search of the "mysterious G-spot."

Further, why is the university spending so much money teaching students to do something they're doing anyway? It's not like 50 years from now people will be talking about the "Great Orgasm Famine of 2013." Young people seem to be doing just fine on their own — it's not like figuring out sex is akin to solving the mystery of cold fusion.

Additionally, for most people, it would seem the challenge isn't giving or receiving sexual pleasure. The real challenge is giving or receiving sexual pleasure with someone else in the room. Isn't sex kind of the easy part? Once you have found someone willing enough to form a meaningful overnight bond with you, you're really 98% of the way there. Teaching some guys sexual "techniques" is about as useful as teaching a hedgehog the works of P.G. Wodehouse.

Clearly, universities have determined that sex is important to their students — but think about how important sex is to men already. In order to get it, they are willing to do anything: buy nice cars, imperil their marriages, jeopardize their presidencies and, worst of all, pretend they like eating vegetarian dishes.

And even if we concede that "kink" is an important lesson for students, aren't there enough private-sector options for them to pursue? Like picking up a Cosmopolitan magazine, each of which contains the Top 500 Ways to Please Your Partner.

Finally, speaking from a man's perspective, sex is important not because of the act of sex itself but because it allows a man to say the following:

"I can't believe I found someone willing to let me do that to her!"

You see, despite your slovenly lifestyle, marginal paycheck and questionable looks, suddenly you found someone willing to ignore all of that to engage in the most intimate of acts with you. And that fact alone is awesome. You wake up the next morning fully expecting a ceremony in which you're awarded a gold medal for "tricking a woman into thinking you're worthwhile." It's a validation of your lifestyle — a measuring stick to see where your street value currently stands.

Yet universities will continue to waste money on teaching students how to please their partners, not about the wonders of the emotional bond that should accompany the act. Somehow, our university curriculum has become indistinguishable from a junk email. Perhaps next semester, UW will host a seminar on "how to invest millions of dollars with a Nigerian prince."

Milwaukee Journal Sentinel

GOVERNMENT FUELING THE STUDENT DEBT BUBBLE

January 13, 2016

When the financial crash tragicomedy "The Big Short" hit theaters last month, critics rushed to explain what an important movie it was. Based on Michael Lewis' book of the same name, the film was described as "tragic and frightening" by Brad Wheeler of Globe and Mail. Tom Long of the Detroit News called it "ominous," and Peter Travers of Rolling Stone pegged it as "a slapstick tragedy that makes us wish we could see every character in it behind bars."

In retrospect, it's easy to see the financial markers that should have warned of the impending housing crisis. But it seems we're also turning a blind eye to what could be the next financial bubble to burst: the student loan debt bubble.

Just as the housing bust was precipitated by banks stuffing homeowners into loans they couldn't possibly afford, more and more college students are taking on loans that they can't pay back. Between 2001 and 2012, yearly student loan originations increased from $53 billion to $120 billion; the current $1.2 trillion in outstanding loans is the second-largest category of debt in America, behind mortgages. And one in six of all student loan borrowers is either delinquent or in default.

One could argue that students need to take out more loans to keep up with rapidly rising university tuition; indeed, tuition at public universities has quadrupled (to nearly $10,000 per year in 2014 dollars) over the past 35 years. As Paul F. Campos pointed out last April in The New York Times, if car price increases had kept up with the rate of tuition increases, the average new car would now cost $80,000.

But it isn't tuition that is driving the recent explosion in student loan issuance. In fact, it is exactly the other way around — the availability of easy money flooding the market in the form of loans has allowed college administrators to hike tuition to soak up this excess cash.

In this way, the college student loan crisis shares one important feature with the housing market crash; both were instigated by federal government programs intended to generate more customers. Just as when Fannie Mae and Freddie Mac were using governmental power to back subprime loans, stuffing consumers with bad credit into mortgages they couldn't afford, students are now facing financial hardship when their federal loan repayment schedule eventually kicks in. In fact, federal loan programs have accounted for more than 90% of all student loan originations since the 2009-'10 school year.

This had led politicians to pitch all kinds of "debt forgiveness" plans to help students pay back the loans they signed up for. Wisconsin's Sen. Tammy Baldwin has introduced her own bill to allow students to refinance their student loan debt; Hillary Clinton has pushed a similar measure.

But such a plan mostly helps students with the most ability to pay back their loans. In 2014, the Brookings Institution found that the richest 25% of families hold 40% of the total student loan debt, while the bottom 25% would get less than one-fifth the benefit from a refinancing plan. While those with high debt loads may have the most about which to gripe, they tend to graduate from the most prestigious programs and have the greatest ability to pay off those loans.

Thus, instead of treating a symptom of increased college costs, politicians should look to treating the actual cause — tuition itself. To those on the left, "college affordability" typically means either pumping more taxpayer money into universities or making loans more available. Affordability never means keeping tuition down, as that deprives universities of revenue — even though Department of Education data shows a 60% growth in university administration between 1993 and 2009. This is nearly 10 times the growth in tenured faculty positions over the same time frame.

As Oscar Wilde once said, "Whenever a man does a thoroughly stupid thing, it is always from the noblest motives." Getting people in homes and allowing them to attend college are both noble causes; but in the end, government has only served the purpose of bailing us out from the government.

Milwaukee Journal Sentinel

HERE COMES THE FEDERAL SPEECH CODE

July 26, 2013

Back in 1988, the University of Wisconsin-Madison was at the forefront in the national battle over political correctness. That year, the campus governing bodies passed speech codes for both students and faculty that prohibited anyone from making gestures or statements that "demean" students on the basis of race, gender, sexual orientation, culture and handicapped condition.

The code, passed with support of then-Chancellor Donna Shalala, itself became a national laughingstock. The speech regulations chilled free expression on campus, leading several professors to be investigated for merely tackling controversial subjects.

The student code was overturned by a federal court in 1991; the faculty Senate finally invalidated its own rule in March 1999. (The final straw was an episode in which a student complained about a professor using the word "niggardly," as she was unaware that the word is completely benign.)

Yet for those who enjoy hairspray, Rubik's cubes and being afraid of Russia, the 1980s are suddenly back in vogue. In an attempt to cut down on sexual harassment on campuses around the country, the U.S. Justice Department and the Department of Education's Office of Civil Rights (OCR) have jointly issued new regulations for universities that include restrictions on "sexually harassing speech."

Groups such as the Foundation for Individual Rights in Education and the American Civil Liberties Union have blasted the new federal "blueprint," pointing out how shockingly broad the regulations are. The new regulations outlaw "any unwelcome conduct of a sexual nature," including "verbal conduct."

Thus any action that makes a student uncomfortable immediately could become grounds for a complaint. (If awkward date offers were a crime, I'd likely be serving five consecutive life sentences.)

After an immediate public outcry, OCR "clarified" the plan, saying that it never meant to classify things such as jokes, rumors and gestures as "assault." But the OCR did maintain that such things should be "reportable," as they might, in totality, lead to a "hostile environment."

The new federal rules require university employees to report speech for investigation and allow for punishing the offending students before an investigation is even completed. Students and faculty could be deemed guilty until proven innocent, as the thought police roam the halls looking for violations.

404

Of course, students should be protected from sexual harassment, and assaults should be treated seriously. But we've been here before with speech codes, and the results aren't pretty. If anything, the new codes will ostensibly create more harassment violations on campus, as behavior that was legal before will be reported and stick to a student's record.

UW-Madison professor Donald Downs, one of the national leaders in opposing speech codes, says the new blueprint is part of a "misguided feminist agenda." Downs says he "brandishes liberal feminist credentials," but that the new rules insult women, as the standard "implies that women are essentially victims, not responsible agents who can handle 'unwelcome' ideas that fall short of constituting harassment reasonably and objectively defined."

Downs also objects to the new standard by which offenders are being found in violation of the code. In the past, defendants had to be found guilty "by clear and convincing evidence," which is a standard just below the "beyond a reasonable doubt" used in the court system.

Yet many schools are now only requiring a panel to find an offender guilty by "a preponderance of the evidence," essentially meaning "more likely than not." Not only is it becoming easier to accuse someone of impropriety, it is easier to find that person guilty, as well.

We all encounter unwelcome sexual material in our everyday lives. I'd like to sue someone any time I hear any news about "Carlos Danger."

But the UW System has lived through this debacle before. It should resist implementing the new federal regulations, even if the feds threaten to withhold funding for non-compliance. The UW wants the citizens of Wisconsin to think it is a place where free speech and viewpoint diversity are valued. Now is the university's chance to prove it.

Milwaukee Journal Sentinel

'THE CONCEPTUAL PENIS' BATTLES THE WOKE MOBS

January 29, 2019

In our era of absurdity, it is both fitting and depressing that the professor behind a study that exposed how preposterous research papers could find their way into prestigious academic journals now finds himself in hot water. Peter Boghossian, author of the so-called "Grievance Studies Hoax," is the academic version of a whistle-blower — but now he's the one facing backlash.

Boghossian and his partners, researchers James Lindsay and Helen Pluckrose, teamed up in 2016 to draft outlandish papers that analyzed rape culture in dog parks, blamed "the conceptual penis" for climate change,

405

and suggested silencing white males in college classrooms. (This paper counseled they should be made to sit on the floor in chains to experience "reparations"). The trio's papers demonstrated that literally anything can earn the imprimatur of "research" as long it adheres to a certain progressive narrative.

The group's coup de grace was tricking a feminist journal into accepting a paper using exact phrases from Adolf Hitler's Mein Kampf with "fashionable buzzwords switched in." (The words "Our Struggle is My Struggle" appeared in the bogus paper's headline, offering an overt clue as to its provenance.)

Of the 20 papers authored by Boghossian and his partners, seven were accepted, four were published, and seven more were still "in play" when their cover was blown.

The paper that purported to show that research conducted at dog parks suggested training men like dogs in order to reduce "rape culture" in society received rave reviews: One peer reviewer called the study, submitted under a female pseudonym, "incredibly innovative, rich in analysis, and extremely well-written and organized given the incredibly diverse literature sets and theoretical questions brought into conversation." This paper was not only published, it was cited as one of the best 12 works in the 25-year history of the academic journal Gender, Place, and Culture.

Naturally, Boghossian's hijinks have not been viewed kindly by the academic community they skewered. In December, Portland State barred Boghossian from leading further research for allegedly violating "human subject" research rules by not gaining prior consent from his institutional review board. According to the university, the academics who reviewed the papers weren't told they were being studied, and thus a research rule was violated. Boghossian was told to cease all research until he completes "human subjects research training."

Yet research is conducted regularly in which an academic misrepresents some aspect of his or herself in order to test society's reaction to a variable; for example, one recent study by a Harvard University researcher sent out 1,600 resumes for entry-level job openings – some of the resumes were "whitened" to determine whether employers were more or less likely to call back minority job applicants if they hid their race. (Spoiler: They were.) Boghossian told me this is how he viewed his research.

"I really didn't want to make this a right-left issue," Boghossian told me, although he conceded it is the left that is driving this faulty social science. "To me, this is not a political issue, it is an issue of scholarship and scholarly rigor."

The Grievance Hoax researchers are still awaiting resolution of charges by Portland State that they "fabricated" research. It is true, Boghossian and his co-authors did not actually inspect the genitals of "nearly 10,000" dogs at the Portland dog park and then ask their owners about the dogs' sexuality.

But the bogus research was the whole point of the study — there is value in knowing what nonsense people will deem true just because it fits their ideological predispositions. (There are, for example, still people who think Mexico is going to pay for a border wall. But I digress.) Further, none of the research was going to be allowed to stand once the study was complete.

Given universities' stated allegiance to "academic freedom," further sanctions against Boghossian by Portland State would be unconscionable. He exposed the fraud and corruption within the publishing arm of academia, where the "publish-or-perish" culture forces faculty into, in his words, "pushing a kind of social snake oil onto a public that keeps getting sicker."

Boghossian believes what the university does with him "will tell you what kind of university they want to be."

"Do they want to be a social justice university," he asked, rhetorically, "or do they want to be a truth-seeking university?"

A study successful in rooting out fraudulent scholarship should not itself be attacked as shoddy research. These academics are wasting taxpayer money and university resources in their quest for intellectually homogenous campuses, and yet they rest comfortably outside the public's glare. Exposes such as Boghossian's should be embraced, not shamed.

The Bulwark

BERNIE SANDERS' FREE COLLEGE PLAN FLUNKS COMMON SENSE

February 10, 2016

After enough time passes, there's no limit to the things that cease to shock us. Take, for instance, parrots. I feel like a larger portion of our daily interactions should be dedicated to discussing the fact that there's an animal that can talk. And yet there it sits, our unspoken secret, while we discuss less important things over coffee, such as religion and politics.

But even politics has its own unspoken conversational grenades. For example, a leading contender for the presidential nomination of one of our major parties is currently shopping an idea so bizarre, it should warrant at least half the space in any discussion about him. I am talking, of course, about Bernie Sanders' plan to provide free public college tuition in America.

Sure, Donald Trump's "terrific" plan to build a wall between the United States and Mexico and have the Mexicans pay for it warrants a mention in the "bat-excrement crazy" category. But at least people are calling for a wall to curtail illegal immigration; before Sanders started promising "free" college, even students figured it was fair for them to at least pick up a portion of their tuition.

Naturally, to socialists (not an insult — how Sanders actually describes himself), "free" merely means "someone else pays for it." Estimates put the price tab on Sanders' plan at $70 billion, per year, until campus costs rise, then the taxpayers' tab balloons.

What's particularly puzzling about Sanders' plan is that he wants to take a scarce resource — taxpayer money — and spend it on people who can most afford to pay for college. For someone so concerned about income inequality, Sanders wants to hand the wealthy a huge college tuition subsidy. When you subsidize college costs across the board, you're paying just as much for the children of millionaires to attend college as you are for the truly needy. Why would we pay $70 billion a year for Donald Trump's kids to go to college while food shelters struggle to keep the homeless fed?

Free tuition also would structurally change the way colleges in America work. For one, the private university system would collapse; if given the choice between attending an expensive private college or a top-flight public university, many of the best students will opt for the taxpayer subsidy. That would squeeze middling students out of college altogether, as their slots would be taken up by those fleeing private colleges.

And once college essentially becomes the "Federal Department of Higher Education," look for far less innovation and flexibility. The University of Wisconsin-Madison has been experimenting with distance and online learning; when that authority has to be authorized by Congress, good luck modernizing anything on campus.

More generally, it makes sense for students to have skin in the game. If a student is paying for his or her own tuition, books and rent, he or she has the incentive to see it all the way through. Sure, students who are given full-ride scholarships often do very well, but they usually got the scholarship because they're self-motivated. Just handing free money to everyone, regardless of academic interest, is a recipe for substandard academic performance and massive dropouts.

Sanders' bizarre plan never will happen, and it is horrifying that anyone even proposing such an impossibility is taken seriously as a candidate. Even Hillary Clinton now looks like the third Koch brother, having repeatedly denounced the plan. Thankfully, the Founding Fathers explicitly set up Congress as a firewall against plans hatched in a cloud of marijuana smoke, so the public should be safe.

During election season, candidates throw a lot of ideas around in the washing machine, sloshing to and fro. But Sanders' fatuous free college plan should be the red sock that stains the rest of his campaign.

Milwaukee Journal Sentinel

THE ADULTS ARE BOTH JUVENILE AND DELINQUENT

April 22, 2016

In February of 1940, students at small Young Harris College in Georgia staged an uprising. Among their demands of the Methodist institution were the right to hold school dances, to liberalize campus dating practices and for each student to be given an additional sandwich on the Sunday menu.

In responding to the students' demands, college president T. Jack Lance said that the "faculty will not tolerate Bolshevism." Such student activism long has been a part of college campuses. But in modern America, we are paying the price for appeasing young people, who are now more prone to fabricate controversies. In the Internet age, symbolic outrage has gone viral.

At the University of Wisconsin-Madison last week, students decided to party like it's 1969 and held protests in support of a black student who was arrested for vandalizing campus property, causing $4,000 worth of damage. In one incident, the student was accused of telling a bystander trying to stop him from spray painting anti-racism messages on building walls that he "would kill them if they called police."

A week ago, that student was pulled from class and questioned about the campus vandalism. Evidently enough, delicate UW students were so traumatized by the presence of a police officer in their classroom that the campus police chief issued an apology to the students.

That wasn't enough to pacify the campus' theatrically aggrieved, however, who decided to stage a class walkout on Thursday. Protesters complained that the black student's rights had been violated, even though police had made every effort to contact the student at home and via phone. They knew he would be in that classroom, and they rationally took action.

But the flop taken by activists on campus has been enough to make a European soccer star envious. Before shutting down traffic on a busy Madison street, protesters delivered a list of "demands" to the university administration. Among the demands were for all charges against the student to be dropped, for the arresting officer to be fired and for greater "community control" over the campus police department.

To her credit, UW-Madison Chancellor Rebecca Blank is having none of it. On Thursday, Blank issued a statement saying she "has taken appropriate steps to respond to our community's concerns."

But this may all be too little, too late after years of universities acquiescing to the demands of groups such as Black Lives Matter. It's difficult not to enjoy a little bit of schadenfreude when arguably the most progressive campus in America is forced to confront the victimization that such leftism has wrought. These are the progeny of the "ism" culture — young people who believe racism and sexism are everywhere, leaving them incapable of dealing with actual transgressions when they occur.

If anything, appeasing counterproductive behavior among young black students is its own brand of racial paternalism, as is expecting less of students of color. In 2014, Michigan State professor Dorinda Carter Andrews told Wisconsin State Journal reporter Molly Beck that, "When you're not tough on me and you accept less from me, I see it as a lack of respect and a lack of care."

But groups on campus are trying to bully the adults into expecting less of them, even accusing UW of promoting "white supremacy." It's actually a sleight-of-hand. In this case, a student allegedly vandalized buildings with messages about white supremacy on campus, got arrested for property damage, and provoked more accusations of white supremacy. It's the self-fulfilling grievance.

I'm not going to name the student accused of defacing property. Young people make mistakes and sometimes don't deserve to have their names plastered across Google searches in perpetuity. Let's hope that in the future, he can look back and realize how silly this all was. But that will happen only if the adults in his life stop excusing the kind of things he is accused of doing.

Milwaukee Journal Sentinel

INSTRUCTING CAMPUSES ON DUE PROCESS

September 8, 2017

In decades past, amid conservative calls for new laws to regulate "morality," progressives frequently argued that our private bedrooms were no place for the government. Yet if you are a student on a college campus in modern America, if you ask someone over to "Netflix and chill," you better make sure you make enough room on the couch for your second guest, the federal government.

Starting in 2011, new rules by the federal Department of Education's Office for Civil Rights strong-armed colleges into regulating sexual activities by their students. Under Title IX, a law originally passed in 1972 to deal with gender discrimination in public education, President Barack Obama's administration unilaterally decreed new procedures for how colleges adjudicate sex cases on campus.

New OCR guidelines dictated that in cases dealing with sex, universities lower the standard of proof to one of a "preponderance of evidence," or anything greater than 50% probability, rather than the traditional "clear and convincing" standard.

In many cases, students or professors accused of sexual impropriety are denied basic constitutional due process rights; they may be denied legal counsel, the right to cross-examine their accusers, and the right to impartial fact-finding. Instead, colleges may use a "single investigator" model, making one individual the judge, jury and executioner when a crime of sexual misconduct is alleged. According to a recent study by the Foundation for Individual Rights in Education, nearly half of America's universities require that these fact-finders be impartial, and nearly three-quarters of the nation's top schools have no presumption of innocence in disciplinary matters.

Last week, Secretary of Education Betsy DeVos announced a new process that would alter some of the Obama era's Title IX guidelines, arguing that protecting due process for the accused is "the foundation of any system of justice that seeks a fair outcome."

Naturally, DeVos was immediately charged with "blaming the victim" in campus sex cases, making it easier for men who assault women to walk away free of punishment.

But many of her progressive critics are the same ones who would argue vehemently, for example, that defendants in murder or drug trials be granted all the legal protections available to them. Sexual assault is, indeed, a heinous crime — but the heinousness of an alleged crime increases the need for a fair trial, not the other way around.

Further, Title IX hysteria on campuses has completely warped what students consider to be a "sexual" violation. According to a group of Harvard Law School faculty members challenging the university's new Title IX rules, Harvard's new definitions of misconduct "go way beyond accepted legal definitions of rape, sexual assault and sexual harassment."

These new rules have produced some mind-boggling outcomes, ranging from the serious to the absurd. Male students have seen reputations and educational opportunities destroyed based on what they believed at the time to be consensual sex, only to later have a charge filed against them. According to aforementioned Harvard professors Jeannie Suk Gersen and her husband Jacob Gersen, "conduct classified as illegal" on college campuses "has grown substantially, and indeed, it plausibly covers almost all sex students are having today."

And there is no shortage of ridiculous examples of where the new rules have gone wrong. After writing a newspaper article detailing "sexual paranoia" on campus, Northwestern professor Laura Kipnis was hit with a Title IX investigation on the basis of complaints made by two graduate students — one of whom argued Kipnis' article had a "chilling effect" on students' ability to report sexual misconduct. In July, Howard University law professor Reginald Robinson was found guilty and sentenced to sensitivity training after he included a hypothetical question about bikini waxing on one of his exams.

Just this week, an 18-year old man was arrested after being accused of entering a women's dormitory on the University of Wisconsin-Madison campus and taking pictures of women in the restroom. Because he was arrested by police, he will likely go to trial, where he will have all the protections our Constitution affords alleged criminals. We should extend these basic rights to all suspects, regardless of who's making the accusation.

Milwaukee Journal Sentinel

PHONY CAMPUS CRISES LAY GROUNDWORK FOR POWER GRAB

February 7, 2018

As a broke college student in the mid-1990s, I learned every trick in the book to keep myself fed. I'd wake up at noon every day so I could skip breakfast. I'd get part-time jobs exclusively at restaurants so I could eat for free on the job. On a given day, if a scholarship athlete friend wasn't using the meal plan the university provided him at restaurants around the city, I'd impersonate him and eat the food he was passing up. (This frequently worked despite the fact I bore no resemblance to a left tackle.)

At no point did I feel like it was the job of government to step in and make sure I was plied with roast beef sandwiches. But that is the recommendation of Professor Sara Goldrick-Rab at Temple University, who complains too many college students are suffering from "food insecurity."

Writing in The New York Times recently, Goldrick-Rab complains that with the cost of college spiking dramatically, more students are struggling to find money for food, and thus their learning is impaired. Leaning heavily on her own research, Goldrick-Rab concludes that it is "impossible to learn when you're starving."

(Goldrick-Rab recently moved to Temple from the University of Wisconsin-Madison, where she once said the number of similarities between Republican Gov. Scott Walker and Adolf Hitler were "terrifying." Presumably, her contract with her new employer provides her with a daily plate of spaghetti and meatballs to prevent her from saying such uninformed things.)

The idea that a university is in charge of feeding its students fuels a problematic cycle: The more we ask colleges to do for students, the higher tuition gets, and then we ask them to do even more for students who are forced to pay more to go to school.

In fact, the modern university is now asked to be everything to every student. Campuses are set up like full-service county governments, forced to provide a range of human services. Colleges are expected to provide housing and healthcare, oversee their own police forces and run their own judicial systems to either mediate disagreements between students or punish faculty.

And the list of services colleges are expected to provide is growing. Last week, the California Senate passed a bill requiring state universities to provide free "morning after" abortion pills to students; a group of private donors is trying to raise $20 million to set up abortion centers on California campuses. Across the nation, groups are demanding university administrators take new measures to manage racial diversity. UW-Madison students even get free bus passes to go anywhere in town.

Which may lead a lot of parents to throw their hands up and say, "Dude, just teach my kid."

It makes sense for universities to feed students that are in their care; at most colleges, students in the dorms have meal plans to keep them full.

But the desire to have colleges fulfill every need of every student is pushing their development into adults past their graduation dates. It's basically as if we are extending high school, where the school truly is in charge of its pupil's welfare, up the ladder through college. Recent studies have suggested that the human brain doesn't actually mature to adulthood until 25 years old, but this is nonsense — self-sufficiency can be taught as soon as a child is able to talk.

Also worth noting is the government's role in making college less affordable. A 2015 study by the New York Federal Reserve found that for every dollar of loans provided to students, tuition increased by 58 cents. Colleges see young adults flush with student loan cash and adjust their tuition upwards to get their hands on it. (And start all sorts of new social programs to justify the money grab.)

Asking universities to expand their roles in students' lives exacerbates the perception of college campuses as bubbles that insulate young adults from the real world. College should be a time when our kids learn to do things for themselves, and that means keeping themselves fed.

And for the current college students who are hungry and trying to learn, take it from those of us who have been through it. We're now old and fat and don't feel any smarter.

USA Today

CHAPTER SEVEN:
GOD'S COUNTRY

WISCONSIN'S GOVERNOR IS FISCALLY MODEST, POLITICALLY BOLD

February 19, 2011

As tens of thousands of protesters continued to gather at the Wisconsin State Capitol in Madison, the story quickly transitioned to the actions of the protesters themselves. Lost was a discussion of the reason they came from all over the state (and nation) in the first place.

If the union protesters continue to call the governor's bluff, there will be fewer of them in the future.

In an effort to close a $3.6 billion budget gap (about 14 percent of the state's total general fund budget), new Republican Gov. Scott Walker asked state and local government workers to contribute more for their health care and pension benefits. Currently, the overwhelming majority of public sector workers pay nothing toward their pension benefits; Walker is requiring a 5.8 percent contribution, which is matched by the government. Walker is also doubling the amount state employees pay for their health care benefits, from 6 percent of their premium currently, to 12 percent of their premium.

In the fall, Walker campaigned on these issues, and for good reason; a poll conducted by the Wisconsin Policy Research Institute in November 2010 indicated that 80 percent of Wisconsin citizens supported public workers contributing to their own pensions. In that poll, 23 percent of respondents identified themselves as Republicans, while 33 percent said they were Democrats.

Clearly, the public has begun to recognize the largess of the Wisconsin pension system. According to a Wisconsin Policy Research Institute report in February of 2010, a private sector worker would have to earn $70,000 per year to earn the same pension as a public sector employee that makes $48,000. The average employer contribution for private sector plans is 5.3 percent of payroll, compared with the Wisconsin Retirement System, in which the employer contribution ranges between 10.55 percent and 13.3 percent of payroll.

Walker has said his plan, which limits public employee union collective bargaining primarily to wages, will prevent government worker layoffs numbering in the tens of thousands. According to Governor Walker, workers can accept modest changes to their benefits, or face losing their jobs.

On Friday, the leader of the state's largest public employee union said he would accept Walker's financial demands in exchange for retaining the right of the unions to collectively bargain those issues in the future. Walker quickly declined their offer.

Many benefits the governor is trying to reduce are the result of the increase in public sector unionization in Wisconsin in the early 1970's. Between 1958 and 1974, public teacher pay increased an average of 6 percent a year. After a bitter 1974 teachers' strike in the small town of Hortonville that galvanized public unions, teacher pay increased an average of 7 percent annually for the next 16 years. It was also during this time that the state and local governments began paying the full amount of public employees' pension benefits.

So far, Walker's plans have been fiscally modest, but politically bold. Public employee unions will continue to protest, even though the governor is the first politician who has told them the truth in ages. If government workers continue to call his bluff, their protests will likely be much smaller in the future.

New York Times

THE INCREDIBLE SHRINKING PROTEST

June 15, 2011

Madison — Between February 14 and June 14 of this year, stocking caps and scarves have given way to sundresses and cargo shorts, but protesters still languidly stroll around the Wisconsin state capitol in Madison. They have come by the thousands on this warm June day to demonstrate against Scott Walker's plan to curb public-sector-union power, although the crowds are only a small fraction of what the state experienced months ago. The college students have gone home, and public school teachers clearly are much more inclined to protest on days when school is actually in session.

Outside the capitol, there are still drums going and the chants are all the same, albeit with fewer participants and less enthusiasm. In February, the protesters were working to stop Walker's plan — in June, they appear to be simply expressing their disgust at the inevitable. After Walker's plan was struck down by a Madison-based judge on the basis of a perceived open meetings violation, the Assembly announced it was going to re-pass the measure today as a budget amendment. This brought another round of street theater down to the Wisconsin capitol.

Down the sidewalk from the west wing, random speakers take turns holding court at a rigged-up PA system. A rotund woman with a large knee brace, clutching an American Federation of Teachers sign, starts a semi-lucid, profane speech in which she urges the crowd to "do your f—ing homework" at campaign time. For some people, P.J. O'Rourke once noted, free speech is a curse. Her screed is made even more bizarre by a small machine spitting out liquid soap bubbles. Circling the stage is a tall gentleman made even taller by the giant paper-mâché Scott Walker head he has crafted.

Upon entering the capitol, visitors are greeted by a large sign explaining all the items they are forbidden to carry in. Someone unfamiliar with the February protests would be flummoxed as to why some of these items show up on the list, but the list itself tells the story of what happened when hundreds of protesters took up residence in the statehouse a few months ago. Among the verboten items: snakes, crockpots, massage chairs, mattresses, and balloons, plus a catch-all ("... other items that may be considered inconsistent with a plan to depart the building at the posted closing time or whose use is considered a threat to public health or safety").

In the capitol rotunda, around 100 people are gathered, watching the beginning of the assembly session on large monitors that have been set up for their benefit. At the height of the protest, over 6,000 people were reported to be crammed into this space. Resident irritant and multiple-arrestee Jeremy Ryan, who has earned the sobriquet "Segway Guy," slowly makes his way around the crowd perched atop his two-wheel mobility device.

Soon, three men wearing pink tunics appear. "We Are Walker's Pink Slips!" they begin chanting loudly. "If you have to chant what your protest costume is, it's probably not a good one," cracks a nearby lobbyist.

At noon, the crowd is joined by the "Solidarity Singers," a group which congregates every day to sing at the top of their lungs in the rotunda. Last week, an American Red Cross blood drive had to leave the capitol because of the irritating cacophony produced by the singers. A woman weaves her way through the crowd, handing out song books so everyone can sing along. The books include many union favorites, tailored to the Wisconsin struggle. (For instance, "We Shall Overcome" now apparently references the effort to recall Scott Walker.)

There are some catchy new tunes, too, including one called "Scotty, We're Comin' For You:"

First they came for the unions,
Saying that you should have less
Business needs more, you people aren't poor
Stop whining, buck up like the rest
And then they came for the children,
Hard to believe but it's true
Schools and good health

Might take from their wealth
So tell me what are you gonna do?
Scotty, we're coming for you!
The giant has only been sleeping
Now the sun shines on morning dew
From under the sheets, it came into the streets
So tell me, what is it gonna do?
Scotty, we're coming for you!

As they sing, a young woman with a mohawk dances with another woman wearing a Batman mask. The pink-tunic trio has been joined by other pink-sheet-wearers and they are all dancing. Everyone there is likely puzzled as to how none of this has changed Scott Walker's mind.

Later, the assembly announced they wouldn't be convening at all on the budget until Wednesday. Outside, a team of girls wearing tight-fitting shirts puts on a hula-hoop show, which draws an inordinate amount of interest from capitol law enforcement. (Thankfully, the crowd is safe from any hula-hoop related catastrophe.)

The crowd is a mere echo of the days when 100,000 people showed up in the cold and snow to march on the capitol. It has been distilled to the most ardent believers in the cause, and then further distilled to those believers in the cause that wouldn't rather be golfing on a beautiful 80 degree Wisconsin day. Clearly, the thrill of the spectacle has worn thin.

Around 5:00 p.m., the Supreme Court issued an order upholding Walker's collective-bargaining law. After the ruling, protesters formed a ring around the capitol, singing. The legislature would no longer need to re-vote on the provision that so many came to protest against.

Under normal circumstances, the state's citizens would begin to move on. Yet as a result of the months-long conflict, nine state senators now face recall elections through the summer. So while Walker's supporters claimed victory on this Tuesday, it may still just be the end of the beginning.

National Review Online

SOFTBALL POLITICS

June 30, 2011

June 29 was the day that Wisconsin was to be no more. The streets were going to be deluged with sewage. Children would begin pouring bleach into their cereal, as they would cease to learn otherwise in school. The state would devolve into a fiery Mad Max–style wasteland, where people feast on squirrels and barter their pelts. For it was the day that Governor Scott Walker's plan to scale back public union collective bargaining took effect.

Yet there was no apocalypse on display at Madison's Henry Vilas Park on Wednesday night, as the Republican members of the Wisconsin assembly gathered for the annual staff-versus-legislator softball game. Warm weather, sun, and high skies greeted the staffers and legislators as they sought to escape the tumult of the marble capitol walls. Since the collective-bargaining bill was introduced in February, this group has endured intense pressure — screaming, profanity, death threats, endless drums, property damage, picketing at their homes — and they appeared ready to exorcise those ghosts with some alcohol-soaked recreation.

In a sign of Wisconsin's fractured state of affairs, it was the first year in memory that Democrats declined to play in the game. In previous years, it was a chance for legislators and staff to engage in some bipartisan socializing. But no more.

In fact, assembly Republicans had to keep news of the affair as quiet as possible, to avoid drawing protesters to the game. Traditionally the game had been held right down the road from the capitol at Olin Park, but it was secretly moved to avoid attention. "We told people to keep details of the game off Facebook," said one of the staffers that organized the event.

As the game begins, it is clear that many of the participants have been enjoying the beer and weather in equal amounts well in advance of the 5:30 start time. Pink noses, ribald jokes, and slurred speech are already in abundance as the first pitch is thrown.

For the non-players gathered around the keg, the conversation naturally steers toward politics. There is much discussion of "Chokegate," in which state supreme court justice David Prosser is alleged to have been involved in a physical confrontation with fellow justice Ann Walsh Bradley. Before the incident, organizers had wanted to ask Prosser to serve as umpire for the game — he is an avid baseball fan — but for obvious reasons, he has recently been preoccupied. At one point in the game, someone tells a female staffer to "choke up" on the bat, to make it easier to swing. "I want a police investigation," yells someone in the crowd, leading to muffled laughter.

The nine recalls of state senators brought on by the union controversy is also a common topic. 2011 has unexpectedly become an election year in Wisconsin, as six Republicans and three Democrats risk being yanked from the Senate over the union imbroglio. "I hope nobody dies running the bases today," says assembly staffer Kristy Curry. "We already have enough special elections around here these days."

At one point, Representative John Murtha sends a foul ball through the crowd of onlookers. "I'm paying for my health care now, might as well use it," cracks one staffer.

As the game continues, the usual japery ensues. Someone gets hit with a slow pitch, and mockingly charges the mound. A runner is incorrectly called out and epic histrionics follow. Two staffers wear t-shirts emblazoned with "Escape to Fitzwalkerstan" — a sobriquet given the state by Democrat assemblyman Mark Pocan, referring to the reign of Governor Walker and legislative leaders Scott and Jeff Fitzgerald.

The legislators pump line drive after line drive into the outfield, scoring at a rate that would impress even Anthony Weiner. They chug their ample beer bellies around the bases as if they were being chased by picketers. Left-handed-hitting freshman Representative Paul Farrow launches a bomb into the fenceless expanse of right field, and as he rounds third base, he is taunted with chants of "Come on, Governor!" (A recent magazine article on the legislature's up-and-comers said Farrow had the charisma to be governor one day, and his colleagues have ribbed him mercilessly about it ever since.)

By the end of the game, the staffers have taken to employing 17 fielders to thwart the legislators' scoring onslaught. Staff, who are easily an average of 15 years younger than their bosses, concede that the legislator team is better than in past years, as they now have 59 members from which draw. It turns out that the 2010 election was the best softball recruitment tool possible.

On the day that all knowledge in Wisconsin was supposed to end, something at Vilas Park was abundantly clear: As long as the state has summer nights, softball, and beer, everything will be just fine.

And the final score? Legislators 40, staffers 13. Perhaps the staffers should flee to Illinois before next year's rematch.

National Review Online

THE SECOND BATTLE OF WISCONSIN

May 28, 2012

Manitowoc, Wis.— Last year, thousands of people passed by the front doors of Madison's Bartell community theater on their way to the Wisconsin capitol to protest the state's government-employee-compensation reforms. More recently, the theater lowered the curtain on its latest sold-out hit — a play written in the "Fakespearean" style entitled "The Lamentable Tragedie of Scott Walker, Govnour of Wisconsin."

The denouement of the play (which was originally titled "F*** You, Scott Walker") occurs when Walker escapes the mob by climbing to the top of the capitol, only to be thrown to his death while the fool yells "Sic semper tyrannis!" The play's author, Doug Reed, claims he is a "committed pacifist," but says he had to stay true to the form; as he notes, "the title characters in Shakespeare's tragedies never survive to the end of the play."

On this late Monday morning in April, the real Governor Scott Walker, very much alive, is standing in front of a bright orange, $250,000 snowplow belonging to the Manitowoc County Highway Department. Walker is beginning a tour of the state in which he will tout the $1 billion that Wisconsin governments have saved as a result of his hard-won reforms. The governor, 44, is fighting for his political life, as he faces a June 5 recall election instigated by public-employee unions. The race is widely regarded as the second most important American election in 2012.

Yet you couldn't grasp the magnitude of the election by observing the size of the crowd in the spacious garage that houses the snowplow. As Walker speaks at a small brown podium, there are about 14 people on hand, four of whom appear to be under the age of ten. Walker's campaign team has to keep public attendance at press events extremely limited; in every corner of the state, protesters lurk, waiting for their chance to scream an obscenity, on camera, at the governor they have labeled a "dictator."

Prior to Walker's reforms, state and local-government employees paid nothing or very little toward their pensions and paid only slightly more than 6 percent of their health-care premiums. According to the Wisconsin Taxpayers Alliance, the average Wisconsin government employee earned $71,000 in total compensation in 2011. That same year, average total compensation for employees of the state's largest school district, Milwaukee Public Schools, reached $101,091. Walker helped close the state's $3.6 billion deficit by requiring public employees to pay 5 percent of their salaries toward their pensions. He also required state employees to pay 12.6 percent of their health-insurance premiums — less than half the average both in the private sector and for federal-government employees.

But the most controversial part of Walker's plan was its sharp curtailing of union power, and in particular collective bargaining. Prior to Walker's law, all government workers were required to join unions and pay dues, and unions were able to negotiate all conditions of employment — wages, benefits, work rules. Walker made union membership optional, eliminated the automatic deduction of union dues, and ended collective bargaining for everything but wages. Today, the unions are still able to negotiate wages for all employees (including non-members), but governments may decide for themselves how to handle work rules and other forms of compensation, and employees may decide for themselves whether to give money to the unions.

President Barack Obama immediately jumped into the fray, calling Walker's plan an "assault" on unions. Yet not only do the overwhelming majority of federal employees not bargain collectively, but Obama himself unilaterally imposed a pay freeze on civilian federal workers just months before he accused Walker of stripping workers of their collective-bargaining "rights."

These reforms propelled the state into chaos for a good portion of 2011. The capitol was occupied by, to steal a term from Mark Twain, the "great hive" of public employees, who banged drums, blew vuvuzelas, and camped on the marble floors. Fourteen Democratic senators fled the state for weeks to block a vote on the bill; Walker was the victim of a prank call from someone pretending to be David Koch, one of the billionaire Koch brothers. (Walker's willingness to take the call provided the Left with a prominent talking point: that Walker was beholden to corporate America and that the Koch brothers were secretly writing Walker's legislation.) A government-employee union issued a press release comparing Walker to "Adolph Hilter." No one batted an eye when a camel was seen walking around the frozen capitol square.

Throughout the mayhem, Walker stood firm.

Walker is often compared to Wisconsin congressman Paul Ryan — the two are young stars of the national Republican Party, and Walker just happened to grow up "right down the road" from Ryan. Yet their styles are very different.

Ryan unceasingly warns of a coming fiscal apocalypse, making his listeners want to grab a flashlight and canned goods and ride out the federal-debt Armageddon in their basements. Walker, on the other hand, speaks with subdued precision. He has spent a full year explaining how his reforms are working for Wisconsin; for instance, property taxes have declined for the first time in twelve years. School districts whose contracts previously forced them to buy expensive health insurance from the unions' own health-care company are saving tens of millions of dollars, because Walker's law opened up their contracts to competitive bidding. Large-scale teacher layoffs are occurring only in the few districts that chose not to implement Walker's plan requiring increased health-care and pension contributions.

Wisconsin's history created a substantial headwind against Walker. It is the state that birthed "Fighting Bob" La Follette and the Progressive movement at the turn of the 20th century. It is where the union AFSCME was first incorporated, and in 1959 it became the first state to allow collective bargaining by government employees. Madison's infamous Vietnam-era protests included the bombing of a University of Wisconsin building, an attack that killed a young researcher.

More recently, on the other hand, Wisconsin has been a laboratory for conservative reforms; Milwaukee boasts the nation's oldest private-school voucher program, and in the early 1990s Republican governor Tommy Thompson implemented a welfare-reform program that became the model for national welfare reform a few years later. But when Walker was elected, it had been twelve years since the state had elected a Republican governor and 26 years since it voted for a Republican presidential candidate. (George W. Bush lost by a scant 0.22 percentage points in 2000 and 0.48 percentage points in 2004.)

Walker's opponent in the recall election is Milwaukee mayor Tom Barrett, whom he defeated in the 2010 gubernatorial race by six percentage points. In the months leading up to the May 8 Democratic primary, Barrett and former Dane County executive Kathleen Falk were locked in an internecine struggle to demonstrate their obeisance to organized labor. Falk, who has now lost three statewide races, was the first to announce she was challenging Walker. While meeting with the state's largest public-employee unions in January, Falk pledged to veto any future budget that didn't fully restore the unions' collective-bargaining power. She was quickly endorsed by all the major unions, which ended up spending an estimated $5 million in television ads on her behalf.

Walker says he "always thought she would be bought and paid for by the unions," and that Falk's pledge "just proved it." Falk's union deal appeared to be too much for Democratic voters to stomach, and Barrett pulled away in the final weeks of the primary.

Barrett, unlike Falk, had trouble connecting with the unions, a failure that forced him to lurch leftward in an attempt to earn their imprimatur. As mayor of Milwaukee, Barrett actually used many of Walker's reforms to balance his own budget; the Milwaukee Journal Sentinel reported that the city came out $10 million ahead thanks to the governor's plan. A Web video sent out to AFSCME supporters early in the campaign blasted Barrett for supporting passage of Walker's bill, and a number of his early campaign appearances were picketed by union workers.

Yet according to Walker, Barrett's tangles with public unions shouldn't lull voters into thinking he's a moderate on labor issues. "I don't think anybody should mistakenly think that means that Tom Barrett is any less extreme on this," Walker says, adding, "He was just more politically prudent to not let it get out publicly. To me, it's pretty clear that while he had enough political sense not to publicly let out that he was doing this private pledge, the reality is that he'll be just as bought and paid for."

Increasingly, it looks like Walker is winning the argument over the proper role of public-union power. A Marquette University poll conducted the week before the June 5 election showed Walker with a 52 percent to 45 percent lead over Barrett. Since the beginning of April, 16 public polls have been conducted; Walker has led in every one. In the Marquette poll, independents favored Walker by 14 percentage points — the same margin by which respondents favored Walker's plan to scale back public-union collective bargaining.

On the hour drive south from Manitowoc to the Milwaukee suburb of Brown Deer, Walker tilts his head back and nods off for ten minutes. He claims his hectic schedule demands such catnaps; he usually sets the alarm on his BlackBerry for ten minutes, and always wakes up 30 seconds before the alarm goes off. It is clear that he considers this a kind of skill.

When Walker reaches Brown Deer, he receives a brief tour of Dean Elementary School before he sits down to read to a class of fourth-graders. After finishing the book, he takes a few questions from the students before moving on to a press event in the library. (Sample question: "How tall are you?" Answer: Six feet.)

At his press event in the library, Walker moderates a roundtable of local-government officials, who take turns praising his reforms. Racine County executive Jim Ladwig explains how unions had for years blocked the use of prisoners to mow the county's medians, so mowing occurred only once a year; now the grass stays cut. Brown Deer schools superintendent Deb Kerr says that her district is now able to build a new $22 million school, 68 percent of which will be funded by savings realized through Walker's reforms. Brown Deer's finance director, Emily Koczela, follows up by saying Walker's law "turned us loose in terms of talking about every dollar with regard to children."

Following the school event, Walker retreats briefly to his campaign's "victory center" in Wauwatosa, a city just west of Milwaukee, where volunteers are making nonstop phone calls on his behalf. In a corner office, Walker discusses why he, of all the governors in the nation making changes to government-worker benefits, is the one facing a recall election. He mentions Rhode Island, New York, New Jersey, and California as states in which Democrats are actually encouraging substantial changes to government benefits, leaving Wisconsin Democrats out of touch with the national party.

In criticizing Walker's plan, Wisconsin Democrats have targeted the rollback of collective bargaining, saying their opposition to the plan "isn't about the money." Of course, it is about little else. Walker believes it was the end of compulsory union membership and automatic dues deductions more than the end of collective bargaining in itself that prompted the unions' crusade against him.

"I think in the end . . . they would have sold their members out in a heartbeat for double the pension contributions or anything else if they only could have gotten their hands on those automatic dues deductions," says Walker. "That's what makes a difference for them, because that's what they care about. They don't care about the workers, they don't care about collective bargaining, or pensions. . . . I mean, they do, but I don't think it was really about those things — it was about the raw power and money they felt was at risk here because we gave people freedom to choose."

Walker shifts topics, ripping his opponents for their lack of a plan to balance the state budget. During the primary, both Barrett and Falk refused to say how they would have balanced the budget, and failed to offer any hints as to how they would fund the repeal of Walker's collective-bargaining law, something they both vowed to do. Walker boasts that he was able to increase funding for Medicaid by $1.2 billion without raising taxes, thanks to his benefit changes.

"Either they don't have a plan, or the real answer is, they would raise taxes," Walker says. "Two people who are part of a movement that claims that they want to undo what we did in this past year can't tell us what they would do instead." One of the primary critiques of Walker is that he didn't campaign on rolling back collective bargaining in 2010; ironically, it appears the people trying to replace him are just as unwilling to reveal the details of their biggest reform plans before voters put them in power.

Walker asserts that his opponents want to take Wisconsin down the disastrous path that Illinois has traveled over the past year. In January of 2011, Illinois governor Pat Quinn raised taxes in the state by $7 billion; yet, according to City Journal's Steven Malanga, Illinois's lavish government-employee benefits sucked $5.7 billion from the state budget, a number that was only $2.7 billion as recently as 2008. Even with the tax hikes, the state was left with a $9 billion deficit. Consequently, Quinn has proposed to reduce Medicaid eligibility and coverage and drop the rates Medicaid pays to physicians.

"[In Illinois] they're now shutting down state facilities, laying off tons of public employees, and cutting Medicaid, while we added money to Medicaid and avoided massive layoffs," Walker says. He points out that Illinois's credit rating was recently lowered, and is now the worst in the country; that Wisconsin's pension system is fully funded, while Illinois's is less than half funded; and that Illinois's unemployment rate is 8.8 percent, while Wisconsin's is 6.8 percent.

Sipping from a plastic water bottle, Walker says the entire recall effort is "intellectually dishonest." He notes a recent interview given to Mother Jones by Graeme Zielinski, spokesman for the Democratic party in Wisconsin, in which Zielinski admitted that "collective bargaining is not moving people"; he urged Democrats instead to focus on Walker's "war on women" and an ongoing investigation of Walker's former county-executive office.

The investigation, which began in May of 2010, has netted several criminal charges against former Walker aides. Walker's former deputy chief of staff, Timothy Russell, has been charged with stealing $21,000 in contributions meant for Operation Freedom, a picnic that honors veterans. Russell's domestic partner, Brian Pierick, has been charged with two felony counts of child enticement. Two former Walker aides have been charged with doing campaign work on government time. The investigation is ongoing, and Democrats are hoping a charge comes down before the election that ties Walker to criminal wrongdoing.

Walker says he doesn't "think they know anything" about what's being investigated. He notes that it was his office that initially asked for the probe.

When asked about the vituperative attacks by union activists he has endured over the past year, Walker shrugs. He is disappointed that his two high-school-aged sons have been targeted on Facebook; he said someone began screaming at his septuagenarian mother in a grocery store last year. "There's gotta be more wrong with your life than whether you agree with me or not" to do something like that, he says. (Early in his campaign, his sons appeared in one of his television ads; they looked as if they had been forced to participate via court order.)

One Sunday last November, Walker and his sons were raking leaves in their front yard when a car on the street honked at them. Walker looked over to see the car's window roll down, a hand jut out, and a middle finger extend. Three minutes later, Walker heard another honk, and saw two different cars on his street. This time, two arms emerged from the cars' windows, and both flashed him a thumbs-up signal before driving off. While he says that should have comforted him, he adds, "I think it just means I should start raking at night."

Walker isn't alone; for more than a year, it has been open season on Republican legislators in Wisconsin. E-mails threatening death and physical harm poured into legislative offices faster than the police could investigate them. GOP representative Robin Vos had a beer dumped on his head. For much of the period of the demonstrations, legislators had to escape the capitol through an underground tunnel, then get on a bus that took them to their cars. One night the bus was spotted and protesters rocked it back and forth as the legislators held on inside.

But it is Walker's young lieutenant governor, Rebecca Kleefisch, who has drawn the worst of the Left's vulgarisms. The comely redhead is like catnip to angry protesters; they simply can't help themselves. One liberal Madison radio talk-show host ridiculed Kleefisch's recent bout with colon cancer and suggested she got her job by performing sex acts. Following a recent Walker speech, a protester turned to Kleefisch's husband and screamed, "Your wife is a f***ing whore!"

Despite all the vitriol, the Wisconsin imbroglio is earning Walker new fans around the country. When the Republican presidential candidates campaigned in Wisconsin in early April, each one tried to top the others in gushing support for the governor. At an April speech before the Illinois Policy Institute, a woman invoked a recent movie on education reform in asking Walker whether he was the "Superman" she was waiting for. Walker demurred, saying that he was partial to Batman.

Walker says he handles the pressure of newfound fame by hopping on his 2003 Harley-Davidson Road King and hitting the open road. He says the bike gives him "freedom"; his Harley dealer is trying to get him to install a cell-phone communications system, but he bristles at the notion. "Why would I want that?" he says. "The whole reason I ride my motorcycle is for people to not be able to get me on my phone."

He also enjoys the egalitarianism of the Harley culture. He says that when he rides, he might have the CEO of a major company on one side and a janitor on the other, "and nobody knows, nor do they care."

Walker says he learned political fortitude by studying the travails of Ronald Reagan. He has read numerous Reagan biographies, and lists Dinesh D'Souza's Ronald Reagan: How an Ordinary Man Became an Extraordinary Leader as his favorite. "[Reagan] is a guy who was obviously well liked, but who, early on, faced tremendous challenges, major pushback, had a lot of people, including people in his own party, telling him to back off," he says. "But he knew who he was, he knew where he wanted to go, and he knew how he was going to get there, and he didn't back off."

Walker says that if he wins on June 5, the state will begin to come together. He doesn't believe a recall victory will give him a new mandate; it will merely reaffirm the mandate he believes he was given on the day he was elected in 2010.

"If Tom Barrett wins, it doesn't end the 'civil war,' it just opens it all up again," he says. Barrett, he argues, is "going to go to extreme lengths to try to repeal the reforms we have passed, which means you're going to have this debate all over again. If people just want to move on, the easiest way to do that is to see me elected."

When I hand the Lamentable Tragedie playbill to Walker, he chuckles. When informed of his gruesome theatrical demise, he rolls his eyes. "How pleasant," he says. But he does not minimize the national implications of the recall election — the serious effects it could have on states that are attempting to rein in excessive employee pay and benefits. To those states, a Walker loss on June 5 would be the unkindest cut of all.

National Review

THE SPEECH WALKER WOULD RATHER GIVE

January 22, 2014

On Wednesday night, Gov. Scott Walker will give his fourth "state of the state" speech. The following is the speech the reserved Walker might give if he could say what he really wanted — or if he was a cornerback for the Seattle Seahawks.

Hey there, everybody! I'm Scott Walker — you may remember me as the governor you dopey Democrats turned into a national star after you tried to yank me out of office mid-term. In fact, here's a picture of me on the cover of my book, "Unintimidated," which is still for sale in bookstores and on the Internet. In fact, as long as you guys clearly want to talk about my book, let me mention that for every 10,000 jobs you create, you get half off a copy. And if you create 20,000 jobs, I'll get you a copy signed by Paul Ryan.

Look, we all know everybody at home is watching "American Idol," so let's keep this real.

First, let's talk about my billion-dollar budget surplus. Remember the deficit-ridden days when my predecessor, Democrat Jim Doyle, would walk up to this podium looking like Eeyore, listing all the ways he was going to cut programs? Now I got almost a billion-dollar surplus. That's "billion" with a "b" — almost enough money to pay for a Mary Burke snowboarding vacation. (Winks.)

And like any purchase, it's time to give the taxpayers their change back. It's their money, not government's — so all you taxpayers can expect a check in the mail on or around Monday, Nov. 3. Also included in the envelope will be a coupon to purchase my book, "Unintimidated." Coincidentally, I just heard someone in this very chamber talking about it only a minute ago.

Let's talk about jobs. Apparently, some of you think the governor can just wave a magic wand and increase employment. And so what if I allegedly "pledged" to create 250,000 jobs? You'd rather have a governor too weak to shoot high, even if he falls a little short.

As I recall, the 2010 election was between me and Milwaukee Mayor Tom Barrett. Right now, the state unemployment rate is 6.3%, while it's 9.4% in Milwaukee County. Is 9.4% greater than 6.3%? Let me pull out my calculator here — oh, look, turns out it is.

And what's your answer to create jobs, Democrats? To raise the minimum wage, making it harder for businesses to employ people? Here, let me pull that bill off the "fresh ideas" pile for you — it's right here under the bill allowing women to vote.

You think some millionaire snowboarding hippie is going to figure out how to create jobs?

As for education, allow me to issue a special invite to my Democratic friends. Under my union reforms, statewide scores are up and poor families around the state have access to the best schools. As it happens, the cook at the mansion is serving up crow tonight; you're all invited over to enjoy a big, delicious bowl of it.

I know some of you think you're going to take me down with these bogus John Doe investigations, but keep in mind I'm like the blob. Keep shooting me, and I get bigger and stronger. In fact, as soon as you wrap up this current phony investigation, how about you pile Fred, Velma and Shaggy into the Mystery Machine and go figure out who's been spooking the goats down by Old Man Thompson's farm?

A lot of my supporters have been asking what my plans will be after November. Let's face it; we all know I'm going to win. Be honest; nobody can envision a Wisconsin come November where Dom Capers has a job and I don't. I mean, have you seen me on "Meet the Press" and all the national shows?

Ah, yes — but after November. You think I'm stupid enough to actually tell you my plans? I wouldn't dare insult the extremely intelligent and extraordinarily good-looking voters of Iowa and New Hampshire by making an announcement before it's time. All I've said is that the 2016 Republican candidate should be a governor of a Midwestern state, be 46 years old, should ride a Harley, should wear the same blue shirt and red tie combo all the time and was nicknamed "The Desperado" in high school. Could be anyone, really.

Looks like I'm out of time. For the rest of my agenda, you can join the almost tens of thousands who have bought my book, which I hear is still available for purchase.

Support the troops. Polar vortex. Ronald Reagan. And I'm out. (Drops microphone.)

Milwaukee Journal Sentinel

A TRIP THROUGH SCOTT WALKER'S BRAIN

March 1, 2015

Imagine for a moment you are a thought in Gov. Scott Walker's brain. It's a pretty good gig - lately, you've been getting a lot more attention from people around America.

But recently you've had some jealousy heaped on you from your friends because you're the thought Walker summons when he wants to talk about Act 10, his 2011 victory over public sector unions. And with Walker's presumptive presidential run, he's been calling on you an inordinate amount. On one side of you lives your neighbor, "tax cuts," and on the other side lives the much quieter "traditional marriage." Down the street lives the guy nobody knows anything about, "common core." The house across the street from you was mysteriously vacated a week ago; nobody's really offered an explanation why "Obama's Christianity" skipped town in such a hurry.

Word has recently come down, however, that Walker would be speaking at the 2015 Conservative Political Action Conference, a nationally talked about showcase for presidential contenders. This is your time to bask in all the glory you worked so hard to earn; without you, Walker probably wouldn't even be invited to that stage. You start jogging and doing push-ups to get ready.

Finally, your day to show off is here. Word comes down that Walker's speech has begun, so you begin stretching. Suddenly, your phone rings, and you're ordered to make the short sprint down to Walker's mouth to boast of your accomplishments. You run down there and slay the crowd. The conservative attendees hoot and holler at your appearance, thinking you've justified Walker's front-runner status.

When your time is up, you make the triumphant trip back home, hoping every one of your appearances is this successful. Scuttlebutt on the block is that all your friends are killing it. "Concealed carry," "voter identification," "elected three times in four years," and "right-to-work" are all earning rave reviews. But you know, deep inside, that you are the star of this show. You simply must make an encore performance. The crowd demands it.

With your new neighbor "we need to be tough on ISIS" currently on stage, you decide to head back down to Walker's tongue. You start the leisurely stroll downward, so confident in yourself that you miss some warning signs on the route. On one side of the road are Walker's staffers, yelling and screaming for you to stay up in his brain. On the other side of the road are magazines showing the butchery and barbarism in which ISIS terrorists engage. Yet you remain blissfully unaware.

As you get closer, you pass "we need to be tough on ISIS" on her way back. She asks you where you're going. When you say you're making a return performance, she squints her eyes. "Are you sure that's a good idea?" she asks. "If you go out there now, people are going to think you're comparing me with you, even if you don't mean it."

"What's wrong with just saying you showed courage in one instance, so you're prepared to show courage in another instance, even if it's not as serious?" you say.

"You know exactly what is going to happen," she says. "It will be portrayed as ungenerously as possible by the media. They will write every headline saying 'Walker compares dealing with protesters to dealing with ISIS' just to make him look like an idiot. Just look what happened when 'Obama loves America' took a vacation day last week."

You brush her aside. What does she know? She's only lived in the neighborhood for a few weeks - you've been a star for four years now. She wouldn't even exist without your prodigious strength.

And off you go. You step into Walker's mouth one more time to let the crowd's cheers wash over you.

"We need a leader with that kind of confidence," Walker says, bidding goodbye to the previous speaker. "If I can take on 100, 000 protesters, I can do the same across the world."

You're the show stopper - it will be the thing he proudly ends with. But as you turn around to head home, you see a number of puzzled people furiously tapping away at their phones.

On the trail back home, you see a dark figure that you've come to know much better in the past three weeks. As he moves closer to you, you can see he's carrying a dustpan, a broom, and a bottle of Windex. You know that in order for Walker to mount a plausible presidential candidate, you'd better see a lot less of this dark figure in the future.

"Oh, hello 'clarification,' you say.

Milwaukee Journal Sentinel

WE MUST HONOR FEINGOLD'S 18 YEARS IN THE SENATE

August 2, 2015

Being the etiquette enthusiast I am, I recently looked up the protocol for addressing former elected officials. According to the book "Honor and Respect: The Official Guide to Names, Titles, and Forms of Address," tradition requires that "former senators keep the honorific in retirement."

Thus, in keeping with tradition, it is incumbent on Wisconsinites to honor Sen. Russ Feingold with his rightful title as he once again runs for the U.S. Senate. To do otherwise would be to disrespect the 18 years Senator Feingold spent in the Senate. I mean, 18 years is a long time. If Senator Feingold's career in the Senate were a person, it could smoke cigarettes, go to war, and actually vote for Senator Feingold.

The loquacious Senator Feingold, however, has been somewhat bashful about being honored in this way. According to recently minted state Democratic Party chair Martha Laning, Senator Feingold's campaign has requested his supporters never refer to him as "Senator Feingold."

"They want us to say 'Russ' because the last campaign - it was all about '16 years, 16 years, 16 years, he's there too long,' "Laning recently told a group of Door County Democrats. "And so they want to say, 'He's just one of us.' We want to go back to Russ being Russ." (Laning, misspoke - Senator Feingold actually spent 18 years in Washington, D.C.)

Laning added that, "Second one is we never want to say 'go back' to the Senate. We just want to say 'electing' him to the Senate. They want to totally get away from all that."

What humility from Senator Feingold! Why wouldn't he want people to know all about his 18 years serving in a Congress that currently enjoys a 16% approval rating? Why would Senator Feingold not boast of the fact that he first ran for public office in 1982, a robust 33 years ago?

And if Senator Feingold was truly interested in joining the federal Senator Witness Protection Program, why not really commit? Grow a beard and pretend to be Russian oil magnate "Ruslan Feingoldovich." (Unfortunately for Senator Feingold, "Don Draper" was already taken.)

Perhaps Senator Feingold is now sitting in his office thinking up new ways to describe what he did in Washington for nearly two decades. Instead of "U.S. senator," Senator Feingold's resume probably now reads "senior voter service manager, 1993-2011." All references to "Congress" will be changed to "that law-talking place." (Under "Special Skills," it will read, "competent in Word, Excel and having major campaign finance reform legislation overturned time after time in the U.S. Supreme Court.)

Even though Senator Feingold shouldn't be ashamed of his three terms in the U.S. Senate (for the record, he was elected in 1992, 1998 and again in 2004), he is clearly skilled at the campaign arts. If he weren't a U.S. senator for 18 years, he very easily could have been a director in the way he has stage-managed his supporters. Remember in 2010, when Senator Feingold's campaign invented a woman ("Elizabeth Ackland") who claimed to have benefited from the expensive stimulus plan? What genius to concoct a dream woman out of thin air! It's almost as if Senator Feingold was the inspiration for the 1985 movie "Weird Science"!

Or during his two decades in Congress, when he claimed to want money out of politics, but then used his political action committee as a slush fund to pay himself and his cronies? A command performance!

Senator Feingold's humility, however, seems destined to fail. In a recent poll, 39% of Wisconsin voters hadn't even heard of the man who beat Senator Feingold in 2010, Sen. Ron Johnson. Walk around the streets of Milwaukee and ask random people who their U.S. senator is at this moment, and half would probably say "Russ Feingold." But that's what happens when you spend nearly a quarter of a century in the U.S. Senate (as Senator Feingold did, if I hadn't mentioned it.)

We do drink a lot in Wisconsin, but not enough for us to forget Senator Feingold's 18 glorious years in the U.S. Capitol. In order to truly honor his service, we should all make sure he never forgets it.

Milwaukee Journal Sentinel

REHNQUIST, FORGOTTEN BADGER

October 23, 2015

When reporting on Rep. Paul Ryan's likely ascendance to the position of U.S. speaker of the House, the Journal Sentinel's Craig Gilbert noted that Ryan "would be the highest-ranking officeholder ever from this state." Of course, being speaker would make Ryan third in line in the presidential order of succession, which pings back and forth between the legislative and executive branches.

But the succession order ignores the ever-important third branch, in which U.S. Supreme Court justices often prove themselves to be the nation's most powerful officeholders. For those who doubt the Supreme Court's muscle, just ask opponents of either abortion or Obamacare.

As it happens, Wisconsin birthed one of these mystical chief justices of the Supreme Court. In fact, he served on the high court for 33 years. William Rehnquist was from Shorewood. He passed away in 2005, and was replaced by Justice John Roberts, who currently serves as chief justice.

If one accepts that being the chief justice is the most important job in America, then a Milwaukee native held that job for 19 years. And yet his memory seems to have all but vanished from our collective consciousness. Imagine if a Wisconsinite had held the presidency for 19 years (22nd Amendment notwithstanding, of course.) We'd be holding a ticker-tape parade annually for him or her.

Tommy Thompson missed his best chance to run in 1996, when he was revered as America's most innovative governor. Scott Walker's run at the White House this year was shorter than a Kardashian marriage. "Fighting Bob" LaFollette merely ran for president, and he still retains cult-like status among progressives in the state. Half of the public land in Wisconsin is named after Gaylord Nelson, and he never even sought the presidency.

Yet here we have Rehnquist, during whose tenure the court's temperament shifted dramatically. In a 2006 visit to Milwaukee, Justice Antonin Scalia reflected on Rehnquist's tenure, saying the Rehnquist court's true legacy is a movement toward "neutral, non-substantive and more easily ascertainable" methods of interpreting both laws and the Constitution. In other words, rather than deciding cases based on changing community standards or legislative history, justices more often use textualism. During his tenure as chief justice, Rehnquist's court would decide landmark cases dealing with virtually every salient constitutional issue - from the proper exercise of the Commerce Clause, to gay rights, to free speech, to support for school vouchers.

Of course, as in the case of any public official, there were some missteps along the way. The time and thought Rehnquist put into how many stripes he should have on the robe he wore during President Bill Clinton's impeachment hearing is sadly the first line in his biography for some political observers. And he wasn't exactly the most dynamic public speaker, although personal eloquence is hardly a requirement to apply the law consistently and fairly. Conservatives may have some gripes about some of the cases his court refused to overturn (Roe vs. Wade, Miranda vs. Arizona), although Rehnquist personally dissented in many of the cases upholding those controversial opinions.

Regardless, the fact remains that Rehnquist was perhaps the most powerful man in America for two decades, and Wisconsin has yet to pay him the proper respect. The fourth-longest serving chief justice in U.S. history is one of our own, yet since his death, his name has appeared in only a handful of stories in the Journal Sentinel - mostly in reference to Scalia's visit in 2006. While Scalia may be more bombastic and Justice Clarence Thomas more controversial, it is not an overstatement to say that

Rehnquist may have been the most consistent conservative voice in American jurisprudence in the past 30 years.

One wonders whether Rehnquist would be lionized by the media had he shifted the court to a more activist role, in the mold of Chief Justices Earl Warren and Warren Burger before him. As it stands, it seems Rehnquist already has been cast into the bin of Great Forgotten Wisconsinites. (In Heaven, he is no doubt commiserating with Donald K. "Deke" Slayton, one of the original seven Mercury astronauts, who hailed from Sparta.) This is unfair treatment for a man who even Justice Thurgood Marshall would call "a great chief justice." He deserves better.

Milwaukee Journal Sentinel

DELIVERY ROOM CONFIDENTIAL

June 26, 2006

My best friend's wife just had a baby girl. I had a great time talking to him on the phone about becoming a daddy for the first time, because a lot of our childbirth experiences were virtually identical. I had wanted to do a post about what becoming a daddy for the first time is like, but they had the kid before I got around to doing it. I've seen a lot of articles about what childbirth is like for women, but few about what it's like for men. So here it is.

All the time leading up to the birth of the child is spent focused on the mother's needs. They learn what to buy, how to breathe, what to pack for the hospital, how to nurse, etc. I actually decided to go for the Husband of the Year Award and show up to the breastfeeding classes, just to support my wife. When I walked out of the room after the class, I was clutching my chest because my nipples hurt so much just from watching the breastfeeding movies. If men had to breastfeed, the human race would have died off about a hundred thousand years ago and a pterodactyl would be sitting at your desk doing your job right now.

As much as you prepare for the actual moment you have to go to the hospital, you will completely lose your mind when it happens. You scramble around the house like a hamster on Red Bull to get your bags together and thrown into the car. The only upside is that you get to drive like a complete maniac on the way to the hospital, just like they do on TV – my driving was so bad, I'm surprised the baby didn't jump out to tell me to slow down (nothing more irritating than a nagging inter-uterine driver).

When you get to the hospital, they will put you in a little waiting room where they do a preliminary check to make sure you're really having a baby and you're not just there pulling an elaborate ruse to get the free mini-

Pepsis from the OB snack bar. After they check the mother out, they will tell you that there's a chance that despite your rush to get to the hospital, the baby may not be ready to come out and you may have to go home for a few hours. At that point, you will tell them that you are leaving the hospital with a baby, whether it's yours or someone else's.

Soon, they put your wife on drugs to try to induce the child to come out. This is far more effective than your idea of dangling two free Packer tickets down between her legs. Now is the time to take pictures, as within hours she will have convinced the staff at the hospital that you are an active al-Qaeda operative. Once the contractions start, you and your wife will enter an entirely new phase of your relationship. For details, see any Bill Cosby standup routine from the last 30 years.

Obviously, during this time your wife is in extraordinary pain, and any man that suggests otherwise is secretly shipped off to a remote internment camp for insensitive men and never heard from again. But you will feel a deep sense of utter helplessness, and it's hard. Standing before you is the person you care most about in the entire world in extreme pain – and the most you can do is offer her the occasional ice cube. Jokes are not appreciated. The only thing that would possibly make her feel better would be the sight of a pack of rabid dingoes attacking your crotch.

During the entire night, hospital staff is running in and checking your wife's progress. There are doctors, nurses, interns, and other staff that have an all-access pass to her womb. It won't surprise you a bit to find out that some guy examining your wife's cervix is the Pepsi machine mechanic just coming in to see if everything was alright.

Finally, it's time for an epidural, which will numb her from mid chest down and completely change the trajectory of the evening. For one, you will find out that your relationship may not be as strong as you thought after she proposes on the spot to the anesthesiologist. She will treat this guy like he's George Clooney handing her an Ann Taylor credit card with no limit. You instantly become the fifth most important person in the room (behind the doctor, your wife, the baby, and the soft drink mechanic, who won't leave for some reason).

Finally, it comes time to push the baby out. You rush to your wife's side and grab her hand, reminding her to breathe. She's pushing as hard as she can, swearing that she can't push any more. If you had half this much determination, you'd be running your company instead of sitting on your butt reading anonymous blogs all day. For some reason, you bend your knees and get in an athletic crouch, not unlike how your little league coach told you to stand when you played shortstop (it may also be helpful to wear a cup to protect yourself in this situation, too). This may make you feel like you're helping, but really has nothing to do with whether the baby is coming out or not.

When the baby refuses to come out, the doctor will ask you to grab your wife's leg and pull it back to get her in a better position. You jump right in, not realizing that this isn't exactly what you signed up for when you joined your health plan. Later, you will ask the doctor for a discount since you had to do some of the work yourself. Seriously – if I'm getting a new muffler and have to bring my own screwdriver, it better not be full price.

And finally, within a split second, your life will change forever. You'll hear the most important sound you'll ever hear – that of your child crying. You'll be in such shock, that you won't even notice when the doctor asks you if you want to cut the umbilical cord, and you actually do it – despite being completely grossed out by the concept an hour earlier.

You look around the room and see your wife's blood, and you will be scared out of your mind.

You'll look at her and suddenly your entire relationship will flash before your eyes. In an instant, you'll think of the night you met. You'll think about your first date, when you stayed up all night laughing nervously, wondering if she really liked you or not. You'll remember the night at the UW Memorial Union Terrace when you finally realized that this was the woman that you wanted to spend the rest of your life with, and how you proposed to her on that spot. She'll be laying there with tears in her eyes, drenched in sweat and hair messed up, but at that instant, you will never have seen a woman so beautiful in your life.

You can't believe that any woman would ever have so much faith and trust in you that she would go through such excruciating pain to deliver a child. Fortunately, in case you forget that, you will be reminded of it approximately 8,345 times over the next twelve months. You thank the Lord that you could be there to witness the birth of this child, seeing as there's really only an even-money chance you were there for the conception.

You fumble around for your camera to try to get pictures. You start sobbing like Richard Simmons after meeting an 800 pound guy that has to be removed from his house with a crane. Your wife starts breast feeding the baby, and you try to get a picture of it without getting too much of the breast in the picture (your friends will be looking at these, after all). It is incredible that babies have the innate ability to breast feed right out of the womb – much like you were born with the uncanny ability to watch the Brewers, listen to music, and scratch yourself all at the same time.

Apparently unaware of your court record, the doctors hand your baby over to you. It is at this point precisely that you are overwhelmed with about 100 feelings simultaneously. You can't believe this is all real, and that something so great could happen to you. I mean, you are the guy, after all, who used to throw lawn furniture off the top of your fraternity house to see if it would break. You're the guy who would have girls drop you off three blocks away from your house after a date so they wouldn't find out exactly where you lived. You're the guy that used to get drunk and wash all the cars on your block at three o'clock in the morning, hoping some hot chick would appreciate the gesture.

And here in your hands is the greatest thing that God ever created. It feels like you are now the first person ever to figure out procreation – that nobody could have ever done this before. You can't believe that somehow this actually sometimes occurs without the father being involved. Sure, you may be a sap, but it's inconceivable to you that fathers leave and don't come back, or don't even know that one of their children is born at all.

It is at that point that suddenly you realize your life has a purpose. As listlessly as you may have lived your life, now you are responsible for another human being. Sure, it took you an extra year or two to finish college, and you may never have gotten the job you really wanted, but suddenly all of your personal ambitions and travails seem trivial. Your life is clear as day now – I have to take care of this baby, and do the best job I possibly can. And that's it, really. Nothing else even comes close.

For years, you have been wondering whether anyone will ever remember you when you're gone. What have you ever done that's really affected anyone in any real way? You never wrote a hit screenplay, never played in the NBA, never volunteered at the Boys and Girls club. You're afraid that if you were to disappear, nobody would even know you were there at all. Now, all at once, you realize what your legacy will be – you know that by raising this kid to be a kind, generous, and hard-working adult, you've given the world the best possible gift you can.

What you don't realize at the time, however, is the fact that you are no longer writing your own life story. Those days of going boozing with the boys? Done. Movies? What are those? You won't ever eat in a restaurant again that doesn't offer you the option of "Biggie Sizing." You will soon come to recognize that you are now relegated to a bit part in your own autobiography. The seven pound, four ounce conspirator in your arms has now taken over as head writer of your life story. And you will never mind a bit.

The digital clock above you says 7:12 A.M. You've now been awake all night waiting for this moment. It's time to catch what little sleep you can before your life starts all over again. You doze off thinking how great it is to be a dad. And wondering if you have to prove the baby's yours for the hospital to validate your parking ticket.

THIRD PARTY ANIMALS

Spring 2008

On the evening of November 5, 2002, the election results began to roll in. A rainy election day had come to wash away the grime from an often-brutal gubernatorial race in Wisconsin, which had seen the candidates refer to each other as "crooked" and "absolutely disreputable." Incumbent Republican Governor Scott McCallum, who had been in office scarcely two years, faced a strong challenge from long-time Democratic Attorney General Jim Doyle. The race was a crucial turning point for Wisconsin, as it represented the first time in sixteen years iconic Governor Tommy Thompson was not on the ballot.

Merely a year earlier, Republican officials could only have dreamed about Doyle pulling a paltry 45% of the vote on election night. McCallum had suffered in Thompson's shadow after Tommy had left to be Secretary of Health and Human Services in the Bush Administration. McCallum, saddled with a large budget deficit, sought to cut spending to local governments to make up the difference. Naturally, local officials, many of them Republicans, appeared all too willing to defenestrate McCallum in favor of the Democrat.

Yet on election night, Doyle's poor showing did little to cheer up the GOP faithful. While the Democrat had fallen well short of the magic 50% mark, McCallum had pulled in a woeful 41%, losing to Doyle by nearly 66,000 votes. For the first time in sixteen years, Wisconsin would be led by a Democrat – and a long time bitter Thompson foe, at that.

The reason both major candidates together could only muster 86% of the total vote could be found in bucolic Tomah, Wisconsin (pop. 8,400). Former boxer, professional card player, tavern owner, and Tomah Mayor Ed Thompson had decided a year earlier to run for Governor in 2002. Thompson, a short, stout man with glasses so thick they looked like they could plausibly protect him from a bullet, had signed on with the Libertarian Party of Wisconsin in order to make his third party charge toward the state's highest office. His sole qualification for the office of governor appeared to be that he once emerged from the same womb as his brother, Governor Tommy Thompson.

440

Thompson's 2002 run for governor represented a perfect storm for a third party candidacy in Wisconsin. The Legislature was in the midst of a scandal that eventually led to leaders of both houses being convicted of felonies for crimes such as extortion, bribery, and using state offices for fundraising. The economic downturn of 2001 left voters skeptical of either party's ability to deal with their financial troubles. By September 2002, 45 percent of Wisconsin residents felt the state was on the wrong track, up from 20 percent only three years earlier. Seventy-five percent of citizens believed lobbyists had more say in how the government spent money than voters did.

Of course, Thompson's last name didn't hurt either. As the brother of the state's most beloved political figure, Ed Thompson had immediate name recognition throughout the state. Plus, it's not entirely impossible that some voters may have actually confused Ed Thompson with his famous brother. Confusion over names at the polls isn't exactly unprecedented—it is believed by some historians that Wisconsin's first African-American legislator, Lucien Palmer, was elected in 1906 because voters confused him with another political Palmer, who was white. Lucien Palmer only lasted one two-year term, which may have been just enough time for voters to figure out their "mistake."

Perhaps the most famous example of mistaken identity in Wisconsin politics occurred in 1970, when a Sheboygan gas station attendant Robert A. Zimmerman ran as a Democrat for the position of secretary of state. At the time, the incumbent secretary of state happened to be a popular Republican, Robert C. Zimmerman. Robert A. Zimmerman, who wasn't allowed to speak during the campaign by his mentor Edmond Hou-Seye, won the Democratic primary against up-and-comer Tom Fox, presumably because voters confused him with the incumbent secretary. (Fox went on to become commissioner of insurance in Wisconsin.) Zimmerman, the mute gas station attendant, went on to lose to Zimmerman the secretary of state. Hou-Seye went on to run several ill-fated races for statewide office himself, coining the phrase "journalism is the science of distortion" along the way.

Wisconsin historically has been a sanctuary for third parties. It was in Wisconsin where Robert M. LaFollette, Jr. split the Progressive Party off from the GOP in 1934. That year, the Progressives won a landslide of state offices, including Philip LaFollette winning the governor's office for the first time as a Progressive candidate. Milwaukee famously elected three Socialist mayors in the first half of the twentieth century, the only major city in the U.S. to have done so.

In recent years, third parties in Wisconsin have continued to affect statewide elections. In 2000, Vice President Al Gore defeated Texas Governor George W. Bush by 5,708 votes in Wisconsin. Gore's margin of victory was actually less than the 6,640 Wisconsin votes cast for Libertarian Harry Browne for president in that same election. In the 2000 election, third party presidential votes numbered 116,445 in Wisconsin—nearly 20 times the size of Gore's margin of victory. Everyone remembers the vote count debacle and subsequent court action in Florida following that presidential election, yet that charade would not have occurred had a small fraction of third party voters in Wisconsin shifted their votes to George W. Bush.

Strong third party voting in Wisconsin held true to form in 2004, when Senator John Kerry beat Bush by 11,384 votes. In that election, Wisconsin saw 26,397 votes cast for third party candidates. While well below the 2000 third party vote (due mostly to a drastically diminished Ralph Nader effort), the third party total still greatly exceeded the final margin of victory for Kerry.

Naturally, Ed Thompson wasn't the only third party candidate in the field in 2002. Thompson was joined by 34-year-old Aneb Jah Rasta Sensas-Utcha Nefer-I, who insisted that he was already governor of Wisconsin. "I was born to rule, because God's judgment will judge all unrighteousness," said Sensas-Utcha, a native of Milwaukee. "I'm the damn governor of the State of Wisconsin." To back up this claim, Sensas-Utcha pointed to several bills regarding E Coli that he had passed earlier. Unfortunately, he was unable to describe the details of this important legislation, claiming the press might be able to use it against him. Despite his previous hypothetical electoral success, Sensas-Utcha was only able to muster 929 votes statewide in November.

Thompson was also joined as a third party gubernatorial candidate by Mike Mangan, who campaigned wearing a gorilla suit. Mangan, a self-employed energy consultant from Waukesha, waged what he called a "guerilla attack against state spending." Mangan criticized the state's "King Kong deficit," which is quite a coincidence since he happened to own a gorilla mask. (Fortunately for Mangan, the deficit wasn't the size of a turtle, as he would have had to scramble for a new costume.) Mangan was actually a fan of Ed Thompson's run, seeing it as a breakthrough for third parties in future races, saying, "I think he's opening doors."

These independent candidates represent only a small sliver of the colorful history of third party politicians in Wisconsin. In 1974, flamboyant West Milwaukee used car dealer James Groh legally changed his name to "Crazy Jim" to run for governor as an independent. Crazy Jim was a staunch advocate of legalized gambling, and frequently spun a tale of how he once played cards with Frank Sinatra in Las Vegas. At the time, the concept of legal gambling in Wisconsin seemed to be far-fetched—yet Crazy Jim turned out to be a visionary, as Wisconsin adopted a state lottery and welcomed almost unlimited Indian casino gambling by the 1990s. Crazy Jim lost to incumbent Patrick Lucey 629,000 votes to 12,100; but his family said he took solace throughout his life in the fact that he carried Waushara County. (Although he did not—records show he only garnered 47 votes in Waushara County, which placed him a distant fifth.) Crazy Jim died in 2002 of a heart attack.

In Madison, self-described "futurist" Richard H. Anderson has run for numerous offices, including state assembly, mayor, and city council. Anderson routinely ran on an "anti-mind control" platform, believing the government had planted a cybernetic chip in his brain. A self-described bisexual, Anderson fought for better treatment of minorities and, as a surprise to exactly no one, for legalized marijuana. "Just because I'm a pot head doesn't mean I'm not qualified to hold office," he once said. Unfortunately, the government rarely used mind control to direct voters to vote for him, as he once mustered a scant six votes in a race for the state Assembly against now-Congresswoman Tammy Baldwin. Naturally, the Progressive Capital Times newspaper said Anderson had "made a good impression."

(One has to wonder what a debate between a "pro-mind control" and "anti-mind control" candidate is like. Presumably, the "anti" candidate would get up to speak, the "pro" candidate would glare and point his finger at them, and the "anti" candidate would sheepishly sit back down without saying a word.)

Yet the candidacy of Ed Thompson in 2002 represented a breakthrough for independent candidates, who had previously been relegated to the scrap heap of oddities, curiosities, and also-rans. In early 2001, Thompson was a man without a party. Without the backing of a more established third party, a Thompson candidacy could have been viewed as a fringe endeavor and may have lost traction quickly.

Early that year, Thompson met with notorious independent Governor Jesse "The Body" Ventura of Minnesota, who had been carried by his nationwide wrestling fame to victory in 1998. (Thompson would later joke that he should be called Ed "The Belly.") The meeting was arranged by Bob Collison, leader of the Libertarian Party of Wisconsin. Soon thereafter, Thompson signed on as the official Libertarian candidate for governor of Wisconsin. It was a symbiotic relationship—the Libertarian tag gave Thompson the legitimacy his campaign needed, while Thompson gave the

Libertarians a big enough name to finally make a splash in state politics.

Yet there remained an internecine struggle within the party between Libertarians who fundamentally subscribed to the Libertarian principles of limited government and those looking for statewide legitimacy in the electoral process. Clearly, Ed Thompson wasn't a dyed-in-the-wool Libertarian, although he espoused many of the dangers of government police powers. In the late 1990s, Thompson's Tee Pee supper club was raided by authorities and four nickel slot machines were confiscated. He refused to cut a deal and plead guilty, and the charges were dropped when the county district attorney was voted out of office over the raid. Thompson said that one of his motivations for running for governor was to beat then-Attorney General Jim Doyle, whom he believes had ordered the raid on the Tee Pee.

However, this desire for deregulated gambling alone wasn't enough to make him a Libertarian. As mayor of Tomah, Thompson governed as if he were any mayor of any small town in Wisconsin. His gubernatorial platform included more environmental regulation to preserve Wisconsin's natural spaces and more money for the University of Wisconsin system. Thompson's supporters bred more distrust among philosophical libertarians when they bitterly complained about Thompson not receiving enough public tax money to run his campaign—a concept anathema to those truly interested in restricting government spending.

Furthermore, as his running mate, Thompson signed up retiring Democratic Assembly Representative and former Ladysmith Mayor Marty Reynolds. While Reynolds described himself as socially liberal and fiscally conservative, throughout his twelve years as a representative he represented a reliable vote for Assembly Democrats when they sought to expand taxes and spending. Yet, as is required of Northern Democrats in Wisconsin, Reynolds was staunchly in favor of individual rights with regard to firearms and property. Before picking him as his running mate, Thompson said he had never actually met Reynolds—he had only read an editorial the representative had written decrying the "corruption" at the State Capitol. Thompson praised Reynolds' experience as a legislator, saying he would be an "active participant" in his administration, instead of "playing basketball all the time"—a thinly veiled shot at McCallum, who was known for his hard court wizardry during his brother's administration.

On November 15, 2001, at the State Capitol, Thompson officially announced his candidacy for governor of Wisconsin. He posited himself as the everyman candidate, saying:

I am no big time Charlie. I'm just a common hard-working man who is dedicated to serving the hard-working people of Wisconsin. I'm a fighter. I've been in the ring many times as a boxer and there is nothing I like better than a good fight. This is the biggest fight of my life, and I plan on winning it.

Having announced he was running, it was time for Thompson to mobilize his supporters. This included Libertarian Party of Wisconsin President Bob Collison, who had introduced Thompson to Jesse Ventura. Collison had recently garnered press attention for his opposition to the U.S. Census, believing the questions asked on their survey were too personal. (Collison would later leave the Libertarian Party to make an unsuccessful run for the Wisconsin State Assembly.)

Also in the mix was Wisconsin Libertarian Vice Chair Rolf Lindgren, who in November 2003 was accused of stealing $50 out of a bar apron at the Irish Waters Tavern in Madison. After being accused of stealing the cash, Lindgren was arrested for his fourth drunk driving violation. At his trial, he pleaded insanity, testifying that the stress caused by the police accusations related to the Irish Waters incident caused him to blow a .23 on the breathalyzer (11 times the legal limit for someone with three prior drunk driving arrests).

Lindgren also said he was feeling anxiety over appearing in a documentary about Ed Thompson's life the next morning, and suggested that his arrest was retribution for his attempt to recall Jim Doyle from the governor's office. Said Lindgren, "it doesn't really matter why they [filed charges]. What really matters is that they did do it. If I were a black person, I'd be charging racism. What are they saying, all white people look alike?"

The charge against Lindgren for stealing the $50 from the tavern was dropped, as the Dane County District Attorney said the prosecuting attorney needed more time to prosecute the drunk driving charge. In 2006, a jury rejected Lindgren's insanity plea and he was sentenced to five months in jail for driving while intoxicated.

With his campaign team mobilized, Thompson hit the road in his beat-up, 20-year-old motor home. In the week following his campaign announcement, he visited Waukesha, Wausau, Superior, Eau Claire, and Sparta. On the trail, Thompson's policy agenda began to round into shape. He espoused the benefits of lower taxes and more local government control. He pushed for legalization of marijuana and for the release of nonviolent felons from prison. He argued for term limits that would limit governors and legislators to eight years in office.

However, Thompson most often used what he thought was his most powerful talking point—that government was corrupt and it was time for a third party candidate to change it. Eventually, discussion of policy issues merely faded into the background in favor of his corruption speech. When Thompson launched his first radio ads in April 2002, they focused on the ongoing criminal investigation of the Legislature. "Our state government is being tarnished by corruption," Thompson boomed in the ad. "Enough is enough. It's time to put the people's interests above special interests. We need common sense and accountability in government," he said.

At one point in May 2002, students at a campaign appearance at Rice Lake High School asked Thompson what a Libertarian was. "It means you have the right to live your life as you want, as long as you don't physically hurt someone and no one physically hurts you," he said. "It takes the business attitude of the Republican Party and the social attitude of the Democratic Party and improves them," he added.

Later that day, at Bob's Grill in Rice Lake, an 81-year-old patron asked Thompson what life was like in Washington D.C. "No, that's my brother," Ed Thompson politely replied. He then mentioned that he's three years younger but ten years smarter than Tommy, and definitely better looking.

As the campaign wound into the oppressive Wisconsin summer months, Thompson was able to set himself apart from the other candidates in one regard: his yard and highway campaign signs seemed to outnumber his opponents' by a fifty-to-one ratio. By September, Thompson had 850 large highway signs and 9,000 yard signs out the door. Thompson's close ties to the Wisconsin Tavern League virtually guaranteed a black and yellow Ed Thompson sign would be in front of every bar in the state. In rural Wisconsin, those bars are often the centers of civic debate. Tommy Thompson's exploits in local bars are often credited with catapulting him to statewide recognition. It seemed his little brother may be able to capture a little of the same plainspoken magic.

Meanwhile, the race between the major party candidates raged ahead. McCallum ran a television ad that accused Attorney General Doyle of being "crooked" for not aggressively pursuing corruption in the Legislature. Doyle volunteers held a "bingo party" at a Kenosha home for the developmentally disabled where there also conveniently happened to be absentee ballots available for residents to fill out on site.

As election day grew nearer, Thompson was finding it harder and harder to take his "common man" message to the voters. For one, he was having difficulty working his way into debates, which required a candidate to earn six percent of the total vote in the primary. Since Thompson ran unopposed in the Libertarian primary, he didn't garner enough votes. He argued, accurately, that rather than waste their vote on him, his supporters likely voted in the contested primaries between the major candidates.

Eventually, Thompson filed a complaint with the State Elections Board, arguing his exclusion amounted to an illegal campaign contribution to the major candidates. He lost the complaint, but went on to take part in minor debates throughout October. Finally, on October 29th, he participated in a debate broadcast statewide. But by that point, the race between Doyle and McCallum had turned bitter and personal, and Thompson was left without much time to speak between the bickering.

When the dust settled on election night a week later, Thompson had received 10.5% of the vote. While it wasn't nearly enough to win, it was the largest percentage any third party candidate for governor had received in sixty years. Watching the results at the Tee Pee, Thompson seemed upbeat. "We changed the face of politics in Wisconsin," he beamed, adding, "We've made the third party viable." Furthermore, reaching the 10% vote level meant that the Libertarian Party would be validated by having an official representative on the State Elections Board.

Thompson's supporters, however, were confused as to why their candidate didn't fare better. Following the election, Rolf Lindgren wrote an editorial claiming that Ed Thompson hadn't been beaten by the voters; he had instead been beaten by the polls. In the column (in which he listed his credential as "1986 UW-Madison Mathematics Graduate,") Lindgren expressed disbelief that Thompson only received 10.5% of the vote, when a poll prior to the election had Thompson's approval rating at 39%. Since a candidate merely had to receive 34% to win the three-way election, Lindgren was confused as to why Thompson wasn't able to garner enough support to emerge victorious. Apparently, he was unaware that approval ratings measure a candidate's popularity against only themselves, while actual elections pit candidates against each other.

Lindgren went on to argue, as only a 1986 mathematics graduate could, that polls published during the campaign that showed Thompson with single digit support actually depressed his popularity. Lindgren believed the polls showing (accurately, as it turned out) Thompson with little support drove away individuals that normally would have been supporters. "In hindsight, if he had done a few more polls at key moments, and put out a few more polls-related press releases, he might have won the election," said Lindgren.

The debate still rages in Wisconsin about whether Ed Thompson handed the state over to Jim Doyle by stealing votes from McCallum. Conventional wisdom tells us that since Libertarians are further to the right, they steal votes from Republicans. Thus, the GOP immediately groused that Thompson's 10.5% vote total may have swung the race to the incumbent Governor had "Fightin' Ed" not run.

The numbers seem to indicate that, even had Thompson not run, a McCallum victory would have been a long shot. When Thompson's 185,000 votes are divided up, McCallum would have had to win 67.7% of them to overcome Doyle's 66,000-vote margin. While it is true that Thompson did extremely well in GOP-dominated counties like his home Monroe County (Thompson 45%, McCallum 27%, Doyle 26%), Thompson also pulled substantial votes out of the city of Madison, likely due to his support for legalized marijuana. (It is estimated Thompson received 100% of the vote from the much sought-after "dudes who make late night trips to Taco Bell" demographic.)

Additionally, rather than merely being a Libertarian, Ed Thompson was a once-in-a-generation cult of personality. There's no evidence that his votes were from people who lean Libertarian. It's possible his votes were comprised of voters sick of the two parties generally and who recognized his family name as a safe haven for their vote. His addition of Marty Reynolds to the ticket may have made it even easier for Democrats to vote for him.

On the other hand, it is possible that Thompson pulled more votes from Republicans than Democrats. Aside from the votes on election day, Thompson's entry into the race drew other types of resources away from the major candidates—he was able to raise and spend over $400,000, which may have favored McCallum, had Thompson not been able to get his hands on it. Furthermore, the curiosity of Thompson's campaign took up media time that may have changed the face of the race had he not been in it (although given the press McCallum was getting at the time, it might have been better for him to get less coverage throughout the campaign).

Whether Ed Thompson gift-wrapped the 2002 election for Democrat Jim Doyle, we can never really know (although Doyle did defeat a strong Republican challenger, Republican Congressman Mark Green, in 2006). What we do know is that third parties in Wisconsin are a force to be reckoned with. While many regard third parties as a motley group of political nutballs, they have what the major candidates need—votes.

Given the proclivity of Wisconsin voters to cast their ballots for a third party, the 2008 presidential election could hinge on how well candidates relate to these third party voters. With Wisconsin's traditional razor-thin margins of victory, the major candidate who appeals most to third party voters could be the one who emerges victorious. Senators John McCain and Barack Obama need to tap into the wealth of Wisconsin votes that could easily stray into third party territory. With big names like Former Congressman (and star of "Borat") Bob Barr running as a Libertarian, Former Congresswoman Cynthia McKinney seeking the Green Party nomination, and Ralph Nader doing whatever it is he does, independent voters could very well decide Wisconsin, and therefore the presidency.

In 2005, three years after his gubernatorial run, Ed Thompson was elected to the city council back in Tomah. The problem was, he didn't know he was running. Thompson had benefited from a write-in vote effort of which he was unaware. After receiving 31 of 34 votes, he begrudgingly took office. In 2007, Thompson flirted with the idea of running for president himself after aligning himself with a group of "9/11 Truthers" who believe the U.S. government had a role in the September 11, 2001, attacks. In 2008, he was once again sworn in as Mayor of Tomah, assuming the comfortable position he had left to run for governor. It appears he is now content to be an important footnote in Wisconsin's political history— one that major candidates should not soon forget.

Wisconsin Interest Magazine

CHAPTER EIGHT:
SUNDRY FLIMFLAMMERY

JUST WAIT UNTIL MY COWORKERS SEE MY NEW BATHROBE

November 21, 2017

[Ed. note: In late 2017, one of the most respected men in television news, Charlie Rose, was exposed as a sexual predator and immediately thrown off the air. I wrote this piece to ridicule him, and it was accepted by McSweeney's. Before it ran, I asked some people whether the issue was still too hot for a humor piece, and a number of people I trust told me it was – so I asked that it be pulled. It appears here for the first time.]

Honestly, it is easy to feel a modicum of pity for my female co-workers. They clearly all have deep feelings for me, yet have not had the appropriate opportunity to express their desire to be swept away in my love tornado.

But that has all changed. Wait until my coworkers get to see my new bathrobe.

In the past, an affirmative desire for sex was expressed verbally, when people said things like, "yes, I would like to have sex with you," or "I will meet you for a job interview," or "what's in this drink?" But these days, women have become much coyer about letting men now their true intentions.

For instance, yesterday some local teenage ruffians I ran into after buying some traveler's checks told me the best way to attract a woman was to send her an unsolicited picture of my package – but I do not know how to work a digital camera, so why not eliminate the cyber-middle man and simply inflame the womanly passions in person?

This can be achieved by offering an innocent conversation starter, such as wearing my soft, comfortable new robe during business meetings and job interviews. Then, just as the boring talk starts, I shed the robe, letting the young woman scan every glorious inch of my 65-year old male physique. Surely, no woman could resist the naked body of a near-septuagenarian, especially after I explain that I have a member but no club for it to join.

Imagine the delight of these young twenty-somethings when they realize I have just interrupted our planning meeting to take a shower! Just a year ago, they had an uneventful, thankless job at a local one-camera television station, and now they get to hear me berate them as I lather myself in soap! Surely no one will question why I have had showers installed in my office, conference room, television studio, and several prominent restaurants around town.

While unconventional, this will surely prove more effective than my previous tactic of throwing tomato soup on my pants, then suggesting I immediately shed them. After six such attempts with my assistant Tiffany, she suspected something was awry and left me to work in a more comfortable workplace for women, at Fox News.

One day the world will applaud me for allowing these women, some of whom are 40 years younger than me and have only met me once, to pursue their shared feelings for me. As long as these pert young innocents recognize the power of the bathrobe, there will always be a position for them on my staff.

I have to go now – my assistant tells me the Washington Post is on the phone...

LETTER FROM THE FRONT LINES OF THE 2019 CIVIL WAR

October 1, 2019

Way back in September of 2019, President Donald Trump declared a new Civil War in America over accusations he had pressured the Ukrainian president to supply him with damaging information on Democratic presidential candidate Joe Biden. Constitutional scholars have debated whether a president can declare war via Twitter and whether it counts if he spells it "Sivil Wore."

Nonetheless, a letter from one of the troops fighting for the president's forces has been unearthed and is now housed at the Biggest, Perfect, Most Beautiful Museum Ever (known in 2019 as the Smithsonian Institution).

Dearest Melanie:

I hope this WhatsApp message finds you safely. I am stationed here at the front lines of the Civil War, which began late in September after being declared by President Donald Trump via Twitter. As we would all soon find out, deadnaming people via tweet would be enough to get you thrown off Twitter, but presidents declaring civil wars seemed to be well within the site's terms of service.

Red baseball hat? You're on my side.

I hope you have not lost too much sleep while I have been away. Morale is good, as General Giuliani has kept things light with his winning, ebullient personality. He has convinced us all that we are fighting the most valuable battle since the last Civil War — clearly the eradication of owning human beings as slaves is morally on par with people saying mean things about President Trump.

However, like you, I am a bit perplexed as to how this particular Civil War is supposed to be won. In 1860, the adversaries were identifiable by geographic region — the North battled the South by marching and firing cannonballs at the rebels. In the Great War of 2019, where Trump loyalists mingle comfortably among the despised "NeverTrumpers," the battle fronts are … literally everywhere. It is safe to assume that anyone not wearing an ill-fitting red baseball hat is suspect.

There are only so many drag queen story hours where the insurgents can be smoked out!

Yet I can say without hesitation that our side is now enjoying a great number of glorious victories! Just yesterday, when a cuck corporal defamed our great president by suggesting Republicans would have lost their minds if President Barack O-Bummer had solicited foreign help to destroy a political opponent, I tweeted him a crippling "Orange Man Bad" meme. After my 12 followers see it, he will certainly never be heard from again!

Chick-fil-As seized, provisions low

Further, I have been reassured by Commanders Diamond and Silk that we are winning the intelligence war on the ground. Our greatest minds have been sent to hipster coffee shops to surreptitiously overhear what liberal caffeine enthusiasts might be saying about troop movements and strategies. Word is they are very adept at trying to trick people into filing sexual harassment lawsuits against the hated liberal leaders, which will surely mark their downfall!

I am sad to report, however, that provisions are running low. Leftist freedom fighters have seized all of the Chick-fil-A franchises, leaving conservative warriors all suffering from a waffle fry deficiency.

Countermeasures were taken soon thereafter when a MAGA soldier disguised himself in an Elizabeth Warren for President T-shirt, stood outside a Starbucks and yelled, "I found a high school picture of Mike Pence in blackface!" When the coffee shop patrons sprinted outside to see the nonexistent photo, Pepe Team 6 swooped in and commandeered the shop, seizing all of the unsold Alanis Morissette CDs prominently displayed by the register.

Yet no victory was as satisfying as the Battle of Yale, where a single Trump supporter walked on campus wearing a mildly provocative Halloween costume, leaving dozens of students dead. Who knew the "free speech is violence" people were right all along?

Gearing up for the Battle of Instagram

I'm sorry — I have actually just received an emergency message from President Trump's most brilliant strategic mind, Admiral Stephen Miller, telling me he needs my IMMEDIATE assistance. I stand ready to serve in this war to defend our truth-telling president, and will do ANYTHING to see him rightfully exonerated — even by checking the "$25 DONATION" box as the letter asks me to do.

I must say, Melanie, that I miss your smell. I crave the touch of your skin. I can only assume it is coincidence that I have not gotten to experience either since I told you 18 months ago that I voted for Donald Trump. I can promise you that those three days we dated were the most eventful of my life, and I yearn to feel your embrace once again while I sweetly whisper to you about how Hillary Clinton's email server is clearly to blame for all this anti-Trump hate.

I must go now, as our company is gearing up for the Battle of Instagram. I have to get some sleep so I can be up early arming our troops with dangerously witty hashtags.

Yours always,

Private Jeff

P.S. — I have some suggestions about who should play me in the inevitable Ken Burns miniseries.

USA Today

WHY I AM SUPPORTING MOMO IN 2020

April 15, 2019

You may know Momo as the terrifying, bird-faced creature that convinces children on the internet to commit suicide. But open your mind a little and you'll see something much more important: a potential SWAMP-DRAINER-IN CHIEF!

Sure, the "Momo challenge" turned out to be a hoax—there were actually no reports of any children harming themselves because they saw the demonic, large breasted chicken-human hybrid on their computer screens.

But think of all the free media Momo generated! Surely she must be a genius, playing 14-dimensional chess! She played the press like fools, driving them all to report FAKE NEWS for weeks on end!

Imagine how angry CNN would be if Momo took office—the dumbfounded look on Brian Stelter's face would be PRICELESS. It's time we own those clowns at MSNBC—let's make the rivers run with Maddow's tears!

Momo even got KIM KARDASHIAN to tweet about her—only a truly all-knowing leader could ever pull off such a partnership!

In Momo, I figure I must have a candidate, because everybody who's coming out against her are all corrupt, and she's an OUTSIDER. She has spent her life pursuing and eating young children, NOT as part of the swamp. With her crazed homicidal ways, Momo is going to be so disruptive, so outside the norm, that the swamp will drain because the swamp can't stand her and how she is running things.

Nobody controls Momo—she's beholden only to herself and even though I don't know any of her positions on anything, she has to be better than the corrupt system we have now! Those dunces Paul Ryan and Mitch McConnell never did anything—they couldn't even trick Barack Obummer into repealing Obamacare, his signature accomplishment that bears his name!

I admit, I'm a former Obama voter who believed he was a fresh face who was going to change things. But me and the boys down at the tiny Michigan-based plastic dinosaur factory haven't seen a wage increase in YEARS. Who knew other countries could make miniature pterodactyls? Just through fear and intimidation Momo can bring those American jobs back.

Obviously the system is RIGGED and needs to be shaken up!

You may say to yourself, "aren't you a God-fearing Christian? Why would you support grotesque Satanic poultry?"

Sure, she feasts on adolescents, but who among us doesn't have flaws? If you are focused so much on the next life, you are not worried about what is happening in this life, and that's sad.

Towards the middle of the second Obama term I was like, "Oh my God, the end of this can't come soon enough." He keeps doing damage. He keeps doing irreparable damage to our country, financially.

America was just out of control and everybody started expecting everything can be free. Free cell phones, free college, free health care, it was just like people were just excited about anything they got free. The entitlement was crazy.

Momo is not a politician. She is not part of the system, a system that has been failing a lot of people. She is her own person (except for the bird part), with her own style. And honestly, for the first time in the 50 years I've been able to vote, I'm excited to vote.

Finally, I definitely think there should be more coverage of Obama/Momo voters. More people should write books explaining how deeply savvy we are about politics and how our attempt to graft our hopes and dreams on to a horrifying candidate aren't entirely self-serving. So far, I've only been interviewed for 14 books explaining the Midwest swing voter!

You can throw all the facts you want at me, but the bottom line is, Momo is detested by the same lamestream media that made her a star. Nothing can shake my support in her.

As long as she doesn't hire Stephen Miller. That dude is creepy.

The Bulwark

I AM ALSO NOT DATING JANE KRAKOWSKI

January 26, 2021

[Edit. note: In 2021, a rumor broke out that MyPillow founder and armed insurrection enthusiast Mike Lindell was dating 30 Rock actress Jane Krakowski, leading Lindell to issue a statement denying the only thing that would make him seem like a reasonable human being.]

FOR IMMEDIATE RELEASE

In the past few weeks, I have had any number of insults directed at me. I have been called a "traitor," a "liar," and been accused of "treason." But I want to distance myself from perhaps the most insidious calumny that may soon be hurled my way: I have never dated beloved actress Jane Krakowski.

If I were to be accused of such a misstep, it would no doubt overshadow all the good I have done for the last year, from inciting an armed insurrection against the nation's government to spreading lies about the security of voting machines, to pitching miracle cures for the COVID-19 virus. My run of positive media coverage simply couldn't take the hit if I were accused of once having romanced the beautiful and winsome star of such shows as "30 Rock" and "The Unbreakable Kimmy Schmidt."

Think of the damage such a rumor could do to my persona as the leader of unimpressive white men! Just the other day, a young man with tears in his eyes approached me and said "please tell me you haven't been involved with the multi-talented host of "Name that Tune" airing at 9 ET/8CT on FOX." I slapped him in the face for even making the suggestion, and he thanked me effusively, indicating he now had a reason to continue living.

I have had one acquaintance suggest to me that an unfounded accusation of being a stone cold lover that beds starlets may be a boon to my public persona. "Nonsense!" I yelled to him as he handed me a sampling of Vienna sausage on a toothpick. I didn't care who in Costco was aware of my displeasure!

If the FAKE MEDIA is allowed to go around and destroy powerful men by accusing them of bedding starlets, will there be no end to the witch hunt? Innocent men in offices across America will no doubt be brought down for an unfounded suggestion that they once took Tootie from the "Facts of Life" to Applebee's!

In fact, I already had to fire one employee simply for admitting he once had amorous feelings for Janice from Dr. Teeth and the Electric Mayhem band!

Clearly, being tied to a charming and funny personality would be a catastrophe for the three employees at my company, MyCravat. It's a neckerchief, but...slightly different! And on the strength of nonstop late night television ads, we have sold almost several!

Yet for some reason, our products have recently been pulled from most big box stores, forcing me to sell MyCravats in Bed, Bloodbath and Beyond, the nation's largest retailer of products for anti-government-based domestic terrorists. It's your lucky day when you've been taken hostage using their lavender-scented zip ties!

To prove I am serious, I have sent up a charity to fend off others who may have been accused of dating Jane Krakowski. With any contribution of $100,000 or more, you will receive one free MyCravat and a complimentary visit from the FBI to search your home.

AN OPEN APOLOGY TO THOSE WHO WON'T GET TO MEET ME BECAUSE OF COVID-19

April 20, 2020

A SHORT STORY

We can all agree – since the virus hit, we've been missing out on a lot. No symphony of clinking cups in our favorite coffee shops. No eye contact with strangers, as sidewalk passersby treat us with suspicion. Some of us won't even have a job to return to when we all escape home confinement.

But trust me – the thing you'll miss most is meeting me.

I am so sorry.

Sometime next week, we were both going to lock eyes at a show put on by an up-and-coming singer-songwriter at a tiny local bar. You were going to stroll up to me and compliment my ironic "Lordy, Lordy, Look Who's 40" t-shirt I bought last week at Goodwill, hoping it would draw attention from someone just like you. We would have begun talking, and you'd strategically never ask my real age (26), impressively ducking the most obvious conversation starter.

Instead, I would have casually mentioned I have a podcast and pretended to accidentally throw out my Instagram handle. You would have then walked back over to huddle with your friends, obviously perusing my Insta feed to confirm I wasn't a creepster. My phone would then buzz with your friend request, and I would know I had earned the votes of the valuable concerned-best-friend demographic.

A week later, we would have met up at a grimy local restaurant, pretending it was fine dining. You'd say "no" when the gum-snapping waitress offered you gravy on your fries, which was standard at this hole-in-the-wall.

That night, we would have kissed for the first time, but you wouldn't have let me stay over. Two nights later, I would have slept at your apartment, and the next morning we would have laid together all day talking – you'd pretend you like dogs and I'd pretend I care about the environment. I would have teased you for how you arranged the books on your shelves by color; you would have joked that I was just lazy.

I would have held your hand over the weeks as we took walks on the lakefront, watching the weather turn from summer to fall. I would have eaten with your family at Thanksgiving, even though your brother, Brad, who I just met, would have kept calling me "smelly nuts."

That is SO Brad.

We would have gone ice skating together, even though my balance is awful and I wobble terribly.

You would have put on my long-sleeved shirts when you got cold, a thing that turned me on, but which I would never admit to you.

One night, we would have settled on the couch and I'd suggest we watch something by noted film actor Edward Norton.

"Oh, we should watch Keeping the Faith, the one where he plays a priest," you would have said. "That's his best role."

"Wait a minute," I would have said. "Clearly, Ed Norton was best in Fight Club."

"Fight Club is flaming garbage," you would have said. "Who wants to pay money to watch a cinematic ode to white male rage?"

"I do," I would have said. "I enjoy the film's commentary on the perils of rampant consumerism, I never see the surprise ending coming, and I also believe Meat Loaf is excellent in it," I would have said.

"The surprise ending?" you would have yelped. "The idea that one person is actually two people is one of the oldest literary devices in history. Have you ever read Dostoevsky's 'The Double?' Were you aware that in medieval times, seeing one's double was a sign of impending death? Your 'surprise' ending is about as old as the discovery of gunpowder."

"I was just saying Ed Norton is wonderful as the neurotic narrator," I would have said.

"Ed Norton isn't really that great," you would have said.

"What?" I would have said. "Ed Norton is one of the finest actors of the past two decades," I would have cried.

"He is fine in Rounders," you would have said. "And passable in The Illusionist."

"He was the best Hulk – way better than Mark Ruffalo," I would have said. "And, of course, that doesn't even account for his three Oscar Nominations, one for Birdman or (The Unexpected Virtue of Ignorance), one for American History X, and one for 1996's Primal Fear."

"He lost to that goofball Italian guy in the Holocaust movie in 1999," you would have said. "He was just nominated for American History X because he put on so much weight."

"You're putting on a lot of weight and I have yet to see you give an acceptance speech," I would have said.

"You're an asshole," you would have said.

"How can you not enjoy the everyday charm of Ed Norton!" I would have pleaded. "He was so endearing in Grand Budapest Hotel. And as the voice of Rex the dog in Isle of Dogs!"

"Do NOT act like he is Meryl Streep!" you would yell. "He was in Death to Smoochy for the love of Christ!"

"That is it!" I would have screamed. "I will not stand here and listen to America's most relatable and versatile acting talent be disparaged in such a manner! You are even forgetting his comedic turns in 2012's The Dictator and as Sammy Bagel Jr. in the groundbreaking animated film Sausage Party! You must leave!"

Over the next few weeks, the issue of Edward Norton's merits as an actor would continue to burn inside you as you begun to slowly poison my food. When I was finally rendered incapacitated, you would saw off my arms, legs, and head, put them all in a garbage bag, and drive them out to a marsh to bury my detached body.

Rather than haunt you for eternity (you were right about me being lazy), my ghost would have avenged my death simply by turning you in to the local police, at which point you would be arrested without incident. After weeks of testimony, you would have been sent to prison on a light sentence from a sympathetic judge who was ambivalent about Edward Norton's performance as a scoutmaster in Moonrise Kingdom.

Upon release from prison, the only job you would have been able to procure would be at a local drive-in theater selling popcorn and hot dogs. One night, the theater would have showed Fight Club, at which point you would have realized that Ed Norton is, indeed, one of the finest film actors of our day and that I was completely right.

And as I said before, COVID-19 has robbed you of the glory of this realization.

And for that, I am so sorry.

BUT WHAT ABOUT ALL THE AMERICANS TRUMP DIDN'T TELL TO GO BACK TO AFRICA?

July 16, 2019

Dear fellow MAGA patriot:

Once again our Genius President Donald J. Trump is under attack for speaking the truth! Yesterday America's Greatest Leader boldly told a handful of women of color in Congress to "go back and fix the totally broken and crime infested places from which they came."

Clearly Trump is a playing a game here that the lamestream media can't even understand! It's like Sudoku but without being given ANY OF THE NUMBERS.

The Dummycrats and Destroy Trump media are trying to say the president is being racist by telling people of color to go back to another country. But they are lying to you! They are painting him as racially insensitive because he used words like "Democrat" and "Congresswomen" and "who" and "originally" and "came" and "from" and "countries" and "whose" and "governments" and "are" and "a" and "complete" and "and" and "total" and "catastrophe." I imagine many of us use some combination of those words daily!

Even if the media are right, these are just four people! America has tens of millions of people of color—just imagine all the African-Americans, Hispanics, and Muslims Trump has NOT told to leave the country. He'd have to be president for 400 years before he even got to the cast of Hamilton!

In fact, the evidence Trump is making huge progress with African-Americans is everywhere.

Just look at the visit he received from his good friend, the very emotionally stable Kanye West. During their whole press conference, not once did Trump tell Kanye to return to the land of his African ancestors. Nobody ever mentions THAT.

Sure, George W. Bush was pals with Condoleezza Rice – but Trump has black friends everywhere. No other president has made the time to be friends with both Diamond AND Silk!

In fact, I hear that Trump is planning on having Frederick Douglass to the White House soon, so he can get the recognition he deserves for traveling back in time and conquering the airports during the Civil War!

If you've had enough, then just follow this simple playbook and you'll DESTROY lie-berals who want to argue about Republicans and race: Stand up and yell "but we freed the slaves!" And then run out of the room.

Liberals may be entitled to their dumb opinions, but they aren't entitled to their own facts. And that's just a FACT. This proud legacy of our party is why an overwhelming one in ten African-Americans consider themselves Republicans today.

Don't believe any of the hoaxes out there about Trump being a racist. They're just FAKE NEWS. That time he suggested Federal Judge Gonzalo Curiel would rule against him because he was from a small village in Mexico known as "Indiana?" Just think of all the destitute migrants that would pour over the border and, like Curiel, steal federal judgeships from hard-working American lawyers!

And the time Trump took out ads in the New York Times urging the death penalty for a group of young, black men who were later found not guilty of a brutal rape in Central Park? Just look at how the media is always moving the goalposts: He didn't tell those gang-bangers to go back to Africa —he just wanted them to be electrocuted!

Once again, Trump has shown his superior political skills by making liberals like "Cryin' Paul Ryan" weep like infants. He should either deport Ryan to Ireland or force him to become ambassador to some shithole country that's full of people with dark skin.

You know, the kind of country where, unlike a good old American white supremacist rally, there aren't very fine people on both sides.

The Bulwark

A LETTER FROM THE BATTLEFIELD

July 17, 2017

[Edit. note: Wonder Woman is a movie that came out in 2017.]

Digging through some of my great-grandfather's old personal belongings, I found the following note:

December 17, 1918

My dearest Mabel:

I hope this letter finds you in good spirits. For nearly a year here on the Western front, I have longed to once again gaze upon your honeyed visage. As the nights fall to below freezing in our fetid trench, my memories of you are all I have to warm my heart. And I cannot say how long that will be enough to keep me alive during this, the greatest of all wars.

As we continue to pound away at the German lines, the unmistakable specter of death has us surrounded. The food we are being fed isn't for consumption by any living thing. My company loses a dozen men a day from German cannon fire, sniper attacks, disease, or from the cold. The only positive thing to happen in the past month was the time a barely-clothed woman leapt from our trench and defeated an entire German battalion by herself armed with only a shield, a sword, and some bullet-resistant arm cuffs.

Otherwise, the smell of corpses is beginning to overwhelm our trench. Desperation has taken hold of our men – even late at night, we can still hear the cries of our brothers left wounded on the battlefield, begging for their mothers and wives. Their final pleadings are close enough to hear, yet they are too far to attend to. It is almost enough for some healthy men to wish for a swift death themselves, rather than having to endure another day in this nightmare.

Perhaps I should provide some more clarification about my previous reference to the comely, near-naked woman who ended up killing hundreds of Germans by herself. It was a very curious event; she shed her jacket, then walked straight into no-man's land while donning a glittering crown and some very alluring boots, all while defending herself against thousands of bullets being sprayed her way. Having drawn the attention of the Hun, we were able to then attack and defeat their heavily fortified line, providing the Allied powers with a rare victory indeed.

Yet despite this temporary victory, few men have hopes of ever winning the war. The Germans will stop at nothing to crush France, Britain and the United States on their path to world domination. To many, this was a war begun by the assassination of a worthless archduke nephew of an equally worthless emperor; and yet troops are seeing their best mates cut down in the prime of their lives. We can only hope that the Lord blesses our mission with his divine grace to stop the barbarism being inflicted on Europe by the Kaiser.

The weird thing is, why were the Germans shooting at the most beautiful woman in the world while she was completely unarmed? I mean, she's twice as hot as any of the flamethrowers they've been using on us. If you looked hard enough, you could see a pretty solid side-boob – why would an entire battalion rain all their gunfire on this glorious figure while completely ignoring the hundreds of Allied troops carrying their own guns and rushing towards the German trench?

Anyway, I may have gotten sidetracked there for a moment. It is a question left only for the history books. Hopefully future volumes will tell of the heroism of the men fighting in the Great War and the blood they have shed to free the world from the shackles of imperialism. I am willing to die for our cause – with God on our side, what glory awaits!

My pencil is getting dull, so one final note – once the war is complete, my commander has commissioned me and several of my comrades on a mission to Themyscira, an island that is…um… evidently very dangerous and is of vital strategic importance. As it is the birthplace of this wondrous woman, it must be defended at all costs, as there are no men on the entire island. It is a mission of such prestige, literally every man in my battalion has volunteered for service! What a brave sacrifice we are all willing to make!

I must leave you now, dear Mabel. Please do not weep if you do not hear from me again. In my remaining days, my mind will be busy thinking of you, my own mortality, the morality of war, and what it would be like to perform battlefield CPR on literally the most unbelievable woman in the world.

U.S. Corporal S. Schneider
Veld, France

FROM A CENTURY AGO, A MESSAGE FROM PRESIDENT TRUMP

February 26, 2016

A century ago, as a bloody war waged on the battlefields of Europe, America was still noncommittal about joining the effort. In late February of 1916, the catastrophic Battle of Verdun began on the Western Front, in northeastern France. At the time, U.S. President Donald Trump gave the following speech to the American people to outline the threat the Germans faced:

"My fellow Americans — believe me, nobody knows more about the mess in Europe than I do. I know even more than the French and the Germans. Kaiser Wilhelm is so low-energy — such a not-good guy. And all my generals went to the finest military college in the world — Trump University. Trust me, my generals would have kept that choker Archduke Ferdinand from being shot. Only losers get shot, my friends. I prefer world leaders who don't get gunned down.

Just ignore that fat loser Teddy Roosevelt, who's trying to get me to send American troops to France. Have you seen how much this guy sweats? Watch how often he wipes perspiration drops off that mustache of his — definitely not presidential material. Oh, he was president once? Well, I wasn't in politics then, wasn't really paying attention.

My advisers tell me that so far, this has been a very not good war. But believe me, when we decide to get into it, it's going to be the greatest, classiest war ever. From that point on, people are going to call it the 'World War' because it'll be the best war the world has ever seen. Tell the people of Belgium they're done getting schlonged by the Kaiser who's a total lowlife. Bad!

When our troops get to Europe, you're all not going to believe how much winning we're going to do. I read in the paper that the Germans are starting to use poison gas and flamethrowers on the battlefield. Well, our flamethrowers are going to burn twice as hot, and our gas will be 10 times as poisonous. When the Germans see our gold-plated tanks, they'll throw down their guns, come over to our side, and apologize by cooking meals for our soldiers and giving them back rubs.

But the first thing we need to do is round up all the Germans in America and send them home. You have all these Kaiser-lovers walking around eating their sauerkraut and owning dachshunds. Well, no more — they and their traitor dogs are all going to be on a boat headed back to Berlin, baby. And restaurants here in America won't be serving kraut, we're going to call it "liberty cabbage." People in America won't even be allowed to have the name 'Wilhelm' — we'll make them change it to something far more wholesome, like 'Adolph.'

When we win the war, we're going to build a wall around Germany to keep them in. And for every German who escapes, we're going to build the wall 10 feet higher. It's going to be the most spectacular wall you've ever seen — the whole country is going to be turned into a casino, and the name will be changed to 'Trump Presents Germany.'

And all the best-looking women in France will be so thankful we won the war for them. American men will be fighting them all off. I'm talking about all the classiest French women, here — all the '9s' and '10s.' In fact, any French woman deemed an '8' or below by my Department of Hotness will be sent to Germany to work in the casino.

In closing, Americans, you're all tremendous. At least 30% of you think I have a 200% chance of winning this war!"

As the history books have noted, one month later, America was invaded by Germany. So let us all celebrate the 100th anniversary of Occupation Day! Prost!

USA Today

WELCOME TO THE WHATABOUTISM MUSEUM

October 23, 2019

Welcome, tourists, to the new Whataboutism Museum, built back in early 2020 to honor America's bravest public figures – those who risked their own dignity by bringing up a completely unrelated issue in order to change the subject away from something politically damaging.

At the beginning of the tour, I'd like to thank the philanthropists at the Two Wrongs Definitely Make a Right Foundation for their generous financial contribution.

As you can see, the Whataboutism Museum now inhabits the stately structure that once held the Newseum near the U.S. Capitol in Washington, D.C. The story is well worn, but it's worth telling again: In late 2019, the American public rightly determined that the actual actions of our elected officials weren't worth knowing; instead, the real story was everything the media refused to cover. What wasn't news was now the only news.

On our left, you can see the museum's most recent acquisition, a large copper statue of Maggie Haberman rolling her eyes while a Donald Trumpist-funded website lectures her on how reporting works. As you all remember, Haberman and her ilk at the New York Times actually believed it was newsworthy that the President of the United States was the subject of a criminal investigation by an independent prosecutor at the same time two FBI agents might have been carrying on an illicit affair.

On our right is the crown jewel of our collection, an entire wing dedicated to a golden era when personal shame vanished into the ether and whataboutism became the dominant argumentative ploy. I'm talking, of course, about October of 2019, a month that will forever be newsworthy, at least until someone points out a different month that is more deserving of coverage.

If you look to your left, you'll see video of Golden State Warriors head coach and China money enthusiast Steve Kerr defending China's authoritarian regime by equating that country's enslavement of millions of Muslims with America's Second Amendment to the Constitution.

Kerr, a world-renowned expert in both geopolitics and pointing at places on a basketball court and telling players to run there, thought the real story wasn't the NBA's capitulation to a brutal communist regime in order to keep money flowing to him and the league's players, but instead the "human rights abuses" perpetuated by America's founders by protecting the right of this nation's citizens to own firearms.

On your right is a video display of a column written on October 10 by Republican U.S. Senator Ron Johnson entitled "We need answers to questions mainstream media won't ask about Democrats." As you all may remember, the column was issued in the heat of an impeachment controversy in which President Trump clearly asked foreign governments for help in finding damaging information on his domestic political opponents. It was as if, after escaping an inquiry into whether he colluded with the Russian government during the 2016 election, Trump said, "I'll show you people what real collusion is."

Yet Johnson, dogged by questions about whether Trump's actions were proper, thought the real story was a conspiracy theory straight from the amygdala of Sean Hannity – that the Democratic "deep state" had been conspiring against Trump all along. Johnson claimed he had "never seen a new president face such resistance," which provoked an angry tweet from the ghost of James A. Garfield, who was felled by an assassin's bullet six months into his first term.

However, Johnson was insistent an election that took place three years prior, and which a president of his party won, be re-litigated. Failing at this attempt, Johnson instead had the words "Hunter Biden" tattooed on his forehead.

Downstairs is our historical archive, where you can see audio/visual presentations of Republicans in the early 1970's defending President Richard Nixon against Watergate charges by claiming Ted Kennedy's involvement in Chappaquiddick was worse. You can see Soviet leaders defend their mass murders and gulags by invoking America's history of slavery and poor treatment of Native Americans.

You can watch the video of the 2016 presidential debate where Trump defended himself against sexual assault allegations by hauling women who had accused President Bill Clinton of similar actions to the debate. You can pore over tweets from current Republicans who claim they cannot possibly be racist because the Republican Party freed the slaves in the 1860s.

You can relive the time that Trump supporters defended him against charges that he didn't know why the Civil War was fought because President Barack Obama once said there were 57 states. Remember when Trump shared classified information with Russia during an impromptu conversation? Well, what about the time Barack Obama shared information with Cuba?

On the way out, be sure to swing by the gift shop, where you can buy one of our signature "To Quoque" t-shirts – just head to the register and pay Rudy Giuliani at the register. Granted, each shirt costs $500,000 (or barter for 5 Javelin missiles), but the good news is that you'll be able to fire one American ambassador by the end of the day.

The Bulwark

THE NOVEL CORONAVIRUS PRAISES THE PLAN TO REOPEN AMERICA

May 6, 2020

Thank you all for joining me today. I just wanted to tell you all what a great year it's been and what a huge success I am. When people were downplaying my importance back in February, I worried about making a splash in the greatest economy on Earth, but I never had any doubt it would be big.

In spite of those who ignored me, I've literally grown from zero to a million cases in two months – I've basically gone platinum.

And people can't get enough of me! Now Americans are cramming into state capitols, shopping malls, and public parks to lobby on my behalf! Some people are actually bringing guns to protect their right to pass me around from person to person. A literal armed militia has risen to defend me!

And I've been able to achieve all this with 95 percent of the media against me. Seriously – how many pro-COVID-19 stories do you see? Nobody has been treated this unfairly since the Spanish Flu.

The fake news media aren't giving me nearly enough credit. Even your president, Donald Trump, called me a "very brilliant enemy" and said I was a "genius!" Sure, I'm microscopic, but I have a very big brain.

Just think of all the wonderful things that have come about since I showed up. People are baking bread and sewing masks and playing Monopoly and talking to their children. Nature is healing!

And just look at the ratings I'm getting! I'm not saying this, but I've heard other people say, that the press conferences the president is holding rival those of the Bachelor finale and Monday Night Football!

And just think of all the things I haven't done. I haven't suggested people drink bleach (I don't even have a brain and that's the dumbest thing I've ever heard), and I haven't Tweeted well wishes to Kim Jong Un. That guy's an asshole.

Anyway, it's clear the people want more of me. Some of the president's favorite supporters have tweeted that the states' stay-at-home orders are like "slavery" and that they'd refuse to take any vaccine once it's developed. In the meantime, I can get millions of dollars' worth of free public relations. Name someone else born from a medium-rare bat that could achieve that!

See, Americans love an underdog – I'm like the nerdy kid that catches the game-winning touchdown in that Charlie Sheen movie Lucas from the '80s. (Shout out to Charlie Sheen – a big supporter of the anti-vax community.)

What can I say – I agree with Donald Trump's optimism that great times are ahead. Re-opening America is more than any infectious disease can ask for. All I ask from America is that you keep manufacturing phony drama between Doctors Birx and Fauci and Trump – getting rid of the experts will be the viral equivalent of sending me out on tour.

In closing, I would like to thank all the impatient Americans for their support. If anyone ever challenges you on your love of the virus, just compare not being able to eat in a restaurant to Japanese internment camps during World War II, yell "herd immunity!" and run out of the room.

I have provided a complimentary Clorox smoothie for all of you on your way out.

The Bulwark

CHAPTER NINE:
HORTONVILLE

Young anchor Tom Brokaw breaks news of the Hortonville strike

HORTONVILLE

At one o'clock in the afternoon on Saturday, April 20, John Blosser dropped to the ground. Blosser, a 42-year old teacher from Lakeland Union High School in Minocqua, Wisconsin, was in the small town of Hortonville picketing in support of the district's striking teachers. While carrying a picket sign outside the Hortonville Education Association (HEA) headquarters, Blosser was allegedly hit by a car driven by Francis Jamison, a Hortonville School Board member.

Only no one actually saw any car hit Blosser. Several witnesses told a reporter that he had faked the collision. An ambulance came from nearby Appleton and transported Blosser the 15 miles back to St. Elizabeth hospital for treatment. But Blosser was not admitted to the hospital, and the police never had any evidence to charge the school board member with striking him. Many saw it as an attempt to embarrass the school board, with whom the striking teachers had been feuding for over a month.

In August, four months after the Blosser incident, a group of Hortonville residents huddled around a table at McHugh's Tap, known for being the headquarters of the anti-striking teacher movement. A group of local men, who dubbed themselves "The Vigilantes," complained to a reporter that Blosser's "accident" was just one of dozens of "dirty tricks" being played by the striking teachers on the residents of Hortonville, who overwhelmingly opposed the teachers' daily picketing. (The Vigilantes chose their name after considering other options, such as "The Minutemen" and "the Untouchables.")

Over the clinking of beer bottles at McHugh's, the Vigilantes, in their thick Northern Wisconsin accents, ticked off a list of all the petty pranks for which they accused the teachers of being responsible. They said the teachers were harassing school board members by ordering Playboy Magazine subscriptions sent to their homes without paying for them. They accused the teachers of making 3 A.M. wakeup calls and sending roses and pizzas to replacement teachers' homes, leaving the "scabs" on the hook to pay.

One day, the striking teachers and their sympathizers from around the state parked all their cars on Main Street and abandoned them, blocking any patrons from being able to shop. One Vigilante said it was like "a ghost town." Another merchant complained that protesters would come into his grocery store and start moving merchandise around: candy to the medicine aisle, medicine to the cereal aisle, cereal to the meat aisle. (One Vigilante pointed out that the protesters "did buy some meat" - six hot dogs, he thought.)

What angered the Vigilantes the most, however, was the teachers' condescending attitude towards people whose jobs involved manual labor. Until March 1974, Hortonville was a sleepy town of 1,524 citizens. Senator Joseph McCarthy was still revered in the heavily conservative town, as he had grown up a mere 12 miles away in Grand Chute. The town's residents were actually outnumbered by the 1,900 public school students that attended elementary and high school there.

Many of the children were sons and daughters of small business owners, dairy farmers, paper mill workers, and farm implement salesmen. As is typical in rural Wisconsin it took some kids a bumpy bus ride of over an hour to get to the school.

It was this cultural divide that exacerbated the intractable strike. One newspaper reported a striking teacher yell "I'm not going to let any dumb farmers tell me how much I'm going to make." When the teachers went on strike the morning of March 18th, 1974, it was clear that the conflict was going to be about a lot more than simply educator salaries.

The Hortonville teachers' strike of 1974 was one of the longest, most bitter work stoppages in the history of American education. Before it was over, the small town would be flooded with thousands of union activists and would draw the attention of the nationwide media. Consequently, it forever changed the way the State of Wisconsin and its local governments would bargain with public employees, bargaining strategies that would become the model for the nation.

It's difficult to remember a time when teachers' unions were not major political players in state and national politics.

In 1959, Wisconsin was the first state in the U.S. to pass a law permitting collective bargaining for public employees. In 1964, the Milwaukee Teachers' Education Association became the first certified teachers' bargaining agent. Slowly, more school district teachers began to organize. Wisconsin was one of eleven states in the late 1960s and early 1970s where statewide teachers' unions were formed. Finally, in 1969, Ashwaubenon teachers became the first WEA-local members to strike, when 83 teachers walked out for four days.

Soon, WEA transformed into the Wisconsin Education Association Council, which had the authority to bargain on behalf of teachers all over the state. In 1972, WEAC first began to collect funds from its members ($3 apiece) to spend on supporting political candidates. According to WEAC, 88% of the candidates it supported in the 1974 elections won, which, they believe, demonstrated their newfound clout.

On the frontlines, local unionized teachers were routinely flexing their muscle through 1960's-style mass demonstrations. Between 1969 and 1974, teachers struck 50 times. While striking was against the law, there were no penalties prescribed for striking teachers; thus, WEAC leadership frequently convinced its members to ignore the state's prohibition.

Then, in March 1974, Hortonville happened. And everything changed.

The Hortonville teachers' strike, in which 88 teachers went on strike and 84 were permanently fired as a result, sent shock waves through the state. It led to a reconstituted, more strident WEAC, and triggered new collective bargaining laws for public employees in Wisconsin – laws which eventually led to hundreds of thousands of state workers descending on the Capitol in 2011 when Republican Gov. Scott Walker proposed changing them.

Eventually, the strike ended up in the hands of the United States Supreme Court.

On the morning of March 18, 1974, a fleet of 25 buses full of children showed up for school in Hortonville. But instead of walking inside, they saw 88 of their teachers marching up and down the street holding picket signs.

At 8:30 AM, Hortonville superintendent Marvin Obry packed all the kids back on the buses and sent them home. Obry didn't officially close school until the teachers didn't come inside. "At different instances, it seems the teachers had said they were going to strike, but didn't," he said at the time. That day, Obry announced the last school activity to be held would be the Future Farmers of America-sponsored donkey basketball game that evening.

The previous Wednesday evening, the Hortonville teachers had approved the strike by a 9-1 vote. The teachers had used other tactics earlier in the year to force a settlement, including refusing to handle any duties during after school hours in late afternoon and evening and conducting "informational" picketing before school started in the morning.

In their negotiations, the school district and Hortonville Education Association (HEA) were unable to agree on a base salary for the 1974-75 school year. According to both sides, the contract for the 1973-74 school year was all but agreed to. The board and HEA had agreed to $7,550 base salary for teachers for 1973-74, up from $7350 for 1972-73. The previous contract had expired in June of 1973.

But the teachers made acceptance of the current year contract contingent on a contract for 1974-75. It was the contract for the following year that remained the insurmountable bargaining point.

For 1974-75, the board offered a $7,800 base salary for teachers with 4-year degrees and $8,450 for teachers with master's degrees. Maximum pay would be $12,012 and $13,013, respectively. The teachers initially asked for a $8,800 base salary (an increase of 16.5%), then reduced their offer to $8,600 before finally settling on $8,200 – still an 8.2% increase of the $7,550 base agreed to for 1973-74.

The board said its offer would cost $63,000 more on a base budget of $960,000. They believed that the teachers' offer, when benefit increases were included, would increase the budget $135,000, or 15%.

That didn't satisfy the HEA, which decided to follow nearly 50 other local teacher bargaining units to the picket lines. While technically illegal, most teacher strikes were settled fairly quickly. There was no reason to believe a strike in Hortonville would be any different.

In fact, Hortonville was tight-knit community where neighbors knew each other well. HEA president Mike Wisnoski, who taught junior high science for seven years at Hortonville, once took board chairman Roger Weihing's oldest son on a camping trip to Canada in 1972. Superintendent Marvin Obry's daughter had both Wisnoski and HEA chief negotiator Kenneth Couillard as teachers.

As the teachers hit the picket lines, Wisnoski thought teachers should get credit for the civility in their strike, saying their signs merely said "HEA on Strike," and not "sarcastic placards." He said the matter was serious to teachers and that they should "act like professionals."

In the early days of the strike, the teachers weren't exactly seasoned in the picketing arts. At times, teachers would grow bored with the traditional oval formation. "Let's do a figure eight," suggested one woman, only to be shot down by a man in the group. "Oh, God – we'd really get confused," he said.

On March 19, the day after the strike began, the school board filed for an injunction to end the strike, citing its illegality under state law. Obry directed teachers to return any school materials they had in their possession, including room keys, lesson plans, and class records. Wisnoski said the teachers would be "glad" to comply with the request to return materials, "but only when they are back in the classroom."

Wisnoski also complained that the school was locked up tight, saying he believed chaining the doors to the school shut constituted a fire hazard.

Three days after the strike began, Superintendent Obry had to figure out how to get the school open again. He began hiring substitute teachers, who were to be paid $45 a day, $25 above the normal daily substitute rate of $20. The picketing teachers immediately took offense, calling the substitutes a "glorified babysitting service."

The new substitutes also got mileage allowances for travel over 25 miles, and some were rumored to be coming from over 100 miles away. The HEA claimed many of the substitutes didn't have certification and that they were released from other school districts for incompetence. Several striking teachers reportedly told their students that the grades given out by replacement teachers were invalid, so the students didn't have to pay attention to what their "scab" teachers were telling them.

In order to turn the town's residents against the substitute teachers, some striking teachers played on the residents' distrust of outsiders. Incredibly, one housewife opened up to a reporter about her true fears regarding the replacements that were being hired. "Before the strike, the teachers said they would be replaced by niggers from Milwaukee," she told the reporter. "People around here didn't like that because most of them have never seen or talked to black people."

On the evening of March 21, four days after the strike had begun, the school board and teachers met for three and a half hours to continue contract negotiations. Progress appeared to be afoot when the teachers dropped their salary request to $8,100 and the board upped theirs to $7,900. A scant $200 per teacher stood between the two parties and labor peace.

But the bonhomie didn't last long. The strike went on, and despite the hiring of substitute teachers, the school remained closed. Local resident Mrs. Kettner had to stay home with a living room full of her ten children as a result of the strike. She said having them home wasn't too bad, but that on the first day "little Jeff cut his thumb off." A performance by "Just Us," one of Kay Jacobsen's music groups, was cancelled, as was the Band-O-Rama competition.

On March 24th, a reporter from the Appleton Post-Crescent began walking around town, talking to residents about what they thought about the now-week old strike. It was the first attempt to gauge the public's temperature regarding the picketing – and it quickly became clear that the town's residents overwhelmingly disapproved of the teachers' walk-out.

Only five of the 35 citizens the reporter talked to believed the teachers should get what they want. One elderly man walking down the street was asked his reaction. "Let 'em strike," he said, adding, "We don't learn nothing in school but how to cheat."

That same day, the HEA was about to get some reinforcements from Madison. Lauri Wynn, the stylish, afro-wearing president of WEA appeared, and snowmobile suit-clad teachers showed up to hear her speak truth to power.

476

"We work because we want to teach children, not because we want to be servants," she defiantly told the group.

On March 25, school reopened with the substitutes and limited class offerings. Mike Wisnoski, HEA president, said the school board, in reopening the school, "isn't thinking of the kids at all."

Superintendent Obry said the school had a full staff, but before the doors actually opened, some of the subs were threatened by the teachers. As a result, 12 substitute teachers reportedly backed out at the last minute after confrontations with picketers.

With Wynn's appearance, people in the community began to get the idea that the Hortonville strike was being used as a proxy for teacher union fights all over the state. It appeared that Hortonville was where WEA was going to plant its flag. Wisnoski disagreed, saying it was the school board that brought someone in from Madison to negotiate for them, so they started it.

Once school opened, local law enforcement officers began to worry about confrontations between the striking teachers and the replacement teachers attempting to get to the school. A dozen Hortonville policemen and Outagamie County Sheriff Calvin L. Spice were on hand in case there was trouble. One striker took photographs of the subs as they pulled in, and others jotted down license plate numbers.

Kenneth Couillard, who negotiated on behalf of the teachers, said the school shouldn't be open for safety reasons. "We encourage parents to check in on their [children's] continued safety while in the school," he said, ominously. Soon, parents of children in class would begin patrolling entrances to the school during the day.

Once the school was reopened, Obry said 90% of the high school students and 80% of the elementary students attended classes. Eventually 80 children would withdraw from the school to be taught in other schools or by a tutorial program run by striking teachers.

Couillard said with substitute teachers in place, the students were not actually getting an education in the school.

"Games, coloring, movies, past lesson plans and lectures comprised the major activities of the day," Couillard said. "It was observed that 30 minutes after school started one group was outside for recess," he added.

Couillard tried to assuage the local residents by showing concern about out how expensive the strike was for the taxpayers – yet it was these same taxpayers that would be footing the bill for higher teacher salaries had the strikers gotten their way. Even in the early days of the strike, extra law enforcement and mileage reimbursement for substitute teachers was getting to be expensive.

On March 28, ten days after the strike began, harbingers of the acrimony to come began to emerge. 31-year old John Sasse was arrested by Outagamie County police for written threats against several people, including Lauri Wynn. At the beginning of the next week, teachers were sent checks with deductions made for the days they have been out on strike. Being docked pay for time out of the classroom was the first time strike began to take a financial toll on the teachers.

On the day of Sasse's arrest, classes were cancelled due to an unseasonably harsh snowstorm, but the school board extended the closing for the first three days of the next week in order to have disciplinary hearings with each of the 88 striking teachers.

Bruce Ehlke, Madison-based legal counsel for the teachers, charged that the hearings were "illegal" because they weren't part of the teachers' contract. Ehlke said the meetings were an attempt to "coerce and intimidate" the teachers. He said the teachers would not agree to individual hearings, preferring instead to be treated as a group.

On April 2nd, the Hortonville school board fired 86 teachers that refused to return to work. Each teacher was notified with a letter mailed to their homes, with an offer to re-apply for their jobs. The board announced that substitute teachers would serve out final nine weeks of the school year.

The stunning decision came on Tuesday after lengthy closed-door school board meeting. The HEA contended the firing was illegal because they were denied due process; the board countered that they offered up individual disciplinary hearings, and the teachers opted out of the process by boycotting the hearings.

At the same time, legal actions from both parties began to work their way through the courts. The board sued teachers to return valuable class materials that were considered property of the school district. The teachers sued the board to force them to accept their proposed contract.

The day after the firings were announced, a three-and-a-half hour negotiating session followed, with no progress made. The teachers claimed they made concessions: they gave up the $5 pay they received when being required to take another teacher's class during their free or preparation hour; they gave up the 20 teacher days per year they requested for association time; they dropped their request for liability insurance for transporting students in one's personal car, and ended their demand for increased dental insurance.

Determined to show that the school year was going on without interruption, the board began announcing that several events were going on as planned. For instance, on April 5th, Obry announced the Junior

Prom would still take place – good news to everyone except pimply young boys who had hoped the year would end without anyone noticing they couldn't find a date.

With the firings looking more and more like they would stand, tensions heightened exponentially on both sides. On the morning of April 7th, Marvin Obry walked out his front door to get the newspaper and found two spent 20 gauge shotgun shells on his doorstep.

When Obry was working as an administrator in the Shiocton school district several years earlier, he had one the windows in his home shot out after expelling several students. He said it was "disgusting" that someone would do it and called the perpetrator "sick."

Across town, a dummy was found hung in effigy from the Hortonville water tower. The teachers believe it was supposed to represent either Wisnoski or Couillard. The Vigilantes also hung banners on Main Street across from the teachers' headquarters that said "HEA – Half Educated Adults."

Soon thereafter, Wisnoski received a letter containing a death threat, but the sender of the letter was arrested. He claimed he simply shrugged the threat off.

Even though tensions were escalating among the local citizens, soon things would get even worse when the teachers began calling in what they called "reinforcements." On April 8th, teachers across the state were beginning their spring recess, and many chose to visit Hortonville to picket with the fired teachers. Or, as one visiting teacher said, "just to make their presence known."

The influx of teachers from around the state demonstrated that the strike was no longer simply a local issue; due to the mass teacher firings, the issue now spread to the state borders. "What happens to the teachers here will have a lot to do with what happens to others in the state," said Wynn, signaling that Hortonville was the place WEA was going to make their stand. WEA couldn't legally provide direct strike assistance to the HEA teachers because of the state statute against teacher strikes, but Wynn said money was flowing in from individual teachers across the state.

That morning on the picket lines, a controversy erupted when Wynn was found riding for a half a mile on the hood of a substitute teacher's car that had arrived to the school. The woman driving the car, Mrs. Floyd Grode (in a conservative community, women still spoke to the media using their husband's names) said her car was completely stopped when Wynn jumped on. Wynn said she did not want to bring charges against the driver, while Grode said had plenty of eyewitnesses, and she'd be happy to go to court.

A day later, Wynn complained to the media about the direction the picketing had taken. She decried the "anti-union" attitude of the community, and the "twinges of violence" on the line.

Aside from the Wynn joyriding incident, picketers were growing more aggressive, bolstered by the influx of reinforcements. Police often intervened when abusive language and the blocking of driveways became common. ("They were using all kinds of four letter words and shit," one Vigilante would say later.)

All the while, Sheriff Calvin Spice sat in his car at the periphery, looking on as law enforcement tried to quell the incidents.

The next day, about 30 residents showed up to escort the substitute teachers in and out of the parking lot. The Vigilantes tussled with the teachers before law enforcement was able to bring order. Spice called the situation a "powderkeg," and petitioned the village board for more law enforcement officers. Merchants began to worry about possible property damage or harm. Teachers worried about violence against their members. They feared someone would try to invade their strike headquarters on Main Street.

The next day, a man brandishing a six-shooter in a "big western-style holster" walked into the HEA headquarters. Wisnoski claimed the man had been drinking.

Later, while interviewed at McHugh's Tap, the bar known as the Vigilante headquarters, he said he had taken out the firing pin, and just walked in to say hello to some teachers he knew. He couldn't understand why anyone would at all object to his armed excursion behind enemy lines.

On April 9th, an offer by the HEA to go to binding arbitration was rejected by the board. Ronald W. Scheid of the Appleton Federation of Labor Unions proposed the idea that was taken to the board. Scheid said he didn't normally support binding arbitration, but "it is apparent that neither side is in a position to bring your situation to a reasonable conclusion."

At the same time, the teacher lawsuit challenging their firings was ongoing, before substitute Circuit Court Judge Allen Deehr. During their testimony before Deehr, many of the teachers said they never expected to actually be fired. Many said they were already suffering economically.

In an interview around that time, Lauri Wynn admitted that WEAC had succeeded in getting two "plants" hired as substitute teachers. While their "moles" passed themselves off as replacements, they were secretly collecting information about what was going on in the school and passing it on to union leadership.

"Our plants indicated the school board will hire anyone to teach and pay them $45 a day," Wynn said. "The board said the substitutes are certifiable, rather than certified." She said she believed it was much less ethical to use "scabs" than to use plants.

Wynn complained about the "dangerous climate of fear" surrounding the strike, which she compared to 19th century America. She claimed that "armed vigilantes" were riding the streets and guarding stores.

On April 11th, Judge Deehr denied the teachers' attempt to halt the use of replacement teachers. Since teacher strikes were technically illegal, Deehr said the teachers came into court with "dirty hands."

The state Wisconsin Employment Relations Commission couldn't get involved because both parties had to be willing to compromise. Wisnoski, experienced in the devoutly religious nature of Hortonville's citizens, appealed to God, saying "If the board is acting in a Christian manner, it is time they show it."

Sensing heightened tensions, more police were sent out to monitor picketing. By April 11th, over 75 officers were stationed at the school, to monitor 35 picketers, mostly women, and 100 Vigilantes that stood across the street yelling obscenities.

Air was let out of the tires of a striking teacher, and paint was thrown on the homes of three teachers the previous evening. 38 year-old Morris Andrews of Monona, executive director of WEA, was arrested for obstructing police, along with two other out-of-town picketers. According to Sheriff Spice, he had just warned Andrews about improper picketing, when Andrews ran back to the line and grabbed Deputy Sheriff James Ring as Ring was assisting a vehicle through the pickets.

Law enforcement had more to worry about, as Easter vacation approached. Sheriff Spice had heard rumors that busloads of teachers were headed to Hortonville from all over the state. Spice recommended the board shut down school for the entire week, hoping it would lessen confrontations between the out-of-towners and the Vigilantes. Obry declined to close school, however, citing all the days that had been lost already. Plus, several weeks before, the number of out-of-towners showing up fell well short of the 5,000 that had been expected.

On the early morning of April 14th, State Highway 15 was blanketed with the rumbling of buses coming from all over the state. A large cadre of protesters were headed to Hortonville from Madison, where protesting was a profession; to Madisonians, picketing had been refined to an art form. Many had taken place in the famous Dow Chemical protests on the University of Wisconsin-Madison campus in October of 1967, which led to students being clubbed and tear-gassed by police.

On many of the buses, teachers were handed blank checks and told to use them to post bail once they were arrested. Many merchants chose to close their stores with the influx of teachers heading their way.

That Monday morning, 31 protesters were arrested, none of them from the Hortonville area. Many of them came from over 250 miles away. They were peacefully hauled to the Outagamie County Courthouse after sitting in the road and blocking traffic at the intersection of Olk and Nash streets.

Later in the day, three more teacher sympathizers were arrested, but alleged excessive force by the police. One of those who alleged police brutality was Morris Andrews, who was arrested for the second time in as many weeks. According to news reports, Andrews was struck in the groin by one riot-stick wielding officer after asking to see the identification of an officer who had arrested one of his cohorts.

The first day of the heightened protests, Spice had 200 police officers armed and ready. The next day, there were 190 officers; yet estimates put the crowd at about one-third as large as the previous day.

Despite the prediction of heavy turnout, police estimates put the Tuesday crowd at about 150 to 200 teachers picketing. One teacher from St. Francis said he thought a lot of teachers didn't feel like getting up at 4 A.M. to picket, and expected turnout to improve as the day wore on. Soon, the total tab for police protection would exceed $100,000, sparking arguments about which governmental bodies were on the hook to pay for it all. Some Hortonville aldermen proposed billing the school board directly for the $17,000 per day extra cost for law enforcement.

The major confrontations, of course, took place as students and substitute teachers entered and exited the school. On the 15th, strikers yelled to children on buses "get sick, stay home!"

As substitute teachers walked out of the school toward their cars, picketers outside the lot yelled "we're waiting for you, scabbies!" and "Judas, Judas, Judas!"

Spice and his officers held the picketers back while 52 cars exited the lot – one picketer threw his sign over the officers and struck a car. While the officers worked to get the teachers out, a skirmish broke out between protesters and Vigilantes about a quarter mile from the school. It led to three picketers being arrested, as town citizens stood a few feet away, across a ditch, and cheered the police on.

By April 17th, 71 total people had been arrested related to the teachers' strike. But a court order issued that day by Outagamie County Judge Urban P. Van Susteren (father of cable news host Greta) severely restricted ongoing picketing activities. The order restricted the number of picketers allowed to 50, and prohibited "loud and provocative hollering."

In his decision, the Van Susteren said his overriding concern was for the children and that "to see the teacher hollering provocatively and boisterously would cause irreparable damage to the respect students have for their teachers."

Yet the protests continued, getting more and more elaborate. On April 17th, the protestors took part in some "shows" at the school entrance and played "hide and seek" with police officers.

At about 2:30 PM, striking teachers staged a mock "rush" at the parking lot entrance. From about 40 feet from the school's south entrance, the picketers all dropped their signs and sprinted en masse towards the gate. The police ignored them, and the teachers resumed their usual picketing, reading aloud passages of author Jack London's poem, "The Scab."

Soon, residents recognized that Van Susteren's order may have had the unintended effect of pushing the protests into the town, where activists couldn't be regulated by police.

Sheriff Spice told the media he had heard of cars with their license plates removed braking suddenly in front of school buses. Lauri Wynn threatened to sue him for $800,000 unless he retracted his accusation within 12 hours. Within days, Spice had cut the number of officers at the school to 30, as fewer protesters picketed at the school itself. He also apologized to Lauri Wynn for his accusation, as he said the complainants wouldn't come forward.

Some of the picketing began taking place not in the controlled environment outside the school, but at substitute teachers' homes. One group of strikers figured out where a substitute teacher lived by following a pizza delivery truck to her home. Many of the substitute teachers were getting late night phone calls, waking them at all hours.

One replacement teacher, anticipating trouble, stayed up until 2:30 A.M. one night to keep people away from his home. The next morning, the word "scab" was spray painted on three sides of his house.

Yet, for many of the substitute teachers, the intimidation tactics had the opposite effect.

"The more I see them act like that, the more I feel they shouldn't be allowed to act like that," said one substitute teacher whose house was picketed. "They're trying to intimidate me, but I think they're just a bunch of immature children playing games. There's no way they're going to keep me from going back."

As the strike moved past its one-month anniversary, Spice thought the number of strikers was dwindling. Yet other unions kept joining in the HEA's cause. On April 18th, representatives at a WEA meeting in Appleton recommended by a 74-16 vote that teachers all over Wisconsin stage a "chalk cough" – a one-day walkout to show their solidarity with HEA.

That same day, James Harris, the president-elect of the NEA, came to Hortonville to support the teachers, touring their headquarters and carrying a picket sign. During his visit, he decried the law making teacher strikes illegal, and urged Wisconsin to pass a binding arbitration law similar to one that had just passed in Iowa.

Also showing up in Hortonville was young Madison Mayor Paul Soglin, who had been a central figure in the Dow Chemical protests on the UW-Madison campus. Teachers from around the state also began to contribute to a strike fund for the Hortonville teachers. Wisnoski said the teachers had received around $20,000 from state teachers, while teachers from Antigo sent $1,000 and 1,000 pounds of potatoes.

Back at the school, the picketing became more theatrical. Teachers staged a "death march" down Main Street and around the school on Friday, the 19th. Striking teachers walked slowly up and down the street while bound and gagged, with other teachers banging together garbage can covers, hubcaps, and other loud objects. One teacher read off the names of each of the 84 teachers who had been fired as a result of the strike. The Vigilates claimed it scared the school kids.

Yet Wynn said the picketing may be running its course, and threatened to step things up a notch. "Picketing is an ordinary sort of thing," she said. "The ordinary sort of things, we believe, we tend to get tired of. Our feet are tired from Hortonville."

Wynn kept quiet about their future plans, saying "a certain degree of apprehension is created" with the element of surprise. "That's what we want."

In the meantime, replacement teachers kept showing up for work under extreme duress. Despite the claims of the HEA, all the replacement teachers were either certified or had their applications for certification in. The Hortonville board said they had to pick through over 300 applications to replace the striking teachers, which led the board to believe kids were being taught by quality educators. There had been a statewide oversupply of teachers, which had left many of them without jobs or underemployed for long periods of time.

In fact, according to an analysis by the Appleton Post-Crescent, there were more teachers with master's degrees than there were before the strike. The substitute teachers interviewed bristled at the teachers' contention that they were merely "day care."

"Those of us who are spending hours and hours each night to make up lesson plans are hardly babysitters," one replacement teacher said. "I would feel I was cheating the school board if I took attendance and just rapped with the kids."

The replacements also thought the strike had permanently damaged relations between the picketing teachers and their students. One substitute complained: "I would like to raise my children in a decent setting. Have I no rights? Can I trust my children to those teachers who were screaming obscenities at me?"

The fired Hortonville teachers continued to pick up support from national unions, from sectors both public and private. They received pledges of solidarity from the Milwaukee Federation of Labor and the Milwaukee Professional Police Association. Even Cesar Chavez, president of the Farm Workers of America, sent a telegram to the HEA, promising his support and urging HEA members to keep faith.

April 21st featured a rally put on by the United Auto Workers in support of the teachers. Over 300 supporters attended and heard UAW District 10 director Raymond Majerus promise more manpower and financial assistance. Vernon Plamann of Greenville, who had two children in the Hortonville school, sat back and watched the rally.

"If ignorance could be turned into gold, this would be a rich community," he cracked.

Some of the speeches were interrupted by bearded, sleeveless motorcyclist who pulled up near the podium and gunned his engine in an attempt to drown out the songs and speeches. The cyclist stayed to trade insults with the protesters, suggesting the teachers all get a job at a foundry that he knew was hiring. After about five minutes, he peeled out, leaving teacher sympathizers choking on his exhaust.

Teachers across the state had to decide whether to accept the recommendation of the WEA and walk out for a day in support of the HEA. Eleven local school districts, including Appleton, voted in favor of a walkout. Madison Mayor Paul Soglin, who picketed on behalf of the HEA, said he would not support a sympathy strike – but indicated no action would be taken against any Madison teachers that participated.

The 6,000 member Milwaukee Teachers Education Association, the largest unit in WEA, voted against a sympathy strike. Kaukauna and Fond du Lac voted against it, while school boards in Madison, Rice Lake,

Menomonie, Burlington, Sheboygan, La Crosse and Janesville all supported the one-day walkout.

By April 24th, 27 districts had voted in favor of the walkout and 33 had voted against it. Governor Lucey denounced the sympathy strike, saying "it would extend the crisis to the boundaries of the state." Lucey also said the strike in Hortonville was "dramatic evidence that the present law prohibiting strikes by public employees does not work."

On April 22, Outagamie County Judge Thomas Cane said he might use his powers to force binding arbitration and end the strike. Multiple court proceedings kept moving through the system, as the board continued to seek an injunction against the strike. The teachers challenged Van Susteren's anti-picketing order, claiming it violated their First Amendment rights.

While their public actions demonstrated strong group solidarity, the striking teachers began to individually struggle. By April 24th, 80 of the 84 teachers had visited the Outagamie County Department of Social Services in Appleton to check on their eligibility for welfare assistance. County Welfare director James Stampp said none of the teachers had actually applied for aid, but he said "quite a few appear to be eligible" and might apply later.

On April 24th, a glimmer of hope appeared. The teachers made a surprise offer which would have returned most of their members to the classroom. Bruce Ehlke, the Madison attorney for the teachers, said the HEA would accept the "tentative contract" for 1973-74 and the board's final offer for 1974-75. In addition, Ehlke said the teachers would be willing to accept "legitimate suspensions" or firings as a result of strike-related activities. Ehlke made the offer after consulting with Couillard in the hallway outside the courtroom at 8:45 in the morning before proceedings started.

At the moment Couillard made his decision, a busload of 50 University of Wisconsin-Madison teaching assistants joined the picket line. Embroiled in their own labor issues on campus, Spice called the TAs "much louder and much more nasty" than he had previously seen. He said some had told children they would "turn into scabs" if they entered the school.

April 25th rolled around, the day scheduled for the statewide teacher walkout. 85 law enforcement officers in riot gear lined the street outside the school, expecting thousands of striking teachers from around the state to join the picket lines.

But they never came. The night before, Lauri Wynn called off the statewide walkout, citing the fact that only 25% of the state's teacher associations agreed to join in the sympathy strike.

"Unlike other unions, we can't take mass action unless the rank and file agrees," Wynn said. Later, Wynn would say she needed at least 40% to 50% of the locals to approve the sympathy strike to move ahead with it.

Donald Dickinson, Appleton WEAC representative, spun the news positively. He said 25% statewide support for a teacher walkout was "tremendous," and said support would have been greater if they had more time to prepare. Teachers around the state had supported them financially, as the strike fund climbed to over $50,000 with a $10,118 donation from the Oshkosh teachers. A candlelight vigil was held in Madison at the State Capitol, drawing 500 people.

Perhaps sensing weakness, the board rejected the teachers' offer to return to work. Jack Walker, attorney for the board, said that the striking teachers had been replaced, and that there were only five positions open. They did, however, offer to talk with the teachers about the five open positions. HEA representatives said the board's rejection of the offer showed they never planned on negotiating in good faith. Even Sheriff Spice was disappointed at the board's unwillingness to take the teachers back. "There was bullheadedness on both sides. Now they've just backed themselves into a corner," he said.

Soon, the right for public unions to strike became a statewide campaign issue. State Senator Tom Petri, about to enter a race for the U.S. Senate against Gaylord Nelson, was opaque regarding his position on teacher strikes. Petri merely said the Hortonville strike caused "an unhealthy situation." That year "Remember Hortonville!" became a rallying cry in political campaigns. Despite the law against teacher strikes, the state Democratic Party voted support for the striking teachers, citing the board's "unwillingness to negotiate for a bargain in good faith."

As the strike dragged on, it began harming Wisconsin's industries. The state Coalition of Public Employees, AFL-CIO, began discussing a statewide boycott of dairy products, thinking the Wisconsin Farm Bureau was too supportive of the Hortonville school board. The proposal was scuttled, however, as the labor coalition thought a boycott would hurt sympathetic organizations like the National Farmers Organization.

While the teachers thought the ongoing contract dispute was the central issue, the real issue had become the strike itself. The strike had severely fractured a community that was heavily against the teachers to begin with.

Board president Roger Weihing said the district would flatly refuse to rehire any teachers it didn't want, or who were involved in what the board considered "misconduct" during the strike, including trying to run cars off the road and making harassing phone calls. Weihing said the board was keeping copious notes detailing individual teachers' behavior during the strike, and worried that if the teachers were allowed back, many more parents would pull their children out of school.

On April 29th, the board did offer jobs to four of the striking teachers. Three rejected the offer, preferring to show solidarity with their colleagues. The one that accepted was a man nearing retirement and in jeopardy of losing his pension benefits.

Hiring for the 1974-75 school year was underway, however. The board issued an ultimatum to the teachers – break the strike and apply for your jobs for next year as individuals, or none of them would be hired back. Wisnoski said "all of us will return to work or none of us will." The HEA charged that the board had made this hiring decision at an illegal meeting that failed to give proper public notice.

HEA teacher Tom Nadeau presciently saw the big picture for unions in the state, and urged the teachers to stand strong. He said he believed public employees "would eventually look back at Hortonville as the turning point in their battle for equal rights."

In May, determined to get negotiations moving, Outagamie County Judge R. Thomas Cane ordered the board to come up with list of names of teachers it would be willing to hire back, and a list of those it would not due to strike misconduct. Under Cane's order, if offered jobs, teachers would have to accept them, a move that Ehlke said would "bust the union." Neither side was happy, but both sides obeyed the order.

The three teachers offered jobs the previous week accepted them. This irked the board, saying they had just given HEA a "Trojan horse," as those teachers would be able to report the daily goings-on in the school back to the union.

As the strike continued through May of 1974, Hortonville continued to get national media attention. On May 27th, TIME Magazine featured an article about the "Hortonville 84," referring to the fired teachers. The article highlighted how the strike had ripped apart the small town's fabric. "Such a hatred has grown. The scars will be a long time healing," said Hortonville resident Ann Milleren.

Images of teachers being dragged away from school entrances by heavily armed policemen would make their way into local papers across the nation. The New York Times ran a brief on the arrests; Ayoung NBC anchor named Tom Brokaw would deliver updates on the strike to a national audience.

In June, one of the replacement teachers entered as a contestant in the annual "Alice in Dairyland" competition, a beauty pageant put on by the state's agriculture department. Yet when Robin Rae Miller showed up to compete in the pageant, the picketers were there to greet her. They jeered her throughout the competition and she eventually lost.

The striking continued for months, even in unlikely venues. In July, the National Football League veterans went on strike. As the giant football players carried picket signs and chatted with fans outside the Green Bay Packers' practice facility near Lambeau Field, they were joined by a small group of Hortonville teachers expressing union solidarity (and likely getting autographs.)

Picketing also continued near the school. The Vigilantes were always there, sometimes wielding axe handles. They believe the teachers' condescending attitude towards blue-collar workers fomented class conflict. They cited one picketer, who yelled out "I'm not going to let any dumb farmers tell me how much I'm going to make!"

One day, Kevin Quinn walked into his backyard and found his pet beagle dangling lifeless from its own chain. The Vigilantes understood that killing a man's hunting dog is a declaration of war. "Those striking teachers did it," they all agreed.

At that point, it was the teachers' cause that had lost all signs of life. In July, Judge Deehr deemed all the teacher firings legal. The Wisconsin Supreme Court found in favor of the teachers, saying the Due Process Clause required that the teachers' conduct and the board's response be evaluated by an impartial decision maker other than the board.

The case went all the way to the U.S. Supreme Court, which found in favor of the board in a 6-3 decision. (Wisconsin's own Justice William Rehnquist sided with the majority against the teachers.)

Chief Justice Warren Burger penned the decision, in which he laid out the justification for firing the teachers:

> "Permitting the Board to make the decision at issue here preserves its control over school district affairs, leaves the balance of power in labor relations where the state legislature struck it, and assures that the decision whether to dismiss the teachers will be made by the body responsible for that decision under state law."

When school opened for the 1974-75 year, the lawsuits were still working their way through the courts. Yet with the school still staffed primarily by replacements, the picketing continued, even with the teachers' grievances apparently rendered moot.

In September of 1974, the HEA filed a lawsuit in federal court against local law enforcement for failing to protect picketers when school began in the fall. According to the teachers, 30 members of the Hortonville Vigilante Association were waiting for them on the first day of school, some of them carrying firearms. (The notion of a "vigilante association" seems somewhat oxymoronic.) Police Chief Douglas Jones said he found no evidence of any Vigilantes bearing firearms.

Eventually, the strikes stopped, but the hard feelings did not. Hortonville turned out to be one of the longest strikes in the history of U.S. education. For years, friends would walk out of their way to avoid meeting, and acquaintances would mutter curses under their breath instead of "hello." As one substitute teacher said, "How will anyone be able to look each other in the eye again?"

Of the 84 fired teachers, 51 eventually went on to work in other school districts. To this day, the teachers that went on strike rarely visit Hortonville. As of 2004, former Superintendent Marvin Obry was retired and occasionally drove a school bus for the district. Michael Wisnoski never returned to the classroom. He founded a pension firm, which he sold upon retirement. In 2007, Wisnoski said his lasting lesson from the strike was that "you never get 64 women mad at the same time."

The cost of litigation totaled $300,000 for both the HEA and the school board. The board's initial offer to the HEA would have cost $64,000; the teachers' offer was pegged at $135,000. To this day, WEAC will not allow the local Hortonville union to be affiliated with them until every one of the original replacement teachers in the town has retired.

When asked about whether it was wise for WEAC to push all its poker chips in Hortonville, Morris Andrews says, flatly, "I would have chosen a better place." But Andrews was able to turn the Hortonville disaster into a long-term victory for teachers around the state.

Andrews was able to parlay the Hortonville imbroglio into a stronger WEAC, which flexed its muscle in getting the 1978 a new mediation-arbitration law passed. The new law imposed a system known as "entire package final offer arbitration," meaning an arbitrator had to pick the entire offer made by one of the parties without amendment. Through "pattern bargaining," or the use of comparable school district data, Andrews was able to strong-arm arbitrators into accepting healthy pay and benefit increases for teachers across the state.

Interestingly, some union leadership stalwarts, such as John Matthews of the Madison teachers union, loathe the med-arb law, preferring the old style of bare-knuckle bargaining. "I'd rather have our fights on the street," Matthews told Milwaukee Magazine. "We'll go and block school entrances. We'll tell people they shouldn't be taking our jobs."

In December 2010, executive director of AFSCME Council 24 Marty Beil, warned of impending job action by public employees when Gov. Walker proposed many of the post-Hortonville union gains be rolled back. Beil warned of the potential of "labor unrest," saying, "when you push a person to the corner and there's no escape, he'll push back."

While the Hortonville strike was a short-term embarrassment for teachers' unions, labor redoubled its efforts and scored some important long-term victories. WEAC's post-Hortonville muscle led to passage of a 1977 mediation-arbitration ("med-arb") law that guarantees the settlement of deadlocked collective bargaining disputes.

The new law had the effect of essentially eliminating public employee strikes. According to the Wisconsin Employment Relations Commission, 111 municipal employee strikes have taken place in the state since 1970. Most of those, 90%, occurred prior to the 1977 med-arb law took effect.

Even with the case having been settled, the damage to the town still lingers. To this day, people still have difficulty speaking about it.

For the teachers' union, the rulings were a short-term defeat. But in the longer term, unions in Wisconsin and across America redoubled their efforts and became major political players both locally and nationwide. After Hortonville, public funding for education in the U.S. skyrocketed as states implemented laws requiring public teachers to be members of a union. It was repeal of these laws provoked hundreds of thousands of public employees to occupy state capitols around America in 2011 and 2012.

But perhaps most notably, the strike further exacerbated the urban-rural divide which once again took center stage in the 2016 presidential election. The county including Hortonville went to Donald Trump by 14 percentage points, showing that blue collar workers still harbor animosity towards government elites directing their lives.

Ultimately, as a final insult, the board gave principals, administrators, and replacement teachers substantial raises.

And in an ironic twist, the Hortonville replacement teachers mobilized to form their own union.

ACKNOWLEDGMENTS

I started this book with a Mark Twain quote, so I'll end with one.

"At forty a man reaches the top of the hill of life and starts down the sunset side," he once said, reflecting on his own life. "The ordinary man, the average man, not to particularize too closely and say the commonplace man, has at that age succeeded or failed; in either case he has lived all of his life that is likely to be worth recording."

Of course, Twain lived a full life until the age of 75, finding much more to document for us to enjoy.

I am now 48 years old, and still feel like I'm just getting started. But it took a lot of help to get even to this modest place where I reside, well below "superstar columnist" but somewhere above "digging half-eaten burritos out of the trash at Chipotle."

First, a special thanks to Morgan, my wife of 20 years, and my children, Mara, Cole, and Finn. They have shown much patience and support throughout the years, even if they still think their dad's job is to stare, forlornly and with glassy eyes, at a computer screen for days at a time.

Thanks to my mom and dad, who I still surprise on a daily basis by managing to not get arrested.

Thanks to my former office mate Jack Jablonski, who first suggested I should start a blog about politics, then spent the next fifteen years pretending he didn't know me.

Thanks to Jim Miller and George Lightbourn for hiring me at the Wisconsin Policy Research Institute, where I truly got my start writing for a living. Thanks to Charlie Sykes for seeing that writing and publishing it in his magazine, then having me on television and radio to talk about it.

Thanks to Rich Lowry at National Review for giving me the opportunity to take my writing national, where it was seen by other publications. One of those publications, the Milwaukee Journal Sentinel, became my home for almost seven years after I was hired by Marty Kaiser and David Haynes to be a staff columnist. Special thanks to Ernie Franzen for championing my columns even if they probably made his eyes roll out of his head.

Thanks to my editors at USA Today, Jill Lawrence, David Mastio, and Thuan Le Elston, for always supporting my work there and for adding me to the Board of Contributors, which makes me sound pretty important.

Thanks to John J. Miller for offering me the chance to write for The College Fix, documenting the weird world of higher education. It is a topic that never gets old.

Also, thanks to Steven Hayes, Jonah Goldberg, Rachael Larimore, and the folks at The Dispatch who are creating a reporting-first based website of which they should be proud.

And to everyone who've I ever been nice to on social media, thank you for paying attention. I love you all. Except you, over there.

ABOUT THE AUTHOR

Christian Schneider is a member of the USA Today Board of Contributors. He has also spent time at the Milwaukee Journal Sentinel and National Review. His op-eds have been featured in The New York Times, the Wall Street Journal, the Washington Post, the Weekly Standard, The Dispatch, and The Bulwark. He holds a Master's degree in political science from Marquette University. He lives in Madison, Wisconsin.